PENGUIN BOOKS

FISH, FISHING AND THE MEANING OF LIFE

'Top anthology, and great for friends who enjoy dipping into books is *Fish, Fishing and the Meaning of Life* ... I've never fished in my life but this quirky compendium bubbling with snippets about trout-tickling, maggot-growing, eel-switching, and using live frogs as bait, made me want to rush out and buy a fishing rod' – Val Hennessy in the *Daily Mail*

'Any book about fishing must be judged by how well it reproduces that journey into magic ... *Fish, Fishing and the Meaning of Life* does this extra ordinarily well' – Andrew Brown in the *Independent*

'A well-researched guide book which will lead the reflective angler past the deeper drifts of angling verbiage and on to more rewarding waters ... Paxman introduces each chapter with an essay, which ... are excellent, larded with his quick humour and sharp observation' – James Freeman in the *Herald*

'A splendid anthology' – Louise Guinness in the *Evening Standard*

'My anthologist's gold star is awarded [to *Fish, Fishing and the Meaning of Life*] ... Jeremy Paxman has revelled in his task of qualifying and categorizing "the art of piscatorial", fossicking about among double-barrelled lieutenant-colonels, Augustan clergymen and poet-anglers to the Elizabethan Thomas Bastard, bemoaning the decline of the sport because "fishes decrease and fishers multiply"' – Jonathan Keates in the *Observer* Christmas Books

D1147857

ABOUT THE AUTHOR

Jeremy Paxman was born in Yorkshire and educated at Cambridge. He is an award-winning journalist who spent ten years reporting from overseas, notably for *Panorama*. He is currently the presenter of *Newsnight* and *University Challenge*. His other books, the bestselling *Friends in High Places: Who Runs Britain?* and *The English*, are also available from Penguin.

Fish, Fishing
and the
Meaning of Life

JEREMY PAXMAN

PENGUIN BOOKS

PENGUIN BOOKS

Published by the Penguin Group
Penguin Books Ltd, 27 Wrights Lane, London W8 5TZ, England
Penguin Putnam Inc., 375 Hudson Street, New York, New York 10014, USA
Penguin Books Australia Ltd, Ringwood, Victoria, Australia
Penguin Books Canada Ltd, 10 Alcorn Avenue, Toronto, Ontario, Canada M4V 3B2
Penguin Books (NZ) Ltd, Private Bag 102902, NSMC, Auckland, New Zealand

Penguin Books Ltd, Registered Offices: Harmondsworth, Middlesex, England

First published by Michael Joseph 1994
Published in Penguin Books 1995
8

Copyright © Jeremy Paxman, 1994
All rights reserved

The moral right of the editor has been asserted

Printed in England by Clays Ltd, St Ives plc

Except in the United States of America, this book is sold subject
to the condition that it shall not, by way of trade or otherwise, be lent,
re-sold, hired out, or otherwise circulated without the publisher's
prior consent in any form of binding or cover other than that in
which it is published and without a similar condition including this
condition being imposed on the subsequent purchaser

Contents

ACKNOWLEDGEMENTS   vii

INTRODUCTION   xi

1. *Idylls*   1
2. *Fish*   77
3. *Tactics*   125
4. *Rods, Reels and Bottles of Gin*   203
5. *Ones That Got Away*   243
6. *Ones That Didn't Get Away*   291
7. *The Dangers of Fishing*   345
8. *Fish That Bit Back*   391
9. *Fishing Inns and Fishing Accomplices*   427
10. *The Ethics of Fishing*   473

BIBLIOGRAPHY   541

INDEX   549

ACKNOWLEDGEMENTS

The greatest debt of any anthologizer is to those who have written the books from which he draws his extracts. After that come the people who help you to find the material. Pre-eminent among them are the staff of the British Library, who see all kinds of eccentrics trying to prove the Chancellor of the Exchequer is a visitor from the Planet Zog, and treat all inquiries with the same courtesy.

I should also thank Justin Knowles, publisher of *The Fly Fisher's Classic Library*, for introducing me to many of the great British fishing books and for putting me in touch with Kevin Mackenna, currently compiling the definitive bibliography of Irish angling literature, who in turn pointed me in the direction of books I'd never even heard of. David Zincavage, one of the great authorities on American angling literature, suggested half-a-dozen transatlantic authors. My brother and fishing companion, James Paxman, lent me his favourite books. David Stocker, despite a previous long and occasionally fractious correspondence, volunteered a list of candidates for inclusion. Jocelyn Godley and Ed Hill each independently pointed me to the delights of 'Robert Traver', a Michigan judge with an eye to the important things in life. Brian Harris at London Zoo answered queries about dangerous fish. Bruce Sandison put me in touch with Robert Howden, factor at Berriedale, Caithness, who supplied the hilarious French newspaper account of George V's fishing prowess. Matthew Fort, the food writer and fishing fanatic, rifled through his collection of fishing books for interesting or amusing recipes. His brother Tom, collector of fishing books, shared his enthusiasms with me while we were both on a pretty unsuccessful trip to try to catch dorado in Brazil. Brod Sullivan, fabled boatman of Lough Currane, recited the angler's prayer after much drink one night on the Kola peninsula. John and Penny Mortimer provided their photocopier and plentiful good company. Christopher Butterworth, president of the Flyfishers' Club, gave me lunch and then allowed me rare access to the club library, to which the librarian, John Morgan, has written an exhaustive catalogue.

Most of all, I thank the many people with whom I have shared the pleasures of fishing. There's an awful lot of tosh talked about what Walton called the 'brotherhood of the angle'. But it does exist.

The Angler – E.T. Reed, *Punch*, 1892

PERMISSIONS

The author and publishers would like to thank the following for permission to reprint copyright material:

Illustrations: to Mary Evans Picture Library for the illustrations on pages viii, 207, 244, 292, 346, 393 and 477.
'B.B.': to David Higham Associates Ltd for *The Naturalists' Bedside Book* (Michael Joseph, 1980), *The Wayfaring Tree* (Hollis & Carter), *The Fisherman's Bedside Book* (White Lion Books, 1993), *The Idle Countryman* (Eyre & Spottiswode), *Fisherman's Folly* (Boydell & Brewer); H.E. Bates: to Laurence Pollinger Ltd on behalf of the estate of H.E. Bates for 'The Little Fishes' from *Sugar for the Horse* (Michael Joseph Ltd); Elizabeth Bishop: to Farrar, Straus & Giroux Inc. for 'The Fish' from *The Complete Poems 1927–1979* by Elizabeth Bishop. Copyright © 1979, 1983 by Alice Helen Methfessel; Edmund Blunden: to Peters Fraser & Dunlop Group Ltd for *The Face of England* and 'The Pike' from *Collected Poems*; W.H. Canaway: to Curtis Brown Ltd for *A Snowdon Stream*, copyright © W.H. Canaway 1958. Reproduced by permission of Curtis Brown Ltd, London on behalf of the copyright owner; Raymond Carver: to Capra Press for 'Deschutes River' and 'Bobber' from *At Night the Salmon Run*, copyright © 1976 by Raymond Carver; Charles Chevenix-Trench: to Longman Group Ltd for *The Poacher and the Squire*; Victor Coppleson: to Harper Collins Publishers (Australia) for *Shark Attack* (Angus & Robertson); David Day: to Routledge Kegan Paul for *The Whale War*; Negley Farson: to *Country Life* (IPC Magazines Ltd) for *Going Fishing*; *The Field*: to *The Field* for selected letters and prose extracts; John Gierach: to Pruett Publishing Company for *Trout Bum* (1986); Zane Grey: to Dr Loren Grey for *Adventures in Fishing*; Arthur Grimble: to John Murray (Publishers) Ltd

for *A Pattern of Islands*; Bill Hammond: to the author for *An Irish Salmon Gilly*; Seamus Heaney: to Faber & Faber Ltd for 'The Pulse' from *Seeing Things*; Ernest Hemingway: to Charles Scribner's Sons, an imprint of Macmillan Publishing Company, for 'Big Two-Hearted River' from *In Our Time*, copyright 1925 by Charles Scribner's Sons. Copyright renewed 1953 by Ernest Hemingway; to *The Toronto Star* Syndicate for 'The Best Rainbow Trout Fishing in the World' (28 August 1920); Robert Hughes: to Time Inc. for 'Blissing out in Balmy Belize', *Time*, 22 April 1991; Ted Hughes: to Faber & Faber Ltd for 'Night Arrival of Seatrout' from *River*; William Humphrey: to Random House UK Ltd for *My Moby Dick* (Chatto & Windus, 1979); T.C. Kingsmill Moore: to Colin Smythe Ltd for *A Man May Fish*; G.D. Luard: to Faber & Faber Ltd for *Fishing Fortunes and Misfortunes*; A.A. Luce: to Hodder Headline Ltd for *Fishing and Thinking*; C.B. McCully: to Carcanet Press Ltd for *Fly-Fishing: A Book of Words*, 1993; Norman Maclean: to The University of Chicago Press for *A River Runs Through It*; George Orwell: to A.M. Heath & Company Ltd, the Estate of the late Sonia Brownell Orwell and Martin Secker & Warburg Ltd for *Coming Up For Air*; Anthony Pearson: to Michael Joseph Ltd for *Fisherman* (Michael Joseph, 1970) copyright © Anthony Pearson, 1970; Pliny: to Penguin Books Ltd for *Natural History: A Selection*, translated by John F. Healy (Penguin Classics, 1991), copyright © John F. Healy, 1991; François Poli: to Presses de la Cité for *Sharks are Caught at Night*; Ezra Pound: to Faber & Faber Ltd for 'Fish and the Shadow' from *Collected Shorter Poems*; Arthur Ransome: to Random House UK Ltd for *Rod and Line* (Jonathan Cape, 1929); Charles Ritz: to Random House UK Ltd for *A Fly Fisher's Life* (The Bodley Head); Byron Rogers: to the author for an article from the *Daily Telegraph Magazine* (11 June 1976); Bruce Sandison: to Harper Collins Publishers for *The Sporting Gentleman's Gentleman*; Frank Sawyer: to A & C Black (Publishers) Ltd for *Keeper of the Stream*; G.E.M. Skues: to A & C Black (Publishers) Ltd for *Itchen Memories* and *The Way of a Trout With a Fly*; David Thomson: to Random House UK Ltd for *Nairn in Darkness and Light* (Hutchinson, 1987); Robert Traver: to the estate of Robert Traver for *Trout Madness*; Bernard Venables: to Merlin Unwin Books for 'Over the Volcano' from *The One that Got Away*; David Webster: to Reed Consumer Books Ltd for *Myth and Maneater*; T.H. White: to David Higham Associates Ltd for *England Have My Bones*; Christopher Yates: to Michael Joseph Ltd for *Casting at the Sun* (Michael Joseph, 1986), copyright © Christopher Yates, 1986.

Every effort has been made to trace or contact copyright holders. The publishers will be glad to rectify, in future editions, any amendments or omissions brought to their notice.

INTRODUCTION

I think the happiest days of my life have been spent fishing. It was my grandfather who taught me. I was ten or eleven; he, I suppose, seventy; his big frame stooped by old age and his eyes pale and watery.

We used to go to the River Ure, a few miles from Ripon. I haven't been there for twenty years or more, but I remember it as if it were yesterday. Beside the bridge, a few cottages, beyond them the church. On the upstream side, a high cliff on one bank and beeches and willows on the other. Between them, the river babbling from pool to stream was the colour of dry sherry. In my memory, the sun always shone those days. The trees dappled the water and, however badly you tossed your Treacle Parkin into the stream, you always seemed to catch a trout or grayling.

We had travelled there in his big old Rover. It was a rare treat to be allowed to ride in the front seat beside my grandfather, in the collar and tie he always wore even to spend the day standing alone in the middle of a river, miles from anywhere. However old it was, that car never lost the sweet smell of leather. Sometimes on the way we'd call in at one of the farms, where Mrs Spence still churned her own butter, her great ham-like arms pumping away as she told my grandfather about the prices they had got for the cattle they had sold at market last month. He would sit and sip his tea and nod knowledgeably, although I suspect most of the minutiae of farming passed him by – he had made his money in the canning business and bought the farms as an investment after the war when land prices were low.

Yet the man I saw when he was setting out on these jaunts was a different person from the sombre, moustached figure of a few hours earlier, hidden behind the *Financial Times*. I recognize the transformation now in myself. It is the prospect of imminent freedom.

For the rest of the world, angling is an occupation for slow-witted ruminants. Robert Louis Stevenson once looked at a line of anglers on a riverbank watching their floats and decided that 'you might have trepanned every one of their innocent heads and found no more than so much coiled fishing line below their skulls.'

This was a strange observation for him to make, since he was a fisherman himself and must have known how wrong was the popular misconception that fishing is no more than a matter of tossing a worm or fly into the water and waiting for a fish to bite. If that were so, the mind would still be in chains. Any angler knows that casting your fly to a rising trout or watching your float intently for the slightest hint of a nibble focuses the mind so intensely that you can't worry much about anything else.

The fisherman's quarry is a stupid, cold-blooded creature, so far down the evolutionary scale that his pursuit seems an absurd waste of the talents of *homo sapiens*. Yet these primordial beings have such quicksilver reflexes and such discriminating senses that the fisherman's only chance of outwitting them is to make himself inconspicuous – by somehow inserting himself into the natural environment by keeping the sun on his face, hiding behind trees and creeping through the undergrowth. No wonder it seems so comic.

On our way down to the river, my grandfather would often call at the hatchery, a series of ponds in the ground hidden in the trees behind a wattle fence.

'Let's have a word with Mr Sturdy.'

There was a terrible stink about the place, because there was always the carcass of a dead sheep lying around. I think they fed it to the trout, but maybe Mr Sturdy, the keeper, had something to do with the local hunt kennels too. Anyway, grandpa seemed not to notice the smell, and I did my best to control my heaving stomach.

Mr Sturdy, as his name suggested, was built like a Charollais, bristling arms bulging out of his white shirt, thick tweed trousers tucked into his permanent wellington boots. Keepering the river ran in the family. His uncle had had the job before him and designed his own pattern of fly – pale hackle, herl body and red tag – which was terrific against grayling in the autumn.

'They've been coming well to the Black Spider,' he'd say, and my grandfather would reach into his grubby old fishing bag and see if, among the hundreds of flies, he had this particular combination of starling feather and brown silk.

Mostly, the flies we used were very old-fashioned. There was the ubiquitous Greenwell's Glory, first tied for Canon William Greenwell on the River Tweed over a century earlier, and doubtless part of the secret of his long life. (He once wrote to a friend 'at the age of $92\frac{1}{2}$, I have caught one hundred trout this season, weighing $117\frac{1}{2}$ lb' – how perfectly the childlike details of his own age and the precise weight of his fish capture the mania of fishing.) We took March Browns and Blue Duns. A local pattern, the Yellow Sally, first described by John Jackson of Tanfield Mill in 1853, never did me much good but grandpa never went anywhere without at least one in his box. And a Wickham's Fancy, a Snipe and Purple and a Tup's Indispensable. It was some years before I realized that the distinctive pink tinge to the body of this last fly was because the wool was snipped from around the genitalia of a ram. The wool has a special greasiness which makes it seem to shine in the water. Or so they say.

Days with my grandfather invariably ended with his having caught half-a-dozen trout, most of them taken on the dry fly from lies so far under the overhanging branches you couldn't understand how anyone could have cast onto the water and not got hooked up in the trees.

If, as was more likely than not in the early days, I had caught nothing by the evening, he would take me down to his 'special place', and within a few casts I might have a fish. It was around the time that I saw the joke about the Tup's Indispensable that I realized his special place was right below the outfall from the hatchery, where homesick fish would lurk in nostalgia for bits of dead sheep. Mr Sturdy was obviously in on the trick, and sometimes when one of my brothers, too small to be able to cast a fly, was there, Mr Sturdy would take him off with a pocketful of worms to break the club rules about banned fishing methods.

Those dappled sunlit days introduced me to a world I would never otherwise have known. When the loudest sound was the babbling of the river, creatures went about their lives undisturbed. Grey and yellow wagtails bucked their way across the rocks. Water rats would drop into the pools with a sudden 'plop'. Otters would glide noiselessly in and out of the water. One time an eel slithered across the toes of my boots. Sandpipers called 'twee-wee-wee' as they flew over the water, and, where the river had cut high banks in the soft earth, sandmartins popped in and out of their honeycomb colonies. Then, from nowhere, the air would be split by a flash of sapphire, as a kingfisher tore down the river, six feet or so above the water. As evening fell and more and more flies hatched on the water surface, swifts flew tireless aerobatics.

Every day cannot have been this idyllic. It must have rained occasionally. There must have been days when there was no chance of catching a fish, when you stepped in so far the water poured down the inside of your boots, or you fell in. But I don't recall them. Pursuing fish is to return to the wilderness. The magic of fishing is something to do with the primeval challenge of our hunting ancestry; something to do with peace and solitude and utter concentration upon the unimportant, with time to watch the world turning around you. Even the later days when everything ended in disaster – one time I nearly drowned, smashed my reel and got bitten to death by midges – I look back on them with affection and would be happy to suffer again, for the chance of a day on the river.

But it was only recently that I realized that fishermen always live in this sort of nostalgia. Just as each day's fishing begins as an adventure, so each season ends in a warm glow of recollected challenges and triumphs and failures. There is an associated lugubriousness. Conditions, the angler perennially laments, are worse now than they have been for years. If it isn't poaching, it's pollution; mink or seals or disease; drift-netting on the high seas or drought in the rivers. Anyone who took up the sport since the war has become accustomed to tales of how much better things used to be in our grandparents' or great-grandparents' time.

Yet in his 1960 reminiscences *A Man May Fish*, Kingsmill Moore was complaining that 'The great days of (Lough) Corrib were over before 1926 when I started to visit it.' In 1890 Andrew Lang was lamenting in his *Angling Sketches* that 'even then, thirty years ago (1860), the old stagers used to tell us that the water was overfished.' And as far back as 1598 Thomas Bastard was moaning that 'the fishes decrease and the fishers multiply.' The only realistic conclusion from the systematic evocation of an earlier Golden Age is that 1. fishermen are natural moaners and 2. they will reach for any alibi they can to explain their failure to catch fish.

But it would be unfair to characterize anglers as natural pessimists. That spring in the step as they set out for a day on the riverbank is the perpetual triumph of hope over experience. The chances are that something or other will be wrong. The river will be too high. Or too low. Or too coloured. The sun will be too bright. Or it will be too cold. There will be no hatch of fly, or, if there is a hatch of fly, it will be quite unlike any of the patterns you have in your flybox. There will be a wind blowing force eight straight downriver. And so on, and so on.

Why do the anglers bother when the odds seem so stacked against them? A week of salmon fishing, with accommodation and transport costs thrown in, may cost thousands of pounds, which makes the single fish caught almost as expensive as its weight in caviar. And there are plenty of people who spend thousands in a season and don't catch anything at all.

The answer is that anyone who asks that sort of question doesn't understand the essential point about fishing: it has to be difficult. There is certainly no pleasure in the kill itself, which reduces a creature of flashing silver or glorious stipple to an inert, dead thing. The skin darkens, the body stiffens, the bright slippery sheen becomes a glutinous jelly. It is the chase, the matching of artifice to challenge, the successful act of deceit which gives the pleasure. The harder the challenge, the greater the achievement.

The superiority affected by the grander British rivers and clubs is based on the belief that 'game' fishing is inherently above 'coarse' fishing only partly because game fish, like salmon and trout, are wilder, freer and harder to catch. It is also to do with technique, because fly fishing is more dainty, more predicated upon observation of the natural world, requiring greater precision and skill. The numinous properties of fly fishing are held to embody some Platonic ideal of angling.

Though there is nothing to match fly fishing for sheer exhilaration, the vindication of artifice when a fish breaks the water to seize your imitation, the earliest English fishing literature makes no claim that some techniques are superior to others. All methods seem to have been treated much the same way. By the early seventeenth century, at least one author (Lawson) was proclaiming that 'the trout makes the angler the most gentlemanly and readiest sport of all other fishes. If you fish with a made fly, this is the chief pleasure in angling.' And, by the 1650s, two distinct schools of angling seem to have emerged. Robert Venables' *The Experienced Angler* (1662) distils a lifetime's familiarity with fly fishing, while it is abundantly clear from *The Compleat Angler* (1653) that Izaak Walton was more at home with a worm.

It is with the emergence of the cult of dry-fly fishing towards the end of the nineteenth century that the gradations of social hierarchy in fishing become clear. At the top (in his own estimation, at least) came the dry-fly purist, who would only fish by trying to drop something which looked like a natural fly onto the water upstream of a feeding trout. He looked down on the wet-fly fisherman, who had cast his line downstream, so that it swung round below the surface with perhaps three flies attached. He in turn affected scorn for the fisherman who used a worm or grub. Yet, as late as 1843, William Scrope was cheerfully describing how to drift a boat down the Tweed in low water, stabbing salmon with a leister, an object like a pitchfork.

Few sports have been more written about. The first accounts in Western literature come in Homer. Odysseus's companions were swept up by Scylla 'even as a fisher on some headland' catches a fish and 'flings it writhing' to the ground. Martial (*c.* 40–104 AD) writes about fish 'killed by fraudful flies'. Aelian (*c.* 170–235 AD) describes the first *artificial* flies – the Macedonians 'fasten red wool round a hook and fix on to the wool two feathers which grow under a cock's wattles and which in colour are like wax.'

The earliest references in English literature seem to be by that master of Old English, the Abbot of Eynsham, Aelfric, in the late tenth or early eleventh century. From then onwards, from Geoffrey

Chaucer to Ted Hughes and Seamus Heaney, fishing had become such a commonplace activity that English literature is packed with accounts of it either as a pursuit or a metaphor. Writing specifically about fishing is the literature of obsession, produced by men who will spend the night pasting their lawns with mustard and water to raise worms which they keep in their pyjama pockets, or who will strip off and swim across a river when a salmon takes their line around a patch of weed.

All things we do for pleasure can exercise a hypnotic hold. But few seem to have the pull of fishing. Football or even cricket may have more followers. But no British sport has as many participants – four million or so at the last guesstimate. And, as Arthur Ransome noted, most anglers spend their summers fishing and their winters thinking about fishing. When Britain's greatest sailor, Horatio Nelson, had his right arm shot off at the elbow, he learned to cast with his left hand. When Lord Grey was saddled with the burden of British foreign policy at the height of empire, he would scurry off through the gloom of Whitehall to catch the last train to his beloved Hampshire. Even now, Eric Clapton will spend thousands of pounds just to have the opportunity of a few days' trout fishing in each season.

From Herodotus on, most writing about fishing has been either descriptive or instructive. Herodotus was teaching how to catch crocodiles, since when thousands of lesser talents have taken it upon themselves to teach how to catch everything from minnows to whales. In the most famous fishing book of all, Izaak Walton maintained that 'angling may be so like the mathematics that it can never be fully learnt,' and then went on to spend the rest of the book telling his readers how they could indeed learn to fish.

There is such an abundance of 'how to do it' advice that I have had to be pretty selective. My principle has been to try to cover some of the main forms of fishing, but only if the accounts have some historical or literary merit. Or if they're fun.

Sadly, the heyday of British writing on fishing seems to have passed. From Izaak Walton onwards, a succession of writers managed to combine instruction with something more profound. By the middle of the nineteenth century half the British population was living in cities or towns, which meant that what had a generation or so ago been a matter of finding something to put on the table became an escape from the mechanistic drudgery of making a living. The railways gave easier access to the countryside and writers gave advice on how to enjoy leisure. Soon, books on salmon fishing were coming out at the rate of one a year and the sport had developed into its own distinct genre.

The authors of this period are men with solid, upholstered names like W. Bromley-Davenport or H. Cholmondeley-Pennell. They loved their sport and they had the wealth to pursue it. If some of their methods seem unsporting today, we can be sure that they would as soon have cheated at cards or seduced their neighbour's wife as knowingly poached a chap's water. To this period belong the great, precise observations of fly and animal life on the riverbank, the most exhaustive catalogues of the life histories of species of fish. Some of the finest writing, from people like William Scrope and the splendid 'The' O'Gorman, is shot through with humour. But just as Queen Victoria's splendid Diamond Jubilee procession of stiff-backed Guardsmen, victorious generals and rajput princes had marked the high-water of empire some time after it had actually begun to fall apart, so the flowering of British writing on fishing – in Sir Edward Grey's *Fly Fishing*, or the protracted spat between Halford and Skues on the demands of the dry fly – referred back to a more glorious period. Much of British fishing literature is essentially Victorian in its values and its assumptions about the world.

By the early twentieth century vast acres of forest were being felled to enable the production of angling memoirs by Marmaduke Garsington-Smythe and his family. These accounts of how Marmaduke or whoever had upset his hostess by some solecism, like peppering his egg at breakfast, always include stories of the prodigious numbers of salmon slain in a day, matched only by the Somme-style slaughter of grouse, pheasants and partridges. (As T.H. White observed of the Archduke Franz Ferdinand's feat of killing four thousand birds in one day – a pheasant every ten seconds for twelve successive hours – 'the unfortunate man had practically stunned himself with gunpowder, long before they bagged him at Sarajevo.')

As late as the 1950s retired colonels from the colonial service were still writing stirring accounts of battles with obscure fishes in The Dark Continent, as their grandfathers had done before them. The best of them are terrific. The worst succumb to adjectival exhaustion by page four. There are, after all, only so many ways you can describe a fish; restaurants overdraw the description bank daily. Much fishing literature is, frankly, awful. After twenty-five pages of dedication and four 'recommendatory poems' introducing *Northern Memoirs* (1658), that prize Cromwellian booby Richard Franck promises to 'manduct' the courteous reader 'through the slender margin' of his 'uncultivated book'. He didn't talk about the start of spring but said that the Vernon Ingress smiles. A hackle fly had an 'indigency of wings'. Prolix isn't the word. Unfortunately, Franck's descendants are alive and well and churning out deathly angling columns every week. A few decades ago they wrote about the 'finny throng'. Nowadays, they talk about epic battles which end in a 'bar of silver' being brought to the bank. The fisherman-writer reclines on a bed of self-satisfied cliches.

Much of the best modern writing about fishing is American. The new set of ethics they have developed in the last forty years, built around the idea of 'catch-and-release', seems to be more in touch with global worries about the future of the environment, which the British are still only beginning to grapple with. Most excitingly, there is a freshness about much of American angling writing which blows off the page like the breath of a Colorado mountain wind.

It has also taken on mystical overtones. Not since early English writing proclaimed the spiritual benefits of fishing as a consolation for the soul have we seen such an emphasis on the metaphysical side of fishing, as in books like Norman Maclean's *A River Runs Through It*, Hemingway's *Big Two-hearted River* or even Howell Raines' recent *Fly Fishing Through the Midlife Crisis*. Despite their detail, these books are 'about' fishing in much the same way as *Lady Chatterley's Lover* is about gamekeeping. They are about other things, about the relationship between man and his environment, about love and families and innocence. It may, in time, become unfashionable to write about these subjects in this context, bathetic and laboured even. But my bet is that the best of this new wave will never pall.

Much post-war British writing on fishing has failed to match these exciting American authors, preferring to concentrate on how-to-do-it. It is time for a renaissance.

One is bound to ask, of course, whether the world really needs another fishing book. Once, much later in my research than would have been the case if I'd been sensible, I looked up 'fish' and 'fishing' on the British Library computer database. There were 6,803 of them. As the titles scrolled by – histories of angling in Iceland, dreary mountains of European Union regulations on the size of fishing fleets, entirely unnecessary reprints of *The Compleat Angler*, I realized how banal most of it is. Reading about fishing is only a poor substitute for the real thing, but then plenty of fishermen think sex compares unfavourably. Yet you do begin to wonder how long it will be before we get *The Joy of Maggots: Mr Pooter's Guide to Fishing Success*.

So *Fish, Fishing and the Meaning of Life* is an attempt to redress the balance, to bring together some of the most entertaining writing about fishing. The best anthologies, like Lord Wavell's marvellous collection of poetry, *Other Men's Flowers*, are an auction of the furniture of someone's mind, accumulated, like all furniture, as presents, happy discoveries, inheritances. I have included the famous and the unknown, some pieces I have known for years, many I had never come across before starting on this anthology. It does not pretend to be an exhaustive collection: my only guiding principle has been that the pieces should be entertaining. I hope you enjoy them. They may not be as much fun as going fishing. But they may be the next best thing.

CHAPTER ONE

Idylls

*A*ll fishing days begin in dreams. Most end in tall stories and strong drink. But occasionally they end dreamily, too.

These happy days aren't necessarily just to do with the number of fish caught, although blank days are rarely idyllic. They often involve the pursuit of particular fish, but not necessarily. Mostly, they are summer days, although not the height of summer; crisp winter mornings, when the cold seems to freeze the joints of your fingers, can be the most memorable of the lot.

These are the days that live on in the mind's eye and keep you going through the long months when there's no fishing to be had. At times like that you remember the drowsy afternoons when the big old trout you'd been after for months was rising under the willow and sipping down mayflies and, in a one-in-a-thousand cast, you managed to flick your fly four inches above him, and he came to it.

They are, by definition, remembered days, often recalled at great distance. For many fishermen and women the recollection of great days fishing is really the recollection of youth. Advancing years tend, inevitably, to give halcyon days an even more rosy glow. It is, perhaps, because the remembrance of things past is such an indicator of present shortcomings, that so many fishing writers tend always to think that things were better then that they are now.

Perhaps they were. Certainly, the modern angler who reads the accounts of previous generations staggering home under the weight of trout in the creel, or who gasps at the casual depiction of a day in which a dozen or more salmon were brought to the bank, can only conclude that, objectively, things have got much worse.

But the best of these accounts of idyllic days aren't so much about the numbers of fish caught as the evocation of a mood or a moment. For all the thumping of the heart when a fish takes, the recollections of perfect days are recollections of peace, when, away from everyday cares, you had time to stand and stare, to spend twenty minutes watching the water-ousels or the otter which plays along the far bank. It's then that you realize the greatest privilege of fishing is the obligation it puts upon you to be quietly part of a world we spend the rest of our lives trying to defy, control or ignore.

Taking it Easy – W. Senior, *Waterside Sketches*, 1875

Testament of a Fisherman

I fish because I love to; because I love the environs where trout are found, which are invariably beautiful, and hate the environs where crowds of people are found, which are invariably ugly; because of all the television commercials, cocktail parties, and assorted social posturing I thus escape; because, in a world where most men seem to spend their lives doing things they hate, my fishing is at once an endless source of delight and an act of small rebellion; because trout do not lie or cheat and cannot be bought or bribed or impressed by power, but respond only to quietude and humility and endless patience; because I suspect that men are going along this way for the last time, and I for one don't want to waste the trip; because mercifully there are no telephones on trout waters; because only in the woods can I find solitude without loneliness; because bourbon out of an old tin cup always tastes better out there; because maybe one day I will catch a mermaid; and, finally, not because I regard fishing as being so terribly important but because I suspect that so many of the other concerns of men are equally unimportant – and not nearly so much fun.

ROBERT TRAVER, *Trout Magic*, 1960

Chub Fishing on Christmas Morning

It was a typical Christmas morning of the good old-fashioned sort; a slight misty haze, aided by a frost, had clothed the trees and hedges in a fantastic garb of glittering, scintillating white. Scarcely a breath of wind was blowing, but what there was brought with it in the face of the early morning sportsman a taste of the coldness of the north. The sun was just rising above the spur of a range of low hills that flanked the south-eastern horizon, and gleamed with a dull misty red, throwing a series of strange lights and shadows across its track, and lighting up in a brilliant silvery sheen the tops of the distant trees. Underfoot the grass crunched with every step, and all along the river's edge, and clinging lovingly to the lowest twigs of the overhanging scattered bushes, was a thin skim of ice, that swayed and dipped with every swirl of the current.

It most certainly was not a morning for a butterfly fisherman to be out, whose idea of fishing was green trees and leaves, to be lulled into sleep by a lazy drone from a thousand insects, under a cloudless sun. I was a bit younger and more hardy on the day that I have in my mind's eyes just now, and rather gloried in the beauties of a keen winter's morn, and considered a day's chubbing under the conditions of that day the very beau-ideal of a sportsman's life; for be it known to all and sundry that our leather-mouthed friend the chub is the sporting fish par excellence of a keen and frosty day, pike and grayling not excepted, by me at any rate.

I had left the people of the house that Christmas morn – the women folk, at any rate – a clear field and no favour to prepare the turkey, the plum-pudding, and the various indigestible items that go to make up that time-honoured meal known as the Christmas dinner. Strict orders and sundry injunctions had been given as to the time to return, and an hour later I stood in the valley of the grand old river Trent, watching the wintry sun climbing slowly up the distant hill, and lighting up the whole landscape in a glorious halo of dancing white. The river flowed along, curling under the roots of those old bushes, ever and anon swirling with a gurgling splash as an eddy was sucked underneath the hollow clay bank, then swirled on again until finally lost under the dark shadows of a distant bough. It was extremely inviting, in spite of its somewhat wintry aspect. The water was just tinged with a very faint colour: a stone on the bottom could be detected about two feet down.

Chub are a fish that can be found in a suitable place during very cold and frosty weather, even when the place is not more than three or four feet deep. It is a mistake to think that chub can only be found in very deep water during the cold weather; I have found them at all depths, when the float had to be fourteen feet away from the hook, and when it was only two feet away. This particular part of the river, under the boughs and overhanging banks, varied from two to five feet in depth, and contained some pretty fair fish, as previous visits and experiences had more than once clearly proved, and I looked forward to an enjoyable, not to say an exciting time.

If there is one bait more than another that I swear by for the fish now under notice, when weather is cold and frosty, that bait is bullock's pith, raw, for the hook, and bullock's brains, boiled hard and finely minced, for ground-bait, if that particular operation can be called ground-baiting. It was rather a difficult job, getting that bait on Christmas Eve, but by great good luck a butcher friend obliged me with a set. The brains were well washed and cleaned, all the blood and impurities being carefully removed; they were then tied up in a square of calico and boiled for nearly an hour, until they became tough and hard.

The pith itself, which I suppose I need not say is the spinal cord of the beast, was skinned, divided into short ropes as it were, and well washed and cleaned. This is all that is required; the inner fine skin is useful for holding the bait more firmly on the hook, the coarse, rough outside skin only being removed.

It was a morning made for chub fishing – water in the very best condition, and a stream running that was strong enough to carry the float and tackle onward without check or hindrance. This combination of affairs suggested an enjoyable time, and something to show for it at the end. The first place I tried was along the front of a low overhanging bank, crowned with a couple of bushes whose lowest boughs touched the water some four feet out in the stream: water about the same number of feet deep.

Taking out the shell and scissors, I put a bit of the boiled brains about the size of a large walnut in the former and clipped it up as small as ever I could, then putting sufficient water in the shell to cover the brains, well stirred and mixed them together, finally throwing the contents of the shell a few yards higher up stream, so that it would reach midwater or a little deeper by the time it got to the bushes, taking care that it sank a foot or so in front of the boughs and whirled about the stream in tiny fragments. If you are careful where you throw the clipped-up brains and mix and stir well in a little water, they will sink attractively, exactly where you want them.

My pith was in short ropes about six or eight inches long, and say half an inch thick. Clipping a bit off about three quarters of an inch long, I inserted the hook two or three times, until the bait was worked up the shank, and no more long ends hanging loose below the bend than could possibly be helped.

Then I stood well up above the stream, gently tossing out the tackle so that the float would travel some foot or eighteen inches in front of the boughs, with the bait about six inches above the bottom (hitting that distance nicely), taking care that the float did not travel quite so fast as it would have liked to do. This gentle holding back of the float causes the bait to travel a little in advance, and the strike, when a fish takes it, is more sharp and direct. Now this is most important in any sort of stream-fishing, when the float must of necessity be a good distance below where you stand: the bait must not trail behind the float.

Steadily onward went that float, three quarters of an inch of its red tip showing above the water, until it reached about the centre of the first bush, when it shot suddenly downwards with that sideways glide so characteristic of a chub bite when he means business. An instantaneous response from the rod-point resulted in a heavy plunge and a tackle as fast as a thief in a mill, which no amount of sawing this way and that could loosen. I have heard my old friend, the late Tom Sunman, say that a chub hardly ever takes bait the first time it goes past him; he simply looks out for a convenient stump or root, and next time, seizing the bait, dashes headlong round its chosen retreat.

Anyhow, there it was, a bad start; the first swim down had resulted in a lost fish and a broken tackle. Luckily the hook itself only had gone, so it was very easy to repair the damages.

The swim being hopelessly disturbed for the time being, I went on to a nice little eddy that curled inside a hollow shelving bank. Repeating the operation that had led to such a disastrous result before, the bag speedily had its first occupant. Ten more minutes' careful trail there failed to add a companion to its lonely condition. The three next swims and more than half an hour's work also failed to produce any results whatever, and I began to think that after all the bag would be extremely light.

A little lower down stream, at the corner of a small spinney, was a short length of old decaying camp-shedding, with one or two rather dangerous fasteners projecting from it. This swim was a little deeper than the usual run just there, and it looked so tempting that I determined to give it a little extra ground-bait and a more extended trial, in spite of the fine skins of ice that encrusted every rotten timber and threatened to cut asunder the line if the fish bolted for that particular bit of cover. I got here the best brace of the day, both well over the three pounds, and had two rather bad smashes among these villainous piles, stones, sunken timber, and old iron bolts.

About fifty yards lower down stream the bank suddenly rose to a height of nine or ten feet; a heavy flood some time or other had there swept out a little sheltered bay, into which the stream raced with considerable force, forming a beautiful umbrella-like eddy that curled and dimpled round and round, edging a mass of yeast-like foam six inches up the steep bank on the opposite corner. This swim was about three feet deep, and always worth trying. But now a two-pounder only rewarded my very best efforts.

A distant village clock, through the clear winter atmosphere, now chimed out the hour, and reminded me that our Christmas fishing trip was rapidly drawing to a close, and that it would soon be time to pack up and away. There was just time to try the bushes where four hours earlier I had had my first mishap; so I retraced my steps, passing the succession of curling eddies, dipping boughs, old wooden camp-shedding, and rattling streams that had afforded me such delight during the short hours of that winter's day. This time I managed, by exercising a quick and sudden pressure, to land the brother chub to the one hooked and lost in the morning.

The rooks were homing slowly overhead, a cloud of pigeons were whirling up the slope of a distant wooded hill, and a flock of green plovers were alternately showing their black and white as they turned from side to side during their flight across the meadow on the opposite bank, when I turned away for the hour's homeward march that lay between me and that Christmas dinner, for which the day and its results had given me such an appetite. The bag contained six chub weighing close on fifteen pounds – the largest nearly three and a half pounds, smallest just under two pounds.

J.W. MARTIN, *My Fishing Days and Fishing Ways*, 1906

A First Salmon

I can't begin describing to-day. The rainbow last night was a good sign, and I woke up feeling that it was going to be a massacre. But the window was wet and the slate sky icy. Still, it might clear at noon. We started on the Mill Pool straight away, on the assumption that one never knew. There might be. And so we cast slowly down, and the east wind blew the rain through everything, and the river was higher still (it has not yet been in good condition) and the more we cast the more it grew upon us that hope was dead. From 8.30 till 1.15 we wandered on the banks, like lost souls staying for waftage. It didn't clear at noon. We tried the Crooked Pot; we tried the Ardgalleys; we tried up above the snipe marsh to the bitter end. I cracked off one of my two Kessler's Fancies. The east and watery wind blew Macdonald's casts on to the bank, to my secret joy. My mackintosh was torn at the back. I only had a cap, and that was a cold poultice. I wore it back to front, in the vain effort to keep the rain from running down my neck. I paid out a sticking line with slippery, frozen fingers: the horrible and slightly rasping stickiness of cold wet deer's fat. I snapped off one of Macdonald's flies, using the salmon rod, by catching it in the bank. I found it again, and tied on in an ague.

At 1.15 we had lunch. We didn't talk much. Macdonald says that witchcraft *was* practised about here, but it has died out. There were three curlew and a thing like a black water rat: probably a form of were-wolf.

From 1.45 to 2.30 we draggled miserably back towards the Mill Pool. By now Macdonald was fishing in front with the fly and I was coming after him, hand-lining a minnow off Cheese's rod. It became really impossible to go on. I couldn't feel the line. I forgot whether it was hail then or sleet. I asked Macdonald if he would mind my using his spinning rod. It was a case of wanting something to do, but being unable to go on hand-lining. I had four casts, and caught the bottom. By now I was accustomed to this, and didn't strike. At the sixth cast I caught it again, but it was a little different. It just seemed to move: an inch, a millimetre. I struck. It couldn't be what it seemed. The line cut the water, not quite in the usual way. I could have felt, I thought, I did feel that it was moving towards me. But I was not going to tell Macdonald, not yet. It was a salmon. Oh, God, it was a salmon, and it would obviously get off at once. I pulled and waited and it was coming and it didn't seem to get off. It was deep. It stayed deep.

I shouted to Macdonald, who came, thinking I was snagged. I said: 'I think I have a fish.'

He looked at me to see if I was mad, then at the line to see if he was. He said: 'You have. Yes, certainly you have.' Then he began to become hysterical. If it had been his own fish he wouldn't have minded. But he had been wanting one for me for three days, and he was terrified I would lose it. He was in agony because he said I was holding it too hard. He beseeched me to let it go. I assured him that it was quite all right. I talked conversationally about different ways of killing salmon. I asked him to look at the time.

Then the fish came up for a second. Macdonald said: 'It's a big trout,' and my heart went down.

I said: 'Thank God it isn't an eel.'

He said: 'But no trout would hold you down like that. It would come up and flutter on the surface.'

It was only the reddish water, the aftermath of the spate, which had made him look rusty. I played him. I was hard on him, except when he had to go. He only took me 20 yards down the bank. Macdonald kept pleading for kinder treatment, but I wouldn't. I didn't know how long it was going to go on, or what was likely to happen, but I was going to hold him tight. I became aware of the moment when the cast would snap supernaturally, and let him off at that moment.

I brought him up, and we could get a good look. He was lovely and terrible, like a shark. I knew we couldn't possibly have him. He sloughed in the water. Then he was weaker and came towards us. Then he was off. And then back slowly, but still too strong. Twice more, and he was swimming just below Macdonald. Macdonald slashed at him, and *missed*. I said, agonised, 'No hurry,' and took him off for another circular tour. At last he was floating on his side, exactly below the executioner. This time there was no mistake. The gaff pulled like lightning: he was on the bank!

My first salmon. 10½ pounds. 13 minutes.

Incredible, but killed. I stuffed a pound into Macdonald's pocket, against his will, nearly cried, and went on fishing. Occasionally I peeped at the salmon. For some reason I didn't like to give it a close look. It would have been a kind of hubris to look at it closely. It might have vanished.

Thinking back over this incredibly wonderful experience, the only time I shall ever kill my first salmon again, several things become vivid. There was the way he took me. I understand now what fishing writers mean by a 'determined pull.' There was no grab, like a trout's. He simply *took* hold of me, not *caught* hold, and held me down. It was as if I were a small boy that he was going to spank. It was a determined outrage on my minnow, nothing wild or flashy about it at all. Then there was the extraordinary and unforced calm which descended when I knew he was on. I felt happy and interested, as if I had been condemned to death. This changed once, when my line jammed on the handle of the reel. Then I said: 'Oh, it's jammed.' It was a lamenting squeal, and I heard my own voice. I also remember Macdonald saying: 'Well, if we can only get this one on the bank, we can call it a guid day.' The important thing was the weather. Just for that twenty minutes the wind veered west and the sun shone. It woke the salmon up and they began to move up once more. But before moving they felt lively and took. I am sure that I hooked this fish during the only three or four minutes when it would have been possible to take fish by any means. The sun went in again, the wind went east, the rain came down: but there was a silver cock salmon on the bank. The first from Craigenkillie this year.

When people talk about salmon here they call it 'a fish.' Trouts are just trouts. A fish means a salmon. Quite right.

T.H. WHITE England Have My Bones, 1936

Fly-tying in Winter

No doubt the proper place for tying flies is at the waterside and the proper time is just before fishing, when, after seeing what fly is on the water, the perfect fisherman takes out his dubbing bag and ties one like it, 'and if he hit to make his fly right, and have the luck to hit also where there is store of trouts, a dark day, and a right wind, he will catch such store of them as will encourage him to grow more and more in love with the art of fly-making.' But perfection is hard to come by, and exact knowledge of flies and the assiduity of professional fly-tyers have made it less urgently desirable than it used to be, at least in this matter. Your fisherman is not very likely to find the trout feeding on a fly which has not got its place in every tackle-maker's catalogue. He wastes no time in tying one for himself, but takes one ready from his box and with it, let us hope, catches such store of trouts as will encourage him to buy more flies at the same shop.

Though the proper time for fly-tying may be the moment before fishing, the time when this art is likely to yield the greatest pleasure is out of the trout season altogether, when the disconsolate trout-fisher knows that another two months or so must pass before he may even try to catch a trout. Then fly-tying is the next best thing to fishing; it is the sort of licking of the lips that eases a thirsty man in a desert. You may renew the whipping on your rod, take your reels to pieces and oil them and put them together again, varnish the ring of your landing-net (a thing often left undone until it is too late), strip your line and air it; you may do all these things, but not one of them will bring you so near to fishing as the looking through of the scraps of fur and feathers that are meant for fishes' mouths. And though it is decidedly good to go through your fly-boxes, it is not so good as to make new flies. A lover cannot for more than a moment or two contemplate a lock of his mistress's hair, but he can happily spend a deal of time in carving a table for her. Inspection cannot be prolonged without uncomfortable idleness. There is a limit to the number of times you can rearrange a fly-box without finding yourself out.

But in winter it is dark early. We must tie flies by artificial light, and this is likely to yield strange results if we do not pick out our silks and feathers beforehand, by day. Nor, since we can get no models, is winter the time to experiment in new dressings. We must make flies like those we have already tried and of patterns that we know will be useful. We can do, for example, with a dozen of Greenwell's Glory, and this, with its starling wing, dull-waxed yellow silk, gold thread, and coch-y-bondhu hackle, is a fly about which we are not likely to make mistakes, even by the light of a candle. Black Spiders, too: there is always sense in filling up our stock of them, with red, black, orange, or orange and gold bodies, hackled with plain black cock's hackles or, better, the soft metallic blue-black hackles from the head and neck of a cock pheasant. A neighbour sent me the best feathered cock pheasant I have had for many years, and ever since, in spare moments after dark, I have been turning out the flies that I know I shall need during next season, pheasant tail and hare's ear (a good variety of stone-fly) and spiders of all kinds. J.W. Dunne's series of dry flies can be made in artificial light by a man who has seen no models if he has bought the materials, which are all described and sold by letters and numbers. 'Silk, blended M. and L.; Hackle, so many turns of J.12.' But the mathematical precision of such a recipe detracts from the pleasure of the cook. Something should be left to chance and taste and for winter tying I prefer old simple dressings; 'badger hackle, pheasant wings, and mallard whisks' – with such a recipe the cook has a latitude wholly desirable. The other way is like counting the plums that are to go into a pudding.

Too much precision catches at the mind just when it should be free for distant flights far from the circle of light in which, indoors, in winter, after dark, the fingers are shaping wings, twisting hackles, spinning the down of a hare's ear on a thread of lightly, wetly varnished silk. As you tie a fly you are already fishing it, and, while your fingers are busy under the lamp, it is only the Grand Vizier of your mind who superintends them. The Caliph, you, has moved in time and space. A summer stream laps about your knees, there is a noise of water in your ears, flies are hatching and floating down before your eyes, and there, just where the ripple turns to smooth, you see the flash of a trout. Will he take in June the fly your fingers are still making in January? Of course he will. He does, and you strike. It is the trembling of your fingers that brings you back to winter lamplight. This will never do. That hackle must be unwound and preened and wound again. But long before it is fairly wound and made fast the Vizier is again alone and the Caliph, you, is once more far away, this time six months younger and by another stream, catching, with a fly the very spit of this that is all but finished, the best trout you put in your basket last year.

It is waste of time, I say, to experiment in winter. Make, as well as you can, the flies that you can trust, partly because such flies have a past, of which they give you the freedom while you tie them, partly because you will otherwise never use them. A natural disposition to distrust new flies, together with a natural diffidence, will lead you, in summer, when the trout are rising, to try every fly you have in your box before risking the loss of a fish by offering some unorthodox, half-accidental mongrel tied by yourself. This, of course, applies particularly to flies for river fishing. Lake flies have a wider margin of permissible fantasy. But even for lake fishing, when I am tying them by lamplight, I prefer to make flies of the patterns I know I shall need. Some of them may, what with the Caliph's happy absences, be rough, but

'How poor a thing I sometimes find
Will captivate a greedy mind.'

And if you run out of a standard pattern, Greenwell's Glory for example, losing your last in a good fish, you are happy to find even a poor specimen in a corner of your box. Poor as it may be, it has its family prestige. Even if it catch no fish in summer it has caught plenty' in winter, while it was still in the vice. It has already the glamour of victory. You fish it with confidence and therefore well, and if it is your tail-fly you may at least get a trout on the dropper.

ARTHUR RANSOME, *Rod and Line*, 1929

Bobber

On the Columbia river near Vantage,
Washington we fished for whitefish
in the winter months of November,
December and January; my dad, Swede –
Mr Lindgren – and I. They used belly-reels,
pencil-length sinkers, red, yellow, or brown
flies baited with maggots.
They wanted distance and they got out there,
clear up to the edge of the riffle.
I fished near shore with a quill bobber and a cane pole.

My dad kept his maggots alive and warm
Under his lower lip. Mr Lindgren didn't drink.
I liked him better than my dad for a time.

He let me steer his car, teased me
about my name 'Junior', and one day
said I would grow into a fine man,
remember all this and fish with my own son.
But my dad was right. I mean
he kept silent, stroked his chin,
and went on pissing an arc into the river.

                    from *At Night the Salmon Run*, RAYMOND CARVER, 1976

The American Dream

A true angler is generally a modest man; unobtrusively communicative when he can impart a new idea; and is ever ready to let a
pretentious tyro have his say, and good-naturedly (as if merely
suggesting how it should be done) repairs his tackle, or gets him
out of a scrape. He is moderately provided with all tackle and
'fixins' necessary to the fishing he is in pursuit of. Is quietly self-
reliant and equal to almost any emergency, from splicing his rod or
tying his own flies, to trudging ten miles across a rough country
with his luggage on his back. His enjoyment consists not only in the
taking of fish: he draws much pleasure from the soothing influence
and delightful accompaniments of the art.

With happy memories of the past summer, he joins together the
three pieces of his fly-rod at home, when the scenes of the last
season's sport are wrapped in snow and ice, and renews the glad
feelings of long summer days. With what interest he notes the
swelling of the buds on the maples, or the advent of the blue-bird
and robin, and looks forward to the day when he is to try another
cast! and, when it comes at last, with what pleasing anticipations he
packs up his 'traps,' and leaves his business cares and the noisy city
behind, and after a few hours' or few days' travel in the cars, and a
few miles in a rough wagon, or a vigorous tramp over rugged hills
or along the road that leads up the banks of the river, he arrives at
his quarters! He is now in the region of fresh butter and mealy
potatoes – there are always good potatoes in a mountainous trout
country. How pleasingly rough everything looks after leaving the
prim city! How pure and wholesome the air! How beautiful the

clumps of sugar-maples and the veteran hemlocks jutting out over the stream; the laurel; the ivy; the moss-covered rocks; the lengthening shadows of evening! How musical the old familiar tinkling of the cow-bell and the cry of the whip-poor-will! How sweetly he is lulled to sleep as he hears

> 'The waters leap and gush
> O'er channelled rock, and broken bush!'

Next morning, after a hearty breakfast of mashed potatoes, ham and eggs, and butter from the cream of the cow that browses in the woods, he is off, three miles up the creek, a cigar or his pipe in his mouth, his creel at his side, and his rod over his shoulder, chatting with his chum as he goes; free, joyous, happy; at peace with his Maker, with himself, and all mankind; he should be grateful for this much, even if he catches no fish. How exhilarating the music of the stream! how invigorating its waters, causing a consciousness of manly vigor, as he wades sturdily with the strong current and casts his flies before him! When his zeal abates, and a few of the *speckled* lie in the bottom of his creel, he is not less interested in the wild flowers on the bank, or the scathed old hemlock on the cliff above, with its hawk's nest, the lady of the house likely inside, and the male proprietor perched high above on its dead top, and he breaks forth lustily – the scene suggesting the song –

> 'The bee's on its wing, and the hawk on its nest,
> And the river runs merrily by.'

When noon comes on, and the trout rise lazily or merely nip, he halts 'sub tegmine fagi,' or under the shadow of the dark sugar-maple to build a fire and roast trout for his dinner, and wiles away three hours or so. He dines sumptuously, straightens and dries his leader and the gut of his dropper, and repairs all breakage. He smokes leisurely, or even takes a nap on the green sward or velvety moss, and resumes his sport when the sun has declined enough to shade at least one side of the stream, and pleasantly anticipates the late evening cast on the still waters far down the creek. God be with you, gentle angler, if actuated with the feeling of our old master! whether you are a top fisher or a bottom fisher; whether your bait be gentles, brandling, grub, or red worm; crab, shrimp, or minnow; caddis, grasshopper, or the feathery counterfeit of the ephemera. May your thoughts be always peaceful, and your heart filled with gratitude to Him who made the country and the rivers; and 'may the east wind never blow when you go a fishing!'

THADEUS NORRIS, *The American Angler's Book*, 1865

Possessing Quietness

No life, my honest scholar, no life so happy and so pleasant as the life of a well-governed angler; for when the lawyer is swallowed up with business, the statesman in preventing or contriving plots, then we sit on cowslip banks, hear the birds sing, and possess ourselves in as much quietness as these silent silver streams, which we now see glide so quietly by us.

IZAAK WALTON, *The Compleat Angler*, 1676

'You Might Have Trepanned Their Heads'

It was a fine, green, fat landscape, or rather a mere green water-lane going on from village to village. Things had a settled look, as in places long lived in. Crop-headed children spat upon us from the bridges as we went below, with a true conservative feeling. But even more conservative were the fishermen, intent upon their floats, who let us go by without one glance. They perched upon sterlings and buttresses and along the slope of the embankment, gently occupied. They were indifferent like pieces of dead nature. They did not move any more than if they had been fishing in an old Dutch print. The leaves fluttered, the water lapped, but they continued in one stay, like so many churches established by law. You might have trepanned every one of their innocent heads and found no more than so much coiled fishing line below their skulls. I do not care for your stalwart fellows in india-rubber stockings breasting up mountain torrents with a salmon rod; but I do dearly love the class of man who plies his unfruitful art forever and a day by still and depopulated waters.

ROBERT LOUIS STEVENSON, *An Inland Voyage*, 1878

A Painter Recalls Golden Days in Brittany Before The First World War

The nature of a fisherman's joy is a subtle quality. It cannot be adequately expressed in written characters, nor is it occasioned by the mere catching of fish. Birds come into it, and flowers and the spring sunshine, and there is nature-magic, too, which even winged words would fail to touch. If, therefore, we may share only a little of our joy with brothers of the blood, what fragment of its fringe will others find – our other friends who do not fish? 'But isn't it rather dull?' they ask, remembering Paris, and vaguely a long line of fishers, motionless and vigilant, who guard the river Seine. 'It would require too much patience.' For them it would, and doubtless we are wise to keep a golden silence, thankful for waters yet not over-fished, and friends who still respect a patient, meditative turn of mind, even when they find us odd and very dull. Perhaps, however, that philosophic and contemplative mood which is necessary to perfect contentment in angling only comes with years. Youth is so full of the fever of pursuit, that there is no time to put the rod down even for five minutes while we light a ruminative pipe. Unfortunately, some of us never grow up. We are too keen on excitement. We change our fly often, and rush on from pool to pool, harassed and worried, spoiling what should be the joy of a summer's day. Yet none of us can quite spoil it. Sooner or later we begin to realise a sense of freedom, of mental detachment. We find emotional elbow-room – time to think, to rediscover the things in life which really count. Mother Earth is very near in those hours by the water-side, that are so long and golden.

It was not for nothing that a canon law of the ancient Church prescribed fishing for the clergy as being 'favourable to the health of their body, and specially of their soules'.

Jean Pierre will have it that all good fishermen are good fellows, and that no really bad man ever cares for fishing: *Et vous savez il faut avoir foi dans la pêche, car la foi est un don du bon Dieu.* Apparently the one exception to the rule is the miller of Kerval. But, then, Jean maintains that the miller is no fisherman.

With all this elevated matter in mind, it were, perhaps, as well to turn for a while to the more material aspect of a fisherman's experience, recalling the sheer joy of successfully landing a big fish on fine gut and with an eight-ounce rod; also that unregenerate moment when an even greater trout lies under the shadow of a may-tree sucking down flies, while our own is fixed firmly in the lowest branch a foot above his neb. If only we dared to break off that fly. The slightest pull on the line is certain to scare the fish and put him down, but it is our last resort. We try it, snapping the cast just as the fish turns after his rise. He has not seen us. He is still feeding! On all fours we creep back to the safety of the long grass. Hurriedly we adjust a fresh fly, while every nerve is strung, our fingers trembling. Surely there is something primitive and pagan about all this, yet it is delightful all the same.

Then, too, there is that sensuous and very human feeling which possesses a man after a long day's fishing. He has dined. He is very tired, but he still retains an extraordinary consciousness of well-being. His slippered feet are warmed by a generous wood-fire, and he remembers! . . . No need to fetch that gleaming dish of fish reposing in the dim coolness of the larder. He has them all. That big trout in rough water nearly weeded him, and this plump fellow of the withy-bed. What bungling had been there! That was a case of nerves; nerves, slack line, and luck. It is not by heavy bags alone that we count happy days at the river-side. There are many minor incidents, trifling in themselves, which, when bunched together one by one, will bloom again in fragrant retrospect.

Yet we found no flavour in that moment when we moved a step too far, flooding our waders, cut an inch too short. Nor in those weary hours when we trudged home belated, nor in those tangled thickets, trackless wastes, through which we crawled, torn, tired, hungry, in the dark. Strange that the poignancy of such distress can pass, to leave only the keen savour of fried eggs at supper-time. As for those waders, their chill clamminess is gone; while our wood-fire crackles we keep only the sweet warm scent of clover buds, the ripple of the river as it passed a great flat stone, a yellow bush of gorse, whereon inverted waders hang, steaming in hot sunshine.

ROMILY FEDDEN, *Golden Days: From the Fishing Log of a Painter in Brittany*, 1919

A Spring Day in the Highlands

24. iv. xxxiv.

Fishing by 8.30 in an easterly blizzard, alone. All the lures failed in the Catloupe and I wandered up to the Mill Pool in some sorrow, trying a minnow here and there on the way. The water was already slightly up and it rained continuously. Hand-lining the minnow (left on from the last attempt at my friend in the Catloupe) was bitter work. Fished the Mill Pool with fly and then with minnow. I went back to fly at the Crooked Pot (all this meant casting in the teeth of the east wind) and reached the Lower Ardgalley just before noon. The sixth cast had him, undeservedly, on a bellying line, at precisely twelve o'clock. I had naturally left the gaff at the Crooked Pot, being far too wet and frozen to expect a fish. I was alone.

Well, it was a grand run. I had to take him over the rapids, back to the Crooked Pot, which was fortunately downstream, and to cross a foot-bridge myself in the process. Not knowing the snags in the river well, I was in agony all the way over the rapids, piloting him between stones with frantic care. When we got there he was still on, and as I picked up the gaff Macdonald hove over the horizon. But I was not going to be cheated of the full laurels at this stage. At exactly ten minutes past twelve I gaffed him out by myself, and he was 12¾ lbs. The fly was the Bulldog, on the 13-ft. rod and light salmon cast.

We re-fished all the Ardgalleys, and the Crooked Pot, and the Mill Pool, both fly and minnow, whilst the weather became steadily more arctic. Then lunch, wrapped in coats and mackintoshes, with the rain down our necks. Then we did it all over again. Then we lay on the bank and became torpid, hibernating in the showers. At about five o'clock Madonald shewed signs of wanting to go home. The river was several inches up and there seemed to be no prospects. I said I would come too, just throwing a quick fly over the Upper

Crombie, Lang's Pot and the Catloupe. On the way down, the lambs were playing in the opposite fields: absolutely lovely: thirteen or fourteen of them charging up and down their special playground, whilst a Nannie sheep looked on like a nurse in a poem by Blake. They ran races, all together, butted each other, and occasionally made tentative attempts to mount. A brave new world, about a month old.

The Upper Crombie was in bad order and blank. When we reached Lang's Pot, Macdonald said: 'You fish the top end with the fly and I'll fish the bottom with a minnow: then we'll have two fish.' I thought to myself: 'It'll be odd if we do get two,' and began. I think I deserved my fish. It was not a splash and a dash. I covered the whole surface without a blemish, and hooked him, striking with him, at about the twentieth cast, far out. For some reason he looked a monster, and the rod had evidently been weakened by my efforts in gaffing my own fish in the morning. I had scarcely looked at my watch and got up to the foot-bridge, when there was an ominous crack. The rod had been broken once before, rebound, and now was sprung. I lowered the pressure at once; and brought the fish to gaff in eight minutes, with one of the canes gone. Weight 10 lbs. only: fly again the Bulldog. This fly has now killed $38\frac{3}{4}$ lbs. of fish. If he tops the 40 I will retire him, and he shall live a life of ease and luxury in an envelope of transparent paper stuck to a page of this book.

After this triumph I stopped fishing, and, when Macdonald had covered the Catloupe, we came home.

If only there was a pub to go to, and English draught beer for my evening, this would be the most perfect day of my life. Walking back to the post office I passed a terribly crooked man, twisted into fantastic shapes by excessive labour. It was past seven o'clock, but he was still topping turnips. I thought how much happier than he I was, and for no known reason. Of course the rational remedy for this is communism: but then the rational remedy for the agonies of the fish is to give up fishing. So much for reason.

T.H. WHITE, *England Have My Bones*, 1936

The Pulse

The effortlessness
of a spinning reel. One quick
flick of the wrist
and your minnow sped away

whispering and silky
and nimbly laden.
It seemed to be all rise
and shine, the very opposite

of uphill going – it was pure
duration, and when it ended,
the pulse of the cast line
entering water

was smaller in your hand
than the remembered heartbeat
of a bird. Then, after all of that
runaway give, you were glad

when you reeled in and found
yourself strung, heel-tip
to rod-tip, into the river's
steady purchase and thrum.

SEAMUS HEANEY, from *Seeing Things*, 1991

Victorian Paradise

The sun was shining an hour ago. It is now raining; it rained all
yesterday; the clouds are coming up from the south and the wind is
soft as oil. The day is still before us, and it is a day made for trout
fishing. . . .

No river in England holds finer trout, nor trout more willing to
be caught. A day's fishing at Cheneys means a day by the best water
in England in the fisherman's paradise of solitude.

The water-keeper is at the window – best of keepers – for he will accept a sandwich perhaps for luncheon, a pull from your flask, and a cigar out of your case, but other fee on no condition. The rain he tells me has raised the water, and the large fish are on the move, the May-fly has been down for two days. They were feeding on it last evening. If the sky clears they will take well in the afternoon; but the fly will not show till the rain stops.

Breakfast over, I start for the lower water. I have my boy with me home for the holidays. He carries the landing net, and we splash through the rain to the mill. . . .

The small fish take freely – some go back into the water, the few in good condition into the basket, which, after a field or two becomes perceptibly heavier. The governor, a small humble bee, used to be a good fly at Cheneys, and so did the black alder. Neither of them is of any use to-day. The season has been cold and late. The March brown answers best, with the never-failing red spinner. After running rapidly through two or three meadows, the river opens into a broad smooth shallow, where the trout are larger, and the water being extremely clear, are specially difficult to catch. In such a place as this, it is useless to throw your fly at random upon the stream. You must watch for a fish which is rising, and you must fish for him till you either catch him or disturb him. It is not enough to go below him and throw upwards, for though he lies with his head up-stream, his projecting eye looks back over his shoulders. You must hide behind a bunch of rushes. You must crawl along the grass with one arm only raised. If the sun is shining and the shadow of your rod glances over the gravel, you may get up and walk away. No fish within sight will stir then to the daintiest cast.

I see a fish close to the bank on the opposite side, lazily lifting his head as a fly floats past him. It is a long throw, but the wind is fair, and he is worth an effort – once, twice, three times I fail to reach him. The fourth I land the fly on the far bank, and draw it gently off upon his very nose. He swirls in the water like a salmon as he sweeps round to seize it. There is a splash – a sharp jerk, telling unmistakably that something has given way. Large fish may break you honestly in weeds or round a rock or stump, and only fate is to blame, but to let yourself be broken on the first strike is unpardonable. What can have happened? Alas, the red spinner has snapped in two at the bend – a new fly bought last week at ——'s, whose boast it has been that no fly of his was ever known to break or bend.

One grumbles on these occasions, for it is always the best fish which one loses; and as imagination is free, one may call him what weight one pleases. The damage is soon repaired. The basket fills fast as trout follows trout. It still rains, and I begin to think that I have had enough of it. I have promised to be at the mill at midday, and then we shall see.

Evidently the sky means mischief. Black thunder-clouds pile up to windward, and heavy drops continue falling. But there is a break in the south as I walk back by the bank – a gleam of sunshine spans the valley with a rainbow, and an actual May-fly or two sails by which I see greedily swallowed. The keeper is waiting; he looks scornfully into my basket. Fish – did I call these herrings fish? I must try the upper water at all events. The large trout were feeding, but the fly was not yet properly on – we can have our luncheon first.

How pleasant is luncheon on mountain side or river's bank, when you fling yourself down on fern or heather after your morning's work, and no daintiest *entrée* had ever such flavour as your sandwiches, and no champagne was ever so exquisite as the fresh stream water just tempered from your whisky flask. Then follows the smoke, when the keeper fills his pipe at your bag, and old adventures are talked over, and the conversation wanders on through anecdotes and experiences, till, as you listen to the shrewd sense and kindly feeling of your companion, you become aware that the steep difference which you had imagined to be created by education and habits of life had no existence save in your own conceit. Fortune is less unjust than she seems, and true hearts and clear-judging healthy minds, are bred as easily in the cottage as the palace. . . .

Below the shallow there is a pool made by a small weir, over which the flood is now rushing – on one side there is an open hatchway, with the stream pouring through. The banks are bushy, and over the deepest part of the pool the stem of a large ash projects into the river. Yesterday, when the water was lower, the keeper saw a four-pounder lying under that stem. Between the weir and the trees it is an awkward spot, but difficulty is the charm of fly-fishing. The dangerous drop fly must be taken off; a drop fly is only fit for open water, where there is neither weed nor stump. The March brown is sent skimming at the tail of the casting line, to be dropped, if possible, just above the ash, and to be carried under it by the stream. It has been caught in a root, so it seems; or it is foul somewhere. Surely no fish ever gave so dead a pull. No; it is no root. The line shoots under the bank. There is a broad flash of white just below the surface, a moment's struggle, the rod springs straight, and the line comes back unbroken. The March brown is still floating at the end of it. It was a big fish, perhaps the keeper's very big one; he must have been lightly hooked, and have rubbed the fly out of his mouth.

But let us look closer. The red spinner had played false in the morning; may not something like it have befallen the March brown? Something like it, indeed. The hook has straightened out as if, instead of steel, it had been made of copper. A pretty business! I try another, and another, with the same result. The heavy trout take them, and one bends and the next breaks. Oh! —— ——! Well for Charles Kingsley that he was gone before he heard of a treason which would have broken his trust in man. You in whose praise I have heard him so often eloquent! You never dealt in shoddy goods. You were faithful if all else were faithless, and redeemed the credit of English tradesmen. You had not then been in the school of progress and learnt that it was the buyer's business to distinguish good from bad. You never furnished your customers with cheap and nasty wares, fair looking to the eye and worthless to the touch and trial. In those days you dealt with gentlemen, and you felt and traded like a gentleman yourself. And now you, too, have gone the way of your fellows. You are making a fortune as you call it, out of the reputation which you won honourably in better days. You have given yourself over to competition and semblance. You have entered for the race among the sharpers, and will win by knavery and tricks like the rest. I will not name you for the sake of the old times, when C.K. and I could send you a description of a fly from the furthest corner of Ireland, and by return of post would come a packet tied on hooks which Kendal and Limerick might equal, but could not excel. You may live on undenounced for me; but read C.K.'s books over again; repent of your sins, go back to honest ways, and renounce the new gospel in which whosoever believes shall not be saved.

But what is to be done? Spite of the rain the river is now covered with drowned May-flies, and the trout are taking them all round. I have new May-flies from the same quarter in my book, but it will be mere vexation to try them. Luckily for me there are a few old ones surviving from other days. The gut is brown with age – but I must venture it. If this breaks I will go home, lock away my rod, and write an essay on the effects of the substitution of Political Economy for the Christian faith.

On then goes one of these old flies. It looks well. It bears a mild strain, and, like Don Quixote with his helmet, I will not put it to a severe trial. Out it shoots over the pool, so natural looking that I cannot distinguish it from a real fly which floats at its side. I cannot, nor can that large trout in the smooth water above the fall. He takes it, springs into the air, and then darts at the weir to throw himself over. If he goes down he is lost. Hold on. He has the stream to help him, and not an inch of line can be spared. The rod bends double, but the old gut is true. Down the fall he is not to go. He turns up the pool, he makes a dart for the hatchway, – but if you can stand a trout's first rush you need not fear him in fair water afterwards. A few more efforts and he is in the net and on the bank, not the keeper's four-pounder, but a handsome fish, which I know that he will approve.

He had walked down the bank pensively while I was in the difficulty with my flies, meditating, perhaps, on idle gentlemen, and reflecting that if the tradesmen were knaves the gentlemen were correspondingly fools. He called to me to come to him just as I had landed my trout. He was standing by the side of the rapid stream at the head of the mill pool. It was as he had foretold; the great fish had come up, and were rolling like salmon on the top of the water gulping down the May-flies. Even when they are thus carelessly ravenous, the clearness of the river creates a certain difficulty in catching them in ordinary times, but to-day the flood made caution superfluous. They were splashing on the surface close to our feet, rolling about in a negligent gluttony which seemed to take from them every thought of danger, for a distance of at least three hundred yards.

There was no longer any alarm for the tackle, and it was but to throw the fly upon the river, near or far, for a trout instantly to seize it. There was no shy rising where suspicion balks the appetite. The fish were swallowing with a deliberate seriousness every fly which drifted within their reach, snapping their jaws upon it with a gulp of satisfaction. The only difficulty was in playing them when hooked with a delicate chalk-stream casting-line. For an hour and a half it lasted, such an hour and a half of trout-fishing as I had never seen and shall never see again. The ease of success at last became wearisome. Two large baskets were filled to the brim. Accident had thrown in my way a singular opportunity which it would have been wrong to abuse, so I decided to stop. We emptied out our spoils upon the grass, and the old keeper said that long as he had known the river he had never but once seen so many fish of so large size, taken in the Ches in a single day by a single rod. . . .

The storm has passed away, the dripping trees are sparkling in the warm and watery sunset. Back then to our inn, where dinner waits for us, the choicest of our own trout, pink as salmon, with the milky curd in them, and no sauce to spoil the delicacy of their flavour. Then bed, with its lavender-scented sheets and white curtains, and sleep, sound sweet sleep, that loves the country village and comes not near a London bedroom. In the morning, adieu to Cheneys, with its red gable ends and chimneys, its venerable trees, its old-world manners, and the solemn memories of its mausoleum. Adieu, too, to the river, which, 'though men may come and men may go,' has flowed and will flow on for ever, winding among its reed beds, murmuring over its gravelly fords, heedless of royal dynasties, uncaring whether Cheney or Russell calls himself lord of its waters, graciously turning the pleasant corn mills in its course, unpolluted by the fetid refuse of manufactures, and travelling on to the ocean bright and pure and uncharged with poison, as in the old times when the priest sung mass in the church upon the hill and the sweet soft matins bell woke the hamlet to its morning prayers.

J.A. FROUDE, Cheneys and the House of Russell, 1879

A Mayfly Hatch

Then we came out and lay among the meadow grass and watched the mayflies dancing. We were right down among the buttercups, the shiny yellow goblets were above us, and overhead floated the mayflies, *up*, with a flitting of gauze-like wings, *down*, which a parachute motion, their long thread-like tails turned upwards. A small heath butterfly appeared and chased one of them, the twain went dancing away over the flowers.

Then all at once the mayflies seemed tired of dancing, they all settled on the grass and looking up the course of the brook I saw that all the countless thousands had done the same, barely one insect was on the wing.

But after about five minutes the dance began again, as far as the eye could see, all up the course of the Folly. Some locked together in mid-air fell into the grass, others, whose brief life was over, winged back to the stream, closing their wings and falling on the surface of the pool. I watched one mayfly struggling, resting and struggling again, as it was borne slowly away by the current, sending minute rings outwards. A dim shape appeared beneath, there was a flash of silver, and a fat roach sucked it down. This happened to several other exhausted insects that drifted by.

What a lovely summer dream it is when the mayflies dance! For two years these fairy-like creatures have been living a worm-like grub existence in the sand and mud of the stream bed. Millions of other grubs must even now be below, the water, waiting for just such another glorious summer day next year. Ice has roofed them in, covered with snow, the bitter winds of winter have blown across the dreary fields, long winter nights have given place to grey days. Two years for this, the mating dance in the June sunshine, this brief hour of glory!

'B.B.', *The Idle Countryman*, 1955

Eternal Mysteries

When the Wise Man laid it down that there were three things which were too wonderful for him – yea, four which he knew not – he came to the climax with 'the way of a man with a maid'. Some future Solomon will end with a fifth – the way of a trout with a fly – for it combines the poise of the eagle in the air, the swift certainty of a serpent upon a rock, and the mystery of the way of a ship in the midst of the sea, with the incalculableness of the way of a man with a maid. Our aviators seem to be on their way towards a solution of the way of an eagle in the air. The mystery of the way of a ship in the midst of the sea has yielded all its secrets to the persistence of modern man, but the way of a man with a maid and the way of a trout with a fly remain with us to be a delight and a torment to thousands of generations yet unborn.

G.E.M. SKUES, *The Way of a Trout with a Fly*, 1924

The Delights of the Chalk Stream

In these happy valleys each season has a charm of its own. If you are so lucky as to be there in early April you have the added attraction that spring and summer are in front of you, five solid months of fishing. What matter if there be no rise? There will come days in May when the olives will sail down in fleets. What matter that you know that your total days in the year will be few? Never mind, you will have some: the glories of the summer are still to come, and you feel the same deep inflowing happiness which you experience when you are on the river early on a June morning and know that the whole long day is before you.

The valley early in April is quite different from its aspect in June. The willows are only just green, the oak and the poplar still bare. The dead rushes and sedges, washed by the winter rains, give the landscape a peculiar bleached look, and the water by contrast looks dark and rather forbidding. Not many flowers are out, but the kingcup is everywhere: in waste places where last year's reeds lie thick and yellow it glows beneath them like flame beneath firewood. The grass too in the water-meadows is the dark glossy grass of early spring, unlike any other colour in the world and quite different from the grass of summer. Ever since January the water has been let in to trickle among the roots of the herbage, and now when ordinary fields have not begun growing the water-meadows have a thick crop. The sheep will soon be penned on it and their busy teeth will eat every scrap down to the roots, until the field looks a faded yellow. Then the water will be run in again, and in June the haymakers will be at work.

As April runs into May, the valley changes greatly. It becomes green everywhere; so of course do other landscapes, but its special character is that it shews so many different shades of green, and shews them all together. The yellow green of the young willows, the bright green of the reeds, the blue green of the iris, the vivid green of some water weeds – these are seen simultaneously. But perhaps the chief cause of the valley's beauty is reflected light. Light is reflected at all angles off the glancing water, and gives the leaves an airy and translucent appearance, which you do not get elsewhere. May too is the month of the hawthorn, and thorn trees flourish particularly well on the chalk. Then also the birds come, and sedge and reed warblers make the banks musical. Opinions will differ as to whether May or June is the best month. May has the charm of novelty not yet worn off, but June has that of perfect fulfilment. And to the chalk-stream fisherman June is the best month of all, for who would not if he could choose a windless day in June? It is the month of the meadow flowers, and though the different shades of green are less marked and are merging into their summer sameness, the yellow iris makes the banks a garden, the wild rose stars the hedges, and the guelder rose hangs its cream-coloured lamps over the carriers.

As summer goes on and the rest of the world grows dry and dusty, the valley remains green and cool. Running water is everywhere: racing in a miniature trout stream by the road side; filling deep brimming carriers, rivers in themselves; trickling and percolating over the fields. The valley is a delight all the year, but perhaps it is never quite the same after the summer grass has been mown, for it loses something never regained, and you see signs that the best of the year is passing. Still, July and August have their attractions. A new set of flowers appears. The comfrey and the thick clusters of purple loosestrife and the golden mimulus may not equal the June flowers. They may not compare with the wild rose, the guelder rose, and the yellow iris, perhaps the loveliest of British flowers. But they are suitable to the time, and their solid colours fit in with hot days. July and August too are fishing months whose excellence is often overlooked. On late rivers such as the Kennet you get good fishing right into September. By August another feature of the valley appears, the Great Sedge is in flower. Until June the sedge forest is composed of the tall yellow stalks of last year's growth. The green shoots as they grow slowly push them off, but they remain late in the summer and it is not till August that the new growth is complete. Then they are a glaucous green, with feathery purplish heads, beloved of night-flying moths. The forest is as tall as a man, and so thick that you have to force your way through it.

As September runs to its end, some of the special features of the valley disappear. It becomes more like other landscapes; beautiful still, but less individual. If you like you can stay on for the grayling fishing and watch the trees take on their autumn colours. You can if you like. For myself I do not care to. So by September, if you take my advice, you will quit the valley, taking with you memories which will never leave you. Another year has passed, and you are lucky to have spent any of it by the river. You will not regret your 'idle time, not idly spent.'

J.W. HILLS, A Summer on the Test, 1924

The River God

Repent, then; and come with me, at least in fancy, at six o'clock upon some breezy morning in June, not by roaring railway nor by smoking steamer, but in the cosy four-wheel, along brown heather moors, down into green clay woodlands, over white chalk downs, past Roman camps and scattered blocks of Sarsden stone, till we descend into the long green vale where, among groves of poplar and abele, winds silver Whit. Come and breakfast at the neat white inn, of yore a posting-house of fame. The stables are now turned into cottages; and instead of a dozen spruce ostlers and helpers, the last of the postboys totters sadly about the yard and looks up eagerly at the rare sight of a horse to feed. But the house keeps up enough of its ancient virtue to give us a breakfast worthy of Pantagruel's self; and after it, while we are looking out our flies, you can go and chat with the old postboy, and hear his tales, told with a sort of chivalrous pride, of the noble lords and fair ladies before whom he has ridden in the good old times gone by – even, so he darkly hints, before 'His Royal Highness the Prince' himself. Poor old fellow, he recollects not, and he need not recollect, that these great posting-houses were centres of corruption, from whence the newest vices of the metropolis were poured into the too-willing ears of village lads and lasses; and that not even the New Poor Law itself has done more for the morality of the South of England than the substitution of the rail for coaches.

Now we will walk down through the meadows some half mile,

While all the land in flowery squares,
Beneath a broad and equal-blowing wind
Smells of the coming summer,

to a scene which, as we may find its antitype anywhere for miles round, we may boldly invent for ourselves.

A red brick mill (not new red brick, of course) shall hum for ever below giant poplar-spires, which bend and shiver in the steady breeze. On its lawn laburnums shall feather down like dropping wells of gold, and from under them the stream shall hurry leaping and laughing into the light, and spread at our feet into a broad bright shallow, in which the kine are standing knee-deep already: a hint, alas! that the day means heat. And there, to the initiated eye, is another and a darker hint of glaring skies, perspiring limbs, and empty creels. Small fish are dimpling in the central eddies: but here, in six inches of water, on the very edge of the ford road, great tails and back-fins are showing above the surface, and swirling suddenly among the tufts of grass, sure sign that the large fish are picking up a minnow-breakfast at the same time that they warm their backs, and do not mean to look at a fly for many an hour to come.

Yet courage; for on the rail of yonder wooden bridge sits, chatting with a sun-browned nymph, her bonnet pushed over her face, her hayrake in her hand, a river-god in coat of velveteen, elbow on knee and pipe in mouth, who, rising when he sees us, lifts his wideawake, and halloas back a roar of comfort to our mystic adjuration, –

'Keeper! Is the fly up?'

'Mortial strong last night, gentlemen.'

Wherewith he shall lounge up to us, landing-net in hand, and we will wander up stream and away.

CHARLES KINGSLEY, *Chalk Stream Studies*, 1903

A Bobbing Reed

On a day in August some fifteen years gone I had fished upstream with but modest success until about three o'clock, when I arrived at a big red-brick bridge spanning my chalk stream, standing below which on the right bank I saw the current setting strongly against the pier on the far side, carrying all flotsam swiftly along the brickwork into the tumbling hurly-burly of the eddy below – an eddy which was often the haunt of big trout; but they seldom seemed to venture up under the bridge.

For an hour or more not a dimple had marked the surface and I recalled my forgotten sandwiches and took my seat upon a cattle fence commanding a view of the eddy and the river under the span. Often on days following rain I had heard the drip of water through the arch on to the surface; but there had been a spell of drought, and this was a dry day. So, when presently I heard a sound like the fall of a drop of water on the surface, and presently another, I looked to see where it could be falling. I did not see another falling, but presently I heard the sound again, and, after an interval, again; but still no splash. A little intrigued, I watched, and again I heard the sound, but saw nothing to suggest a cause. I seemed, however, to place it near the lower end of the arch, and there, caught against the pier on the far side, I saw a long spear of giant rush, and when the dripping sound recurred I saw the rush give a little jump, as if rebounding after the drop of water struck it. Still not satisfied, I kept my eye on the reed, and presently became aware of a tiny pale dun being swung along the current, close to the arch, hugging the brickwork, then alongside the reed, and then the reed bobbed again and the dripping sound recurred. Just long enough I waited to see the incident recur. Then, knotting on a pale pattern of Tup's Indispensable on a No. oo hook, I began to let out line. Presently I thought I had enough to cover the eighteen or twenty yards of water between me and the farther pier of the bridge, and I let my

Indispensable down on the water. It was, of course, a sheer fluke, and I daresay I should not have done the same thing again in a hundred, perhaps not in a thousand, casts, but the fly lit within an inch of the reed about two-thirds of the way up it. The current took it swiftly down – again there was that dripping sound, again the bobbing reed – and in a moment a beautiful yellow trout leapt a yard into the air and fell back with a resounding smack. He did not, however, shake out the hook, and presently I laid him, decently wrapped in a napkin, along with his predecessors of the morning. He was only one pound five ounces, but somehow his capture gave me extraordinary satisfaction.

G.E.M. SKUES, *The Way of a Trout with a Fly*, 1921

A Chalk-Stream Keeper Feels Guilt

One day I released a head of water to wash clear the cut weed in a lower reach. During the previous three weeks the sluices had been regulated to maintain a constant high level in the upper reach and when this impounded water was set free the river down-stream quickly rose bank high. As I stood on a bridge just below the sluice gates, a movement at the edge of the river caught my eye. I thought a fish had risen and watched the spot to see if the movement was repeated. A few seconds passed, then up through the water came a water vole. Something about its head looked unusual. I looked closer as it came swimming down towards me and landed at the base of an old withy pollard. Then I could see it had a young one in its mouth. Quickly it scrambled into a hole amongst the roots.

After a few moments the vole came out without the baby and, running rapidly along the bank, dived into the water at the spot where I had seen its first appearance. Soon it was up again with a second baby. The same route as before was taken to the tree-root. Then twice more the procedure was repeated. After waiting about ten minutes for the little animal to reappear, I decided she had taken in the last of the family. She was only just in time. The rising water had by then spread over the river bank and all but the tall grass at the river edge was submerged.

Going quietly to the tree I peered down into the hollow of its trunk. I could hear rustlings and tiny squeaks and, as my eyes became accustomed to the dim light, I could see the mother vole crouched amongst a litter of dried grass and rushes, busily pulling the material around her. As she worked so now and then she exposed one of the young ones as they wriggled about beneath her. I watched with interest, but eyes other than mine were also watching for there, humped up on a ledge, was a male vole. It was his couch she had taken over for her family in time of need. He made no attempt to help or to interfere, but his senses were keenly alert. I suppose I made some sound or quick movement. Like a flash he plopped into the water beneath him while she, for a moment, looked straight into my eyes. She froze and then leapt out of the nest to follow the male into the water. There exposed in the hollow nest were four little pink bodies trying to nestle into each other for warmth.

Poor little creatures, I thought. They were only a day or two old, and to be dragged rudely through water at this age they were indeed starting early to be water voles. I moved away quietly. It had been my fault. My lifting of the sluices had upset the calculations of this little family – the flooding was something for which they had been unprepared.

FRANK SAWYER, *Keeper of the Stream*, 1952

The Charm of Birds

For the angler, birds are not merely zoological specimens of interesting habits, of special form, of particular colour, laying a spotted or a spotless egg, they are his friends, whom he looks forward to meeting at the waterside. 'You remember the day the kingfisher perched on my rod? You remember the day we found the green woodpecker's burrow full of eggs in the pollard willow?' – this is how the angler's days are numbered. Can he ever forget his first introduction to the dipper? How she bobbed her plump white breast to him from out the gloom where a great beech tree's mossy roots overhung the burn – a white spot in the dark – a pale, twinkling star? Ever quitting him as he moves forward, gently preceding him as he slowly fishes his way upstream, for the wading angler alone she shines. A wanderer on the bank cannot see this low pale star. Sometimes with lively, eager glide she will run into and under the water, seeking food in the flooded mosses; then, landing on a neighbouring stone, will again begin her friendly little bobs: whilst nearer and nearer draws the angler searching with his fly along each bank; behind each stone, in each tiny pool and narrow run, until – see! higher up a fish's head and tail make a silhouette against the bright reflected sky – he hurries on – nearer and nearer he draws, one eye on the fish, one on the bird. One last bob, then with a cheery chirp a black ball swings from the bank out over the water and, turning, shoots further upstream; suddenly a new star shines out from under the far bank – a moment – and the best fish of the day is netted, 12¾in. from the tip of its nose to the tip of its tail, with many bright red spots adown its sides.

Last year I waded under the low wooden bridge, the sturdy little bridge across which, in small trolleys, stone is carried from the quarry under the cliff to the high road; I waded under it believing I could thus pass it most easily, but I found the water deep, and whilst bending low to avoid a beam I suddenly felt a cold trickle like a knife thrust down my left leg. I reacted violently, stumbling into deeper water. Nothing could save me. Fate ordained I must obey, and flood both my waders. But Fate is not wholly unkind; she will sometimes mix an ace with the low cards, and she dealt me one then: something fluttered out close to me, darkening for a moment the window of the arch, and, looking up, I saw in the dim light a great ball of moss neatly filling a niche in the wood-work – the dipper's nest. Within, hidden warm and cosy like precious pearls concealed in velvet case, were spotless eggs which, by now I hope, a mother's warmth and tender care have reared to four white bobbing breasts: it was a hot, bright, sunny spring day, when church bells ring clear, when a faint green veil is first drawn across grey winter's cloak, when every piercing blade of grass and bursting bud is promising beauty and saving: 'Wait only a little while and I will spread for you fragrant fields of hay and gay hedgerows,' when every second calls: 'Dance, dance, be happy, be merry, for winter and sorrow have passed' . . .

The greenfinch grates in a white mist of blackthorn bloom, the rookery resounds with noisy caws of young birds clamouring for food and parents gruffly ordering them away. How could I be angry then? Besides, is not a dipper's nest worth a ducking? Waders are soon emptied, garments soon wrung out. To lie in the sun, to listen to the earth, to smoke an idle pipe while the clothes are drying on a thorn bush, these are all in a day's fishing; they *are* a day's fishing.

J.C. MOTTRAM, *Fly-Fishing – Some New Arts and Mysteries*, 1915

A Parsifalian Quest

Fishing makes rivers my corrective lens; I see differently. Not only does the bird taking the mayfly signify a hatch, not only does the flash of color at the break of the riffle signify a fish feeding, but my powers uncoil inside me and I must determine which insect is hatching and what feeding pattern the trout has established. Then I must properly equip myself and properly approach the fish and properly present my imitation. I am engaged in a hunt that is more than a hunt, for the objects of the hunt are mostly to be found within myself, in the nature of my response and action. I am on a Parsifalian quest. I must be scientist, technician, athlete, perhaps even a queer sort of poet.

NICK LYONS, *Bright Rivers*, 1977

A Rabbit

A good deal later in the day and a good way farther up-stream, feeling not nearly so clever and very hot and bothered with the unravelling of many tangles and the reconstruction of a many-times-broken cast, I stood in meditation beside a nice pool with steep banks, but fairly approachable from a shallow at its tail. It was a hopeful-looking pool and I decided to await events there and go no farther. I don't know how long I had stood there when a rabbit came out of the bushes on the bank and, loping out into the field, began to nibble the grass. He was so near to me that I could study his large and fearful eye and reflect what it must be like to be a rabbit and live always under the shadow of fear. Probably, in actual fact, though it is difficult to believe, especially when one is looking into that eye, the rabbit is quite unperturbed till danger approaches; but that we can never know for certain. Another rabbit appeared ten or fifteen yards farther up-stream and cantered to a spot some distance from the bank; and, as the sun drew near to the horizon, the field became populated with feeding rabbits. Because I did not move, they accepted me as part of the scenery – rabbits seem to me to have little sense of smell – and they all nibbled away contentedly. I watched most closely the first, which was also the nearest to me. Now and again he stopped nibbling grass to sit up and listen, but he heard nothing to worry him. What a pity it is that these engaging little creatures are farm pests and, inevitably, outlaws.

A strange movement of rabbit number two caught my eye. He fell over on his side, and the next moment I saw the white of his under-parts and his four legs in the air. My first thought was that he was entangled in a wire noose, and my first impulse to let him out. But it seemed an unlikely spot in which to set a wire, and, fortunately, I checked the impulse to move just in time. Remaining still as I was, I saw something I had never seen before. The rabbit resumed a normal position, then again rolled over, and it was perfectly clear that he was just rolling, like a horse. Three times he had a good hearty roll – perhaps he had more than his normal quota of fleas – and then he resumed his evening meal.

The sound of a sucking chop came to me from the direction of the pool. I saw the ripple of a good rise. It was nearly time to go. There was one half-pound fish in the bag; I had better try to make it a brace. So I turned; the rabbits vanished and I slipped cautiously down the bank to the shallow. By a lucky shot I rose and hooked that fish at once, and he weighed three-quarters of a pound. I seem to have made myself a reputation – a brace weighing 1¼ pound is a good brace from this water. I am glad about the fish; but I am more glad that I have watched a rabbit rolling for all the world like a horse.

HENRY MAURICE, *Sometimes an Angler*, 1947

The End of a Day's Dapping in Ireland

We wait and watch the sunset. These Lough Derg sunsets are indescribably glorious. The sun hangs low in the west – a great crimson ball swinging in ultra-marine deepening to darkest sapphire. He drops lower and lower, and his reflection streams across the black water – a broad pillar of fire. A cloud swims in front of him and the whole western sky is red, and the waters turn blood-colour, reminding us of the legend from which Lough Derg derives its name. And the mountains to the west stand out black as ebony, with a fringe of fire, and the eastern hills light up in the after-glow; and then the gorgeous spectacle fades away, and Danny shivers and says: 'It's time to go home, sir!' So we go home; and no sound breaks the stillness of the night save the creaking of the thole-pins, and the gurgle of the yielding water at the bow, or the far-off lowing of the cattle on the Galway shore.

And then the grey seabirds come. They come from the east, and they go to the west. Why? No man knows. But they come, and float over us, following some inscrutable law of their own. They come from the east, they vanish in the west like wraiths; without a sound, without a trace – they are gone.

I think of them as the spirits of the many races that have lived and loved and warred and passed away over this mystic land. Fomorians, Milesians, Celts, Danes, Normans and Saxons – they have all left their traces here for those with eyes to see. We carry on our dapping – and this to me is almost its greatest attraction – in a region inconceivably rich in legendary lore: of Maeve, and Finn, and Oisín; of Bryan of Kincora, when he crushed the hosts of Asmond, and the Leinster men broke before the Dalcassian battle-axes. Of the wars of the Geraldines and the Butlers, of Confederates and Covenanters; and even still in the homes of the people they tell of Sarsfield and his irresistible dragoons. And so my story ends.

Next morning Danny and I exchange regretful but not hopeless farewells.

'Ye'll be back for the dapping next year, sir?'

'Please God, Danny. Good-bye.'

He returns to his fruit trees and his flowers – and I to noise and smoke and civilisation!

SIR THOMAS GRATTAN ESMONDE, Hunting Memories, 1920

The End of the Day

The June evening is almost over. The rosy light fades from the oaks, and from the willows the voices of the doves are ceasing; out of the nettles that hide the angler's lair comes one talking to himself. It seems natural in this light with the bats wheeling capriciously in the air. We follow him and his wicker basket along the footpath separating the wood and weed from plantations of young fruit trees, newly fenced with tall tarred stakes.

His walk, and ours, emerges into a lane, and he goes into a large white house with a quince tree by its gate – outpost to a few thatched cottages, an alehouse, a workshop, and a duck pond with the ducks asleep on the shore. We envy him the wide diamond window where he will be sitting a little later to enjoy the look and presence of the night.

The time is happy and serene, the darkness not that forbidding shroud which falls so often when there is no moon, but sweetly awake, luminous; the far-stealing dawn seems already to be glancing on the horizon of rounded hills and rising orchards. At times from the woods by the river, or woods by rivers of another world, a sigh passes through the element, and dimly answered by our trees for a brief moment is lessening away towards the horizon. We may fancy in such a night that it is the spirit of the wild cherries among the woods by the river, communing with their kindred sheltered here about the hamlet. The small, child-like complaint of birds awakened by fear is still again; and to us the hawthorn thickets round cattle-waterings far away at the end of the pastures are made as clear as though seen at noonday by the eclogues of nightingales.

Then comes your little suspecting owl to alight on the gate and at last discovers us. The pheasant's clamour, the fox's bark, do not disturb this world of dewy tranquillity. The whistle of the trains on the main line comes transformed into a voice of reverie, the rushing wheels only send us a murmur like the songs of the little waterfall below this gloom of fragrant interweaving boughs.

EDMUND BLUNDEN, *The Face of England*, 1932

Henry Thoreau on the Pond at Night

Occasionally, after my hoeing was done for the day, I joined some impatient companion who had been fishing on the pond since morning, as silent and motionless as a duck or a floating leaf, and, after practising various kinds of philosophy, had concluded commonly, by the time I arrived, that he belonged to the ancient sect of Coenobites. There was one older man, an excellent fisher and skilled in all kinds of woodcraft, who was pleased to look upon my house as a building erected for the convenience of fishermen: and I was equally pleased when he sat in my doorway to arrange his lines. Once in a while we sat together on the pond, he at one end of the boat and I at the other; but not many words passed between us, for he had grown deaf in his later years, but he occasionally hummed a psalm, which harmonised well enough with my philosophy. Our intercourse was thus altogether one of unbroken harmony, far more pleasing to remember than if it had been carried on by speech. When, as was commonly the case, I had none to commune with, I used to raise the echoes by striking with a paddle on the side of my boat, filling the surrounding woods with circling and dilating sound, stirring them up as the keeper of a menagerie his wild beasts, until I elicited a growl from every wooded vale and hill-side.

In warm evenings I frequently sat in the boat playing the flute, and saw the perch, which I seemed to have charmed, hovering around me, and the moon travelling over the ribbed bottom, which was strewed with the wrecks of the forest. Formerly I had come to this pond adventurously, from time to time, in dark summer nights, with a companion, and making a fire close to the water's edge, which we thought attracted the fishes, we caught pouts with a bunch of worms strung on a thread, and when we had done, far in the night, threw the burning brands high into the air like sky-rockets, which, coming down into the pond, were quenched with a loud hissing, and we were suddenly groping in total darkness.

Through this, whistling a tune, we took our way to the haunts of men again. But now I had made my home by the shore.

Sometimes, after staying in a village parlour till the family had all retired, I have returned to the woods, and, partly with a view to the next day's dinner, spent the hours of midnight fishing from a boat by moonlight, serenaded by owls and foxes, and hearing, from time to time, the creaking note of some unknown bird close at hand. These experiences were very memorable and valuable to me – anchored in forty feet of water, and twenty or thirty rods from the shore, surrounded sometimes by thousands of small perch and shiners, dimpling the surface with their tails in the moonlight, and communicating by a long flaxen line with mysterious nocturnal fishes which had their dwelling forty feet below, or sometimes dragging sixty feet of line about the pond as I drifted in the gentle night breeze, now and then feeling a slight vibration along it, indicative of some life prowling about its extremity, of dull uncertain blundering purpose there, and slow to make up its mind. At length you slowly raise, pulling hand over hand, some horned pout squeaking and squirming to the upper air. It was very queer, especially in dark nights, when your thoughts had wandered to vast and cosmogonal themes in other spheres, to feel this faint jerk, which came to interrupt your dreams and link you to Nature again. It seemed as if I might next cast my line upward into the air, as well as downward into this element, which was scarcely more dense. Thus I caught two fishes, as it were, with one hook.

HENRY THOREAU *Walden, or Life in the Woods*, 1854

Ernest Hemingway Discovers 'The Best Rainbow Trout Fishing in the World'

Rainbow trout fishing is as different from brook fishing as prize fighting is from boxing. The rainbow is called *Salmo iridescens* by those mysterious people who name the fish we catch and has recently been introduced into Canadian waters. At present the best rainbow trout fishing in the world is in the rapids of the Canadian Soo.

There the rainbow have been taken as large as fourteen pounds from canoes that are guided through the rapids and halted at the pools by Ojibway and Chippewa boatmen. It is a wild and nerve-frazzling sport and the odds are in favor of the big trout who tear off thirty or forty yards of line at a rush and then will sulk at the base of a big rock and refuse to be stirred into action by the pumping of a stout fly rod aided by a fluent monologue of Ojib-wayian profanity. Sometimes it takes two hours to land a really big rainbow under those circumstances.

The Soo affords great fishing. But it is a wild nightmare kind of fishing that is second only in strenuousness to angling for tuna off Catalina Island. Most of the trout too take a spinner and refuse a fly and to the 99 per cent pure fly fisherman, there are no one hundred per centers, that is a big drawback.

Of course the rainbow trout of the Soo will take a fly but it is rough handling them in that tremendous volume of water on the light tackle a fly fisherman loves. It is dangerous wading in the spots that can be waded, too, for a mis-step will take the angler over his head in the rapids. A canoe is a necessity to fish the very best water.

Altogether it is a rough, tough, mauling game, lacking in the meditative qualities of the Izaak Walton school of angling. What would make a fitting Valhalla for the good fisherman when he dies would be a regular trout river with plenty of rainbow trout in it jumping crazy for the fly.

There is such a one not forty miles from the Soo called the – well, called the river. It is about as wide as a river should be and a little deeper than a river ought to be and to get the proper picture you want to imagine in rapid succession the following fade-ins:

A high pine covered bluff that rises steep up out of the shadows. A short sand slope down to the river and a quick elbow turn with a little flood wood jammed in the bend and then a pool.

A pool where the moselle colored water sweeps into a dark swirl and expanse that is blue-brown with depth and fifty feet across.

There is the setting.

The action is supplied by two figures that slog into the picture up the trail along the river bank with loads on their backs that would tire a pack horse. These loads are pitched over the heads onto the patch of ferns by the edge of the deep pool. That is incorrect. Really the figures lurch a little forward and the tump line loosens and the pack slumps onto the ground. Men don't pitch loads at the end of an eight mile hike.

One of the figures looks up and notes the bluff is flattened on top and that there is a good place to put a tent. The other is lying on his back and looking straight up in the air. The first reaches over and picks up a grasshopper that is stiff with the fall of the evening dew and tosses him into the pool.

The hopper floats spraddle legged on the water of the pool an instant, an eddy catches him and then there is a yard long flash of flame, and a trout as long as your forearm has shot into the air and the hopper has disappeared.

'Did you see that?' gasped the man who had tossed in the grasshopper.

It was a useless question, for the other, who a moment before would have served as a model for a study entitled 'Utter Fatigue,' was jerking his fly rod out of the case and holding a leader in his mouth.

We decided on a McGinty and a Royal Coachman for the flies and at the second cast there was a swirl like the explosion of a depth bomb, the line went taut and the rainbow shot two feet out of water. He tore down the pool and the line went out until the core of the reel showed. He jumped and each time he shot into the air we lowered the tip and prayed. Finally he jumped and the line went slack and Jacques reeled in. We thought he was gone and then he jumped right under our faces. He had shot upstream towards us so fast that it looked as though he were off.

When I finally netted him and rushed him up the bank and could feel his huge strength in the tremendous muscular jerks he made when I held him flat against the bank, it was almost dark. He measured twenty-six inches and weighed nine pounds and seven ounces.

That is rainbow trout fishing.

The rainbow takes the fly more willingly than he does bait. The McGinty, a fly that looks like a yellow jacket, is the best. It should be tied on a number eight or ten hook.

The smaller flies get more strikes but are too small to hold the really big fish. The rainbow trout will live in the same streams with brook trout but they are found in different kinds of places. Brook trout will be forced into the shady holes under the bank and where alders hang over the banks, and the rainbow will dominate the clear pools and the fast shallows.

Magazine writers and magazine covers to the contrary the brook or speckled trout does not leap out of water after he has been hooked. Given plenty of line he will fight a deep rushing fight. Of course if you hold the fish too tight he will be forced by the rush of the current to flop on top of the water.

But the rainbow always leaps on a slack or tight line. His leaps are not mere flops, either, but actual jumps out of and parallel with the water of from a foot to five feet. A five-foot jump by any fish sounds improbable, but it is true.

If you don't believe it tie onto one in fast water and try and force him. Maybe if he is a five-pounder he will throw me down and only jump four feet eleven inches.

ERNEST HEMINGWAY, The Toronto Star Weekly, 28 August 1920

Brilliant Rainbows

I caught a tremendous fish
and held him beside the boat
half out of water, with my hook
fast in a corner of his mouth.
He didn't fight.
He hadn't fought at all.
He hung a grunting weight,
battered and venerable
and homely. Here and there
his brown skin hung in strips
like ancient wallpaper,
and its pattern of darker brown
was like wallpaper:
shapes like full-blown roses
stained and lost through age.
He was speckled with barnacles,

fine rosettes of lime,
and infested
with tiny white sea-lice,
and underneath two or three
rags of green weed hung down.
While his gills were breathing in
the terrible oxygen
– the frightening gills,
fresh and crisp with blood,
that can cut so badly –
I thought of the coarse white flesh
packed in like feathers,
the big bones and the little bones,
the dramatic reds and blacks
of his shiny entrails,
and the pink swim-bladder
like a big peony.
I looked into his eyes
which were far larger than mine
but shallower, and yellowed,
the irises backed and packed
with tarnished tinfoil
seen through the lenses
of old scratched isinglass.
They shifted a little, but not
to return my stare.
– It was more like the tipping
of an object toward the light.
I admired his sullen face,
the mechanism of his jaw,
and then I saw
that from his lower lip
– if you could call it a lip –
grim, wet, and weaponlike,
hung five old pieces of fish-line,
or four and a wire leader
with the swivel still attached,
with all their five big hooks

grown firmly in his mouth.
A green line, frayed at the end
where he broke it, two heavier lines,
and a fine black thread
still crimped from the strain and snap
when it broke and he got away.
Like medals with their ribbons
frayed and wavering,
a five-haired beard of wisdom
trailing from his aching jaw.
I stared and stared
and victory filled up
the little rented boat,
from the pool of bilge
where oil had spread a rainbow
around the rusted engine
to the bailer rusted orange,
the sun-cracked thwarts,
the oarlocks on their strings,
the gunnels – until everything
was rainbow, rainbow, rainbow!
And I let the fish go.

> ELIZABETH BISHOP, 'The Fish', from *The Complete Poems*,
> 1955

The Delight of the Unknown

It is the unknown which constitutes the main charm and delight of every adult human creature's life from very childhood; which life from the beginning to the end is, I maintain, one continued gamble. Uncertainty is the salt of existence. I once emptied a large fish-pond, which, from my youth up, I had held in supreme veneration and angled in with awe, lest some of the monsters with which it was supposed to abound, especially one ferocious and gigantic pike, which a six-foot gamekeeper gravely asserted to be as big as himself, and to have consumed endless broods of young ducks, should encounter me unawares, and the result was a great haul of small and medium sized fish of all kinds, a few obese fat-headed carp, and the conspicuous absence of the monster pike.

I refilled the pond but never fished in it again; I knew what was in it, and also what was *not* in it. Its mystery, and with it its glory, had departed. So it is with shooting – I hate to know how many pheasants there are in a wood, how many coveys in a partridge beat, how many birds in a covey. So it is, of course, with everything else in life. Whatever is reduced to a certainty ceases to charm, and, but for the element of risk or chance – uncertainty in short – not only every sport or amusement, but even every operation and transaction of this world, would be tame and irksome. If we foreknew the result we would seldom do anything, and would eventually be reduced to the condition of the bald, toothless, toeless, timid, sedentary, and incombative 'man of the future' foreshadowed recently by a very advanced writer. How few would even marry a wife if the recesses of her mind were previously laid as bare as my fish-pond! And how few women would accept a husband under similar circumstances! So that the elimination of the element of uncertainty would perhaps lead to universal celibacy. Still possessing it however, and far from any approximation to this latter result, let me sing the praises of that sport which ranks next to fox-hunting in its utter absence of certainty – the prince and king of all the angling domain – salmon-fishing. Delightful in itself, this regal sport conducts its worshippers into the grandest and wildest scenes of nature.

WALTER BROMLEY DAVENPORT, *Sport*, 1885

The Angler's Invitation

I.
Come when the leaf comes, angle with me,
Come when the bee hums crossing the lea;
    Come with the wild flowers,
    Come with the mild showers,
Come when the singing bird calleth for thee!

II.
Then to the stream-side gladly we'll hie,
Where the grey trout glide temptingly by;
    Or in some still place,
    Over the hill-face,
Cast, ever hoping, the magical fly.

III.
Then when the dew falls, homeward we'll speed
To our own loved walls down on the mead;
    There, by the bright hearth,
    Holding our night mirth,
We'll drink to sweet friendship in need and in deed!

THOMAS TOD STODDART, *An Angler's Rambles*, 1866

A Foreign Secretary's Escape From London

It is impossible to live in London without great sacrifice. Happily it is possible to go away, if not to home, at any rate to some country retreat at the end of the week, and to combine the best of dry fly fishing with this on Saturday. Where this can be done, the prospect of the escape on Saturday till Monday is a great consolation in all moments of leisure during the week. It is borne about with us like a happy secret; it draws the thoughts towards it continually, as Ruskin says that the luminous distance in a picture attracts the eye, or as the gleam of water attracts it in a landscape.

If our work will let us escape on Friday evening, it is luxury; but even if we belong only to those in the middle state of happiness, who work till midnight or later on Friday, and can have the whole of Saturday and Sunday in the country, we may still be splendidly well off, provided that we are careful to miss nothing. The earliest trains leave Waterloo, the usual place of departure for the Itchen or Test, either at or just before six o'clock in the morning. To leave London it is possible once a week, even after late hours, to get up in time for these early trains, and if you have no luggage (and you need have none if you go to the same place week after week), you will not find it difficult to get to the station. There are places where hansoms can be found even at these hours of the morning; they are not numerous, and they seem quite different from the hansoms that are abroad at more lively hours, but they can be found if you will look for them at certain places. The best plan, however, is to live within a walk of Waterloo, and as you cross the river in the early summer morning, you may feel more reconciled to London than at any other time, and understand Wordsworth's tribute to the sight from Westminster Bridge. I pass over the scene at Waterloo station, which at this hour is very different from the usual one, and the journey on which perhaps one sleeps a little, though I have found that, while it is very easy to sleep sitting up in the late hours of the evening, it is necessary to lie down, if one wishes to sleep in the early hours of the morning. At some time between eight and nine o'clock, you step out of the train, and are in a few minutes amongst all the long-desired things. Every sense is alert and excited, every scent and everything seen or heard is noted with delight. You are grateful for the grass on which you walk, even for the soft country dust about your feet.

Let me again be free to choose the day, and let it be bright and cloudless without wind this time. A warm day with a maximum temperature of 75° in the shade; rather trying weather for a wet fly angler, but not at all bad for dry fly fishing at this season, and the sooner the angler can satisfy himself with breakfast and be by the water the better. On such a day in mid-June some fish should be found rising at any time after eight o'clock, and this is said without prejudice to what may happen before eight o'clock, of which I have no experience. There are thirteen hours of daylight after eight o'clock in the morning, and that is enough for a full day's fishing. But the rise will probably be quite different in character to the rise in May. It will be much more prolonged, but more quiet, and the beginning and end of it will not be so clearly defined. You may expect the fish to take best, and to find most fish rising between ten o'clock and two o'clock in the day; but both before and after these hours, there should be some trout feeding. The rise of fish corresponds of course to the rise of fly, and there will probably be some duns upon the water all day, but at no time in such quantities as during the few hours into which the hatching is concentrated earlier in the season and in colder weather. This is what makes June such a good month: the fishing is spread over a much longer period of the day. It is true that the trout are not so greedy, but on the other hand, partly for this very reason and partly because the flies are less numerous at any one time, they are not so likely to do nothing but rush about after *larvae*, and it is better to be casting over the most fastidious trout which is taking flies on the surface, than over the hungriest one that is 'bulging.' On a bright warm day such as this, the angler will go very quietly, watching the water, always expecting to see a rise, but knowing that a trout may be well on the feed and yet rising slowly at comparatively long intervals of time. The little light coloured places with a gentle swirl of water immediately below a patch of weed are very favourite spots, and in these it is often possible to see a fish very clearly. On a bright day, the angler should therefore not only look for a rise, but look also for the fish, and many a trout will be discovered lying on the watch for flies before it is actually seen to take one. There is not much difficulty in telling by its attitude in the water, whether a trout is worth trying for. Between the appearance of a trout that is resting motionless and dull upon the bottom, and one that is poised in the water near the surface, there is all the difference in the world; the very attitude of the latter, still as it may be for the moment, seems to have something watchful and lively about it.

In June the trout should be at their very best and strongest, and the angler should be ambitious and go to the water, where he knows there are large ones, to match his skill and his fine gut against them in bright weather. Many a big trout will be seen, risen, and hooked, but the weeds as well as the fish are strong now, and where two-pounders are common and taking well, there are sure to be catastrophes in a long day's fishing. On the other hand, except on very unlucky days, what triumphs there are! what moments of suspense as the fly is floating to the place where one feels sure, either from the sight of the rise or of the very fish itself, that a great trout is feeding! Often in the case of these large trout my rod trembles visibly as the fly comes to the spot, perhaps after all not to be taken. I cannot say which is the more exciting, to have seen only the rise, or to be watching the movement of the fish.

SIR EDWARD GREY, Fly Fishing, 1899

Old Buffers See Paradise

Hunting, shooting and fishing (i)

SIR, Three years ago I was fishing for salmon in the late autumn on that delightful river, the Fowey, in Cornwall. Having had trouble with the brightly-coloured leaves floating down the river and catching my fly, I decided to go up the bank and have my lunch.

It was one of those splendid autumn days with the weak sun showing up the colouring of the trees. I had just taken a sandwich in my hand when I noticed a line of guns – standing down the side of a tree plantation to my left – over the river. I was saying to myself that I had never seen such a grand sight. All that was required to complete the picture was a hunt. At that moment a pack of hounds streamed across the valley in full cry and away over the hill.

I do not claim to have hunted, fished and shot all in one day, but to see all these sports going on around one, at the same time, in the space of eating *one* sandwich, surely must be rare. Despite leaves and no fish that sight made my day.

    W.F.L.H. Devonshire.

Hunting, shooting and fishing (ii)

SIR, Reading your correspondents' letters in *The Field* (24 October and 7 November) reminded me of a recent experience of my own. I was out with beagles last March, soon after the foot-and-mouth restrictions were lifted, hunting near the south bank of the Trent not far from Nottingham.

Our hare took us to an open piece of flat grassland bounded on one side by the river. Here at the same time I could see the following: two rowing eights practising on the river, fishermen on the bank, riders out hacking, as well as one game of hockey and another of rugby. All these, as well as the beagles, were at one time within a radius of two hundred yards.

    G.R.C.B. Nottinghamshire.

      Letters to *The Field*, from *Pig Overboard!*, MERRILY HARPUR,

            1984

A War Reporter Decides to go Home

The young Italian was called Luigi Ferrari. He was short and stocky, very dark-skinned with a scar running from his left eye to the corner of his mouth which made him look sinister. He wasn't. He was young and full of life and the sort of man you liked at once.

Luigi Ferrari was a passionate fisherman. I met him in the Congo in 1960. We were walking down a road towards Elizabethville and there was a lot of shooting so we dived into the bush and waited for a while. When the shooting stopped, we went on. As a correspondent I had no real privileges and no one cared much about me. I carried a Belgian FN rifle and a Colt .38 police special in a small holster on my belt and these two guns were the only privileges I had. The day before I had seen my friend, Jack Allan, strafed across the chest with heavy MG bullets. He was trying to see what it was all about so he could tell the people who didn't care anyway, except with the usual morbid interest people have in those sort of small wars – how many women were raped? Were they white or black? How do the Baluba kill prisoners slowly? No one was interested how Jack Allan died. He was just a casualty of war. I hugged my FN and determined I would not be another.

When we rounded the bend and came to the place where the fight had been there was this little Italian sitting on a big rock. Three or four Simbas and one white mercenary were dead in the road. Ferrari had the red and white Katanganese flashes on the shoulder of his para jacket and he was holding a Gustav light machinegun. The other mercenaries had gone when they knew the U.N. troops were coming. Mercenaries were really illegal then. Luigi was finished so he just sat and waited and when we came round the bend he threw away his machinegun and held up his hands.

On the way back to base he told me he had joined up as a mercenary to make enough money to buy a boat for fishing in the Gulf of Akaba. The fishing there was maybe the best in the whole world and was untouched. He had enough money in a bank in Geneva to do it and he didn't see much point in going on with the Katanga Commando and getting himself shot up – or worse – by either the U.N., or the Simbas. I didn't see him again for close on eight years.

I had business with my friend Marcel Huas and for this business we were in Egypt and we needed a fast boat. We went to a place called Haja and there I met Luigi Ferrari again. He had a very good fast boat with a low keel and shallow draught, ideal for the work we had in mind. He told me he had not done so good with the fishing because there were not so many tourists especially now there was a war on and it was difficult working in the Gulf during the day because the Israeli troops were always after fadayeen commandos and they kept on arresting Luigi and accusing him of running supplies to the fadayeen (which in fact he was doing). He told me he would take me out to fish for tuna, but he never did because that same night he ran across the Gulf with some cargo of Marcel's and got caught up in the searchlights while he was too close inshore on the Israeli side. He got a burst of machinegun bullets in his stomach. Before he died he told me he was saving up to buy a house and get married and it was all going so well. I watched him die. He was bleeding badly and his blood soaked through my cord trousers and para jacket as Marcel blasted the boat away from the machinegun fire. 'You know,' Luigi said to me 'they've gone and shot my balls off. Isn't it rotten. We never did go fishing.' And he died. And all he wanted to do was go home. And I did.

ANTHONY PEARSON, *Fisherman*, 1970

The Cleveland Wrecking Yard

My own experience with the Cleveland Wrecking Yard began two days ago when I heard about a used trout stream they had on sale out at the Yard. So I caught the Number 15 bus on Columbus Avenue and went out there for the first time.

There were two Negro boys sitting behind me on the bus. They were talking about Chubby Checker and the twist. They thought that Chubby Checker was only fifteen years old because he didn't have a mustache. Then they talked about some other guy who did the twist forty-four hours in a row until he saw George Washington crossing the Delaware.

'Man, that's what I call twisting,' one of the kids said.

'I don't think I could twist no forty-four hours in a row,' the other kid said. 'That's a lot of twisting.'

I got off the bus right next to an abandoned Time Gasoline filling station and an abandoned fifty-cent self-service car wash. There was a long field on one side of the filling station. The field had once been covered with a housing project during the war, put there for the shipyard workers.

On the other side of the Time filling station was the Cleveland Wrecking Yard. I walked down there to have a look at the used trout stream. The Cleveland Wrecking Yard has a very long front window filled with signs and merchandise.

There was a sign in the window advertising a laundry marking machine for $65.00. The original cost of the machine was $175.00. Quite a saving.

There was another sign advertising new and used two and three ton hoists. I wondered how many hoists it would take to move a trout stream.

There was another sign that said:

THE FAMILY GIFT CENTER
GIFT SUGGESTIONS FOR THE ENTIRE FAMILY

The window was filled with hundreds of items for the entire family. *Daddy, do you know what I want for Christmas? What, son? A bathroom. Mommy, do you know what I want for Christmas? What, Patricia? Some roofing material.*

There were jungle hammocks in the window for distant relatives and dollar-ten-cent gallons of earth-brown enamel paint for other loved ones.

There was also a big sign that said:

USED TROUT STREAM FOR SALE
MUST BE SEEN TO BE APPRECIATED

I went inside and looked at some ship's lanterns that were for sale next to the door. Then a salesman came up to me and said in a pleasant voice, 'Can I help you?'

'Yes,' I said. 'I'm curious about the trout stream you have for sale. Can you tell me something about it? How are you selling it?'

'We're selling it by the foot length. You can buy as little as you want or you can buy all we've got left. A man came in here this morning and bought five hundred sixty-three feet. He's going to give it to his niece for a birthday present,' the salesman said.

'We're selling the waterfalls separately of course, and the trees and birds, flowers, grass and ferns we're also selling extra. The insects we're giving away free with a minimum purchase of ten feet of stream.'

'How much are you selling the stream for?' I asked.

'Six dollars and fifty cents a foot,' he said. 'That's for the first hundred feet. After that it's five dollars a foot.'

'How much are the birds?' I asked.

'Thirty-five cents apiece,' he said. 'But of course they're used. We can't guarantee anything.'

'How wide is the stream?' I asked. 'You said you were selling it by the length, didn't you?'

'Yes,' he said. 'We're selling it by the length. Its width runs between five and eleven feet. You don't have to pay anything extra for width. It's not a big stream, but it's very pleasant.'

'What kinds of animals do you have?' I asked.

'We only have three deer left,' he said.

'Oh . . . What about flowers?'

'By the dozen,' he said.

'Is the stream clear?' I asked.

'Sir,' the salesman said. 'I wouldn't want you to think that we would ever sell a murky trout stream here. We always make sure they're running crystal clear before we even think about moving them.'

'Where did the stream come from?' I asked.

'Colorado,' he said. 'We moved it with loving care. We've never damaged a trout stream yet. We treat them all as if they were china.'

'You're probably asked this all the time, but how's fishing in the stream?' I asked.

'Very good,' he said. 'Mostly German browns, but there are a few rainbows.'

'What do the trout cost?' I asked.

'They come with the stream,' he said. 'Of course it's all luck. You never know how many you're going to get or how big they are. But the fishing's very good, you might say it's excellent. Both bait and dry fly,' he said smiling.

'Where's the stream at?' I asked. 'I'd like to take a look at it.'

'It's around in back,' he said. 'You go straight through that door and then turn right until you're outside. It's stacked in lengths. You can't miss it. The waterfalls are upstairs in the used plumbing department.'

'What about the animals?'

'Well, what's left of the animals are straight back from the stream. You'll see a bunch of our trucks parked on a road by the railroad tracks. Turn right on the road and follow it down past the piles of lumber. The animal shed's right at the end of the lot.'

'Thanks,' I said. 'I think I'll look at the waterfalls first. You don't have to come with me. Just tell me how to get there and I'll find my own way.'

'All right,' he said. 'Go up those stairs. You'll see a bunch of doors and windows, turn left and you'll find the used plumbing department. Here's my card if you need any help.'

'Okay,' I said. 'You've been a great help already. Thanks a lot. I'll take a look around.'

'Good luck,' he said.

I went upstairs and there were thousands of doors there. I'd never seen so many doors before in my life. You could have built an entire city out of those doors. Doorstown. And there were enough windows up there to build a little suburb entirely out of windows. Windowville.

I turned left and went back and saw the faint glow of pearl-colored light. The light got stronger and stronger as I went farther back, and then I was in the used plumbing department, surrounded by hundreds of toilets.

The toilets were stacked on shelves. They were stacked five toilets high. There was a skylight above the toilets that made them glow like the Great Taboo Pearl of the South Sea movies.

Stacked over against the wall were the waterfalls. There were about a dozen of them, ranging from a drop of a few feet to a drop of ten or fifteen feet.

There was one waterfall that was over sixty feet long. There were tags on the pieces of the big falls describing the correct order for putting the falls back together again.

The waterfalls all had price tags on them. They were more

expensive than the stream. The waterfalls were selling for $19.00 a foot.

I went into another room where there were piles of sweet-smelling lumber, glowing a soft yellow from a different color skylight above the lumber. In the shadows at the edge of the room under the sloping roof of the building were many sinks and urinals covered with dust, and there was also another waterfall about seventeen feet long, lying there in two lengths and already beginning to gather dust.

I had seen all I wanted of the waterfalls, and now I was very curious about the trout stream, so I followed the salesman's directions and ended up outside the building.

O I had never in my life seen anything like that trout stream. It was stacked in piles of various lengths: ten, fifteen, twenty feet, etc. There was one pile of hundred-foot lengths. There was also a box of scraps. The scraps were in odd sizes ranging from six inches to a couple of feet.

There was a loudspeaker on the side of the building and soft music was coming out. It was a cloudy day and seagulls were circling high overhead.

Behind the stream were big bundles of trees and bushes. They were covered with sheets of patched canvas. You could see the tops and roots sticking out the ends of the bundles.

I went up close and looked at the lengths of stream. I could see some trout in them. I saw one good fish. I saw some crawdads crawling around the rocks at the bottom.

It looked like a fine stream. I put my hand in the water. It was cold and felt good.

I decided to go around to the side and look at the animals. I saw where the trucks were parked beside the railroad tracks. I followed the road down past the piles of lumber, back to the shed where the animals were.

The salesman had been right. They were practically out of animals. About the only thing they had left in any abundance were mice. There were hundreds of mice.

Beside the shed was a huge wire birdcage, maybe fifty feet high, filled with many kinds of birds. The top of the cage had a piece of canvas over it, so the birds wouldn't get wet when it rained. There were woodpeckers and wild canaries and sparrows.

On my way back to where the trout stream was piled, I found the insects. They were inside a prefabricated steel building that was selling for eighty cents a square foot. There was a sign over the door. It said:

INSECTS

RICHARD BRAUTIGAN, *Trout Fishing in America*, 1967

Night Fishing For Bass

For the most part, we fish the flowing tide, although the ebb often yields fish and if it comes to a choice between fishing the flood in daylight and the ebb at night, most of us would choose the latter. I like best to arrive a little before dusk just before the young flood begins, so that my tackle will be set up in time for me to fish the first hour just as the light is failing. The low rocks are uncovered completely at low water and the waves are breaking on sand and beginning to run up the gullies between the rocks.

In the ordinary way of things, this hour gives the best chance of fish. The first movement of the tide excites every inshore creature (as you will see if you observe a fair-sized rock pool just before the tide reaches it, so long as you are careful to keep out of sight). The bass move into the rocks and feed on what the surf has washed out of the crevices; and the fisherman lets his bait roll slowly across the sandy patches; taking the risk that the hooks might catch in the rocks, for during the rest of the tide he will not be so sure of where the fish are, for when the rocks are covered they will spread out along the beach. His rod must be held high to keep as much of the line as he can from falling slack and snagging in the rocks that the tide is obscuring. The sand channels are narrow, and as the tide rises, he has to rely on a precise mental picture of their positions when he casts again. Landing a fish is fraught with difficulties: the water is shallow and the bass makes bewildering changes of direction which often lead to the line being taken around the rocks . . .

There is not much of this fishing. The sand gullies peter out and the rocks behind are too uneven to yield a sure line of retreat. In a way it is a relief to move across to the clear sand, even though the fish are not so concentrated there. At this stage of the tide, one is still on the seaward side of the long sand bar which runs across the beach, the fish still close in, and it is possible to stay until the tide begins to cut around on either side, making it necessary to retreat to the far side of the bar, and to accept a pause in the fishing. On these shallows, the surf begins to break much farther out, so that only a very long cast will be effective until the water deepens over the bar and the bass move in again. Very roughly, this sterile period occupies the two middle hours of the tide, and I accept it as a welcome break. I go on fishing, but only through the proxy of my rod set in its rest, and this is the time for me to eat and drink, put my tackle in order and establish a base camp above the high water mark, because soon there may be no time for such things, for the top of the tide, when the water deepens as it reaches the steep bank is the time when it is most likely that a big bag will be made. Though the fishing is a good deal less consistent than that of the early run between the rocks, when the bass are present they are there in numbers. The surf becomes much shorter here, in the sense that it begins to break much closer in, so that there is no need to cast very far. Sometimes, especially when the sea is quiet, the fish are within a few feet of the shore and it is easy to cast into barren water beyond them.

Once, a young friend of mine, Terrence Thomas, broke a spring in his reel early on in the tide. All he had as an alternative was a stiff old Nottingham reel that had languished for months at the bottom of his fishing bag, and stubborn and oil-less as it was, he had to use it if he wanted to go on fishing. It was only possible to lob the tackle ten yards out, and until the last hour of the tide he caught nothing. Then, one after the other, he landed four good fish, while I was as fishless as he had been before. Although I was swift to follow his example and bring my bait closer in, the fish had by that time gone. . . .

The beach at night is full of sound, noisy even. Against the roaring of the sea there is the intimate sound of the wet sand beneath thigh boots, and at intervals the hysterical piping of flocks of oyster-catchers that seem to become more active at night, though this is no more than a casual impression of mine. There is sometimes a rustling of life near the high tide mark, more distinct and loud than the millions of tiny sand-hoppers could make, though a flash of torchlight shows every strand of weed and twig and driftwood covered with them so that the outline of each is blurred and shifting with life. The noise in the dry wood is made by the shore rats that live in the rabbit burrows left uninhabited after myxamatosis. They are great fish stealers, and now the fishermen are careful to stow away the bass they have caught after losing many. Sometimes, when I reach the beach at last light I disturb a fox beach-combing, and he too is a fish thief. . . .

As the sun rose, the waves looked like common water, not pregnant in any way with life. The light made my eyelids feel gritty and my feet dragged in the sand as I walked across to where John was fishing, as unsuccessfully as we had been. We had thought to fish with a float from the rocks when the tide went back, and so we did, but it was a mechanical business. It would have been sheer altriusm on the part of any bass to allow himself to be hooked under those conditions. When I looked round, Terrence was lying asleep on the hard rock, his shoulder and arm obliviously in a tide pool. Now was the time to go.

The walk back and the cliff-climb was leaden toil, for the sun was hot and the coarse bents made traps for our boots unless we lifted them high. The eventual feel of the hard road under them was luxurious. After that there was the waiting for my wife who had promised to drive out for us. We dozed in the long warm grass at the roadside hearing the surf and the gull noises, and everywhere around us the ecstatic singing of larks.

We were not there for much more than half an hour, but in that time I had as intense an experience of the kind of *catharsis*, of being completely drained and recreated, that arduous and exhausting sea-fishing expeditions sometimes bring. 'Rest after toil, port after stormy seas', is an over-simplification. There is more than the simple satisfaction of rest. There is a calm and conscious happiness which comes from a feeling of achievement, even though the achievement is small as it was on that day. To some degree it is a feeling of mastery. There were only seven fish between the three of us, but we had taken them from a sea that yields nothing easily, sending out long tenuous probes of nylon into the alien surf with skill and knowledge. It is by no means an inevitable reaction; at times there is nothing but fatigue and flatness of spirit; most commonly there is a feeling of ordinary satisfied pleasure.

CLIVE GAMMON, *A Tide of Fish*, 1962

Chasing Dace in Edwardian Suburbia

The angler might travel very much farther and fare very much worse. That is my thought every time I visit Isleworth fly-rod in hand, and it is strange if September or October does not find me there at least once in each year. I have made the expedition pretty often now, but the charm of it never fails; it is like nothing that I know in the way of fishing near London. Nowhere else can one feel that one is literally cheating Fate out of a few happy hours. When one goes farther afield, to the Colne, perhaps, at West Drayton, Uxbridge, or Rickmansworth, there is the sense of an undertaking about it; one is earning the right to enjoyment by dint of railway travelling, by having made 'arrangements', by being burdened with a landing-net and possibly lobworms – one is definitely out for the day. But Isleworth is a simple, unpremeditated sort of matter. At luncheon-time one has a sudden conviction that too much work is telling on one's health, and that an afternoon off is the right medicine. A glance at the paper tells one that the tide was high at London Bridge at half-past nine; a simple calculation proves that, since it is an hour later at Richmond, the Isleworth shallows will begin to be fishable at about two.

A light ten-foot rod, a reel, fly-box, and basket take no long time to collect; the rubber knee-boots stand ready in their corner. One is equipped and away almost as soon as the idea has been formed.

It matters little that the train stops at all stations, and that the carriages are primitive almost to archaism. *En route* for Richmond these things are just and proper. One likes to see people getting in and out full of business. Even if one does not quite understand why anyone living in Gunnersbury should apparently be in such a hurry, so impatient to get to Kew Gardens and urgent affairs, this does not mar the sense of personal emancipation; rather it enhances it by contrast.

One could get out at Kew Gardens oneself, by the way, walk down to the towpath, and fish up to Isleworth, and I have done this once or twice. But I prefer on the whole to go on to Richmond now and walk downstream. Richmond has made efforts of late to get into line with the times, but mercifully its fascination will not easily be destroyed. Modernity mellows there by the side of age better than in almost any place I know. As a matter of fact, one sees little of the town, for almost opposite the station yard is a gate leading to the old deer park. It is about ten minutes' walk across the park to the towpath, which one strikes just above the lock, and yet ten minutes more to the church ferry at the bottom of Isleworth eyot. Above the lock there are always anglers, but I have never yet seen one of them actually catch anything at the time of my passing. From below it one can see the weir, the only one on the Thames which has not moved in me the desire of trout. At high water, however, it looks if it ought to hold one or two, and there certainly are trout in the reach, though systematic trout-fishing does not seem to go on there. I remember once seeing a big trout feed at the head of the eyot, but whether he is still in existence I know not. Almost any day at low water, however, below the eyot there are alarms and excursions to be seen among the dace, which argue fish of prey of considerable size, trout probably. Occasionally, too, a trout is caught by a dace-fisher, but it is usually a small one.

Arrived at the ferry, it is well to cross over and fish on the other side, and the knowledgeable make their way down for a third of a mile or perhaps rather more to the point where the river is shallowest, just above a slight but recognizable bend in the stream. Here, they say, are the biggest dace, the six-ounce fish, which, when caught, are to be found at the top in each man's basket, like half-pound trout in Devonshire. But I should say that there is a fair sprinkling of these big dace all the way down, the difficulty being to catch them. Some men hold by big flies, coachmen, black gnats, yellow duns, etc., on No. 1 or even No. 2 hooks being considered about right, and more than once I have been tempted to the same opinion. Lately, however, the big fly has not served me well. On my last visit nothing but a black spider on a tiny hook would do any good. That afternoon also upset another theory, or, rather, taught me something new. My belief had been that you could catch the Isleworth dace in two ways – one with the dry or semi-dry fly, in which case the fish usually took it on the drop or half volley, as some authority puts it, or wet and drawn along more or less rapidly under water. For a while they confirmed me in this belief, and I caught several with the dry fly, while I missed a good many in the other way.

Then they ceased to come up to it at all, either wet or dry, until I accidentally got a rise in recovering the fly as it floated. This led to experiments, and I found that, by letting the fly fall dry and then dragging it for a few inches along the surface, I got plenty of rises, and pretty bold ones too. The fish came at it before it had gone six inches or not at all, and for an hour I had quite a brisk bit of sport, so much so that on reaching the ferry I did not hesitate to estimate the number of fish kept as three dozen. I was really surprised, on counting tails afterwards, to find that there were only a dozen and a half. It had seemed to me that for a time I was catching them as fast as I could. Three dozen would be a very fair basket for a good day, though takes of eight or ten dozen are made once in a way. Six inches is the size limit, and the majority of fish caught are about seven. If your three dozen average three ounces apiece, you have done very well indeed, and if you have three or four six-ounce fish you may be proud. There are plenty of these big ones in the water, but they are difficult to tempt.

It is worth while catching a dish of these little dace, if only for the pleasure of looking at them afterwards. They make a brave silvery show when laid side by side, and though individually at time of capture they have not the looks of brook trout, collectively in the evening they have the advantage. Brook trout lose their gold, but dace preserve their silver. One good angler informed me (rather apologetically), that he proposed to have his catch to breakfast. No apology was needed, for, bones admitted and extracted, dace are good meat – as good as many trout.

But dace are not the whole of Isleworth fishing. There is the daily wonder of the great river shrinking away so that a man may go dry-foot (or practically so) along its gravel bed, to see only a clear, shallow stream where a few hours back was a deep, turbid flood; there is the awful pleasure of imagining what would happen if one were caught suddenly by the turn of the tide, for one is so low down in the world that it seems wellnigh impossible to climb up that steep bank through the mud to the grounds of Zion House;

there is the wonderful solitude almost within sound of London – a small human figure or so up at the ferry, perhaps, and about the brown-sailed barges at the distant quay, but for the rest no sign of life except a gull or two wheeling round, some rooks exploring the naked river-bed, and the dace dimpling the surface of the quiet stream.

Then, when the tide has turned (and may you be not too far from the ferry when that happens!), there is a late tea at the London Apprentice, the quaint old inn near the church. The view from its billiard-room window up stream and down is alone worth the journey. After it there is the return in the ferry-boat, with a long backward look at the riverside street and the old church beneath their canopy of crimson sky; the meditative walk back along the towpath under the great trees, almost each one sheltering its couple of shy lovers who are making believe that the world is as they would have it be; the crossing of the old green, with its circle of fair dwellings; and lastly, the extraordinary blaze of light as one gets to the corner of the green and looks up towards the town. This is a fitting end to a day of impressions that one does not easily forget.

H.T. SHERINGHAM, *An Open Creel*, 1910

The Harbingers of the Fishing Season

Every angler knows that his feet are never put to the ground with such alacrity and right good-will, as when tramping to the river – rod in hand – full of hope and expectation, on a fine April morning. Serenely happy, he then proclaims a universal amnesty to every created being (except an opposition angler), and feeling internally at peace with himself, the world, and all mankind, every object that meets his view seems to wear the same sunny smile that gilds his own happy reflections. I have often beguiled the dreary days of winter, when spotless snows formed nature's universal winding-sheet, by longing for the appearance of the yellow catkins of the sallow, the buds of the woodbine, the maiden notes of the thrush, borne by the breeze from the top of some tall pine, or the hoarse croack of the frog. For well I know them to be sure harbingers of the time when the speckled trout, recovered from his winter's torpor, would again breast the sparkling streams, and recall me from the closed room and sweltering hearth, to gather bodily health and vigour from the pure breath of the mountains.

A.S. MOFFAT, *The Secrets of Angling*, 1865

The Oldest Fishing Book on the Joys of Angling

All other manner of fishing is also laborious and grievous, often making folks full wet and cold which many times hath been seen cause of great infirmities. But the angler may have no cold nor no disease nor anger, but if he be causer himself, for he may not lese at the most but a line or an hook of which he may have store [in] plenty of his own making as this simple treatise shall teach him. So then his loss is not grievous, and other griefs may he not have, saving but if any fish break away after that he is taken on the hook, or else that he catch nought which be not grievous. For if he fail of one he may not fail of another if he doeth as this treatise teacheth, but if there be nought in the water. And yet at the least he hath his wholesome walk and merry at his ease, a sweet air of the sweet savour of the mead flowers that maketh him hungry. He heareth the melodious harmony of fowls; he seeth the young swans, herons, ducks, coots and many other fowls with their broods, which me-seemeth better than all the noise of hounds, the blasts of horns and the scry of fowls that hunters, falconers and fowlers can make. And if the angler take fish, surely then is there no man merrier than he is in his spirit. Also whoso will use the game of angling he must rise early which thing is profitable to man in this wise: that is to wite, most to the heele of his soul.

from the *Treatyse on Fishing with an Angle*, 1496

The Essential Bait

I early learned that from almost any stream in a trout country the true angler could take trout, and that the great secret was this, that whatever bait you used, worm, grasshopper, grub, or fly, there was one thing you must always put upon your hook, namely, your heart; when you bait your hook with your heart the fish always bite; they will jump clean from the water after it; they will dispute with each other over it; it is a morsel they love above everything else. With such bait I have seen the born angler (my grandfather was one) take a noble string of trout from the most unpromising waters, and on the most unpromising day. He used his hook so coyly and tenderly, he approached the fish with such address and insinuation, he divined the exact spot where they lay; if they were not eager he humored them and seemed to steal by them; if they were playful and coquettish he would suit his mood to theirs; if they were frank and sincere he met them half way; he was so patient and considerate, so entirely devoted to pleasing the critical trout, and so successful in his efforts – surely his heart was upon his hook, and it was a tender, unctuous heart, too, as that of every angler is. How nicely he would measure the distance, how dexterously he would avoid an overhanging limb or bush and drop the line in exactly the right spot: of course there was a pulse of feeling and sympathy to the extremity of that line. If your heart is a stone, however, or an empty husk, there is no use to put it upon your hook; it will not tempt the fish; the bait must be quick and fresh. Indeed, a certain quality of youth is indispensable to the successful angler, a certain unworldliness and readiness to invest yourself in an enterprise that don't pay in the current coin. Not only is the angler, like the poet, born and not made, as Walton says, but there is a deal of the poet in him, and he is to be judged no more harshly; he is the victim of his genius; those wild streams, how they haunt him; he will play truant to dull care, and flee to them; their waters impart somewhat of their own perpetual youth to him. My grandfather when he was eighty years old would take down his pole as eagerly as any boy, and step off with wonderful elasticity toward the beloved streams; it used to try my young legs a good deal to follow him, especially on the return trip. And no poet was ever more innocent of worldly success or ambition. For, to paraphrase Tennyson, –

'Lusty trout to him were scrip and share,
And babbling waters more than cent for cent.'

He laid up treasures, but they were not in this world. In fact, though the kindest of husbands, I fear he was not what the country people call a 'good provider,' except in providing trout in their season, though it is doubtful if there was always fat in the house to fry them in. But he could tell you they were worse off than that at Valley Forge, and that trout, or any other fish, were good roasted in the ashes under the coals. He had the Walton requisite of loving quietness and contemplation, and was devout withal. Indeed in many ways he was akin to those Galilee fishermen who were called to be fishers of men. How he read the Book and pored over it, even at times I suspect nodding over it, and laying it down only to take up his rod, over which, unless the trout were very dilatory and the journey very fatiguing, he never nodded.

JOHN BURROUGHS, *Locusts and Wild Honey*, 1879

An Old Border Fisherman Remembers

These are the waters with which our boyhood was mainly engaged; it is a pleasure to name and number them. Memory, that has lost so much and would gladly lose so much more, brings vividly back the golden summer evenings by Tweedside, when the trout began to plash in the stillness — brings back the long, lounging, solitary days beneath the woods of Ashiesteil — days so lonely that they sometimes, in the end, begat a superstitious eeriness. One seemed forsaken in an enchanted world; one might see the two white fairy deer flit by, bringing to us, as to Thomas Rhymer, the tidings that we must back to Fairyland. Other waters we knew well, and loved: the little salmon-stream in the west that doubles through the loch, and runs a mile or twain beneath its alders, past its old Celtic battle-field, beneath the ruined shell of its feudal tower, to the sea. Many a happy day we had there, on loch or stream, with the big sea-trout which have somehow changed their tastes, and today take quite different flies from the green body and the red body that led them to the landing-net long ago. Dear are the twin Alines, but dearer is Tweed, and Ettrick, where our ancestor was drowned in a flood, and his white horse was found, next day, feeding near his dead body, on a little grassy island. There is a great pleasure in trying new methods, in labouring after the delicate art of the dry fly-fisher in the clear Hampshire streams, where the glassy tide flows over the waving tresses of crow's-foot below the poplar shade. But nothing can be so good as what is old, and, as far as angling goes, is practically ruined, the alternate pool and stream of the Border waters, where

> The triple pride
> Of Eildon looks over Strathclyde,

and the salmon cast murmurs hard by the Wizard's grave. They are all gone now, the old allies and tutors in the angler's art – the kind gardener who baited our hooks; the good Scotch judge who gave us our first collection of flies; the friend who took us with him on his salmon-fishing expedition, and made men of us with real rods, and 'pirns' of ancient make. The companions of those times are scattered, and live under strange stars and in converse seasons, by troutless waters. It is no longer the height of pleasure to be half-drowned in Tweed, or lost on the hills with no luncheon in the basket. But, except for scarcity of fish, the scene is very little altered, and one is a boy again, in heart, beneath the elms of Yair, or by the Gullets at Ashiesteil. However bad the sport, it keeps you young, or makes you young again, and you need not follow Ponce de Léon to the western wilderness, when, in any river you knew of yore, you can find the Fountain of Youth.

ANDREW LANG, Angling Sketches, 1891

A Pair of Otters at Work

I had sat in the oak for about half an hour, with my eyes fixed on the stream, and my back against the elastic branch by which I was supported, and rocked into a sort of dreamy repose, when I was roused by a flash in the upper pool, a ripple on its surface, and then a running swirl, and something that leaped, and plunged, and disappeared. . . .

Presently I saw two dark objects bobbing like ducks down the rapid between the two pools, but immediately as they came near distinguished the round, staring, goggle-eyed heads of two Otters, floating one after the other, their legs spread out like Flying Squirrels, and steering with their tails, the tips of which showed above the water like the rudder of an Elbe 'scuite'. Down they came as flat as floating skins upon the water, but their round, short heads and black eyes constantly in motion, examining with eager vigilance every neuk and rock which they passed. I looked down into the pool below me – it was as clear as amber – and behind a large boulder of granite in about eight feet of water I saw three salmon – a large one lying just at the back of the stone and two smaller holding against the stream in the same line. They were sluggish and sleepy in the sunshine, without any motion except the gentle sculling of their tails.

The Otters were steering down the pool, bobbing and flirting the water with their snouts, and now and then ducking their heads till they came over the stone. In an instant, like a flash of light, the fish were gone, and where the Otters had just floated there was nothing but two undulating rings upon the glossy surface. In the next instant there was a rush and swirl in the deep, under the rock on the west side, and a long shooting line going down to the rapid, like the ridge which appears above the back fin of a fish in motion. Near the tail of the pool there was another rush and turn, and two long lines of bubbles showed that the Otters were returning. Immediately afterwards the large salmon came out of the water with a spring of more than two yards, and just as he returned the Otter struck him behind the gills and they disappeared together, leaving the star of bright scales upon the surface. The skill with which they pursued their game was like that of well-trained greyhounds in a course. Whenever they came to the throat of the pool they pressed the fish hard to make him double into the clear water, and one was always vigilant to make him rise or turn, the increased effort of which exhausted his strength. With equal sagacity they worked him at the tail of the pool to prevent him descending the rapid. With this race the fish began to tire, and the Otters continued to press him, until at length, one of them having fixed him by the shoulder-fin, he was dragged up the bank, apparently quite dead.

JOHN STUART, *Lays of the Deer Forest*, 1869

Tarpon Fishing in Belize

The ideal day for flat fishing is cloudless, calm and roasting hot. The guide poles the skiff along the flats in a predatory silence, and you stand on the bow platform, with line stripped out, sweating through the sunblock lotion, ready to cast. Tarpon fishing is stalking. You must see the fish and cast to it. Hence its peculiar excitement, which far exceeds trout or even salmon fishing. 'Look, look, out there, about 30 meters, in the white spot, a big one, he's coming, ooh, thrreee of them!' You peer and scan and peer again, and see nothing. Then you do: a dark gray bar under the green ripples, ghosting along.

What the guide expects you to do is shoot the line out 20 m or 22 m, drop the fly (a vulgar tuft of feathers and Mylar) some $1\frac{1}{2}$ m in front of the tarpon's snoot and start stripping it in. The fish will then charge the fly, you will strike, and it's showtime! So much for utopia.

This being the real world, one of several things will happen. Flustered by the sight of the fish, which is so much larger than anything you imagined catching on a fly before, you bungle your cast and land the line in a tangled hurrah's nest far short of the fish, which glides away. Or you drop the fly on its nose, so that it spooks and heads for Cozumel. Or you get it right, and the fish takes off like a drag racer, at which point you find you were standing on a loop of the fly line, and it is knotted around your ankle.

But, at last, when you have run out of spare leaders and foul language and are cooked by the sun, you hook one. The sight is amazing. The fish looks, a friend of mine said after striking his first one, like a silver man rising straight out of the water: an apparition.

Now your troubles have only started. Tarpon are inordinately strong. To subdue a big one on a one-hand, 10-weight fly rod takes an hour and a half and teaches you what a sore arm can be. It is like cutting mahogany, but with the additional likelihood that the tree will escape. The tarpon has a mouth like a cinder block, in which the hook seldom holds: generally, only one fish is brought to boat for every 10 that are hooked.

While other anglers lie about the size of their fish, tarponers lie about the number of minutes they had it on before it threw the hook. The fish makes long reel-burning runs, and jumps repeatedly, a thick column of mercury twisting in the spray. It lands with a smacking splash that can be heard a kilometer away. 'Bow to the fish!' cries the guide, wanting you to drop your rod tip. Bow? You feel like prostrating yourself. And then it is gone. In five days I saw perhaps 150 fish, hooked four and boated one – 11 kg, a mere minnow.

No matter. The 40-kilo jumpers will still be there next year.

ROBERT HUGHES, 'Blissing Out in Balmy Belize', in *Time*, 22 April 1991

His Brother's Last Day on the River

Father slowly rose, found a good-sized rock and held it behind his back. Paul landed the fish, and waded out again for number twenty and his limit. Just as he was making the first cast, Father threw the rock. He was old enough so that he threw awkwardly and afterward had to rub his shoulder, but the rock landed in the river about where Paul's fly landed and at about the same time, so you can see where my brother learned to throw rocks into his partner's fishing water when he couldn't bear to see his partner catch any more fish.

Paul was startled for only a moment. Then he spotted Father on the bank rubbing his shoulder, and Paul laughed, shook his fist at him, backed to shore and went downstream until he was out of rock range. From there he waded into the water but now he was far enough away so we couldn't see his line or loops. He was a man with a wand in a river, and whatever happened we had to guess from what the man and the wand and the river did.

As he waded out, his big right arm swung back and forth. Each circle of his arm inflated his chest. Each circle was faster and higher and longer until his arm became defiant and his chest breasted the sky. On shore we were sure, although we could see no line, that the air above him was singing with loops of line that never touched the water but got bigger and bigger each time they passed and sang. And we knew what was in his mind from the lengthening defiance of his arm. He was not going to let his fly touch any water close to shore where the small and middle-sized fish were. We knew from his arm and chest that all parts of him were saying, 'No small one for the last one.' Everything was going into one big cast for one last big fish.

From our angle high on the bank, my father and I could see where in the distance the wand was going to let the fly first touch water. In the middle of the river was a rock iceberg, just its tip exposed above water and underneath it a rock house. It met all the residential requirements for big fish – powerful water carrying food to the front and back doors, and rest and shade behind them.

My father said, 'There has to be a big one out there.'

I said, 'A little one couldn't live out there.'

My father said, 'The big one wouldn't let it.'

My father could tell by the width of Paul's chest that he was going to let the next loop sail. It couldn't get any wider. 'I wanted to fish out there,' he said, 'but I couldn't cast that far.'

Paul's body pivoted as if he were going to drive a golf ball three hundred yards, and his arm went high into the great arc and the tip of his wand bent like a spring, and then everything sprang and sang.

Suddenly, there was an end of action. The man was immobile. There was no bend, no power in the wand. It pointed at ten o'clock and ten o'clock pointed at the rock. For a moment the man looked like a teacher with a pointer illustrating something about a rock to a rock. Only water moved. Somewhere above the top of the rock house a fly was swept in water so powerful only a big fish could be there to see it.

Then the universe stepped on its third rail. The wand jumped convulsively as it made contact with the magic current of the world. The wand tried to jump out of the man's right hand. His left hand seemed to be frantically waving goodbye to a fish, but actually was trying to throw enough line into the rod to reduce the voltage and ease the shock of what had struck.

Everything seemed electrically charged but electrically unconnected. Electrical sparks appeared here and there on the river. A fish jumped so far downstream that it seemed outside the man's electrical field, but, when the fish had jumped, the man had leaned back on the rod and it was then that the fish had toppled back into the water not guided in its reentry by itself. The connections between the convulsions and the sparks became clearer by repetition. When the man leaned back on the wand and the fish reentered the water not altogether under its own power, the wand recharged with convulsions, the man's hand waved frantically at another departure, and much farther below a fish jumped again. Because of the connections, it became the same fish.

The fish made three such long runs before another act in the performance began. Although the act involved a big man and a big fish, it looked more like children playing. The man's left hand sneakily began recapturing line, and then, as if caught in the act, threw it all back into the rod as the fish got wise and made still another run.

'He'll get him,' I assured my father.

'Beyond doubt,' my father said. The line going out became shorter than what the left hand took in.

When Paul peered into the water behind him, we knew he was going to start working the fish to shore and didn't want to back into a hole or rock. We could tell he had worked the fish into shallow water because he held the rod higher and higher to keep the fish from bumping into anything on the bottom. Just when we thought the performance was over, the wand convulsed and the man thrashed through the water after some unseen power departing for the deep.

'The son of a bitch still has fight in him,' I thought I said to myself, but unmistakably I said it out loud, and was embarrassed for having said it out loud in front of my father. He said nothing.

Two or three more times Paul worked him close to shore, only to have him swirl and return to the deep, but even at that distance my father and I could feel the ebbing of the underwater power. The rod went high in the air, and the man moved backwards swiftly but evenly, motions which when translated into events meant the fish had tried to rest for a moment on top of the water and the man had quickly raised the rod high and skidded him to shore before the fish thought of getting under water again. He skidded him across the rocks clear back to a sandbar before the shocked fish gasped and discovered he could not live in oxygen. In belated despair, he rose in the sand and consumed the rest of momentary life dancing the Dance of Death on his tail.

The man put the wand down, got on his hands and knees in the sand, and, like an animal, circled another animal and waited. Then the shoulder shot straight out, and my brother stood up, faced us, and, with uplifted arm proclaimed himself the victor. Something giant dangled from his fist. Had Romans been watching they would have thought that what was dangling had a helmet on it.

'That's his limit,' I said to my father.

'He is beautiful,' my father said, although my brother had just finished catching his limit in the hole my father had already fished.

This was the last fish we were ever to see Paul catch. My father and I talked about this moment several times later, and whatever our other feelings, we always felt it fitting that, when we saw him catch his last fish, we never saw the fish but only the artistry of the fisherman.

NORMAN MACLEAN, *A River Runs Through It,* 1976

Reflections in Winter

In a short while now, a very short while, those black bare trees will be a wall of impenetrable green, and somewhere out of sight the turtle doves will be crooning. The slow sure wheel of the seasons is such a comforting thing, so methodical, almost mechanical, but one never senses this. Each spring is a new spring and the leaves seem to be unfolding for the first time from twigs which have always been naked and black.

Each season a large family is born and grows to maturity in my little wood and pond: insects, birds, fish, animals, and plants. The badgers will have young, the fox cubs will play round the dark cavern of the earth. At least twenty woodpigeons will be born, and more than half that number will fly and go out into the world. Twenty odd blackcaps will be hatched. Eight bullfinches will build and lay, but only eight or more of the young will leave the nest. These shy and lovely rosebud finches suffer much from enemies who climb the thorns and rape the nest of eggs and young.

Thirty or more blackbirds, about the same number of thrushes, will hatch and fly safely. All these are only a tithe of the various creatures which find annual sanctuary by Thorney Pond. And yet I think, as I stand in the sun by the water side, how strange it is that all these warm, pulsing creatures are as yet out of the scheme of things, or rather, that they are impatiently awaiting life as the sleeping peacock butterfly awaits the sun.

I cannot compute the numbers of froglings which will eventually crawl laboriously away from Thorney Pond on the big Adventure, nor the millions or insects which will hatch and enjoy their brief hour.

Down in the mud at the bottom of the pond the big carp move and stir, revolving in their dull cold brains the magic of awakening summer.

Some are no doubt destined to feel the prick of a hook, and will fight a gallant battle, but the ponderous twenty-pounders (which I like to think are down there out of sight), they will no doubt have an uneventful summer. I wish them plenty of fat grubs and a good season for ground-bait – with all my heart I do.

But sun has gone at last, a wind stirs among the oak tops, ruffling the skin of clear cold water. We are all of us waiting, waiting, and the sun and season is in no hurry. It is time to look over my rods, to look to my lines and reels. There is time yet to read a good book, to enjoy the warmth of friendship and a log fire.

We are all of us waiting, and I, being an angler, am used to waiting. The peacock butterfly, the tight-closed buds, the roots of the meadow grasses, all are awaiting God's good time. The chiffchaff, which I shall so surely hear, is at this moment no doubt hopping in an orange-grove in the sun of Spain, the gentle turtle doves are busy in an African jungle. But soon there will come to them uneasy restless thoughts, and perhaps – who knows? – into their diminutive craniums, so delicately wrought, will steal a vision of a little green wood, set in a pleasant meadow, a still dark pool, where fish lie basking, the very place where they themselves first entered into this lovely life, and where sometimes an idle man sits and fishes and gives thanks to God.

'B.B.', *Fisherman's Folly*, 1987

CHAPTER TWO

Fish

*F*ish are remarkably unsophisticated creatures to have captured the imagination of such a large proportion of *homo sapiens*. They do not, as a rule, speak. Dolphins apart, they cannot be trained to do tricks. They make remarkably undemonstrative pets. Which just goes to prove, say the sceptics, what a silly, futile and loathsome pursuit fishing is.

Yet there is something utterly enthralling about these cold-blooded creatures. It may have something to do with the fact that they cannot survive in our element nor we in theirs. It certainly has something to do with the lustre of their squamous beauty. Most of all, it has to do with fact that, for all their dull-witted remoteness, they remain unknowable. This is how D.H. Lawrence summed it up in his poem, 'Fish':

They are beyond me, are fishes.
I stand at the pale of my being
And look beyond and see
Fish, in the outerwards,
As one stands on a bank and looks in.

I have waited with a long rod
And suddenly pulled a gold – and greenish, lucent fish from below,
And had him fly like a halo round my head,
Lunging in the air on the line.

Unhooked his gorping, water-horny mouth,
And seen his horror-tilted eye,
His red-gold, water-precious, mirror-flat bright eye:
And felt him beat in my hand, with his mucous, leaping life-throb.

And my heart accused itself
Thinking: *I am not the measure of creation.*
This is beyond me, this fish.
His God stands outside my God.

For all that science can tell us about the life-cycles of creatures, it cannot explain the urge that drives a salmon thousands of miles across the oceans, to return again to the very stream in which it was spawned. It cannot explain why eels make a similar journey. What is behind the desperate determination that drives a salmon to thrash itself time after time into a waterfall until finally it makes it over the top, or the march of eels across fields to the river estuary? And if our ignorance is so profound about these more visible creatures, how much deeper is our benightedness about fish we never see?

It is because they exist beyond the frontiers of the comprehensible that we imagine the most extraordinary things about them. Pliny believed that a goby, or sea-gudgeon – a full couple of inches in length – could stop a trireme at full pelt, just by fastening itself on to the rudder. Tales of sea-monsters abound throughout folk literature and Loch Ness is not the only big landlocked lake to boast a real or imagined monster: in fact, the harder task is to find a great lake which doesn't have some primeval mystery.

The monster is the ultimate expression of our fascination with the unfathomableness of water. Olaus Magnus, medieval Bishop of Upsaala, writes of great square-headed sea-monsters off the coast of Norway and others which stand high in the sea, spouting enough water to drown a fleet. He writes of sailors landing on a fish so big they took it for an island, until they lit a fire on its back and the creature grumpily slid down into the depths, leaving them to drown.

It is small wonder, then, that mermaids and mermen became a staple of mythology, from ancient Greece to Babylon: the human who could thrive in this mysterious and dangerous element was a wonder. Hindu mythology depicts Vishnu in one of his incarnations emerging from the mouth of a fish. Apparently serious historians record that in 1404 a mermaid was caught in a storm at Edam, Holland. In a demonstration of the superiority of Western civilization, she was said to have converted to Christianity and died a good Catholic. A century later, Rondelet describes a sea-monster captured off Norway which had the face of a monk. At least this fish didn't suffer the indignity of the one taken near Orforde in Suffolk in 1187, which bore such a close resemblance to a man that it was kept for six months in the local castle and taken to church every Sunday, where, unfortunately, 'he showed no signs of adoration'.

Laugh as we may at medieval credulity, such stories do illuminate man's enduring fascination with this enigmatic element. Science has not yet answered all the mysteries and probably never will.

Chau of Windermere.

Gwyniad, or Schelly of Hawes Water.

Charr of Hawes Water.

– Sir Humphry Davy, Bart., *Salmonia; or Days of Fly Fishing*, 1851

Fun With Lampreys

In northern Gaul all lampreys have seven spots on their right jaw arranged like the constellation of the Great Bear; these spots have a golden colour while the fish is still alive, but disappear when it dies. Vedius Pollio, a knight of Rome and member of the Council under the late Emperor Augustus, used this creature as a means of proving his cruelty: he threw condemned slaves into tanks of lampreys, not because land-beasts were unable to carry out the punishment, but because only with the lamprey could he watch a man being completely torn to pieces as it happened.

PLINY THE ELDER (23-79 AD), *Natural History*, translated by
John Healy

Pliny's Belief in the Extraordinary Power of a Two-Inch Sea-Gudgeon

Yet even though all these forces may drive in the same direction, they are checked by a single goby, a very small creature. Gales may blow and storms rage but this fish controls their fury, restrains their tremendous force, and compels ships to stop – a thing unachievable either by hawsers or even by dropped anchors, which cannot be drawn back because of their weight. The goby holds off their attacks and tames the fury of the universe with no effort or resistance of its own other than suction. This diminutive fish is strong enough – against all those forces – to prevent vessels from moving. War fleets carry towers on their decks so that men may fight as if from city walls even when at sea. How pathetic men are, when one considers that those rams, equipped with bronze and iron for striking, can be held fast by a little fish some 2 inches long. It is said that at the Battle of Actium this fish brought Antony's flagship to a halt when he was touring his fleet to encourage his men – until, that is, he changed his ship for another. For this reason Octavian's fleet straight away made a more concerted attack. Within living memory a goby stopped the Emperor Gaius' ship on his voyage back from Astura to Antium.

In the event this little fish proved to be an omen, for very soon after Gaius' return to Rome he was struck down by his own men. His delay occasioned surprise only for a little while, since the cause was immediately discovered. As his quinquereme alone of all the ships in the fleet was not making any headway, men immediately dived overboard and swam round the ship to ascertain the cause. They found a goby attached to the rudder and showed it to Gaius who was furious that such a thing had held him back and prevented 400 rowers from obeying his orders.

Accounts agree that what particularly annoyed him was that the fish had stopped him by attaching itself to the outside of the ship, yet did not have the same power when brought inside. Those who saw the goby then, or subsequently, say that it looked like a large slug.

PLINY THE ELDER (23–79 AD), *Natural History*

The Steelhead

The rest of the world's trout may be taken in summer, to the sound of birds and the pleasant hum of insects, but the steelhead – the big, sea-going rainbow of the Northwest coasts – is winter's child. To know him you must gird as for war and wade the rivers when they are bitter cold – in sleet-filled gloom, or in freezing blue weather when the leafless alders gleam in pale sunlight along the streams, and ice forms in the guides of your rod. To know the steelhead, you should hurt with cold and nurse a little fear of the numbing current which pushes against your waders; it can pull you down and make you gasp and drown you, as steelhead streams methodically drown a few of your fellow fishermen with every passing year.

The steelhead may be pursued in fairer weather, and in easier ways. He runs as far south as the Sacramento River in California. Some of his number run in the early spring, and, in such rivers as the Snake and Oregon's famed Rogue, he runs in the summer, too. But he is a northern fish; when he leaves the sea to spawn, he comes mostly to the rivers of Oregon, Washington, British Columbia, and Alaska, and he migrates chiefly during December, January, and

February. The fisherman who has not met him when it is cold has not been properly introduced. Winter sets the stage for him and makes him unique.

There is ominous drama in the very look of a chill, green river on a dark and stormy afternoon, and a man fighting cold and snow to wade it is being properly conditioned for his moment of revelation. For the steelhead is a fish which makes an impact upon the adrenalin-producing glands rather than the intellect. He is always big (six to thirty pounds), and he burns with savage energy from the limitless feed of the ocean he has left behind. He can hurtle into the air a split second after he is hooked, and flash hugely out in the murk, like the sword Excalibur thrust up from the depths – at once a gleaming prize and a symbol of battle. At that sight, and at the first astounding wrench of the rod, the fisherman is rewarded for his hardihood: he is suddenly warm and reckless, and simultaneously possessed of mindless desperation and rocketing hope.

Men in the grip of this atavistic elation sometimes find themselves doing extraordinary things. A steelhead out in moving water at the end of a six-pound test leader and a nine-pound monofilament line transmits a horrifying sense of power to the rod. Many an otherwise conservative fellow has found himself heedlessly following his fish downstream – laboring wildly along a gravel bar while up to the waist in icy water, body half buoyant, weightless feet feeling desperately for bottom, bucking rod held high and numbed hands working the reel with reverence to get back precious line.

Men have tripped, gone down with a splash, and come up with hardly a change of expression to carry on the struggle; they have run along river banks, hurdling rocks and thrashing out into the water around log jams, in their effort to turn, control, and finally dominate their trout. A lot of them have lost. A few have literally hurled their rods into the stream at the awful second when the line went irrevocably slack. But of course a lot of men – and women, too – have won battles with a big fish in bad water, have guessed when it was time to say, 'Now it's you or me,' have increased the pressure, controlled the startling submarine disturbance at the end of the line, have endured the trout's last jump and its surface splashing, and have finally reached it – silver, iridescent, and enormous – on shelving gravel or frozen sand and have reached for its gills like a prospector bending at last over the mother lode. And afterwards have relaxed, before an evening fire, in a glow of weariness and euphoria.

PAUL O'NEIL, *Sports Illustrated*, 1957

Night Arrival of Seatrout

Honeysuckle hanging her fangs.
Foxglove rearing her open belly.
Dogrose touching the membrane.

Through the dew's mist, the oak's mass
Comes plunging, tossing dark antlers.

Then a shattering
Of the river's hole, where something leaps out –

An upside-down, buried heaven
Snarls, moon-mouthed, and shivers.

Summer dripping stars, biting at the nape.
Lobworms coupling in saliva.
Earth singing under her breath.

And out in the hard corn a horned god
Running and leaping
With a bat in his drum.

TED HUGHES, 'The River', 1983

Summoned by Bells

Mr Bradley, a great observer of fish, relates an instance of carp tameness: – 'At Rotterdam, in a garden belonging to M. Eden, I had the pleasure,' he says, 'of seeing some carp fed, which were kept in a moat of considerable extent. The occasion of my seeing these creatures was chiefly to satisfy me that they were capable of hearing. The gentleman having filled his pocket with spinach seed, conducted me to the side of the moat. We remained quiet for some time, the better to convince me that the fish would not come till he called them. At length he called in his usual way and immediately the fish gathered from all parts of the moat in such numbers that there was hardly room for them to lie by one another.'

The same sort of thing may be noticed in the waters of some public gardens near Rotterdam.

In these ponds the carp are also in the habit of following visitors about, in expectation of food; and one immense fellow, with a side as broad as a flitch of bacon, and an appetite that seemed insatiable, actually pursued us for nearly a hundred yards along the side of the bank until our stock of bread being exhausted, we were fain to try experiments with some paper pellets, when he sailed off in magnificent disgust. The fish must have weighed at least 15 lbs.

It is not to be supposed, however, from these instances, that carp are the only fish which are capable of being tamed, or are sensible to the influence of external sounds. At Sir J. Bowyer's, near Uxbridge, Mr Bradley tells us, there is, or was, a pond full of tame pike, which could be called together at pleasure. Mr Salter was acquainted with a person who for several years kept, in a waterbutt, a perch, which came to the surface for its food whenever the owner tapped on the side of the butt. According to Ælian, the chad was lured to its destruction by the sound of castanets. Professor Renni states that in Germany this fish is still taken by nets hung with rows of little bells arranged so as to chime in harmony; and, without going back to the story of Amphion and the Dolphins, or the old Scottish harper, who, according to the ballad, 'harped a fish out of the salt water,' we may find hundreds of well-authenticated anecdotes pointing to the conclusion that fish have a very considerable perception of external sounds.

H. CHOLMONDELEY-PENNELL, *Fishing Gossip*, 1866

A Tame Trout

The following instance of longevity appeared, some years since, in the *Westmoreland Advertiser*: –

'Fifty years ago, Mr W. Hossop, of Bond Hall, near Broughton, in Furness, when a boy, placed a small fell-beck trout in a well, in the orchard belonging to his family, where it remained till last week, when it departed this life, not through any sickness or infirmity attendant on old age, but from want of its natural element, water, the severe drought having dried up the spring that supplied the well, a circumstance that has not happened for the last sixty years. His lips and gills were perfectly white; his head was formerly black, and of a large size. He regularly came, when summoned by his master, by the name of Ned, to feed from his hand on snails, worms, and bread. This remarkable fish has been visited, and considered a curiosity by the neighbouring country, for several years.'

T.C. HOFLAND, *The British Angler's Manual*, 1834

Jaws

The Shark is the most voracious and terrific fish of the ocean: its teeth are disposed in rows, some of which are moveable, and others fixed: it has generally five spiracles at the sides of the neck, of a semi-lunar shape: the body is oblong, rather cylindrical and rough, with tender prickles. These animals are never found in rivers and lakes; they inhabit the sea only, and carry terror and destruction wherever they appear.

There are no less than thirty-four species of the Shark; but the terrific kind, of which only we speak, is called by naturalists *Squalus carcharios*, or the White Shark. These sometimes attain the length of thirty feet, and weigh three or four thousand pounds: they occasionally emit a phosphoric light, which is visible by night. They produce their young alive, and several at a time; but every one enclosed in a transparent hornlike substance, lengthened at the extremity into a thread, which attaches to fixed substances, such as rocks or weeds. They are fierce and rapacious in the extreme; seizing whatever they find with the greatest avidity, and following in the wakes of ships for the sake of every thing that is thrown from them. When an unfortunate mariner slips from his hold on the rigging, into the sea, the Sharks are seen to tear him to pieces, with all the violence of competition; and, in the deep waters of warm latitudes, the sailors can never bathe without imminent danger: for many writers assert, that a full-sized Shark can swallow a man entire.

ATKINSON HOWITT, *Foreign Field Sports, Fisheries and Sporting Anecdotes*, 1814

A Shark Feeding Frenzy

One of the most nightmarish aspects of shark behaviour is the so-called feeding frenzy. It is known that blood and certain other substances attract sharks from great distances. They are known to be able to home in on blood and fish oil from a distance of at least a quarter of a mile. When a number of sharks close in, a pattern of behaviour may be trigged that can only be described as manic. They bite and tear at anything, including themselves and each other. Throw tin cans into the water and they will be gobbled up. Reports exist of sharks being ripped open by gaff hooks during a feeding frenzy and turning around to eat their own entrails. It is evident that nothing could survive such an onslaught. The lack of survivors from downed aircraft and sunken ships almost certainly results from behaviour of this kind in some instances. Sharks are known to be attracted by explosions in or on the water. No repellent is of use during these frenzied mass attacks.

The author had read of this mass-feeding pattern a number of times and set out to witness it firsthand. With three friends, he chartered the shark-fishing boat of Frank Mundus of Montauk, New York. Mundus has earned a worldwide reputation as a shark fisherman. The forty-five-foot *Cricket II* sailed from the tip of Long Island at 6.30 A.M. on Saturday, September 22, 1962. The plan was to drift with the current, periodically ladling chopped-up fish, or 'chum,' over the side. Drifting away and sinking at the same time, the chum would pave a neat path of fish oil from the sea bottom to the boat. The mate never had a chance to start the chumming. Within thirty seconds after the engine was cut, a ten-foot blue shark passed beneath the stern. A minute or so later it was followed by three or four others. Within ten minutes, there were at least twenty big blue sharks circling the boat. Before the group gave out from exhaustion, they took five sharks, on 50-pound test line, totaling nearly 1,300 pounds. Some fought for over an hour, while others were brought to gaff in a matter of a few minutes. As the sharks were brought in close enough to gaff and lasso, others closed in so rapidly that it was impossible to tell which shark was on the line and which were trying to eat it. As the diesel winch pulled the captured specimens out of the water, others grabbed hold and were pulled clear of the surface as they hung on and shook loose huge chunks of meat from their still-living hunting partners. Six of us aboard the boat leaned over the side and beat sharks on the head with gaff hooks, chum ladles, rifle butts, and anything else that could be used as a club. The author shot several through the head at a range of a foot and a half with 9-mm pistol as they tore at our hard-won prizes. One that was hit between the eyes went over backwards and started to sink with a few convulsive flicks of its tail. Before the water it splashed landed on the deck, two other sharks closed in on it. Frank Mundus leaned over and grabbed one by the tail. Infuriated, it struck out at another shark that brushed against it. Mundus stabbed one in the face, drawing blood and condemning it to be eaten alive. A shark that had been caught, gaffed and roped, grabbed another and started to tear out a chunk of meat while it was being dragged backwards around the boat to where the pulley and winch could lift it out of the water. This was an unusual experience where all of the sharks were large – mostly around ten feet long. It was easy to picture what would happened to anyone who fell overboard at such a time.

ROGER CARAS, *Dangerous to Man*, 1976

Mark Twain's Tale of How a Shark Made a Fortune

I have a tale to tell now which has not as yet been in print. In 1870 a young stranger arrived in Sydney, and set about finding something to do; but he knew no one and brought no recommendations, and the result was that he got no employment. He had aimed high, at first, but as time and his money wasted away, he grew less and less exacting, until at last he was willing to serve in the humblest capacities if so he might get bread and shelter. But luck was still against him; he could find no opening of any sort. Finally his money was all gone. He walked the streets all day, thinking; he walked them at night, thinking, thinking, and growing hungrier and hungrier. At dawn he found himself well away from the town and drifting aimlessly along the harbour shore. As he was passing by a nodding shark-fisher, the man looked up and said, 'Say, young fellow, take my line a spell and change my luck for me.'

'How do you know I won't make it worse?'

'Because you can't. It has been at its worst all night. If you can't change it, no harm's done; if you do change it, it's for the better, of course. Come.'

'All right, what will you give?'

'I'll give you the shark, if you catch one.'

'And I will eat it, bones and all. Give me the line.'

'Here you are. I will get away now for awhile, so that my luck won't spoil yours; for many and many a time I've noticed that if – there, pull in, pull in, man. You've got a bite! *I* knew how it would be. Why, I knew you for a born son of luck the minute I saw you. All right – he's landed.'

It was an unusually large shark – 'a full nineteen footer,' the fisherman said, as he laid the creature's stomach open with his knife.

'Now you rob him, young man, while I step to my hamper for a fresh bait. There's generally something in them worth going for. You've changed my luck, you see. But my goodness, I hope you haven't changed your own.'

'Oh, it wouldn't matter; don't worry about that. Get your bait, I'll rob him.'

When the fisherman got back, the young man had just finished washing his hands in the bay, and was starting away.

'What, you're not going?'

'Yes. Good-bye.'

'But what about your shark?'

'The shark? Why, what use is he to me?'

'What *use* is he? I like that. Don't you know that we can go and report it to Government and you'll get a clean solid eighty shillings bounty? Hard cash, you know. What do you think about it *now*?'

'Oh, well, you can collect it.'

'And *keep* it? Is that what you mean?'

'Yes.'

'Well, this is odd. You're one of those sort they call excentrics, I judge. The saying is you mustn't judge a man by his clothes, and I'm believing it now. Why yours are looking just ratty, don't you know; and yet you must be rich.'

'I am.'

The young man walked slowly back to the town, deeply musing as he went. He halted a moment in front of the best restaurant, then glanced at his clothes and passed on and got his breakfast at a 'stand-up.' There was a good deal of it, and cost five shillings. He tendered a sovereign, got his change, glanced at the silver, muttered to himself, 'There isn't enough to buy clothes with,' and went his way.

At half past nine the richest wool-broker in Sydney was sitting in his morning-room at home, settling his breakfast with the morning paper. A servant put his head in and said:

'There's a sundowner at the door wants to see you, sir.'

'What do you bring that kind of a message here for? Send him about his business.'

'He won't go, sir. I've tried.'

'He won't go? That's – why, that's unusual. He's one of two things, then; he's a remarkable person, or he's crazy. Is he crazy?'

'No, sir. He don't look it.'

'Then he's remarkable. What does he say he wants?'

'He won't tell, sir; only says it's very important.'

'And won't go. Does he *say* he won't go?'

'Says he'll stand there till he sees you, sir, if it's all day.'

'And yet isn't crazy. Show him up.'

The sundowner was shown in. The broker said to himself, 'No, he's not crazy; that is easy to see, so he must be the other thing.' Then aloud: 'Well, my good fellow, be quick about it; don't waste any words; what is it you want?'

'I want to borrow a hundred thousand pounds.'

'Scott! (It's a mistake; he *is* crazy. No – he *can't* be – not with that eye.) Why, you take my breath away. Come, who *are* you?'

'Nobody that you know.'

'What is your name?'

'Cecil Rhodes.'

'No, I don't remember hearing the name before. Now then – just for curiosity's sake – what has sent you to me on this extraordinary errand?'

'The intention to make a hundred thousand pounds for you and as much for myself within the next sixty days.'

'Well, well, well. It is the most extraordinary idea that I – sit *down* – you interest me and somehow you – well, you fascinate me; I think that that is about the word. And it isn't your proposition – no, that doesn't fascinate me; it's something else, I don't quite know what; something that's born in you and oozes out of you, I suppose. Now then – just for curiosity's sake again, nothing more – as I understand it, it is your desire to bor –'

'I said intention.'

'Pardon, so you did. I thought it was an unheedful use of the word – an unheedful valuing of its strength, you know.'

'I knew its strength.'

'Well, I must say – but look here, let me walk the floor a little; my mind is getting into a sort of a whirl, though *you* don't seem disturbed any. (Plainly this young fellow isn't crazy; but as to his being remarkable – well, really he amounts to that, and something over.) Now, then, I believe I am beyond the reach of further astonishment. Strike, and spare not. What is your scheme?'

'To buy the wool crop – deliverable in sixty days.'

'What, the *whole* of it?'

'The whole of it.'

'No, I was not quite out of the reach of surprises, after all. Why, how you talk! Do you know what our crop is going to foot up?'

'Two and a half million sterling – may be a little more.'

'Well, you've got your statistics right, anyway. Now, then, do you know what the margins would foot up, to buy it at sixty days?'

'The hundred thousand pounds I came here to get.'

'Right once more. Well, dear me, just to see what would happen, I wish you had the money. And if you had it, what would you do with it?'

'I shall make two hundred thousand pounds out of it in sixty days.'

'You mean, of course, that you *might* make it if –'

'I said "shall."'

'Yes, by George! you *did* say "shall." You are the most definite devil I ever saw in the matter of language. Dear, dear, dear – look here! Definite speech means clarity of mind. Upon my word, I believe you've got what you believe to be a rational *reason* for venturing into this house, an entire stranger, on this wild scheme of buying the wool crop of an entire colony on speculation. Bring it out – I am prepared – acclimatised, if I may use the word. *Why* would you buy the crop, and *why* would you make that sum out of it? That is to say, what makes you think you –'

'I don't think – I know.'

'Definite again. *How* do you know?'

'Because France has declared war against Germany, and wool has gone up fourteen per cent. in London, and is still rising.'

'Oh, indeed? *Now* then, I've *got* you! Such a thunderbolt as you have just let fly ought to have made me jump out of my chair, but it didn't stir me the least little bit, you see. And for a very simple reason: I have read the morning paper. You can look at it if you want to. The fastest ship in the service arrived at eleven o'clock last night, fifty days out from London. All her news is printed here. There are no war-clouds anywhere; and as for wool, why, it is the low-spiritedest commodity in the English market. It is your turn to jump now . . . Well, why don't you jump? Why do you sit there in that placid fashion, when –'

'Because I have later news.'

'Later news? Oh, come – later news than fifty days, brought steaming hot from London by the –'

'My news is only ten days old.'

'Oh, Mun*chausen*, hear the maniac talk! Where did you get it?'

'Got it out of a shark.'

'Oh, oh, oh, this is *too* much! Front! call the police – bring the gun – raise the town! All the asylums in Christendom have broken loose in the single person of –'

'Sit down! And collect yourself. Where is the use in getting excited? Am I excited? There is nothing to get excited *about*. When I make a statement which I cannot prove, it will be time enough for you to begin to offer hospitality to damaging fancies about me and my sanity.'

'Oh, a thousand, thousand pardons! I ought to be ashamed of myself, and I *am* ashamed of myself for thinking that a little bit of a circumstance like sending a shark to England to fetch back a market report –'

'What does your middle initial stand for, sir?'

'Andrew! What are you writing?'

'Wait a moment. Proof about the shark – and another matter. Only ten lines. There – now it is done. Sign it.'

'Many thanks – many. Let me see; it says – it says – oh, come, this is *interesting*! Why – why – look here! prove what you say here, and I'll put up the money, and double as much, if necessary, and divide the winnings with you, half and half. There now – I've signed; make your promise good if you can. Show me a copy of the London. "Times" only ten days old.'

'Here it is – and with it these buttons and a memorandum book that belonged to the man the shark swallowed. Swallowed him in the Thames, without a doubt; for you will notice that the last entry in the book is dated "London," and it is of the same date as the "Times" and says, "Per Consequentz der Kriegeserklärung reise ich heute nach Deutschland ab, auf dass ich mein Leben auf dem Altar meines Landes legen mag" – as clean native German as anybody can put upon paper, and means that in consequence of the declaration of war, this loyal soul is leaving for home *to-day*, to fight. And he did leave, too, but the shark had him before the day was done, poor fellow.'

'And a pity, too. But there are times for mourning, and we will attend to this case further on; other matters are pressing now. I will go down and set the machinery in motion in a quiet way and buy the crop. It will cheer the drooping spirits of the boys. In a transitory way – everything is transitory in this world. Sixty days hence, when they are called to deliver the goods, they will think they've been struck by lightning. But there is a time for mourning, and we will attend to that case along with the other one. Come along, I'll take you to my tailor. What did you say your name is?'

'Cecil Rhodes.'

'It is hard to remember. However, I think you will make it easier by and by, if you live. There are only three kinds of people –

commonplace men, remarkable men, and lunatics. I'll classify you with the remarkables, and take the chances.'

The deal went through, and secured to the young stranger the first fortune he ever pocketed.

MARK TWAIN, *More Tramps Abroad*, 1897

Small Boys' Breakfasts

Roach and Rudd are inedible because their myriad small bones defeat the most hardened ichthyophagist. Very small roach caught by very small boys may be boiled in a pie dish with vinegar, peppercorns, onion, etc., and served cold as a breakfast side dish, but only the small boy should be obliged to eat them.

MAJOR HUGH B.C. POLLARD, *The Sportsman's Cookery Book*, 1926

The Salmon's Life Story in a Single Sentence

As the salmon is a monarch and king in the freshes, so he is the ultimate result of the angler's conquest. This royal game (all the summer-time) has his residence in the rapid and forcible streams in rivers; but the sea is his sanctuary most months in the winter: So that a man may rationally conclude, without a parenthesis, that he is always to be found, though not always in season. Besides, the salmon is incident, as other fish are, to various accidents; more especially if we consider the female fish, who in the spring (as other females do) drops her eggs (but some call it *spawn*) which makes her infirm: and if it so happen that she lags behind her natural mate in the fall of the leaf, she is then prohibited the benefit of salt-water to bathe her fins, and carry off her slimy impurities, which is the natural cause of her kipperish infirmity, that alters her delicate proportion of body, and blots out the beautiful vermilian stain and sanguin tincture of blood, which vividly and transparently shines through her rubified gills; so that now she begins to look languid and pale, her fins they fag, and her scales by degrees lose their natural shining brightness; as also her regular and well-compos'd fabrick of body, looks thin, lean, and discoloured: and her head that grows big and disproportionable, as if distemper'd and invaded with the rickets; over whose chaps hangs a callous substance, not much unlike to a falcon's beak, which plainly denotes her out of season, and as plainly as any thing demonstrates her kippar.

RICHARD FRANCK, *Northern Memoirs*, 1658

Carp Explained

The carp grows sometimes to the length of a yard and a half, and a proportionate thickness. In 1739, a pretty large one was caught in the Thames, near Hampton Court, which weighed thirteen pounds. Willoughby affirms that the largest weigh twenty pounds. The colour of this fish, especially when full-grown, is yellow; the scales are large, the head short, and like that of a tench; the mouth is of a middle size; the lips flat, fleshy, and yellow. It is without teeth, but there is a triangular bone in the palate and two other bones in the throat, which serve for the same purpose. On the upper lip, near the corner of the mouth, are two yellow appendages, which may be called mustachios, from their situation. The fins are large; the tail is broad, a little forked, and of a reddish black. The lateral line is straight, and passes through the middle of each side.

It has no tongue, but in the room thereof nature has provided a fleshy palate, which being taken out of the mouth looks like a tongue, and some persons pretend to be positive that it is one.

Some imagine it is only the small carp that are the breeders, but this is a mistake. A gentleman in Cheshire cleansed his moat, and stored it with large carp, imagining, as the larger sort did not breed, they would feed well; but, in a very small time, the moat was all alive with carp spawn.

They spawn several times a year, but the principal are in May and August, in which months they are lean and insipid, and consequently out of season. The females drop their spawn as they swim along, and are generally followed by thirteen or fourteen males who impregnate it as it falls, yet a great deal of it perishes. They are said to live to a great age, and to spawn from two years old to thirty.

===

One thing observable in a carp is, that it lives the longest out the water of any other fish; and Mr Derham assures us, that in Holland they hang them up in cellars, or other cool places, in a small net, full of wet moss, with only their heads out, and feed them with white bread soaked in milk for many days.

RICHARD BROOKES, *The Art of Angling*, 1790

Alternatives to Cooking

A recent survey showed that roughly two-thirds of all fishermen never eat fish. This should surprise nobody. Fish is brain food. People who eat fish have large, well-developed brains. People with large, well-developed brains don't fish. It's that simple.

The question a fisherman faces, then, is how to get rid of the fish he has caught. There are several schools of thought on this problem.

The Pilgrim Fathers buried a dead fish in each hill of corn to make it grow. Unfortunately, few fishermen have access to cornfields. Most farmers would sooner have a cyclone.

Some fishermen try to palm off their catch on kindhearted friends and neighbors. Naturally, it doesn't take *those* folks long to learn that when a trout has been lugged around all day in a hot creek, it is poor competition for a pork chop.

Other methods of fish-disposal are (1) stuffing them in a corner mailbox when nobody is looking, (2) hiding them under potted palms, (3) checking them at the Union Depot and throwing away the check, (4) hurling them from fast-moving cars on lonely roads late at night, (5) mailing them to the Curator of the Museum of Natural History, requesting an identification of the species and giving a phoney name and return address, and (6) baiting walrus-traps with them.

None of these methods is satisfactory. (1) Is probably illegal, (2), (3), (4), and (5) are in lousy taste, and (6) brings up the problem of walrus-disposal. Walrus-disposal makes fish-disposal seem like child's play.

My friend Walt Dette throws back all the trout he catches in the Beaverkill, and keeps only chubs to feed to his seven Siamese cats.

===

This is dandy for people who have (a) sense enough to put back trout for future sport and who also have (b) seven Siamese cats. Few fisherman have both. Both, hell. *Either*.

ED ZERN, *To Hell With Fishing*, 1945

Herodotus Misunderstands Things

Fish that go in shoals are not often found in rivers, but, being bred in lakes, these are their habits: When the desire for procreation comes on them, they swim out in shoals to the sea. The males lead the way, emitting their milt; the females follow them and swallow it, and are impregnated in this way. When they find themselves well filled, and in the sea, they swim back, each to their usual haunts; but the males no longer lead the way; this time the females do so. They lead the way in shoals, acting in the same way as the males did previously: they keep emitting their roe, a few eggs at a time, and the males following devour them. These eggs are really fish. But from the spawn that escapes, and that is not devoured, the fish that grow up are produced. Any of these fish that may be captured during their passage towards the sea will be found to have bruises on the left side of the head; those that are taken on their way back have bruises on the right. The reason of this is as follows: When they swim out to sea they keep close to the land on the left; when they swim back, they go close to the same shore, hugging it and keeping in contact with it as much as possible for fear that the current might make them lose their way. When the Nile begins to overflow, the lower parts of the land and also the marshes near the river, first get filled, as the river water percolates through the ground. As soon as these hollows are filled, they immediately swarm with little fish. This is the reason of it, as I think: The preceding year, when the Nile retired, the fish that had spawned on the marshy ground went away with the last of the flood, but when in the course of time the flood-season returned, these eggs immediately produced fish. This is all I have to say about fish.

HERODOTUS (?485–?425 BC), *The Histories*, translated by J.A. Prout, 1858

The Wondrous Whale

The whale is a wondrous life form, not just because of its size but also because of the unbelievable speed of its growth. Measuring its growth from the ovum at conception, through eleven months of gestation, until it reaches one year of age and 26 tons, the blue whale is the fastest growing organism – either plant or animal – on earth.

As any enthusiast will tell you, whales are the Grand Canyon and the Mount Everest of the animal world. The blue whale weighs as much as 2,000 men. The brain of the sperm whale, at 20lb, is six times the size of the human brain. The bowhead whale has a mouth as wide as an interstate ferry ramp, which would allow two semi-trailer trucks to enter side by side. The humpback whale sings arias that can be heard over a thousand miles of open ocean. The grey whale has a 7,000-mile migration pattern – the longest of any mammal on earth – ranging from the Arctic waters of Alaska and Siberia to the Baja Gulf in Mexico. The killer whale propels itself beyond the explanation of science at speeds of 40 miles per hour and is the fastest animal in the sea.

With the whales we seem to enter the realm of an ancient and long-vanished world, or a fairy-tale world that never was. But the time is now, and the living whale is a reality that dwarfs the dinosaurs of prehistoric times and even the mythical giants and dragons of our imagination.

DAVID DAY, *Whale War*, 1987

How Whales Make Love

The penis of the whale is of a tendinous nature, and is six, seven, or eight feet long, according to the bigness of the fish: it lies in a doubling of the skin, just like a knife in the sheath when the haft only appears. The pudendum of the female is shaped like that of a mare, or cow. On each side of it grow two udders with nipples, like those of a cow; some of these are all over white, some are speckled with black and blue spots, like a lapwing's egg. When they have no young ones their udders are small. In the act of coition they stand upright with their heads out of the water, embracing each other with their fins.

It is supposed they never have more than two young ones at a time, because there have never been found more than two in their bellies when they have been cut open. How long they go with young, is altogether uncertain.

RICHARD BROOKES, *The Art of Angling*, 1790

St Anthony's Sermon to the Fishes

When the heretics would not regard his preaching, St Anthony betook himself to the seashore, where the river Marecchia disembogues itself into the Adriatic. He here called the fish together in the name of God, that they might hear his holy word. The fish came swimming towards him in such vast shoals, both from the sea and from the river, that the surface of the water was quite covered with their multitudes. They quickly ranged themselves, according to their several species, into a very beautiful congregation, and, like so many rational creatures, presented themselves before him to hear the word of God. St Anthony was so struck with the miraculous obedience and submission of these poor animals, that he found a secret sweetness distilling upon his soul, and at last addressed himself to them in the following words.

'Although the infinite power and providence of God (my dearly beloved Fish) discovers itself in all the works of his creation, as in the heavens, in the sun, in the moon, and in the stars, in this lower world, in man, and in other perfect creatures; nevertheless the goodness of the Divine Majesty shines out in you more eminently, and appears after a more particular manner, than in any other created beings. For notwithstanding you are comprehended under the name of reptiles, partaking of a middle nature between stones and beasts, and imprisoned in the deep abyss of waters; notwithstanding you are tost among billows, thrown up and down by tempests, deaf to hearing, dumb to speech, and terrible to behold: notwithstanding, I say, these natural disadvantages, the Divine Greatness shows itself in you after a very wonderful manner. In you are seen the mighty mysteries of an infinite goodness. The holy scripture has always made use of you, as the types and shadows of some profound sacrament.

'Do you think that, without a mystery, the first present that God Almighty made to man, was of you, O ye Fishes? Do you think that without a mystery, among all creatures and animals which were appointed for sacrifices, you only were excepted, O ye Fishes? Do you think there was nothing meant by our Saviour Christ, that next to the paschal lamb he took so much pleasure in the food of you, O ye Fishes? Do you think it was by mere chance, that when the Redeemer of the World was to pay a tribute to Caesar, he thought fit to find it in the mouth of a fish? These are all of them so many mysteries and sacraments, that oblige you in a more particular manner to the praises to your Creator.

'It is from God, my beloved Fish, that you have received being, life, motion, and sense. It is he that has given you, in compliance with your natural inclinations, the whole world of waters for your habitation. It is he that has furnished it with lodgings, chambers, caverns, grottoes, and such magnificent retirements as are not to be met with in the seats of kings, or in the palaces of princes. You have the water for your dwelling, a clear transparent element, brighter than crystal; you can see from its deepest bottom everything that passes on its surface; you have the eyes of a lynx, or of an argus; you are guided by a secret and unerring principle, delighting in everything that may be beneficial to you, and avoiding everything that may be hurtful; you are carried on by a hidden instinct to preserve yourselves, and to propagate your species; you obey, in all your actions, works and motions, the dictates and suggestions of nature, without the least repugnancy or contradiction.

'The colds of winter, and the heats of summer, are equally incapable of molesting you. A serene or a clouded sky are indifferent to you. Let the earth abound in fruits, or be cursed with scarcity, it has no influence on your welfare. You live secure in rains and thunders, lightnings and earthquakes; you have no concern in the blossoms of spring, or in the glowings of summer, in the fruits of autumn, or in the frosts of winter. You are not solicitous about hours or days, months or years; the variableness of the weather, or the change of seasons.

'In what dreadful majesty, in what wonderful power, in what

amazing providence did God Almighty distinguish you among all the species of creatures that perished in the universal deluge! You only were insensible of the mischief that had laid waste the whole world.

'All this, as I have already told you, ought to inspire you with gratitude and praise towards the Divine Majesty, that has done so great things for you, granted you such particular graces and privileges, and heaped upon you so many distinguishing favours. And since for all this you cannot employ your tongues in the praises of your Benefactor, and are not provided with words to express your gratitude; make at least some sign of reverence; bow yourselves at his name; give some show of gratitude, according to the best of your capacities; express your thanks in the most becoming manner that you are able and be not unmindful of all the benefits he has bestowed upon you.'

He had no sooner done speaking, but behold a miracle! The fish, as though they had been endued with reason, bowed down their heads with all the marks of a profound humility and devotion, moving their bodies up and down with a kind of fondness, as approving what had been spoken by the blessed Father St Anthony.

The legend adds, that after many heretics, who were present at the miracle, had been converted by it, the saint gave his benediction to the fish, and dismissed them.

ST ANTHONY OF PADUA (1195–1231), translated by Joseph
Addison in *Remarks on Several Parts of Italy*, 1705

Laying Down Sardines

Just as many famous vintages are now in short supply, because so many people are putting down wine as an investment, so the epicures are putting down sardines. But, if you want to start a collection in a more modest way, the best of the Portuguese sardines (brands like *Marie Elizabeth*) are likely to turn out just as well with ageing as the more expensive. They are also more readily available.

Once upon a time the French packers matured the fish themselves before they put them on the market. Now, with increasing world demand, the most expensive brands are shipped as soon as the tins are sealed. Some of the packers are said to have a secret method of part-grilling the fish. But, if you want the old standards today, you must, as in so many other activities, do it yourself.

When you lay down a collection of sardines, it is a good plan to vary them as you would a selection of wines. You will then learn which develop best. Every tin should be labelled with the month and year in which you bought it. Connoisseurs claim that the best vintages for sardines coincide with the best vintage years for wine!

You should turn over the tins every subsequent month after acquiring them. This will keep the oil moving about the fish. After a few years, anything from three to five, the oil will melt all the bone.

At intervals you should add to your reserve to keep up a regular supply of properly ripened fish. Inside the tin they will keep indefinitely, and improve.

Never buy sardines which are packed in anything other than pure olive oil. Sauced sardines, or sardines in any oil less than olive, are plonk.

MACDONALD HASTINGS, *Wheelers' Fish Cookery Book*, 1974

Disdain For the Chub (and the Portuguese)

They are cowardly, inasmuch, that if you once turn them, they are presently dispirited, and you manage them as you please. For this reason some waggish, merry Anglers compare them to Portuguese Soldiers, who have very little inclination to fighting at any time, even tho' the defence of their Country requires them, and if their enemy make a vigorous attack, they immediately turn tail, and it is twenty to one if you can prevail with them, by any means to face about.

From *The Gentleman Angler*, 1726

Cromwellian Verbosity About the Roach

As the roach is no costly fish, so is he not over-curiously enquired after. He that seeks him, without difficulty finds him as early for breakfast, as the sun salutes the creation; whose habitation is found bordering upon banks, in eddies, small turns, and meandring streams; and where there's a bush in the suburbs of the streams, there you shall find him sheltring himself, when recruits of rain force down the freshes, and drive the soil from off the fertil fields; for then you may fish him, and not go far to find him: when at other times, more especially near the approaching winter, he houses himself in the more solitary security of can-docks and bull-rushes, in depths of the water. But whilst we paraphrase and discourse the roach, we but decipher and interpret the rud; since nature's laws are alike to both, for both have but one fate and period, though of different complexion in fin, having natural inclination to long and warm days, to small and trilling streams, yet neither of them lovers nor admirers of travel: by which you may guess, that seldom or rarely they are found far from home.

RICHARD FRANCK, *Northern Memoirs*, 1658

Fish and the Shadow

The salmon-trout drifts in the stream,
The soul of the salmon-trout floats over the stream
Like a little wafer of light.

The salmon moves in the sun-shot, bright shallow sea . . .
As light as the shadow of the fish
  that falls through the water,
She came into the large room by the stair,
Yawning a little she came with the sleep still upon her.
'I am just from bed. The sleep is still in my eyes.
Come. I have had a long dream.'
And I: 'That wood?
And two springs have passed us.'
'Not so far, no, not so far now,
There is a place – but no one else knows it –
A field in a valley . . .
    Qu'ieu sui avinen,
Ieu lo sai.'

She must speak of the time
Of Arnaut de Mareuil, I thought, '*qu'ieu sui avinen*'.

Light as the shadow of the fish
That falls through the pale green water.

EZRA POUND

The Tench and the Pike

The Tench is the physician of fishes, for the Pike especially, and that
the Pike, being either sick or hurt, is cured by the touch of the
Tench. And it is observed that the tyrant Pike will not be a wolf to
his physician, but forbears to devour him though he be never so
hungry.

IZAAK WALTON, *The Compleat Angler*, 1676

A Legendary Tench

A piece of water, at Thornville Royal, Yorkshire, which had been
ordered to be filled up, and wherein wood, rubbish, &c. had been
thrown for years, was in November 1801, directed to be cleared out.
Persons were accordingly employed, and almost choaked up by
weeds and mud, so little water remained, that no person expected to
see any fish, except a few Eels, yet nearly two hundred brace of
Tench of all sizes, and as many Perch, were found. After the pond
was thought to be quite free, under some roots there seemed to be
an animal, which was conjectured to be an otter; the place was
surrounded, and on opening an entrance among the roots, a *Tench*
was found of most singular form, having literally assumed the shape
of the hole, in which he had of course for many years been
confined. His *length*, from fork to eye, was *two feet nine inches*; his
circumference, almost to the tail, was *two feet three inches*; his *weight*,
eleven pounds nine ounces and a quarter; the colour was also singular, his
belly being that of a Charr, or a vermillion. This extraordinary fish,
after having been inspected by many Gentlemen, was carefully put
into a pond; but either from confinement, age, or bulk, it at first

merely floated, and at last, with difficulty, swam gently away. It is now alive and well.

To this account some *Sceptics* have demurred, and have expressed their doubts, in *prose* and *verse*, as follows.

The Tench of Thornville House,
A TRUE STORY!!!

O' the marvellous,
    At *Thornville House*,
We read of feats in plenty,
    Where with *long bow*
    They hit, I trow,
Full nineteen shots in twenty!

Their fame to fix,
    'Midst other tricks,
In which they so delight, Sir,
    These blades, pray know,
    The *hatchet throw*
Till it is out of sight, Sir!

Of beast and bird
    Enough we've heard,
By *cracks* as loud as thunder;
    So now they dish
    A monster *Fish*,
For those who *bite at wonders*!

The scullion wench
    Did catch a *Tench*,
Fatter than Berkshire hogs, Sir,
    Which, pretty soul,
    Had made his hole
Snug shelter'd by some logs, Sir!

Sans *water* he
   Had liv'd, d'ye see,
Beneath those roots of wood, Sir!
   And there, alack,
   Flat on his back,
Had lain since NOAH's flood, Sir!

   Now he's in stew,
   For public *goût*,
And fed with lettuce-cosse, Sir;
   In hopes the Town
   Will gulp him down
With good *humbugging* sauce, Sir! NIM.

But notwithstanding the *squibs* and *witticisms* of incredulity, the
account is authentic.

THE REVEREND WILLIAM DANIEL, *Rural Sports*, 1802

The Enigma of the Eel

The eel is the most mysterious of all fishes of Thames and not of
Thames. The mysteries of the eel are more than the mysteries of
the salmon. The eel. is a miracle; God has made it the most
wonderful of all creatures of the waters. *What* instinct sends the eel
up Thames to the mill-cutting at Mapledurham where we caught
those two tench the other day? The mill-cutting where the river
débris collects and disintegrates and, in flood time, tumbles over
the lasher and away to Caversham on the big waters? And *why*
comes the eel?

We know why the salmon comes back to Balathie on Tay and
passes up the Troughs at Makerstoun on Tweed. We recognize the
call of the head-waters and the springs and the spawning redds
below Braeriach who bears the infant Dee. We guess at the urge,
the impulse, that moves the winged legion of birds southward to
follow the sun and, perhaps, to draw therefrom some element
necessary to life and hedge-sparrows' eggs in an April hazel copse at
home. But the eel?

But the eel one morning, an October morning when the days go by like a flight of macaws and the woods above the weir pool are heathen palaces and *teocallis* of gold, comes to the shallow water on the lasher's lip where the bulrush grows and whither that big trout followed your spinning-bait last May. And there the eel sees the heathen goldenness of things and perhaps remembers. Anyhow he says 'hey, for the Gulf of Mexico' and he wriggles through the reed bed, pitches over the lasher and into the pool, crosses the shallows under the mill eyot, picks up the stream, turns the corner into the main river and has gone.

An eel in a hurry lands and takes short-cuts to the Gulf of Mexico and makes nothing of so doing. Mr Eric Parker tells me of how a correspondent of his met two hundred eels marching down a dry, gritty road at ten-thirty of a summer night. The watcher rubbed his eyes, a white owl hooted, the moon winked at the waking Stour, and the procession moved on for Mexico via the Sargasso Sea.

And when the eel goes to sea it travels fast. But first it changes its dress from yellow-belly to 'silver.' I do not mean that it becomes a creature of pure and unsullied argent, for all it does is to change the tint of its mustard-coloured underneath for a shade of white which is by courtesy called silver. And even then it is not a bonny fish or a beautiful and so the eel can, for all its mystery and romance, never be quite the same to the angler as the salmon is. For anglers, and most other men and women, judge by appearances, and personal beauty goes a long way with us all.

PATRICK CHAMBERS, *At the Tail of the Weir*, 1932

The Love Lives of Eels

With regard to the generation of eels, authors are divided in their opinions; for Aristotle assures us, that he could find no difference of sexes. Pliny affirms, that, though there are neither male nor female, they will rub themselves against rocks and stones, and by that means detach particles or scales from their bodies, that quicken by degrees, and afterwards become small eels. Some maintain that they couple, and at the same instant they shed a kind of viscosity, which, being retained in the mud, gives birth to a great number of same animals.

Rondeletius informs us, that he has seen eels cling together; and he thinks they cannot want the parts of generation, since, at the lower part of the body there is a vulva in the female, and semen in the male; but then these parts are so covered with fat, as well as the spawn, that they do not appear.

Boecler, and other moderns, think that they proceed from eggs; for though they are brought forth alive, and on that account may be said to be viviparous, yet it does not follow from thence that they may not be produced from eggs in their bodies.

Some Cheshire fishermen confidently affirm, that in January, where the Mersey joins the sea, they have seen eels linked together in the act of copulation: and that, on cutting open the bellies of large eels, they have found perfect little elvers, or eels, about the bigness of a small needle, which appeared to be lively, and were inclosed in a skin like a bladder, which stuck to the backbone of the fish. These are supposed to be the eel-brood, which in the spring months swim on the sides of the said river as high as Warburton, where the poor people catch them in scoops, in order to store fish-ponds, or sometimes to scald, and make eel-pyes with. Nay, so great plenty is there near Northwich, that the farmers catch them, in order to feed pigs with.

RICHARD BROOKES, *The Art of Angling*, 1790

A True Story About a Big Eel

Sometime ago in the last century, the farmers near Yeovil, whose fields lay contiguous to the river, suffered greatly by losing vast quantities of hay; for which several people were taken up on suspicion of stealing the same; what added to the surprise of every one was, that the hay missing did not appear to be cut, as it usually is, but pulled out as if by some beast, but that appeared a little improbable, as several loads were lost in the space of a few nights; a circumstance so alarming to the farmers induced them to offer a considerable reward to any who should discover how their hay was destroyed.

A company of soldiers quartered then at Yeovil, some of them for the sake of the reward, undertook to find out the affair. They made their intention known to the people injured, who readily accepted their offer; and a night was fixed on, to begin their watching, in order to make a discovery. The appointed time came, and a dozen of the soldiers after eating and drinking plentifully at the respective farmer's houses, went on their new enterprise with bayonets fixed, and muskets charged, as if going to engage an enemy. They had not been long in ambush before one of them espied a monstrous creature, crawling from the side of the river, towards one of the stacks of hay; he instantly told his comrades. A council was immediately called, and they all unanimously agreed, if the bear devoured any of the hay, that two of them should get behind the stack, and fire at it, while the others dispersed themselves at different parts of the field, in order to intercept it, if it escaped their comrades vigilance; but the precaution was needless, for the soldiers fired their pieces with such dexterity that they soon laid the monster sprawling. This done all ran to see what was slain; but the moon not shining very bright, their curiosity could not be satisfied; though some of them said it must be the devil, in the shape of a snake. Highly pleased with this exploit, they hastened to the farmers and made known how well they had succeeded in their enterprise.

Next morning all the neighbours round, with the farmers, their servants, and the soldiers, went to see this amazing creature, and to their no small astonishment, found it to be a prodigious eel, which, it is supposed, not finding subsistence in the river, came out (ox-like) and fed on the hay. Its size was such, that the farmers ordered their men to go and harness eight of their best horses, in order to draw it to one of their houses, which with difficulty they did. When they got it home, the soldiers desired leave to roast it, there being a large kitchen with two fireplaces. This request was granted; and after cutting it in several pieces, fastening each piece to a young elm tree, by way of spit, they put it down to roast. It had not been above an hour before the fire, until there was as much fat run out of it, as filled all the tubs, kettles, &c., in the house, which put them under the necessity of going out to borrow; but at their return they found the inundation of grease so prodigious, that it was running out at the key-hole and crevices of the door.

R. TAYLOR, *The Wonders of Nature and Art*, 1780

Pining Perch

It has been remarked elsewhere that fish are capable, under certain circumstances, of exhibiting considerable attachment for others; and this is often seen in the case of fish kept for some time together in the same receptacle. When thus situated they not unfrequently contract a strong affection for one another, insomuch that, if by any chance they are separated, they mope, or refuse their food, and in some cases actually die of grief. An instance of this attachment in the Ruffe species is mentioned in the 'Philosophical Transactions,' vol. ix.: –

'Two Ruffs were placed by Mr Anderson in a jar of water about Christmas, and in April he gave one of them away. The fish that remained was so affected that it would eat nothing for three weeks, until, fearing that it might pine to death, he sent it to the gentleman on whom he had bestowed its companion. On rejoining the other it ate immediately, and very soon recovered its former briskness.' This, if the fish were of different sexes, may possibly have been the 'pining away for love, and wasting lean,' alluded to by Burton in his 'Anatomy of Melancholy;' but if of sexes similar, then clearly it was the passion of friendship in its most platonic phase.

H. CHOLMONDELEY-PENNELL, *The Angler-Naturalist*, 1868

The African Tiger-fish

Tiger-fishing. What memories the words bring back! Wide, tropic rivers lying smooth as polished metal in the blazing sunshine, the gunwales of the canoe too hot to touch with comfort, the dural of your reel scorching, the sweat running out of your shirt sleeves and down your neck and into your eyes. The heat is terrific, and the glare off the water worse, and you are deeply thankful for the sissyfied dark glasses that the tough old African explorers never deigned to wear. You have trolled for hours, and never a touch, and you are bored with the whole show, and – Bang! your rod is pulled down flat, and the reel is screaming, and away, far away it seems, astern of the canoe a great fish flashes out into the sunlight, thrashing frantically, and falls back with a smash of spray. Madly you reel up, to get the line tight again; and again the handles are dragged from your fingers by a savage, heavy run, and again up he comes, lashing and quivering with fury. Gradually you get him under control; the rushes are shorter now, the leaps less furious, until you have him close to the canoe, the hot sunlight shining through the brown water and lighting up his glimmering silver flanks and crimson fins and tail. He's done. And then, as you get the gaff ready, he plays the last card; from four feet down, that powerful tail shoots him up – up in a last defiant leap, flashing in the sunshine in a burst of glittering spray; you have a split-second glimpse of the spoon sailing past your head, and he is down again, sousing into the river with a wallowing splash. For an instant he lies there, almost within your reach, gasping, immobile, ten or twelve or fourteen pounds of first-class fighting fish; just for a long moment only, and then with a final flick of his strong, red-tipped tail he dives, and the river closes over him, and he is gone.

That's tiger-fishing.

v. FOX-STRANGEWAYS, *Wandering Fisherman*, 1955

The Alaskan Dallia Pectoralis

This species is probably the most abundant of all the fishes which occur in the fresh and brackish waters of the northern part of Alaska. It is known to the whites as 'Black-fish,' to the Russian speaking population as '*Chórnia Reeba*,' and to the Eskimo as '*Ē máng ŭk*'.

It is found in all the small streams of the low grounds, in the wet morasses and sphagnum-covered areas, which are soaked with water and which at times seem to contain but sufficient water to more than moisten the skin of the fish. In the low grounds or tundra are many, countless thousands, small ponds of very slight depth, connected with each other by small streams of variable width, of few feet to those so narrow as to be hidden by the overlapping sedges or sphagnum moss. These smaller streams are said to have been made by the muskrats and mink, which travel from pond to pond in search of food. These narrower outlets of the ponds are at certain seasons so full of these fish that they completely block them up. The soft, yielding sphagnum moss above is pushed aside, and under it these fish find a convenient retreat. Here the fish are partially protected from the great cold of winter by the covering of moss and grass. In such situations they collect in such numbers that figures fail to express an adequate idea of their numbers. They are to be measured by the yard. Their mass is deep according the nature of the retreat. If it is a pond overgrown with sedges and mosses which by their non-conductivity of heat allows only a slight depth to be thawed out in the short Arctic summer, the fish mass will completely fill it up. The natives repair to the places, which are known to be the refuge of these fish, and set a small trap constructed after the following manner: A number of small splints of spruce wood are carefully bound together so as to make a conical-formed weir some eight feet in length, the smaller end of which is opened about two to three inches. This communicates with a large basket-shaped trap, which is so placed that when the fish enter the small orifice next the trap they will scarcely find it by which to make their exit. . . . The fish push on until the basket is filled, their number prevent those within from moving outward until the whole trap is a mass of living fish. The natives remove the basket every day or two to relieve the pressure on it and to supply their own wants and those of their dogs. Nearly every head of a family has a trap, and during the greater part of the year, from May to December, tons and tons of these fish are daily removed. . . . When taken from the traps the fish are immediately put into baskets and taken to the village, where the baskets of fish are placed on stages, or *caches*, out of the way of the dogs. Here the fish are exposed to the severe temperature and cold winds. The mass of fish in each basket is frozen in a few minutes; and when required to take them out they have to be chopped out with an ax or beaten with a club to divide them into pieces of sufficient size to be fed to the dogs, or put into the pot to boil.

The vitality of these fish is astonishing. They will remain in those grass-baskets for weeks, and when brought into the house and thawed out they will be as lively as ever. The pieces which are thrown to the ravenous dogs are eagerly swallowed; the animal heat of the dog's stomach thaws the fish out, whereupon its movements soon cause the dog to vomit it up alive. This I have *seen*, but have heard some even more wonderful stories of this fish.

L.M. TURNER, *Contributions to the Natural History of Alaska*, 1886

India's Mighty Mahseer and its Role in the First World War

Colonel J.S. Rivett-Carnac, on the 28th December 1919, fishing with rod and line (using 'ragi' paste bait) on the River Cauvery, South India, killed a mahseer (*Barbas Torassullah*) and succeeded in landing it in thirty minutes. The fish was a spent female decidedly out of condition, weight 119 lb. This is the biggest authentic record for India, caught on rod and line.

Another mahseer of 110 lb. was killed on the River Cubbany (South India) on the 22nd of October 1938, by Mr A.E. Lobb, using a similar bait, but it took him three hours and fifty-five minutes to land it – a hen fish in good condition. Still larger fish have been caught on rod and line in Iraq. Major H.L. Colan killed one on the Diala River (a tributary of the Tigris) in September 1918, which weighed 125 lb. Major Colan was using a 14 ft. rod, bait *ata* paste, and it took one and a half hours to land.

One yet bigger was caught by Major F.B. Lane on the Tigris at Samarra on the 21st of September 1915. This fish weighed 140 lb. and was killed on a rod, the bait being a two-inch spoon. Both the above varieties have been identified as *Barbus Seich*.

The writer has also been fortunate in witnessing many battles with big fish of this type which have broken him (an all too common occurrence.)

Far bigger fish than any of these mentioned have been caught by the troops but *not* on rod and line. In some cases I have been able to take measurements and photographs.

The normal battles took place as follows: During the war 1914–

1918, a lot of stout telephone cable, abandoned by the Turks, was salvaged by the men. This made excellent line, all that was required being a mighty hook, usually fashioned by the unit's armourer, the bait used being meat, or more frequently, a large pear-shaped blob of *ata* paste. Once a big fish took this bait the unfortunate angler was sometimes seen rapidly disappearing into the water. His friends, rushing to his assistance, joined in the tug-of-war until the monster was dragged on to the bank and despatched with a crack on the head. Cases of the angler being drowned did occur when, in his excitement, he hung on too long until he was swept away in the dangerous currents.

One of these fish (photographed) weighed 167 lb., and another from the Euphrates at Massiriyah scaled 213 lb. This weight was vouched for by some staff officers of the 15th Indian Division, 1918.

Still bigger fish lie in the rivers of Iraq and also in India, Burma and Malaya, but it is difficult to get accurate weights for very heavy scales are rarely carried when in camp. Most anglers who have done much mahseer fishing will be able to record first-hand experiences of battles with these monsters, which, incidentally, are usually hen fish.

Unfortunately, the rivers are so large and the currents so strong that it is often impossible to follow up your fish owing to bad ground. The battle has probably lasted for hours until the angler is completely exhausted.

So it is not surprising that sooner or later a break will occur, rendering an authentic record impossible, although the thrill of the fight will remain for ever in the mind of the angler.

LIEUTENANT-COLONEL R.B. PHAYRE MC, *The Fisherman's Bedside Book*, 1945

The Pike

The pike bears the same relation to the finny tribes that the hyena and jackal do to animals, the vulture to birds, or the spider to insects. ... Some pike were turned into a pond in England, the largest of which weighed two and a half pounds. Four years after, the water was let off, when one pike of nineteen pounds, and others of from eleven to fifteen, were found. Mr Jesse, in his Gleanings of Natural History, relates certain experiments by which he shows that the growth of pike is about four pounds a year, which corresponds with the growth of those before stated.

The various books on sporting give numerous instances of pike weighing from thirty to forty pounds, taken in England, though an instance is mentioned in Dodsley's Register for 1765, of an enormous pike weighing one hundred and seventy pounds, which was taken from a pool near Newport, England, which had not been fished in for ages. In Ireland and Scotland, they are found larger than in England. In the Shannon and Lough Corrib, they have been found from seventy to ninety-two pounds in weight. At Bradford, near Limerick, one was taken weighing ninety-six pounds. Another was caught by trolling in Loch Pentluliche, of fifty pounds; and another in Loch Spey, that weighed one hundred and forty-six pounds.

BENTLEY'S MISCELLANY, July 1851

A Young Pike

A slim young pike, with smart fins
And grey-striped suit, a young cub of a pike
Slouching along away below, half out of sight,
Like a lout on an obscure pavement . . .

D.H. LAWRENCE, 'Fish'

The Pike's Prodigious Appetite

The pike is of a long and roundish body, has a plain, smooth head, is covered with small scales, of a whitish colour, the body is sprinkled on both sides with yellowish spots, the young ones are more green, the upper and lower jaw are full of teeth, and three rows of teeth upon the tongue; he's the tyrant of fresh-water-fish, and reckon'd a longer liver than any other fish, except a Carp; he is very chargeable to his owners; the chief of his subsistence being upon other fish, even those of his own species; he will bite at a dog or any other creature he sees in the water, of which many instances might be given. A very particular one I shall relate as follows: my father catcht a Pike in Barn-Meer, (a large standing water in Cheshire) was an ell long, and weigh'd 35 pounds which he brought to the Lord Cholmondley; his Lordship ordered it to be turn'd into a canal in the garden, wherein were abundance of several sorts of fish; about 12 months after his Lordship draw'd the canal and found that this overgrown Pike had devour'd all the fish, except one large Carp that weighed between 9 and 10 pounds, and that was bitten in several places; the Pike was then put into the canal again together with abundance of Fish with him to feed upon, all which he devoured in less than a year's time, and was observ'd by the Gardiner and Workmen there to take the ducks and other water-fowl under water; whereupon they shot Magpye and Crows and throw'd them into the canal, which the Pike took before their eyes; of this they acquainted their Lord, who thereupon order'd the slaughterman to fling calf's-bellies, chicken's-guts, and such like garbage to him to prey upon, but being soon after neglected he dyed, as suppos'd for want of food. It is the general opinion that no other fish will associate themselves with this water-tyrant, for he always swims alone, and is the most bold and daring of all our fresh-water fish, knowing no other pleasure, as we conjecture, than prey or rest.

CHARLES BOWKLER, *The Art of Angling, c.* 1746

The Pike's Menu

Amongst a great variety of *objets de consommation* the following have been ascertained to be most to their taste – a swan's head and shoulders, a mule's lip, a Polish damsel's foot, a gentleman's hand (probably, however, no objection would be made to a lady's); plump puppies just opening their eyes, and tender kittens paying the penalty of a mother's indiscretion; together with every kind of fish that comes to the maw, with the few exceptions just noticed.

Fraser's Magazine, October 1853

The Pike

From shadows of rich oaks outpeer
The moss-green bastions of the weir,
Where the quick dipper forages
In elver-peopled crevices,
And a small runlet trickling down the sluice
Gossamer music tires not to unloose.

Else round the broad pool's hush
    Nothing stirs.
Unless sometimes a straggling heifer crush
Through the thronged spinney where the pheasant whirs
    Or martins in a flash
Come with wild mirth to dip their magical wings,
While in the shallow some doomed bulrush swings
At whose hid root the diver vole's teeth gnash.

And nigh this toppling reed, still as the dead
    The great pike lies, the murderous patriarch
     Watching the waterpit sheer-shelving dark,
Where through the plash his lithe bright vassals thread.

The rose-finned roach and bluish bream
And staring ruffe steal up the stream
Hard by their glutted tyrant, now
Still as a sunken bough.

He on the sandbank lies,
    Sunning himself long hours
With stony gorgon eyes:
    Westward the hot sun lowers.

Sudden the gray pike changes, and quivering poises for slaughter;
   Intense terror wakens around him, the shoals scud awry,
      but there chances
   A chub unsuspecting; the prowling fins quicken, in
     fury he lances;
And the miller that opens the hatch stands amazed at the whirl
  in the water.

EDMUND BLUNDEN, 1940

A Frog's Revenge on a Pike

But before I proceed further, I am to tell you that there is a great antipathy betwixt the Pike and some frogs: and this may appear to the reader of Dubravius, a Bishop in Bohemia, who, in his book 'Of Fish and Fish-Ponds,' relates what he says he saw with his own eyes, and could not forbear to tell the reader. Which was: –

'As he and the Bishop Thurzo were walking by a large pond in Bohemia, they saw a Frog, when the Pike lay very sleepily and quiet by the shore-side, leap upon his head; and the Frog having expressed malice or anger by his swollen cheeks and staring eyes, did stretch out his legs and embraced the Pike's head, and presently reached them to his eyes, tearing with them and his teeth those tender parts: the Pike, moved with anguish, moves up and down the water, and rubs himself against weeds, and whatever he thought might quit him of his enemy: but all in vain, for the Frog did continue to ride triumphantly, and to bite and torment the Pike, till his strength failed: and then the Frog sunk with the Pike to the bottom of the water: then presently the Frog appeared again at the top and croaked, and seemed to rejoice like a conqueror, after which he presently retired to his secret hole. The Bishop, that had beheld the battle, called his fisherman to fetch his nets, and by all means to get the Pike, that they might declare what had happened: and the Pike was drawn forth, and both his eyes eaten out; at which when they began to wonder, the fisherman wished them to forbear and assured them he was certain that Pikes were often so served.'

IZAAK WALTON, The Compleat Angler, 1676

A Grateful Pike

When the late Dr Warwick resided at Dunham, the seat of the Earl of Stamford and Warrington, he was walking in the park by a pond where fish were temporarily kept for the table; and a pike of about 6 lbs. weight, when it observed him darted hastily away, and in doing so struck its head against a tenter-hook in a post, one of several placed in the pond to prevent poaching; and, as it afterwards appeared, fractured its skull and turned the optic nerve on one side. The anguish suffered by the fish appeared, to be intense; it rushed to the bottom, boring its head into the mud, writhing about, and for a short interval was almost lost to sight; then plunging about the pond, at length threw itself out of the water on to the bank. The doctor on examining it found a small portion of brain was protruding from the fracture in the skull. He carefully replaced this, raised the indented portion of skull, and replaced the pike in the pond. It appeared at first a good deal relieved, but in a few minutes again plunged about and threw itself a second time out of the water. Dr Warwick again did what he could to relieve it, and put it back into the water. But as the fish several times continued to throw itself out, he with the assistance of the keeper made a kind of bandage or pad for the fish, which was then left in the pond to its fate. Upon the doctor making his appearance there the next morning, the pike swam to the edge of the water, the doctor examined the fish's skull and found it going on all right. He then walked backwards and forwards along the edge of the pond for some time, and the fish continued to swim up and down, turning whenever he turned; but being blind on the wounded side of the skull, appeared to be agitated when it had that side towards the bank, as it could not then see its benefactor. The next day the doctor took some friends down to see the fish, which came to him as before, and at length he actually taught the pike to come to him at his whistle and feed out of his hands. Dr Warwick thought this a remarkable instance of gratitude in a fish for a benefit received; and as it always came to his whistle, it also proved, what he had previously disbelieved, that fishes are sensible to sound.

ALFRED JARDINE, Pike and Perch, 1898

Meetings With Remarkable Congers

Recently I came on a young conger eel in a rock pool. He was a small one and I let him slither away unmolested because I had no particular need of him alive or dead. He could not have been more than a pound in weight and, accidents barred, he had much growth to make, for he could easily end up as a 40- or 50- pounder and still fall far short of the British record.

A conger is not everybody's idea of a synonym for charm in the world of Nature, though I suppose that if one could make a sufficiently impersonal assessment one might admire such suppleness combined with such strength. But the bigger they get the less graceful they become, for their girth increases proportionately faster than their length and they lose their svelte figures.

At what poundage they acquire an ability to bark is not known, but perhaps they always have this intimidating talent, though only adults can do it loud enough to make themselves heard by human ears. Lest I be called a liar I must make it clear that I do not claim to have heard them baying at the moon, but so many people claim to have heard them bark that I accept the fact.

I have never caught a large conger and I have no wish to, for I gather from those who have that such are apt to get very rough in play. I base this belief on the tale of the eel-of-my-uncle, a true tale and not a bilingual exercise like the plume-of-my-jardinier.

He hired two Mauritians to take him out into deep water and in due course he hooked a vast eel. Apparently, the monster was more than obliging once it had been fought up to the boat, and skinned aboard with alacrity, where it proceeded to put a point of view with appalling vigour.

It raged around so savagely that it swiftly penned my uncle in the bows and the boatmen in the stern, where they conducted a Custer's-last-stand, backs-to-the-bulwarks type of defensive battle, banging it with oars and boathooks and making no great impression on it. My uncle said that only the fear of meeting the creature's twin stopped him from going overboard, but eventually it was persuaded to return to its element and a frightened boat's crew made all haste back to land.

I asked him how big it was, but he could only say that he had been too busy to measure it, and his impression was that it was about 20 ft. long with a head like a bull terrier at each end. Laying off a bit for wind, it might have been half that size, for a 12-footer has been taken in Australian waters and there are scientific grounds for thinking that far bigger ones exist.

Both conger and freshwater eels start life as curious little leaf-like transparencies which, when about 3 in. long, alter to become the miniature eels which we know as elvers, and then grow to maturity.

Link that fact to another and you get a startling conclusion. In the Marine Biological Laboratory at Charlottenlund, Denmark, is preserved just such a juvenile eel (or *leptocephalus*) which is slightly over 6 ft. long. If its adult size had borne the same ratio to its early dimensions as that of an ordinary eel it would have reached 60 ft. or 70 ft.

Perhaps they were correct as well as wise to bundle the eel-of-my-uncle overboard. No true sportsman keeps undersized fish.

C.C.L. BROWNE, *The Field*, 1965

Cod as Messengers

SIR, A Norwegian newspaper, *Faedrelandsvennen*, is responsible for this remarkable story of a cod fish carrying a letter from Bergen, in Norway, down the North Sea to the Dogger Bank, where the fish was caught, to the Fish Market at The Hague, where the letter was extracted from its stomach.

'Something like a fortnight ago the postmaster at Bergen received a communication from his colleague at The Hague, enclosing a letter to a man residing at Bergen. The letter, it was explained, had been found in the stomach of a cod fish at the Fish Market at The Hague. The envelope and missive inside it were in a fair state of preservation, and the address could be deciphered with ease, in spite of its strange adventures.

'When handed to the man whose name it bore, he had no difficulty in recognizing his property. He explained that the letter fell into the water at Skudevigen, Bergen, early in January, wherefore his astonishment can be understood on having it handed back to him. He was still more amazed on learning that a cod fish

had made a meal of it, and most likely suffered from indigestion until it was caught on the Dogger Bank and killed at The Hague. It is well known that a hungry cod fish will swallow anything that shines in the water.

'Something like a month elapsed from the date of losing the letter until its return to the owner.'

R.T. London.

Letter to *The Field*

Carp and Cognac

The secretary of the National Fish Culture Association lately tried the experiment of endeavouring to revive with brandy some carp which had been left eight hours out of water. Of this experiment the *Daily Telegraph* publishes an amusing account.

The actual facts, as may be found stated in the *Fish Culture Journal*, are these. Two Prussian carp were taken out of a tank of the South Kensington Aquarium and put into two separate dry cans, and one of the fish, to distinguish it from the other as a carp of temperate habits, was decorated with a piece of blue ribbon. They were left in their wretchedness until they were to all appearance quite dead, the teetotal fish succumbing half an hour after the other. To make sure of decease the corpses were left alone for four hours, after which they were both restored to their proper element, it was then obvious that the floating things were as thoroughly defunct as need be. The Secretary, being satisfied of this, then took out the fish without the ribbon – the Licensed Victualler we will call it – and gave it a dose of brandy with a feather, and put it back into the water. The effect was amazing, for the carp in a very few minutes pulled itself together, and though a trifle groggy in its movements at first, began to swim about. Meanwhile the other – which for distinction's sake we may call the Teetotaller – continued dead, and, the experiment being considered complete, it was taken out of the water and thrown away. A dead carp, even though it may have died of excessive abstinence, is not worth much, at any rate not as a carp.

About four hours later, however, it occurred to the Secretary that perhaps it was all pride on the part of the Teetotaller that made it go on being dead; that it would not commit itself to anything that might seem to countenance the tippling of its companion; that, in fact, it persisted in keeping its eyes shut to the important facts transpiring before it out of sheer obstinacy of principle. With this in his mind, the Secretary took up the representative of temperance and – we shudder as we write it – poured some brandy down its throat. There was no feather used this time. He simply opened the Teetotaller's mouth and let the spirits run down. The fish was then restored to the water for the second time, and for five minutes refused to confess that the brandy had done it any good. It floated helplessly on its side. All of a sudden, however, it thought better of it – a live toper is, after all, something better than a dead teetotaller – and wagged its tail. The motion was very feeble, a mere apology of a wag – a waggle; but, still, it was a beginning. Then it moved a fin, and then it gaped, and finally, turning itself right side uppermost, proceeded to swim. Both fish are now alive and well.

H. CHOLMONDELEY-PENNELL, Fishing Gossip, 1866

Death by Natural Causes

The natural end of a trout is starvation – starvation brought about by blindness. Death comes slowly but very surely and the last stage of a trout's life may extend for two or three years. First, he reaches the pink of condition. He grows quickly to three years old then, with few exceptions, he spawns annually. Rich summer feeding is needed to make up for loss of feeding during winter and for the strength he expends in spawning, but during the summers following the first three spawnings he is able to mend his condition and add a little to length and to girth. But at six years old he finds the balance – the rich feeding of spring and summer does no more than compensate for the loss of condition through spawning. And so it continues.

He may live on for several years – losing weight in winter, gaining it again by the following autumn – but slowly, though

surely, he finds it more difficult to maintain the balance. As he ages, so his eyesight fails. Younger fish are more active in taking the food supply. Spawning saps his strength, and no longer can he live where the maximum food supply is to be found. A year or two may pass and though he goes to the spawning grounds, he no longer takes an active part. Summer feeding becomes more and more difficult and soon he is forced to feed by sense of smell. Gradually he gets thinner, and now weighs no more than he did at three years old. He seeks the backwaters and quiet places about the river – places where he need no longer use his fins and strength to maintain a position.

Weeks and months pass along and sightless eyes are in a head that is out of all proportion to the body, and soon all desire to feed is gone. With the instinct of the wild creature he seeks a place to die and with his last remaining strength pushes his way into some cover, on, or near, the river bed. Little flesh is now left upon his bones and no air contained within his body. There he lies concealed from the view of his fellow creatures and then, with a few gasping movements of the gills, his life is over.

So ends the life of a trout, but Nature cannot allow his emaciated body to pollute the stream. To the scavengers of the water comes the scent of death. Crayfish and shrimps gather to do their work, and soon the bones of a once noble fish are scattered over the river bed.

FRANK SAWYER, *Keeper of the Stream*, 1952

CHAPTER THREE

Tactics

Anglers are not, by and large, a showy lot. Quite at home in a filthy old jacket and smelly boots, the best of them do not take easily to dishing out advice. Unless asked, of course, in which case some will dole out nostrums faster than you can say 'another large one?' They will swear blind that the only fly which will catch fish on this river is a bizarre concoction you've never seen before and certainly don't have the means to tie for yourself; that you cannot catch anything at all in a north-east wind; that the secret of a full creel is never to fish on a Thursday afternoon from the right bank before six o'clock unless there's an 'R' in the month. Their audience, if they are wise, say nothing. Some might raise an eyebrow. But tomorrow afternoon, when they've all caught nothing and they think they're alone, each will be giving the saloon bar prophet's techniques a go, 'just out of interest'.

Reticence does not, however, come easily to the people who write about fishing. That writing which is not about the author's heroic struggles with monster fish consists mostly of instructions to the rest of us on how we ought to be going about things. Since the principles of fishing are easily understood, this advice is often as useful as a swizzle stick at a temperance wedding. Fishing cannot be learned from books.

But this simple fact has not stopped people trying to tell the rest of us what to do. Sometimes this advice is genuinely useful, the product of a lifetime's experience, packed with ideas you might never have thought of, like Lee Wulff's suggestion of throwing stones into a pool. Other times, it's the consequence of obsession. Imagine the sight of three middle-aged men standing in a river firing shotguns into the riverbank to settle an argument over fishes' hearing. Or squatting beside a stream, spitting flies coated with cayenne pepper onto the water to test their sense of taste. Imagine just collecting the houseflies in the first place and then painting them with pepper and mustard. Yet not only have these experiments, and numerous others in similar vein, been carried out in all seriousness, they have been the subject of obsessive dissertation.

Admittedly, much of the rest of fishing advice tends to be an account of something which worked once upon a time and from which a whole new Law of Fishing has been spun. This is seized upon avidly. Magazine proprietors support ocean-racing yachts, pseudo-Tudor manor houses and Chelsea Harbour love-nests on the angler's appetite for more tips on how to do better.

It can all get terribly confusing. For years, I thought Izaak Walton's advice to fish 'fine and far off' was a principle to be followed by all modern anglers. In some circumstances it is, but if you can get closer without spooking the fish, it makes it a heck of a lot easier to cast a fly. Walton had no choice because he was fishing without a reel, with the line tied to the top of his rod. It would have been helpful to have realized that before trying to follow his method.

The most famous dispute about fishing tactics, the one which initiated the class distinctions in fly fishing which exist to this day, is the debate about the 'superiority' of dry-fly fishing. True, there is no more exciting way to catch a fish. It is certainly also more difficult. But we should do well to remember that it was originally brought in and refined as a way of catching *more* fish rather than fewer. W.C. Stewart, who extolled the merits of upstream fishing in *The Practical Angler* (1867), used to catch 12 lbs of wild trout in a day.

Whoever was the first to try systematically to catch his trout by floating his fly on the surface of the stream, the technique was certainly well established by the middle of the nineteenth century, particularly on the southern English chalk streams. It took Frederick Halford to elevate it into a religious faith. It was something of a help, to say the least, that he was able to retire from business at the age of forty-five, to devote the rest of his life to refining the techniques of insect-imitation culminating in the dry-fly fisherman's bible *Dry Fly Fishing in Theory and Practice*. Halford's role as the Archbishop of dry-fly fishing has been sneered at frequently since, notably for his insistence on a tactic which is simply not appropriate at all times and in all places. Much of Halford's theory is merely repetition of ideas put forward three or four decades earlier. But he was the first to appreciate fully the overwhelming importance of entomology and for that reason all subsequent writers have written in his shadow.

The intensity with which the most famous tactical dispute was fought – that between the dry-fly purists and the rest – seems extraordinary. *Dry Fly Fishing in Theory and Practice* was published in 1899; G.E.M. Skues' counterblast, *Minor Tactics of the Chalkstream*, in 1910. While Europe was blundering into war, this Lilliputian tussle consumed Skues in particular for years. And trout fishermen of either persuasion affect superiority at their peril – it is the huge appetite of this fish which makes it so catchable.

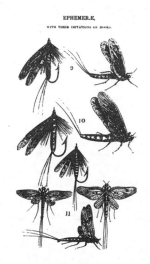

EPHEMERÆ,
WITH THEIR IMITATIONS ON HOOKS.

– Sir Humphry Davy, Bart., *Salmonia; or Days of Fly Fishing*, 1851

There are hundreds of books telling you how to catch fish, so the extracts which follow have been chosen not necessarily because they represent the most precise distillation of advice but more out of curiosity. Few of us are likely to be lucky enough to be invited to fish for mahseer in India, fewer still to join an Eskimo fishing party. But if you are, you should get the basic principles from the extracts which follow. As for live frog fishing, I can take it or leave it.

Well, Not Exactly (A French Newspaper Reporter Gets Overexcited by George V's Fishing)

He is an angler of the first force, this King of Britain. Behold him there, as he sits motionless under his umbrella patiently regarding his many coloured floats. How obstinately he contends with the elements. It is a summer day of Britain. That is to say it is a day of sleet, and fog and tempest. But what would you? It is as they love it, those who follow the sport.

Presently the King's float begins to descend. The King strikes. My God, how he strikes! The Hook is implanted in the very Bowels of the salmon. The King rises. He spurns aside his footstool. He strides strongly and swiftly towards the rear. In due time the salmon comes to approach himself to the bank. Aha! The King has cast aside his rod. He hurls himself flat on the ground on his victim. They splash and struggle in the icy water. Name of a dog! But it is a braw laddie! The Ghillie, a kind of outdoor domestic, administers the coup de grâce with his pistol. The King cries with a shrill voice, 'Hip-Hip-hurrah!' On these red letter days His Majesty George dines on a Haggis and a whisky grog. Like a true Scotsman he wears only a kilt.

AUTHOR UNKNOWN (luckily for him), 20 July 1917

Catching an Octopus in Ancient Rome

Trebius Niger also adds that no animal is more savage in killing a man in the water: it struggles with him, embracing him with its tentacles, swallows at him with its many suckers and pulls him apart; it attacks shipwrecked men or men who are diving. If, however, the octopus turns over, its strength diminishes; for when these creatures are on their backs they collapse inwardly. The other facts recounted by Niger may appear rather bizarre.

At Carteia an octopus used to come from the open sea into the uncovered tanks of the fish-farms and there forage for salted fish. All sea-creatures are powerfully attracted to the smell of salted fish, and for this reason baskets used in catching fish are smeared with salted fish. In view of the continual theft, the overseers became exceedingly angry. Fences were put up to obstruct the octopus, but it used to climb these by means of a tree. It could be caught only by employing dogs with a keen scent. These surrounded the octopus as it was returning at night and roused the overseers, who were terrified by its strange appearance. Its size was unheard of and likewise its colour; it was smeared with brine and had a dreadful smell. Who would have expected to find an octopus there, or to recognize it against such a background? They seemed to be locked in a struggle with something out of this world, for it nauseated the dogs with its terrible breath, lashed them with the ends of its tentacles, and then struck them with its stronger arms, which it used in the manner of clubs. After great trouble, it was dispatched with the aid of many tridents.

Lucullus was shown the octopus's head, which was as big as a jar and had a capacity of well over 90 gallons. In the words of Trebius himself, its cluster of tentacles, round which one could scarcely put both arms, were knotted like clubs and almost 30 feet long; it had suckers, or cups, like 3-gallon basins; and teeth in keeping with its size. The octopus's remains, which were kept as a curiosity, weighed 700 pounds.

PLINY THE ELDER (23–79 AD), *Natural History*, translated by
John Healy

Octopus Fishing in the Gilbert Islands

But that very quality of the octopus that most horrifies the imagination, its relentless tenacity, becomes its undoing when hungry man steps into the picture. The Gilbertese happen to value certain parts of it as food, and their method of fighting it is coolly based upon the one fact that its arms never change their grip. They hunt for it in pairs. One man acts as the bait, his partner as the killer. First, they swim eyes-under at low tide just off the reef, and search the crannies of the submarine cliff for sight of any tentacle that may flicker out for a catch. When they have placed their quarry, they land on the reef for the next stage. The human bait starts the real game. He dives and tempts the lurking brute by swimming a few strokes in front of its cranny, at first a little beyond striking range. Then he turns and makes straight for the cranny, to give himself into the embrace of those waiting arms. Sometimes nothing happens. The beast will not always respond to the lure. But usually it strikes.

The partner on the reef above stares down through the pellucid water, waiting for his moment. His teeth are his only weapon. His killing efficiency depends on his avoiding every one of those strangling arms. He must wait until his partner's body has been drawn right up to the entrance of the cleft. The monster inside is groping then with its horny mouth against the victim's flesh, and sees nothing beyond it. That point is reached in a matter of no more than thirty seconds after the decoy has plunged. The killer dives, lays hold of his pinioned friend at arms' length, and jerks him away from the cleft; the octopus is torn adrift from the anchorage of its proximal suckers, and clamps itself the more fiercely to its prey. In the same second, the human bait gives a kick which brings him, with quarry annexed, to the surface. He turns on his back, still holding his breath for better buoyancy, and this exposes the body of the beast for the kill. The killer closes in, grasps the evil head from behind, and wrenches it away from its meal. Turning the face up towards himself, he plunges his teeth between the bulging eyes, and bites down and in with all his strength. That is the end of it. It dies on the instant; the suckers release their hold; the arms fall away; the two fishers paddle with whoops of delighted laughter to the reef, where they string the catch to a pole before going to rout out the next one.

Any two boys of seventeen, any day of the week, will go out and get you half a dozen octopus like that for the mere fun of it. Here lies the whole point of this story. The hunt is, in the most literal sense, nothing but child's play to the Gilbertese.

ARTHUR GRIMBLE, *A Pattern of Islands*, 1952

American Indians Taking Catfish

They have a surprising method of fishing under the edges of rocks, that stand over deep places of a river. There, they pull off their red breeches, or their long slip of stroud cloth, and wrapping it round their arm, so as to reach to the lower part of the palm of their right hand, they dive under the rock where the large cat-fish lie to shelter themselves from the scorching beams of the sun, and to watch for prey: as soon as those fierce aquatic animals see that tempting bait, they immediately seize it with the greatest violence, in order to swallow it. Then is the time for the diver to improve the favourable opportunity: he accordingly opens his hand, seizes the voracious fish by his tender parts, hath a sharp struggle with it against the crevices of the rock, and at last brings it safe ashore. Except the Choktah, all our Indians, both male and female, above the state of infancy, are in the watery element nearly equal to amphibious animals, by practices and from the experiments necessity has forced them to, it seems as if few were endowed with such strong natural abilities, – very few can equal them in their wild situation of life.

JAMES ADAIR, *The History of the American Indians*, 1775

Singing For Your Supper

In the straights of Sicily, every year, at the month of May, and no other time of the year, they fish in an extraordinary manner, not in use in any other part of Europe, for a large sea-fish, called sword-bearers, because they have a bone which resembles a sword with teeth.

A fisher sings certain words, made to a particular tune, adapted to the purpose, in order to allure the fish, and enchant it with this music; as soon as ever it appears upon the surface of the water, it is taken. One of the most experienced fishermen, as well as strongest, fastens a three-pointed iron to the end of a rope, one end of which he ties about his arm, and then stands upright upon the fore part of the boat, while another man who stands by him, calls and allures the fish with words, songs, and antic gestures. No sooner does the fish hear him, but it mounts to the surface of the water, and as soon as ever it appears, the other fisherman darts his iron at it with his whole force, and with admirable dexterity, throwing out the cord at the same time. When he has caught the fish he lets it move, and flounce about in the water, till it has lost all its blood, and is so exhausted as to be able to swim no longer. Then he draws it up into the boat, where the other fisherman deprives it of the remains of life.

ROBERT BLAKEY, *Historical Sketches of the Angling Literature of All Nations*, 1856

Caribbean Turtle Fishing

In some parts of the South Seas, a curious method is employed to catch Turtle: the party proceed in boats cautiously towards the Turtles, which are observed floating on the surface of the water during the great heats in the day-time. As the least noise would disturb them, at a convenient distance the most expert diver lowers himself into the water, and swims beneath the surface towards the Turtle he intends to seize; then, rising just behind it, he takes hold of the buckler near the tail, and forcing the hinder part of the animal beneath the water, he raises the head, and prevents it from diving; in this situation he continues to hold it, until his companions arrive with the boats, and secure it.

Foreign Field Sports, 1814

Eskimos Do It Through a Hole in the Ice

When the ice in November has set, small holes of a few inches in diameter are cut through it. ... The hook used by the Eskimo consists of a piece of slightly curved bone, ivory, or deer horn. A small piece of metal (preferably copper, as this will not be so easily broken as steel or iron) is sharpened and firmly set in the concave side of the shaft of the hook. No barb is used, as the weather is so cold in winter that the hands would be frozen in removing the fish, which the presence of the barb would render necessary. ... The great secret is to keep the line taut, so that in drawing it to the surface the fish has no chance to become detached, but does so as soon as the line is slackened. The bait used is generally a piece of fresh fish of any kind. ... The line is generally made of whalebone (baleen), cut into long strips, and polished so that the water will not cling to it and freeze. The lower part of the line next the hook is sometimes made of strips of the shaft of the quill of a gull, goose, or swan, or the sinew from the wing of a swan is also used. Several of these snoods may be used on one line, and during times of abundance of fish each hook will have a fish on it. . . .

A sinker is seldom used, excepting in summer fishing, and then may be a grooved stone from the beach, or often a piece of ivory is cut in imitation of a fish and tied on the line with the tail upward. This serves two purposes, one to represent a fish going down to seize the bait and make the live, big fish hurry up and bite, and secondly, to make less resistance when the line is drawn from the water. . . .

The Eskimo fisherman, or woman, goes out early in the morning to the hole, which has been made the day before, for while cutting it out the fish are frightened away from it and nothing will be caught that time. The person takes a grass sack or basket along to carry the fish home in. A piece of old sealskin or grass mat is taken to sit on. . . . Ere many seconds one or two fish will be drawn out and slung high in the air; and, as they slap down on the ice they invariably become detached from the hook. The native is now in good humor, as an abundance of fish is indicated by their taking the hook when first put down. He takes off his glove and contentedly reaches behind his right ear for the quid of tobacco, which has lain there for the last twelve hours, covered by his abundant locks of hair; and, thrusting it far back between the teeth and cheek, calmly lets it soak while he pulls out dozens (of fish).

L.M. TURNER, *Contributions to the Natural History of Alaska*,
1886

Indian Salmon Fishing in British Columbia

When the salmon are running you can find a Siwash village in the night – blindfold. The stench is unbelievable. The reason is that their villages of unpainted board shacks with the grotesque, carved totem poles standing outside them, are nearly always established near a shallow reach of river in which the salmon can be speared. The men stand there, throwing spears into slamon, throw the ten- or fifteen-pound fish to their squaws; the squaws slit them open, jerk out their insides, and throw these over their shoulders up the bank. The overpowering effect of some thousands of salmon interiors putrefying in the hot sun leaves you searching for words. It is appalling.

These particular Siwash were using a spear with two steel barbs on a Y-shaped tip. The barbs each had a little lanyard holding them to the main shaft. And the shaft had a lanyard which the thrower attached to his little finger. They threw the spear in the way the ancient Greeks threw the javelin – *not* held in the middle, but propelled from fingers placed against the butt. They thus threw it into the air in a parabola – letting it *fall* into a fish, not throwing it into him.

This distinction must be grasped in order to appreciate their skill. Because they not only had to allow for refraction – which makes you think the salmon is further away from you than he actually is – but also for the speed of the fish, allowing the spear to drop as the salmon was passing under it. Yet they hardly ever missed.

I, seizing the spear by the middle – and throwing well under where the water-refraction made him appear to be – drove both barbs deep into my first salmon – and merely aroused smiles. A patient Siwash, when I drew the fish in, politely showed me how my clumsy, strong-arm method had merely succeeded in ruining a salmon for smoking. Not only had I broken its back; I had mucked the fish about with the spear driven half through him.

NEGLEY FARSON, *Going Fishing*, 1942

Leistering in the Borders

Under the old code the leister might be used in any form during the open season by those who had the right to unchartered water. One system was called 'clodding.' This was practicable only in shallow water, and for a few weeks before close time when some of the earlier fish were beginning to frequent the spawning beds. The 'clodder' used a very heavy leister (I have seen one which weighed 16 lbs.) with a very short shank. One end of a fine rope was tied to the cross portion of the spear, and the rope itself was coiled up on the ground. The leister was thrown at the fish, and if pierced, the sportsman seized the rope, and gradually and cautiously pulled the fish to the bank as it was carried down the water. The art was difficult to acquire, and not very generally practised. I have seen a man ascend a tree to look over a stream, then come down and spear a salmon twenty yards from the bank, whence the fish could not be seen. A more exciting system was to frighten the fish in a pool and make them seek shelter behind large stones near the side, or in holes in the banks. A clear, sunny day and a shrunken river were most suitable, and several persons were required. While the leisterers stationed themselves at the points to which former experience had taught them the disturbed fish would run, others threw heavy branches of trees, covered with their foliage, or large white clothes, such as bedsheets, into the top of the stream. When these came in sight of the salmon lying in the throat they dashed wildly down the pool or towards its sides, and were speared whenever they came within reach of the leisterer. One day I saw six fish taken by this method from a favourite pool into which the Leithen flows as it joins the Tweed. It was very fair sport on a good day, but much less exciting than another way of leistering which I have seen pursued during daylight on the Liddel and on the Ewes, a tributary of the Dumfriesshire Esk, and in other of the smaller Border rivers. Out of a party of, say a dozen, two were armed with the murderous weapon and six with poles. The poleman dragged the throats or rummaged below the grassy turf hanging over the margin of pool and stream, and if their pole struck a sea-trout the alarmed fish rushed wildly about and was thus brought under the eye of the leisterer. In most cases certain death followed, but sometimes a trout would escape the first aims of the spearman and rush headlong down the shallow stream below the pool. Those of the party on the bank followed it shouting to the spearman and polemen, who rushed pell-mell in pursuit, splashing and hallooing. If the poor fish had found a shelter before its assailants were up to it, the polemen usually soon hunted it out again and it was captured at last. Three or four miles of river made a good day's sport and gave zest to the wearied hunters's enjoyment of cheese and ale in the country inn on their way home.

'River Poaching on the Borders' in *The Fishing Gazette*,
26 April 1878

The Life of an Eighteenth-century Whale Hunter

They likewise agree to attend prayers morning and evening, on pain of a forfeit at the discretion of the Captain; nor to get drunk, or draw their knives, on forfeiture of half their wages; nor fight, on forfeiture of the whole. They are not to lay wagers on the good or ill success of the fishing, nor buy nor sell with the condition of taking one or more fish, on the penalty of twenty-five florins. They are likewise to rest satisfied with the provisions allowed them; and they are never to light candle, fire, or match, without the Captain's leave, on the like penalty.

After the reading this regulation, the crew are called over, who receive the customary gratuity before their setting out, with an assurance of another at their return, in proportion to the success of the voyage.

Each vessel of three hundred tons has six shaloops, each shaloop is allowed a harpineer, and five sailors to row it; in each shaloop there are seven lines of three inches circumference, five of them in the fore part of the vessel, and two behind. The five lines together make six hundred fathom, and with the addition of the other two, the whole amounts to eight hundred and fifty fathom. If the whale dives deeper, or runs further under the ice, the line must be cut, to prevent the loss of the boat.

The instrument wherewith the execution is done, is a harping-iron, or javelin, five or six feet long, pointed with steel in a triangular shape, like the barb of an arrow.

The harpineer, standing at one end of the shaloop, as soon as he is at a proper distance from the whale, flings the harping-iron, with all the force he is master of, against the whale's back, and if he is so lucky as to penetrate through the skin and fat into the flesh, he lets go a string fastened to the harping-iron, at the end whereof is a dry gourd, which swimming on the water discovers whereabout the whale is, who, as soon as he is struck, plunges to the bottom. The gourd is made use of when they have not line enough to pursue the whale in its career. However, great care is taken that they may have line enough; and if the cargo of one shaloop is not sufficient, they throw the end of the cord to another, and from thence to another, if there should be occasion.

The cord in running out so swiftly would often take fire, if it was not kept wetting with a mop or a swab.

As soon as the whale rises again for breath, the harpineer gives him a fresh wound with a launce, and so do the rest of the crew, as they have an opportunity; for when he begins to faint with loss of blood, they can approach near him, and then they plunge their launces into various parts of his body, which soon dispatch him. When the carcase begins to float, they cut off the fins and tail, and tow him to the ship, where they fasten ropes to keep him from sinking, and when it is cold they begin to cut it up.

In order to do this, three or four men go down upon the whale, with irons upon their boots to keep them from slipping. They begin to open him on the side, and proceed downwards towards the belly, cutting off all the fat into pieces of three feet broad, and eight long: besides the fat on the sides, they frequently cut off that on the throat and the under lip, leaving the lean behind. They next proceed to the whalebone, which they cut off, with hatchet made for that purpose, from the upper jaw of the fish. The fat and bone thus procured, they leave the carcase for the bears, who are very fond of it.

As fast as the large pieces of fat are cut off, the rest of the crew are employed in slicing them smaller, and picking out the lean.

When this is prepared, they stow it under deck till the fat of all the whale is on board; then cutting it still smaller, they put it up in tubs in the hold. or bottom of the vessel, cramming them very full and close; this done, they sail homewards, where the fat is to be boiled, and melted down into train oil.

As to the produce of this fishery, it is different in different years. In 1697, the most fortunate year that ever was known, one hundred ninety seven vessels took one thousand nine hundred and sixty-eight whales.

RICHARD BROOKES, *The Art of Angling*, 1790

Shooting Pike With Bow and Arrow

My friend, who has travelled practically round the whole world, had a great many sporting experiences, his chief pastimes being shooting and fishing, having specially reduced the latter to a fine art.

I had always known him as a man of many surprises, but I think the surprise he gave me that evening topped the list.

To my amazement he suddenly looked at his wrist-watch and thereafter ordered the gillies to remove the luncheon baskets and then dismissed them for the day, just as I was in the act of preparing to embark for another spell on the loch.

'Why are you doing this?' I ventured to ask him. 'Never mind,' said he, 'you will find out later. There is no time to be lost' – and commanding the gillies to take away all the fishing gear to his house – some two miles distant – he beckoned me to follow him, which I did.

'I am now going to show you how to catch pike without either rod or net,' he whispered, 'if you don't mind accompanying me.' 'Not a bit,' I said, somewhat taken aback, wondering to myself if he had suddenly taken leave of his senses. Of course, being his guest, I could hardly do otherwise than fall in with his very mysterious suggestion.

On reaching his car by the side of the road he started up the engine and soon we were speeding along in the opposite direction to which we had come. We had motored roughly three or four miles when he suddenly pulled up at an old wooden gate, and on opening it, we drove about a quarter of a mile along a sort of cart track and parked the car beside a rough strip of wood, which seemed alive with young birds, opposite a clover field, above which hovered a kestrel.

Getting out of the car, he turned to me with a grin on his face and said: 'We shall now proceed to look for our fish with the keen eye of the hunter and when we spot them we will shoot them.'

'Shoot them!' I exclaimed in astonishment, 'with a charge of dynamite or what?'

'No, not even with a gun,' replied my friend, 'but with the skill of archery' – and leaning over the side of his car he produced two bows and arrows.

As the month had been a dry one, my friend commented that it was a very favourable time to shoot fish, as the waters were low and clear, in consequence of which the fish would be more easily observed in the water from the bank.

Between the chains of lochs I have already referred to, there are sluggish streams with occasional deep pools and shady shallows fringed with reeds, from the sides of which one is able to stalk one's fish.

My friend explained he had learned his theory of angling by archery some years ago from a certain tribe of Indians, while he was in North America, to whom rods and nets are practically unknown articles, and that he had been taught by them how to construct his own bows and arrows from hard wood; and the bow he handed to me was about four and a half feet long, and cane arrows with barbed metal points about the same length.

It would be about 4 p.m. as we made our way, bows in hand, walking breast high through the tall grasses and sedges overlooking a deep pool, on the opposite side of which was a sandbank surrounded by rushes, and although the sun was still bright enough to give us plenty of light, the surface of the water was freed from fiery reflection, as we took up our position in a grassy hollow such as lovers are wont to sit in, in the moonlight.

Lying flat on our stomachs, we gently manoeuvred our way towards the bank in front of us. My friend slipped an arrow on to his bow and crawled cautiously forward a foot or two in advance, all the while keeping his eyes glued on the surface of the water, every now and then giving me a signal to halt or follow him.

His bow bent slowly, and with a 'ping' of his bow-string an arrow ripped into the water, and disappeared into the depths, reappearing some moments later about twenty yards downstream, almost vertical and vibrating violently, and then it commenced to sink gradually below the surface again. In a few seconds the top of the arrow reappeared about fifty yards downstream, pulsating as if alive only to disappear again.

By this time we were on our feet, and wasting no time hurried to a point on the bank opposite where we had last observed the throbbing shaft. Hardly had we reached the water's edge when we observed the top portion of the arrow again break the surface of the water, forming in its manoeuvres a series of semicircles. The excitement by this time was tense, and being unable to restrain my feelings any longer I approached to the very water's edge, and bending over the stream with bow in hand, took careful aim, like a veritable Cupid, and allowing for the refraction, discharged my arrow right into the body of the sickly fish a few feet from where I stood. On being struck at almost point-blank range, the fish gave a wild rush towards the opposite bank, and after a somewhat futile struggle, turned on its side and floated quietly in midstream towards the deeper waters at the head of the loch.

In an instant my friend was almost waist deep in water, and following him, I waded out to seize our prize, which my friend clutched by the tail, and in no time our captive lay kicking his last among the tall grasses on the bank of the stream with both arrows still deeply embedded in its side, when a jab with the knife through the brain ended its sufferings.

The pike we 'shot' weighed roughly ten pounds, but we had the satisfaction of knowing that, although caught in this seemingly unsporting manner, it would never be mourned, for the pike is recognised as the most rapacious fish in the British Isles, and I think I am correct in stating that a pike of ten pounds or so is quite worth writing about.

R. MACDONALD ROBERTSON, *In Scotland With a Fishing Rod*,
1935

How to Snare a Pike

Fish-poaching is simple and yet clever in its way. In the spawning time jack fish, which at other periods are apparently of a solitary disposition, go in pairs, and sometimes in trios, and are more tame than usual. A long slender ash stick is selected, slender enough to lie light in the hand and strong enough to bear a sudden weight. A loop and running noose are formed of a piece of thin copper wire, the other end of which is twisted round and firmly attached to the smaller end of the stick. The loop is adjusted to the size of the fish – it should not be very much larger, else it will not draw up quick enough, nor too small, else it may touch and disturb the jack. It does not take much practice to hit the happy medium. Approaching the bank of the brook quietly, so as not to shake the ground, to the vibrations of which fish are peculiarly sensitive, the poacher tries if possible to avoid letting his shadow fall across the water.

The poacher, having marked his prey in the shallow yonder,

gently extends his rod slowly across the water three or four yards higher up the stream, and lets the wire noose sink without noise till it almost or quite touches the bottom. It is easier to guide the noose to its destination when it occasionally touches the mud, for refraction distorts the true position of objects in water, and accuracy is important. Gradually the wire swims down with the current, just as if it were an ordinary twig or root carried along, such as the jack is accustomed to see, and he therefore feels no alarm. By degrees the loop comes closer to the fish, till with a steady hand the poacher slips it over the head, past the long vicious jaws and gills, past the first fins, and pauses when it has reached a place corresponding to about one-third of the length of the fish, reckoning from the head. That end of the jack is heavier than the other, and the 'lines' of the body are there nearly straight. Thus the poacher gets a firm hold – for a fish, of course, is slippery – and a good balance. If the operation is performed gently the jack will remain quite still, though the wire rubs against his side: silence and stillness have such a power over all living creatures. The poacher now clears his arm and, with a sudden jerk, lifts the fish right out of the stream and lands him on the sward.

So sharp is the grasp of the wire that it frequently cuts its way through the scales, leaving a mark plainly visible when the jack is offered for sale. The suddenness and violence of the compression seem to disperse the muscular forces, and the fish appears dead for a moment. Very often, indeed, it really is killed by the jerk. This happens when the loop either has not passed far enough along the body or has slipped and seized the creature just at the gills. It then garottes the fish. If, on the other hand, the wire has been passed too far towards the tail, it slips off that way, the jack falling back into the water with a broad white band where the wire has scraped the scales. Fish thus marked may not unfrequently be seen in the stream.

With such a rude implement as this some fish-poachers will speedily land a good basket of pike. During the spawning season, as was observed previously, jack go in pairs, and now and then in trios, and of this the poacher avails himself to take more than one at a haul. The fish lie so close together – side by side just at that time – that it is quite practicable, with care and judgment, to slip a wire

over two at once. When near the bank two may even be captured
with a good withy noose: with a wire a clever hand will make a
certainty of it. The keeper says that on one occasion he watched a
man operating just without his jurisdiction, who actually succeeded
in wiring three jacks at once and safely landed them on the grass.

RICHARD JEFFERIES, *The Gamekeeper at Home*, 1878

Izaak Walton's Notorious Humbug About Frogs and Pike Fishing

And thus use your frog, that he may continue long alive:

Put your hook into his mouth, which you may easily do from the
middle of *April* till *August*, and then the frogs mouth grows up, and
he continues so far at least 6 months without eating, but is sustained,
none but he whose name is Wonderful, knows how: I say, put your
hook, I mean the arming wire, through his mouth, and out at his
gills, and then with a fine needle and silk sew the upper part of his
leg with only one stitch to the arming wire of your hook, or tie the
frogs leg above the upper joynt, to the armed wire; and in so doing,
use him as though you loved him, that is, harm him as little as you
may possibly, that he may live the longer.

And now, having given you this direction for the baiting your
ledger hook with a live Fish of frog, my next must be to tell you,
how your hook thus baited must or may be used: and it is thus.
Having fastened your hook to a line, which if it be not 14 yards
long, should not be less than 12; you are to fasten that line to any
bough near to a hole where a Pike is, or is likely to lie, or to have a
haunt, and then wind your line on any forked stick, all your line,
except ½ yard of it or rather more, and split that forked stick with
such a nick or notch at one end of it, as may keep the line from any
more of it ravelling from about the stick, than so much of it as you
intend; and choose your forked stick to be of that bigness as may
keep the Fish or frog from pulling the forked stick under the water
till the Pike bites, and then the Pike having pulled the line forth of
the clift or nick of that stick in which it was gently fastened, he will
have line enough to go to his hold and pouch the bait: and if you
would have this ledger bait to keep at a fixt place, undisturbed by

wind or other accidents which may drive it to the shore side, (for you are to note, that it is likeliest to catch a Pike in the midst of the water) then hang a small Plummet of lead, a stone, or piece of tile, or a turf in a string, and cast it into the water, with the forked stick, to hang upon the ground, to be a kind of Anchor to keep the forked stick from moving out of your intended place till the Pike come. This I take to be a very good way, to use so many ledger-baits as you intend to make trial of.

Or if you bait your hooks thus with live Fish or Frogs, and in a windy day, fasten them thus to a bough or bundle of straw, and by the help of that wind can get them to move cross a *Pond* or *mere*, you are like to stand still on the shore and see sport presently if there be any store of *Pikes*; or these live baits may make sport, being tied about the body or wings of a *Goose* or *Duck*, and she chased over a *Pond*: and the like may be done with turning three or four live baits thus fastened to bladders, or boughs, or bottles of hay or flags, to swim down a River, whilst you walk quietly alone on the shore, and are still in expectation of sport.

IZAAK WALTON, The Compleat Angler, 1653

Live Frog Fishing for Large-Mouth Bass

I know it sounds inhumane. But a 'frog-fisher' always looks down on the man who uses the mechanical lures, sneering that he is 'fishing with machinery!' And to cast a live frog correctly required a skilled and gentle hand. For many years I fished with one of the finest 'frog-casters' in the United States. At any rate, he made it almost a matter of course to win every prize given by the big sporting magazines.

But this doctor did not fish for prizes. He was a Southerner, from the Deep South, and a gentleman of the purest heart. He both looked and talked like the old President Theodore Roosevelt, who, he asserted, was what an all-round man should be. And, although he had just enough to keep him comfortable, this fine old doctor didn't care a whoop for either money, fame, even medical distinction; he lived the year round for just one month – July.

Every morning in July, except Sunday, a local man arrived at the doctor's door with 75 small, live frogs in a box. Then the doctor got into his old-fashioned car. Back he would come at sunset, red as a strawberry; and some dozen or so monster bass would be lying under a wet gunnysack. Where he got them from, such a continual supply of big ones, the neighbourhood never could make out. And then, too, the neighbours were not particularly interested; for, as I have said, this was in the money-making age, and most of the wealthy men who had their summer homes around that lake were merely tolerant of the doctor, liking him, but thinking him rather a fool – to go off fishing in the hot sun that way.

But he baited me so often about my 'fishing with machinery' that I took to frog-casting in sheer self-defence. I caught his fever.

There was a shallow, sandy-bottomed lake that it took us some hours to get to. A mite too slack, this reedy-marged expanse, for the vigorous small-mouth. There was a sort of back-bone of willows that seemed to grow almost out of the water along the centre of it.

'Negley,' the old doctor would say, baiting a fresh frog through its lips, 'the big old bass, the wise ones, lie under the shade of those willows in the heat of the day. Now there's one . . . just . . . there . . . that I've stirred once or twice . . .'

As he said 'just there' the doctor made his cast – plenty of line already stripped off the reel over the fingers of one hand; the *dressed* silk line, in this case, 'shooting' easily through the guides. The art is to cast your frog so that there is no jerk. You mustn't kill him, or take the life out of him, by jerking his head about. You must drop him gently *on the willows*.

'Y-e-e-s . . .' said the doctor, reminiscently; 'he must be at least five pounds . . . that fellow under there.'

And as he said that he was gently coaxing the frog off the willow branch into the water. The frog dropped. Instantly, it began to swim – with kicks. If the bass didn't take it then, the doctor pulled the line in, strip fashion, so that each pull straightened out the frog's legs, and each pause gave it time to kick again. But usually a big waiting bass was ready for it.

There was a swirl – and the swimming frog was taken under.

'*But you don't strike now, Negley!*'

No, the doctor explained; that would only mean that you pulled the frog out of the bass's mouth. 'Because these large-mouth always take a frog, first, sideways. Then they swim off and down a bit, blow it out, then take it in head-on!' So, while he was saying this, I watched with apprehensive stare the line sliding through the big guides of the Leonard rod. The doctor made no attempt to stop it; on the contrary, he was obediently paying it out – so that the bass should feel no pull.

Then there was a pause when the line stopped moving. The doctor's jaw muscles began to set. Then the line started slowly moving out again. Carefully, oh so carefully, the doctor gently took in all the slack; then he leaned back – *struck*!

Well, if you have ever stirred a paddle around in a bath tub, you can imagine the rumpus that was aroused. A huge bass – five, six, possibly eight pounds, had had the hook driven deep into him. He was wild. He came from the surface, the spray flying away from him, arched, turned like a fighting plane in a dog-fight – and crashed back into the water again.

'Away!' shouted the doctor; 'get me away from those willows! Work out into the lake! For God's sake – keep your side to him. Wait – don't move – he's making a run! Ah – got you, you beauty!'

The fish had flung out into the sunny air, crashed back again. And, in all these contradictory commands, I had won the valuable space between us and the shore. The art of frog-casting will make you dissatisfied with the artificial lures. Its drama is more visible, because you are watching your frog for most of the time – a thing you seldom get the chance of doing when you are fishing with a live minnow. Always, after the doctor and I had killed a few satisfactory fish, we would deliberately chance losing one merely for the opportunity of watching the bass handle the frog; they always did what the doctor said – took it from the side, then swam off and down to blow it out. You never came closer to watching a fish *thinking* than when you saw one of these deep-shouldered bass eye the frog . . . and bear down on it to swallow it head-on. Then, when you struck, at these close distances, you witnessed all the frantic energy you had set in motion.

As to the cruelty of this sport, it cannot be any more unpardonable than baiting a live minnow through the back and letting the doomed thing swim. Sometimes the frogs would come back with their 'trousers' ripped off, or long triangular rips in their green and white skin; this meant that a pike or pickerel had taken a snatch at it, with their long rows of slanting teeth. We always killed these frogs immediately and threw them ashore. The doctor, too, had a sense of fair play, even with frogs; he never used one for more than four casts. 'Then he's served his time,' he would say with a smile, looking at me over the tops of his spectacles; 'he's a free frog.' So, when we pulled ashore under some shady tree for luncheon, the old man always released a dozen or so lively little ones. *His* gentle casting had not hurt them. A less-skilled man might kill the frog in two casts. And they would grow up, said the doctor, reminding me of Uncle Remus, to sing the booming bull-frog song: 'Doncher-believe-'um! Doncher-believe-'um!'

NEGLEY FARSON, *Going Fishing*, 1942

Bad News For Geese

Huxing Pike is also done by fixing an armed hook baited, at such a length as to swim about mid-water, to the leg of a *Goose* or *Duck*, and then driving the birds into the water. It was thus formerly practised in the *Loch* of *Monteith* in Scotland, which abounds with very large Perch and Pike. 'Upon the Islands a number of *Geese* were collected by the Farmers, who occupied the surrounding banks of the *loch*, after baited lines of two or three feet long had been tied to the *legs* of their geese, they were driven into the water; steering naturally homewards, in different directions, the baits were soon swallowed; a violent and often tedious struggle ensued, in which, however, the *geese* at length prevailed, though they were frequently much exhausted before they reached the shore.' This method has not been so long relinquished, but there are old persons upon the spot, who were active promoters of the amusement.

THE REVEREND WILLIAM DANIEL, *Rural Sports*, 1802

Pity The Mullingar Goose

I cannot well omit acquainting you with one manner of fishing used for diversion on this Lough. They take into their boat a goose, and about her body, under her wings, they tie one end of their fishing line, the hook being covered with some bait at the other. Thus they throw the fishing-goose into the water, who sports and preens herself with seeming pleasure enough, until some unmannerly fish seizes the baited hook and interrupts her diversion by giving her a tug which douces her almost under water, this commonly frightens her so as to put her to the wing, but if the fish be heavy she is forced to float upon the water, and though in romance the knight generally slays the giant, yet if the pike be of the larger sort Mrs Goose without the assistance of the spectators is sometimes like to go down to the pike instead of the pike coming up to her.

Extract from a letter by JOHN DONTON, travelling in Ireland
circa 1690

Darned Elusive Tench

The tench is a very curious fish in his habits. You may see a pond which is stocked with good tench, and look over it narrowly, and even do so many times, without having the slightest idea that there is a fish in it. I have known ponds which have been supposed to be fishless for years, by the merest accident to be discovered to contain large numbers of fine tench in them. In many places tench are very peculiar also in their times of feeding; on some days they will feed well, while at other times you will not manage to get a fish in a week; and though this is not *always* the case, they are yet usually more or less capricious. As an illustration of the above, I may state that I once knew a little pond in Hampshire, which was not perhaps more than about twenty yards square. I had many times seen it, but never saw a fish in it, when one day the person to whom it belonged, knowing that I was fond of fishing, asked me if I would not like to catch some of the tench in the pond. I had no idea there were any in it, but as he assured me there were, and as I had nothing else to do one afternoon, I got a bag of worms and walked down to the pond with my rod. I put up a small light cork float, and a couple of hooks, one four or five inches above the other, baited with red worms, threw in some broken worms, and waited. Presently I caught a little eel; then another; then a little tench of less than half a pound weight; then one or two more eels; and although I kept on throwing in the broken worms I did no more, and finally I threw in the rest of my worms and went away disgusted, not having seen another fish move. Still the proprietor assured me there were good tench in the pond, and urged me to try again, and the next afternoon, being inclined for a lazy hour or two, I took my rod, a book, and my pipe, and walked down to the pond. I pitched in my float as usual, and sat down behind a bush, lighted my pipe, and began to read, when on looking up I found that my float had disappeared, and was 'making tracks' for the middle of the pond. Thinking it was only a small eel, I got up lazily, took up the rod and struck, when to my surprise, I found that I had hold of something a good deal larger than I bargained for, and after a tolerable tussle, I got out a fine tench of a pound and a half. The book was at once consigned to oblivion, and I set to work carefully, and barely was my float settled, when 'wriggle, wriggle, wriggle,' it went, and after the usual preliminary gyrations and bobs which the tench generally communicates to it, off it went; I struck again, and got another fine tench of nearly two pounds: after this the fun grew fast and furious. Unfortunately, I did not keep score of the fish I caught, as, finding I was having such great sport, I was afraid of clearing the pond out, so I put most of them in again, merely keeping three brace of two-pounders; but I should imagine that I must have captured about thirty fine tench, not one of which would be under a pound and a quarter, and many of them topped two pounds and a half. Where all these large fish could have packed themselves in this mite of a pond without ever attracting notice, I could not imagine. Tired of pulling them out, I left off in the evening while the fish were yet biting freely. I went there again the next day, and caught *one* tench of three-quarters of a pound; but, though I fished there many times since, *I never caught a tench afterwards*. Tench at times feed freely enough all day; but the favourite feeding-time is at dusk, and when you can barely see your float – then they will take if they take at all.

FRANCIS FRANCIS, *A Book of Angling*, 1867

Fly-Fishing for Chub

No nets will exterminate these spawn-eating, fry-eating, all-eating pests, who devour the little trout, and starve the large ones, and, at the first sign of the net, fly to hover among the most tangled roots.

There they lie, as close as rats in a bank, and work themselves the farther in the more they are splashed and poked by the poles of the beaters. But the fly, well used, will – if not exterminate them – still thin them down greatly; and very good sport they give, in my opinion, in spite of the contempt in which they are commonly held, as chicken-hearted fish, who show no fight. True; but their very cowardice makes them the more difficult to catch; for no fish must you keep more out of sight, and farther off. The very shadow of the line (not to mention that of the rod) sends them flying to hover; and they rise so cautiously and quietly, that they give excellent lessons in patience and nerve to a beginner. If the fly is dragged along the surface, or jerked suddenly from them, they flee from it in terror; and when they do, after due deliberation, take it in, their rise is so quiet, that you can seldom tell whether your fish weighs half a pound or four pounds and a half – unless you, like most beginners, attempt to show your quickness by that most useless exertion, a violent strike. Then, the snapping of your footlink, or – just as likely – of the top of your rod, makes you fully aware, if not of the pluck, at least of the brute strength, of the burly alderman of the waters. No fish, therefore, will better teach the beginner the good old lesson, 'not to frighten a fish before you have tired him.'

For flies – chub will rise greedily at any large palmers, the larger and rougher the better. A red and a grizzled hackle will always take them; but the best fly of all is an imitation of the black beetle – the 'undertaker' of the London shops. He, too, can hardly be too large, and should be made of a fat body of black wool, with the metallic black feather of a cock's tail wrapped loosely over it. A still better wing is one of the neck feathers of any metallic-plumed bird, *e.g. Phlogophorus Impeyanus*, the Menaul Pheasant, laid flat and whole on the back, to imitate the wing-shells of the beetle, the legs being represented by any loose black feathers – (not hackles, which are too fine). Tied thus, it will kill not only every chub in a pool (if you give the survivors a quarter of an hour wherein to recover from their horror at their last friend's fate), but also, here and there, very large trout.

CHARLES KINGSLEY, Chalkstream Studies, 1903

===

A British Airman Reflects in a German Prisoner-of-War Camp

The golden rule for striking salmon is 'don't'. With a sunk fly and line the temptation to strike isn't quite as great as with a greased line. If the rod point is kept low and a finger on the line the fish will hook itself by turning against the tight line, and when a steady pull is felt all that is needed is to raise the rod point slowly. With a greased line most people like to have a few feet of loose line between the reel and the first ring: When a fish takes they let this line go. An alternative is to have the check of the reel set very light and allow it to turn a couple of times before raising the rod point. It is difficult to stop oneself striking, especially when the fish takes with a head-and-tail rise, but I can usually manage it and watch the line stealing away across the water without any violent reaction. They say it is fatal to strike at once and I believe it is, but when the fish spits the fly out again before he is hooked, I sometimes wonder whether a good quick strike mightn't have done the trick and hooked me a salmon. This happened on the last day's salmon fishing I had before I was *abgeschossen* and the Germans who pulled me out of the Zuider Zee said, 'The war for you is ended, yes?' I was fishing the long stream on the Rutherford beat of Tweed in the autumn. The river was fairly low so I was using a greased line and small fly. I can still see the line begin to move away across the water as I let him have the slack line I was holding, but before he took it all up he let go. If I had struck should I have had him? I have plenty of time to think it over anyway.

STEPHEN JOHNSON, *Fishing From Afar*, 1947
(written in Stalag Luft III in 1943)

Other Baits for Chub

The Chub will take *Gentles, Wasps-Maggots*, (which must be baked in an oven before used,) *Paste* of fine new white bread, (without being made *wet*,) worked up in the hand, and tinged with *Vermilion* as near as possible to the colour of *Salmon's Roe*; from the hook this paste will not easily wash off, and is a most killing bait; but the best baits for *bottom* or *float*-fishing for this fish, are, *old Cheshire* cheese, (such as without crumbling will mould in the hand,) and the *Pith*

===

from the back bone of an *Ox*, with the *outward* so carefully taken off, as not to bruise the *inward* skin. At every season of the year the former of these is good, but the *latter end* of *Summer* and *all* the *Winter*, are the preferable times for both.

THE REVEREND WILLIAM DANIEL, *Rural Sports*, 1802

An Oxford Plumber's Son

The strike is the roach fisherman's art, for roach have tiny suspicious mouths and love to nibble at a bait or take it in and eject it so quickly that the movement scarcely shows in a quiver on the float. Such playful creatures were never safe with Tom. His eyes were hard on his float, and his whole body was hunched towards it, keeping the rod top as nearly as possible above it right through the length of the swim. The tiniest check meant a swift, sure strike and generally a fish securely hooked. I watched him many times before going off with my fly rod to look for chub, and occasionally I tried my hand with his tackle. Whenever I did so, I learned humility; again and again I would strike too late or too hard or fail to strike at all. And Tom would take the rod and show me. 'There. You see 'ow easy it is. Just keep your eye on the quill and 'it 'im as soon as it checks.' As he spoke, he would have struck to a check that only his spirit could have seen – his eyes were no better than mine and I had not seen it – and be fast in a good fish. He played them as he fished for them, with a minimum of fuss and movement, generally on a tight line and following the runs and struggles of the fish by keeping his rod top as nearly as possibly directly over it. With the fish on the bank, he would say, 'You could do it, easy, if you'd keep at it. It ain't nothing but practice and a little patience. You'll come to it when you're older and not so flighty.'

RODERICK HAIG-BROWN, *A River Never Sleeps*, 1942

A Crane Divines the Secret of Angling

'*Though to my feathers in the wet,*
I have stood here from break of day,
I have not found a thing to eat

For only rubbish comes my way.
Am I to live on lebeen-lone?'
Muttered the old crane of Gort.
'For all my pains on lebeen-lone?'

King Guare walked amid his court
The palace-yard and river-side
And there to three old beggars said,
'You that have wandered far and wide
Can ravel out what's in my head.
Do men who least desire get most,
Or get the most who most desire?'
A beggar said, 'They get the most
Whom man or devil cannot tire,
And what could make their muscles taut
Unless desire had made them so?'
But Guare laughed with secret thought,
'If that be true as it seems true,
One of you three is a rich man,
For he shall have a thousand pounds
Who is first asleep, if but he can
Sleep before the third noon sounds.'
And thereon, merry as a bird
With his old thoughts, King Guare went
From river-side and palace-yard
And left them to their argument.
'And if I win,' one beggar said,
'Though I am old I shall persuade
A pretty girl to share my bed';
The second: 'I shall learn a trade';
The third: 'I'll hurry to the course
Among the other gentlemen,
And lay it all upon a horse';
The second: 'I have thought again:
A farmer has more dignity.'
One to another sighed and cried:
The exorbitant dreams of beggary,
That idleness had borne to pride,

Sang through their teeth from noon to noon;
And when the second twilight brought
The frenzy of the beggars' moon
None closed his blood-shot eyes but sought
To keep his fellows from their sleep;
All shouted till their anger grew
And they were whirling in a heap.

They mauled and bit the whole night through;
They mauled and bit till the day shone;
They mauled and bit through all that day
And till another night had gone,
Or if they made a moment's stay
They sat upon their heels to rail,
And when old Guare came and stood
Before the three to end this tale,
They were commingling lice and blood.
'Time's up,' he cried, and all the three
With blood-shot eyes upon him stared.
'Time's up,' he cried, and all the three
Fell down upon the dust and snored.

'Maybe I shall be lucky yet,
Now they are silent,' said the crane.
'Though to my feathers in the wet
I've stood as I were made of stone
And seen the rubbish runabout,
It's certain there are trout somewhere
And maybe I shall take a trout
If but I do not seem to care.'

W.B. YEATS, 'The Three Beggars', in *Collected Poems*, 1914

Shark-fishing in the Gilbert Islands

Although safety first is the rule when tiger-shark are about in
numbers, plenty of Gilbertese are ready to fight a lone prowler in its
own element. Owing to his great girth, a tiger cannot turn quickly;

once launched on its attack, it thunders straight forward like a bull; there lies the hunter's advantage in single combat. Out sailing with a Tarawa friend one day, I pointed out a cruising dorsal fin. 'That's a tababa,' he said, 'watch me kill him.'

We lowered sail and drifted. He slid overboard with his knife and paddled around waiting to be noticed. He soon was. The fin began to circle him, and he knew he was being stalked; he trod water; it closed in gradually, lazily to fifteen yards.

He held his knife right-handed, blade down, the handle just above the water, his crooked right elbow pointed always towards the gliding fin. He would have a split second to act in when the charge came. It came from ten yards' range. There was a frothing swirl; the fin shot forward like an arrow; the head and shoulders of the brute broke surface, rolling as they lunged. My friend flicked aside in the last blink of time and shot his knife into the upswinging belly as it surged by. His enemy's momentum did the rest. I saw the belly rip itself open like a zip-fastener, discharging blood and guts. The tiger disappeared for a while, to float up dead a hundred yards off.

That kind of single combat used to be fairly common. It was rather like a nice score of fifty at cricket in England; the villagers applauded but did not make a great song about it.

ARTHUR GRIMBLE, *A Pattern of Islands*, 1952

To Catch a Sturgeon

In 1925, when the Rumanians were shocking the world with their organised murdering of the Russians they were inducing to escape across the Dniester (and then shooting them as they crossed the river to Kichenev) I got into Bessarabia without a permit. I lived with some Russian sturgeon fishermen in the frozen marshes of the Danube delta, sleeping in their clay hut on the top of their clay stove. The Russian peasant is outrageously courageous when it comes to talking; he says everything that is on his mind – if it is a complaint – even though he knows he might get killed for it. And I almost had to shut these people up when they began pouring out what they knew about the Tartar Bunar massacre which had just taken place – Bessarabia was a land of terror in those days.

To get them to the stage of intimacy where they would begin to talk I first had to go out to fish sturgeon with them in their black sailing lodka in the choppy yellow waves of the Black Sea. The days were so cold that I thought my spine would become nothing but a strip of ice. They caught the sturgeon on long lines of bare hooks that lay like a rake before the shallow entrance of this mouth of the Danube. The sturgeon, feeling his way up along the bottom, met these obstructive hooks, gave a flip – and the next instant he was involved in a whirl of hooks – pinioned. With the ice coating the black skiff these three men pulled a sturgeon almost as big as a man into the boat. Then they beat him to death with wooden clubs. Remember, the sturgeon has armour-plated sides and a head hard as a stone, built that way to meet the rocks of the bottom up which he must travel against the swift currents. These hooks, made in Norway, had needle-sharp points. With them flying around my head as the sturgeon flung himself about the skiff, I can truthfully say I have seldom had a more terrifying experience in my life.

Rumanian sentries, with fixed bayonets – also sharp as needle points – challenged us from every bit of solid land in the marsh. But it was so bitterly cold that they did not take their mittens off to examine our papers. A good thing for me – for I had none.

These persecuted fishermen had to 'sell' all their sturgeon to the Fish Control – a horrible piece of Government graft – and the big one was duly taken up to the market at Wilkowo; but a smaller one was walking around all that afternoon, cut up in small pieces, in the fishermen's pockets and down inside their boots. That night we made a rich, red soup of him; and we all ate it with the same wooden spoon. It was considered good manners to lick the spoon clean before you passed it on. We drank the last of my vodka, and they suddenly produced some red wine from a blue tea-pot. The hut steamed. The ice boomed and cracked in the moonlit marshes. They sailed me down the Black Sea the next day, where I was arrested at Sulina. But their story had corroborated a story of official terrorism that I had been putting together ever since I left Bucharest. Later, I wired it from Constantinople – with never a hint of these courageous sturgeon fishermen. And it was with a satisfied mind, on my last night with them, that I stretched myself out on their warm stove –

to dream of the mighty sturgeon, feeling his way up the Danube, with his cold moonstone eyes.

NEGLEY FARSON, *Going Fishing,* 1932

Eel-switching in Ireland

The eel-switch is a long, thin, gaff-stick. To the end is lashed a knitting needle, and on to the knitting needle is lashed a cod hook. On the still days, when there was no wind or ripple, one drifted silently over the water, the switcher kneeling on the bottom of the boat with his eyes glued on the bed of the lake till he saw an eel, either inert, stretched at full length or curled up, or with his head under a weed or stone, and his tail and body waving in the water as he hunted for worms or shrimps. Then the switch went over the side very cautiously till the hook was within an inch or two of the eel's body. A sudden jerk, and (if the switcher was an expert) up came the switch and a writhing, astonished eel was wriggling amidst our feet.

It seemed to me incredible that the hook should go into that slippery, narrow strip of indiarubber as if it were butter – but so it was, when an expert wielded it. Even I got one occasionally, though the owner of the lake switched four to my one – and mine were always those that were still. He could switch them as they moved, or strike at exactly the right place in an unseen body when only a tail showed from under the weeds. He was even quick enough, on rare occasions (remember this was Ireland, the home of poachers), to switch a trout. He never miscalculated his distance in the clear water, as I did, and struck above his quarry: he never timed his strike too soon, and caught a weed – or barked his knuckles on the gunnel, or let the eel drop off the hook as he brought it up.

And he was equally good at the night switching, which was even more exciting, as is anything done in the dark; and more difficult, because the eels are more lively at night and apt to be scared by the electric torch. For eel-switching at night requires, not only a dead calm but an electric torch, held downwards on to the water by an assistant, who searches the bottom and keeps it steady on the eel while the switcher makes his stroke. We sometimes got as many as a dozen eels, though never any very big ones. But, of course, the smaller they were, the more difficult they were to switch. Apart from the skill required and the pleasure of picking one's prey suddenly out of the deep, the great merit of this form of eel-fishing is that there is no extracting of the hooks from the inside of the eel, and no unravelling of a slimy line.

MAURICE HEADLAM, A Holiday Fisherman, 1934

Bobbing for Eels

There are two ways of fishing for Eels, proper and peculiar to that fish alone; the first is termed by some, angling for Eels, which is thus: take a short strong rod, and exceeding strong line, with a little compassed, but strong hook, which you must bait with a large well-scoured red worm, then place the end of the hook very easily in a cleft of a stick, that it may very easily slip out; with this stick and hook thus baited, search for holes under stones, timbers, roots, or about flood-gates; if there be a good Eel, give her time, and she will take it; but be sure she has gorged it, and then you may conclude, if your tackling hold, she is your own.

The other way is called bobbing for Eels, which is thus: take the largest garden worms, scour them well, and with a needle run a very strong thread or silk through them from end to end; take so many as that at last you may wrap them about a board, for your hand will be too narrow, a dozen times at least, then tie them fast with the other two ends of the thread or silk, that they may hang in so many long bouts or hanks; then fasten all to a strong cord, and something more than a handful above the worms, fasten a plumb of lead, of about three quarters of a pound, making your cord sure to a long and strong pole; with these worms thus ordered, you must fish in a muddy water, and you will feel the Eels tug strongly at them; when you think they have swallowed them as far as they can, gently draw up your worms and Eels, and when you have them near the top of the water, hoist them amain to land; and thus you may take three or four at once, and good ones, if there be store.

ROBERT VENABLES, The Experienced Angler, 1662

Whistling for Eels

The Chinese are reputed to call their goldfish for their food by whistling. Sir Joseph Banks and Sir Francis Bacon were both in the habit of summoning their fish to be fed by ringing a shrill bell, while Dr Alfred Smee, F.R.S., describes how his goldfish used to come up mouth-out-of-water when he gave a high-pitched whistle. There is of course always the possibility that the fish caught sight of the persons about to feed them or were conscious of approaching footsteps. But it seems incredible that men of the intellectual and scientific calibre of those mentioned would have been so easily deceived, seeing that a few simple tests would have cleared up any doubt about the matter.

The practice of whistling for eels and other fish seems to be world-wide, and is prevalent in Northern India. Here is another case of which I chanced to be an eye-witness. The scene was a big river in a mountainous district. Except in mid-stream the water was shallow and strewn with big rocks, evidently fallen from the slopes above. After doing a lot of heavy wading I was taking a rest on the bank when I noticed in the distance a motionless, blanketed figure stooping over a rock. I walked over out of curiosity and found that the strange figure was a fisherman from a neighbouring village. In one hand he held a stick with a hook and a worm at its business end, and moving from boulder to boulder he dipped it in the water close to one of the rocks, always on the downstream side. Meanwhile he kept on whistling shrilly at short intervals. On questioning him I discovered that he was after eels.

'Why,' I asked, 'don't you put your stick in upstream so that the eels can smell the worm?'

'No, no,' he replied. 'The eel will hear and will run away.'

He explained that if he whistled long enough the eels poked their heads out and spotted the worm. He had been standing still, doubled up for a long time, whistling incessantly. Suddenly he called out: 'It is coming,' and pulled out an eel about 2 ft. long. Anxious to get to the bottom of the puzzle I asked him what would happen if he didn't whistle. His answer was short and pithy. 'No whistle no eel,' he said.

If there is nothing more in this practice than whistling for a wind, it is strange that it is so universal.

JOSCELYN LANE, *Fly-Fisher's Pie*, 1954

Why Dumb People Catch More Trout than Smart People

If you hang around Charley's Hotel Rapids on the Brodheads Creek, or Frank Keener's Antrim Lodge on the Beaverkill, and pay close attention to the inmates, you will notice that the lamer the brain, the heavier the creel.

The reason for this is very simple. When a fisherman gets to the stream he looks it over and decides where he would go if he were a fish. Then he takes out his worm can or his fly-box and decides which worm or which fly he would prefer if he were a fish.

Then he drifts his worm or casts his fly into the spot he has decided on. If he catches a fish, he is very proud, because he knows he thinks like a fish. And naturally, fishermen who think like fish catch more trout than fishermen who think like armadillos or duck-billed platypuses or mongooses.

Of course, the reason a fish thinks the way he does is that his brain is very tiny in relation to his body. So the tinier the fisherman's brain the easier it is for him to think like a fish, and catch trout right and left.

The same principle explains why fishermen with big mouths catch the most large-mouth bass, and fishermen with banjo eyes catch the most walleyed pike, and fishermen with jaundice catch the most yellow perch, and so forth.

The virgin sturgeon has never been caught on rod and reel.

ED ZERN, *To Hell With Fishing*, 1945

Advice on Escaping

A trip is an adventure, and on an adventure things should be allowed to happen as they will. Still, I have developed some guidelines.

Bad camp cooks are okay as long as you can keep them away

from the food, but bad cooks who mix cans of spaghetti and chile together in the same pan as a way of continuing to punish their mothers for something should be avoided, as this tendency may show up in nonculinary areas as well.

Whiners of all sorts should not come along. People who cannot deal with the standard adversities – either real or imagined – can throw a serious clod in the churn.

Compulsive score keepers should be avoided: people who refuse to have had a good day unless they've hit some preconceived mark, like '25 fish boated' or 'at least one 20-incher.'

Never go fishing with someone else's kid unless you enjoy kids a lot more than you do fishing.

People who claim to own 'fishing dogs' are all blinded by love. There's no such thing as a good fishing dog. Most of these beasts are retrievers who think they can do to trout what they've been trained to do to ducks. It may sound cute, but it's not. Stay away from people who take their dogs fishing.

Do not go fishing with someone who is so set on being back at a certain time that he will refuse to invent a case of car trouble to keep you on the water an extra day.

Don't travel in large or even medium-sized groups. A typical gang of six fishermen will include a bad cook, a whiner, a score keeper, someone who absolutely has to be back by Thursday noon, his five-year-old son, and his dog, Gonzo.

In the end, it's probably best to travel with established fishing partners, no more than two at a time. The old hands are like your regular brand of beer – less than perfect, perhaps, but predictable.

And never say exactly when you'll be back; that way it's not possible to be late.

JOHN GIERACH, *Trout Bum*, 1986

Stealing Children's Toys

A child's boat, either clockwork steamer or sailing boat, is useful for carrying out your baited line to a tantalising area of water which is out of reach by casting from the bank.

When your offspring is out of the way raid the toy cupboard. On reaching the waterside coil the line twice on the decking with the bait hanging over the side. Wind up the clockwork ship, adjust the rudder, or, in the case of a sailing boat trim the sails correctly, and with a fervent prayer, speed the craft upon its way. When the vessel has reached the exact spot – gently pull your fishing line. The bait will then drop into the water and the ship (we hope) sails on its mission completed. The rightful owner may then be sent to the other side of the pond to retrieve it.

If the boat goes aground afar off or becomes marooned in a lily bed, then that's just too bad – you will have to buy him (or her) another one.

Toy balloons, leaves, and logs, also make good 'carriers' but unless there is a wind they are, of course, useless.

In every pond there always seems to be one enchanted area which by normal methods you can never reach. It is always there the big fish lie, basking in security. Hence the above suggestion, which I have tried myself, and found most effective. Whether it is a strictly sporting method I leave for you to decide for yourself.

The devil may suggest attaching spinners to the stern and a fine line to the bow, but don't listen to him. I know a keeper's son who caught a large trout in a forbidden water by swimming across it with a spinner attached to one of his legs. This method is chilly and tedious.

'B.B.', *Fisherman's Folly*, 1987

Drugging Fish

Take the leaves and fruit of the spurge (*Euphorbia*), throw both in a fish-pond or in other water where many fishes are, which fishes eat of this herb or weed and become so drunk by it that they turn their belly up as if they were dead, only they come back to themselves and that does not injure them. Then throw them in fresh water, and they recover; thus they are taken with the hands.

DIT BOECXKEN, Antwerp, circa 1492

A Scottish Poacher Remembers a Poisoning

The older fish poachers rarely go in for poisoning. This is a cowardly method, and kills everything, both great and small, for miles down stream. Chloride of lime is the agent mostly used, as it does not injure the edible parts. The lime is thrown into the river where fish are known to lie, and its deadly influence is soon seen. The fish, weakened and poisoned, float belly uppermost. This at once renders them conspicuous, and they are simply lifted out of the water in a landing-net. Salmon and trout which come by their death in this way have the usually pink parts of a dull white, with the eyes and gill-covers of the same colour, and covered with a fine white film. This substance is much used in mills on the banks of trout-streams, and probably more fish are 'poached' by this kind of pollution in a month than the most inveterate moucher will kill in a year.

It is only poachers of the old school that are careful to observe close times, and they do their work mostly in summer. Many of the younger and more desperate hands, however, do really serious business when the fish are out of season. When salmon and trout are spawning their senses seem to become dulled, and then they are not difficult to approach in the water. They seek the highest reaches to spawn and stay for a considerable time on the spawning beds. A salmon offers a fair mark, and these are obtained by spearing. The pronged salmon spear is driven into the fleshy shoulders of the fish, when it is hauled out on to the bank. In this way I have often killed more fish in a single day than I could possibly carry home – even when there was little or no chance of detection. There is only one practicable way of carrying a big salmon across country on a dark night, and that is by hanging it round one's neck and steadying it in front. I have left tons of fish behind when chased by the watchers, as of all things they are the most difficult to carry. The best water bailiffs are those who are least seen, or who watch from a distance. So as to save sudden surprise, and to give timely warning of the approach of watchers, one of the poaching party should always command the land from a tree top.

The flesh of spawning fish is loose and watery, insipid and tasteless, and rarely brings more than a few pence per pound. In an out-lying hamlet known to me, poached salmon, during last close time, was so common that the cottagers fed their poultry upon it through the winter.

JOHN WATSON, *Confessions of a Poacher*, 1890

Self-poaching Salmon

Salmon are remarkable for their strength and activity, and, as the spawning season advances, they shoot up the rapid stream with great velocity, and are not easily retarded in their progress, as they spring over wiers, or falls of water, called salmon-leaps, of the height of from seven to ten feet. Sometimes, when they meet with a wier, or a cascade, which they cannot surmount, they will make repeated efforts, even till they die on the spot. Many fish are taken by the fishermen during their attempts to spring over these impediments.

It is said that one of the wonders, which the Frazers of Lovat, who are lords of the manor, used to shew their guests, was a voluntarily cooked salmon at the Falls of Kilmorac. For this purpose a kettle was placed upon the flat rock on the south side of the fall, close by the edge of the water, and kept full and boiling. There is a considerable extent of the rock where tents were erected, and the whole was under a canopy of overhanging trees. There the company are said to have waited till a salmon fell into the kettle, and was boiled in their presence; a mode of entertainment I confess myself incapable of coveting, being too much of a sportsman, and too little of an epicure, to desire conquest so unworthy, and cookery so unnatural.

T.C. HOFLAND, *The British Angler's Manual*, 1834

Night Lines for Trout

Most poached trout are probably taken on night lines. Of these there are several types. A stout line, attached to a stake or tree root, may be baited with a worm and left in a deep pool for the old cannibal trout who seldom feeds by day. More effective is the line, attached to two stones sunk in the stream, to which several droppers are attached, each appropriately baited. This is almost impossible for the keeper to detect; but the poacher, knowing exactly its position, can easily retrieve it with a hooked stick or grapnel. In a weedy stream, a night line can be placed in a gap in the weeds, held in place by a bullet through which it passes; a split shot on each side of the bullet ensures that the bait stays where it has been put. A trout, taking a bait in such a place, will certainly go to weed; the keeper, walking along the bank, will see nothing suspicious; but the poacher, knowing exactly where to look will, if his bait has disappeared, haul on the line and drag the trout from the weed-bed.

When the water is going down after a flood, trout tend to lie at the edge of the stream, feeding on worms and grubs washed from the bank. At such a time a poacher can set half a dozen short lines, and then withdraw and smoke a pipe. When he comes back twenty minutes later, he will probably find one or two fish hooked.

A modern variation of the night line is a fly-spoon attached to a length of nylon which is tied to a whippy branch trailing in a fast stream. The fish hooks and plays himself until exhausted, and the device is almost invisible unless one knows exactly where to look.

CHARLES CHEVENIX-TRENCH, *The Poacher and the Squire*,
1967

Taming a Mahseer

Who cares to pull out a dead pike on a night line? The pot-hunter, not the sportsman. To battle with a heavy salmon, or kill a good game trout on a very light line, is quite another matter. From this point of view it is that I say a Mahseer shows more sport than a salmon. Not that you can kill more of them, which you may also do, but that each individual Mahseer makes a better fight than a salmon of the same size. I am prepared to expect that on this point, as on most others not capable of being proved to demonstration, some will disagree with me. . . . For my own part I can only say that my prejudices were all in favor of the salmon, both as being a salmon, a sort of lion of the waters, whom I had grown up looking on with respect from my childhood, and as being a fellow-countryman. But the Mahseer compelled me to believe in and honor him in spite of my prejudgment to the contrary. I came to the conclusion that though he might not make so long a fight of it as a salmon, he yet made a much more difficult one, because his attack was more impetuously vehement, his first rush more violent, all his energies being concentrated in making it effective, though his efforts were not, and from that very cause, could not be, so long sustained. Trying to account for this I had the curiosity to measure and compare the size of his tail and fins with that of his body, and I found that the superficial area of his propelling and directing power amounted together to as much as the superficial area of the whole of the rest of his body. The proportion which the tail and fins of a salmon bear to the rest of his body is very much smaller. The Mahseer having then so much greater means of putting on steam and having also the habit of always putting it on at once energetically and unsparingly, it is readily intelligible that his first rush is a mighty one, and that, that made, his strength is comparatively soon exhausted. Other rushes he will make, but his first is the dangerous one. Then it is that the final issue of the campaign is practically decided. Be one too many for him then, and you may be grimly satisfied that all else he can do will not avail him; you may count on making him your own. Then it is that you must wait upon him diligently. If you have not got all free, the connection between you and your new friend will be severed within a moment of your making each other's acquaintance. If you have carelessly allowed the line to get a turn round the tip of the rod, or let any slack near the hand become kinked ever so little, or twisted over the butt, or hitched in the reel or a button, then it is that not a moment's law is given you for the readjustment of this little matter; there is a violent tug, and an immediate smash. ... You must fish in a state of constant and careful preparedness for this sudden and impetuous rush; for there is no use in hooking a fish if he is to break you immediately. Even your very reel must be looked to that it runs easily, that it is not fouled and clogged by use, that no treacherous sand has got in from laying down your rod and reel by the river side, for when a heavy fish goes off with race horse speed, he will take no denial, and woe betide you if you cannot promptly oblige him with the line he wants.

HENRY SULLIVAN THOMAS, *The Rod in India*, 1873

Tickling Trout

Selecting a quiet spot, just above a hole beneath the bank – a likely resort for the spotted beauties – the operator lies down flat and gently places his open palm on the surface of the water, keeping it there hardly kissing the liquid. Presently a gentle touch will announce the presence of a trout – unable, like woman, to restrain her curiosity at the strange object. Patience and a delicate touch are all that is required for the operation; as the fish gradually becomes more and more tame, and comes time after time to rub his back or his sides against the innocent-looking hand, the operator may gradually feel his way forward to the gills, close his fingers gently downwards round the trout's neck, gingerly tickling him the while, when a sudden grasp will secure the prize in the only part of its body that can be securely held, viz., the gills, and the trout may be hauled out in triumph, unless the tickler, in his excitement, has overbalanced himself and fallen ignominiously into the stream.

From *The Fishing Gazette*, 11 January 1878

Getting a Grip

The movement of fingers beneath the body of a fish will cause it to rise in the water; continual gentle movement will bring it to the surface, where it can quickly be swept out on to the bank. But it is not because the fish is in any state of coma, as one soon discovers if any quick movement is made in getting the fish to the surface, it is just because the trout has no weight in water, and the movement of the fingers, however gentle, is sufficient to propel it to the top of the water. Neither is it because the human fingers have any peculiar quality of their own, for a trout can be raised equally well with a short stick.

Although most people who write about trout tickling explain that the procedure is carried out in shallow water – beneath the river or stream banks, under tree stumps and roots and in the river vegetation – they seldom explain the fact that, while in such places, the fish have cover over them, and therefore feel secure. Actually they are in one of their many holts where they spend many of the daylight hours. These holts are often used by several fish of varying size and in many cases the trout are lying side by side, across and above each other, so that one is continually touching another. Small fish may wriggle beneath the body of a larger one and so pass to the other side. The movement causes no alarm, they are accustomed to it, and so when human fingers, chilled to the same temperature as the water, slide beneath their bodies, they take no notice. . . .

Though tickling trout may sound romantic, actually there is no necessity to tickle at all. Gentle movement of the finger tips acts as a lever, and will lift the fish high enough from the river bed to allow the hands to slide to positions at head and tail, when a firm grasp can be obtained. Trout (and for that matter any other fish) have great difficulty in struggling forcibly if the mouth and gills are held closed, and if a grip is also held on the tail part of the body, the fish is powerless. In such manner a trout can be held firmly, lifted from the water and carried, without in any way damaging it.

And so the trout can be taken from his holt, unaware that the gentle movement beneath his body is other than caused by natural events. He lies quiet in the shaded light while what he thinks is part of one of his brethren moves gently to his head and his tail. He may wriggle a bit, unwilling to be jostled from his position, but until the firm grip of the human hand fastens and traps him, he has no idea anything is wrong.

FRANK SAWYER, *Keeper of the Stream*, 1952

How to Tickle a Tench

Everyone has heard of tickling trout: the tench is almost equally amenable to titillation. Lying at full length on the sward, with his hat off lest it should fall into the water, the poacher peers down into the hole where he has reason to think tench may be found. This fish is so dark in colour when viewed from above that for a minute or two, till the sight adapts itself to the dull light of the water, the poacher cannot distinguish what he is searching for. Presently, having made out the position of the tench, he slips his bare arm in slowly, and without splash, and finds little or no trouble as a rule in getting his hand close to the fish without alarming it: tench, indeed, seem rather sluggish. He then passes his fingers under the belly and gently rubs it. 'Now it would appear that he has the fish in his power, and has only to grasp it. But grasping is not so easy; or rather it is not so easy to pull a fish up through two feet of superincumbent water which opposes the quick passage of the arm. The gentle rubbing in the first place seems to soothe the fish, so that it becomes perfectly quiescent, except that it slowly rises up in the water, and thus enables the hand to get into proper position for the final seizure. When it has risen up towards the surface sufficiently far – the tench must not be driven too near the surface, for it does not like light and will glide away – the poacher suddenly snaps as it were; his thumb and fingers, if he possibly can manage it, closing on the gills. The body is so slimy and slippery that there alone a firm hold can be got, though the poacher will often flick the fish out of the water in an instant so soon as it is near the surface. Poachers evidently feel as much pleasure in practising these tricks as the most enthusiastic angler using the implements of legitimate sport.

RICHARD JEFFERIES, *The Gamekeeper at Home*, 1878

Manhandling a Salmon

Catching salmon by hand is a far more difficult matter; it is a rare art, and I am indebted to a senior officer of the Salvation Army for an account of a notorious salmon poacher who used no 'engines' but an electric torch and a sack to carry away his bag. He operated in shallow streams which he knew well. Wading upstream, sometimes waist-high, on dark nights, he flashed his torch into any likely salmon's lie; as the fish, inquisitive, rose slowly towards the light, the poacher thrust his hands into the gills and, after a violent struggle, dragged it ashore. His conversion by the Salvation Army was very gratifying to magistrates and riparian owners, but a disappointment to the poor of the town whom he had often supplied with fresh-run salmon at fourpence a pound.

CHARLES CHEVEUNIX-TRENCH, *The Poacher and the Squire*,
1967

Deadly Live Baits

I shall now communicate to the reader, a method which I have taken more pikes and Jacks with, than any other way. The hook which you must use, is to be the first hook that I have mentioned, with this exception only, that the lead of a conical figure must be taken away, then before you fix the swivel on the bottom of the line, put on a cork-float that will swim a gudgeon, then put on your swivel, and fix your hook and gimp to it: put a swan shot on your gimp, to make your float cock a little, and of such a weight, that when the hook is baited with the gudgeon it may do so properly. Your gudgeons must be kept alive in a tin kettle: take one, and stick the hook either through his upper lip, or back fin, and throw him into the likely haunts before mentioned, swimming at mid-water. When the pike takes it, let him run a little, as at the snap, and then strike him. In this method of pike fishing, you may take three kinds of fish, viz. pikes, pearch and chubs. It is so murdering a way that the generous angler should never use it, except he wants a few fish to present his friends with.

THOMAS BEST, *A Concise Treatise on the Art of Angling*, 1787

More on Worms

You must not ev'ry worm promiscuous use,
Judgment will tell thee proper bait to choose;
The worm that draws a long immod'rate size
The trout abhors, and the rank morsel flies;
And if too small, the naked fraud's in sight,
And fear forbids, while hunger does invite.
Those baits will best reward the fisher's pains,
Whose polish'd tails a shining yellow stains;

Cleanse them from filth, to give a tempting gloss,
Cherish the sullied reptile race with moss;
Amid the verdant bed they twine, they toil,
And from their bodies wipe their native soil.

JOHN GAY, *Rural Sports*, 1713

Or You Could Send Your Dog . . .

One day I witnessed a very strange thing, the action of a dog, by
the waterside. It was evening and the beach was forsaken; cartmen,
fishermen, boatmen all gone, and I was the only idler left on the
rocks; but the tide was coming in, rolling quite big waves on to the
rocks, and the novel sight of the waves, the freshness, the joy of it,
kept me at that spot, standing on one of the outermost rocks not yet
washed over by the water. By and by a gentleman, followed by a
big dog, came down on to the beach and stood at a distance of forty
or fifty yards from me, while the dog bounded forward over the
flat, slippery rocks and through pools of water until he came to my
side, and sitting on the edge of the rock began gazing intently down
at the water. He was a big, shaggy, round-headed animal, with a
greyish coat with some patches of light reddish colour on it; what
his breed was I cannot say, but he looked somewhat like a sheep-
dog or an otter-hound. Suddenly he plunged in, quite disappearing
from sight, but quickly reappeared with a big shad of about three
and a half or four pounds weight in his jaws. Climbing on to the
rock he dropped the fish, which he did not appear to have injured
much, as it began floundering about in an exceedingly lively manner.
I was astonished and looked back at the dog's master; but there he
stood in the same place, smoking and paying no attention to what
his animal was doing. Again the dog plunged in and brought out a
second big fish and dropped it on the flat rock, and again and again
he dived, until there were five big shads all floundering about on
the wet rock and likely soon to be washed back into the water.

The shad is a common fish in the Plata and the best to eat of all
its fishes, resembling the salmon in its rich flavour, and is eagerly
watched for when it comes up from the sea by the Buenos Ayres
fishermen, just as our fishermen watch for mackerel on our coasts.

But on this evening the beach was deserted by every one, watchers included, and the fish came and swarmed along the rocks, and there was no one to catch them – not even some poor hungry idler to pounce upon and carry off the five fishes the dog had captured. One by one I saw them washed back into the water, and presently the dog, hearing his master whistling to him, bounded away.

W.H. HUDSON, *Far Away and Long Ago*, 1918

If You Don't Have a Dog, a Badger Will Do

SIR, With reference to 'A Fisherman's Notebook' (January 14) and a pig taking a salmon, this may be of interest. I have had a tame badger since she was a few weeks old last April. Then she was unable to walk and had only had her eyes open for a few days. She was bottle-reared.

During the summer she would come fishing with me, following me until the water was up to her shoulders. Sometimes she would slip out of her depth in a hole, but she always extricated herself without help.

When I caught a trout, killed it, took it off the hook and threw it near her in the water, she would at once retrieve it and take it up the bank. After pushing it about with her nose, she would come back to stand behind me again.

But if she was within 250 yards of the Land Rover, she would carry the trout by the back of the neck or tail to undeneath the Land Rover, which apparently was the earth for the afternoon, and start eating it, always by the head.

E.M.H. Herefordshire

Letter to *The Field*, 1963

And if You Have Neither Dog Nor Badger . . .

When you have after all this divertisement brought him to the Bank, you will find something to do, before you can confidently call him your own; for if you go unadvisedly to take him out, either by the Back or the Tail, or any part of his Body, though you may think his best is past, and his dancing days are done, yet he may cut you another Capor; and if he has had a little breathing time, he may give another leap, when you do not expect it; the best way then, is to use fair means, and invite to the land by persuasions, not compulsions, taking him by the Head, and putting your fingers into his Eyes, which is the fastest hold. If the Water be low, so that the Bank rises some distance from it; you must not fear catching an Ague, by laying your Belly level with the ground, especially if you have no contrivance to guide him out to a more commodious place: some will adventure to take him by the Gills, though that hold is neither so secure nor so safe for the Fisher; because the Fish in that heat of passion, may accidentally take revenge upon his Adversary, by letting him blood in his Fingers, which way of Phlebotomizing is not esteemed so good, because some are of opinion, that the teeth of a Pike are Venomous, and those Wounds very difficult to be healed.

ROBERT HOBBES, *The Compleat Troller*, 1682

Using a Dolphin to Catch Mullet

In the province of Gallia Narbonensis and the region of Nemausus there is a marsh called Latera where dolphins and men co-operate to catch fish. At a fixed season a huge number of mullet rushes through the narrow mouth of the marsh into the sea, after watching for a turn of the tide that prevents nets from being stretched across the channel.

When the fishermen see this and a crowd collects, as they know the time and are keen on this sport, the whole population shouts as loudly as it can from the shore, calling on 'Snubnose' for the finale of the show. The dolphins soon hear their wish and at once hurry to the spot to help.

Their battle-line appears and immediately takes up position where the fray is to commence. They put themselves between the open sea and the shore and drive the mullet into shallow water. Then the fishermen set their nets and lift the fish out of the water with two-pronged spears. The speed of some of the mullet enables them to leap over the barriers, but the dolphins still catch them. But satisfied for the moment with killing them, the dolphins put off their supper until complete victory has been achieved.

The battle hots up. The dolphins press on very bravely and do not mind being caught in the nets, and, fearing that this may encourage the enemy's flight, they slip out gently between boats, nets and swimming fishermen to avoid opening up ways of escape. None tries to get away by leaping out of the water, which in other circumstances they like doing, unless the nets are placed beneath them.

PLINY THE ELDER (23–79 AD), *Natural History*, translated by
John Healy

First Principles of Fly Fishing

You may also observe, what my own experience taught me, that the fish never rise eagerly and freely at any sort of fly, until that kind come to the water's side; for though I have often, at the first coming in of some flies, which I judged they liked best got several of them, yet I could never find that they did much, if at all value them, until those sorts of flies began to flock to the rivers sides, and were to be found on the trees and bushes there in great numbers; for all sorts of flies, wherever bred, do, after a certain time, come to the banks of rivers, I suppose to moisten their bodies dried with the heat; and from the bushes and herbs there, skip and play upon the water, were the fish lie in wait for them, and after a short time die, and are not to be found: though of some kinds there come a second sort afterwards, but much less, as the orange-fly; and when they thus flock to the river, then is the best season to angle with that fly. And that thou may the better find what fly they covet most at that instant, do thus:

When you come first to the river in the morning, with your rod beat upon the bushes or boughs which hang over the water, and by their falling upon the water you will see what sorts of flies are there in greatest numbers; if divers sorts, and equal in numbers, try them all, and you will quickly find which they most desire. Sometimes they change their fly; though not very usual, twice or thrice in one day; but ordinarily they do not seek another sort of fly till they have for some days even glutted themselves with a former kind, which is commonly when those flies die and go out. Directly contrary to our London gallants, who must have the first of every thing, when hardly to be got, but scorn the same when kindly ripe, healthful, common, and cheap; but the fish despise the first, and covet when plenty, and when that sort grow old and decay, and another cometh in plentifully, then they change; as if nature taught them, that every thing is best in its own proper season, and not so desirable when not kindly ripe, or when through long continuance it begins to lose its native worth and goodness.

ROBERT VENABLES, *The Experienced Angler*, 1662

The Class Structure of Trout Fishing

Trout are fished for at three depths: upper, middle, and lower. It is not immaterial that society, as we know it, is divided into the same layers. Three families of artificial flies exist, one for fishing at each of these depths. They represent the natural insect in three successive, and ascending, stages of its life cycle. The complete fly fisherman ought to be adept with all three, and to know when to use which. In practice it does not work out that way. A man is drawn to wet-fly fishing – why is as mysterious as why some men take up the viola instead of the violin. He becomes a good wet-fly fisherman, and his loyalty to the wet fly turns him to it at times when one of the other two kinds might work better. Another man becomes a good nymph fisherman; that is the depth at which he likes to catch fish: when they are feeding on insects after these have left the stream bed and before they have hatched on the surface. He would almost sooner not catch them than catch them in another way. Upon hatching, the insect spreads its wings to dry and rides downstream for a moment before either taking flight or being eaten by a trout. It is this winged stage that the dry fly imitates. The dry-fly fisherman is the most stubbornly loyal of all to his way and he is the snob of snobs among fishermen. He believes that his way entitles him to the topmost rung of the social ladder of fishing mentioned earlier. The odd thing is, the other kinds of fishermen agree with him on this, and defer to him. They acknowledge him their superior in fishing finesse. On second thought, is that so odd? The assertion of social superiority is usually all that is needed to make others accord it to you. The reason that all other kinds of fishermen look up to the dry-fly purist is not that he catches more fish than they; on the contrary, it is because he catches fewer. His is the sport in its purest, most impractical, least material form.

The wonderful obstinacy of the dry-fly purist! The odds which he knows are against him, and despite this – or because of it – his pertinacity, his lofty indifference to mere gross success, his concentration upon means, not ends! Let him be on public water, water without restrictions as to tackle and baits. Along comes a worm fisherman, his creel heavy with fish. The dry-fly man not only does not envy him his catch, he despises the oaf. Along comes a spin fisherman, one whose outfit allows him to fish bushy places where the fly fisherman cannot penetrate, and who, with his metal lures, has taken his limit. 'Hardware merchant,' is the dry-fly man's contemptuous name for him. Along comes (we are ascending, rung by rung, that social ladder, reader) a man who fishes with flies, but with streamer flies, which imitate not insects but minnows. Big fish feed on minnows, and so this fisherman also has filled his creel. Along comes a wet-fly fisherman; wet flies imitate insects but are fished underwater. This fisherman, too, has fish, for a statistical reason presently to be explained. With differing degrees of intolerance, the dry-fly man looks down upon them all. For him, in the words of an old song, it ain't what you do, it's the way what you do it. His creel may be empty (he may not even carry a creel: he may belong to that most select group of all: those who would never dream of killing a trout, who put back all they catch) yet he will not switch, though he knows as well as any of them, indeed, better than any of them, that big fish, the kind he too is after, seldom stir themselves for a morsel of food that would require a diamond merchant's scale to register its microscopic weight, and he knows that all trout, even little ones, take only about ten percent of their food on the surface of the water, where he is fishing. And the strange part is, that though they regard him as daft, and subject him to much joking, down deep those other varieties of fishermen have a sneaking admiration for his quixotry and yield him without grudge his place at the top of the ladder.

WILLIAM HUMPHREY, *My Moby Dick*, 1979

The Principle of Dry-Fly Fishing

The art of dry-fly fishing is to present a fly that floats – and floats perfectly – to the notice of a rising fish in such a manner that it is mistaken for the natural *ephemera* which is hatching out, and in the result is accepted as such by the fish. To lure *Salmo Fario* successfully after this manner it is necessary that the angler should have skill; be very observant; have the patience of Job, and, beyond all, be properly equipped for the task.

Hardy Brothers Catalogue, 1907

Casting a Fly

When a fish has just risen at a natural object it is well for the fisherman to try to throw into the curl occasioned by the rise and left as a mark for him, but should the undulations have nearly died away, before he can throw to the spot, then he should throw as nearly as he can judge a yard or two above it and allow the flies to float down to the supposed place of the fish; if a rise does not occur it may be concluded that the fish has removed without seeing the flies; he may then try a yard or two on each side of the place where the curl appeared, when he may probably have a rise and may possibly hook the fish providing he has the knack of striking, which knack like all other is only acquired by practice.

ALFRED RONALDS, *The Fly Fisher's Entomology*, 1836

How Far to Cast?

It is impossible to lay down adequate instructions in acquiring the art of casting. That can alone be learned by practice. A few hints, however, may not be out of place on the use of the rod. It is well to begin with a short line and cast towards a particular spot. This is good practice in accuracy. A cast must be regarded faulty which does not reach the desired spot, or, if it does succeed in that particular, falls with a splash in the water. Salmon are timid fish, and any bungling in placing the fly over them is punished by their hasty retreat. They frequently lie close to the bank or near to the anchored boat from which one is fishing. A short line, therefore, is all that is necessary. The reel line, which is much thicker and more conspicuous, is very often over the fish instead of the fly. It is common experience for a salmon to be tempted when only a yard or two of line is drawn. On one occasion, fishing the Galway river, I carelessly threw the casting line and its two flies on the water, preparatory to drawing off a few yards of line from the reel. The moment the tail fly touched, a salmon seized it, and dived with his imagined prize with such vigour that it was a wonder that the top of my rod was not broken. He hooked himself in the act and rushed across stream like a thing possessed, lengthening the few yards that separated me from him by quite fifty. Every young angler imagines that all the salmon are far off and the only chance of sport is to be secured by throwing a long line.

JOSEPH ADAMS, *Salmon and Trout Angling*, 1923

The Dry-Fly Apostle Makes His Case

In treating of the advantages of dry-fly over wet-fly fishing, I am most desirous of avoiding any expression which should tend to depreciate in any way the skill exhibited by the experienced and intelligent followers of the wet fly. They require not only most undoubted judgment of the character of water frequented at various times of the day and season by feeding fish, not only a very full knowledge of the different species and genera of insects forming the food of the fish, not only a full perception of the advantages of fishing up-stream under one set of conditions and of fishing down-stream under others; but, in addition to all this, great skill in placing their flies accurately in the desired position, and allowing them to drift down in a natural manner and without any drag or check over the precise spot they wish to try. There is far too much presumption of superior scientific knowledge and skill on the part of the modern school of dry-fly fishermen, and I should be the last to wish to write a line tending to encourage this erroneous assumption of superiority, or to depreciate in any way the patience and perseverance, coupled with an intuitive perception of the habits of the fish, requisite for a really first-rate performer with the wet fly. The late Francis Francis said that 'the judicious and perfect application of dry, wet, and mid-water fly-fishing stamps the finished fly-fisher with the hallmark of efficiency'. This sentiment is to my mind pre-eminently characteristic of its author, and worthy of repetition by any of his admirers in later times.

Under certain circumstances the dry fly has in every stream great advantages over the wet, and in rivers where it is not generally used has the further advantage, that, from the fish being unaccustomed to see anything but the *natural* fly floating down cocked over them, they are altogether unsuspicious of the artificial, and take it with such confidence as to render their being hooked, if not their capture, almost a certainty. To define the circumstances specially suited to the dry fly is not difficult. When a fish is seen to be feeding on the surface, when the angler can ascertain the species of insect on which the fish is feeding, when he can imitate it, when he can present this imitation to the fish in its natural position and following precisely the course taken by the natural insect, and when he can carry out all these conditions at the first cast, so as to delude the fish before he has any suspicion of being fished for, the rising and hooking of the most wary trout or grayling is almost a foregone conclusion for the dry-fly fisherman.

It must be remembered that the only possible means of establishing a satisfactory connection between the fish and the fisherman is the medium of sight. A fish's sight is much more highly developed than any other sense, it being questionable whether he has any hearing, or whether his power of smell with surface food is sufficient to guide him in discriminating between the natural and artificial fly. Hence keeping out of sight is a most essential point to study; in fact, as before said, the fish should be hooked before he has any suspicion of being fished for. On the other hand, where no rising or bulging fish are to be seen, and whence it may be inferred that the fish are not taking surface food at all, the conditions are favourable for the use of the sunk fly. Even under these conditions it will sometimes occur that the floating fly is more efficacious than the wet.

F.M. HALFORD, *Dry Fly Fishing in Theory and Practice*, 1889

The Thrill of the Dry Fly

In what does its charm lie? Partly in the fact that all the moves in the game are visible. Just as a stalk is much more interesting when you can see your stag and watch his slightest movement, so with a fish. If you see him your eyes never leave him: if not, you watch for his rise. If it does not occur with its accustomed regularity, you have put him down. If you can see him, you watch every motion. Then you see your fly too. Nothing is hid. When the fly comes over him, you see him prepare to take it – or treat it with stolid indifference. You see him rise and take. The whole drama is played out before your eyes.

Then again you attack him when the odds are most in his favour. On a hot still day in June he is far more alert than on a blowing April morning. He has lost the exuberance of spring. The water is low and clear, and the surface unruffled. Weeds are thick and handy. Your gut must be the finest, your fly the smallest. He is hungry, it is true, but particular. Not only must your fly not fright him, it must please his lazy senses. When he pokes his nose at it and refuses, it may be that the reason is daintiness, not distrust.

His size too is an added attraction. No dry fly fishing is good where fish do not run large, and a big fish is a prize. Shooting gives no such trophy. You do not find one grouse three times the size of another, and if you did he would be easier, not harder, to hit. But the trout gets craftier as he gets bigger: his cunning grows with his girth.

The casting too has its fascination. On your day – and such days come to all of us, to make up for the many when we are either maddened or drugged and stupefied by our incurable ineptitude – how delicately and how surely you throw. You mean your fly to fall four inches above the fish, and sure enough it does, not an inch more or less. Nothing is too difficult: drag has no terrors: head wind is a friend, not an enemy, for does it not enable you to put a curve on your gut, which brings your fly over the fish first? You know exactly what to do, and you do it. Wherever the fish may be rising, your fly sails over him, hardly touching the water, wings up, floating like a cork, following every crinkle of the slow current. You gain an extraordinary sense of power. Your rod and line, right down to the fly, are part of yourself, moved by your nerves and answering to your brain.

J.W. HILLS, *A History of Flyfishing for Trout*, 1921

G.E.M. Skues Meets Frederick Halford, High Priest of the Dry Fly, and is Less Than Impressed

We had heard on the day of our arrival in Winchester that the great man was putting up at The George and was nightly welcoming his worshippers at that hotel to hear him expound the pure and authentic gospel of the dry fly – which no one would dream of questioning. So that evening found us, after our meal, among the humble listeners. It came to our ears on that occasion that we were to have the great man's company on the Abbots Barton water, the lessee having invited him for a week. With becoming reverence we listened to his words of wisdom until it became necessary that the session be broken up.

On the following day we were on the water a quarter of an hour or so before our mentor's arrival – taking the side stream, my friend above in the Ducks' Nest Spinney, I a couple of hundred yards further downstream, thus leaving the main river, the fishing of which was reputed the better, to the great man. He was not long behind us and presently we saw him casting on Winnel Water, the main river. Soon afterwards he crossed the meadow which divided the two streams and accosted me from the left bank of the side stream to advise us kindly on the fly to put up, and to make his advice clearer he cast his fly to light on the right bank of the side stream, having first ascertained that I had mounted a fly of George Holland's dressing, known as the quill marryat. He insisted that his fly, which was an india-rubber olive, was the right fly. My selection was based on little pale duns seen on the water. I took a look at his fly and was not a little shocked to see how coarse was the gut on which his fly was tied, but I was also too polite or timid to venture on such a comment.

We met at lunch-time and he inquired how I had done. I said two and a half brace. He had one trout only, but congratulated me civilly and offered to put me up for the Flyfishers' Club, then recently formed. Not expecting, despite my additional thirteen pounds in ten days, to live long enough to make it worthwhile, I declined and did not in fact seek membership till the autumn of 1893, when a voyage to the Cape and back had gone a long way to re-establishing my health.

Halford only fished the Abbots Barton length for three more days of his week, but just as I had been profoundly shocked to do better than the great master did on the first day, I was fated to be similarly shocked on each of his three other days. Yet it encouraged me to rely most on my own observations and not to attach undue importance to authority.

G.E.M. SKUES, *Itchen Memories*, 1951

Fish Autopsies

An autopsy is made, from an angler's point of view, to ascertain the gullet and stomach contents, but note should also be made of any parasite or disease, the sex and condition of the fish. An autopsy should be made as soon as the fish has been killed and weighed, because digestion continues after death, and a fish that has been cleaned at once will keep very much longer. Two instruments are required to perform this operation artistically, a pair of blunt-pointed scissors and a pair of small forceps; a knife is a very useless weapon. Open the fish by cutting with the scissors from the vent up to where the gill covers meet.

In the upper end of the incision will be seen the triangular pink heart, which, if the fish has recently been killed, will be found beating; do not be alarmed, for the heart of any cold-blooded animal will continue to beat for many hours, even after it has been removed from the body, provided it be kept in a damp, cool atmosphere. Just behind the heart will be found a dark red organ, the liver, and behind this the stomach, usually somewhat hidden in fat; the intestine, which occupies the space between the stomach and vent, is usually a short, straight tube; on either side of the stomach in the case of a female fish will be seen the roes. All these organs except the heart, but with the swimming bladder, which lies beneath the stomach, should be removed together in this way: holding the stomach with the forceps, and pulling it downwards will separate the liver and heart, and between these will be seen deep down a white tube, the gullet; cut through this: now the whole of the abdominal contents will come away, and snipping through the intestine close to the vent will complete the removal. The fish may now be placed in the basket. Do not wash it, as by so doing most of its blood, which is a very good preservative, will be lost.

Now to examine the contents of the stomach. ... The larger descending or cardiac limb will contain the more recently taken food; the gullet, if any, the most recently; the ascending or pyloric limb, food which has undergone partial digestion, and will seldom repay examination. To display the contents: with the forceps hold the cut end of the gullet, then slit up with the scissors both gullet and stomach. Usually the nature of the contents can be at once recognised; but if the contents are of much interest, or of such small insects, &c., as not to be easily recognised, some or all of the contents should be put into a small bottle of dilute formalin, which should be carried for this purpose, so that a more careful examination may be made with a lens at home.

The following remarks apply to trout only, and I think show how autopsies add much to the interest of fishing and increase the chance of success, and I believe would especially do so when bottom or wet-fly fishing. The staple food may be said to consist of snails, shrimps, small fish, caddis, duns, and nymphs; less commonly spinners or one of the diptera, and occasionally special flies such as grannon or sedges form a meal. Besides these, odd things are frequently found, such as two leeches, a lampern, two or three black beetles, a wasp, three or four bluebottles, a spider, &c. These odd things are often found in a stomach full of duns or black gnats, and in my opinion explain why a trout feeding on duns will often take a large fancy fly. For this reason I believe it is wise to try a large trout in a weedy stream with a large fancy fly, so that if he takes it the great advantage of a big hook may be had. There is a trout which I call the 'hold all.' He usually lives under a tree and takes anything that drops off; his stomach will contain a very mixed collection of flies, beetles, spiders, small bees, wasps, gall-flies, sallies, and sedges. After a heavy shower in a stream overhung with trees the fish often rise ravenously, and their stomachs are found to contain a similar miscellaneous collection of insects beaten by the rain from the foliage.

J.C. MOTTRAM, *Fly-Fishing – Some New Arts and Mysteries*,
1915

Seventeenth-Century Advice on Catching a Salmon

I will now show you the way to take a salmon.

The first thing you must gain must be a rod of some ten foot in the stock, that will carry a top of six foot pretty stiff and strong, the reason is there must be a little wire ring at the upper end of the top for the line to run through, that you may take up and loose the line at your pleasure; you must have your winder within two foot of the bottom to go on your rod made in this manner, with a spring, that you may put it in as low as you please.

The salmon swimmeth most commonly in the midst of the river . . . [and] if you angle for him with a fly which he will rise to like a trout, the flie must be made of a large hook, which must carry six wings, or four at least; there is judgment in making those flies. . . . You must be sure that you have your line of twenty six yards in length that you may have your convenient time to turn him; but if you turn him you are very like to have the fish with small tackles; the danger is all in the running out both of salmon and trout, you must forecast to turn the fish as you do a wild horse, either upon the right or left hand, and wind up in your line as you find occasion in guiding your fish to the shore, having a good large landing hook to take him up.

THOMAS BARKER, *The Art of Angling*, 1657

It Takes a Special Sort of Fortitude to Become a Salmon Fisher

Composure, patience, and perseverance are indispensable qualifications for all the followers of this art, but more especially for the Salmon Angler. He must lay his account with frequently beating the waters in vain exertion; in being long wet and weary, ere he can (to use the fisher's expression) move a fin; and when he does, to be perhaps then only mocked with a wanton rise, or a false bite; or should he at last prevail in luring the Salmon to his fly, and after working and playing him through many streams, and through many pools, he brings him within his reach, and then thinks he is to take possession of his prize, in a moment the tackle snaps, and all is gone. Such, with many other disappointments, await the Angler; but these ought not to make him fretful, nor give up the pursuit; he must persevere in hopes of better sport. In this point of view, the course he has to steer is a fine practical lesson in the economy of human life.

Many writers on Angling have given various directions for the dress that should be worn, how to counteract the effects of moisture, and what drink to take while you are employed in this amusement. These are principally to use water-proof boots and shoes, and, to make them the more secure, to lard them well with mutton suet, in order to keep the feet and legs perfectly dry; to sit upon a piece of coarse woollen cloth, doubled two or three times; and while warm, to avoid the drinking of small liquors. Such advices may well suit float and gudgeon fishers, but the Salmon Angler must laugh at such ideas; he had better indeed never begin the occupation, if he has not a constitution strong enough to wade in deep and rapid rivers, during all the hours of the day, and be able to bear every vicissitude and eager extremity of both sky and water.

GEORGE BAINBRIDGE, *The Fly-fisher's Guide*, 1816

The Truth About Casting a Salmon Fly

It is impossible on paper to teach the tyro how to cast a salmon-fly. Nothing but practice will do it. Even actual showing and demonstration are not of much use until he can command the rod to some extent. Let him note how it is done, and then flail away to the best of his ability for a day or two until he can pitch the line out somehow. Then let him get some adept to instruct him how to get it out properly, and to correct any fault in his manipulation. After that, practice, practice, practice, and watching a performer now and then at work, will do the rest.

Another rule of great importance I would here emphatically lay down, and that is, never use more strength or vigour in making a cast than is absolutely necessary, for all beyond that is not only downright waste of power, but positively defeats the end the fisher has in view. Let him study, not how much noise he can make by 'swooshing' his rod through the air, but whether he cannot avoid making any at all. And if any old angler, who has been accustomed to adopt the former plan, will only try the latter a few times, I am confident that the result will positively amaze him. It is astonishing how hard it is at times, with all your force, to send a fly against or through the wind truly and fairly, and how easy it really is to do with little or no force at all. When I hear an angler's rod 'swooshing' through the air on a windy day, as one often may hear it seventy or eighty yards away, I think it very extraordinary that he should never by accident have discovered that all that force and noise is not only superfluous, but mischievous; and how that without it he would cast an infinitely better line, and not strain his rod, particularly the ferrules, as he is doing. In very long throws, of course, a good deal of force must be employed; but in ordinary ones, no matter what the weather or wind, or which way it blows, it is absolutely unnecessary. I have often surprised myself by seeing how beautifully straight the fly goes, without doubling or bagging, through the wind, by merely letting the top do the work it was intended for. The angler should consider that he does not cast with the butt or main joints of his rod, and need not therefore try to bring them into play. The part of the rod which sends the fly home is the most pliable part; why not, then, let that do its duty, instead of trying to make the less pliable parts take its place, which they cannot and do not do?

FRANCIS FRANCIS, *A Book of Angling*, 1867

Striking a Salmon

I unhesitatingly assert that there is no single moment with horse or gun into which is concentrated such a thrill of hope, fear, expectation, and exultation as that of the rise and successful striking of a heavy Salmon. *I have seen men literally unable to stand, or to hold their rod, from sheer excitement.*

And indeed in this very excitement – in the impetuosity of spirit it engenders – lies almost the only real difficulty of Salmon-fishing. Two causes combine to make the moment of striking a critical one: In the first place the Salmon is so large and bright, and in the second so comparatively slow-moving, owing to his bulk, that the eye almost certainly perceives him in the water before he has actually taken the fly; when a premature stroke, an almost instinctive tightening of the muscles and line, at once snatches the fly from the fish, and the fish from the creel. The art is to resist for a moment the inclination to strike; only for one moment, but long enough to allow the fish to take and turn down again with the fly; and then strike if you will: not a slight hesitating blow like the tap of a lady's fan – for there is often a long line and a heavy strain on it between the Salmon and his would-be captor – but a strong, steady, determined stroke bringing the line up as flat as a knife, and driving the tapering hook-point well in over the barb.

Next to the number of Salmon lost through striking too quickly, are those lost from striking too feebly. I repeat, therefore, strike strongly and hard, as I have described, and *repeat the stroke* by way of making sure. If the tackle will not stand this strain it is a clear proof that it is not fit for Salmon-fishing. A weak stroke is worse than useless, because whilst it fails to make the hook penetrate, it provokes the fish to a sudden violent effort to rid himself of it, and thus lessens the chance of his hooking himself.

If the above mode of striking is adopted, not more than one fish in five which fairly take the fly in open water ought to escape. I kept a register for some time of my losses and takes, and I found this to be a fair average.

H. CHOLMONDELEY PENNELL, *The Modern Practical Angler*,
1870

If At First You Don't Succeed . . . Throw Stones

There comes a time to every angler when he is stymied. None of his regular tricks will bring any results. It is at these moments that some new slant or technique may turn a blank day into a successful one. These are the times to experiment.

TRIMMING DOWN FLIES

When the trout or salmon refuse all your wet flies, or when they swirl at your smallest flies without actually taking them, start trimming material off the fly, trying it again after each reduction. I recall fishing for a school of feeding sea-run brook trout that paid no attention to my flies. It was obvious from their actions that they were feeding, but on something very tiny. I started whittling down a Number 16 wet fly. I ended up with a bare hook, and, fishing it like a nymph, I was able to take a dozen trout. Apparently the bare brown hook, because of its color, shape and size, was a close approximation to the nymphs the trout were feeding on. Fish have no knowledge of a hook. A hooked trout has no way of telling whether it is the feathers of the fly or the metal that hurts him. He may shun the fly in the future but the hook in itself represents nothing he is afraid of. Too many anglers grant their quarry a greater knowledge of things that are commonplace to us than it is possible for them to possess.

STONING

When the waters of a stream grow warm the fish are likely to congregate in the deeper pools and grow listless, feeding little. When hours of casting over this type of water fails to bring results, if there are no other anglers to be bothered by it, try stoning the pool. This is one of those last resorts that should be employed only when fishing in seldom-fished water. Throw stones into the water frightening the fish in all sections of the pool. This stirring up of the fish sometimes raises their appetites and results in better fishing thirty minutes or an hour later when their fear has passed. I have seen this procedure worked on both trout and Atlantic salmon.

BIG FLIES

When the fish refuse all your flies get out the largest fly you have and false cast it repeatedly over the water to interest the fish that lie in a pool. Let it drop occasionally for a normal retrieve, or if it is a dry fly a normal float, and you may be surprised by a wild rush from a fish. I have seen trout, salmon and bass try to get a wildly waving fly that was being false casted over them, coming clear of the water in a vain effort. Even though they may never actually take the big fly you use as a teaser it may excite some interest that will lead them to take a fly of more normal size later.

LEE WOLF, *Handbook of Freshwater Fishing*, 1939

Or Try a Recitation

The senseless and the unreasonable, in fishing as in much else, are infinitely attractive to me. I watch my life being corrupted by superstition as I fish; I will insist, for example, on sitting on a particular stone for lunch by a pool, because once, years back, I caught a fine trout after sitting on that stone for lunch. Or when the fish are not rising I recite long, sonorous pieces of poetry to them in a loud voice, bellowing into the wind. There is nothing that bores trout so completely – Herder, Milton, Spenser and Victor Hugo are the best – and they become quite distracted, yawn, and so make, for them, the fatal mistake. This method is also recommended for dour Scottish lochs when boat fishing; though one may recall, perhaps, that recitation also serves to keep oneself awake when, for hour after hour, one casts and casts with no response. It means that when a trout comes, at least one is at home to greet it.

JOHN INGLIS HALL, *How to Fish a Highland Stream: The Truim*, 1960

Captain Mainwaring Praises Dynamite

Watching the river one sultry summer's day, it occurred to me that the reason fish refused to take in such weather might be because they were all half asleep like myself, and that possibly a brick-bat or two in their midst might make them sit up and take notice. This theory I ventilated in the 'Field,' incurring the usual derision that invariably greets any novelty of ideas.

On the day in question the Colonel and I started fishing in the Quarry Pool. For a quarter of an hour we fished most carefully, but then we had to stop, for a workman came to tell us they were about to explode a charge of dynamite in the quarry. Watching the blue smoke curling away from the fuse, I found myself wondering what the fish would think of the concussion, and remembered my own remarks on stirring them up. Now whether the workmen had put in an extra charge for our benefit I do not know, but the explosion seemed a mighty one as the huge rocks, riven from their hold, rose slowly into the air only to descend again into the field with a mighty thud. One block, at least twice the size of a man's head, fell with a thundering splash into the very middle of the river not forty yards from where we had been fishing. 'Now is the time,' quoth the Colonel, 'to prove your precious theory.' The ripples caused by this bolt from the blue had barely subsided as I made my next cast, and felt a pull at the shrimp. In another cast or two he came again, and I killed a fifteen pounder. *Verbum sap.*

ARTHUR MAINWARING, *Fishing and Philandering*, 1914

Salmon Fishing With a Worm

As to the worms best adapted for salmon fishing, I require to say little. The lob or large dew-worm is esteemed the favourite. This is easily obtained in the desired quantity from almost any piece of garden ground. It is met with, stretched at length on the earth during mild nights, and especially after a shower when the surface of the soil is damp. Besides the lob-worm, the large button-worm is sometimes used, and possesses this advantage, that it is easily scoured and becomes tougher and redder than the other. It is not, however, found in such great abundance or in all localities, and with respect to size is decidedly inferior to the lob-worm.

In baiting the hook, two, sometimes three worms are made use of. These are attached in the following way: Holding one of them betwixt the thumb and forefinger of the left hand, insert the point of your hook a short way below the head of the worm, which, I shall suppose, measures in length 8 or 9 inches; run the bend of the wire carefully along through the bait, to the full extent of an inch, in the direction of the tail; bring the point out again, and passing over an equal portion of the worm, re-enter it further on, drawing up, as you do so, what has already been transfixed, along the shank of the hook, then, as before, bring out the point an inch lower down. Repeat this proceeding a third time, and at its completion pull the worm up quite free from the hook to the gut above. Select a second worm, and insert, as formerly, the barbed wire below the head; run it along underneath, until the shank, bend, and point are completely concealed. Then, with your finger and thumb, press down the first bait close against the shank, so as to hang over in small loops or folds.

In the event of a third worm being thought necessary, string on the one preceding it in the manner I have already described, and use the worm in question to cover the hook. . . . The performer requires to use a long, stiffish rod, 18 feet and upwards, such as is employed for pike trolling. The rings should be large, allowing the line to pass through them without the smallest restraint, and the reel itself ought to be facile in the extreme, having neither catch nor multiplicator. With regard to the quantity of line employed in casting, it should not greatly exceed the length of the rod itself. Considering the manner in which it is weighted, and the mode of using it I am about to point out, it is difficult to manage more.

Having baited his hook, let the angler take his place at the head of the cast or salmon-stream he intends fishing. Immediately on commencing operations, there is a matter of observance to which he must pay particular attention. It forms, in fact, to some extent the secret of the successful worm-fisher, and is embodied in this simple piece of instruction, viz.: Let him draw out with his hand, over and above what he uses in casting, a yard or so of line from off the reel, allowing the same to hang loosely down towards the butt-end of his rod. The intention of this is, that he may afford instant and unresisting compliance with the movements of the fish, on first seizing the bait. Should the least check occur in the running off of the line, the salmon will, in most cases, quit before gorging . . . I have placed the angler at the head of a cast or salmon-stream. Let him heave his bait across, and, in some measure, with the current, which I take to be so heavy or rapid as to bring round the weighted line, at a deliberate rate, until it attains its full stretch or tension. It is necessary, during this circuit, that the worm travel deep, in contact almost with the channel of the river, otherwise it will not prove attractive to the fish. On completing its range, the angler should allow it to hang, as it were, for a few seconds in subjection to the current, and when recovering, in order to renew the cast, should do so with extreme caution and deliberation.

When a check occurs, no matter from what cause it may, on the instant, be imagined to proceed, he ought at once to give line, not merely exhausting what he has in preparation, but dealing out ungrudgingly a further supply from his reel, and this by means of the hand, so that it may run off easily, and, as it were, humour the movements of a supposed fish. The check itself may very possibly be occasioned by collision of the plummets with some stone or jut of rock, or it may proceed from the interference of a trout or eel, but this being quite uncertain, the angler has himself to blame, should he, by dealing with it as such and uncircumspectedly, give opportunity for a good fish to escape. In general, however, I may remark, a mere check or stoppage is not the usual indication of a fish having seized the worm. What takes place has more the nature of an attack, quick and vigorous as is that of the pike on a running bait. The progress of the hook downwards is disturbed by a violent jerk or pull, sometimes in the direction of the current, but as frequently to the side, towards the lair or retreat of the salmon. Should this attack on the bait be met with unresistingly by the angler, and sufficient line allowed on the occasion, it will generally, after a short pause, become repeated, with less violence indeed, but with more earnestness and effect. In the interval between the charges, however, care must be taken to sustain and give an animated appearance to the worms. If allowed to drop to the bottom, the salmon will no longer assail them. Accordingly, recover line with the hand, and be a little more chary than at first of yielding it when the fish renews the attack. At this point it is, that a slight measure of resistance will act as a provocative; previously its effect was to alarm and beget suspicion.

The salmon will now, after two or three successive assaults, bolt the bait; and his doing so may be inferred from a peculiar strain upon the line, more fixed and continued in character than any it had yet been subject to, during the attack. The resolute and quick elevation of the rod will suffice to fix the hook deep among the entrails of the fish, and nothing further is left to be done but to fatigue and land him.

THOMAS TOD STODDART, *The Angler's Companion*, 1847

The Joy of Trolling

Trolling with par for large trout is a glorious pastime, especially on a Highland loch, circled with mountain scenery – the craft of nature by incantation wrought, when the morning stars sang together. It needs intellect to enjoy it well, and a poet's heart to know its luxury. Take with you some choice and idle spirit, a rower he must be, that can manage your airy shalop as the winds do a weathercock – can chant a ballad of yore, of ladye and chieftain, and pranksome elf and kelpie wild – can speak to the echoes and to yourself, cheering you with wit and wisdom, and admiring your science and skill, and the gorgeous fish you are playing, twenty fathoms off, with a strong and steady hand; your heart 'high fluttering the while, like woman's when she loves.'

THOMAS TOD STODDART, *An Angler's Rambles*, 1866

An Irish Gilly Remembers a Record

'One of the best years, I ever knew on the river at Careysville was 1927, if me memory serves me right. That was the year the present Duke's grandfather landed two hundred and fifty fish in a few months. A great fisherman he was, as were all the other members of the family. There was another successful angler I remember well, a Major Ashley Cooper, who landed twenty-three on a bait in one day a few years ago; and in the year 1952 he landed twenty-four on a fly in one day.

'Of course if you were to pick the times when really huge catches were landed, you would have to go back to the old days when they fished with crosslines. You never hear of crosslines now, but great yokes they were for killing fish.

'On a crossline you had two rods, with an angler on each bank; that's where the double bank fishing at the Ville came in handy. You fished from and to each other, with eight flies tied to eight six-foot droppers, four feet between each dropper, making the gear about thirty-two feet long.

'Well do ye know what, with them eight flies in the water I often saw the poor fish scratching their heads and saying, "In honour of God which one will I take?"

'Well it was with a crossline that I landed what must have been a record catch with one cast. But sit back Bill, and I'll be telling ye how it happened.

'I was fishing one day with another young gilly, Maurice Mc-Sweeney, who was in his first year in the business and still very green at it. We had five fish on the line at the time and they were nearly played out, I was starting to pull back to gaff one when a 30-Pounder gave a sudden whip and fouled the reel on Maurice.

"What will I do now, Billy?" he shouted.

'I thought for a second and then called back; "Cut the line and leave them to me."

'He did what I told him, and there I was with the five salmon, that no one will ever have again, on one line.

'The tackle at that time was strong stuff, so when I had one played, I put the rod down, and used the line like a handline. Then, when I had the fish near the bank, I gaffed him and cut the dropper. One by one I played the five of them to the bank and flung them over my head until they were safely landed. It was an experience I'll remember to me dying day.'

BILL HAMMOND, *An Irish Salmon Gilly*, 1984

Herodotus on How to Catch a Crocodile

To some of the Egyptians crocodiles are sacred objects; to others not so, and they treat them as enemies. Those who live in the neighbourhood of Thebes and of Lake Moeris think them very sacred; the inhabitants of both places keep a crocodile, training it to be quite tame, putting earrings of crystal and of fused gold into their ears, and bracelets on their front feet; they give them prescribed and sacred food, and treat them as handsomely as possible whilst they are alive; they embalm them when they are dead, and bury them in sacred vaults. The people who live in the neighbourhood of Elephantine eat them and do not consider them sacred. They are not called crocodiles by the Egyptians, but champsae. The Ionians named them crocodiles because they thought them like the lizards – which are called crocodiles – that breed in the hedges or stone walls.

There are many and various methods of capturing the crocodile, but I will only describe the methods that seem most worthy description. The fisherman, as soon as he has baited a hook with the chine of a pig, lets it down into the middle of the river; he holds a live young pig close to the brink of the river and beats it; the crocodile, hearing its cries, hurries towards it, and coming across the chine of pork, he swallows it. Men haul it to land. As soon as it is drawn ashore, the first thing that the hunter does is to plaster up its eyes with mud; this done, everything else is managed very easily, but he has a great deal of trouble until he has done this.

HERODOTUS, *The Histories*

And How They Did It Under The Raj

Crocodiles are very shy, and not to be caught, except by night line. A simple way of setting this is to get a bamboo of full thickness, and 10 or 22 feet in length. To one end of it tie a hook with only a foot of line between hook and bamboo. I used three large sea hooks tied together like a treble hook. The line should not be a single cord, which the crocodile can bite in two, but fifteen or twenty pieces of common twine tied together at the ends, but not twisted at all. These will get between his teeth, and escape being bitten, and their united strength will hold him fast enough. Bait the hook, which must be a large and very strong one, with a bull frog, or a fowl's entrails, or a couple of crows, or any meat, and push the whole out into the lake, pool, or fort moat in which the crocodiles are, and leave it for the night. If there is a slight current, it is easy enough to attach a stone, by way of anchor, by a long string to the other end of the bamboo, and to drop it in. The line between the bamboo and the hook being so short, the bait is kept near the surface, and is not liable to be concealed amongst weeds, etc., at the bottom; when the crocodile takes the bait and turns down with it, the shortness of the line, and the ready opposition of the floating bamboo, quickly strikes the hook into him, and the more he tries to get down the more stoutly the bamboo resists him, for it is full of air from end to end, and is a very powerful buoy. As long as he keeps to the water the bamboo plays him well, and if he tries the land he will soon be brought up with a round turn by the bamboo getting hitched amongst bushes. As far as my experience goes they always take to the land eventually.

I have been told that good fun can be had out of the crocodile by baiting as above in the daytime, and setting a man to watch from a distance in concealment. The man must be very still, and well concealed, and at a distance, or not a crocodile will be hooked, for they are very wary. Directly one is hooked he gives the information. Then into small boats quick, one man in each prow with a hog spear, start fair, and 'ride' or 'off' for first spear. As he sees the boats coming, down goes the crocodile, and up stands the bamboo, more and more upright the deeper he goes, so that the more he tries to avoid you the more conspicuous becomes his course. Follow him up, for if the bamboo is a big one, as it should be, it will be so strongly buoyant that he must come to the top soon. There, now, the bamboo is beginning to slope, showing that he is coming to the surface. Now is your time for a spear. But look out for his tail – it is very powerful. If he upsets you, he has big brothers about, and they may reverse the sport.

HENRY SULLIVAN THOMAS, *The Rod in India*, 1873

Some Advice Masquerading as a Sonnet, or Vice Versa

Go, take thine angle, and with practised line,
    Light as the gossamer, the current sweep;
    And if thou failest in the calm still deep,
In the rough eddy may a prize be thine.

Say thou'rt unlucky where the sunbeams shine;
 Beneath the shadow, where the waters creep,
 Perchance the monarch of the brook shall leap –
For fate is ever better than design.
Still persevere; the giddiest breeze that blows,
 For thee may blow with fame and fortune rife;
Be prosperous – and what reck if it arose
 Out of some pebble with the stream at strife,
Or that the light wind dallied with the boughs?
 Thou art successful; such is human life.

THOMAS DOUBLEDAY, 1818

The Importance of Weather

When the night proves dark, cloudy, or windy, and the moon shines little, or not at all, next day there will be little or no sport, except for small fish: For trout and great fish then range about to devour others.

RICHARD BROOKES, *The Art of Angling*, 1790

How to Predict the Weather

Sounds, such as bells, noise of water, beasts, birds, heard distinctly from a great distance, portend *rain*. If the earth or any *fenny* places, yield any extraordinary scents, or any disagreeable smells arise from drains, *rain*. A *white* frost, *rain* within three days; the more than usual sinking of *rivers*, presages *rain*. The speedy *drying* of the *surface* of the earth denotes a *northerly* wind and *fair* weather, and its becoming *moist, southerly* wind, and *rain*; for the *air* sucks up all the moisture on the surface, even though the sky be overcast, and that is a sure sign of fine weather; but if the earth continue damp; and water stands in shallow places, no trust should *be put* in the *clearest* sky, for in this case it is deceitful.

 If Cattle or Sheep feed greedily, and faster than ordinary when it rains, it is a sign of the *rains* continuance, and when *Sheep* skip and play wantonly, rain is at no great distance. In the mountainous part of Derbyshire, called the *Peak*, the inhabitants observe, that if the *Sheep* wind up the *hills* in the morning to their pasture and feed near the *tops*, the weather, altho' cloudy and drizzling, will clear away by degrees and terminate in a fine day; but if they feed in the bottoms, the rain will continue and increase. *Geese* and *Ducks* more noisy, and washing and diving more than usual, *rain*; *Cock* crowing in the middle of the day, and *Peacock* squalling much, *rain*; *Kites* hovering high in the air, *fine weather*; *Owls* screaming frequently in the evening when foul, *fair* and *frosty*; *Larks* rising high and singing long, *fine*; *Redbreasts* singing loud in the open air, *fine*; faintly under cover, *rain*; when the *Moor game* and other birds quit the mountains, and betake themselves to the lower lands; *rain; Crows* are more earnest after their prey before *rain*. PLINY remarks that 'it is a sign of rain when the land fowl, especially *Crows*, are clamorous near waters, and wash themselves.' HORACE likewise describes this bird, as prophetic of impending showers. When they and *Ravens* stand gaping towards the sun, it foretells extreme heat. *Swallows* skimming the surface of water, *rain*; so long as they keep aloft their prey, the sky is serene, but when they descend and flit along the surface of the earth or water, *rain* is not far off, and the remark will for the most part be correct. A drought of three months duration broke up the summer solstice in 1775. The day previous to the rains falling, the Swallows flew very near the ground, which they had never done during the whole period of the dry weather. *Sparrows* chirping much in a fine morning, *rain*; and the *Chaffinch* being loud in his call or note, is a pretty certain signal that wet is fast approaching.

Dogs are by some said to be particularly sleepy, and to eat *grass* before *rain*, but grass is a natural vomit, which nature prompts them to take at all times when their stomachs require such an evacuation, of course it is no proof that the approach of rain alone drives them to seek this remedy; the *dryness* of the dog's *nose* is stated to be a much surer presage of wet weather. Moles throwing up more earth than usual, and its being small and dry, and their appearance sometimes above ground, *rain*; *Worms* creeping in numbers out of the ground, *rain*; and from the same principle, that they as well as Moles, are sensible of the access of something new in the atmosphere, and to the surface of the earth. *Frogs* appearing of a golden hue, fine; dusky colour, rainy; and *Toads* in an evening crawl over the road or beaten path, where they seldom are seen, but when restless, from the expectation of approaching *rain*. Fishes are supposed to be affected, since it is allowed that they cease to bite freely when *rain* is depending. All sorts of *insects* are more stirring than ordinary against *rain*, Bees are in fullest employ, but if likely to rain, confine their industry to where they can reach their hives before the storm arises; when they fly far abroad and stay out late, *fine*; when the common *flesh flies* are more bold and greedy, hovering about the mouths and eyes of persons and cattle, and are peculiarly troublesome, *rain*; when small flies flock together in great numbers about the beams of the sun a little before it sets, *fine*. *Ants* bustle more than usual, move their eggs to dry places, and then retire to their burrows before *rain* falls. *Gnats* playing in the open air in the evening, *heat*; when they collect and dance in the shade, *showers*; and when they sting much, cold and *rain*. *Fleas* biting greedily, *rain*; *Spiders* crawling abroad, *rain*; their *webs* on the ground or floating in the air, *fine*; *Bats* flying more numerously and early in the evening, fine; Glow-worms appearing in unusual numbers, fine.

THE REVEREND WILLIAM DANIEL, *Rural Sports*, 1802

The Anglers' Commandments

First. Thou shalt not fish when the wind is cold, nor shalt thou fish within the length of thy rod and line of thy brother Angler.

Second. Thou shalt not shew thyself to the fish, nor let thy shadow be seen on the water.

Third. Thou shalt not Float-Fish without plumbing the depth.

Fourth. Thou shalt not Fly-Fish, with the wind in thy face; nor shalt thou let thy line or any part thereof, fall on the water; but the fly only, if possible.

Fifth. Thou shalt not fish in troubled water.

Sixth. Thou shalt not take small fish with large hooks.

Seventh. Thou shalt not have good sport, unless thou strikest the moment the fish bites, nor shalt thou strike too hard.

Eighth. Thou shalt not land a large fish without a landing-net, or landing-hook; nor shalt thou be in too great a hurry in so doing.

Ninth. Thou shalt not make paste with dirty hands.

Tenth. Thou shalt not have good sport, without good baits, rods, lines and hooks.

The Angler's Pocket Book, 1805

But Don't Take Any Advice Too Seriously

The more one fishes for trout, then, the more he is forced to the conclusion that no man knows even faintly when or why the fishing will be good or bad. Too often have all of us marched forth hopefully on those rare 'perfect' days when all the licensed fish prophets were for once smiling and nodding in sweet accord – only to return wondering whether all the trout hadn't migrated to Mars. Or again, too often have we braved their collective frowns – and gone out and hit the jackpot. *Why?* I don't know why, otherwise I would set up shop as a swami myself – and henceforth tramp the trout circuits of the world, fishing away like mad on the proceeds of my sage revelations.

While we indeed live in an advanced age of science, and an alarming one at that, many men are too apt to think that therefore *all* the problems of living – and fishing – can be solved by applying the pragmatic methods of science to problems that are perhaps essentially insoluble. The same men laugh at the superstitions of our quaint ancestors and at the leaping witch doctors of present-day primitive tribes, yet themselves gladly swallow enough phony science every day to make even the dizziest witch doctor look like Dr Einstein.

I hasten to add that most trout swamis are a serious, well-intentioned, and dedicated crew who genuinely love to fish; they are often highly intelligent men, perhaps lacking only in the saving perspective offered by a sense of humility and humor, whose pretensions after all cause little harm and possibly save quite a few trout. In a sense they are victims of their own hobbies. And sometimes their predictions are dead right, as they are occasionally bound to be, like a man who always plays the same number in roulette. They can't possibly always be wrong. Their occasional home runs are in fact the thing that keeps them in business.

There's one other thing that helps weld their flocks together. If, rightly or wrongly, a disciple of one of these fanatic fishing faiths *believes* that the fishing is going to be good, in that frame of mind he is naturally going to fish better – and that, too, is still a pretty important factor in all fishing. And should his favorite prophet say nay, the more devoted disciple generally doesn't even dare go fishing, so he is scarecely in a position to convict let alone accuse his holy man of treasonable error. Or if he goes fishing anyway, possibly because he has already planned the trip, his heart isn't in it, he is oppressed by a sense of sin for slumming among the heathen, his decalogue is shattered. One way or another he is less likely to be on the ball. Consequently he is apt to ascribe his subsequent fishing pratfall as still another triumph for his particular fishing saint. Thus, you see, his favorite prophet simply can't lose.

It's the same sort of thing as the fisherman and his 'favorite' fly. The fly became a favorite, of course, because he or a pal once caught or raised a lot of trout with it; therefore he has faith in it, it is a 'good' fly; therefore he fishes it more often and with greater care; therefore he is more likely to continue to take most of his fish on it; and therefore, to complete the vicious circle, he becomes more and more caught in the spell of his favorite fly. Or even take a strange deluded fellow who becomes depressed when he thinks he sees a certain mysterious gun-metal sheen on the water . . .

For my part it will be a sorry day when any character can ever tell me ahead of time what my fishing is going to be. To me the indescribable sense of anticipation and mystery in simply *going* fishing is almost half the fun. It is the beckoning lure of the unknown, the very unpredictability of the enterprise, that draws me on and on. Always I keep telling myself: This may be the big day when I'll get on – and stay on – to Grampaw . . . And if ever some sly superswami comes along who can *really* tell me what I'm apt to do on Frenchman's Pond tomorrow night, he'd better quick gather up his crystal ball and start running. And he'd better not trip on his robes. Because I'm going to crack him and his crystal ball with my stoutest trout priest. I've now given him fair warning.

Have I told you my own new pet theory, the one about the influence of *bald spots* on trout fishing? Boy oh boy, it never fails! It's terrific! Oh, so you don't want to hear about it? So you prefer to worship at that eccentric rival angling church across the street –

the one with bats in its belfry? Very well and *pardon* me. If you still want to blindly embrace such a weird collection of medieval fishing dogma and superstition, hop to it. See if I care. It's a free country. But as for me, *I'll* still cling to my precious bald spots. Because, you see, bald spots are milder. And, lordy, how they do satisfy!

ROBERT TRAVER, *Trout Madness*, 1960

Especially This ...

'Never examine your hook after taking a fish, for, should the point be broken or blunted, it might occasion you the trouble and inconvenience of changing it; and after having had a tolerable number of rises at the imperfect hook, seek out your friends, and complain that "really the fish come uncommon short to-day." Neither pry too closely into the condition of your gut after having used it for some time, nor on a windy day, nor after hooking weeds, trees, and such-like vegetable matters. If you do, you will be sure to find it knotted, twisted, frayed, or in some unaccountable predicament, which will not increase your pleasure or happiness one iota. "Where ignorance is bliss, 'tis folly to be wise."

'When not using your rod by the riverside never stick it upright, but always lay it down; you can then take a quarter-deck promenade ... when you will most probably, unless very lucky, contrive to tread upon it, perchance breaking one of the joints. There's a break for you, not only in the rod, but in the monotony of the day.

'Always "play" a fish well where there are plenty of weeds or roots. It is quite amusing to see a fine trout dash into a heavy bed of weeds, and your wonder will be very considerably increased if you ever see him come out again.'

WHEATLEY'S *Rod and Line*, 1849

CHAPTER FOUR

Rods, Reels and Bottles of Gin

The fisherman loves his tackle. It is an obsessive love and, like most obsessions, irrational. Golfers do not, after all, talk fondly about their three irons; footballers don't hurry home after a game to polish up the ball. Yet anglers will spend hours debating the relative merits of rods, reels, lines, bits of metal, plastic, fur and feather which to any impartial passer-by look nearly identical.

None of these obsessives was born obsessional. Something made them that way. My guess is that they wouldn't be obsessional if it weren't for the sheer fickleness of fishing. Every new device which promises – however bogusly – to stack the deck in the angler's favour offers the prospect of success next time. To visit the tackle shop is to enter the temple of enchantments, where each seductive, plastic-wrapped gizmo suggests there will be no more Ones That Got Away.

I love these places, with their smell of mothballs, rubber and waxed cotton. Sometimes, there's a whiff of something more stomach-churning, usually because someone has bought a stock of maggots or shrimps and then lost them under the counter. In any but the most corrupt or inept, you're sure of a warm welcome. It is the most congenial way to part with your money. Anglers have been drawn to tackle shops ever since Izaak Walton visited the Three Trouts in St Paul's churchyard, perhaps the most appropriate location imaginable for a business dealing in promises.

Yet the staff are no snake-oil salesmen. In the best places they have the worldly-wise attitude of people who have seen it all before. This is usually because they have. The eagerness of fishermen to believe is not seen quite the way a car salesman watches his mark stroke the shiny bonnet. Being anglers themselves, the tackle-shop men share the enthusiasm. They would rather be fishing than working, anyway, and half an hour talking about the state of the river is better than another £50 in the till. Admittedly, they have an easy time of it, for the fisherman's appetite for tackle is unlimited. You have a shoebox full of spinning lures in red and green and yellow and silver? That doesn't mean you don't need another. Even another in exactly the same colour. It's a slightly different size. It swims in a slightly different way. It's lighter. It's heavier. Above all, it's untested, and therefore it promises all things. The conundrum of fishing tackle is how functional objects like hooks or nets or even a bag of purple-dyed shrimps vacuum-packed in salt can be given an imaginative life of their own.

No cricketer makes his own bat, but plenty of fishermen make their own rods. And because all anglers are forever either modifying their tackle or making it themselves (particularly flies for salmon and trout), the tackle shop is where you are allowed entry to the imagination of others, marvelling at how someone else has noticed that if you tie the wings of a trout fly just a little more upright, they look so much better from underneath, or that if you fit a ring to the middle of the net it stops it catching when you climb over barbed-wire fences. It's just the thing. I'll take it.

So it is all the more surprising that fishing tackle took so long to evolve. For most of history, certainly from the time of the ancient Egyptians, anglers fished with their line tied to the top of their rod. Reels, which allowed the angler to control any fish he caught far more effectively than had previously been possible, seem to have become common in Britain during the seventeenth century. They are a pretty simple piece of engineering, giving the opportunity to launch fly or worms into places which would otherwise have been quite out of bounds, so it is surprising that it took three thousand years or so to invent them.

Before that, because the line was attached to the rod tip, if you hooked a big fish the only thing to do was to drop the rod in the water and let the fish wear itself out towing a branch around behind it. Because the rods had to be huge, too. The one described in the earliest British fishing book, the *Treatyse of Fysshynge with an Angle* – conventionally and probably wrongly attributed to Dame Juliana Berners, prioress of Sopwell Nunnery, Hertfordshire – describes one twelve feet long. Izaak Walton's collaborator, Charles Cotton, talks of rods of fifteen or eighteen feet: they had to be that length if the fisherman was to be able to get his fly onto the water.

By the time *The Compleat Angler* was published, the first fishing-tackle shops had appeared. With them came the first of the interminable discussions about the relative merits of different types of rod. Cotton praises Yorkshire rods, made with butts of fir and with six to twelve pieces spliced together, tapering to a fine point. This was usually made of whalebone, the rod itself of hazel or sometimes cane. The line was made from the hairs of a horse's tail, knotted together, again tapering from thick to thin.

By the nineteenth century, with the reel now commonplace, rods were getting shorter. The Caribbean colonies produced a new wood, greenheart, from which mighty great salmon rods were built, stronger and more reliable than previous rods, but exhausting to use. Soon, this too was superseded by split cane, which was lighter, more flexible and therefore more reliable. For fly fishing, lines of greased silk tipped with a gut cast allowed the fly to be floated on the surface of the water. Like most of the breakthroughs in fishing technology, split cane was brought to the highest pitch of refinement in the United States.

Nowadays, most rods are made of fibreglass or carbon fibre – lighter again than split cane and often with a lot more power. They come in all sizes and with all manner of specialist applications. Together with plastic-coated lines which will float, sink, float just under the surface, sink quickly to great depth, and doubtless, in the fullness of time, which will simply do as they're told, the modern fisherman has more choice, more technology and fewer excuses than ever before.

By comparison with earlier fishermen, ours is a cossetted generation. William Scrope, the Victorian salmon fisherman, thought waterproof boots – waders – were strictly for wimps. It was, he said, quite safe to wade out into rivers in shoes and socks until water was lapping the fifth button of your waistcoat. In February on the river Tweed, where it is often cold enough to freeze the line to the rod, 'should you be of a delicate temperament', it might be a good idea to have an occasional glance at your legs. 'Should they be black or even purple, it might, perhaps, be as well to get on dry land.' But if they are merely 'rubicund' (ruddy), you needn't worry.

As the equipment has become more sophisticated, some of the vigour has gone from fishing. It is not that it has become easier – in some ways it is harder now. It is the spirit of the sport which has been damaged: the most heavily fished waters nowadays are holes in the ground into which trout have been poured, fresh from the brood ponds. The 'fishermen' stand on the banks, throw vastly long lines, and strip in 'flies' which bear about as much relation to natural insects as a London bus does to a budgerigar. The name of the game is 'bagging your limit', a form of fishmongery. It requires a great leap of imagination to see any connection with the artistry of Edward Grey.

Fashion in fishing tackle tends to go in cycles. Sometimes, the latest invention turns out to be a new version of something in common use a century ago. Other times, someone dreams up a new weapon and catches fish on it. If it works for him it will work for me, thinks everyone else. So they buy it too. Pretty soon, everyone on the river is fishing for the same fish with the same device. Inevitably, some of them are successful. Whereupon, the deadly efficacy of the fly or spinner, or whatever it is, is confirmed. After a while, the fish have seen enough of the relevant fly to be able to draw an artist's impression in their sleep. Then, some bold soul will, in boredom, desperation or inventiveness, try something else. He catches fish. His fame spreads. And the cycle begins again. Buying fishing tackle is a mug's game. Manufacturing is a millionaire's.

It follows, from much of the above, that of all the gizmos the angler may have inside his fishing bag, the pre-eminent one is his credit card. The two greatest obstacles to fishing are lack of money and lack of time. Zane Grey could tramp the world hunting marlin and sailfish because he had the proceeds of books like *Riders of the Purple Sage*. It *is* still possible to get a day's fishing at little expense on the banks of the Thames, the Severn or the Ouse. But to taste the best that fishing has to offer, the deceit of a brown trout sipping down olives on a gin-clear chalk stream, or the heartstopping exhilaration of a salmon ploughing your line through the water, that costs plenty of money.

At the last count, there were well over three thousand patterns of flies, from delicate imitations of midges as fine as the down on a child's chin to gaudy great trollopes with all the subtlety of a can-can dancer. In Alaska or northern Russia there are flies tied to look like small hedgehogs, in New Zealand there are others which look like voles. Quite how this qualifies as a 'fly' is anyone's guess.

Yet the greatest exhilaration of all, the *ne plus ultra* of fishing, is catching a trout on a home-tied dry fly. At that point, all the elements – guile, skill and the winter's evening at the kitchen table with a boxful of bits of fur and feather coalesce: the angler has thought himself into the environment and got away with it.

Jolly Anglers – *Pierce Egan's Book of Sports*

My fish car is probably one of the most complete fish cars in the world. Perhaps she is *the* completest, but then I don't like to brag. This I do know: All I have to do is to get into her and drive away – and we can stay out fishing for a week. There is no further preparation and nothing I can forget (unless I forget Buckshot herself) because I always leave all of my treasures in her custody. When she and I shove off we are a sort of Abercrombie & Fitch on the march. Here is only a partial list of the gear we *always* carry; it's standard equipment: Four fly rods and a spinning rod, all of which ride snugly on rubber slings suspended from the inside roof; binoculars, a camera, a magnifying glass (for studying the birds and the bees and the stomach content of trout), four sizes of flashlights (from pencil size to Lindbergh Beacon), and even one of those old Stonebridge candle lanterns for emergencies; waders and hip boots and low boat boots, and of course all the usual endless fishing gear (*that* would take a page itself), complete with patching cement, ferrule cement, and all the many odds and ends; eight miles of miscellaneous sizes and lengths of rope; a complete set of detailed county maps of Michigan based upon late air photos and showing all waters and side roads; a bedroll and spare blanket; rain clothes and a complete change of woods clothes; a tarpaulin and pup tent; a Primus stove and nesting cook kit with all the many trimmings; assorted water canteens; a small portable icebox; grub for a week, mostly bottled or canned; and, last but not least, always a supply of beer and a bottle or two of whisky – *always* when I leave, that is.

In addition I carry two spare tires and some extra tubes; enough small spare parts to start a neighborhood garage; a hand-cranked tugger that could yank a Patton tank out of a mudhole, complete with assorted logging chains and snatch blocks and 'come-alongs' and U-bolts and towing cables, together with an old car axle to drive in the ground and use as a towing anchor in treeless terrain. I also carry enough tools and assorted junk to build and furnish a ranch house. On the roof I carry my rubber boat and inside the car the boat gear including anchors, jointed paddles, kapok cushions, air pump, etc. Then I carry two axes, one hatchet, one head-hunting brush knife, two sizes of pruning shears for cleaning out difficult 'hot spots,' an all-size leather punch, two handsaws, nails and hammers, and enough pry bars and wrecking tools to convict me of intended sabotage and burglary. To keep in character for my felonies I usually tote a .38 special revolver. Then, to top it off, there is a six-volt overhead light bulb in the car that is so bright I can read the fine print on a bill of lading without my glasses.

And where does the driver sit? one may sensibly ask. Incredibly enough, I somehow manage to keep *both* front seats free for driver and passenger. Of course with this mound of equipment piled behind us we are usually obliged to converse in guarded whispers, lest our voices jar loose the poised glacier and bury us in the avalanche. Indeed, sometimes I have even managed to squeeze an adventurous small fisherman in the *back* seat, stashing the stuff around him, though I always thoughtfully furnish him a breathing pipe so that he does not perish on the way. 'Fisherman drowned in tidal wave of fishing equipment!' is one headline we seek to avoid.

As I read over this modest inventory I am struck by the number of items I have left out. I haven't even hinted about the assorted barometers, thermometers, and depthometers, the toilet, gaming and first-aid kits, the fishtail propellers, transistor radios, and folding camp stools; nor yet about the red flares and collapsible canvas pails, the crow calls, Audubon birdcalls and Indian love calls – not to mention the aluminum waterscope I use leeringly to watch mermaids. And when my pals and I really go on a prolonged expedition and take along the trailer and all *three* of my boats, that is something to behold. Then I pile most of the gear in the flat-bottomed trailer boat, and lash the third boat on top. *Ship ahoy!* Admiral Dewey is about to steam into Manila harbor.

Last summer as I was about to shove off on big safari, Grace came out on the back porch to see me off. She studied the caravan rather thoughtfully for quite a while. She spoke slowly.

'You look,' she said quietly, 'you look like the addled commander of a one-man army about to launch a rocket invasion of Mars.'

'Nope,' I corrected her. 'I'm the Ringling Brothers on my way to merge with Barnum & Bailey. Good day, Madam. Giddap, Buckshot!'

ROBERT TRAVER, *Trout Madness*, 1960

Some Advice on Literature From an Irishman

As there is nothing so much wanting to a good angler, as proper depositories for his various tackling, I shall proceed without preface to express my thoughts on this most important subject.

Go not, therefore, to a tackle-shop to throw away your money on ill-formed and inefficient pocket-books, where the flies are all made up in small rolls. Nothing can be more distressing to a good angler than the trouble necessary to be taken in straightening the links before fishing with them. Now do as I shall direct.

Try to procure three or four well-bound novels, but lay not your unhallowed hands on the standard ones, and by these I mean the Vicar of Wakefield, Fielding, Smollett's and Sterne's works, Richardson's Clarissa and Sir Charles (though this latter is too much ornamented for my taste), Caleb Williams, many of Scott's – for instance, Old Mortality, Waverley, Rob Roy, Heart of Mid Lothian, Quentin Durward, Peveril of the Peak, Guy Mannering, The Abbot; do as you please with the Monastery (I hate monasteries and nunneries); spare not Scott's rubbish, for there is a great deal of it in prose and verse; spare Anastasius, Cyril Thornton, and most of Bulwer's works; the latter are true pictures of English life; spare Banim's, they are Irish life; spare Lover's, too; spare all Campbell's works, he has written too little; also Moore's, except his paltry Fadladeen prose story, miscalled Lalla Rookh: he is our countryman, and the sacred fire of liberty illumines his works; spare Lord Byron's, except his ode to Napoleon (it has disgraced him) – tear out that ode, and put a parchment in its place. Could he dare accuse Izaak Walton of cruelty, and yet have written such a poem? Melancholy to think that our greatest men should in so many instances have laid themselves open to the charge of cruelty; but, alas! the page of history bears witness against them.

Lord Byron has made some amends by his forgiveness of the spider –

'Go, poor spider, go.
But take care how you bite Sir Hudson Lowe.'

I find myself getting critical, instead of continuing my instructions;
so I must resume.

Tear, then, as many leaves out of any novels which you may find,
on perusal, worthless, or abounding with immoral descriptions, and
fill their places with parchment covers, open at one end, and the full
heighth and size of the binding of the volume – by these means,
your flies can be made up tolerably large, full as large as the breadth
of the book – then for colours, you need only sew some leather
ends to prevent them from flying out, in any of those works that
may be of little or no value as food for the mind. – I perceive, by
the way, that I have been guilty of great remissness in not noticing
some admirable works by women, such as Evelina, by Madame
D'Arblay, and Discipline, by Miss Brunton. As to Self-Control, 'I
shall not presume to control your judgment, reader.' Miss Edge-
worth has also written many admirable works, as have several
others whom your taste will lead you to appreciate as they deserve.

Two or three of the books I allude to will hold your colours,
flies, and hooks.

JAMES 'THE' O'GORMAN, *The Practice of Angling*, 1845

The Bare Essentials

For several sufficient reasons we do not propose to deal fully with
everything that might be included under this heading. This is a
small book and everything is a big subject. Therefore we must limit
our attention to a certain number of items whose importance has
been made manifest by the encomiums of the learned and the
recommendations of the wise. The first, indeed, has not the weight
of such authority behind it, for, so far as we know, it has not
been before set down as an essential part of the angler's equipment.
We have little doubt, however, that a moment's thought will
convince the judicious reader as to the justice of its claim to be
considered.

It is MONEY, money in greater rather than lesser quantity. This extremely useful commodity will enable the angler to rent a salmon river, take two miles of dry-fly water, pay a hotel bill, tip a keeper, travel by rail, join a fishing club, bait up a barbel pitch, have a fish immortalised in a glass case, enjoy the esteem of tackle merchants, and do various other things which are interesting and enjoyable. Without money he will find himself limited in several directions. Credit is good, of course, but it will not altogether supply the place of money. It will not, for example, procure a copy of this book, excessively moderate though its price be. First, therefore, and foremost must be the piece of advice, 'Have some money.'

The next thing that must be mentioned is THE OIL-BOTTLE. The value of this utensil is self-evident; it contains oil. This may be odorous or odourless according to taste. Whether the savour of paraffin is actually attractive to trout depends on their olfactory and degustatory receptivity, the keenness of which has not as yet been sufficiently determined. In close relationship to the oil-bottle is THE BUTTON, to which it is attached by A PIECE OF STRING. Anglers should certainly be provided with these also.

Of considerable importance is THE PIN, which is stuck in the lapel of the angler's coat, being withdrawn for the purpose of coping with the Gordian, turle, and other knots. Owing to the shy nature of the implement, trouble chiefly arises when the pin falls into long grass. It could easily be avoided by the simple expedient of tying a luggage label round the pin's neck, and by writing his name and address thereon the angler would be able to let the world know to whom the property belonged.

COBBLER'S WAX

This is indispensable for many fishing purposes, and it imparts a look of rude health and honest labour to the hands of the user. Fastidious people may get rid of it from their hands by employing the contents of the oil-bottle for that purpose. For getting rid of the smell of paraffin more cobbler's wax may be suggested.

THE LINE-GREASER

Obviously no angler should be without this. The poetry of pleasant places is much enhanced if greased lines are cast in them. Besides, the line-greaser (the up-to-date kind at a shilling) could at a pinch be utilised to hold a spare cigarette, or even two.

THE HALFPENNY
This is to be considered on its own merits, and quite apart from its claim to inclusion under our first heading. It serves as a screwdriver (a thing required by some modern high-powered devices), as a tobacco (or worm) tin opener, and as a composer of the mind. When in doubt as to which fly, which bait, which pool, which – in fact, when in doubt, the angler has only to consult his halfpenny. If his heart should say 'heads,' while his eyes say 'tails,' he can go on consulting the coin till an agreement is reached.

THE COLLECTOR'S NET
With this trifle of gauze and wire the dry-fly man employs the shining hours to good and serious purpose. *Nulla dies sine ephemera* should be his motto. With luck he might even catch a trout as well, in one of the smaller carriers.

THE CORKSCREW
The possession of this implement will give the angler many an opportunity of doing a good turn to his fellow men. Besides, one good turn deserves another.

THE PLUMMET
This is very necessary. Often as it is being drawn up through the water it will attract the notice of the hungry pike or the greedy perch, which will follow and assault it. Such an incident is worth an audience of five to any practised raconteur.

A FRIEND WITH A MOTOR-CAR
We cannot too strongly advise the inclusion of this. For getting to the top of the water or the bottom of the water, for carrying fish or luncheon, and other purposes, the car has no serious rivals. The friend may perhaps be trusted with the landing net when he has done his other work.

It must not be supposed that the foregoing round dozen of necessities exhausts the subject of angling equipment. But for the rest, experience (and the tackle shops) will soon teach all that need be learnt as to triangles, baskets, bags, nets, gaffs, floats, gut casts, leads, fly-books, bait-cans, minnow-traps, weighing machines, electric lamps, fly-vices, eel-spears, rod-rests, kneeling-pads, salmon flies, chub flies, wet flies, dry flies, pike flies, grayling flies, tackle-cases, rod-boxes, tailers, priests, disgorgers, gags, perch hooks, roach hooks, barbel hooks, bream hooks, carp hooks, chub hooks, tench hooks, bottled gudgeon, bottled bleak, bottled eels, bottled prawns, bottled dace, Archer tackle, Stewart tackle, Pennell tackle, Bickerdyke flights, Jardine snaps, swivels, pipe-leads, bullets, paternoster tackle, leger traces, Thames trout flights, split cane, greenheart, hickory, blue mahoe, whole cane, Spanish reed, whalebone, lancewood, spears, buttons, stilettos, line-clearers, line-winders, line-twisters, single hair, files, tweezers, pilots, centre-pins, band brakes, optional checks, silent checks, reversible drums, phantoms, devons, halcyons, spoons, wagtails, salmon rods, trout rods, roach rods, punt rods, pike rods, spinning rods, trolling rods, general rods, portmanteau rods, composite rods, spliced rods, two-handed rods, one-handed rods, spare tops, top cases, rings, fly reels, spinning reels, Nottingham reels, multiplying reels, and the other articles which help to make up a simple list of no great length.

H.T. SHERINGHAM, *Fishing: A Diagnosis*, 1914

What the Fashionable Fisher is Wearing

. . . No angler should look grotesque (if he can help it), and there are two things which he should always studiously avoid, and they are a white straw hat and patent leather boots, as these frighten the fish.

Some angling advertisements lay it down as a rule that anglers should wear 'all wool', and nothing but wool, and that by so doing they will be able to avoid rheumatism and such like ailments; but in my case I got the woollen clothing and rheumatism as well, so this statement is not to be replied upon.

Apart from advertisements, a soft 'Wild West' felt, a loose Norfolk jacket, grey flannel trousers, and a coloured pocket handkerchief seem to me a nice romantic 'rig' for a dry-fly fisherman, especially if he is one of those who like to have a copy of Izaak Walton, or one of the classics, in their pocket (to read when anyone is passing by) as does,

Yours faithfully,

G.F.E.

Journal of the Flyfishers Club, 1918

No Loud Colours

And let your garments russet be or gray,
Of colour dark, and hardest to descry;
That with the rain or weather will away,
And least offend the fearful fish's eye:
For neither scarlet nor rich cloth of ray,
Nor colours dipped in fresh Assyrian dye,
    Nor tender silks of purple, paul, or gold
    Will serve so well to keep off wet or cold.

JOHN DENNYS, *The Secrets of Angling*, 1613

If You Should Have to Swim a Mile or Two . . .

The angler's coat and trowsers should be of cloth, not too thick and heavy, for if they be the sooner wet they will be the sooner dry. Water-proof velveteens, fustians, and mole-skins – rat-catcher's costume – ought never to be worn by the angler; for if he should have to swim a mile or two on any occasion – when overtaken by the tide on Duddon sands, for instance, or across Bassenthwaite or Ullswater, to save going six miles about – he would find them a serious weight when once thoroughly saturated with water; and should he have a stone of fish in his creel, it would be safest not to make the attempt. An elderly gentleman of the Kitchiner school, now sitting at my elbow, who knows the 'Peptic Precepts' better than he does his catechism – which he has long since forgotten, except a phrase or two which he sometimes quotes as St Paul, in religious company – suggests the propriety of anglers wearing *cork* jackets, which if strapped under the shoulders, would enable the wearer to visit any part of a lake, where, in warm weather, with an umbrella over his head, he might enjoy his sport, cool and comfortable, as if in a 'sunny pleasure dome with caves of ice'. The same gentleman thinks that a bottle of Reading sauce, a box of 'peptic pills', and a portable frying-pan ought to form part of every angler's travelling equipage. Having merely noticed these recommendations of the worthy member of the 'Eating-made-easy' club, I leave it to those who may feel so inclined, to avail themselves of the above hints.

STEPHEN OLIVER, *Scenes and Recollections of Fly-fishing in Northumberland, Cumberland and Westmoreland*, 1834

Examine Your Legs

Wading in the water is not only an agreeable thing in itself, but absolutely necessary in some rivers in the North that are destitute of boats; and that you may do this in the best possible style, procure half a dozen pair of shoes, with large knob-nails at some distance asunder: if they are too close, they will bring your foot to an even surface, and it will glide off a stone or rock, which in deep water may be inconvenient. Cut some holes in the upper-leathers of your shoes, to give the water a free passage out of them when you are on dry land; not because the fluid is annoying, for we should wrong you to say so, but to prevent the pumping noise you would otherwise make at every step. . . . When you are wading through the rapids, step on quickly and boldly, and do not gaze down on the stream after the fashion of Narcissus; for running waves will not reflect your beauty, but only make your head giddy. If you stop for a moment, place your legs abreast of each other: should you fancy a straddle, with one of them in advance, the action of the water will operate upon both, trip you up, and carry you out to sea. Observe, I am talking of a heavy stream. The body of a man, who probably lost his life in this manner, was found low down the river when I was fishing. I asked John Haliburton, who was then my fisherman, where it came from. 'I suppose,' said he, 'it travelled all the way from Peebles.' [i.e. about twenty-five miles downstream – ED.]

Avoid standing upon rocking stones, for obvious reasons; and never go into the water deeper than the fifth button of your waistcoat: even this does not always agree with tender constitutions in frosty weather. As you are likely not to take a just estimate of the cold in the excitement of the sport, should you be of a delicate temperament, and be wading in the month of February, when it may chance to freeze very hard, pull down your stockings, and examine your legs. Should they be black, or even purple, it might, perhaps, be as well to get on dry land; but if they are only rubicund, you may continue to enjoy the water.

WILLIAM SCROPE, *Days and Nights of Salmon Fishing*, 1843

The Disadvantages of Wading Boots

Those contrivances certainly protect us in a degree from the direct action of the cold water of the river, and to some extent shield us from its intensity; but it must not be forgotten that at the same time that the water from without is prevented from getting access to our limbs, the moisture exhaled from the pores of the skin within is equally as effectually prevented from escaping; and this, becoming condensed amongst the interstices of our garments, by the cold of the external water, keeps us nearly as thoroughly soaked in wet as if we were at once exposed to the current; the waterproofs in this respect exactly imitating the functions of the condenser of a still. But should it be the will of anyone to protect himself thus from the assaults of cold water, he may use either Macintosh stockings, which reach up to the middle of the thigh or the body, or boots of waterproof leather. The stockings are the lightest and easiest to travel in, and the latter the neatest and most seemly. In using the former, the wearer should bear in mind to put on a pair of long, thick, home-knit hose next his skin, entirely woollen, with short-kneed small-clothes, over which the Macintosh stocking is to be drawn, and over them again a pair of socks, to prevent the shoe (which must be made especially for the purpose, and two or three sizes larger than those usually worn) from abrading it. Although this triplicate costume may render the foot of a smart young sprig of some five feet and a trifle, something larger in dimensions than the 'clodpressers' of the 'Staleybridge Infant' (a noted pugilist of six feet two inches in stature), yet the whole will not be nearly so heavy and fatiguing as a pair of cumbrous leather boots; and should the children of every village through which he passes pursue him with extended fingers and derisive cheers, as will most likely be the case, I would not recommend him on any account to put himself out of temper, but pocket the insult as coolly as possible, and go on his way rejoicing.

A.S. MOFFAT, The Secrets of Angling, 1865

A Small Arsenal for Fishing on Exmoor

In Scotland the angler's ambition is to deceive the trouts and fill his basket.

In Exmoor it is to dodge the trees and economize in tackle.

In Scotland the Golden Rule is 'Keep your flies in the water.'

In Exmoor one is well satisfied if one can get them on to the water at all.

Every form of fishing has its own peculiar problems and for their solution its own peculiar methods. A word or two, therefore, about the Exmoor angler's outfit will appropriately inaugurate this paper.

The first requisite is a ladder. There are many patterns, but the best is one which Messrs Harlow have designed, after suggestions of my own, and list in their catalogue as 'The Exebury.' It is made of aluminium, so as to be light and strong, in sections twelve inches in length, each costing 3s. 6d. Every section is provided with two sockets into which the two points of every other fit easily. Thirty of these (weighing just eleven pounds and four ounces) may be carried in the fishing bag, and it is very rarely that, after joining them up, the angler will find it impossible to recover his fly or flies.

For exceptional cases, however, he will do well to carry an axe. Messrs Harlow make one that I can recommend. It is fitted with a handy clip which enables it to be slung from that ring of the bag to which the landing net is (elsewhere than on Exmoor) usually attached. Axe and ladder together make it unnecessary for any landing net to be carried.

The rod I can most honestly recommend is one that Messrs Harlow purvey, called 'The Qualm.' It is my own design and so I know that it is good. Its length is just twenty-five inches. It is made of solid steel in one piece, and it will bend point to butt without breaking. A few strong slashing strokes with this excellent little weapon will clear a path to the river for the angler through all but the most thickly grown parts of the bank. In such exceptional places the axe may usefully be brought into play.

As regards flies, it will perhaps assist the angler who proposes to make experience of Exmoor fishing if I give a short list of the most useful patterns, together with the number of each which he should take with him for, say, a week's sport.

Blue Uprights - - - - - -	500
Half Stones - - - - - - -	450
March Browns - - - - - -	400
Red Uprights - - - - - -	350
Greenwell's Glories - - - . - -	300
Olive Quills - - - - - -	250
Wickhams - - - - - - -	200
Yellow Uprights - - - - - -	150
Purple Uprights - - - - - -	100
Bolt Uprights - - - - - -	50
Fisherman's Curses - - -	1,000,000,000

He will hardly need more than sixty casts, since Sunday fishing is not allowed in most places.

It is well that all clothing should be strongly made, because the thorns which beset the angler's passage under the banks are only a little less tenacious than barbed wire. Messrs Harlow purvey a cloth both for suits, and, waterproofed, for waders and mackintoshes which I can thoroughly recommend. It is woven of very fine steel thread, which being in two shades, black and white, makes a very trim material hardly distinguishable from Irish tweed.

To protect the head from the briars a trench helmet may usefully be worn, for to leave an ear behind in a bush is an incident of a day's fishing with which most anglers will gladly dispense. Messrs Harlow have a very serviceable model, furnished with a cock band wherein those flies may be stuck which serve to mark off the fly-fisher from his inferiors.

Thus armed and caparisoned the novice in Exmoor fishing may

approach the valleys of the West Country with a reasonable degree of confidence, not only in his own security from laceration or maiming, and in his not running out of tackle before the end of his visit, but also in being able to hold up his head among the other people at his inn. For in Exmoor it is not the fellow who creels the largest number of trout that is esteemed, but he who can declare, at the end of the day, that he has lost no more than twenty or thirty flies, and one, two or three new casts.

WILLIAM CAINE, *Fish, Fishing and Fishermen*, 1927

The Compleat Angler's *Advice on Trout Rods*

For the length of your Rod, you are always to be govern'd by the breadth of the River you shall chuse to angle at; and for a Trout River, one of 5 or 6 yards long is commonly enough, and longer (though never so neatly and artificially made) it ought not to be, if you intend to Fish at ease, and if otherwise, where lies the sport?

Of these, the best that ever I saw are made in *York-shire*, which are all of one piece; that is to say, of several, six, eight, ten or twelve pieces, so neatly piec't, and ty'd together with fine thred below, and Silk above, as to make it taper, like a switch, and to ply with a true bent to your hand; and these are too light, being made of Fir wood, for two or three lengths, nearest to the hand, and of other wood nearer to the top, that a Man might very easily manage the longest of them that ever I saw, with one hand; and these when you have given over Angling for a season, being taken to pieces, and laid up in some dry place, may afterwards be set together again in their former postures, and will be as strait, sound, and good as the first hour they were made, and being laid in Oyl and colour according to your Master *Waltons* direction, will last many years.

The length of your line, to a Man that knows how to handle his Rod, and to cast it, is no manner of encumbrance, excepting in woody places, and in landing of a Fish, which every one that can afford to Angle for pleasure, has some body to do for him, and the length of line is a mighty advantage to the fishing at distance; and to fish *fine, and far off* is the first and principal Rule for Trout Angling.

CHARLES COTTON, *The Compleat Angler*, 1676

How to Make a Rod

The wood for rods should be cut about Christmas, (and some insist that if left in the open air for twelve months afterwards, it will season better, than if stowed in a dry place.) *Hazel* is the wood generally procured for this purpose, and of all the sorts, that of the *Cob-nut* grows to the greatest length, and is for the most part straight and taper; the but end should rather exceed an inch in diameter, but of whatever wood the rod is composed, the shoots for stocks, middle pieces, and tops, must be of proper size, well grown, and as free from knots as possible. The tops should be the best rush ground-shoots, without knots, and proportionally taper; the excrescent twigs are to be cut off, but not close, for fear of hurting the bark, which ought never to be touched with a knife or rasp, for altho' they will dress neater, it considerably weakens them; these pieces are to be kept free from wet until the beginning of the following Autumn, when such as are wanted to form a rod, should be selected, and after being warmed over a gentle fire, set as straight as possible, and laid aside for two or three days, when they must be rubbed over with a piece of flannel and linseed oil, which will polish and fetch off any superfluous bark; they are then to be bound tight to a straight pole, and so kept until the next Spring, when they will be seasoned for use; (some however prefer keeping them from eighteen months to two years before they are made up;) they are then to be matched together in just proportion, in three, four, or more parts, according to the width of the water, or the wish of the maker, taking care that the different joints fit so nicely, if ferruled, that the *whole* rod may move as if it were but one piece. If the parts are not ferruled, observe, that they must be cut to join each other with the utmost exactness, and neatly spliced with *glue*, boiled very gently in strong quick lime water, keeping it stirred until it becomes smooth and all alike, and then are to be whipped over the glued part with waxed thread. When the rod is completed, it should be nicely rubbed with the following varnish: – Half a pint of linseed oil, and a little India rubber scraped fine; put them over a slow fire, and stir them well together until the rubber is dissolved, then boil and skim it; apply it warm, and do not use the rod until quite dry. The appearance upon the rod will be like a fine thin bark, it will preserve the rod from being worm eaten, and from other injuries, and is very durable. As moisture is at all times destructive to wood, it is essential for the Angler to guard all in his power against its influence on his rod; for admitting, that a shower of rain will not spoil it, yet if not protected by a varnish, it may soon be deprived of its elasticity, which is the chief requisite of any, and more particularly of a Fly-rod. Variety of methods are used in preparing varnish, the one here mentioned is said to be excellent; half an ounce of *Shell*, and the same quantity of *Seed-Lac*, powdered fine in a mortar; put into separate vials, with half a pint of good spirits of wine in each, and placed in a sand heat to dissolve; during the process, shake the vials often; when each is dissolved, mix them together in a larger bottle, with half an ounce of *Gum Benjamin*; increase the heat, and the dregs will subside; then warm the wood, and with a Camel's hair brush apply that part of the varnish which is become fine; the third coat will remain on the surface, and securely protect the rod from injury; the rod composed of the Hazel will not do for fly fishing, the least wet being apt to warp, and render it crooked.

THE REVEREND WILLIAM DANIEL, *Rural Sports*, 1802

The Best Horse-Tail Hair For Lines

Elect your Hair not from lean, poor, or diseased Jades, but from a Stone-horse, or Gelding at least, that is fat, strong, and lusty, and of 4 or 5 years old, and that which groweth from the inmost and middle part of his Dock, and so extendeth itself downwards to the Ground, is commonly the biggest and strongest Hair about the Horse, and better than those upon the upper part of, or setting on of the Tail: Generally best Horses have the best Hair.

JAMES CHETHAM, *The Angler's Vade Mecum*, 1681

Turning Hair into Lines

In making *lines*, every hair in every link, should be equally big, round and even, that the strength may be so proportionate, that they will not break singly, but all together; by carefully choosing the hairs, they will stretch and bear a much stronger force, than when a faulty hair is included. Never strain the hair before twisting, the best will easily be selected by the eye, and two or three inches of the bottom part of the hair should be cut off, as it is generally defective. The links should be twisted very slowly, and not to be harsh, but so as to twine one with another, and no more, for a hard twisted line is always weak; by mixing *chesnut, black*, or any other coloured hair, the line may be varied at pleasure.

Sorrel, chesnut, or brown coloured hairs, are best for ground angling, especially in muddy water, as they nearly resemble the colour of the water; white, grey, or darkish white hair is for clear streams. Some use a pale watery *green* for weedy rivers in summer. Black will only do for rivers immediately flowing from *mosses*.

THE REVEREND WILLIAM DANIEL, *Rural Sports*, 1802

Izaak Walton's Technique for Dyeing Horse-hair Lines

Take a pint of strong ale, half a pound of soot, and a little quantity of the juice of walnut-tree leaves, and an equal quantity of alum; put these together into a pot, pan, or pipkin, and boil them half an hour; and having so done, let it cool; and being cold, put your hair into it, and there let it lie: it will turn your hair to be a kind of water or glass-color, or greenish; and the longer you let it lie, the deeper colored it will be. You might be taught to make many other colors, but it is to little purpose; for doubtless the water-color or glass-colored hair is the most choice and most useful for an Angler; but let it not be too green.

But if you desire to color hair greener, then do it thus. Take a quart of small ale, half a pound of alum; then put these into a pan or pipkin, and your hair into it with them; then put it upon a fire, and let it boil softly for half an hour; and then take out your hair, and let it dry; and, having so done, then take a pottle of water, and put into it two handfuls of marigolds, and cover it with a tile, or what you think fit, and set it again on the fire, where it is to boil again softly for half an hour, about which time the scum will turn yellow; then put into it half a pound of copperas, beaten small, and with it the hair that you intend to color; then let the hair be boiled softly

till half the liquor be wasted; and then let it cool three or four
hours, with your hair in it: and you are to observe, that the more
copperas you put into it, the greener it will be; but doubtless the
pale green is best. But if you desire yellow hair, which is only good
when the weeds rot, then put in the more marigolds; and abate most
of the copperas, or leave it quite out, and take a little verdigris
instead of it.

IZAAK WALTON, *The Compleat Angler*, 1676

How to Make Silk Gut

Silk-worm gut, which forms so important a part of the angler's
outfit, is the substance of the worm in an immature state, and is
made by steeping the insect in vinegar or some other acid, a short
time before it is ready to commence spinning its cocoon, stretching
it to the required length, and securing the ends until the strand is
dry. It is then divested of any extraneous substance by rubbing. It is
imported from China, Spain, and Italy, in hanks of a hundred
strands, and sold by all the tackle stores, the price varying according
to its size, length, and roundness. A scientific friend informed me
once, that he had produced the veritable article, by stretching out
the worms after steeping them in vinegar, and securing the heads
and tails in notches made in each end of a shingle.

THADEUS NORRIS, *The American Angler's Book*, 1865

Advice in Verse

But every fish loves not each bait alike,
Although sometime they feed upon the same;
But some do one, and some another seek,
As best unto their appetite doth frame,
The roach, the bream, the carp, the chub and bleak,
With paste or corn, their greedy hunger tame,
    The dace, the ruffe, the gudgeon and the rest,
    The smaller sort of crawling worms love best.

The chavender and chub do more delight
To feed on tender cheese or cherries red,
Black snails, their bellies slit to shew their white,
Or grasshoppers that skip in every mead,
The perch, the tench, and eel, do rather bite
At great red worms, in field or garden bred,
    That have been scoured in moss or fennel rough,
    To rid their filth, and make them hard and tough.

JOHN DENNYS, *The Secrets of Angling*, 1613

Eighteenth-century Carp Baits

A carp exercises the angler's patience as much as any fish, for he is very fly and wary. They seldom bite in cold weather; and in hot, a man cannot be too early or too late for them. Yet when they do bite, there is no fear of their hold.

Proper baits are the red-worm in March, the candew in June, and the grasshopper in July, August and September. But a recent discovery has proved a green pea to be a bait inferior to none, if not the best of all; and that the best method to prepare them for use is by half boiling a sufficient quantity, and covering them with melted butter.

In hot weather, he will take a lob-worm at top, as a trout does a fly: or, between the weeds, in a clear place, sink it with a float, about eight inches in the water, with only one large shot on the line, which is to be lodged on the leaf of some weed: Then retire, keeping your eye upon the shot, till you see it taken away, with about a foot of the line, and then you may venture to strike; but keep him tight, and clear of the weeds. Great numbers of carp have been taken this way.

As before observed, this fish is very cautious, and therefore your float must be small, and you must be sure to keep out of sight. And because, when hooked, he struggles in a violent manner, you must take care that your tackle be very good and strong, otherwise he will break from you.

If you are desirous of angling with a paste, the following is as good as any. Take fine flour, a bit of lean raw veal, a little honey, and cotton-wool sufficient to keep the ingredients together, and beat them in a mortar to a paste. Or white bread mixed with cotton-wool, and worked into paste with some of the water where you are fishing, is not a despicable bait. Carp will take red currants, green figs, or almost any sort of bait. When you fish with a grasshopper you must take off its wings, and let it sink into the water without lead or float. Gentiles, two upon a hook, throwing in at the same time chew'd white bread, is a good method to angle for carp, especially in a pond.

RICHARD BROOKES, *The Art of Angling*, 1790

A Hackney Take-away

Go to Mother *Gibert's* at the *Flower-de-Luce* at *Clapton*, near *Hackney*, and whilst you are drinking of a Pot of *Ale*, bid the Maid make you two or three Penny-worth of *Ground Bait*, and some *Paste* (which they do very neatly, and well); and observing of them, you will know how to make it yourself for any other Place; which is too tedious here to Insert.

WILLIAM GILBERT, *The Method of Fishing in Hackney River*, 1676

On Salmon Roe, the Deadliest Bait of All

This is the most destructive bait that can be used, and many conscientious anglers think it unfair to use it, for more reasons than one. In the first place, the bait can only be procured by the destruction of the salmon, and the roe they contain, just before spawning, and at a time when the fish are out of season; and in the second, the use of it, by some persons, is considered little better than poaching. I have heard of various modes of curing salmon roe, and have tried some of them, but without any great success. It may be procured in the spring, in pots, at two shillings and sixpence each, at most of the London fishing-tackle shops, in great perfection.

In some cases the salmon roe is made into a paste; in others, the round red pellicles of the roe remain unbroken, and in this latter state I prefer it.

The great value of salmon roe is during the increase of a fresh of water, when the stream is large and much discoloured, but it may be employed successfully in the deep eddies by the apron of a mill-tail, or in the deep shady part of a stream, even if the water be bright.

One shot, No. 4, will generally be sufficient to sink your bait, as you must choose the stiller parts of the stream, such as the eddies and holes near the banks. I have taken a dozen trout at a standing, by letting the bait drop gently to the bottom, in the stillest part of the eddy, and leaving it stationary till a tug was felt, when the fish must be instantly struck, or the bait will be lost as well as the fish.

T.C. HOFLAND, *The British Angler's Manual*, 1834

Catching Worms

Lobworms can be found on the lawn at night, when there has been rain or heavy dew. Catching them makes the back ache, but is sport of a mild kind. The sportsman arms himself with an electric torch and a can or small bucket, and then proceeds up and down the lawn, stooping so that the torch throws its light on the grass in front of him. He will soon come on a lobworm lying full length on the grass, and putting the bucket down, will make a grab. At first he will miss his prey, for the worms are very quick at retreating backwards into their holes; but with practice he will learn to seize them with finger and thumb before they can escape. It is well to aim not at the head, which is on the grass, but at the tail, which is usually just inside the hole. Each worm as it is caught is dropped into the can, and on a good evening a couple of hundred can be caught in an hour. Sometimes a worm when seized will be found to cling tight to its hole with its tail. It should not be pulled out forcibly, or it will break in two; but it can generally be 'eased' out by a succession of gentle tugs. A small tub or box filled with fairly moist earth is the best thing to keep a stock of worms in. A few can easily be taken out as they are wanted and put in moss for a day or two before fishing. Dead ones should be thrown away at once.

H.T. SHERINGHAM, *Elements of Angling*, 1930

Tips About Pyjamas

Worms may be induced to come up for air by soaking an area of grass or earth with a mixture of mustard and water. They also come out at night but you will have to become as deft as a thrush to catch them and your wife will raise objections if you arise in the small hours to catch worms in the garden.

I know a man who practised this method and used to put the captured worms in his pyjama pocket. The inevitable happened – he omitted to take all the worms out of his pocket when he came back to bed. He is now divorced. There are some things which even a fisherman's wife will not stand for.

'B.B.', *Fisherman's Folly*, 1987

Scouring Worms

An angler should be always provided with well-scoured worms, as they are more lively, bright, and tough, than when first taken from the earth. There are various modes recommended for scouring worms, but clean moss alone will answer every purpose required. Moss may be easily procured in almost every part of the country, and in London may be purchased in Covent-Garden; it should be well washed and squeezed till nearly dry, and then placed in an earthen pan to receive the worms, which will be ready for use in four or five days. Great care must be taken to keep the moss sweet and clean, by changing it every three or four days, or by well washing it; and if any of the worms are found to be in a sickly state, or dead, they must be removed, or they will destroy the sweetness of the moss, and thereby greatly injure the healthy worms.

T.C. HOFLAND, *The British Angler's Manual*, 1834

For a Fresh Supply of Maggots or Gentles

Take the liver of any animal, and hang it over a barrel half full of dry clay, and as the gentles grow large they will fall into the barrel and scour themselves, and will be always ready for use; OR, if it be required to keep them all the year, procure some dead animal which is fly blown, and when the gentles begin to be alive and stir, bury the carcase and them together in soft moist earth free from frost; these gentles may be dug out as they are wanted, and will be fit for use until March, at which time they will turn to flies.

GEORGE BAINBRIDGE, *The Fly-Fisher's Guide*, 1816

More Tips About Maggots

Maggots are kept with dead flesh, beast's liver, or suet; or, which is better, you may both keep and scour them in meal or wheat-bran. In order to breed them, prick a beast's liver full of holes; hang it in the sun in summer time, and set it under an old barrel, or small firkin, with clay and bran in it: into which they will drop, and cleans themselves, and be always ready for use. In this manner gentles may be produced till Michaelmas: But if you would fish with them from Michaelmas to May-day, you must get a dead cat, kite, or other carrion, at the latter end of September, and let it be fly-blown; and when the gentles begin to be alive and stir, bury it and them together in moist earth, deep in the ground, that the frost may neither kill nor injure them, and they will serve for use till March and April following, about which time they turn to be flesh-flies.

RICHARD BROOKES, *The Art of Angling*, 1790

Harvesting Other Baits

Bark-worms are found under the bark of an oak, ash, alder, and birch, especially if they lie a year or more after they have fallen, you may find a great white worm, with a brown head, something resembling a dore bee, or humble-bee, this is in season all the year, especially from September until June, or mid-May; the Umber covets this bait above any, save fly, and cad-bait; you may also find this worm in the body of a rotten alder, if you break it with an axe or beetle; but be careful only to shake the tree in pieces with beating, and crush not the worm: you may also find him under the bark of the stump of a tree, if decayed.

Dry your wasps, dores, or bees, upon a tile-stone, or in an oven cooled after baking, lest they burn; and to avoid that, you must lay them on a thin board or chip, and cover them with another so supported, as not to crush them, or else clap two cakes together: this way they will keep long, and stick on your hook well. If you boil them hard, they grow black in a few days.

Dry your sheep's blood in the air, upon a dry board, till it become a pretty hard lump; then cut it into small pieces for your use.

When you use grain, boil it soft, and get off the outward rind, which is the bran; and then if you will, you may fry the same in honey and milk, or some strong scented oils, as polypody, spike, ivy, turpentine; for Nature, which maketh nothing in vain, hath given the fish nostrils, and that they can smell, is undeniable; and I am persuaded, more guided by the sense of smelling, than sight, for sometimes they will come to the float, if any wax be upon it, smell at it and go away.

When you see ant-flies in greatest plenty, go to the ant-hills where they breed, take a great handful of the earth, with as much of the roots of the grass growing on those hills; put all into a large glass bottle, then gather a pottle full of the blackest, ant-flies unbruised, put them into the bottle, or into a firkin, if you would keep them long, first washed with honey, or water and honey; ROACH and DACE will bite at these flies under water near the ground.

When you gather bobs after the plough, put them into a firkin, with sufficient of the soil they were bred in, to preserve them; stop the vessel quite close, or all will spoil; set it where neither wind nor frost may offend them, and they will keep all Winter for your use.

At the latter end of September, take some dead carrion that hath some maggots bred in it, which are beginning to creep; bury all deep in the ground, that the frost kill them not, and they will serve in March or April following, to use.

To find the flag-worm, do thus: go to an old pond, or pit, where there are store of flags, or, as some call them, sedges, pull some up by the roots, then shake those roots in the water, till all the mud and dirt be washed away from them, then amongst the small strings or fibres that grow to the roots, you will find little husks or cases of a reddish, or yellowish, and some of other colours; open these carefully with a pin, and you will find in them a little small worm, white as a gentle, but longer and thinner; this is an excellent bait for the Tench, the Bream, and especially the Carp: if you pull the flags asunder, and cut open the round stalk, you will also find a worm like the former in the husks; but tougher, and in that respect better.

ROBERT VENABLES, *The Experienced Angler*, 1662

First Find a Willing Ram – A Bait for Mullet

Put the member of a ram into a new pot, and having covered it with another pot, stop it so that it may have no vent, and send it to the glass furnace to be set on from the morning to the evening, and you will find it become quite tender; then use it for bait.

And One for Luring Fish to an Angling Spot

Take three limpets, that are produced on rocks, and having taken out the fish, inscribe on the shell the words which follow, and you will immediately see the fish come to the same place, in a surprising manner. The words are, 'the God of Armies', and the fishermen make use of them.

CASSIANUS BASSUS, *Geoponika* (?2nd century AD)

Chocolate Biscuits on Lake Nyasa

The fish at Nkata Bay are said to be very hard to catch, and for the first day of our stay they upheld their reputation so stoutly that we were exhausted and dispirited; hours of trolling and casting, at different speeds and depths and with every variety of lure in the bag, had produced one half-pound fish wearing a brown and yellow football jersey and an *ncheni* like a sardine. The infuriating part of it was that the fish could be seen plainly in the clear water, almost in hundreds, and no mere babies either. We gave up trolling and spinning, and tried the drift-line, using the lightest gear we had, with 4x gut, a No. 14 hook, and small pieces of *usipa* as bait. Still no good. We tried throwing in ground-bait, with the baited hook among the pieces; but as they sank slowly through the clear water we could see those high-class fish pick out with unerring instinct all the safe morsels, leaving the spiky one severely alone. What to do? We had no finer tackle; yet baffled and discouraged as we felt, it seemed better to fish on. Then the supply of *usipa* gave out. We tried bread paste from our sandwiches; no good, and that gave out too. Even rock-cake paste was refused; the fish just would not play with us.

And then one angler remembered that in the bag was a tin of chocolate Bourbon biscuits. They were brought out amid jeers and laughter; Bourbon paste was hastily made, and some crumbs thrown in as ground-bait; then in went the baited hook, and whizz-zz! the angler was into a good *chipuzi* of about a pound. On that tackle he put up a marvellous fight, and the shoal might well have been scared; but no, every time the little chocolate pellets went in a fish came out, until the Bourbons were finished and we had twelve good *chipuzi* in the boat. It was a memorable evening; we were fishing the north bay, and it was almost dead calm, and the clear water mirrored the white boat and the passing canoes and reflected flickers of light on to dark green foliage of the surrounding trees. There was no sound at all except the lapping of water round the boat, the occasional cry of a fish-eagle, now and then a screech from the reel or the mutter of an angler hastily baiting up, and the little splashes of fish as they were netted. The *chipuzi* fought magnificently in that deep green water, twisting and flashing far down, and pulling line off the reel in savage tugs, so that the light rod was arched till its tip was nearly pulled under. Two cormorants were fishing busily fifty yards away, sitting on the dead branch of a drowned tree, slipping off it alternately in the cleanest of dives that made never a ripple, staying under for what seemed an impossible time, and coming up again to sit once more on the stump and dry their wings and feathers in that well-known attitude that is at once heraldic and slightly ridiculous. And for once we were doing considerably better than they were.

That Bourbon tip is worth knowing, always take a tin with you when you go to Nkata. If the fish won't have them, so much the better for the anglers.

v. FOX-STRANGEWAYS, *Wandering Fisherman*, 1955

How to Give a Carp a Hangover

Over-night mix bean-flower with a little honey, wet it with rectify'd spirits of wine, and a little oil of turpentine, make it up into little pellets, and such fish as nibble it, when thrown in, will be stupified, so that in the morning coming to themselves a little, they will bite very eagerly, as being after their drunken fit, exceeding hungry.

RICHARD AND CHARLES BOWLKER, *The Art of Angling*, 1674

The Fisherman's Legendary Kindness

    In *Surry* Rises there,
     A branch of *Medway*, where
Store of all sorts of Fish do breed,
To serve for Pleasure and for need,
Well stor'd with Game the Rivers be,
Could they from poaching be kept free:
Once Angling at the Rivers side,
    Observing how the stream
In gentle motions then did slide,
With eager haste to meet his bride,
    And makes his Joys supream;
    By chance I spy'd a Rustick Clown,
A halling something up and down,
    To him I streight repair,
    Aud ask'd his business there.
He told me Fishing for an hour or two,
Lord, how amaz'd was I to see him go,
A bush pul'd from the hedg, his Angling rod
No top, but like a staff with which Men plod,
When driving home full udders to the pail,
Heaven bless me when such tackling can prevail:

His hook ti'd to a string, that to a piece of leather,
A flote just in the place where both were knit together,
Fortune her self that time was double blind,
She could not see and so perforce was kind.
　　For straight he took two *Bleaks*, one *Roach*,
　　　　And last of all a well grown *Perch*,
　　　　　　Who gasping lay upon the ground,
　　　　　　I Judged to weigh at least a pound.
Pleas'd with the fancy I unto him gave,
An Angle, Rod and Line the best I have,
　　And shew'd him where good baits to find
A Cow-turd, ten days old, and newly lin'd,
With *blew-tails* which from homed *Gentiles* spring,
A ready bait and good for every thing,
The Man was Civil, and exprest his mind,
In real thanks, then sought some better luck to find.
　　　　　　JOHN WHITNEY, *The Genteel Recreation*, 1700

On Bread And Paste and Wine and Ox-tongue

And if you have a boy to go along with
you, a good Neats-Tongue (cured ox-tongue – Ed.), and a
bottle of canary (sweet wine – Ed.) should not be wanting:
To the enjoyment of which I leave you.
　　　　　　WILLIAM GILBERT, *The Angler's Delight*, 1676

Keeping Spirits Up on a Visit to New Hampshire

I had often heard of people catching Trout 'as fast as they could haul
'em out:' I had often been assured of the plausibility of such a fact,
but I had my doubts. I knew *I* had fished for Trout, and never 'hauled
'em out' at all, and so I was a sceptic as to any such proceedings as
enthusiastic anglers from the north of the Granite State had repeatedly
affirmed to have been within their daily experience. Taking all things
into consideration, therefore, I determined to try for myself.

There were three of us: our baggage as follows: Item, one bottle of gin, two shirts: Item, one bottle schnapps, two pair stockings: Item, one bottle Schiedam, one pair fishing-pants: Item, one bottle genuine aromatic, by Udolpho Wolfe, name on the wrapper, without which the article is fictitious, one pair extra boots: Item, one bottle extract of juniper-berry; one bottle brandy, long and wide, prescribed by scientific skill for medicinal purposes. Also, rods, flies, tackle in abundance, and a supply of gin; in addition, each of us had a quart-flask in our pockets, containing gin. We also had some gin inside when we started.

Thus prepared, we started by rail from where the gin was purchased, for Littleton, which we reached in the afternoon.

THADEUS NORRIS, *The American Angler's Book*, 1865

The Importance of Tea

I feel bound to emphasise the importance of the angler's tea – with country bread and butter, new milk, and possibly home-made jam. I strongly advise the novice never to neglect this simple meal when he is fishing, and to take some trouble, if need be, to ensure getting it. My reason is partly the pleasure of it – a townsman never more fully realizes the charm of the country than when he is seated in the parlour of some cottage or simple inn, looking out into an old-world garden, and enjoying the scent of the wall-flowers – and partly the use of it. The half-hour's rest after what has in all likelihood been a heated and strenuous day is very necessary if the angler is to make good use of his evening; also the hot tea itself is a mild stimulant, just sufficient to refresh a weary man and set him going again. Let the novice make sure of his tea, wherever he fishes.

H.T. SHERINGHAM, *Elements of Angling*, 1930

As for Flies

I think either for trout, or any other fish, that will rise at flies, those that they rise at most, that season when you fish for them, are the best to take them with; and there are so many, that I cannot (for fear of making my little piece swell beyond its price) stand to name them.

Now as to artificial flies, take only this rule with you; that is, to provide all colours of silk, and feathers, and such things as are convenient for making of them: and never go about to make one, artificially, without a natural one before you, whatever it is you would imitate: But you had better go, or send, to the Three Fishes, over-against the little North Door of St Paul's, in London, where you may find them better and cheaper, than you can make them; and so much for trout.

WILLIAM GILBERT, *The Angler's Delight*, 1676

Why Size Does Matter

Let us grant, then, that the trout's sight is quick; let us concede him a strong sense of colour or texture or both; but is that sight clear? Has the trout even a rudimentary sense of form? There are grounds for doubting it. I am going to get into hot water with the apostles of the 'precise imitation' school, but I am not going to dogmatize, but to call attention to facts.

If we take the most exquisitely dressed Olive Quill or Iron-blue dun and compare them with their prototypes in nature, can we honestly say that the resemblance of form or attitude is marked? We know it is not. We are satisfied if in colour and size the imitation is approximate. If the fly be tied with rolled wings reversed, it is frequently as good a killer as, or even better than, the ordinary pattern. Yet the fly with dense, stiff wings thrown forward is really not, in shape at any rate, a striking likeness of the natural insect, with its wings sloping just the other way. A good instance of this is the Mole Fly – a sedge; instead of having its wings laid back over the body, it presents them flung forward in the opposite direction. Yet it is indubitably a successful pattern. Then, does the trout pay much attention to the fact that the floating fly of commerce is generally able to give the centipede fifty legs and a beating? There are times when he does not. Does he even mind where the legs occur in the anatomy (if one may be pardoned the term) of the artificial fly? They may, as in the Wickham or any of the sedges, be in spirals all down the body, but what does he care? Take the Dotterel dun. This is a hackled imitation of a light yellow-legged dun. The dotterel hackle is a brownish dun feather with yellow tips to the points of the fibres. The dun colour represents the wings, the yellow tips the legs. But does the trout resent being offered a fly with yellow legs at the tips of his wings, and these wings spread mopwise all round his body? If he does resent it, the popularity – the well-deserved popularity – of the Dotterel dun is hard to account for. Making every allowance for some disarrangement of toilet in a natural fly which has become submerged or caught by the current, can we say that it ever has its wings starred all round its head or shoulders in a palpitating mop? Then the honey-dun hen hackle. This is the same thing again. And we know that the honey-dun hen feathers are among the trout-fly dresser's most cherished treasures.

Let us turn to the Iron-blue dun. The natural insect has lead-coloured wings and red feet, and the artificial may be dressed either winged or hackled. If hackled, a dark blue dun feather with copper-red points is an admirable feather to use. But the trout does not mind a bit that your Iron-blue dun has a mop of blue wing all round its head, with a little red foot at the end of each fibre. It is a commonplace of fly dressing that, in translating a winged pattern into its hackled correlative, you select a hackle combining as far as possible the colour of wings and legs, and, so long as you keep the colours, their relative position is of little consequence. As an instance, let me quote the case of the Lead-winged (*i.e.*, starling-winged) Coachman and the Little Chap. Each has a peacock herl body. The dun of the starling wings in the Coachman is reproduced by the dun centre of the hackle of the Little Chap, and the red hackle of the Coachman by the red points of the hackle of the Little Chap. But if they be dressed on the same size of hook, when one will kill, as a general proposition the other will kill. If the artificial fly lay on quite still water it may be doubted whether it would often be taken; but in general the movement of the stream imparts an appearance of motion to the fly, and the trout, catching a general impression of correct size and colouring, absorbs it, hook and all, without too nearly considering the things that belong to his peace. Taking it by and large, the fact is indisputable that the shabbiest, roughest, most dilapidated, most broken-winged fly is as likely to kill as the newest and freshest of the fly-tier's confections – provided size and colour be right.

G.E.M. SKUES, *The Way of a Trout With a Fly*, 1924

Two Moths for Night Fishing

Although the Angling by night has a close affinity to *Poaching*, and as such is beneath the notice of a gentleman, yet as in extreme droughts during the Summer months it may be difficult to procure a dish of fine fish, however urgent the necessity, and as this method is decidely more sportsman-like than the use of the net, a description of the two baits most likely to succeed is subjoined for the benefit of such persons as may chuse, for the sake of a dish of fish, to expose themselves to the heavy dew of a Summer's night.

The wings of the WHITE MOTH are made from the feather of a white owl; the body of white ostrich harl, and a white cock's hackle over it. If a gentle be added, the success will be more certain.

The wings of the BROWN MOTH are to be made from the wings of the brown owl, or the back feathers of a brown hen; the body of dark bear's hair, and a brown cock's hackle over it. A cod-bait, as being nearer the colour of the body, is preferable to a gentle for this fly.

Both these moths are to be dressed rather larger than the green or gray drakes, and may be used until the approach of dawn. The fish will be heard to rise at them very distinctly, at which moment the Angler must strike.

GEORGE BAINBRIDGE, *The Fly-Fisher's Guide*, 1816

The Fast Track to Divorce and Poverty

I took up fly-fishing long enough ago that I don't remember exactly when it was, but I remember I had the novice's ready-made fascination with all the mysterious gear and gadgets. In fact, it was probably the exotic tackle and accoutrements that first attracted me to the sport. I had previously fished with what I now think of as 'nonfly' tackle, but the stuff fly-fishermen carried was both beautiful and serious looking at the same time – like a big, jangling ring of keys to a different reality. I was clearly hooked on the ambiance before I even got started, which is *why* I got started in the first place.

Of course, like all such things, it was more complicated than I first imagined. I remember walking into a store and announcing that I'd come to buy a fly rod.

'What kind?' asked the guy behind the counter.

'You mean there are different kinds?'

I asked for a regular-old, garden-variety fly rod and ended up with a fiberglass $7\frac{1}{2}$-footer for a #6 line fitted with a Pflueger Medallist reel. I passed up the one you could convert to a spinning rod by doing some fancy footwork with the reel seat. After all, I was a purist.

It took me a few trips to the store and a bit more money than I'd planned on – an ominous sign of things to come – but soon I had what I then considered to be the full getup: a small, inexpensive, flimsy vest, some leader material, a bottle of mosquito repellent, a pair of Taiwanese ditchboots, and a box of about a dozen flies, also from somewhere in the Third World. The flies were all nice and big and real pretty.

At first I thought I was in business, but it wasn't long before I started feeling half naked next to the archetypal properly attired fly-fisherman I'd meet on the streams. Some of these guys were pretty impressive; they looked like combinations of tackle stores, biology labs, and hospital emergency wards. The rattling, clanking sound they made when they walked had an authoritative ring to it, and most of them seemed to have evolved elaborate personal systems for balancing a strung-up fly rod, fly box, forceps, micrometer (you can't trust the factory measurements on this tippet material, you know), imported English scissor/pliers, etc.

They'd descend on the stream like information-gathering modules, sprouting collection nets, specimen bottles, and stream thermometers, and could often be heard muttering to each other in some foreign language I later discovered to be Latin: 'Clearly one of the large Ephemerella, probably the doddsi, though possibly the glacialis, easily mistaken for the E. grandis. Better tie on an Adams.'

The only Latin I could remember from college was *cogito ergo sum* ('I think, therefore I am'), I think.

The clincher was that most of these guys seemed to catch more trout than I did, and the only obvious difference between us was all that equipment. I began to suffer from voidophobia – the unreasoning fear of empty vest pockets. I didn't know exactly what I needed, but I clearly needed a lot of stuff, enough stuff to make me clank and rattle when I walked, to strain the single-stitched seams of my cheap vest, enough to put me in the same league with the guys who were catching all the fish.

By this time I'd figured out there were shops that dealt exclusively in fly tackle. (I'd bought my first gear at a place that also sold tires, garden tools, school supplies, Mexican felt paintings, and hot dogs.) I've since worked in fly shops and have cringed to see myself in some of the rosy-cheeked types who came in and asked things like, 'What size fly do I need to catch a 20-inch brown?' or 'How do I tie this little bitty fly to this big fat fly line?'

'Well . . . you need a leader.'

'A what?'

A clerk in the average fly shop spends half his time patiently leading people from the middle back to somewhere near the beginning.

Luckily, I happened to walk into the now-defunct Hank Roberts shop on Walnut Street in Boulder, Colorado. Had I stumbled into the clutches of an unscrupulous tackle dealer, I could easily have been fleeced for my life savings, such as they were. I wanted *stuff*, lots of it.

As it was, I was sold a few flies (Adamses and Hare's Ears), a tapered leader and some tippet material, and one of those fancy double-tapered lines to replace my level 6. I was even treated to a free casting lesson out in the parking lot.

'Look, you're not throwing a rock, you're casting a fly rod. Let the rod do the work.'

'Yeah, right, oof, oof, oof.'

'And by the way, when you get a chance, you might want to get yourself a *decent* rod.'

There were some decent rods back inside, rods with names like Leonard, Thomas & Thomas, and Orvis on them. A few cost more than the pickup truck I was driving, some of the gray smoke from which was still drifting through the open front door. Some of them were made from some kind of blonde-colored wood that was sawed up into six strips.

'Split cane.'

'Huh?'

'Bamboo.'

'Oh, right, I had a bamboo rod when I was a kid.'

'(sigh)'

I didn't know it then, but I'd been treated well. Still, I was disappointed that I didn't clank and rattle any more than I did before, and after spending a fair piece of change, too.

I started reading magazines, and then books on the subject. There was this guy named Ernest something (not Hemingway) who seemed to know a lot about bugs. Well and good, but what size fly do I need to catch a 20-inch brown?

Slowly, gradually, I began to realize what I needed. (In the language of fly-fishing, 'need' is roughly synonymous with 'want.') I needed forceps, scissor/pliers, tweezers (no telling what for), enough leader material to build a hand-tied tapered leader from the butt down, fingernail clippers with a folding knife blade that said 'Henry's Fork Anglers/Last Chance, Idaho' on them (only a rank amateur buys his clippers at a drug store), a combination tape measure and scale, stomach pump, bug net, specimen bottles, fly boxes, leader stretchers, waterproof match holder, wader patch kit, flashlight, two types each of fly float and fly sink, and, well . . .

I learned that getting oneself properly outfitted wasn't cheap, or even acceptable in some circles. I was still married to my second wife at the time, and I can recall the long, serious discussions over the kitchen table at two o'clock in the morning over the relative values of three-hundred dollars' worth of fly tackle (plus eighty dollars for a bigger vest to carry it all in) and, say, getting the leak in the roof fixed.

The fact that I'm single now only illustrates that a sportsman of my caliber can't possibly live with someone whose ducks aren't in a row. She used to say, 'You never take me anywhere!' and I'd answer calmly, logically, 'I took you fishing just last month.'

FISH, FISHING AND THE MEANING OF LIFE

A friend once asked, 'How come a guy who dresses in rags and drives a smoky old pickup can afford such snazzy tackle?'
'It should be obvious.'

JOHN GIERACH, *Trout Bum*, 1986

CHAPTER FIVE

Ones That Got Away

*T*he One That Got Away is the oldest angling joke. Somewhere in the never-never land between the hook and the shore the fish grew mysteriously and acquired a strength and beauty quite unlike any other fish.

It isn't just that what the eye doesn't see the heart feels free to romanticize. The special quality of the fish that lives to fight another day is that it remains in the element from which we tried to wrest it. For a while we were in contact with this cold-blooded enigma. Our attempts at deception had succeeded, for the brief moment of strike we had inserted ourselves into another world. As long as the fish remains on the end of the line, that shudder is a mark of our control. When, inexplicably and without warning, the rod and line cease to pulse with life, we are rendered impotent. The unknowable, untameable quality of water is expressed in the freedom of the fish.

The angler who claims not to be disappointed, however perfunctorily, at the moment when the line goes dead is a liar. Jack-the-Lad characters who've spent a lifetime hooking fish will sometimes have a way of deadpanning the experience. When the American trout fisherman John Gierach tells his friends about losing a big one in the mountains of Oregon, he talks about executing a Long Distance Release on a hawg, but even he admits that, at the time, his heart hit the soles of his boots.

The feeling is every bit as intense as the exhilaration which overtook you when you suddenly felt something alive and unknow-able on the end of your line, shaking its head to throw the hook or boring deep, contemptuous and disdainful in the way it defies your attempts at control. Luckily, it doesn't last long.

Neither does the memory. Mostly, the lumber-room of fisher-men's minds is filled with memories of fish they caught rather than ones that escaped. Some days almost every fish you try for comes short, and there's no way of telling one failure from another.

Strangely, given how much of the angler's life is spent looking backwards to better days, the fish we think about most are the ones we plan to catch. The old trout we've watched all season in his lair under the overhanging willow bough, safely out of range of our flies, or the great pike which lies on the river bed oblivious to the stones thrown by small boys from the bridge and has never been caught, although they say someone once had him on for an hour, until he bit through the line as if it were spiderspin.

Those are the fish which occupy our waking dreams, as we too find ways of catching them. Very occasionally, we might even succeed.

Some Hope – Charles Nuttall, 1910

The Consolation of Strong Drink

2:00 P.M. June 24, 1936. Ordinarily I find Dick Hunt's theory that there is little point in fishing before 10 A.M. a convenient one to adopt. Mornings, I think, are meant to be spent in bed, and there, but for the insistence of my wife and children on being supported, I should always spend them. But on this occasion I had journeyed all the way to the Ausable for just two days of fishing, and I was on the West Branch by eight o'clock. By twelve I was hot and tired; by one I was disgusted and discouraged, and toward two I began to consider a good cold bottle of Lake Placid beer as more to be desired than all the wealth of the Indies.

By this time, however, I had reached a particularly promising pool and on the far side were several feeding fish. Avoidance of drag was practically impossible, so I resorted to a nymph and a prayer, and cast as far as I could.

A native of perhaps nine inches accepted my offering and I horsed him out into the current and into the center of the pool, but I couldn't horse him any further – he wouldn't horse. For an instant I was bewildered and then again he came in readily enough, came in to within six feet of where I was. Then with a WHOOSH there came from the deeper water A BROWN TROUT AS BIG AS LAMONT'S DOG. The nastiest looking brown trout I have even seen, took my native in his cavernous jaws and swam away. And (having never had a similar experience before) there was nothing I could do about it. I went to Placid for my beer and drank Scotch instead.

DANA LAMB, *On Trout Streams and Salmon Rivers*

He Had Never Seen so Big a Trout

Nick felt awkward and professionally happy with all his equipment hanging from him. The grasshopper bottle swung against his chest. In his shirt the breast pockets bulged against him with the lunch and his fly book.

He stepped into the stream. It was a shock. His trousers clung tight to his legs. His shoes felt the gravel. The water was a rising cold shock.

Rushing, the current sucked against his legs. Where he stepped in, the water was over his knees. He waded with the current. The gravel slid under his shoes. He looked down at the swirl of water below each leg and tipped up the bottle to get a grasshopper.

The first grasshopper gave a jump in the neck of the bottle and went out into the water. He was sucked under in the whirl by Nick's right leg and came to the surface a little way downstream. He floated rapidly, kicking. In a quick circle, breaking the smooth surface of the water, he disappeared. A trout had taken him.

Another hopper poked his face out of the bottle. His antennae wavered. He was getting his front legs out of the bottle to jump. Nick took him by the head and held him while he threaded the slim hook under his chin, down through his thorax and into the last segments of his abdomen. The grasshopper took hold of the hook with his front feet, spitting tobacco juice on it. Nick dropped him into the water.

Holding the rod in his right hand he let out line against the pull of the grasshopper in the current. He stripped off line from the reel with his left hand and let it run free. He could see the hopper in the little waves of the current. It went out of sight.

There was a tug on the line. Nick pulled against the taut line. It was his first strike. Holding the now living rod across the current, he brought in the line with his left hand. The rod bent in jerks, the trout pumping against the current. Nick knew it was a small one. He lifted the rod straight up in the air. It bowed with the pull.

He saw the trout in the water jerking with his head and body against the shifting tangent of the line in the stream.

Nick took the line in his left hand and pulled the trout, thumping tiredly against the current, to the surface. His back was mottled the clear, water-over-gravel colour, his side flashing in the sun. The rod under his right arm, Nick stooped, dipping his right hand into the current. He held the trout, never still, with his moist right hand, while he unhooked the barb from his mouth, then dropped him back into the stream.

He hung unsteadily in the current, then settled to the bottom beside a stone. Nick reached down his hand to touch him, his arm to the elbow under water. The trout was steady in the moving stream, resting on the gravel, beside a stone. As Nick's fingers touched him, touched his smooth, cool, underwater feeling he was gone, gone in a shadow across the bottom of the stream.

He's all right, Nick thought. He was only tired.

He had wet his hand before he touched the trout, so he would not disturb the delicate mucus that covered him. If a trout was touched with a dry hand, a white fungus attacked the unprotected spot. Years before when he had fished crowded streams, with fly fishermen ahead of him and behind him, Nick had again and again come on dead trout, furry with white fungus, drifted against a rock, or floating belly-up in some pool. Nick did not like to fish with other men on the river. Unless they were of your party, they spoiled it.

He wallowed down the stream, above his knees in the current, through the fifty yards of shallow water above the pile of logs that crossed the stream. He did not rebait his hook and held it in his hand as he waded. He was certain he could catch small trout in the shallows, but he did not want them. There would be no big trout in the shallows this time of day.

Now the water deepened up his thighs sharply and coldly. Ahead was the smooth dammed-back flood of water above the logs. The water was smooth and dark; on the left, the lower edge of the meadow; on the right the swamp.

Nick leaned back against the current and took a hopper from the bottle. He threaded the hopper on the hook and spat on him for good luck. Then he pulled several yards of line from the reel and tossed the hopper out ahead onto the fast, dark water. It floated down towards the logs, then the weight of the line pulled the bait under the surface. Nick held the rod in his right hand, letting the line run out through his fingers.

There was a long tug. Nick struck and the rod came alive and dangerous, bent double, the line tightening, coming out of water, tightening, all in a heavy, dangerous, steady pull. Nick felt the moment when the leader would break if the strain increased and let the line go.

The reel racheted into a mechanical shriek as the line went out in a rush. Too fast. Nick could not check it, the line rushing out, the reel note rising as the line ran out.

With the core of the reel showing, his heart feeling stopped with the excitement, leaning back against the current that mounted icily his thighs, Nick thumbed the reel hard with his left hand. It was awkward getting his thumb inside the fly reel frame.

As he put on pressure the line tightened into sudden hardness and beyond the logs a huge trout went high out of water. As he jumped, Nick lowered the tip of the rod. But he felt, as he dropped the tip to ease the strain, the moment when the strain was too great; the hardness too tight. Of course, the leader had broken. There was no mistaking the feeling when all spring left the line and it became dry and hard. Then it went slack.

His mouth dry, his heart down, Nick reeled in. He had never seen so big a trout. There was a heaviness, a power not to be held, and then the bulk of him, as he jumped. He looked as broad as a salmon.

Nick's hand was shaky. He reeled in slowly. The thrill had been too much. He felt, vaguely, a little sick, as though it would be better to sit down.

The leader had broken where the hook was tied to it. Nick took it in his hand. He thought of the trout somewhere on the bottom, holding himself steady over the gravel, far down below the light, under the logs, with the hook in his jaw. Nick knew the trout's teeth would cut through the snell of the hook. The hook would imbed itself in his jaw. He'd bet the trout was angry. Anything that size would be angry. That was a trout. He had been solidly hooked. Solid as a rock. He felt like a rock, too, before he started off. By God, he was a big one. By God, he was the biggest one I ever heard of.

Nick climbed out onto the meadow and stood, water running down his trousers and out of his shoes, his shoes squelchy. He went over and sat on the logs. He did not want to rush his sensations any.

He wriggled his toes in the water, in his shoes, and got out a cigarette from his breast pocket. He lit it and tossed the match into the fast water below the logs. A tiny trout rose at the match, as it swung around in the fast current. Nick laughed. He would finish the cigarette.

He sat on the logs, smoking, drying in the sun, the sun warm on his back, the river shallow ahead entering the woods, curving into the woods, shallows, light glittering, big water-smooth rocks, cedars along the bank and white birches, the logs warm in the sun, smooth to sit on, without bark, grey to the touch; slowly the feeling of disappointment left him. It went away slowly, the feeling of disappointment that came sharply after the thrill that made his shoulder ache. It was all right now. His rod lying out on the logs, Nick tied a new hook on the leader, pulling the gut tight until it grimped into itself in a hard knot.

ERNEST HEMINGWAY, *Big Two-hearted River*, 1939

A Night in the Blackout – Tench Fishing in Wartime

I reached the lake after sundown. The day had been hot with little wind and the water was well warmed; it was a perfect sultry summer night. No other angler was there at that late hour, and the only sign of activity was a procession of bombers which passed overhead on their way to give Milan and Turin their heaviest raid of the war. The whole air vibrated with their thunder, each plane showing navigation lights from their wing tips.

It was so dusky by the time I had fixed up my rod that I had some difficulty to fasten the gut cast to my line. Night fishing is a tiresome business. But I knew that tench, the really big fish, feed at night when other anglers are well upon their homeward way to bed, and here was I to prove the statement.

Where I stood in that little corner screened by sallows and tall reeds the ground was beaten iron hard, fissured in many directions by the long, hot summer heats.

Furtive squeaks and rustlings sounded in the sedges as numberless water rats scurried hither and thither. Departed anglers had left crusts and refuse from their picnic lunches scattered about. I thought of the hours and hours that had been passed at that spot, of the intense concentration on floats; some of these fishermen come from long distances and sit all day and never get a bite.

Somehow their inexhaustible patience and persistent concentration seemed to be imprinted on my surroundings.

These men are mostly publicans, hairdressers, mechanics, factory hands, with a sprinkling of 'gentlemen fishers,' solicitors, retired service men, and so forth. The bulk are humble, hard-working fellows who look forward all the week to a few hours by the lakeside. I have seen a faraway look in the eyes of my barber as he cuts away; he is thinking of his camp stool and fishing basket. The hateful 'snip, snip' of scissors is replaced by the lap of water in the reeds. I can nearly always tell a coarse fisherman by his face. At heart your true angler is a 'lazy' man; he is the inactive-minded fellow who will sit for hours, immovable as a heron, lost in a dreamy contemplation of his painted quill. Many take up fishing as a means of 'passing the time,' others fish for the fun of catching a creel-full of small roachlings, and are quite content if they catch nothing bigger than a quarter-pounder. But your true fisherman is he who takes a pride in his tackle and really tries to come to conclusions with the big fish, and he will take as much care in the cooking of his catch as in the capture of it. In short, he is a real 'hunter,' a true brother of the angle.

Now, at this hour, thought I, the tench will surely begin to gather and converge upon my corner. For do not departing fishers, with a gesture of either disgust or despair, empty their worm tins and the contents of paste rags into the inscrutable waters ere they leave?

I seemed to see those huge and shadowy shapes nosing through the weeds like questing pigs, seeking what they might devour, confident of an undisturbed meal; assuredly darkness is the time for the big tench!

Fixing a feather in the rubber band of my float I cast forth. The feather cocked up blackly in the dim water; had I not fixed that 'tell-tale' I could never have seen my float.

I had a fine silk line on an Allcock's reel. Even in daylight so fine a line was hard to see; now I only saw the upright black feather sitting on the water.

Ducks quacked and string after string took wing, passing out to their stubble gleaning. A sudden puff of wind ruffled the reeds and sank to stillness.

More bombers throbbed overhead on their deadly evening flight. In an hour or so they would be crossing the moonlight alps, with ghastly glaciers and snow fields below, where no life is, from one year's end to another. Queer, thought I, and here was I enjoying peace and security by this still lake, the shocked-up harvest fields about me, and a hunting owl hooting from a clump of distant giant willows.

Then the feather seemed to dim and blur. The light was going, I had to strain the sight now to see even that black tell-tale.

Suckings and sloshing came from the reeds about. Were they rats or big fish on the prowl? Far away I hear the sound of tipsy singing as the pub emptied and the licentious soldiery quartered in the village came beerily forth from the 'Rose and Crown.'

At a little after half-past ten the tip of the black feather majestically sank from view, and a faint whispering sound told that the coiled line was paying out. I had a bite!

It is not well to strike too soon with big tench. For all their bulk they have small mouths, so I let this fellow take his time, and the worm.

The tip of the feather appeared again, moving along three-quarters submerged, heading for the centre of the lake. It was time to strike, I struck. And the sudden heavy weight told me I was into the grandfather of all tench. Then the pressure eased and I thought he had gone, but no! he was still there, moving in now towards me, boring eight feet down in the dark weeds. The rod point jerked as he took a sudden plunge, I had him firmly hooked. But why keep my reader in suspense?

I began to reel in gently again; there came another vicious tug, as though I had hooked a sluggish whale, and the rod point flew up. He was off.

Nearly crying with vexation and disappointment I reeled in to inspect the damage. This tench had snapped the silk line off just below my float and had departed with eight feet of gut, plus sinkers, and the blue-headed worm. Trailing this cumbersome appendage he was most probably now hurrying away as swiftly as his ponderous bulk allowed, leaving me to mourn upon the darkling bank among the squeaking water rats.

Of course I cast out again (after a suitable interval of twenty

minutes in which I fumbled with invisible gut and line), but I had
no other bite. Once you lose one of these giants you will rarely get
another nibble; one might as well give them 'best' and pack up or
move to another tench hole. And now there was no light in the sky
and only very little on the water. But even through that deep gloom
I could see circling bats skimming above the surface of the lake as
they hawked for flies.

I shall try again one warm night before August is out, and
perhaps may hook that self-same fish; on the other hand . . . I may
not.

'B.B.', *The Wayfaring Tree*, 1948

Escapes After Capture

Preston Lake is another beautiful sheet of water near Norwich,
which reminds us of a night adventure. A couple of us had visited it
for the purpose of taking pike by torch-light, having brought our
spears and dry-pine all the way from Norwich in a one-horse
wagon. It was a cold but still autumnal night, and as we tied our
horse to a tree in an open field, we had every reason to anticipate a
'glorious time.' So far as the fish were concerned we enjoyed fine
sport, for we caught about a dozen pike, varying from one to four
pounds in weight; but the miseries we subsequently endured were
positively intolerable. Not only did we work an everlasting while to
make our boat sea-worthy, but in our impatience to reach the
fishing grounds, we misplaced our brandy bottle in the tall grass,
and were therefore deprived of its warming companionship. About
midnight a heavy fog began to arise, which not only prevented us
from distinguishing a pike from a log of wood, but caused us to
become frequently entangled in the top of a dry tree, lying on the
water. Our next step, therefore, was to go home, but then came the
trouble of finding our 'desired haven.' This we did happen to find,
for a wonder, and having gathered up our plunder, started on our
course over the frosty grass after our vehicle and horse. We found
them, but it was in a most melancholy plight indeed. Like a couple
of large fools, we had omitted to release the horse from the wagon
as we should have done, and the consequence was that he had

released himself by breaking the thills and tearing off the harness, and we discovered him quietly feeding a few paces from the tree to which we had fastened him. What next to do, we could not, in our utter despair, possibly determine; but after a long consultation we both concluded to mount the miserable horse, and, with our fish in hand, we actually started upon our miserable journey home. Our fish were so heavy that we were compelled, at the end of the first mile, to throw them away, and as the day was breaking, we entered the silent streets of Norwich, pondering upon the pleasures of pike fishing by torch-light, and solemnly counting the cost of our nocturnal expedition.

Bentley's Miscellany, July 1851

A Victorian MP Loses a Salmon in Norway

Five o'clock p.m. – we have eaten the best portion of a Norwegian sheep, not much bigger than a good hare, for our dinner, and the lower water awaits us. Here the valley is wider, the pools larger and less violent. It is here that I have always wished to hook the real monster of the river – the sixty or seventy-pounder of tradition – as I can follow him to the sea if he don't yield sooner, which from the upper water I can't, because impossible rapids divide my upper and lower water; and if I had not killed this morning's fish where I did I should have lost him, as it was the last pool above the rapids. We take ship again in Nedre Fiva, a splendid pool, about a mile from my house, subject only to the objection which old Sir Hyde Parker, one of the early inventors of Norway fishing, used to bring against the whole country: – 'Too much water and too few fish!' I have great faith in myself to-day, and feel that great things are still in store for me. I recommence operations, and with some success, for I land a twelve and a sixteen-pounder in a very short space of time; after, which, towards the tail of this great pool, I hook something very heavy and strong, which runs out my line in one rush almost to the last turn of the reel before Ole can get way on the boat to follow him, and then springs out of the water a full yard high; this feat being performed some 120 yards off me, and the fish looking even at that distance enormous. I have no doubt that I have at last got fast to my ideal monster – the seventy-pounder of my dreams. Even the apathetic Ole grunts loudly his 'Gud bevarr!' of astonishment. I will spare the reader all the details of the struggle which ensues, and take him at once to the final scene, some two miles down below where I hooked him, and which has taken me about three hours to reach – a still back-water, into which I have with extraordinary luck contrived to guide him, deadbeat. No question now about his size. We see him plainly close to us, a very porpoise. I can see that Ole is demoralised and unnerved at the sight of him. He had twice told me, during our long fight with him, that the forty-three-pounder of this morning was 'like a small piece of this one' – the largest salmon he had ever seen in his fifty years' experience; and to my horror I see him, after utterly neglecting one or two splendid chances, making hurried and feeble pokes at him with the gaff – with the only effect of frightening him by splashing the water about his nose. In a fever of agony I bring him once again within easy reach of the gaff, and regard him as my own. He is mine now! he *must* be! 'Now's your time, Ole – can't miss him! – now – now!' He does though! and in one instant a deadly sickness comes over me as the rod springs straight again, and the fly dangles useless in the air. The hold has broken! Still the fish is so beat that he lies there yet on his side. He knows not he is free! 'Quick, gaff him as he lies. Quick! do you hear? You can have him still!' Oh, for a Scotch gillie! Alas for the Norwegian immovable nature! Ole looks up at me with lack-lustre eyes turns an enormous quid in his cheek, and does nothing. I cast down the useless rod, and dashing at him wrest the gaff from his hand, but it is too late. The huge fins begin to move gently, like a steamer's first motion of her paddles, and he disappears slowly into the deep! Yes – yes, he is gone! For a moment I glare at Ole with a bitter hatred. I should like to slay him where he stands, but have no weapon handy, and also doubt how far Norwegian law would justify the proceeding, great as is the provocation. But the fit passes, and a sorrow too deep for words gains possession of me, and I throw away the gaff and sit down, gazing in blank despair at the water. Is it possible? Is it not a hideous nightmare? But two minutes ago blessed beyond the lot of angling man – on the topmost pinnacle of angling fame! The practical possessor of the largest salmon ever taken with a rod! And now, deeper than ever plummet sounded, in the depths of dejection! Tears might relieve me; but my sorrow is too great, and I am doubtful how Ole might take it. I look at him again. The same utterly blank face, save a projection of unusual size in his cheek, which makes me conjecture that an additional quid has been secretly thrust in to supplement the one already in possession. He has said not a word since the catastrophe, but abundant expectoration testifies to the deep and tumultuous workings of his soul. I bear in mind that I am a man and a Christian, and I mutely offer him my flask. But, no; with a delicacy which does him honour, and touches me to the heart, he declines it; and with a deep sigh and in scarcely audible accents repeating – 'The largest salmon I ever saw in my life!' – picks up my rod and prepares to depart. Why am I not a Stoic, and treat this incident with contempt? Yes; but why am I human? Do what I will, the vision is still before my eyes. I hear the 'never, never' can the chance recur again! Shut my eyes, stop my ears as I will, it is the same. If I had only known his actual weight! Had he but consented to be weighed and returned into the stream! How gladly would I now make that bargain with him! But the opportunity of even that compromise is past. It's intolerable. I don't believe the Stoics ever existed; if they did they must have suffered more than even I do in bottling up their miseries. They *did* feel; they *must* have felt – why pretend they didn't? Zeno was a humbug! Anyhow, none of the sect ever lost a salmon like that! What! 'A small sorrow? Only a fish!' Ah, try it yourself! An old lady, inconsolable for the loss of her dog, was once referred for example of resignation to a mother who had lost her child, and she replied, 'Oh, yes! but *children are not dogs!*' And I, in some sort, understand her. So, in silent gloom I follow Ole homewards.

Not darkness, nor twilight, but the solemn yellow hues of north-ern midnight gather over the scene; black and forbidding frown the precipices on either side, save where on the top of the awful Horn – inaccessible as happiness – far, far beyond the reach of mortal footstep, still glows, like sacred fire, the sleepless sun! Hoarser murmurs seem to arise from the depths of the foss – like the groans of imprisoned demons – to which a slight but increasing wind stealing up the valley from the sea adds its melancholy note. My mind, already deeply depressed, yields helplessly to the influence of the hour and sinks to zero at once; and despondency – the hated spirit – descends from her 'foggy cloud' and is my inseparable companion all the way home.

WALTER BROMLEY-DAVENPORT, *Sport*, 1885

'The Weight was Pulling Him Back' – Salar the Salmon is Finally Hooked

On the bank the fisherman sat down and perplexedly re-examined his rows and rows of flies. He had tried all recommended for the water, and several others as well; and after one short rise, no fish had come to the fly. Mar Lodge and Silver Grey, Dunkeld and Black Fairy, Beauly Snow Fly, Fiery Brown, Silver Wilkinson, Thunder and Lightning, Butcher, Green Highlander, Blue Charm, Candlestick Maker, Bumbee, Little Inky Boy, all were no good. Then in one corner of the case he saw an old fly of which most of the mixed plumage was gone: a Black Dog which had belonged to his grandfather. Grubs of moths had fretted away hackle, wing, and topping. It was thin and bedraggled. Feeling that it did not matter much what fly was used, he sharpened the point with a slip of stone, tied it on, and carelessly flipped it into the water. He was no longer fishing; he was no longer intent, he was about to go home; the cast did not fall straight, but crooked; the line also was crooked. Without splash the fly moved down a little less fast than the current, coming thus into Salar's skylight. It was like the nymphs he had been taking, only larger; and with a leisurely sweep he rose and turned across the current, and took it, holding it between tongue and vomer as he went down to his lie again, where he would crush and taste it. The sudden resistance of the line to his movement caused the point of the hook to prick the corner of his mouth. He shook his head to rid himself of it, and this action drove the point into the gristle, as far as the barb.

A moment later, the fisherman, feeling a weight on the line, lifted the rod-point, and tightened the line, and had hardly thought to himself, *salmon*, when the blue-grey tail of a fish broke half out of water and its descending weight bended the rod.

Salar knew of neither fisherman nor rod nor line. He swam down to the ledge of rock and tried to rub the painful thing in the corner of his mouth against it. But his head was pulled away from the rock. He saw the line, and was fearful of it. He bored down to his lodge at the base of the rock, to get away from the line, while the small brown trout swam behind his tail, curious to know what was happening.

Salar could not reach his lodge. He shook his head violently, and, failing to get free, turned downstream and swam away strongly, pursued by the line and a curious buzzing vibration just outside his jaw.

Below the pool the shallow water jabbled before surging in broken white crests over a succession of rocky ledges. Salar had gone about sixty yards from his lodge, swimming hard against the backward pull of line, when the pull slackened, and he turned head to current, and lay close to a stone, to hide from his enemy.

When the salmon had almost reached the jabble, the fisherman, fearing it would break away in the rough water, had started to run down the bank, pulling line from the reel as he did so. By thus releasing direct pull on the fish, he had turned it. Then, by letting the current drag line in a loop below it, he made Salar believe that the enemy was behind him. Feeling the small pull of the line from behind, Salar swam up into deeper water, to get away from it. The fisherman was now behind the salmon, in a position to make it tire itself by swimming upstream against the current.

Salar, returning to his lodge, saw it occupied by another fish, which his rush, and the humming line cutting the water, had disturbed from the lie by the sodden log. This was Gralaks the grilse. Again Salar tried to rub the thing against the rock, again the pull, sideways and upwards, was too strong for him. He swam downwards, but could make no progress towards the rock. This terrified him and he turned upwards and swam with all his strength, to shake it from his mouth. He leapt clear of the water and fell back on his side, still shaking his head.

On the top of the leap the fisherman had lowered his rod, lest the fly be torn away as the salmon struck the water.

Unable to get free by leaping, Salar sank down again and settled himself to swim away from the enemy. Drawing the line after him, and beset again by the buzzing vibration, he travelled a hundred yards to the throat of the pool, where water quickened over gravel. He lay in the riffle spreading away from a large stone, making himself heavy, his swim-bladder shrunken, trying to press himself into the gravel which was his first hiding place in life. The backward pull on his head nearly lifted him into the fast water, but he held himself down, for nearly five minutes, until his body ached and he weakened and he found himself being taken down sideways by the force of shallow water. He recalled the sunken tree and it became a refuge, and he swam down fast, and the pull ceased with the buzz against his jaw. Feeling relief, he swam less fast over his lodge, from which Gralaks sped away, alarmed by the line following Salar.

But before he could reach the tree the weight was pulling him back, and he turned and bored down to bottom, scattering a drove of little grey shadows which were startled trout. Again the pull was too much for him, and he felt the ache of his body spreading back to his tail. He tried to turn on his side to rub the corner of his mouth on something lying on the bed of the pool – an old cartwheel – again and again, but he could not reach it.

A jackdaw flying silent over the river, paper in beak for nest-lining, saw the dull yellow flashes and flew faster in alarm of them and the man with the long curving danger.

Fatigued and aching, Salar turned downstream once more, to swim away with the river, to escape the enemy which seemed so much bigger because he could not close his mouth. As he grew heavier, slower, uncertain, he desired above all to be in the deeps of the sea, to lie on ribbed sand and rest and rest and rest. He came to rough water, and let it take him down, too tired to swim. He bumped into a rock, and was carried by the current around it, on his side, while the gut cast, tautened by the dragging weight, twanged and jerked his head upstream, and he breathed again, gulping water quickly and irregularly. Still the pull was trying to take him forward, so with a renewal by fear he turned and re-entered fast water and went down and down, until he was in another deep pool at a bend of the river. Here he remembered a hole under the roots of a tree, and tried to hide there, but had not strength enough to reach the refuge of darkness.

Again he felt release, and swam forward slowly, seeking the deepest part of the pool, to lie on the bottom with his mouth open.

Then he was on his side, dazed and weary, and the broken-quicksilvery surface of the pool was becoming whiter. He tried to swim away, but the water was too thick-heavy; and after a dozen sinuations it became solid. His head was out of water. A shock passed through him as he tried to breathe. He lay there, held by line taut over fisherman's shoulder. He felt himself being drawn along just under the surface, and only then did he see his enemy – flattened, tremulant-spreading image of the fisherman. A new power of fear broke in the darkness of his lost self. When it saw the tailer coming down to it, the surface of the water was lashed by the desperately scattered self. The weight of the body falling over backwards struck the taut line; the tail-fin was split. The gut broke just above the hook, where it had been frayed on the rock. Salar saw himself sinking down into the pool, and he lay there, scattered about himself and unable to move away, his tail curved round a stone, feeling only a distorted head joined to the immovable river-bed.

HENRY WILLIAMSON, *Salar the Salmon*, 1936

The Discipline of Carp

You cannot, of course, fish for big carp in half a day. It takes a month. So subtle are these fishes that you have to proceed with the utmost precautions. In the first week, having made ready your tackle and plumbed the depth, you build yourself a wattled screen, behind which you may take cover. By the second week the fish should have grown accustomed to this, and you begin to throw in ground bait composed of bread, bran, biscuits, peas, beans, strawberries, rice, pearl barley, aniseed cake, worms, gentles, banana, and potato. This ground baiting must not be overdone. Half a pint on alternate evenings is as much as can safely be employed in this second week. With the third week less caution is necessary, because by now the carp will be less mindful of the adage concerning those who come bearing gifts. You may bear gifts daily, and the carp will, it is to be hoped, in a manner of speaking, look these gifts in the mouth – as carp should. Now with the fourth week comes the critical time. All is very soon to be put to the touch.

On Monday you lean your rod (it is ready put up, you remember) on the wattled fence so that its top projects 18in. over the water. On Tuesday you creep up and push it gently, so that the 18in. are become 4ft. The carp, we hope, simply think that it is a piece of the screen growing well and take no alarm. On Wednesday, Thursday, and Friday you employ the final and great ruse. This is to place your line (the depth has already been plumbed, of course) gently in the water, the bullet just touching the bottom so that the float cocks, and the 2ft. of gut which lie on the bottom beyond it terminating with a bait in which is no fraudful hook. This so that the carp may imagine that it is just a whim of the lavish person behind the screen (be sure they know you are there all the time) to tie food to some fibrous yet innocuous substance. And at last, on Saturday, the thirty-first of the month, you fall to angling, while the morning mists are disputing with the shades of night. Now there is a hook within the honey paste, and woe betide any carp which loses its head. But no carp does lose its head until the shades of night are disputing with the mists of evening. Then, from your post of observation (50 yards behind the screen), you hear a click, click, which tells you that your reel revolves. A carp has made off with the bait, drawn out the 5 yards of line coiled carefully on the ground, and may now be struck. So you hasten up and strike. There is a monstrous pull at the rod point, something pursues a headlong course into the unknown depths, and after a few thrilling seconds there is a jar, a slackness of line, and you wind up sorrowfully. You are broken, and so home.

H.T. SHERINGHAM in *The Field*, 1 July 1911

'Something Wonderful had Happened' – A Tarpon Shows his Beauty

We came to a narrow lane or rather opening in the green bank. Two tarpon were lying on the surface, one with fins out. They appeared to be moving very slightly. Thad stuck his oar in the mud, and taking up my rod he cast the bait right at the very nose of the big tarpon. I watched with immense eagerness and curiosity. And just what I had expected really happened. Roar! Smash! Both tarpon plunged away from there, spreading huge furrows and raising the mud.

'That fellow wasn't asleep,' averred Thad. 'He was scared. But if he'd been asleep he'd taken the bait for a mullet hopping close. An' he'd sure have hopped it.'

We glided into the opening, to find it a small cove, shallow and quiet, where the wind could not ruffle the water. The bottom appeared to be clean sand.

'I see a buster, over there,' said Thad.

'I see one, over here,' I replied.

'Yep. There's another in the middle – good big one, too. All asleep! We'll sure hang one of these birds, as R. C. says. Be careful not to make any noise.'

Very slowly he moved the boat, in fact so slowly that suspense wore on me. Yet I tingled with the pleasure of the moment. Nor was it all because of the stalking of big game! The little round cove was a beautiful place, reposeful and absolutely silent, lonely, some-how dreamy. A small blue heron flew away into a green aisle where the water gleamed dark in shade.

Not for moments did I espy the big tarpon Thad was gliding so carefully toward. When I did see him I gasped. He lay close to the bottom in several feet of water. But I could see every detail of him. He shone brighter, a little more silvery gold than those we had seen out in the larger cove. His back looked black. I could scarcely believe this enormous shadow was really a fish, and a tarpon.

Thad halted about twenty-five feet distant, and with slow deliber-ation gently pushed his oar down into the sand. The boat had not made even a ripple.

'Now I'll hit him right on the nose,' said Thad, with the utmost satisfaction.

He wound up the line until the leader was within a few inches of the tip; then he carefully balanced, and swung the bait.

'Watch. I'm bettin' he takes it,' said Thad.

I was all eyes, and actually trembling. But only with the excitement of the place and the fish. I had not the remotest idea that the tarpon would do any more than wake up and lunge out of there.

Thad cast the bait. It hit with a plop and a splash, not right over the tarpon, but just in front of his nose. It certainly awoke him. I saw him jerk his fins. A little cloud of roily water rose from behind his tail.

Then, to my exceeding amaze, he moved lazily and began to elevate his body. It shone gold. It loomed up to turn silver. His tail came out and flapped on the surface. What a wonderful tail! It was a foot broad.

'He's got it,' said Thad, handing the rod back to me.

'No!' I ejaculated, incredulously.

'Sure. I saw him take it in his mouth. . . . So far so good. Now if he doesn't get leary!'

'Oh, he's moving off with it,' I whispered, breathlessly. Indeed, that seemed the remarkable fact. The long, wide, shadowy shape glided away from the edge of the shade. I hoped it would move away from the boat. But he was going to pass close.

A triangular wave appeared on the water. It swelled. I heard the faint cut of my line as it swept out. I saw it move. My eyes were riveted on it. I pulled line off the reel and held my rod so it would run freely through the guides. What an impossible thing was happening! My heart felt swelling in my throat. I saw that great tarpon clearly in sunlit water not over three feet deep. I saw the checkerboard markings of his huge scales. I saw his lean, sharp, snub-nosed face and the immense black eye. All as he reached a point even with me!

Then he saw the boat, and no doubt Thad and me standing almost over him. Right before my rapt gaze he vanished. Next I heard a quick deep thrum. I saw a boiling cloud of muddy water rising toward the surface.

'He saw the boat!' yelled Thad. 'He's scared. Soak him!'

But swift though I was, I could not throw on the drag, and reel in the slack line, and strike in time to avert a catastrophe. I seemed to freeze all over.

The very center of that placid cove upheaved in a flying maelstrom and there followed a roaring crash. A grand blazing fish leaped into the sunlight. He just cleared the water, so heavy was he, and seemed to hang for an instant in the air, a strange creature of the sea. Then the infinite grace and beauty of him underwent a change. His head suddenly became deformed. The wide gill covers slapped open, exposing the red. He shook with such tremendous power and rapidity that he blurred in my sight. I saw the bait go flying far. He had thrown the hook.

With sounding smash he fell back. The water opened into a dark surging hole out of which flew muddy spray. With a solid, heavy thrum, almost like a roar of contending waters, the tarpon was gone. He left a furrowed wake that I shall never forget.

Slowly I reeled in, unmindful of the language of the usually mild Captain Thad. On the moment, as I recovered from what seemed a stunning check to my emotions, I did not feel the slightest pang. Instead, as the primitive thrills of the chase and capture, and the sudden paralyzing shock of fear and loss, passed away together, I experienced a perfect exhilaration.

Something wonderful had happened. I had seen something indescribably beautiful. Into my memory had been burned indelibly a picture of a sunlit, cloud-mirroring green-and-gold-bordered cove, above the center of which shone a glorious fish creature in the air, wildly instinct with the action and daring of freedom.

Just then, before the exultation vanished, I felt as if I had been granted a marvelous privilege. Out of the inscrutable waters a beautiful fish had leaped, to show me fleetly the life and spirit of his element. And I had sought to kill!

When I laid my rod down and took my chair, motioning Captain Thad that we would go, I knew I had reached the end of this fishing trip. There is always an end to everything, even the longest lane. There is always a place for a story to end.

ZANE GREY, *Adventures in Fishing*, 1952

A 'Cockney' Cocks Things up in Canada

The instant that elapsed before the salmon realised that he was hooked I employed in crawling off the point of the pier to the broader part of it, and doubting very much if I should be able to extricate myself without discredit or the loss of the Judge's tackle from the dilemma of my own seeking. I have a dim recollection of wishing it was the first fish I had fast instead of this one, which was twice the size, and decided that he must be given line enough on his first run – if it was down-stream – to make him unlikely to return and get between the next two piers, which would be fatal, when he made the consideration of that question unnecessary by starting violently up-stream towards the New Brunswick shore, and, after a jump which showed a bright fish of at least thirty pounds, came to a temporary stop about fifty yards above the end of the second pier above me. There was nothing to do but get around to the next pier, if the fish would wait, and this I succeeded in doing, with the assistance of the Judge. Once there, and the salmon remaining in nearly the same position, with the dangerous length of line I had out it became an object to get him started down, if possible between the pier on which I was standing and one of those either to the right or to the left of it. The Judge ran to the bank and returned puffing and blowing with his hat full of stones, and soon the fish, yielding insensibly to the steady pressure of the rod and the current, had worked down near enough to have stones thrown in above him. The third missile struck the water near enough to start him, and to our joy he dashed down between the piers he came from, and stopped directly under the bridge, where there were probably some of his friends, taking their afternoon siesta, to whom he made known his troubles. It was but for a moment, however, and down again he went, I following him the length of the pier, giving no more line than possible, until I reached the bridge, where, instead of holding my rod up I had to hold it down, to keep the strain on the fish and the line from fouling the floor-timbers of the bridge.

The salmon 'cavorted' about for some minutes, and twice I saw the axle of the reel; but at last he came back from the quicker water and sought the bottom in the deep and quiet part of the pool about twenty-five yards below the bridge. We concluded he must be tired enough not to be anxious to renew the fight at once, and that now was the time to get the rod so it could be used from the lower side of the bridge, the whole structure being between me and the fish. To do this it was of course necessary to carry the rod underneath, and as the thickness of the timbers was too great to admit of reaching between the ties and passing it along with the hand, I took hold of the butt, after giving the line a hitch about the handle of the reel, and pushed the point of the rod as far as I could under the bridge. The Judge lay down on the bridge and inserted the point of the gaff between the line and the rod at the last ring of the tip, and I let go the butt, which, to our horror, swung about and hit the reel against the pier, breaking off the handle and a piece from the side, but fortunately not the projecting axle to which the line was fastened. We now had the rod hanging perpendicularly, held by the gaff attached to its tip, rather more than half-way across the bridge, the line of course loose, and the salmon sulking in the deeps below unconscious of his opportunity. I next pulled up the slack of the line between me and the fish, not enough to bring any strain which might rouse him to action, and fastened it to the top of the rod, which enabled the Judge, by a long reach, to gaff the line ten feet nearer the salmon. When he had secured this I let go the tip of the rod I had been holding, and it was hauled up by the Judge, handed to me, and the operation gone through once more, which brought us clear of the lower side of the bridge, but not, as we saw, clear of half-a-dozen telegraph wires which ran along just outside of it, and obliged me to hold the recovered rod with the point down nearly as much as from the pier on the upper side. I found when I got at the reel, that it would render line all right, but owing to the handle being gone I could not wind in. The salmon all this time, probably ten minutes, had not stirred, and with hesitation and anxiety we prepared for a renewal of the interrupted hostilities. Gathering up the slack line with care against future foulings, I felt gently of the fish with no response, then giving a heavier pull, I tapped smartly on the rod with my knife-handle. Nothing more than a short angry tug showed a recognition of this hint, and it was not until a well-aimed stone from the Judge dropped directly above the fish that he showed he meant to give us another fight for freedom. This he did by a dart towards the New Brunswick shore, which, against the heaviest pull I dared risk, was not checked until my line was well-nigh exhausted. He stopped where the water was quite shallow and quick, just above the rapid, and the Judge, who went over to see him, shouted the pleasing intelligence that it was hard for him to retain his position, and he occasionally showed his side. At last he began slowly yielding; I was able to recover some line, and, as he gradually moved down and towards the centre of the stream, he several times came to the surface in his gallant but futile efforts to resist the force he felt was overcoming him. As he reached a point directly in front of me, he gave up beat, and lay helpless on the top of the water on his side, with only an occasional feeble flap of his tail. This of course made it necessary to give him line, as the dead weight of so large a fish, aided by the current – which happily was not very strong just where he was – would soon make something give way. We could not tow him ashore, as the rod wouldn't pass the supports for the telegraph wires, which started from the bridge; but we had another resource in our English friend, whose Indians had brought his canoe near the bridge on the Quebec side, and were watching the contest. I shouted to him, asking him if he would drop down and gaff the fish for me. He grumbled something in reply, of which I fancied I could catch the words 'D—— Yankee,' but did not stir. 'Offer the villain the fish,' said the Judge, which I did with an amiable smile. This proposal was too tempting for him to resist, and he at once started out to the salmon. The canoe was stopped about ten yards above; the noble sportsman placed his gaff in a convenient position, then seized my line and began hauling the heavy fish up-stream towards him, hand over hand. To our shouts and abuse he paid no attention, and so firmly was the salmon hooked, and so good the tackle, that he was nearly dragged to the gaff before the casting-line parted, and the canoe silently dropped down-stream and disappeared behind the island. The Judge and I looked at each other for a moment in silence, and realising that pursuit was hopeless and language inadequate, gathered in the remains of our angling equipment and returned to the house. There we found that the tourist had left for good, and was going to Dalhousie in his canoe to catch the night train for St John, which was probably just as well for some of us.

DEAN SAGE, *Salmon Fishing on the Ristigouche*, 1888

'Something Had to Give' – An Irish Pike

SIR, In your article of December 23, there is mention of a 'very large fish' being spotted on Lough Mask in June, 1963. It was in July that year that I had a battle on Lough Mask with a monster of some sort.

Trolling deep at the top end near Ferry Bridge with a trout of about half-a-pound as bait I was taken by a fish. Though not a young man, I struggled with this object for about three-quarters of an hour and failed to make any impression on it. Every yard of line I recovered was always taken back – and a bit more. The monster never surfaced, but it must have been something fearful as a brown trout of some four pounds jumped wildly out of the water as I was playing my mystery fish.

Clearly something had to give. It was the hook. On recovering the bait, I could see that whatever it was had, unusually, taken the bait sideways on and had been hooked by only one triangle, and only one hook at that. Subsequently I fished with the same bait and landed an eight-pound pike on the same rod and heavy tackle, reeling it in as if it had been a stickleback.

I have caught heavy salmon in various parts of the world in nearly half a century of fishing and can therefore claim to have some knowledge of the 'big one that got away.' I have always supposed that this was a pike, probably a world-record fish of eighty pounds or more. But I am now tempted to think that maybe I was into a monster of some other sort.

V.M. Sussex.

Letter to *The Field* quoted in *Pig Overboard!*, MERRILY HARPUR, 1984

Failing with a Mahseer

Big mahseer rarely take a fly. The following account therefore of a tussle with one that did do so may be worth relating, if only for this reason.

The setting was a gorge in the Himalaya a few miles above the Sacred Pool . . . Here the mahseer fishing is at its best and the river, which in places is a hundred yards wide and strewn with huge boulders, has all the features of an Alpine torrent on a gigantic scale. I was fishing a long pool with a heavy fall at its head, which churned up the water on the far side for a distance of some fifty yards. It was a wild scene and the roar of the fall echoing and re-echoing from the cliffs of the narrow gorge was awe-inspiring. On the near side the current eddied in a deep, glassy backwater at the edge of which stood a rock about the size of a big haystack.

From the top of this I could cover the smoother water with my 16 ft. salmon rod.

As an experiment I was trying a very big salmon fly, a Wilkinson. I had made two or three casts and the fly was swinging round into the middle of the eddy when three great grey shapes rose almost imperceptibly from the depths, gliding slowly upwards side by side towards the fly. I judged the smallest to be a fish of 35 to 40 lbs., and the largest from 50 to 60. What happened next was too quick for me to follow. In my excitement I gave the fly a jerk that nearly brought it out of the water, and whether it was jealousy, or the sudden dart of the fly, that roused them it is impossible to say, but all three made a rush for it. There was a prodigious swirl and one of them took it, almost wrenching the rod, not to mention myself, into the water. The reel did not screech, it shrieked, and fifty yards of line ripped through the eddy in a few seconds and were gone downstream before I could bring the butt to bear. Directly the fish stopped, somehow or other I slid and bumped down the side of the rock and, reeling up as I went, scrambled along the stony beach to a point where the line entered the water about thirty feet from the bank. I could make no impression on the fish or feel anything but the throbbing of the current on the line. Obviously I was fast in a snag. Had I been alone that would have been the end of it, but now my orderly who was with me came to the rescue. Without a word he stripped and very pluckily swam out from one rock to another to try and clear the line. The current proved too strong, and after a dive or two he came back to tell me that the fish had taken the line under a submerged tree trunk which he could not move. Not to be defeated, he went off with his kukri and cut down a forked pole from a tree near by, with which he managed eventually to work the line free.

There was no mistake about the fish being still there. No sooner had the line straightened than he started off on another mad rush downstream, stripping off all the backing I had recovered and much more, while I followed as best I could, trying to keep in touch with him. It was no cross-country canter; it was a breath-taking obstacle race. Boulders, breast high, blocked the way and had to be surmounted before I got abreast of the fish some hundred yards further downstream. Directly I brought side strain to bear on him he changed his tactics and cut straight across the river, making the longest non-stop run of all. Anxiously I watched the lengthening line threading its way between the rocks, till the main current caught and drowned it, sweeping it downstream in a deep curve. The fish ran on irresistibly, only stopping more than a hundred yards away near the opposite bank. I could do nothing but raise the rod as high as possible and hang on. A little further down, steep bluffs barred the way, and from below them came the roar of another pool. What was to happen next? The answer was not long in coming. The rod began to bob in little jerks and an ominous grating sensation passed down it. Suddenly the tension ceased. I reeled in frantically, and then more and more slowly as the loose backing floated down the current; and I knew that all was over. The best man had won.

Is it better to have hooked and lost? Painful though it may be, I think it is. I still have the remnant of the backing, and I still have that reel. It is a reel with a famous name, and to me a perpetual memento of fights such as that described; for one of the cross-bars is scored by the line throughout its length, each score telling of the rush of a big mahseer.

JOSCELYN LANE, *Fly-Fisher's Pie*, 1956

'I Believe You Ompolodged, Boy' – H.E. Bates' Uncle Silas Goes Fishing

On one occasion I noticed that the neck-oil was very light in colour, almost white, or perhaps more accurately like straw-coloured water.

'Is it a new sort of neck-oil you've got?' I said.

'New flavour.'

'What is it made of?'

'Taters.'

'And you've got two bottles today,' I said.

'Must try to git used to the new flavour.'

'And do you think,' I said, 'we shall catch a bigger fish now that you've got a new kind of neck-oil?'

'Shouldn't be a bit surprised, boy,' he said, 'if we don't git one as big as a donkey.'

That afternoon it was very hot and still as we sat under the shade of a big willow, by the side of a pool that seemed to have across it an oiled black skin broken only by minutest winks of sunlight when the leaves of the willow parted softly in gentle turns of air.

'This is the place where me and Sammy tickled that big 'un out,' my Uncle Silas said.

'The one you carried home in a pig trough?'

'That's the one.'

I said how much I too should like to catch one I could take home in a pig trough and my Uncle Silas said:

'Well, you never will if you keep whittlin' and talkin' and ompolodgin' about.' My Uncle Silas was the only man in the world who ever used the word ompolodgin'. It was a very expressive word and when my Uncle Silas accused you of ompolodgin' it was a very serious matter. It meant that you had buttons on your bottom and if you didn't drop it he would damn well ding your ear. 'You gotta sit still and wait and not keep fidgetin' and very like in another half-hour you'll see a big 'un layin' aside o' that log. But not if you keep ompolodgin'! See?'

'Yes, Uncle.'

'That's why I bring the neck-oil,' he said. 'It quiets you down so's you ain't a-whittlin' and a-ompolodgin' all the time.'

'Can I have a drop of neck-oil?'

'When you git thirsty,' my Uncle Silas said, 'there's that there spring in the next medder.'

After this my Uncle Silas took a good steady drink of neck-oil and settled down with his back against the tree. I put a big lump of paste on my hook and dropped it into the pool. The only fish I could see in the pool were shoals of little silver tiddlers that flickered about a huge fallen willow log a yard or two upstream or came to play inquisitively about my little white and scarlet float, making it quiver up and down like the trembling scraps of sunlight across the water.

Sometimes the bread paste got too wet and slipped from the hook and I quietly lifted the rod from the water and put another lump on the hook. I tried almost not to breathe as I did all this and every time I took the rod out of the water I glanced furtively at my Uncle Silas to see if he thought I was ompolodgin'.

Every time I looked at him I could see that he evidently didn't think so. He was always far too busy with the neck-oil.

I suppose we must have sat there for nearly two hours on that hot windless afternoon of July, I not speaking a word and trying not to breathe as I threw my little float across the water, my Uncle Silas never uttering a sound either except for a drowsy grunt or two as he uncorked one bottle of neck-oil or felt to see if the other was safe in his jacket pocket.

All that time there was no sign of a fish as big as a hippopotamus or even of one you could take home in a pig trough and all the time my Uncle Silas kept tasting the flavour of the neck-oil, until at last his head began to fall forward on his chest. Soon all my bread paste was gone and I got so afraid of disturbing my Uncle Silas that I scotched my rod to the fallen log and walked into the next meadow to get myself a drink of water from the spring.

The water was icy cold from the spring and very sweet and good and I wished I had brought myself a bottle too, so that I could fill it and sit back against a tree, as my Uncle Silas did, and pretend that it was neck-oil.

Ten minutes later, when I got back to the pool, my Uncle Silas was fast asleep by the tree trunk, one bottle empty by his side and the other still in his jacket pocket. There was, I thought, a remarkable expression on his face, a wonderful rosy fogginess about his mouth and nose and eyes.

But what I saw in the pool, as I went to pick my rod from the water, was a still more wonderful thing.

During the afternoon the sun had moved some way round and under the branches of the willow, so that now, at the first touch of evening, there were clear bands of pure yellow light across the pool.

In one of these bands of light, by the fallen log, lay a long lean fish, motionless as a bar of steel, just under the water, basking in the evening sun.

When I woke my Uncle Silas he came to himself with a fumbling start, red eyes only half open, and I thought for a moment that perhaps he would ding my ear for ompolodgin'.

'But it's as big as a hippopotamus,' I said. 'It's as big as the one in the pig trough.'

'Wheer, boy? Wheer?'

When I pointed out the fish, my Uncle Silas could not, at first, see it lying there by the log. But after another nip of neck-oil he started to focus it correctly.

'By Jingo, that's a big 'un,' he said. 'By Jingo, that's a walloper.'

'What sort is it?'

'Pike,' he said. 'Git me a big lump o' paste and I'll dangle it a-top of his nose.'

'The paste has all gone.'

'Then give us a bit o' caraway and we'll tiddle him up wi' that.'

'I've eaten all the caraway,' I said. 'Besides, you said you and Sammy Twizzle used to catch them with your hands. You said you used to tickle their bellies – '

'Well, that wur – '

'Get him! Get him! Get him!' I said. 'He's as big as a donkey!'

Slowly, and with what I thought was some reluctance, my Uncle Silas heaved himself to his feet. He lifted the bottle from his pocket and took a sip of neck-oil. Then he slapped the cork back with the palm of his hand, wiped his lips with the back of his hand and put the bottle back in his pocket.

'Now you stan' back,' he said, 'and dammit, don't git ompolodgin'!'

I stood back. My Uncle Silas started to creep along the fallen willow-log on his hands and knees. Below him, in the band of sunlight, I could see the long dark lean pike, basking.

For nearly two minutes my Uncle Silas hovered on the end of the log. Then slowly he balanced himself on one hand and dipped his other into the water. Over the pool it was marvellously, breathlessly still and I knew suddenly that this was how it had been in the good great old days, when my Uncle Silas and Sammy Twizzle had caught the mythical mammoth ones, fifty years before.

'God A'mighty!' my Uncle Silas suddenly yelled. 'I'm a-gooin' over!'

My Uncle Silas was indeed gooin' over. Slowly, like a turning spit, the log started heeling, leaving my Uncle Silas half-slipping, half-dancing at its edge, like a man on a greasy pole.

In terror I shut my eyes. When I opened them and looked again my Uncle Silas was just coming up for air, yelling 'God A'mighty, boy, I believe you ompolodged!'

I thought for a moment he was going to be very angry with me. Instead he started to cackle with crafty, devilish, stentorian laughter, his wet lips dribbling, his eyes more fiery than ever under the dripping water, his right hand triumphant as he snatched it up from the stream.

'Jist managed to catch it, boy,' he yelled, and in triumph he held up the bottle of neck-oil.

And somewhere downstream, startled by his shout, a whole host of little tiddlers jumped from the water, dancing in the evening sun.

H.E. BATES, 'The Little Fishes' in *Sugar For the Horse*, 1957

The Bishop of Bristol Takes up the Story After Three Hours of Battle

It is now half-past three o'clock, and we are rapidly approaching Newburgh. The change of tide seems to make the fish frantic. We are never still for half a minute, and never cease wondering what his size must be if his strength is so enormous and so untiring. Finally, he decides on going up with the tide. The waves become embarrassing, and the boat is no longer easy to manage. A new fiend enters the fish, and makes him play the maddest pranks imaginable. We have for some time discussed the probability of his being a strong fish hooked foul, which would account for some part of his power; but just when the waves are at the highest and the boat is blowing up the river close upon the fish, out he springs two feet into the air, a monster as large as a well-grown boy, with the line leading fair up to his snout. 'Never land that fellow with a couple of trout-lines, or any other line,' is the fisherman's verdict; and as if to confirm it a cry comes the next minute, 'The line has parted!' Sure enough one strand has gone, owing to the constant friction of the wet line running through the rings for so many hours, and within twenty yards of the end of the line there is an ugly place two inches long, with only two strands out of three remaining. There is no longer a moment's safety unless that flaw is kept on the reel; and the necessity of pressing close on the fish leads Jimmy such a life as he will probably not forget. We are hungry and cold and somewhat wet; it is growing very dusk, and if we could not land him with 120 yards of line, how can we with twenty? We have caught a Tartar indeed.

And now night comes on in earnest ... The clock at home strikes seven, and we hear our passenger groaning over the fact that they are just going in to dinner. Lights peep out on the hillsides ... At length a measured sound of oars is heard, and a black pirate-like boat comes down upon us. We state our need. Can he take this gentleman down to the pier, and bring us back some food? 'Na!' And that is all he will vouchsafe to say as he sheers off again. Soon, however, a more Christian boat appears, and with many complicated manœuvres, to keep the line clear of the boat in the dark, we trans-ship our friend about eight o'clock, loaded with injunctions to send off food and a light. The light would be of the greatest service, for a frozen finger and thumb are not sufficiently certain indicators of the passage of the frayed portion of the line from the reel; and as the fish has never ceased to rush from one side to the other, frequently passing sheer under the boat, and requiring the utmost care to keep the line clear of the oars, we think almost more of the coming lantern than of the sorely needed food. It is an hour before the boat returns, with an excellent lantern, a candle and a half, a bottle of whiskey, and cakes and cheese enough for a week. Before setting to work upon the food we attempt to put in execution a plan we have long thought of and carefully discussed. A spare rod, short and stiff, is laid across the seats of the boat, with the reel all clear, and a good salmon-line on, with five or six yards drawn through the rings. We wait till the fish is quiet for a moment or two under the boat, and taking gently hold of the line he is on, pass a loop of it through the loop at the end of the salmon-line. As if he divined our intention, off he goes at once, running the flaw off the reel, and costing us some effort to catch him up again. This is repeated two or three times. At last we get the loop through, get a good knot tied, snap the old line above the knot, and there is our friend careering away at the end of a hundred yards of strong salmon-line, with some seven or eight yards only of the thinner line. When we examine the now innocuous flaw, we find it is seven inches long, and half of one of the remaining strands is frayed through.

Time passes on as we drift slowly up the river towards Elcho. Ten o'clock strikes, and we determine to wait till dawn, and try conclusions with the monster that has had us fast for ten hours. The tide begins to turn, and Jimmy utters gloomy forebodings of our voyage down to the sea in the dark. The fish feels the change of tide, and becomes more demoniacal than ever. For half an hour he is in one incessant flurry, and at last, for the first time, he rises to the surface, and through the dark night we can hear and see the huge splashes he makes as he rolls and beats the water. He must be near done, Jimmy thinks. As he is speaking the line comes slack. He's bolting towards the boat, and we reel up with the utmost rapidity. We reel on; but no sign of resistance. Up comes the minnow, minus the tail hook. Jimmy rows home without a word; and neither he nor the fisherman will ever get over it.

G.F. BROWNE (Bishop of Bristol), *Off the Mill*, 1895

PS The Bishop Adds the Following Note:

– A large fish was taken in the nets at Newburgh the next year which was popularly recognised as the fish of the above account. It had a mark just where I saw the tail hook of the minnow when the fish showed itself once in the strong water above Newburgh. It was the largest salmon ever known to be taken, weighing 74-lbs. as weighed at Newburgh, and 70-lbs. in London the next day.

A Blank Day in Abyssinia

In the afternoon I arranged my tackle, and strolled down to the pool to fish. There was a difficulty in procuring bait; a worm was never heard of in the burning deserts of Nubia, neither had I a net to catch small fish; I was therefore obliged to bait with pieces of hippopotamus. Fishing in such a pool as that of the Atbara was sufficiently exciting, as it was impossible to speculate upon what creature might accept the invitation; but the Arabs who accompanied me were particular in guarding me against the position I had taken under a willow-bush close to the water, as they explained, that most probably a crocodile would take me instead of the bait; they declared that accidents had frequently happened when people had sat upon the bank either to drink with their hands, or even while watching their goats. I accordingly fished at a few feet distant from the margin, and presently I had a bite: I landed a species of perch about two pounds' weight; this was the 'boulti', one of the best Nile fish mentioned by the traveller Bruce. In a short time I had caught a respectable dish of fish, but hitherto no monster had paid me the slightest attention; accordingly I changed my bait, and upon a powerful hook, fitted upon treble-twisted wire, I fastened an enticing strip of a boulti. The bait was about four ounces, and glistened like silver; the water was tolerably clear, but not too bright, and with such an attraction I expected something heavy. My float was a large-sized pike-float for live bait, and this civilized sign had been only a few minutes in the wild waters of the Atbara, when, bob! and away it went! I had a very large reel, with nearly three hundred yards of line that had been specially made for monsters; down went the top of my rod, as though a grindstone was suspended on it, and, as I recovered its position, away went the line, and the reel revolved, not with the sudden dash of a spirited fish, but with the steady determined pull of a trotting horse. What on earth have I got hold of? In a few minutes about a hundred yards of line were out, and as the creature was steadily but slowly travelling down the centre of the channel, I determined to cry 'halt!' if possible, as my tackle was extremely strong, and my rod was a single bamboo. Accordingly, I put on a power strain, which was replied to by a sullen tug, a shake, and again my rod was pulled suddenly down to the water's edge. At length, after the roughest handling, I began to reel in slack line, as my unknown friend had doubled in upon me: and upon once more putting severe pressure upon him or her, as it might be, I perceived a great swirl in the water about twenty yards from the rod. The tackle would bear anything and I strained so heavily upon my adversary, that I soon reduced our distance; but the water was exceedingly deep, the bank precipitous, and he was still invisible. At length, after much tugging and counter-tugging, he began to show; eagerly I gazed into the water to examine my new acquaintance, when I made out something below, in shape between a coach-wheel and a sponging-bath; in a few moments more I brought to the surface an enormous turtle, well hooked. I felt like the old lady who won an elephant in a lottery: that I had him was certain, but what was I to do with my prize? It was at the least a hundred pounds' weight, and the bank was steep and covered with bushes; thus it was impossible to land the monster, that now tugged and dived with the determination of the grindstone that his first pull had suggested. Once I attempted the gaff, but the trusty weapon that had landed many a fish in Scotland broke in the hard shell of the turtle, and I was helpless. My Arab now came to my assistance, and at once terminated the struggle. Seizing the line with both hands, utterly regardless of all remonstrance (which, being in English, he did not understand), he quickly hauled our turtle to the surface, and held it, struggling and gnashing its jaws, close to the steep bank. In a few moments the line slackened, and the turtle disappeared. The fight was over! The sharp horny jaws had bitten through treble-twisted brass wire as clean as though cut by shears. My visions of turtle soup had faded.

SIR SAMUEL BARKER, *The Nile Tributaries of Abyssinia*, 1867

A Famous Eel-Pout

A summer morning. The air is still; there is no sound but the churring of a grasshopper on the river bank, and somewhere the timid cooing of a turtle-dove. Feathery clouds stand motionless in the sky, looking like snow scattered about. . . . Gerassim, the carpenter, a tall gaunt peasant, with a curly red head and a face overgrown with hair, is floundering about in the water under the green willow branches near an unfinished bathing shed. . . . He puffs and pants and, blinking furiously, is trying to get hold of something under the roots of the willows. His face is covered with perspiration. A couple of yards from him, Lubim, the carpenter, a young hunchback with a triangular face and narrow Chinese-looking eyes, is standing up to his neck in water. Both Gerassim and Lubim are in shirts and linen breeches. Both are blue with cold, for they have been more than an hour already in the water.

'But why do you keep poking with your hand?' cries the hunchback Lubim, shivering as though in a fever. 'You blockhead! Hold him, hold him, or else he'll get away, the anathema! Hold him, I tell you!'

'He won't get away. . . . Where can he get to? He's under a root,' says Gerassim in a hoarse, hollow bass, which seems to come not from his throat, but from the depths of his stomach. 'He's slippery, the beggar, and there's nothing to catch hold of.'

'Get him by the gills, by the gills!'

'There's no seeing his gills. . . . Stay, I've got hold of something. . . . I've got him by the lip. . . . He's biting, the brute!'

'Don't pull him out by the lip, don't – or you'll let him go! Take him by the gills, take him by the gills. . . . You've begun poking with your hand again! You are a senseless man, the Queen of Heaven forgive me! Catch hold!'

'Catch hold!' Gerassim mimics him. 'You're a fine one to give orders. . . . You'd better come and catch hold of him yourself, you hunchback devil. . . . What are you standing there for?'

'I would catch hold of him if it were possible. But can I stand by the bank, and me as short as I am? It's deep there.'

'It doesn't matter if it is deep. . . . You must swim.'

The hunchback waves his arms, swims up to Gerassim, and catches hold of the twigs. At the first attempt to stand up, he goes into the water over his head and begins blowing up bubbles.

'I told you it was deep,' he says, rolling his eyes angrily. 'Am I to sit on your neck or what?'

'Stand on a root . . . there are a lot of roots like a ladder.' The hunchback gropes for a root with his heel, and tightly gripping several twigs, stands on it. . . . Having got his balance, and established himself in his new position, he bends down, and trying not to get the water into his mouth begins fumbling with his right hand among the roots. Getting entangled among the weeds and slipping on the mossy roots, he finds his hand in contact with the sharp pincers of a crayfish.

'As though we wanted to see you, you demon!' says Lubim, and he angrily flings the crayfish on the bank.

At last his hand feels Gerassim's arm, and groping its way along it comes to something cold and slimy.

'Here he is!' says Lubim with a grin. 'A fine fellow! Move your fingers, I'll get him directly . . . by the gills. Stop, don't prod me with your elbow. . . . I'll have him in a minute, in a minute, only let me get hold of him. . . . The beggar has got a long way under the roots, there is nothing to get hold of. . . . One can't get to the head

... one can only feel its belly. ... Kill that gnat on my neck – it's stinging! I'll get him by the gills, directly ... Come to one side and give him a push! Poke him with your finger!'

The hunchback puffs out his cheeks, holds his breath, opens his eyes wide, and apparently has already got his fingers in the gills, but at that moment the twigs to which he is holding on with his left hand break, and losing his balance he plops into the water! Eddies race away from the bank as though frightened, and little bubbles come up from the spot where he has fallen in. The hunchback swims out and, snorting, clutches at the twigs.

'You'll be drowned next, you stupid, and I shall have to answer for you,' wheezes Gerassim. 'Clamber out, the devil take you! I'll get him out myself.'

High words follow ... The sun is baking hot. The shadows begin to grow shorter and to draw in on themselves, like the horns of a snail ... The high grass warmed by the sun begins to give out a strong, heavy smell of honey. It will soon be midday, and Gerassim and Lubim are still floundering under the willow tree. The husky bass and the shrill, frozen tenor persistently disturb the stillness of the summer day.

'Pull him out by the gills, pull him out! Stay, I'll push him out! Where are you shoving your great ugly fist? Poke him with your finger – you pig's face! Get round by the side! get to the left, to the left, there's a big hole on the right! You'll be a supper for the water-devil! Pull it by the lip!'

There is the sound of the flick of a whip ... A herd of cattle, driven by Yefim, the shepherd, saunter lazily down the sloping bank to drink. The shepherd, a decrepit old man, with one eye and a crooked mouth, walks with his head bowed, looking at his feet. The first to reach the water are the sheep, then come the horses, and last of all the cows.

'Push him from below!' he hears Lubim's voice. 'Stick your finger in! Are you deaf, fellow, or what? Tfoo!'

'What are you after, lads?' shouts Yefim.

'An eel-pout! We can't get him out! He's hidden under the roots. Get round to the side! To the side!'

For a minute Yefim screws up his eye at the fishermen, then he takes off his bark shoes, throws his sack off his shoulders, and takes off his shirt. He has not the patience to take off his breeches, but, making the sign of the cross, he steps into the water, holding out his thin dark arms to balance himself . . . For fifty paces he walks along the slimy bottom, then he takes to swimming.

'Wait a minute, lads!' he shouts. 'Wait! Don't be in a hurry to pull him out, you'll lose him. You must do it properly!'

Yefim joins the carpenters and all three, shoving each other with their knees and their elbows, puffing and swearing at one another, bustle about the same spot. Lubim, the hunchback, gets a mouthful of water, and the air rings with his hard spasmodic coughing.

'Where's the shepherd?' comes a shout from the bank. 'Yefim! Shepherd! Where are you? The cattle are in the garden! Drive them out, drive them out of the garden! Where is he, the old brigand?'

First men's voices are heard, then a woman's. The master himself, Andrey Andreitch, wearing a dressing-gown made of a Persian shawl and carrying a newspaper in his hand, appears from behind the garden fence. He looks inquiringly towards the shouts which come from the river, and then trips rapidly towards the bathing shed.

'What's this? Who's shouting?' he asks sternly, seeing through the branches of the willow the three wet heads of the fishermen. 'What are you so busy about there?'

'Catching a fish,' mutters Yefim, without raising his head.

'I'll give it to you! The beasts are in the garden and he is fishing! . . . When will that bathing shed be done, you devils? You've been at work two days, and what is there to show for it?'

'It . . . will soon be done,' grunts Gerassim; 'summer is long, you'll have plenty of time to wash, your honour. . . . Pfrrr! . . . We can't manage this eel-pout here anyhow . . . He's got under a root and sits there as if he were in a hole and won't budge one way or another. . . .'

'An eel-pout?' says the master, and his eyes begin to glisten. 'Get him out quickly then.'

'You'll give us half a rouble for it presently . . . if we oblige you. . . . A huge eel-pout, as fat as a merchant's wife. . . . It's worth half a rouble, your honour, for the trouble. . . . Don't squeeze him, Lubim, don't squeeze him, you'll spoil him! Push him up from below! Pull the root upwards, my good man . . . what's your name? Upwards, not downwards, you brute! Don't swing your legs!'

Five minutes pass, ten . . . The master loses all patience.

'Vassily!' he shouts, turning towards the garden. 'Vaska! Call Vassily to me!'

The coachman Vassily runs up. He is chewing something and breathing hard.

'Go into the water,' the master orders him. 'Help them to pull out that eel-pout. They can't get him out.'

Vassily rapidly undresses and gets into the water.

'In a minute . . . I'll get him in a minute,' he mutters. 'Where's the eel-pout? We'll have him out in a trice! You'd better go, Yefim. An old man like you ought to be minding his own business instead of being here. Where's that eel-pout? I'll have him in a minute . . . Here he is! Let go.'

'What's the good of saying that? We know all about that! You get it out!'

'But there is no getting it out like this! One must get hold of it by the head.'

'And the head is under the root! We know that, you fool!'

'Now then, don't talk or you'll catch it! You dirty cur!'

'Before the master to use such language,' mutters Yefim. 'You won't get him out, lads! He's fixed himself much too cleverly!'

'Wait a minute, I'll come directly,' says the master, and he begins hurriedly undressing. 'Four fools, and can't get an eel-pout!'

When he is undressed, Andrey Andreitch gives himself time to cool and gets into the water. But even his interference leads to nothing.

'We must chop the root off,' Lubim decides at last. 'Gerassim, go and get an axe! Give me an axe!'

'Don't chop your fingers off,' says the master, when the blows of the axe on the root under water are heard. 'Yefim, get out of this! Stay, I'll get the eel-pout . . . You'll never do it.'

The root is hacked a little. They partly break it off and Andrey Andreitch, to his immense satisfaction, feels his fingers under the gills of the fish.

'I'm pulling him out, lads! Don't crowd round . . . stand still . . . I am pulling him out!'

The head of a big eel-pout, and behind it its long black body, nearly a yard long, appears on the surface of the water. The fish flaps its tail heavily and tries to tear itself away.

'None of your nonsense, my boy! Fiddlesticks! I've got you! Aha!'

A honied smile overspreads all the faces. A minute passes in silent contemplation.

'A famous eel-pout,' mutters Yefim, scratching under his shoulder-blades. 'I'll be bound it weighs ten pounds.'

'Mm! . . . yes,' the master assents. 'The liver is fairly swollen! It seems to stand out! A-ach!'

The fish makes a sudden, unexpected upward movement with its tail and the fishermen hear a loud splash . . . they all put out their hands, but it is too late; they have seen the last of the eel-pout.

ANTON CHEKHOV (1860–1904) 'The Fish' in *The Cook's Wedding and Other Stories*, translated by Constance Garnett

A Second Chance at a Salmon

'I'm in him!' Dick shouted, and as I leaped to my feet the biggest fish I have ever seen rolled over on the surface, hung there for a moment in full view, then sank out of sight. From the height at which I stood I could see his entire length. He was enormous, half as long again as a 30-pounder he looked. I shouted across to Dick: 'That's a tremendous fish – the biggest I ever saw.'

Thereupon, as if to show his power, he turned and proceeded down-stream at a steady pace, neither very fast nor very slow, but deep in the water and with a kind of irresistible force. Dick said afterwards that he had never felt anything like it. And here I must say that with all its thrills and turns of fortune there seemed to be throughout the fight an uncanny sense of the inevitable.

Fifty yards more were soon gone, but still the line continued to travel steadily out. Dick followed the fish down till the water was well above his waist and within 2 inches of his wader tops. A steady grip on the line made not the least impression, it still ran out. Any increase of pressure only caused an answering exertion of strength from the fish, which obviously had no intention of stopping its downward course. Over 100 yards of line were out, and Dick, unable to go any farther, was shouting frantically for the ghillie and the boat. A faint answering shout showed that he was not far off now, but could he be in time?

Unable to help, I had run down my bank to watch the fish's movements – he was now travelling faster. Then I saw the rod bend slowly right down to the water – a moment of tremendous strain – all the line was out, some 200 yards of it, an extra heave from the fish, the line broke at the reel, swished through the rings, and was gone. At that moment the boat arrived. Dick got in and they set off down-stream, Dick watching the water, gaff in hand, from the bows. I saw them consult, and wondered what they were at. A thrilling idea had come to them – the line was brand new and surely it would float; if so, it could be recovered! Down the river they drifted looking out for the line. At first it seemed a hopeless quest, but luckily the reach was a smooth one, and after some 5 minutes I saw the boat slow up and Dick actually hooked up the line from the water.

Now the threading of the line and the re-attaching of it to the reel. This too was successfully accomplished, thanks to the length of line out. Then came the crucial moment. Was the fish still on? Dick reeled in as fast as he could. Yard after yard came in without resistance – the line began to tighten – still there was no movement. Was it a rock? No, by Jove, he's still there – now we'll have him! But not yet. Annoyed by the pressure, the great fish once more recommenced his heavy downward course, and the boat followed him.

Some hundred yards below there is a deep rocky pool overhung by a great limestone cliff which is deeply undercut by the current. A nasty spot to play a big fish. If once he entered the unknown depths beneath the rock it would be all over. And for this he was obviously making, with a deliberate persistence that seemed almost like reasoned purpose. This was the unusual feature of the battle. I have often thought that if all fish behaved as this one did, salmon fishing would become wellnigh useless.

Dick did everything possible to stop him. As he said later, you might as well have been pulling on an ox; there was nothing to be done, and eventually he left the boat and attempted to get on terms with the fish from the shingle bank opposite to the cliff.

This he afterwards thought was a mistake, and I think it was, though I feel that nothing would have made any real difference. For a few moments it seemed as though he was holding his own, but suddenly the line cut the water in a magnificent curving run, the first turn of speed the fish had shown. Straight under the overhanging rock he ran, then, except for a dull scraping sensation, all movement ceased. The line was immovable. Five minutes passed, then quite quietly the line came away cut clean through well above the cast.

So this mighty fish was lost a second time. A terrible blow, though, as Dick says, he never felt confident that he would bring him to the gaff.

What did he weigh? We often wonder. No great fish was picked up afterwards, as in the case of the Wye fish estimated at between 60 pounds and 80 pounds. But at a conservative estimate he was certainly well over 4 feet long.

G.D. LUARD, *Fishing Fortunes and Misfortunes*, 1942

Irish Leviathans

There are stories of monsters that inhabit the deep holes in the Blackwater, Co. Cork.

About twelve years ago a man of the name of Maurice Hallahan, was trailing a bait out of a boat at a place called Hallahan's Rock, between Clondulane Weir and Fermoy, where the depth of the hole is supposed to be at least forty feet. He hooked a big fish, and having no one to help him put down the oars and held on to the rod, the fish dragging boat and man after him down as far as Ballydoroon stream, up again past the rock as far as Mount Rivers, and back again to the Rock, where, after sulking for hours, he took up the Funcheon River hard by, when, getting into shallow water, Hallahan put the gaff into him, but the fish was so heavy he could not get him into the boat, and was obliged to let go. The fish in his struggles broke the line and made a bolt down the Funcheon again to Hallahan's Rock and was seen no more that year. The year after a gallant Major, quartered at Fermoy, was fishing the same hole and hooked a fish which was gaffed after a long play – Hallahan's gaff still in him and enough wattling growing upon it to make a basket to carry him home!

The weight of the fish was never ascertained, and it is justly supposed it never will be.

'B.B.', *The Fisherman's Bedside Book*, 1945

A Day Both Fishermen and Quarry Lost – Whale Hunting in the Azores

In the Azores, lost in the oceanic vastness of the Atlantic, men go in small open boats to pit themselves against this marine monster – a bull sperm whale whose length may be 65 feet. To this dire engagement they go with weapons pigmy for so great a quarry: nothing but hand harpoons and hand lances. Not for them the easy slaughter obscenely wreaked from the safety of a factory ship. Their encounters, day by day, echo the stark frame that has been nature's since the time of the dinosaurs – the predatory balancing of species against species for the best equity of life on earth. These are gentle men: they harm nothing but the sperm whale; the sperm whale harms nothing but the giant squid which is its prey; the giant squid harms nothing but that which gives it its subsistence.

Necessity impels these Azoreans. They are pitifully poor; they must face fearful dangers for the minuscule rewards which whaling wins. But these are also men of a peculiar aptitude. Their nature is that of their islands – outwardly serene, but beneath the surface a volcano simmers. They are kindly men, child-loving, but with a smouldering passion which the perils of whaling ignite. Such is the danger that any day may see a whale, pitifully pestered by its hunters, rise in vast ferocity, smashing the boat, killing the men. Any day's return from sea is met by wives and children with entwining arms, grateful for one more safe return.

Of those days which I shared with these whalers, this is the story of one.

As the first light of dawn dimmed the stars I was at Castelo Branco. Under the fall of land, between fangs of volcanic rock, there lay two whale boats, 37 feet long. They are called *canoas* (pronounced 'canooa'); they lie ready for the instant's bidding. In the bows there is a cross-plank called a 'clumsy cleat', or thigh board, which has a semi-circular notch to take the bracing of the harpooner's thigh. Before him in the bow's peak are the chocks, a cleft to take the running of the whale line. In readiness beside the thigh board are harpoons and lances. Further back are the thwarts and the mast ready for stepping and in the stern the 'cuddy board'; on that stands the loggerhead, a bollard tapered outward from its base. As an angler plays his fish by line and reel, so the boatheader plays a whale by the giving and taking of line round the loggerhead. On either side below the cuddy board are the standing cleats – straddled on these, the boatheader stands for vision ahead. So standing he can use either the rudder or the 22-foot steering oar – rudder under sail, steering oar when going with oars.

Now we wait, the seven crewmen of the boat and I; we wait for the knell which is to send us to whatever is to be the fate of this day. Here is José Fula, the boatheader of our canoa; Antonio Fula the harpooner, and there are five others, one of them a boy in his mid-teens for whom this is his first trial day. We wait for the lookouts. They, with binoculars, on high vantages round the island of Fayal, have overlapping arcs of vision. So from first light they scan the ocean distances for the blowing of a whale. When sighted, it may be thirty or more miles offshore. We are waiting with such stoicism as we can muster for the signal-rocket which shall rouse us into action.

Across the five-mile strait is the perfect volcanic cone of the island of Pico. In this pallid pause between dawn and sunrise all is held in a sense of unreality. The sea lies quiet; the faint swell catches the light like slashed lead. Minutes accumulate.

An effulgence fans up behind Pico, strengthens, floods up the sky. The rising of the sun releases our worst tension; still we wait. Five o'clock comes and passes, then six o'clock, a little past seven the hush is shattered; a rocket is rising, hissing, rising interminably; it bursts, resounds from the heights and we are running to the boats. Then we are afloat, paddling out to the two tow launches just offshore. This day I am going on the tow launch, not in a canoa as on other days. I go aboard and we take our canoas in tow. The launches' throttles roar, our wakes fold white on the ultramarine sea. The little harbour falls astern. With the east's molten blaze behind us we go arrow-straight due west to where, many miles beyond our seeing, a whale is blowing.

Under Fayal's precipitous plunge to the sea we surge on, the canoas bucketing in our wakes. The men, crowded aft, are silhouettes against the eastern light. At the fall of the first hour we pass under Capelhinos, then the raw red cone of the new volcano is on our beam, soon falling back under the starboard quarter. Now we are taken by the vast blue anonymity of sea and sky.

Fayal drops astern, its craggy heights melt to gossamer; Pico dissolves into the dazzle over the stern. Then both are gone and nothing breaks the horizon's infinite rim.

After four hours, sentiently there is a change; the men stir. A current, part instinct, part experience, possesses them. On each launch a man swarms to masthead. The launches veer apart, casting about. Then from our canoa, *São João Baptista*, there is a cry: '*Bloz*,' they shout and point over our starboard bow. About a mile away, over the swell's recession there – there it is – a stubby, vaporous cloud, mushroom-coloured – the blow of a sperm whale.

We stop; the canoa casts its tow; we roll in the huge silence. *São João Baptista* is stepping its mast, raising sail; the sail hesitates, fills with a slap loud in the silence. The whale blows and blows, idling, secure in its ocean loneliness. Now the men have taken to the paddles and sit on the gunwales facing forward, digging in rapid rhythm. The canoa lifts, almost skims. José at the tiller is on the standing cleats; Antonio, heavy-shouldered at the thigh board, hangs loose arms until the climactic moment shall claim him. Still the whale moves in its slow peace 'having its spoutings out', serene and monstrous in the sun.

The canoa is closing on the whale; seconds pass compressed with fearful elation. Antonio picks up the harpoon, raises it rigidly poised, bracing into the thigh board. Still the whale dallies in its innocence in the sun; it blows with the sound of surf receding over shingle.

José is taking the canoa to the whale *cabeça com cabeça* – head on head – the way of greatest danger, straight towards the great bluff of its head, within the very narrow zone of no forward vision. At the very last second he lays his weight to the steering oar, turning the canoa round the head, into vision, and in towards the body behind the head, judging with such exquisite fineness that it is the boat that lives, not the whale. Antonio doubles in a plunging thrust. The harpoon is in. The whale is fastened.

In a blinding smother the stricken whale throws up mighty flukes, then sounds; line tumbles through the chocks. In the bouncing seethe, stays and halyards are let go, the mast and bundled mainsail let down to lie over the quarter. The plunging line wrenches down the bows, taking water. A hundred fathoms pour away, then two hundred; the whale levels off, slows. José makes a first attempt to snub the line at the loggerhead; the bows wrench down taking on water again. The whale sounds more deeply, runs again.

Now the burning torrent of line slackens, hesitates, wrenches spasmodically. The men stand, straddling the thwarts; they haul, gain line yard by yard by drag of muscle, José coiling it down with exactitude so that no flake shall foul another for fear of disaster. He tempts opportunity to snub it again at the loggerhead, this time holding it. The bow plunges; the shivering canoa in headlong tow runs as if powered, bows sheering the sea. Water is poured on the smoking line lest it take fire at the loggerhead. Now the first frenzy is abating. The line slackens; the whale is lifting.

The sea itself bursts open; a grey enormity of whale wallows, thrashing with flippers and flukes, blowing. The flukes are flung up, the whale rounds out and sounds. But it sounds less deeply; fury so frantic is taking its toll. But still it runs, burning away the tumbling line. It slackens, the whale rises; the men astride the thwarts once more gain line. José snubs it at the loggerhead. The whale is running erratically now in a wild staccato. José gains a few turns at the loggerhead, loses them, gains them again. The relentless line is wearing down the mighty strength, nagging it into weakness. The whale arcs about the boat's axis; beating the sea in pestered confusion. Now the men, standing, take the line in the bow cleat for 'bowing' on the whale, edging in towards its quarter. Antonio at the thigh board waits with a heavy droop of shoulders.

Foot by foot the canoa closes in. Now it is very near; the huge, hurt beast beats the sea. Now is the time of greatest danger – one touch of the enormous flipper would smash the boat.

Now – a pause deadly quiescent – the boat goes in from aft towards the flipper. Antonio is poised with the lance. The canoa touches the whale – wood on black skin. In a second, Antonio's throttled waiting bursts through thighs, buttocks, plunging arms. His lance enters to its shaft. The whale rolls in anguish, flippers and flukes lashing. It seeks to sound, plunges, surfaces, all in awful proximity to the boat's fragility. The oars back water several strokes, Antonio strains on the lance warp for the sucking free of the lance. The whale turns sub-surface and runs beneath the boat, lifting it teetering. Staggering, weaving, the giant once again rises, thrashing the swell. The surf is pink.

Now the canoa, like a predatory animal poised for pouncing, waits on opportunity. It comes during a quiet pause; the canoa goes in. Antonio from two fathoms off lobs his lance. It seems to hang, arrested, then drops, penetrating all the length of its wrought iron shaft. Slowly, beating, the whale rolls and blows. The blow is also pink.

On the canoa, a red waif is hoisted; at its bidding we on the launch close in. The whale labours inconsequentially. The sea is reddening. The canoa closes, lances again. The whale blows; the blow is opaque now – a gout of blood; sighing blow after blow drenches the sea. In dreadful sequence the boat comes in again and again.

Now the whale has lost all purpose; it rolls awash, moving in shuddering spasms. Once it lifts its flukes, slapping them explosively. It is in 'the flurry'; the end is imminent. We wait.

Suddenly resurgent life bursts upon the whale; an enormous convulsive lunge throws it up, half out of the sea. Its flukes are spread out. Then it sounds. The line empties away, vertically – a hundred fathoms, two hundred, and thirty more. At last it stops. No movement now. The line is a vertical iron rod. The whale has dived to die. Apart from rare exceptions, a whale dies at the surface.

Now what depth of stoicism must be summoned? A quarter of a mile beneath the surface lies that immense body. How are seven men to lift it? But the men sit placidly on the thwarts; they smoke, they talk quietly. What shall come shall come.

We wait in the vast blue peace of the ocean; a balm of silence lies upon us. *São João Baptista* is held a little down at the bows by its remote anchorage. So we must wait until help summoned by radio shall come. I lie drowsing on the foredeck of the launch. Time passes beyond conjecture.

Then two bow waves, remote dots, appear out of the haze that is Fayal. They grow to become a tuna boat and a launch towing a canoa. From the canoa go its seven men, from the tuna boat two more, into *São João Baptista* – sixteen men in a craft designed for seven. To the raw wet line they set their hands. In the bows Antonio chants softly to set a rhythm. They begin to haul, foot by foot.

Time passes; Antonio sings. The hauling becomes hypnotic – unless made mindless how could there be faith in an end? They draw six inches at each haul; their hands bleed. One man puts his socks on his hands. Five hours pass; then at last, through the clear water, the whale can be seen, a vague shimmer of a shape, perhaps thirty fathoms down. But how can it be raised from that last depth, horizontally, not vertically, so that a tow warp can be put to its tail?

It is rare for a whale to die this way. By chance we have with us Bruno Vailati who by aqualung diving is here to film whaling below and above surface. He puts on his suit, takes a rope and dives. Now the suspense is drum-taut. We scan for sharks. At last he surfaces; he has bent the rope round the peduncle of the whale's tail.

Now we all haul, sixteen in the canoa, and we on the launch. The harsh line bites at our hands and muscles burn to the limit of bearing. But, at last, it is done. The great grey island of body is awash on the surface. Now with the towing strap about the peduncle, the towing warp is bent to it. The two launches, in line, take the whale in tow. At only two knots it will take all night to gain back those many miles to shore and the whale factory.

Exhausted and grateful, we board the tuna boat. In the dark, five hours later, we drag ourselves from the deck to the harbour quay.

It is morning when we hear that half a mile offshore the tow lost its hold, that the whale had sunk, was lost. Tragically, it was one that got away. For nothing had that pitiful ocean giant lost its life. For nothing had the men endured and faced appalling danger. If the whale is not brought to the factory they receive no money.

BERNARD VENABLES, *The One That Got Away*, 1991

CHAPTER SIX

═══

Ones That Didn't Get Away

*W*e are obsessed by monsters. Not just the great prehistoric leviathans said to lurk in the depths of so many inland seas, but perfectly normal fish grown to abnormal size. True sportsmen and women will tell you that they don't care about the size of the fish they catch. What matters is how difficult they are to catch. They aren't lying when they say this. But they know that catching really big fish, the great God-if-I-lose-this-I'll-never-see-anything-like-it-again lunkers, is a special kind of benefaction.

The very biggest fish of all defy imagining. The 103 lb creature taken from the nets in the Forth in 1902 was said by the old soldier who poached it to be 'the ugliest great brute I ever saw . . . black on the head and with an immense hook on its jaw.' It must have looked astonishing on the kitchen table, if it ever got there before being cut up and flogged off around the back doors. But it is the record Atlantic salmon caught on rod and line which are the most remarkable. Postmaster Henrick Henricksen's 79-pounder on the Tana-Elu in July 1928. The Earl of Home's 69-pounder on the Tweed in 1730. Georgina Ballantine's 64-pounder on the Tay in October 1922. 'Tiny' Morrison's 61-pounder from the Deveron in October two years later. Doreen Davey's 59-pounder from the Wye in March 1923.

It is noticeable that they were all caught generations ago. No one knows why we don't see them any more but common sense says it has something to do with numbers. The average size has dropped as

═══

the number of people trying to catch them has risen. Rod-and-line anglers take only a small proportion of the fish population, it is true, but they hammer the water more relentlessly than ever before. And at sea and in the estuaries, vast quantities of salmon are taken by boats equipped with ever-better machines for detection and slaughter. It is reasonable to assume that there are fewer big salmon about because more of them get caught before they have the chance to reach great size.

If, despite everything, the salmon fisher does manage to hook a monster, honesty must force him to confess it is largely a matter of luck. The real exercise of skill lies in getting the thing as far as the net, particularly if fishing with delicate tackle. In the lakes and reservoirs where most stillwater trout fishing is practised nowadays, the size of fish has more to do with the science of the fish-farmer than the fisherman.

For the lure of the big fish is not a simple matter of size. True, when you read Zane Grey, and some other big-game fishermen, they seem to be obsessed by sheer brute poundage. (In the end, the fish had their revenge on Grey: he might have lived longer had his heart not been weakened by the intense strain of breaking off from writing Westerns to fight leviathans.) But the mystique cannot be

American Indian Salmon Fishing With a Dip-net – 1903

measured on a spring balance, a mere ascendancy of numbers. It has to do with the tackle used, too. With a strong enough rod and line, there is precious little chance of losing any fish, once it's properly hooked, so tackle has something to do with it. But Richard Walker's ingenuity in getting not one but two chub of over 6 lbs from the Ouse is cause for applause not because of the objective size of the fish but because of the way he went about trapping them. The same is true of the obsessive carp fishers who will groundbait a lake for days, stand scarecrows on the bank to accustom the fish to the apparent sight of humans, or lurk in trees and bushes for days.

The real challenge of the big fish is the outsmarting of wisdom, the deceit of the fish which has seen it all before. To see the big old fish lurking deep under the bank, grown comfortable on the fruits of safety, and then to trick him into taking your bait, when he has seen and dismissed countless others, *that* is a triumph.

Hunting 'Mocha Dick', the White Whale Which Inspired Moby Dick

This renowned monster, who had come off victorious in a hundred fights with his pursuers, was an old bull whale, of prodigious size and strength. From the effect of age, or more probably from a freak of nature, as exhibited in the case of the Ethiopian Albino, a singular consequence had resulted – *he was white as wool*! Instead of projecting his spout obliquely forward, and puffing with a short, convulsive effort, accompanied by a snorting noise, as usual with his species, he flung the water from his nose in a lofty, perpendicular, expanded volume, at regular and somewhat distant intervals; its expulsion producing a continuous roar, like that of vapor struggling from the safety-valve of a powerful steam engine. Viewed from a distance, the practised eye of the sailor only could decide, that the moving mass, which constituted this enormous animal, was not a white cloud sailing along the horizon. On the spermaceti whale, barnacles are rarely discovered; but upon the head of this *lusus naturæ*, they had clustered, until it became absolutely rugged with the shells. In short, regard him as you would, he was a most extraordinary fish; or, in the vernacular of Nantucket, 'a genuine old sog,' of the first water.

Opinions differ as to the time of his discovery. It is settled, however, that previous to the year 1810, he had been seen and attacked near the island of Mocha. Numerous boats are known to have been shattered by his immense flukes, or ground to pieces in the crush of his powerful jaws; and, on one occasion, it is said that he came off victorious from a conflict with the crews of three English whalers, striking fiercely at the last of the retreating boats, at the moment it was rising from the water, in its hoist up to the ship's davits. It must not be supposed, howbeit, that through all this desperate warfare, our leviathan passed scathless. A back serried with irons, and from fifty to a hundred yards of line trailing in his wake, sufficiently attested, that though unconquered, he had not proved invulnerable. From the period of Dick's first appearance, his celebrity continued to increase, until his name seemed naturally to mingle with the salutations which whalemen were in the habit of exchanging, in their encounters upon the broad Pacific; the customary interrogatories almost always closing with, 'Any news from Mocha Dick?' Indeed, nearly every whaling captain who rounded Cape Horn, if he possessed any professional ambition, or valued himself on his skill in subduing the monarch of the seas, would lay his vessel along the coast, in the hope of having an opportunity to try the muscle of this doughty champion, who was never known to shun his assailants. . . .

'There she *spouts*!' screamed a young greenhorn in the main chains, 'close by; a mighty big whale, Sir!'

'We'll know that better at the trying out, my son,' said the third mate, drily.

'Back the main-top-s'll!' was now the command. The ship had little headway at the time, and in a few minutes we were as motionless as if lying at anchor.

'Lower away, all hands!' And in a twinkling, and together, the starboard, larboard, and waist-boats struck the water. Each officer leaped into his own; the crews arranged themselves at their respective stations; the boat-steerers began to adjust their 'craft;' and we left the ship's side in company; the captain, in laconic phrase, bidding us to 'get up and get fast,' as quickly as possible.

'Away we dashed, in the direction of our prey, who were frolicking, if such a term can be applied to their unwieldly motions, on the surface of the waves. Occasionally, a huge, shapeless body would flounce out of its proper element, and fall back with a heavy splash; the effort forming about as ludicrous a caricature of agility, as would the attempt of some over-fed alderman to execute the Highland fling.

'We were within a hundred rods of the herd, when, as if from a common impulse, or upon some preconcerted signal, they all suddenly disappeared. "Follow me!" I shouted, waving my hand to the men in the other boats; "I see their track under water; they swim fast, but we'll be among them when they rise. Lay back," I continued, addressing myself to my own crew, "back to the thwarts! Spring *hard* ! We'll be in the thick of 'em when.they come up; only *pull* !"

'And they did pull, manfully. After rowing for about a mile, I ordered them to "lie." The oars were peaked, and we rose to look out for the first "noddle-head" that should break water. It was at this time a dead calm. Not a single cloud was passing over the deep blue of the heavens, to vary their boundless transparency, or shadow for a moment the gleaming ocean which they spanned. Within a short distance lay our noble ship, with her idle canvass hanging in drooping festoons from her yards; while she seemed resting on her inverted image, which, distinct and beautiful as its original, was glassed in the smooth expanse beneath. No sound disturbed the general silence, save our own heavy breathings, the low gurgle of the water against the side of the boat, or the noise of flapping wings, as the albatross wheeled sleepily along through the stagnant atmosphere. We had remained quiet for about five minutes, when some dark object was described ahead, moving on the surface of the sea. It proved to be a small "calf," playing in the sunshine.

'Pull up and strike it,' said I to the third mate; 'it may bring up the old one – perhaps the whole school.'

'And so it did, with a vengance! The sucker was transpierced, after a short pursuit; but hardly had it made its first agonized plunge, when an enormous cow-whale rose close beside her wounded offspring. Her first endeavor was to take it under her fin, in order to bear it away; and nothing could be more striking than the maternal tenderness she manifested in her exertions to accomplish this object. But the poor thing was dying, and while she vainly tried to induce it to accompany her, it rolled over, and floated dead at her side. Perceiving it to be beyond the reach of her caresses, she turned to wreak her vengeance on its slayers, and made directly for the boat, crashing her vast jaws the while, in a paroxysm of rage. Ordering his boat-steerer aft, the mate sprang forward, cut the line loose from the calf, and then snatched from the crotch the remaining iron, which he plunged with his gathered strength into the body of the mother, as the boat sheered off to avoid her onset. I saw that the work was well done, but had no time to mark the issue; for at that instant, a whale "breached" at the distance of about a mile from us, on the starboard quarter. The glimpse I caught of the animal in his descent, convinced me that I once more beheld my old acquaintance, Mocha Dick. That falling mass was white as a snow-drift!

'One might have supposed the recognition mutual, for no sooner was his vast square head lifted from the sea, than he charged down upon us, scattering the billows into spray as he advanced, and leaving a wake of foam a rod in width, from the violent lashing of his flukes.

'He's making for the bloody water!' cried the men, as he cleft his way toward the very spot where the calf had been killed. 'Here, harpooner, steer the boat, and let me dart!' I exclaimed, as I leaped into the bows. 'May the "*Goneys*" eat me, if he dodges us *this* time, though he were Beelzebub himself! Pull for the red water!'

'As I spoke, the fury of the animal seemed suddenly to die away. He paused in his career, and lay passive on the waves, with his arching back thrown up like the ridge of a mountain. 'The old sog's lying to!' I cried, exultingly. 'Spring, boys! spring *now*, and we have him! All my clothes, tobacco, every thing I've got, shall be yours, only lay me 'longside that whale before another boat comes up! My *grimky!* what a hump! Only look at the irons in his back! No, don't *look* – PULL! Now, boys, if you care about seeing your sweethearts and wives in old Nantuck! – if you love Yankee-land – if you love *me* – pull ahead, *wont* ye? Now then, to the thwarts! Lay back, my boys! I feel ye, my hearties! Give her the touch! Only five seas off! *Not* five seas off! One minute – *half* a minute more! Softly – no noise! Softly with your oars! That will do – '

'And as the words were uttered, I raised the harpoon above my head, took a rapid but no less certain aim, and sent it, hissing, deep into his thick white side!

'"Stern all! for your lives!" I shouted; for at the instant the steel quivered in his body, the wounded leviathan plunged his head beneath the surface, and whirling around with great velocity, smote the sea violently, with fin and fluke, in a convulsion of rage and pain.'

'Our little boat flew dancing back from the seething vortex around him, just in season to escape being overwhelmed or crushed. He now started to run. For a short time, the line rasped, smoking, through the chocks. A few turns round the loggerhead then secured it; and with oars a-peak, and bows tilted to the sea, we went leaping onward in the wake of the tethered monster. Vain were all his struggles to break from our hold. The strands were too strong, the barbed iron too deeply fleshed, to give way. So that whether he essayed to dive or breach, or dash madly forward, the frantic creature still felt that he was held in check. At one moment, in impotent rage, he reared his immense blunt head, covered with barnacles, high above the surge; while his jaws fell together with a crash that almost made me shiver; then the upper outline of his vast form was dimly seen, gliding amidst showers of sparkling spray; while streaks of crimson on the white surf that boiled in his track, told that the shaft had been driven home.

'By this time, the whole 'school' was about us; and spouts from a hundred spiracles, with a roar that almost deafened us, were raining on every side; while in the midst of a vast surface of chafing sea, might be seen the black shapes of the rampant herd, tossing and plunging, like a legion of maddened demons. The second and third mates were in the very centre of this appalling commotion.

'At length, Dick began to lessen his impetuous speed. 'Now, my boys,' cried I, 'haul me on; wet the line, you second oarsman, as it comes in. Haul away, ship-mates! — Why the devil don't you haul? Leeward side — *leeward!* I tell you! Don't you know how to approach a whale?'

'The boat brought fairly up upon his broadside as I spoke, and I gave him the lance just under the shoulder blade. At this moment, just as the boat's head was laid off; and I was straitening for a second lunge, my lance, which I had 'boned' in the first, a piercing cry from the boat-steerer drew my attention quickly aft, and I saw the waist-boat, or more properly a fragment of it, falling through the air, and underneath, the dusky forms of the struggling crew, grasping at the oars, or clinging to portions of the wreck; while a pair of flukes, descending in the midst of the confusion, fully accounted for the catastrophe. The boat had been struck and shattered by a whale!

'Good heaven!' I exclaimed, with impatience, and in a tone which I fear showed me rather mortified at the interruption, than touched with proper feeling for the sufferers; 'good heavens! — hadn't they sense enough to keep out of the red water! And I must lose this glorious prize, through their infernal stupidity!' This was the first outbreak of my selfishness.

'But we must not see them drown, boys,' I added, upon the instant; 'cut the line!' The order had barely passed my lips, when I caught sight of the captain, who had seen the accident from the quarter-deck, bearing down with oar and sail to the rescue.

'Hold on!' I thundered, just as the knife's edge touched the line; for the glory of old Nantuck, hold on! The captain will pick them up, and Mocha Dick will be ours, after all!'

'This affair occurred in half the interval I have occupied in the relation. In the mean time, with the exception of a slight shudder, which once or twice shook his ponderous frame, Dick lay perfectly quiet upon the water. But suddenly, as though goaded into exertion by some fiercer pang, he started from his lethargy with apparently augmented power. Making a leap toward the boat, he darted perpendicularly downward, hurling the after oarsman, who was helmsman at the time, ten feet over the quarter, as he struck the long steering-oar in his descent. The unfortunate seaman fell, with his head forward, just upon the flukes of the whale, as he vanished, and was drawn down by suction of the closing waters, as if he had been a feather. After being carried to a great depth, as we inferred from the time he remained below the surface, he came up, panting and exhausted, and was dragged on board, amidst the hearty congratulations of his comrades.

'By this time two hundred fathoms of the line had been carried spinning through the chocks, with an impetus that gave back in steam the water cast upon it. Still the gigantic creature bored his way downward, with undiminished speed. Coil after coil went over, and was swallowed up. There remained but three flakes in the tub!

'Cut!' I shouted; 'cut quick, or he'll take us down!' But as I spoke, the hissing line flew with trebled velocity through the smoking wood, jerking the knife he was in the act of applying to the heated strands out of the hand of the boat-steerer. The boat rose on end, and her bows were buried in an instant; a hurried ejaculation, at once shriek and prayer, rose to the lips of the bravest, when, unexpected mercy! the whizzing cord lost its tension, and our light bark, half filled with water, fell heavily back on her keel. A tear was in every eye, and I believe every heart bounded with gratitude, at this unlooked-for deliverance.

'Overpowered by his wounds, and exhausted by his exertions and the enormous pressure of the water above him, the immense creature was compelled to turn once more upward, for a fresh supply of air.

And upward he came, indeed; shooting twenty feet of his gigantic length above the waves, by the impulse of his ascent. He was not disposed to be idle. Hardly had we succeeded in baling out our swamping boat, when he again darted away, as it seemed to me with renewed energy. For a quarter of a mile, we parted the opposing waters as though they had offered no more resistance than air. Our game then abruptly brought to, and lay as if paralyzed, his massy frame quivering and twitching, as if under the influence of galva-nism. I gave the word to haul on; and seizing a boat-spade, as we came near him, drove it twice into his small; no doubt partially disabling him by the vigor and certainty of the blows. Wheeling furiously around, he answered this salutation, by making a desperate dash at the boat's quarter. We were so near him, that to escape the shock of his onset, by any praticable maneouvre, was out of the question. But at the critical moment, when we expected to be crushed by the collision, his powers seemed to give way. The fatal lance had reached the seat of life. His strength failed him in mid career, and sinking quietly beneath our keel, grazing it as he wallowed along, he rose again a few rods from us, on the side opposite that where he went down.

'Lay around, my boys, and let us set on him!' I cried, for I saw his spirit was broken at last. But the lance and spade were needless now. The work was done. The dying animal was struggling in a whirlpool of bloody foam, and the ocean far around was tinted with crimson. Stern all!' I shouted, as he commenced running impetuously in a circle, beating the water alternately with his head and flukes, and smiting his teeth ferociously into their sockets, with a crashing sound, in the strong spasms of dissolution. 'Stern all! or we shall be stove!'

'As I gave the command, a stream of black, clotted gore rose in a thick spout above the expiring brute, and fell in a shower around, bedewing, or rather drenching us, with a spray of blood.

'*There's the flag*!' I exclaimed; 'there! thick as tar! Stern! every soul of ye! He's going in his flurry!' And the monster, under the convulsive influence of his final paroxysm, flung his huge tail into the air, and then, for the space of a minute, thrashed the waters on either side of him with quick and powerful blows; the sound of the concussions resembling that of the rapid discharge of artillery. He then turned slowly and heavily on his side, and lay a dead mass upon the sea through which he had so long ranged a conqueror.

'He's fin up at last!' I screamed, at the very top of my voice. 'Hurrah! hurrah! hurrah!' And snatching off my cap, I sent it spinning aloft, jumping at the same time from thwart to thwart, like a madman.

J.N. REYNOLDS, 'Mocha Dick of the Pacific' in *Knickerbocker Magazine*, May 1839

Georgina Ballantine Tells How She Caught the Biggest British Salmon Ever Taken on Rod and Line (*64 lbs*)

On the evening of 7 October 1922, after a rather strenuous day's fishing, which resulted in the capture of three fine salmon, we determined to finish the day on the river. It was the last evening before the hour changed, therefore we were anxious to make the most of our time.

We amounted to Father and myself, he rowing, as Melvin, the boatman, had knocked off at 5 pm. After towing up the boat we started harling, using two rods, the fly 'Wilkinson' on the right, and the dace, which I was plying on the left. The bait was exceptionally well put on with an attractive curl on its tail and spinning along briskly as only Malloch's minnows can spin.

A few turns at the top of 'Boat Pool' as the sun dipped down behind the hill brought no result. Immediately above the 'Bargie' stone Father remarked that we should 'see him here': scarcely were the words spoken when a sudden 'rug' and 'screech' of the reel brought my rod in an upright position. He was hooked! The bait he seized with no unusual violence at 6.15 pm and thinking him an ordinary sized fish, we tried to encourage him to play into the back water behind 'Bargie', a large boulder. Our hopes, however, upon this point were soon 'barkin' and fleein''. Realizing evidently that something was amiss, he made a headlong dash for freedom and flew (I can apply no other term to his sudden flight). Down the river he went in mid-stream, taking a run of about 500 yards before stopping, at the same time carrying with him about 150 yards of line. Quick as lightning the boat was turned, heading down-stream, and soon we overtook and got him under hand and within reasonable distance.

Heading for the north bank, we were in the act of landing about 200 yards above the Bridge when he came practically to the end of the boat. Scenting danger ahead, he again ran out of reach. Leaving the boat, we followed him down, and as chance would have it he passed between the north pier and the bank when going under the Bridge, otherwise we would have been in a dreadful hole. Not once did he show himself, so we were mercifully kept in blissful ignorance of the monster we were fated to fight to the death.

About 200 yards below the Bridge Father thought it advisable to fetch the boat, as the fish obstinately kept out in the current. Evidently our progress downstream was farther than Father had anticipated, as I immediately got into hot water; 'dinna lat the beast flee doon the watter like that, 'ummin'.

With few remarks and much hand-spitting we again boarded the boat, this time keeping in mid-stream for fully half an hour. As time went on the strain of this was getting beyond us; the fish remained stationary and sulked. Then we endeavoured to humour and encourage him to the Murthly bank, but he absolutely refused to move. Again gradually crossing the river we tried to bring him into the backwater at the junction half-way down to Sparrowmuir, where a small break-water juts out. Again no luck attended our movements in this direction, though we worked with him for a considerable time. Eventually we re-crossed over close to the island. By this time darkness had come down, and we could see the trees on the island silhouetted against the sky.

We had hoped by the light of the moon to find a suitable landing-place, but unfortunately a dark cloud obscured her. The fish kept running out a few paces, then returning, but long intervals were spent without even a movement. He inclined always downstream, until the middle of the island was reached, and the light in the cottage window at Sparrowmuir blinked cheerily across the river.

By this time my left arm ached so much with the weight of the rod that it felt paralysed, but I was determined that whatever happened nothing would induce me to give in. 'Man if only the Laird or the Major had ta'en him I wouldna' ha' been sae ill aboot it.' Encouraging remarks such as those I swallowed silently. Once I struck the nail on the head by remarking that if I successfully grassed this fish he must give me a new frock. 'Get ye the fish landed first and syne we'll see aboot the frock', was the reply. (Nevertheless I have kept him to his word and the frock has been ordered.) By this time we were prepared to spend the night on the Island.

Tighter, and tighter still, the order came, until the tension was so great that no ordinary line could have stood the test for any length of time. It says much for both line and tackle in playing such an important part. Nearer and nearer he came until I was ordered to change my seat to the bow of the boat, and by keeping the rod upright Father was thus enabled to feel with the gaff the knot at the junction of line and cast. Having gauged the distance, the remainder was easy, I wound the reel steadily until only the cast (length of cast, $3\frac{3}{4}$ yards) was left. One awful moment of suspense followed -- then the gaff went in successfully, which brought him to the side of the boat. A second lift (no small weight, over $\frac{1}{2}$ cwt) brought him over the end into the floor of the boat, Father, out of puff, half sitting on top of him. Reaching for Mr Moir's 'Nabbie', I made a somewhat feeble attempt to put him out of pain, and was afterwards accused of 'knockin' oot ane o' the puir beast's een!' It is unnecessary to describe the homeward journey; I was ordered to remain in the boat while Father towed it up. We were met at the Bridge by the old lady, my mother, who was considerably relieved to see us back; her greeting showed how perturbed and anxious she had been during our absence; 'Guid sakes I thocht ye were baith i' the watter!'

No time was lost in administering a stiff dose of 'toddy' which I considered a necessary and well-earned 'nightcap'. Thus ended a 'red-letter' day in the annals of the famous Glendelvine beat of the River Tay.

GEORGINA BALLANTINE in the *Fishing Gazette*,
21 October 1922

Guile with Chub

The biggest chub I ever caught came from the Ouse, near Willington, some years ago. At this point of the river there was a system of weirs, overshoots, pools, locks and backwaters, overhung with willows, overgrown with rushes, but with hard gravel-bottomed runs and glides, shallows and deeps, that provided ideal haunts for the many large chub that lived there.

The last time I visited this part of the Ouse, the overgrowing process had made it practically unfishable except in the weir itself, where the big chub seldom went in the days when I used to fish it. Then, it was in the backwaters that we caught chub, and many days saw half a dozen fish in the keep-net that weighed 4 to $5\frac{1}{4}$ lb. Bigger fish than $5\frac{1}{4}$ lb. came to net very rarely indeed.

Local anglers knew, however, that two very big chub inhabited the small pool below the old lock, the lower gates of which were rotten and falling to pieces. But in common with most Ouse anglers, they seldom fished for chub. Roach, bream, perch and pike were what interested them most – fish that could be caught from a seated position, without much care taken to avoid scaring the fish. They did, however, fish the hole where the chub lived, often enough to make them very shy and wary.

The only place from which a line could be got into this pool was from the top of the wall adjacent to the lock-gates, 8 feet above the water and devoid of any cover except for a few tufts of coarse grass. Anglers who fished from there usually did so sitting on the wall with their legs dangling over it, in full view of the fish. No doubt many of them saw the two chub as they arrived, but not for many seconds after. They certainly did not catch, or even hook, those crafty old fish.

As usually happens, sooner or later, enough anglers saw but failed to catch these chub to make their existence widely known. A local lad told me about them and I went to see, like the army, marching on my stomach. There they were, all right. They looked huge.

A plan of campaign was obviously necessary. I made a landing net with a two-piece, 10 foot handle of cane, the net-ring fixed at right-angles. I used a number 6 hook on 6 lb. line, Wallis rod and a 4 inch centre-pin reel. I spent hours fishing for those chub, with various well-tried chub baits like crust, cheese and worms. They refused to be tempted. I came to the conclusion that it didn't need a sight of me to scare them. They became suspicious if even a rod was pushed out beyond the lock-wall.

In the end I caught those chub quite easily. I got hold of two enormous, yellow, dead frogs. I put one on my hook and I went to that lock, keeping well down and not attempting to extend the rod over the water. Instead, I laid it down, drew off sufficient line, and simply lobbed out the frog by hand. I didn't look over; I watched the line and within seconds the reel, with its check engaged, shrieked. I struck and held on hard, inching forward until I could see the water. It was churned to foam. That chub was a really scrappy one – the sort that confounds anglers who say a chub gives up after the first rush. This one fought long and hard, but no fish has much chance of beating a steady pull from straight above. There were several excursions towards the midstream rushes and more than one attempt to get under the willow branches, but I held on hard, the tackle was sound and eventually the fish rolled on its side.

Getting it into the net wasn't easy and I had to hold the rod in the middle to succeed; but it was done, the rod laid down and the net hauled up hand-over-hand. If I'd given that fish a free frog to swallow before I caught it, it would have taken the spring balance over the 7 lb. mark; as it was, the pointer barely scraped to the 6 lb. 14 oz. mark, so I called it 6 lb. 13 oz.

I put the fish in a keep-net above the lock – a typical fat, small-headed Ouse fish of what we call the 'pretty type' – silver sides without much yellowish tinge, bright pink under-fins, a bluish-brown back and a navy-blue tail. There's another sort, of course, a dark-brown fish with pale fins and tail, which grows as big and fights as hard but doesn't look so good.

Then I sat down, ate my sandwiches, drank my flask of coffee, rested for half an hour, and spent an hour or more fishing the sidestream without success, some other anglers having gone over it pretty thoroughly beforehand. In the early evening I returned to the lock and repeated my former tactics with an almost identical result. The only difference was that this second fish was a little smaller, 6 lb. 3 oz.; and I netted it more easily, having learned from experience that it was necessary to hold the rod in the middle to bring the fish within reach.

Those two chub together made a fine sight; I've never seen a bigger pair since, though I have seen solitary fish that looked larger. I didn't think it wise to drop them back in their pool, so I released them in a slack place in the weir-pool, expecting that they would find their own way back. Whether they ever did, I can't say, for circumstances prevented me from going back to see for several years. When I did, the lock-gates were fallen in and the lock-pool was silted up. It looked sad and dreary and chub-less. It is a mistake to revisit the scene of an angling triumph long afterwards.

RICHARD WALKER, *No Need to Lie*, 1964

A (*Self*) Satisfied Customer

DEAR SIRS, – Now that the nineteenth century has come to a close I may as well tell you what your rods, reels, etc. have done for me in it.

The number of the slain appears from my angling record to be as follows: –

560 salmon up to 32 pounds, considerably more than half of which have been killed (and gaffed by myself), with your single handed trout rods, trout casts, and small trout flies.

275 white trout up to $5\frac{3}{4}$ pounds.

20,066 Brown trout up to 4 pounds 14 ounces.

1,040 perch up to $1\frac{3}{4}$ pounds.

150 pike up to $10\frac{1}{4}$ pounds.

Fifty-six eels up to $5\frac{1}{2}$ pounds, or a total of 22,157 fish.

Of the other coarse fish I have kept no record, but had I done so the total would have been considerably increased. Although I have tried your rods hard, for many a time they have been doubled up for nearly a couple of hours, they have stood well, and I believe them to be the best the world can yet show. Last year I had a heavy fish hooked above the tail with a small trout fly, on a 10-foot rod for 3 hours and 5 minutes before I got him to the gaff and the rod came quite straight again. On 5th August, 1895, while fishing in one of my lakes with your 'Gem' $9\frac{1}{2}$-foot rod, a fine trout cast, and three No. 10 trout flies, I hooked at one cast, and successfully landed a salmon of $5\frac{1}{2}$ pounds, a white trout of slightly over 1 pound, and a brown trout of over 6 ounces. After bearing the strain for an hour and threequarters (I had to gaff the salmon myself), the rod came back as straight as ever. On 4th July, 1892, fishing the river in a heavy flood with one of your 14½-foot rods, I hooked twenty-nine salmon of which I landed twenty-three. No breakage occurred.

I have great pleasure in testifying to the excellence of all kinds of tackle with which you have supplied me.

Hardy Brothers Catalogue, 1902

Swimming for Tuna off California

I had the pleasure of introducing the first rod to the fishes of Santa Catalina, and the experiments they attempted with it, the rods they broke, the lines and reels they devastated, in those early days (1886) was pathetic. In due time I found myself angling for tunas. The Tuna Club, which I founded, allowed a twenty-one-thread line, and a rod weighing sixteen ounces; but I was using an eighteen line and a jointed rod, which I had made for yellow-tail, a fish that averages seventeen pounds, and when the strike came the tuna, instead of plunging down and sounding, decided to play me on the surface, and dashed away four hundred feet.

The details of this game at sea are not essential. I played the tuna for forty minutes, then brought it to gaff with my rod slightly buckled. My boatman, Jim Gardner, of Avalon, gaffed it, hauled it in and we were about to give way to exuberance befitting the occasion, when the tuna, as near as I can recall, doubled up, opened out, shot up into the air, and fell upon the rail. As we were standing, we lost our balance, and the next I knew, I was treading water. The boat went down out of sight, then came up bow first, shooting into the air, spilling the oars, gaffs, lines and everything else, into the sea, nearly a mile from shore. I was inclined to take it as a joke, as we had a launch not four hundred yards away; but my companion suddenly announced that he could not swim, and throwing his arms about the bow of the boat, she rolled over in a menacing fashion. Jim and I got him in, but the boat still rolled, being light and shallow; so we tipped her over, bottom up, helped the non-swimmer onto the bottom, where, by remaining perfectly quiet and lying flat, he was safe. I then looked for the launch, and noticed that in the excitement I had dropped my rod, a valuable piece of angling machinery.

The launch had not moved, and we saw that the engine would not work; so I decided to leave my companion, as the boat would not hold more than one, and swim to the launch. Gardner was a professional swimmer, and I was fairly at home in the water, having had many capsizing experiences in Florida; but I was handicapped by a heavy, impossible suit of corduroy, leggings and heavy shoes.

The sea was perfectly calm, and I soon distanced Gardner who, I thought, had not been very active about arranging the boat for my companion, nor did he seem to make much headway for a professional. But it was not exactly the time for criticism, and I took it easily, and was perhaps fifty feet ahead of Gardner, when I saw that the launch had started and was coming for us, the men waving and shouting encouragement.

How far we swam I do not know, but my armor of corduroy was deadly, and I felt relieved to see the launch coming. She had almost reached us, and I was slowing up, when my boatman's wife, who was aboard, raised her voice in a scream that made the welkin ring. It suggested sharks to my somewhat excited imagination, especially as she cried, 'Jim's drowning.' I stopped swimming and turned for a second, treading water, but could see nothing, as my eye-glasses had tipped; when I straightened them, Jim was indeed gone, and way back, seemingly on the horizon, was my angling companion, lying placidly on the bottom of the boat.

I started to swim back, but had not gone five feet, I confess with the fear of sharks in my heart, when Jim's head shot out of water just long enough to grin at me, then went down. As he came up again I shouted, 'What's the matter?' that grin having put sharks out of my mind.

'I've got your tuna, sir,' and down he went again, to immediately reappear.

I could not believe the evidence of my eyes, and could only laugh as he went down up to his eyes, then pulled himself up to the surface. But he had my tuna, had never released his hold on the gaff in all that exciting turmoil, and had held it with his left hand, helping to turn the boat with his right, and when I suggested that we swim, to give the other angler a fair chance, he said nothing but bore on after me; and when he disappeared the tuna had merely rushed ahead, tried to sound, and had dragged Jim down a foot or two, a clever, and too suggestive imitation of a man being jerked down by a shark.

The launch was now alongside, and Jim threw his legs about the propeller, while I was lashed to the shrouds, as the two men could not for the moment haul me in, the corduroy seemed to weigh a ton; then I was taken aboard.

Jim's entire thought was for the tuna; so I leaned over the stern, the men holding me by the legs, and he lifted the gaff until the tuna's head appeared, when I thrust my hand down into its big mouth, and securing a grip on its gill rakers, gave the word. Heave-o-ohoy! came the chanty. The men hauled on my legs, and I pulled the tuna, and in a few seconds dropped it into the cockpit, when we cheered as anglers will; then Jim was hauled in by a rope which had been tossed him by his wife.

All this time we had kept an eye on the angler on the bottom of the boat, and now steamed for him. He was lying so quiet that one might have fancied he was asleep; but he denied the imputation. The sea was covered with wreckage, and Captain Harry Doss, one of the boatmen of Avalon, who had seen the catastrophe, came out from the shore and picked it up. A rope was tossed to my companion, Mr Dennison of Philadelphia, who fastened it about his waist and was hauled aboard. The boat was righted, and with the first tuna of the season we turned toward Avalon, four miles distant, to claim the Tuna Club prize for the event in rods, etc., which of course went to Jim Gardner.

This is enough for the average fish story, in fact, it is as much as the ordinary listener who has his limitations will believe, yet as there *were* three or four disinterested witnesses I will go on. As soon as the launch got under way, I noticed Jim grasping for something, then he cried to the engineer to stop, and stood up, and in his trousers was the hook which caught the tuna; in some way, either during the capsize, or the swim, it had been flung out, and had hooked onto the gaffer. Jim saw that the line led overboard, and to make a very long story short, he hauled in six hundred feet of line, and at the end, up came my rod and reel which had gone to the bottom and slowly unreeled to the end. I have not claimed a

Carnegie hero medal for my boatman, but all anglers will appreciate the cleverness and nerve of this man in saving his patron's fish under what, to put it mildly, were adverse circumstances.

CHARLES HOLDER, *Fish Stories*, 1909

An Eight-year-old Boy and his First Fish

The thought of fishing sent me wild with excitement. Many a time I'd been past the pool at the Mill Farm and watched the small carp basking on the surface, and sometimes under the willow tree at the corner a great diamond-shaped carp that to my eyes looked enormous – six inches long, I suppose – would suddenly rise to the surface, gulp down a grub and sink again. I'd spent hours glueing my nose against the window of Wallace's in the High Street, where fishing tackle and guns and bicycles were sold. I used to lie awake on summer mornings thinking of the tales Joe had told me about fishing, how you mixed bread paste, how your float gives a bob and plunges under and you feel the rod bending and the fish tugging at the line. Is it any use talking about it, I wonder – the sort of fairy light that fish and fishing tackle have in a kid's eyes? Some kids feel the same about guns and shooting, some feel it about motorbikes or aeroplanes or horses. It's not a thing that you can explain or rationalise, it's merely magic. One morning – it was in June and I must have been eight – I knew that Joe was going to cut school and go out fishing, and I made up my mind to follow.

It was a wonderful June morning. The buttercups were up to my knees. There was a breath of wind just stirring the tops of the elms, and the great green clouds of leaves were sort of soft and rich like silk. And it was nine in the morning and I was eight years old, and all round me it was early summer, with great tangled hedges where the wild roses were still in bloom, and bits of soft white cloud drifting overhead, and in the distance the low hills and the dim blue masses of the woods round Upper Binfield. And I didn't give a damn for any of it. All I was thinking of was the green pool and the carp and the gang with their hooks and lines and bread paste. It was as though they were in paradise and I'd got to join them. Presently I managed to sneak up on them – four of them, Joe and Sid

Lovegrove and the errand boy and another shopkeeper's son, Harry Barnes I think his name was.

Joe turned and saw me. 'Christ!' he said. 'It's the kid.' He walked up to me like a tom-cat that's going to start a fight. 'Now then, you! What'd I tell you? You get back 'ome double quick.'

Both Joe and I were inclined to drop our aitches if we were at all excited. I backed away from him.

'I'm not going back 'ome.'

'Yes, you are.'

'Clip his ear, Joe,' said Sid. 'We don't want no kids along.'

'*Are* you going back 'ome?' said Joe.

'No.'

'Righto, my boy! Right-*ho!*'

Then he started on me. The next minute he was chasing me round, catching me one clip after another. But I didn't run away from the pool, I ran in circles. Presently he'd caught me and got me down, and then he knelt on my upper arms and began screwing my ears, which was his favourite torture and one I couldn't stand. I was blubbing by this time, but still I wouldn't give in and promise to go home. I wanted to stay and go fishing with the gang. And suddenly the others swung round in my favour and told Joe to get up off my chest and let me stay if I wanted to. So I stayed after all.

The others had some hooks and lines and floats and a lump of bread paste in a rag, and we all cut ourselves willow switches from the tree at the corner of the pool. The farmhouse was only about two hundred yards away, and you had to keep out of sight because old Brewer was very down on fishing. Not that it made any difference to him, he only used the pool for watering his cattle, but he hated boys. The others were still jealous of me and kept telling me to get out of the light and reminding me that I was only a kid and knew nothing about fishing. They said that I was making such a noise I'd scare all the fish away, though actually I was making about half as much noise as anyone else there. Finally they wouldn't let me sit beside them and sent me to another part of the pool where the water was shallower and there wasn't so much shade. They said a kid like me was sure to keep splashing the water and frighten the fish away. It was a rotten part of the pool, a part where no fish would ordinarily come. I knew that. I seemed to know by a kind of

instinct the places where a fish would lie. Still, I was fishing at last.
I was sitting on the grass bank with the rod in my hands, with the
flies buzzing round and the smell of wild peppermint fit to knock
you down, watching the red float on the green water, and I was
happy as a tinker although the tear-marks mixed up with dirt were
still all over my face.

Lord knows how long we sat there. The morning streched out
and out, and the sun got higher and higher, and nobody had a bite. It
was a hot, still day, too clear for fishing. The floats lay on the water
with never a quiver. You could see deep down into the water as
though you were looking into a kind of dark green glass. Out in the
middle of the pool you could see the fish lying just under the
surface, sunning themselves, and sometimes in the weeds near
the side a newt would come gliding upwards and rest there with his
fingers on the weeds and his nose just out of the water. But the fish
weren't biting. The others kept shouting that they'd got a nibble,
but it was always a lie. And the time stretched out and out and it
got hotter and hotter, and the flies ate you alive and the wild
peppermint under the bank smelt like Mother Wheeler's sweetshop.
I was getting hungrier and hungrier, all the more because I didn't
know for certain where my dinner was coming from. But I sat as
still as a mouse and never took my eyes off my float. The others had
given me a lump of bait about the size of a marble, telling me that
would have to do for me, but for a long time I didn't even dare to
rebait my hook, because every time I pulled my line up they swore I
was making enough noise to frighten every fish within five miles.

I suppose we must have been there about two hours when
suddenly my float gave a quiver. I knew it was a fish. It must have
been a fish that was just passing accidentally and saw my bait.
There's no mistaking the movement your float gives when it's a real
bite. It's quite different from the way it moves when you twitch
your line accidentally. The next moment it gave a sharp bob and
almost went under. I couldn't hold myself in any longer. I yelled to
the others:

'I've got a bite!'

'Rats!' yelled Sid Lovegrove instantly.

But the next moment there wasn't any doubt about it. The float
dived straight down, I could still see it under the water, kind of dim

red, and I felt the rod tighten in my hand. Christ, that feeling! The line jerking and straining and a fish on the other end of it! The others saw my rod bending, and the next moment they'd all flung their rods down and rushed round to me. I gave a terrific haul and the fish – a great huge silvery fish – came flying up through the air. The same moment all of us gave a yell of agony. The fish had slipped off the hook and fallen into the wild peppermint under the bank. But he'd fallen into shallow water where he couldn't turn over, and for perhaps a second he lay there on his side helpless. Joe flung himself into the water, splashing us all over, and grabbed him in both hands. 'I got 'im!' he yelled. The next moment he'd flung the fish onto the grass and we were all kneeling round it. How we gloated! The poor dying brute flapped up and down and his scales glistened all the colours of the rainbow. It was a huge carp, seven inches long at least, and must have weighed a quarter of a pound. How we shouted to see him! But the next moment it was as though a shadow had fallen across us. We looked up, and there was old Brewer standing over us, with his tall billycock hat – one of those hats they used to wear that were a cross between a top-hat and a bowler – and his cowhide gaiters and a thick hazel stick in his hand.

We suddenly cowered like partridges when there's a hawk overhead. He looked from one to other of us. He had a wicked old mouth with no teeth in it, and since he'd shaved his beard off his chin looked like a nutcracker.

'What are you boys doing here?' he said.

There wasn't much doubt about what we were doing. Nobody answered.

'I'll learn 'ee come fishing in my pool!' he suddenly roared, and the next moment he was on us, whacking out in all directions.

The Black Hand broke and fled. We left all the rods behind and also the fish. Old Brewer chased us half across the meadow. His legs were stiff and he couldn't move fast, but he got in some good swipes before we were out of his reach. We left him in the middle of the field, yelling after us that he knew all our names and was going to tell our fathers. I'd been at the back and most of the wallops had landed on me. I had some nasty red weals on the calves of my legs when we got to the other side of the hedge.

I spent the rest of the day with the gang. They hadn't made up their mind whether I was really a member yet, but for the time being they tolerated me. The errand boy, who'd had the morning off on some lying pretext or other, had to go back to the brewery. The rest of us went for a long, meandering, scrounging kind of walk, the sort of walk that boys go for when they're away from home all day, and especially when they're away without permission. It was the first real boy's walk I'd had.

GEORGE ORWELL, *Coming Up For Air*, 1939

An Awful Poem

I.

A BIRR! a whirr! a salmon's on,
　A goodly fish, a thumper!
Bring up, bring up the ready gaff,
And when we land him we shall quaff
　Another glorious bumper![1]
Hark! 'tis the music of the reel,
　The strong, the quick, the steady:
The line darts from the circling wheel,
　Have all things right and ready.

II.

A birr! a whirr! the salmon's out
　Far on the rushing river,
He storms the stream with edge of might,
And like a brandish'd sword of light,
Rolls flashing o'er the surges white,
　A desperate endeavour!
Hark to the music of the reel!
　The fitful and the grating;
It pants along the breathless wheel,
　Now hurried, now abating.

III.

A birr! a whirr! the salmon's off!
　No, no, we still have got him;

The wily fish has sullen grown,
And, like a bright embedded stone,
   Lies gleaming at the bottom.
Hark to the music of the reel!
   'Tis hush'd, it hath forsaken;
With care we'll guard the slumbering wheel
   Until its notes rewaken.

IV.

A birr! a whirr! the salmon's up!
   Give line, give line and measure;
And now he turns, keep down a-head
And lead him as a child is led,
   And land him at your leisure.
Hark to the music of the reel!
   'Tis welcome, it is glorious;
It wanders round the exultant wheel,
   Returning and victorious.

V.

A birr! a whirr! the salmon's in,
   Upon the bank extended;
The princely fish lies gasping slow,
His brilliant colours come and go,
Silver alternating with snow,
   All beautifully blended.
Hark to the music of the reel!
   It murmurs and it closes;
Silence falls on the conquering wheel,
   The wearied line reposes.

VI.

No birr! no whirr! the salmon's ours:
   The noble fish, the thumper!
Strike through his gill the ready gaff,
And bending homewards we shall quaff
   The overflowing bumper!
Hark to the music of the reel!

We listen with devotion;
There's something in that circling wheel
That stirs the heart's emotion!
          THOMAS TOD STEWART, 'The Taking of the Salmon' from
                    The Art of Angling as Practised in Scotland, 1866

A Sickly Russian Schoolboy Catches his First Big Carp (*1801*)

In spite of the alarming nature of my illness, I went on all the time
with my lessons and outdoor amusements also; only, when the
attacks became more severe, I was more moderate in the amount of
exercise I took, and my mother kept a careful eye on me, and would
not let me go far away or for long. Every morning before the great
heat came on, I went out with Yevséitch to fish. Our very best
fishing was in the garden, and almost under our windows, because
there was a mill and a very large pond below Aksákovo in the
village of Kivatsky, and the overflow caused by the dam extended
nearly as far up as our garden. Every sportsman knows how good
the fishing is, under such conditions. Now for the first time I
became acquainted with the fisherman's chief delight – the catching
of large fish. Up till then I had caught only roach, perch, and
gudgeons; it is true that the two former fish often attain considerable
size, but, for some reason, I never happened to hook a very large
one; and if I had, I could not have landed it, as I used thin lines and
small hooks. But now Yevséitch plaited two lines for me, each of
twenty horse-hairs, attached stout hooks to them, and tied the lines
to strong rods; then he took his own line as well, and guided me
through the garden to a pool which he kept a secret from others,
and which he called 'The Golden Pool'. He baited my hook with a
piece of brown breadcrumb about the size of a large hazel-nut, and
cast my line right under a bush in the deep water, while he dropped
his own by the bank near the weed and rushes. I sat quietly, never
daring to take my eyes off my float, as it swayed gently up and
down in the eddy that formed under the bank. Before long, Yevséitch suddenly sprang up and cried out, 'I've got him, *bátyushka*';[1]

---

[1] The word means 'father', but is used as a general title of respect or affection.

then he began to struggle with a big fish, holding the rod in both hands. Yevséitch had no idea of scientific fishing: he merely pulled with all his might, trying to jerk the fish out over his shoulder. But the fish had probably got fixed behind some weed or rushes; the rod was no more than a stick, and the line broke, so that we did not even see what sort of a fish it was. Yevséitch was much excited; and I too, as I watched him, was almost shaking. He vowed that it was the largest fish he had ever hooked in his life; but it was probably a carp or chub of ordinary size, which seemed so heavy to him because it had got entangled in the weed. Then he shook free my other line and cast it as quick as he could into the same spot: 'I believe I was a little too hasty,' he said: 'next time I won't pull so hard;' and down he sat on the grass, to wait for a second bite; but none came.

My chance came next, and fortune resolved to do me a good turn. My float began gradually to rise on end and fall again; then it remained on end and finally disappeared under water. I struck, and a very large fish began to move heavily, as if reluctantly, through the water. When Yevséitch ran to my aid and caught hold of my rod, I remembered what he had just said, and told him again and again not to pull so hard. At last, as the rod, which I never let go, was not very supple, and the line was new and strong, we landed somehow by our united efforts a very large carp. Yevséitch fell on it at full length, crying out, 'Now we've got him, my little falcon; he won't escape now!' In my joy I shook like a man in a fever – indeed this often happened afterwards when I caught a large fish; for long I could not calm down, but kept constantly running to look at my prize, as it lay on the grassy bank at a safe distance from the water. We threw in the line again; but the fish had ceased to take, and half an hour later we went home, as I had only leave to be out a short time. This early success confirmed once for all my passion for fishing. We tied the carp to a branch, and I carried it home to show my father, who liked to fish at times himself. In those days it was not our custom at Aksákovo to weigh big fish; but I believe that I never afterwards caught so large a carp, and that it weighed at least seven pounds.

SERGE AKSAKOFF, A Russian Schoolboy, 1856

A Sturgeon on the Towy

There is an Angler's Prayer you still come across occasionally, painted on old mugs in fishing inns. It is a bit like a river itself, the couplet meandering towards a tired rhyme.

Lord, grant that I may catch a fish so big that even I,
When speaking of it afterwards, may have no need to lie.

This is an account of a man, 'an excellent angler, and now with God,' as Walton put it, who did just that. He caught a fish so big it would have needed two large men, their arms fully outstretched, to give cynics in saloon bars even a hint of its dimensions.

But he did more than that. He went fishing for salmon one day and caught something so peculiar, so far removed from even the footnotes of angling in Britain, that a grown man who was present ran off across the fields. Nobody would have thought it at all odd that day if the fisherman had been found trying to look up his catch in the Book of Revelations.

It needs a photograph. The fisherman is dead. His friends are beginning to die. If a photograph had not been taken few people would now believe what happened. A hundred years ago, ballads and hearsay would have wrecked it on the wilder shores of myth. As it is yellowing cuttings from the local paper, almost crumbling into carbon, are slowly unfolded from wallets. A print is unearthed reverently from under a pile of household receipts. It was on July 28, 1933, that Alec Allen caught his fish, but even that has been elbowed into myth. His obituary (far from the national press) says that it was on July 9. The *Guinness Book of Records* says that it was July 25. But the one contemporary cutting had no doubts. It was July 28. Appropriately it was a Friday.

The photograph is extraordinary. Allen, a short man in a Fairisle pullover and baggy trousers, leans against a wall beside a trestle. It is a typical Thirties snapshot slouch. His hands are in his pockets. There is a cigarette in his mouth. But of course you notice all this a long time afterwards, because of the thing dangling from the trestle.

At first it looks like the biggest herring in the history of the sea. It towers over the man by a good four feet. It is a fish certainly, but the head ends in a dark snout. The body appears to be armoured. The surroundings, a farm gate, the field beyond, underline the oddness. In a farmyard a man is posing beside a thing the size of a basking shark. Alec Allen had caught himself a Royal Sturgeon in the River Towy, at Nantgaredig, near Carmarthen. It was nine feet two inches long, had a girth of 59 inches, and weighed 388 pounds.

Allen was a commercial traveller from Penarth in Glamorganshire. He was a well-known sportsman and hockey referee. In later life he was to referee Olympic matches. But he was then in his early forties, one of that oddly innocent breed who figure in Saki and Wodehouse, but who latterly seem to have become as extinct as the Great Auk, the sporting bachelor. His great delight was fishing, but in him it was more than a delight.

His great friend was Alderman David Price of Nantgaredig, who died last year aged 74. He had known Allen all his life. All they had ever talked about, he recalled with wonder, was fishing.

In 1933 Allen was traveller for a firm of fishing tackle manufacturers. His father, also a great fisherman, was a traveller for a wallpaper firm. Father and son somehow contrived it that they could travel together in the same car. Both their commercial beats were West Wales, but a West Wales wonderfully concentrated between the rivers Wye, Teify and Towy. When their friends talk about the Allens it is with amusement. It was notorious that their business rounds were engineered for fishing.

Off-stage Hitler was ranting. Stalin drawing up lists of victims. Ramsay MacDonald droned his platitudes and the dole queues lengthened. But in West Wales the Allens went their way, in a car full of tackle and wallpaper, their itineraries perfectly arranged to end in fishing inns beside rivers. The thing has an idyllic quality. It may have been a bit tough on you if your wallpaper shop was nowhere near a river, but nobody seems to have complained. In time the son succeeded the father as wallpaper salesman, but the itineraries did not change.

The two had rented a stretch of the Towy since 1928. This included some of the deepest pools in the river. But the summer of 1933 had been dry, and the water level was low. Walking by one of the pools that July, Alec Allen noted enormous waves suddenly cross it. It puzzled him but at the time he would have discounted any suspicion that they had been made by a living thing. After all, it was 15 miles to the sea, and tidal water ended two miles lower down.

A few days later Allen returned to the pool. It was evening and he had a friend with him, Edwin Lewis of Crosshands. There was a third man, his name lost to history, watching on the bank. Allen began fishing. It was a quiet evening. But then he felt a slight tug on his line. He pulled on it but to no effect.

Alderman Price was fond of telling what happened next. 'Alec used to tell me that he though he'd hooked a log. He couldn't see what it was, except that it was something huge in the shadows. Then the log began to move upstream.' A faint smile would come over Price's face.

'Now Alec knew that logs don't move upstream.'

Allen had still no idea of what was in the river. A more imaginative man might have become frightened at that stage. His line was jerking out under a momentum he had never experienced. In the darkness of the pool he had hooked something which moved with the force of a shark.

He played it for 20 minutes, letting the line move out when it went away. When it came back he retreated up the bank. But there was no channel of deep water leading away from the pool. If there had been, no salmon line made would have held his catch. Then he saw it.

Suddenly the creature leapt out of the water. Maddened, it crashed into a shallow run. It was there under them, threshing in the low water. Allen was confronted by a bulk that was just not possible. The sightseer ran shouting for his life.

But Lewis ran forward with the gaff. He stuck it into the fish, but the fish moved. It straightened the steel gaff. Then the great tail flicked up and caught Lewis, and threw him into the air on to the bank. Just one flick, but it nearly broke the man's leg.

There was a large rock on the bank. Allen dropped the rod (it had been a freak catch, the hook snagging in the fish's head, a sturgeon having no mouth) and tugged at the rock. With it in his hands he waded out, and dropped it on the head, lifting it again and pounding at it. The creature began to die. The two men looked down at it. Neither had any idea what it was.

But in death it provided them with an even greater problem; how were they to get it out of the river? Allen ran to a nearby farm. There then occurred one of those rare moments which cannot help but be pure comedy. Allen asked could he borrow a horse and cart. The farmer, naturally, asked why. Allen said he had caught a fish.

It ended with farmer, farmer's friends, dogs, horse, cart and all going back to the bank.

'I can remember it now,' said Alderman Price. 'Alec came running to my house. I had never seen him so excited. All he would say was, "Well, I've caught something this time that you'll never beat." I went back with him. They'd pulled it up on to the trestle you see in the photographs and the news had got round. People were coming in cars and in carts. They were ferrying children across the river.

'It had these big scales, I remember. Very slimy. It was a sort of black and white in colour. No, I wasn't frightened.' He was in the habit of pausing at that point. 'It was dead.'

As the anglers gathered it was determined that the thing out of the river was a sturgeon. Vague memories stirred. Was it not the law that a sturgeon was the King's prerogative?

A telegram was sent to Buckingham Palace inquiring after the King the next day. A stiff little reply came the same day, that the King was not in residence. Such trivia did not deter a man who had hooked the biggest fish in recorded angling history. Allen sold the sturgeon to a fishmonger from Swansea for two pounds ten shillings.

That worked out at something like a penny ha'penny a pound and this at a time when Scotch salmon at Billingsgate was fetching two and six a pound. More than 40 years later Allen's friends who had helped him load the thing on to the train, were still bitter about the deal.

There had been so much caviar in the sturgeon that some of it had fallen on to the farm yard where it was eaten by those of the farmer's pigs with a taste for the good life. History does not relate what happened to the pigs subsequently. But selling the fish did get rid of one problem. There were no refrigerators in the Valley, and 388 pounds of sturgeon was a lot of fish.

Allen fished on until his death in 1972 at the age of 77. In photographs the lean figure became stocky. Spectacles were added. Catches got held up regularly to the camera, something he could never have done that wild July night when he was content just to pose beside his fish. So did he consider the rest of his fishing life to be a sort of epilogue?

Brian Rudge, who now runs the fishing tackle firm on whose behalf Allen meandered through West Wales, knew him well. 'I think he saw the incident as more of a joke than anything. He wasn't a man who was easily impressed. I think, you know, that as far as he was concerned it was a bit of a nuisance. He was out salmon fishing. The sturgeon had got in his way.'

Alderman Price heard Allen talk about it a few times. 'It was usually when he heard anglers going on about their catches. He wasn't a boasting man but sometimes he couldn't resist saying, 'Well, I suppose this would be the biggest fish I ever caught.' And then of course they'd say, 'Good God.'

Yet outside the valley and angling circles it was a small fame. There was no mention of it in the national press that July.

It was a small item even in the *Carmarthen Journal*. The august organ rose to its greatest heights of sensationalism. 'Two anglers had an exciting time while fishing in the River Towy,' the report began.

In March, 1972, Allen died suddenly at the home in Penarth he had shared with a spinster sister. But there was a passage in his will which surprised his friends almost as much as the catching of the sturgeon. Though he had talked little about the incident, he left instructions that his body be cremated and the ashes put into the river at the spot out of which he had pulled Leviathan.

'I called on David Price one day,' said Ronald Jones, the former Chief Constable of Dyfed, and another of Allen's friends, 'and said what a pity it was about Alec.' 'Aye,' said Dai. 'I've got him there on the mantelpiece.' It was the casket, you see. We were all surprised. Nobody's ever heard of anyone wanting that done before.'

'I suppose it was a romantic touch,' said Brian Rudge, 'but he wasn't the sort of man who'd like people to gather round a grave.'

It was a grey wet day when they put the ashes into the water. A dozen of his old friends, contacted by phone or letter, gathered on the bank. No clergyman or minister had agreed to take part, their religion not recognising a river as consecrated ground.

Despite the hymns in the rain, it would seem to have had pagan overtones. Among the first things a people names are rivers. River gods are the oldest. A man who had pulled out of a river its largest living thing would seem to be assuaging something very old in having himself put back in its place.

'We said the Lord's Prayer,' said the Chief Constable, 'as we committed the ashes to the waters he'd fished for 50 years. But then as the wind carried them I saw a trout leap into the air just where they were drifting.

'And I said to Dai: "Look. Alec's there."'

BYRON ROGERS in the *Sunday Telegraph*

A Brilliant Rainbow in Chile

This river was the Laja, racing down from the extinct volcano of Antuco in the far Andes. In the long flat sweeps it was a deep bottle-green . . . but swirling. Then it crashed through the rocks it had rounded through the ages, poured white over ledges, and emitted the continuous low roar of broken water. I remembered what the ambassador had told me in Santiago – 'plenty of backing on your line' – and my heart sank.

At any rate, I told myself, put on the biggest cast you've got (it was a 2X), soak it well . . . and trust to heaven. It was well I did.

I had picked the side of a broad stretch of white falls where the main river swept past in frothing white water and where there was a lee of green water lying along the main current. I felt that if there were any big trout, waiting for something to come down, this was where they would be. It was easy casting, for there was no high brush behind me, and I kept as long a line as I could in the air, hoping to reach the edge of the white water. I think I must have been even more shocked than the fish when, on my very first cast, just as my fly was sweeping down about opposite me, I got that driving pull of a heavy strike. It was the first cast I made in Chile – and it was the best fish.

Without waiting for any more argument he went straight on down the river, sweeping through the white water, where he seemed to rest, or sulk, for a moment in the green water on the other side. It was lucky for me that he did; practically every foot of my line had been taken out. So there we were. I could not get across to him. Neither could I get him across to me. So I gave him the bend of the rod while I stood there and thought about it.

In these parts of Chile there is a very poor brand of peasant, which exists heaven knows how; they come about as close to living without any visible means of support as you would think man could get. There was the brush-board-and-thatched hovel of one of these ramshackle humans behind me now. Its inhabitants had evidently been watching me for some time. Now, seeing me standing there, apparently doing nothing, a small urchin impelled by curiosity came cautiously up to see what I was doing. We spoke no language in which we could communicate with each other; and when I unhooked my landing-net and snapped it open he almost fainted from fright. But he was a quick-witted little fellow, and, somehow, he comprehended what a net was. I made him take it from me.

So there were two of us standing there now. The fish had remained exactly where he was. I gave him a slow pull. The next instant the fish was going down along his side of the river and the boy and I were stumbling down along the boulders on ours. As I said, these strange, volcanic rocks had been rounded by time, and a more tricky, stumbling, infuriating river journey I have seldom made. For I was deep in the river by now, getting as close to the fish as I could get in order to win back some more line. In this fashion I took several yards back from him. Then I reached a high stretch of bank where the water was too deep, and so came back to land. It was now, I said gloomily to myself, that I would lose this fish. I remembered the big sea trout I had had on for two hours and forty minutes, in the Shetlands. Here was to be another broken heart; for, some fifty yards below me, shone a long sloping shelf of white water in the mid-day sun.

Then the fish took it into his head to command operations. To my confused delight and dismay he came directly at me across the white water, so fast that I could barely strip in the line. I had no chance to reel in. Then he went on up the river, taking the line with him as fast as I could pay it out without fouling it. Then, boring against the line, as if he meant to jump the low falls, he again remained stationary over one spot.

This was exactly what the doctor ordered. I could not have asked him to do anything nicer. Reeling in as swiftly as I could, I worked my way up to him. So there, plus one Chilean boy, we were exactly where we had started over twenty minutes before. I knew it was twenty minutes, because twice during our tussle, I had seen Chillan erupt. That 2,000-foot sulphurous jet!

Now began one of the most beautiful battles I have ever experienced. For I had plenty of line in hand now; when he came past I gave him the bend of the rod for all I thought it could stand – determined he should never cross to the other side of that white water again. And every time I checked him. The green water water was so glass-clear that when he swung in the swirls sluicing past me the sun caught and reflected the pinkish stripe along his strong sides. I could watch him fighting the hook. And then he spun in the sun, jumping. He was the very essence of fight. Furious, I think – still not frightened.

There is no doubt that in the ingredients of a fisherman's delight there is nothing comparable to being able to watch a fish fight like this. For I could see him, or his shape, nearly all the time. Chillan erupted once more.

But by now my gallant rainbow was a slow-moving, sullen thing. His tail working heavily, he lay in the green water about twenty yards out from me. And I looked around for the lee of some rocks and slowly worked him in. I had him in a pool. It was almost still water. He was almost resting against the hook. And then, as the bank was high, and I was an idiot, I signalled the little Chilean boy to wade out and slip the net under him. . . .

The boy did. He was an eager boy . . . so eager that he stabbed the net at the fish . . . pushed him with it! Then he tried to scoop him in from the tail. . . . I jumped. As I did, the boy actually got the fish into the net. I seized boy, net, fish, all at the same time, and threw them all up on the bank. There I dived on the fish.

It all goes to prove the hysterical condition into which some fishermen will get themselves. For this rainbow was not much over 6 lb. But he was such a beautiful one! That was the point; that small nose, and those deep shoulders, and those firm fighting flanks. This fish had been living in clean water on crayfish galore. I sat on the bank and looked at him for nearly twenty minutes. I had him.

NEGLEY FARSON, *Going Fishing*, 1942

Richard Walker's Record British Carp

On 12 September 1952, Peter Thomas and I again went to Redmire.

We left home in a downpour, but by the time we had reached our destination the sky had cleared and the stars were shining brightly. It was very cold indeed, but we fished until about two a.m., when we noticed a bank of black cloud coming from the north-west, and decided to pitch our tent before it began to rain again.

We chose a spot on the west side of the lake, in deference to a theory I have that when carp have been driven into deep water at night by lowering temperature, they usually move out of it again in the early morning sunshine. Here we camped, pitching the tent with its open end about three yards from the water and directly facing it. Between the tent and the water's edge a large groundsheet was spread.

Looking across the lake, about a hundred yards wide at this point, we could see a line of trees, which appeared as black shadows. To the left, ten yards along the bank, was a clump of weeping willows, whose branches trailed in the water, and beyond them was the tough pond-weed, of which I spoke when describing the capture of Maurice Ingham's fish. This extended about twenty yards out into the lake, as did another bed of the same stuff on the right of our position. Beyond that, forty yards away, was the dam at the end of the lake, which runs at right angles to the bank from which we were fishing. Halfway along the dam were once some chestnut trees, which have long since been felled, but their stumps still live and a tangled mass of writhing roots trails into the water Immediately to our right, on the bank from which we were fishing, was a mass of brambles hanging in the water and extending to the bottom, concealing an undercut bank hollowed-out to a depth of between three and four feet, a favourite haunt of moorhens and rats.

Having arranged our week-end home, we baited our hooks and cast out to the edge of the deep water, a few yards beyond the pond-weed; Peter's to the left and mine only a few yards to the right of where his bait had landed. Both baits consisted of balanced paste and breadcrust on No. 2 hooks which had been carefully sharpened beforehand; mine was whipped direct to a twelve-pound b.s. plaited nylon line, of which I had a hundred yards on a fixed spool reel.

Rods were the usual Mk.IV carp-rods, which have never failed us yet – ten ounces of hardened split-bamboo can be made to do surprising things. Electric buzzers were clipped to the lines between butt-rings and reels, and all was ready for the carp to bite; to attract them, mashed bread ground-bait was thrown out. By this time, the sky had clouded over completely, and instead of rain there was a decided increase in temperature, but the darkness was intense. I cannot remember ever being out on a blacker night. It was so dark that even the rats were less active than usual, and all I could see were the silhouettes of the trees opposite. The lake was completely still, its surface unbroken by either wind or the movements of fish; and so it remained, except for one heavy splash far out, and a brief spell of 'flipping' by very small fish on the surface, until some time between four-thirty a.m. and five a.m. About that time one of the buzzers sounded, and we were both at the rods at once.

'It's yours,' said Peter. I raised the back of my hand under the rod to feel if the line was being taken, and felt it creep slowly over the hairs, an eerie but satisfactory sensation. In went the pick-up; a pause to make sure the line had been picked up properly, and then I struck hard and far back. I encountered a solid but living resistance, and Peter, needing no telling that a fish was hooked, reeled up his line out of the way. I crouched so that I could see the curve of the rod against the sky – even that was difficult in the extreme darkness – and waited on events. I did not want a fresh lively fish brought too soon into the fifteen-yard wide channel between the weed-beds, and I determined that if possible the battle should be fought in the deep water beyond.

The fish moved slowly and solidly towards the dam. Every few seconds came a tremendous tug; it felt as if the rod had been struck by a sandbag. As the fish neared the dam, I remembered those chestnut roots. Four pounds or forty, it must not get among them, or all would be lost, so I increased pressure. At first it had no effect; then as I bent the rod more, the efforts of the fish became intensified. I knew only a few yards separated it from disaster, and hung on grimly. The rod bent as never before – I could feel the curve under the corks in my hand; but everything held for the two or three minutes that the fish continued to fight his way towards his refuge. Then, suddenly, he gave it up. He turned and forged into the weed-bed between me and the roots, and I was only just able to keep the line taut. Presently he stopped, and all was solid and immovable.

Peter said, 'Take it easy. Wait and see if he'll move.' I did. Nothing happened. I said, 'I'll try hand-lining.' Peter said, 'All right, but take it easy. That's a big fish, you don't want to lose it.'

I had no idea how big a fish it was. I knew it was a good one, but all I could think of then was, 'Maybe another twenty-pounder – I hope!' I pulled off a couple of yards of line, so as to be able to get the rod up quickly if the fish bolted suddenly; then I pointed the rod straight at the fish and began tugging. The first few tugs made no impression; then came a frantic pull, up went the rod, and out went the fish into the deep water again. I let him go well out, and then tightened up firmly again, praying for him to move left; and he did. When he was opposite I gave him the butt and crammed on to the limit; and in he came, grudgingly, pulling and boring every inch of the way, but always losing ground, until at last he came to the surface and rolled three or four yards out.

Peter was ready with the net, and as I drew the fish towards it, he switched on the electric lamp. We saw a great expanse of golden flank as the fish rolled. 'Common carp,' said Peter. The fish rolled again, then righted itself, and suddenly, with a last effort, shot towards me and to the right. I could do nothing to stop it, and to my horror it crashed through the fringe of trailing brambles; in the light of the lamp I could see the swirls as the fish tried to thrust even further under; but though I put the rod-point under water and strained it as hard as I dare, nothing would shift the fish, which eventually settled down into an immovable sulk.

Peter climbed out to the edge of the overhang and put the big net, thong down, over the hole in the brambles where the fish had gone in. Then, feeling carefully down the line with his free hand, he reached the fish's nose and pulled it round, steering it into the net. I saw vaguely a commotion; then Peter began to lift. He stuck halfway and called for me to take his lamp. I slackened the line, put down the rod, and went to his assistance. Once I had the lamp, he could grasp the mesh of the net, and with a tremendous heave he swung net and fish up and over the brambles and on to the bank.

We knelt side by side looking at it. I knew it was big, and suddenly it dawned on me it was more than that. It was tremendous!

I cut a stick, notched its end, and with this Peter extracted the hook which was only lightly lodged in the roof of the mouth. Then we put the fish in a sack and lifted it on my spring balance, which goes up to thirty-two pounds. The pointer came up against the stop with such a thump that we both knew at once that here was a new record; but we could tell no more; so we tied up the mouth of the sack and lowered it into the water.

Then we re-baited out hooks and cast out again. Peter went into the tent; but I knew I could never sleep, and sat smoking and thinking till dawn. It was then that I resolved that, record or no record, that fish should not be killed. Many, many times I had wondered what I should do if I ever caught a record carp; now I had to decide, and kill it I could not.

At about ten-thirty, I was able to telephone Mr H.F. Vinall, curator of the aquarium at the London Zoo. To cut a long story short, a van containing a vast tub, and two good fellows, who gave up their Saturday afternoon for the purpose, came and fetched it; and it arrived alive and well. I asked that it should be accurately weighed on arrival, which was done, and the weight recorded at forty-four pounds. I thought the sack must have been included at first, but the matter was investigated, and it has now been established that the weight really was forty-four pounds to the dot, without the sack or anything else.

RICHARD WALKER, *Still Water Angling*, 1975

The Record is Broken Again

I could see some movement at the top of the shallows. Big fish were stirring the water, making rose-shaped clouds of red mud. I crept up to Quinlans and thought I could see five carp feeding in the murk. One was a five-pounder, three were twenty-pounders and the other was like a sunken rowing boat. But they all kept disappearing into the mud clouds and it was difficult to know where to cast.

I'd baited with three grains of corn, and after squeezing a bean-sized knob of plasticine onto the line, cast out twenty yards to the right. A biggish fish swam in from the island, coming straight for the bait. He hesitated over it, but then cruised off. Then a twenty-pound common began to mill about below the floating algae, only two rod-lengths out. I dropped a bait in front of him and after a minute the line shot tight – only to fall instantly slack again. I cast twice more to the edge of the scummy algae, resting the rod in a twig and sitting back on an old willow stump. However, even though the breeze had died to a whisper, there was still a fair amount of drift, the floating scum caught the line, dragging the bait and so I reeled in and made another cast right in front of the large dark shape that was just then ghosting round the willow on my left. I almost botched it. Casting at that fish was like casting at the sun – I suddenly lost my focus in a fever of anticipation. But it was all right. The bait flew in a perfect arc and the fish must have taken it before it hit bottom.

I put in the pick-up and was just lowering the rod when I saw the line slithering across the surface. I couldn't miss and found myself connected to a fish that swirled round, making a colossal splash, and surged diagonally across the shallows. I let him run, having planned a neat dodge for such a circumstance. As the line brushed against the willow, I jumped in and floundered round to my right, ducking under an alder bough that was actually hanging into the water. I whipped the rod round the branch with the line still streaming off the spool, and waded on until I was standing at the mouth of the feeder stream. Now I wouldn't have to play the fish from the wrong side of a willow tree.

A huge tail had shown above the surface as the carp charged away, so I was fairly sure I'd hooked the rowing boat. Now, as I increased pressure, he answered me with a tremendous burst of power, making a tail-swipe that flattened out all the ripples in an area ten yards square. The explosive splash was heard (I later discovered) right at the other end of the pool. He was almost under the willows on the far bank, but with the line chiming near its breaking point, I swung him clear.

I began to whistle loudly for help, but there was no answer. The rats must be asleep, I thought.

The carp changed direction and made the move I'd feared most, heading back across the shallows towards the big willow branch in the '35' pitch. I saw a bow wave bulge suddenly upwards as he accelerated towards it. I piled on the pressure and the sidestrain swung him round towards me, so that he was now pointing at an even more dangerous snag – that submerged willow where we'd first made contact. I felt the bend going out of the rod as he came steadily towards me. There was no alternative but to suddenly cram on pressure again, hoping he would think I *wanted* him under the tree. He stopped dead and then, with another tumultuous splash, turned in his tracks and headed back down the pool.

I let him go, but he didn't retreat far enough and I had to ease off to a barely taut line. But he insisted on hanging dangerously close to the willow, so I picked up some water-logged branches and threw them at him. He wasn't impressed and wouldn't shift until I let the line fall absolutely slack, then he moved back along the margins until he was nearing the willow, forty yards away, and I had to tighten up and hold him hard. He stubbornly refused, though, to come out into the open water.

I began to shout and eventually John answered me.

'Bring a net!' I yelled.

'Where are you?'

'Up at the top of the shallows.'

John came crashing and thumping along the overgrown west bank, rounded the top of the pool, splashed across the feeder stream and appeared through the trees behind me, puffing, bedraggled and dripping with muddy water. He waded out next to me, but realised the water was too shallow to net a big fish and so squelched onwards through the silt for another few yards.

Suddenly, I felt the carp heading out into the pool again and saw a wave cleaving through the grey ripples. Without a sound or a word Barry had come up under the willows and actually climbed into the half-submerged tree, causing the fish to take flight.

I steered the carp towards us and Barry had a good view of it as it ploughed past him. He said it was the Bishop, but I thought he was joking and laughed – nervously.

'It's a big fish,' said John, as a wave approached him.

A great black back rose higher and higher in the water; then everything stopped. The fish had grounded itself just ten feet from the net.

I tried to drag it a little nearer, but it wallowed round until it was broadside on and I couldn't budge it. John, sinking waist deep into the silt, inched forward and began to slide the net under the fish. I had visions of the mesh catching the line and winced, saying, 'Careful, I don't want him to thrash about now!' He pushed the net until its frame had enclosed the bulk of the carp, then he began to lift. For a moment nothing happened – he stuck, straining, and the mesh wasn't rising up.

'Lift! Lift it!' shouted Barry from the willow.

John heaved and there was a sudden eruption of mud and water. The bend went abruptly out of the rod and I thought for a moment that the fish had gone, but it was there, hammocked in the folds of the big net with a load of mud, scum and weed.

'Bite the line, John,' I said, turning for the shore.

'You must be joking,' he said, 'I can't move!'

Splodging through the ooze and taking his arm I helped him to heave and wrest himself free. Then we began stumbling back to the bank, half falling, staggering under the weight that was in the net.

Barry came hurrying across the marshy field and helped us carry our load through the edge of the trees. He looked at the carp as we lowered it into the wet grass. It was difficult to see it *was* a carp – it looked like a black pig that had been rolling in the mud. He estimated the weight. 'Fifty-three pounds.' There was no emotion in his voice at all.

I can't remember what I was saying, nor what I was thinking. I'd known, as soon as John lifted, that we'd got a monster, a new record, but I can't recall exactly what was in my mind.

I carefully unhooked it, which was tricky as the hold was firmly in the leather-like bottom lip, then I ran for the spring balance and a pan of water to wash the silty flanks. We cleaned off the mud and the carp was revealed in all its glory. My heart gave another lift as I realised that it was not only gigantic, it was also a beautiful specimen. Sleek and bright. Richly coloured – purple, ochre, chestnut, amber. It was tremendously broad and deep, but it wasn't gross ($36\frac{1}{2} \times 34\frac{1}{2}$ inches).

Gently, we slid the carp into a capacious sling and hoisted it onto the balance. The pointer on the dial swung round and stopped, quiveringly, at $51\frac{3}{4}$ lbs. Deducting the weight of the sling left 51 lbs 6 oz. I gazed at the dial for a few moments, then sat back in the grass blinking. After all these years, all those lost fish, *all these diaries*, my line finally led to this great dark-coloured mirror-carp – a fish I'd caught seven years before, when it looked too old and weary to grow bigger – but it had grown; it had become a different fish altogether and was now the monster that I'd called the Bishop. We lay it reverently on the grass and stared at it.

The sky was almost dark, yet over in the west, under the edge of the cloud, a strip of blue showed clear and cool looking, and in its centre, a thin crescent moon. The breeze had long ceased, the evening was perfectly still.

There were a few moments' awed silence as we crouched round the carp. Then Barry broke the spell.

'Yatesy's cracked it!' he laughed.

I stood up and threw my hat across the field.

CHRISTOPHER YATES, *Casting at the Sun*, 1986

A Loch Alvie Pike

As soon as we had recovered from the consternation this accident occasioned, I ordered the boat to cruise about, for the chance of his taking me again, which I have known frequently to happen with pike, who are wonderfully bold and voracious: on the second trip, I saw a very large fish come at me, and, collecting my line, I felt I had him fairly hooked; but I feared he had run himself tight round some root, his weight seemed so dead: we rowed up, therefore, to the spot, when he soon convinced me he was at liberty, by running me so far into the lake, that I had not one inch of line more to give him. The servants, foreseeing the consequences of my situation, rowed, with great expedition, towards the fish, which now rose about seventy yards from us, an absolute wonder! I relied on my tackle, which I knew was in every respect excellent, as I had, in consequence of the large pike killed the day before, put on hooks and gimp, adjusted with great care; a precaution which would have been thought superfluous in London, as it certainly was for most lakes, though here, barely equal to my fish. After playing him for some time, I gave the rod to Captain Waller, that he might have the honour of landing him; for I thought him quite exhausted, when, to our surprise, we were again constrained to follow the monster nearly across this great lake, having the wind too much against us. The whole party were now in high blood, and the delightful *Ville de Paris* quite manageable; frequently he flew out of the water to such a height, that though I knew the uncommon strength of my tackle, I dreaded losing such an extraordinary fish, and the anxiety of our little crew was equal to mine. After about an hour and a quarter's play, however, we thought we might safely attempt to land him, which was done in the following manner: Newmarket, a lad so called from the place of his nativity, who had now come to assist, I ordered, with another servant, to strip and wade in as far as possible, which they readily did. In the meantime I took the landing-net, while Captain Waller, judiciously ascending the hill above, drew him gently towards us. He approached the shore very quietly, and we thought him quite safe, when, seeing himself surrounded by his enemies, he in an instant made a last desperate effort, shot into the deep again, and, in the exertion, threw one of the men on his back. His immense size was now very apparent; we proceeded with all due caution, and, being once more drawn towards land, I tried to get his head into the net, upon effecting which, the servants were ordered to seize his tail, and slide him on shore; I took all imaginable pains to accomplish this, but in vain, and began to think myself strangely awkward, when, at length, having got his snout in, I discovered that the hoop of the net, though adapted to very large pike, would admit no more than that part. He was, however, completely spent, and, in a few moments we landed him, a perfect monster! He was stabbed by my directions in the spinal marrow, with a large knife, which appeared to be the most humane manner of killing him, and I then ordered all the signals with the *sky-scrapers* to be hoisted; and the whoop re-echoed through the whole range of the Grampians. On opening his jaws to endeavour to take the hooks from him, which were both fast in his gorge, so dreadful a forest of teeth, or tusks, I think I never beheld: if I had not had a double link of gimp, with two swivels, the depth between his stomach and mouth would have made the former quite useless. His measurement, accurately taken, was *five feet four inches*, from eye to fork.

COLONEL THOMAS THORNTON, *A Sporting Tour Through the Northern Parts of England and Great Parts of the Highlands of Scotland*, 1804

A Singer Fishes a Chalk Stream

He was a $2\frac{3}{4}$-pounder, and he lived in the splash below the Beehive bridge and the Whitchurch road, where the horses and cows and engines stop for a drink and to cool their feet. He probably knew every inhabitant of the village by name, and he had a profound contempt for me in view of the number of futile shots I had had at him. He was a beautiful fat shiny fish, and I never could make out how he managed to keep in such perfect condition, for his waking hours seemed to be entirely spent in chasing marauders off his beat. Either he was a night-feeder or had some private store of his own; I never saw him burrow for a shrimp or rise at a fly until the time when he made his one fatal mistake. On this particular occasion he had gone down-stream in a fury at an engine, which had not only stopped on the bridge – a matter of indifference to him – but had sucked up water under his very nose, and then illegally chucked cinders on top of his head, and I had faded away with him down-stream with a conviction in my mind that I was somehow or other going to get him this time. He had a regular routine whenever he was disturbed. I knew it by heart. He would drop down about twenty yards to a certain spot by the weeds under the far bank and, when the obstruction was removed, would gently swim up as though butter wouldn't melt in his mouth and dash suddenly into his old beat, scattering the interlopers like rabbits. True to habit he paused for a time down-stream, and then began to move up. He was in an awful temper. He had lost all his serenity and made no pretence of having just arrived from the country. He kept lashing his tail and making short darts at imaginary foes, as though he were bayoneting sacks or punching the ball, working his way gradually up to the splash. I knew that my only chance was to take him on the move, so just before he got there I put a ginger-quill in front of his nose and a little to the right. He turned on it and snapped at it in a fury. I am convinced that nothing was farther from his thoughts than food at that moment, and that he simply meant to 'land one' on anything that came along. He certainly frightened the life out of me. He had been sacrosanct for so long and he was such a bully that I was almost afraid to take him out of the net when the time came. It took about ten minutes to land him, and when I got back to the splash there was another fish almost as big as himself already in his place.

HENRY PLUNKETT GREENE, *Where the Bright Waters Meet*,
1936

Doreen Davey Tells How She Caught the Biggest Spring Salmon Taken in Britain (59½ lbs, River Wye, March 1923)

I fished all day, as did my father, but nothing would respond. At about 5.30 p.m., having lost all hope and fully expecting to have to go home and record another blank day, I was making a few casts while waiting for my father to join me, and I hooked a fish on a small minnow I had put on for a change. I adopted the usual tactics, but the fish just swam about and did more or less what he liked! I believe it is even possible that he growled at me, but a cold north-east wind drowned the noise and so I did not hear it! He had several nice bits of exercise, but he never jumped or let me get a glimpse at him, and I had to do practically what he suggested, for I was unable to make any real impression on him.

After about twenty minutes of this my father came along, and I called to him to take a turn. He put on as much strain as possible, and gave me the rod back again in about ten minutes, saying it was my 'funeral' and so I ought to do the bulk of the work! So I went on again for about ten minutes and then we changed once more and my father did his best to make the fish really annoyed. We did not want him to go down the river any further, and he did not want to go up! We had been taken as far down the river as was safe.

Then we found that we could annoy the salmon best by walking him up the river with very hard pulling, and then running down with him. So we continued doing this as far as we were allowed to do it by the brute. Of course I was constantly varying the angle of the strain, so as to throw him off his balance, but he countered this by varying his position to meet what I was doing. And so it went on, and it grew darker as the twilight faded. I had to fight the daylight as well as the fish! Luckily the fish and the river were west of us and so we could see the line for quite a long time in the twilight.

Then, at last, about seven o'clock, he got quite cross, running down and across the river wallowing along the surface so that we could see him for the first time. Up to now we had only been guessing, but in the fading twilight we could see that it was really a monster reflected on the surface of the water. After this it soon got quite dark, and Jellis, father's chauffeur, had a brainwave! He has been with us for about twenty years, we call him John, and he has gaffed lots of salmon. He started a large fire on the river bank, and got some paraffin and paper from the hut ready for the crucial moment when the gaff should be required. It was a 'desperate fine battle', but the fish now had to do what we wanted him to do more often than when the fight started. We knew that if the hold was good and the tackle did not give out from the long continued strain, 'beauty would defeat the beast'! An onlooker, who had never caught a fish before, gave us quite an amusing turn. He thought it was about time to pour some of our precious paraffin on the fire, thinking we wanted more light. There was no one to stop him, and he did it. I can smell that funny odour of singed cloth even now!

Then my father swore! He was taking a spell at the rod, and I went to feed the fire. The tin of paraffin had been left near with the cork out, and I accidentally kicked it over! I saved enough for the final effort, however, and father quietened down! We were joined by a fishing neighbour, Mr Barret, and Mr Merton's gillie, Charley Donald, who had come to see what the trouble was about, having noticed the fire and the figures moving about. They brought four inches of candle with them – bless 'em!

The fish, by now, was making shorter journeys, and was 'jagging' badly – a most disquieting action to the angler, for it feels as though every jag must break something! The only safe thing to do, I think, is to keep the top of one's rod well up, and rather easy, allowing the top joint to do what it was intended to do.

The end came with almost dramatic suddenness. The fish took a few long lunges, rolled a bit, ran, and was pulled to the right towards the bank. Jellis crept quickly to the right, but the fish saw him cross the firelight for he jinked, ran back and round to my left. He was steered in, and, in a mix-up of splash and spray, the faithful John Jellis with the gaff and Charley Donald with his hands as much round the tail of the fish as he could get them managed to haul him out of the water. The fish was landed at 7.35, and was hooked at 5.40! One hour and fifty-five minutes of concentrated excitement and real hard work! We never gave him a moment's peace, and played him hard the whole time with the sort of strain that will kill a twenty-pound fish in seven or eight minutes . . .

Now with regard to 'the fool at the other end'! I started to fish when I was five years of age. That was with a bread pill for a roach in competition with my father. He used to beat me then. Now, as the Americans say, I have him cold! My father takes tens in boots, smokes Franklyn's Shag and has a catapult in his pocket except when he goes to London, which is not often!

From *The Fishing Gazette*, 31 March 1923

The Sahib Has Dinner While Fighting a Mahseer

Though, for some mysterious reason, I never had good sport in the early morning fishing, still I was up again next morning by sunrise, and we both tried the pool from the boat; I literally did nothing – did not even stir a fish; but A. landed one of 19 lbs. At 3 pm I went up the river and fished the head of a small pool, with a glorious stream running into it, close by some jutting rocks. Here I landed a 4-pounder and a 22-pounder with phantom and spoon. I then tried a stream a little higher up. I suspect the water was rather too heavy – at least, I stirred nothing; so having given the lower stream an hour's rest, I returned to it, and put on a natural bait. I soon hooked and landed one of 14 lbs, when I put on a fresh bait, intending to have a few more casts before it got dark, it being then a quarter to six, and rather cloudy. The bait had just come across the stream and was entering the backwater, when I felt a vigorous tug, and a monster rushed off down stream, with nearly 100 yards of line before I managed to stop him. Then he tried a run up stream to nearly opposite where I was standing, then down again, then opposite me again, but on quite the further side of the river, and there he sulked for the best part of an hour, all of which time I was keeping a very severe pull on him. Unfortunately, I was fishing from a point of rock, and on my left hand, down stream, was what is best described as 'a long bay' of dead water, 50 yards or so across, and between it and the stream was a bar, consisting of huge rocks rising to within 2 feet or 3 feet of the surface, but with intervals varying from 2 feet to 6 feet between them, so that getting below the fish was quite out of the question. At last I managed to move him, and he dashed down stream 70 or 80 yards, and sulked there. Now commenced my task. I soon found that merely keeping a steady pull on him had no effect, especially as he was now below me. The pressure I kept on him was so great that attempting to wind up line simply caused the line to sink between the coils already on the reel; so my only plan was to draw in an inch or so of the line with my hand, and then wind it up on the reel. By dint of perseverance I succeeded in getting him up to within 20 yards or so, and then not another inch could I gain; but I managed to rile him apparently, for off he rushed to the bottom of the stream again. Of course by this time it was pitch dark, or else I should have been tempted to try and effect a passage across the bar, with the almost certainty of going in over head and ears. As it was, prudence carried the day, and I sat down on a rock, put the butt of my rod between my legs, and lit a pipe. I then sent my fisherman off to camp, about two and a quarter miles over very rough ground, to order some dinner to be brought out, besides dry shoes and socks, and a great-coat. By the time the welcome sight of a lantern appeared it was near ten o'clock, and all the time I had been fighting for every inch of line. There was a splice in my line, and the struggle I had to get it on the reel is almost incredible. Time after time I felt it pass through my fingers and just reach the reel, when the fish would shake his head, and pull it half-way down the rod again.

After some little delay in collecting sticks and lighting the fire, I managed to make a very tolerable meal, keeping a tight hold on the line with one hand while I used the other for dinner purposes. Feeling much refreshed by my hasty repast, I devoted all my energies to my enemy with redoubled ardour. After one or two runs, I fancied there appeared to be something wrong with the reel, so, calling for a light, I examined it, and found to my discomfort that the two screws which connect the reel with the bar that was tied on to the rod were gone, and, of course, on the same side as the handle; the consequence was that the mere act of winding up caused the reel to gape very considerably at this opening. I tried various methods for remedying this mishap, such as getting my fisherman to hold it as firmly as possible in his hands while I wound up line, etc; but I found none of them so satisfactory as crossing my legs as I sat on the rock, and pressing the reel against my left knee. This answered tolerably well, but it was a somewhat awkward position to remain in for long. To make a long story short, however, about 2 a.m. I prevailed on my fish to cross the bar and have a swim in the deep, still pool. He gave two furious runs up and down, I luckily just preventing him from returning to the stream, and then I hauled him into a nice little shallow creek. The fisherman carefully handled him, and he was secured. I made my man carry the captive some yards from the water and deposit him in a safe place, and then a most pleasant sensation of triumph filled my heart, as by the light of the lantern I gloated over the splendid fish which had fought so bravely and pluckily for eight hours and a half. By this time it was 2.30 a.m., so my servants shouldered the fish, pots and pans, and we started off home, floundering about over the two miles and a half of boulders and shingle in pitch darkness, as the lantern had burned out. On arrival I, of course, routed up A., and we weighed the fish. He just turned the scale at 52 lbs, and was 4 feet 5 inches in length, which I must confess rather disappointed me, as I had landed in the previous year one of 57 lbs that had not given anything like the sport of this one.

'κ', *The Field*, October 1869

Taking a Record California Tuna

We could almost feel the premonitory crash; every nerve was tingling with expectation; then twenty feet from the bait there was a rush, the tunas had sighted them, and for several feet they raced along, for there were two (generally the case), hurling the water, arrows aimed at the baits. They had been deflected from the flier, and while the water swirled astern, the cry of two reels rose on the morning air. Vainly the leather thumb brakes were pushed upon the line; the latter slipped beneath it in feet and yards, then one reel became silent, the slack line telling the story of a flaw, or possibly too much thumb power, or a rusty leader. Despite every effort the tuna tore the line from the reel, the boatman backing with all his strength, endeavoring to force sternway on the boat before the line was fully exhausted. Five hundred feet had slipped away and the boat was sliding through the water at a rapid rate when suddenly the line slackened, the game was gone. No, the line was doubling in, and springing to my feet I witnessed a splendid movement of the gamy fish, one which I have never seen repeated. The tuna had turned and was literally charging the boat, *el toro* of the sea, coming on like a gleam of light, its sharp dorsal cutting the water. I reeled with all my speed, knowing that if I was caught on the turn with an unknown amount of slack line, the end might come; but fifty feet had not been gained before the tuna was within fifteen feet of the boat, then seeing me it turned and was away like an arrow from a bow. The big reel groaned as the crash came, but the brake was thrown off and my thumb played upon the leather pad with rare good luck, with just sufficient force to prevent overrunning. I gained enough line during this spectacular performance to stop the fish at three hundred feet, and held it by the thread of line while it towed the boat out to sea. A mile it took us, now plunging into the deep heart of the channel, to rise again with throbs which came on the tense line like heartbeats and found an echoing response. I gained ten feet to lose five, then would lose twenty to recover all, and more by vigorous 'pumping,' as the fish sulked and labored at the bottom of the sea. Suddenly I felt the line humming, vibrating like the cord of some musical instrument as the great fish rose, and as it reached the surface with a mighty swerve that gave the boatman active work to keep us astern to the game, it turned and again charged me. I rose, reeling rapidly as I watched the splendid trick; for trick it was, an attempt to take me unawares, running in on the line to break it if possible in the outrush. Again the fish turned hard by the boat and dashed away, this time inshore, towing us a mile or more, and within fifty feet of the rocks and their beard of kelp where I succeeded in turning it, and now gained so rapidly that I had the fish within a short distance of the boat. The boatman was fingering his gaff, when, with a magnificent rush, the tuna tore from the reel three hundred feet of line, undoing the strenuous labor of nearly two hours. The fish appeared to be seized with a frenzy. It rushed around the boat at long range, plunged deep into the blue water as though searching the bottom for some obstacle upon which to rub the line, then rising with a strange bounding motion which was imparted to the rod, again charged the boat.

For three hours I fought this superb fish, during which it towed the boat from near Avalon to Long Point, then several miles in and out, repeatedly charging, never giving signs of weakening, always bearing away with its full force. At the end of three hours I again brought the fish to within fifty feet of the boat, when it again broke away and towed us four miles south, occasionally stopping to rush in, and once carried us out into rough water, towing the boat stern first against the heavy seaway so rapidly that I expected to see her fill; but by sheer good luck I turned the fish, and at the end of four hours brought it to gaff. Slowly it circled the boat and for the first time we saw that the fish was what we had suspected, of unusual size. As it slowly swam along, its big back of a deep blue, its white belly occasionally gleaming as it turned, its finarettes flashing gold, it presented a magnificent spectacle, a compensation for the hardest struggle I had ever made. Nearer it came, then it was turned at the quarter, the boatman's gaff slid beneath, and the big hook struck home. It was a clever gaff, but with a tremendous surge the tuna sounded, shivering the handle in the gaffer's hands, and was away taking the wreck with it. Fortunately I stopped the rush, and a few moments later again had the tuna alongside. This time a new gaff held it, the gamy creature, never conquered, never discouraged, lashing the water, hurling it over us, a last defiance. A nervous gaffer would have lost the fish at this stage, but the boatman held fast, and stepping on the gunwale pressed it down to the water's edge and cleverly slid the quivering, struggling tuna into the boat, where it pounded the planking with such vigorous blows that the small craft trembled from stem to stern. As its fine proportions were revealed, I realized that we had landed the largest tuna ever taken with a rod. Its actual weight was about one hundred and eighty-seven pounds; its scale record weight on shore after bleeding was one hundred and eighty-three pounds; its length was six feet four inches.

CHARLES HOLDER, *The Big Game Fishes of the United States,*
1903

CHAPTER SEVEN

The Dangers of Fishing

*T*his being, on the face of it, about as peaceable a sport as you could find, safe for all ages from eight to eighty, capable of reducing the most inquiring mind to the happy indifference of a turnip, it is hard to talk seriously about its dangers.

Yet, as this and the following chapter reveal, it is a sport replete with hidden hazards. The risks from the fish themselves we shall come to in the next chapter. But among the obvious dangers there is, firstly, the risk from the water itself. Every year, Farlow's, the fishing-tackle shop in Pall Mall, loses a couple of customers who have slipped while wading a river and drowned. At least, that's what the manager claimed last year. I recall that he was trying to sell me a pair of inflatable braces at the time.

Then there is the danger from the tackle. As several owners of carbon-fibre fishing poles have discovered to their cost, when balanced on the shoulder they are so light to carry that you don't realize how long they are until you walk under a high-voltage power line, when you also discover how well they conduct electricity. No one but a fool tries to cast a big salmon fly into a flukey wind without wearing glasses. In the case of my friend Richard, who last summer drove a double hooked Thunder-and-Lighting through his chin, a helmet and visor might be a good idea.

Then there are the dangers on the bank. On Highland streams you may slip down gorges. On meandering floodplains the banks collapse. For some reason farmers think riverbank fields quite the best place to keep their bulls. It is not true, either, that there are no adders north of Inverness. There are, and they love basking in the sunshine in the sort of place you're likely to put your hand when trying to scramble out of the gorge into which you have slid.

And I haven't even mentioned the dangers of obsession, which merely begin with incipient bankruptcy.

Encounter with a Swordfish on the River Usk – 1870

Having creeled the sewin, we sauntered down towards Pont Faen. Just before reaching the private water above the bridge, we met the hero of this chapter. It had started to rain hard, and, since I have permission to fish Mrs Griffiths' stretch, we were going to pass through and regain the road. But the sight before us made us halt abruptly.

He sat on a little canvas stool in the pouring rain, a sodden knitted woollen cap on his head and a cheap rod made from a tubular steel aerial in his hand. He was wearing a gas cape and gum boots. He was gazing at the water with a rapt, intense expression, much too engrossed in his fishing to notice us. I coughed gently, and he looked up.

'My goodness, it's raining!' he exclaimed; and then, 'Good morning.'

We passed the time of day, and showed him our sewin.

My brother-in-law said, 'I caught that one, as a matter of fact. I'm only a beginner, but I must say fishing is extremely interesting. I think I'll buy a rod and fish regularly.'

The stranger said, 'Do you know, I'm a beginner, too.'

That was quite obvious to me, but I took a back seat while this man and my brother-in-law exchanged confidences. I looked at the man's rod, and saw that he was fishing with a thin nylon line. When he reeled it in I noticed that he was using a maggot as bait, rather inefficiently impaled on a No. 12 eyed hook. I showed him how to attach the maggot properly.

'Thank you,' he said, 'but I think I'll walk along with you, if you're going down to the bridge. I've left my car there, and my sandwiches.'

So we went along together, and as we strolled, the rain ceased, and the stranger told us his story.

His name was Peterson, and he lived in Surrey. Shortly before coming away on holiday, he decided that he might amuse himself by doing a little fishing, so he bought the aerial rod and a few odds and ends of tackle. The man in the tackle shop told him that maggots were a very good all-round bait. Peterson went to the Thames the week-end before his holiday started, put on a maggot and dropped it in. A few minutes later he had caught a large chub. That started the rot.

He and his family had booked rooms at a cottage in a remote village. The first night there, he had slept rather badly, and had got up at first light. Taking his rod, he had gone out to a little stream and caught a trout in ten seconds. Since that first morning, he told us, he had been fishing almost without interruption for three weeks. He would start before breakfast near the cottage; and after breakfast he would take the car and fish down the Gwyrfai, arriving home at midnight or thereabouts.

My brother-in-law looked a little doubtful.

'But what do your family think about this?' he asked.

Peterson waved an airy hand. 'Oh,' he said, 'I buy them plenty of wool. They just sit about and knit. They can't do much else because I've got the car, can they?'

'But what do they say?'

'Oh, nothing much,' said Peterson. 'I don't see them very often, you know. They're asleep when I get up, and asleep when I come back. I just leave them plenty of wool. My uncle keeps a wool shop near here.'

'What are they knitting?' asked my brother-in-law. 'Bedspreads?'

'Certainly not,' replied Peterson. 'Useful things. Warm pullovers: it gets chilly on the river at night. Thick socks to wear with gum boots. Caps like this one I'm wearing.'

We talked a little while longer, and Peterson asked us to give his regards to his uncle in the wool shop. I gave Peterson a fly, and advised him to buy some plastic garden line in Boots, stretch each end of it in a deep freeze box, and make himself a double-tapered line. I had no qualms about Peterson. He would learn, and would make a good fisherman by and by.

'You know,' said my brother-in-law, as we drove home. 'That man has had his lot. If that's what fishing can do to you, I don't think I'll buy that rod after all!'

Just how far Peterson had 'had his lot' we discovered when we called at the wool shop to see the uncle. He told us that Peterson had come to Wales on a fortnight's holiday. He ought to have been back in Surrey the previous week, but had stayed on. Fishing had got him, I fear: the angling fever was running in his blood, brightening his eyes and sharpening his senses, teaching him for the first time how to live in the moment, utterly absorbed in the task in hand. While the first onset raged, Peterson was mad indeed with a very pleasant sort of madness. The man who is discovering fishing counts the world well lost. Let the boss wait; let the hectares of knitting accumulate; who cares?

W.H. CANAWAY, *A Snowdon Stream*, 1958

An Age-old Complaint

Fishing, if I a fisher may protest,
Of pleasures in the sweetest, of sports the best,
Of exercises the most excellent.
Of recreations the most innocent.
But now the sport is marde, and wott ye why?
Fishes decrease, and fishers multiply.

THOMAS BASTARD, *Chrestoleros*, 1598

The Delights of Adversity

Fishing is a real test of character. Your spirits are either on top of a mountain or in the depths of a pit, with certain dead-levels of boredom and commonplace, supposing your soul craves for poundage alone. But there are many sufferings and humiliations outside the orthodox annoyances of the atrocious British climate: the fly in the small of your back which you have to undress yourself to get at; the broken Thermos bottle; the disintegrated lunch, bulls, wasps' nests, moor-hens at the wrong moment, cockchafers in your eye, the other man round the corner at the very spot you have been working up to all the morning, the cast which doubles back, the matches which you have left at home and, worst of all, water in your waders. Of all the maddening things the worst is falling into the water. I have fallen into the Spey three times – near the bank each time, fortunately, for the Spey is in such a hurry to get you to the sea that it does not give you any time to stop and think. In fact, I made such a habit of it that I gave up wearing my watch and left it at home. I was not much the worse for it except for badly damaging one of my fingers in an attempt to link up with Mother Earth, but to have your tobacco and cigarettes made into a wet mush and to feel the icy water trickle gradually from your waist to your toes is enough to bolshevise a saint, especially as it means either walking home a couple of miles to change your things or inviting double pneumonia. The wonder is that you can wade in the Spey at all. It runs like a mill-race, and the bottom is covered with rocks varying in size from a parched pea to a Roman encampment and in shape from a marble to a cubist portrait. At low water these are covered with slime, and a limpet or an anemone would slide about on them as on roller-skates. In view of the precariousness of the foothold and the enthusiasm of the water, the Spey wader should be equipped with a Gieve waistcoat, an air-balloon, and a wire hawser attached to a ghillie or a derrick, on shore, and should have a portable hot-coffee machine keeping pace with him on the bank with a spare set of clothes in the oven. As it is, he has to put up with a pole with which to prod the immediate future, and which at one moment runs up against the rock of Gibraltar and the next descends into the bowels of Vesuvius.

HENRY PLUNKETT GREENE, *Where the Bright Waters Meet*, 1936

A Catechism of Dangers and Defences

A BULL

This is one of the worst of dangers. We have known even experienced hunters of lions, rhinoceroses, grizzly bears, and other formidable fauna to go with timid steps past the haunt of an English bull. The best remedy for a bull is undoubtedly a hedge of the largest size and thorniest texture. Screened by this, the angler may have a fairly easy mind.

A deep and wide dyke on the hither side of the animal is also in some sort a protection. But it must never be forgotten that bulls can and do swim and wade across streams, sometimes on very flimsy pretexts. Any dyke, therefore, chosen as a protection should be bridged by a single plank. The exact middle of this is a point of comparative safety. Should the bull be able to get too close to it, the plank may be employed as a means of swift passage from bank to bank. As the bull takes the slower route by water, the angler has a distinct advantage. If the bull shows a preference for the plank, presumably the angler then takes the other route. Or else he waits in the middle of the plank and adroitly pushes the animal off. But the contingency is one of which we have no experience.

Should there be no plank, a heap of stones of assorted sizes on the angler's bank is to be desired, and also a tree which can be easily climbed. If the stones fail to calm the animal, you must take refuge in the tree. You will probably be able to come down after nightfall and slip unostentatiously away.

It sometimes happens that you come upon a bull suddenly and without a moment for thought or plan. Then you must depend on the moral dignity of man, on a haughty brow, and a flashing eye. Do not, however, presume on your manifest superiority. Behave as one gentleman to another. If the bull is right-minded he will move slowly away. If not, if he shows a disposition to contest your passage, you must advance upon him, shouting in a great and terrible voice. If this has no effect, you are obviously in a tight place, and there is but one thing to do. Lie down at once and pretend to be dead. We are informed that bulls do not attack dead persons. Should our information be incorrect, we can only express our regret.

Other methods of managing a bull are: (1) beating him with an iron bar till he repents his sins; (2) taking him by the horns and wrestling with him till you have him at your mercy; (3) twisting his tail till he is calm. It is open to you to select either of these plans if you prefer them to the pretence of death, which, after all, lacks some of the more heroic qualities.

Cows, bullocks, heifers, and calves may be considered as milder varieties of bull. Deference is, as a rule, all that they demand. But it occasionally happens that you have to deal with a charging herd. You may (1) charge back, whooping; (2) take to the river; (3)

pretend to be dead; (4) throw stones or climb a tree (given the necessary facilities). In the case of calves, we act in the manly way suggested first.

A DOG

Stones are here the specific. Nine dogs out of ten have a wholesome fear of the hurt that flies from a distance. The tenth dog is the trouble. When you meet him you may (1) give him your luncheon, murmuring 'Was he, then? A good old fellow! Nice old boy, then!' (2) take your bite, and trust to getting substantial damages out of the dog's owner; (3) catch the dog's head in your landing-net, and waltz round with him till the matter is settled one way or the other. We do not know which way settlement usually goes.

A WASP

Take off your hat and beat with it till the wasp is dead or you are stung. If there are two or three wasps, walk swiftly away to another place. These creatures are, happily, infirm of purpose and do not follow very far. If you come upon a nest, walk away twice as swiftly, whirling your hat as you go.

THUNDER AND LIGHTNING

It is not necessary to take any precautions against thunder which is quite harmless, being all bark and no bite. Lightning, however, is another matter, for fishing rod is nothing more or less than an invitation to it. We are not in a position to give statistics as to the number of anglers who have been abolished by lightning; but no doubt there are such statistics. Nor, unfortunately, are we able to give instructions as to warding off attack. It would be well to consult an electrician.

In the event of the electrician being far away and the lightning close at hand, we should advise the angler: (1), to spike his rod 100 yards from the river, and leave it; (2), to find a portion of the river not more than 3 ft. deep and lie down in it, immersing all but his nose and eyes; (3), to duck his head when a flash comes. He should thus be able to escape notice.

THE DANGERS OF FISHING

All snakes are not adders, but against this consoling fact has to be set the consideration that all adders are snakes. This should induce the angler to order his goings with great care, and to examine bits of stick, coiling ivy roots, and the like, before he places his hand on them. Beyond this we do not think any elaborate precautions are required. Snakes are of a retiring disposition. Let them retire.

ANTS
The industrious ant busies itself in making fair-seeming seats for anglers, but these seats, like those of the new art, are for show, not for use. Mr Chesterton's example, 'when I find a country seat, I sit in it,' admirable in all other respects, should not be held to apply to those seats mentioned. A few minutes of rest and meditation are dearly purchased at the expense of a frantic undressing in the teeth of an unsympathetic east wind. And the ants do not mind the east wind. The seats that they provide should be left to sluggards.

VAGROM MEN
Anglers do not commonly have their throats cut by bandits and other undisciplined folk, but of course it may occur to them that their traditional mildness and amiability expose them to dangers which do not beset their brethren of the gun, especially in Wales and other outlandish parts where strangers of very hirsute countenance are apt to appear suddenly in lonely places. A crag-like face fringed with red hair, framed in the gap of a hedge or projected over a bush, is, quite reasonably, a matter for apprehension.

But let the angler take heart and also counsel from the old Greek philosopher with his 'Know thyself'. If he studies himself in a glass just before setting out, he will soon see that he has no cause for alarm. Even the face and form of a troglodyte could not hope to vie in terrifying qualities with the be-brogued, be-wadered, be-mackintoshed, be-hatted apparition that the glass reveals. Such a figure seems ripe for the fiercest deeds, and it is almost incredible that the boldest vagabond should wish to provoke its latent ferocity.

H.T. SHERINGHAM, *Fishing, A Diagnosis*, 1914

The Confessions of a Duffer

Some men are born duffers; others, unlike persons of genius, become so by an infinite capacity for not taking pains. Others, again, among whom I would rank myself, combine both these elements of incompetence. Nature, that made me enthusiastically fond of fishing, gave me thumbs for fingers, short-sighted eyes, indolence, carelessness, and a temper which (usually sweet and angelic) is goaded to madness by the laws of matter and of gravitation. For example: when another man is caught up in a branch he disengages his fly; I jerk at it till something breaks. As for carelessness, in boyhood I fished, by preference, with doubtful gut and knots ill-tied; it made the risk greater, and increased the excitement if one did hook a trout. I can't keep a fly-book. I stuff the flies into my pockets at random, or stick them into the leaves of a novel, or bestow them in the lining of my hat or the case of my rods. Never, till 1890, in all my days did I possess a landing-net. If I can drag a fish up a bank, or over the gravel, well; if not, he goes on his way rejoicing. On the Test I thought it seemly to carry a landing-net. It had a hinge, and doubled up. I put the handle through a buttonhole of my coat: I saw a big fish rising, I put a dry fly over him; the idiot took it. Up stream he ran, then down stream, then he yielded to the rod and came near me. I tried to unship my landing-net from my buttonhole. Vain labour! I twisted and turned the handle, it would not budge. Finally, I stooped, and attempted to ladle the trout out with the short net; but he broke the gut, and went off. A landing-net is a tedious thing to carry, so is a creel, and a creel is, to me, a superfluity. There is never anything to put in it. If I do catch a trout, I lay him under a big stone, cover him with leaves, and never find him again. I often break my top joint; so, as I never carry string, I splice it with a bit of the line, which I bite off, for I really cannot be troubled with scissors and I always lose my knife. When a phantom minnow sticks in my clothes, I snap the gut off, and put on another, so that when I reach home I look as if a shoal of fierce minnows had attacked me and hung on like leeches. When a boy, I was – once or twice – a bait-fisher, but I never carried worms in box or bag. I found them under big stones, or in the field, wherever I had the luck. I never tie nor otherwise fasten the joints of my rod;

they often slip out of the sockets and splash into the water. Mr Hardy, however, has invented a joint-fastening which never slips. On the other hand, by letting the joint rust, you may find it difficult to take down your rod. When I see a trout rising, I always cast so as to get hung up, and I frighten him as I disengage my hook. I invariably fall in and get half-drowned when I wade, there being an insufficiency of nails in the soles of my brogues. My waders let in water, too, and when I go out to fish I usually leave either my reel, or my flies, or my rod, at home. Perhaps no other man's average of lost flies in proportion to taken trout was ever so great as mine. I lose plenty, by striking furiously, after a series of short rises, and breaking the gut, with which the fish swims away. As to dressing a fly, one would sooner think of dressing a dinner. The result of the fly-dressing would resemble a small blacking-brush, perhaps, but nothing entomological.

Then why, a persevering reader may ask, do I fish? Well, it is stronger than myself, the love of fishing; perhaps it is an inherited instinct, without the inherited power. I may have had a fishing ancestor who bequeathed to me the passion without the art. My vocation is fixed, and I have fished to little purpose all my days. Not for salmon, an almost fabulous and yet a stupid fish, which must be moved with a rod like a weaver's beam. The trout is more delicate and dainty – not the sea-trout, which any man, woman, or child can capture, but the yellow trout in clear water.

A few rises are almost all I ask for: to catch more than half a dozen fish does not fall to my lot twice a year. . . . My ambition is as great as my skill is feeble; to capture big trout with the dry fly in the Test, that would content me, and nothing under that. But I can't see the natural fly on the water; I cannot see my own fly,

Let it sink or let it swim.

I often don't see the trout rise to me, if he is such a fool as to rise; and I can't strike in time when I do see him. Besides, I am unteachable to tie any of the orthodox knots in the gut; it takes me half an hour to get the gut through one of these newfangled iron eyes, and, when it is through, I knot it any way. The 'jam' knot is a name to me, and no more. That, perhaps, is why the hooks crack off so merrily. Then, if I do spot a rising trout, and if he does not spot me as I crawl like the serpent towards him, my fly always fixes in a nettle, a haycock, a rose-bush, or what not, behind me. I undo it, or break it, and put up another, make a cast, and, 'plop,' all the line falls in with a splash that would frighten a crocodile. The fish's big black fin goes cutting the stream above, and there is a *sauve qui peut* of trout in all directions.

I once did manage to make a cast correctly: the fly went over the fish's nose; he rose; I hooked him, and he was a great silly brute of a grayling. The grayling is the deadest-hearted and the foolishest-headed fish that swims. I would as lief catch a perch or an eel as a grayling. This is the worst of it – this ambition of the duffer's, this desire for perfection . . . I know it all, I deplore it, I regret the evils of ambition; but *c'est plus fort que moi*. If there is a trout rising well under the pendant boughs that trail in the water, if there is a brake of briars behind me, a strong wind down stream, for that trout, in that impregnable situation, I am impelled to fish. If I raise him I strike, miss him, catch up in his tree, swish the cast off into the briars, break my top, break my heart, but – that is the humour of it. The passion, or instinct, being in all senses blind, must no doubt be hereditary. It is full of sorrow and bitterness and hope deferred, and entails the mockery of friends, especially of the fair. But I would as soon lay down a love of books as a love of fishing.

Success with pen or rod may be beyond one, but there is the pleasure of the pursuit, the rapture of endeavour, the delight of an impossible chase, the joys of nature – sky, trees, brooks, and birds. Happiness in these things is the legacy to us of the barbarian. Man in the future will enjoy bricks, asphalte, fog, machinery, 'society,' even picture galleries, as many men and most women do already. We are fortunate who inherit the older, not 'the new spirit' – we who, skilled or unskilled, follow in the steps of our father, Izaak, by streams less clear, indeed, and in meadows less fragrant, than his. Still, they are meadows and streams, not wholly dispeopled yet of birds and trout; nor can any defect of art, nor certainty of laborious disappointment, keep us from the waterside when April comes.

Next to being an expert, it is well to be a contented duffer: a man who would fish if he could, and who will pleasure himself by flicking off his flies, and dreaming of impossible trout, and smoking among the sedges Hope's enchanted cigarettes. Next time we shall be more skilled, more fortunate. Next time!

ANDREW LANG, *Angling Sketches*, 1891

Three Letters to The Field

SIR, I have caught many things with my fly. A volume would not record the things inanimate, but two swifts taken in mid-air, several sparrows neatly picked my Mayfly off the water, and one day I was not quite quick enough to snatch it out of the way of a duck. Yesterday I was out for bigger game. I caught a cow. Throwing back for a longish forward cast, I felt a hitch, turned round, and gave a slight tuck to see where the fly was, when up went the tail of a cow about fifteen yards distant, and away she galloped at full speed. My fly was firmly fixed to her tail. Of course something had to give, and it was not the cow, nor did the hook come away.

E.C. Gloucestershire.

SIR, The entertaining article of June 2 reminds me of an astonishing day with the rod ten or eleven summers ago, on the Rede in Northumberland. In the course of a morning's fishing with fly and minnow, I landed a fourteen-ounce brown trout on March Brown, a stuffed badger and a copy of Mrs Beeton's cookery book, dated 1911, the latter two both on a small silver Devon.

The badger took some landing, but once it was on the bank it soon dried out and gave us the background for many droll practical jokes. *Mrs Beeton* came to hand very easily, with hardly a struggle, and rests on my shelves to this day, rather curled, but completely legible.

D.L. Tyne and Wear.

SIR, Some years before the war, one of my former commanding officers in India was fishing in one of the jungle areas of the Doon valley when his fly suddenly became snagged on the backward cast. Turning round to find out why, he was surprised to see that it was firmly hooked to the ear of a fully-grown tigress, which had been curiously watching his activities from a clump of jungle grass.

Luckily the tigress was even more alarmed than he was and with a roar took to the water. Before the line broke the Colonel found himself involuntarily playing her like an enormous fish.

H.V.R. Devon

MERRILY HARPUR, from *Pig Overboard!*, 1984

Swept Away in the Tay

There was a certain amount of comparatively quiet water near the bank, into which I could possibly wade about fifteen yards, establish myself behind the cover of a good-sized rock, and cast a fishable bait. The current passing the end of this rock was very strong and definitely forbidding. Davy cut me a strong wading-stick, and with my waders as firmly braced as myself I made my way steadily towards the rock and gained some precarious cover behind it. The current felt a great deal stronger than I had expected, and I wondered if it would not be wiser to return immediately. Ah weel! Here I was with an inviting 'Tay Rose' – (a pink sprat of Davy's special dyeing which I had most appropriately christened the previous autumn in honour of its persistent success) – waiting for baptism and the chance of a lively engagement. I spent half an hour behind the rock, not exactly enjoying myself for there was a certain anxiety prevailing regarding my safety and the strain of exercising special care. Yet, with all my care and watchfulness I had moved, unconsciously, an inch at a time, and in the manner one often does when trying to get the lure that little bit farther out, I was at the extreme edge of the boulder, but my foothold was firm against the ledge of a rock below. It was the suction effect of the water passing me that drew my attention to the fact that I had been rather venturesome.

Another cast and I'll away, I thought, but the one already in the water was doing its work. I was into a fish. I did not lift my foot, but just eased the pressure on it the slightest fraction, with the intention of withdrawing well behind the boulder again for safer cover to play the fish. In a split second the undercurrent must have caught my foot, and down I went into the mad, turbulent rush of wild seething foam.

Fortunately, I knew from a previous and precautionary survey that if I did fall in at this point the current might not carry me into the main stream, but should within a quarter of a mile or so, below the Black Stanes, bring me towards the left bank where the water under most conditions forms a strong eddy. Such were my thoughts as I tossed and tumbled along with rod firmly gripped in my right hand – another precautionary measure, based on other experiences, which can be the means of saving one's life when you realise that a good heavy Kingfisher line can catch up and has the strength to hold a man. Apart from this there is, somehow, an incentive to keep your hands and head up while you grip the rod. The butt of a heavy salmon-rod is also strong enough to hold you should it jam broadside between two objects. True, these are just chances, and very remote ones, but they *are* chances.

There was only one thing to do in such an emergency, and that was to keep calm, make no attempt to struggle or swim, and let the current carry me down naturally, thereby conserving every ounce of energy against the time when I should reach easier water and have an opportunity to swim or crawl ashore. Obviously, too, one does not attempt such wading unless he is a strong swimmer and accustomed to heavy waters. I found my full waders no disadvantage in a fast-moving current, they kept my legs down and my torso up. Through the Cradle I went at a speed that alarmed me considerably, and I began to feel the bumps and buffetings as I tumbled among the rapids leading from Clocksden Head. I have a vivid recollection of seeing Davy scrambling along the bank with a gaff in his hand. That gaff! Even in such a predicament the picture flashed through my mind of an incident when Davy forgot to remove the protecting cork and nearly lost me a grand fish. I wondered, too, what his Gaelic mutterings were as he tried to keep up with the speed of the rapids on his uneven rock- and timber-strewn path. I left him behind.

Once on the way I got a complete 'blackout' having struck my head against something. In due course I reached the tail of the Cradle, but was still too far into the stream to make for the bank. I knew, too, that if I didn't turn bankwards during the next hundred yards or so, near the Maggot, there would be nothing for it but the main stream into Upper Stobhall and every prospect of another good wife being widowed.

By this time I was feeling the strain of the buffeting to which I had been subjected, and began to wonder if I had strength enough to make for the bank as I felt myself being whirled steadily into the eddy. I honestly doubt whether I had enough to lift a teacup, but there is a certain reserve of strength that can be called upon in extreme emergency, *if* the will-power and determination to live holds out. I had experienced it all before, and met other men who were almost afraid to speak of it. It is something that gives that impetus to defy the challenge to capitulation. It is a mysterious power that we know nothing about until extreme danger compels us to call upon it. Maybe one takes God more seriously in such circumstances. No human being could convince me with any explanation, since these are incidents that concern just God and the man in trouble.

Suddenly I felt my feet touch bottom. It was only a small plateau which led to a deepish gulf, and where I lost my foothold again, but not before I had been able to give myself a push forward towards the bank and over the narrow gulf. I certainly felt the weight of my full waders in this easier water, and how I covered that twenty yards or so to the bank is something I know nothing about, but I was safely ashore, with the rod-butt resting at my feet, when Davy arrived.

Davy was certainly scared. A gash in my scalp was bleeding most profusely over my face. It was really nothing serious, but no doubt its colourful effects alarmed Davy, who confessed that he thought my head was battered to a pulp.

V. CARRON WELLINGTON, *The Adventures of a Sporting Angler*

A Fearless Test of the Dangers of Waders

Dear Sir,
FISHING TROUSERS. – I always wear these in preference to stockings, but have been somewhat alarmed of late by my friends suggesting that if I were suddenly to slip off a rock into deep water with them on, I must be infallibly drowned; that it did not matter

how good a swimmer one might be, there was no hope of safety. The confined air in the trousers would cause one's legs to stick up almost out of the water, while the head would be kept down. The thought of such a catastrophe was most unpleasant, so I resolved to try the experiment, having a boat at hand in case of need. I therefore put on the trousers, reeving the string at top as usual round my waist, and dived head foremost into deep water. The result agreeably surprised me, for I found that my legs were gently buoyed up in a horizontal position near the surface of the water, while my head was well above it, and I could use my arms freely in swimming.

I swam with the greatest ease for about fifty yards, and it was not for some minutes, and until the water had found its way between the reeving string and my body into the trousers, that I felt any inconvenience from having them on. My legs then began to get heavy, and more depressed in the water, but not so as to prevent my swimming easily.

I am convinced, therefore, that there is no danger in using fishing trousers; on the contrary, if reeved pretty closely at the top, they will act for the first five minutes positively as life buoys. It is not until after they fill with water that they become dangerous. To prevent this, therefore, as long as possible, it is in all cases most advisable to reeve the trousers tightly round the body, you can thus confine the air and exclude the water.

The same may be said of fishing stockings and wading boots; a reeving string round the thigh would in these have the same beneficial effect.

Yours faithfully,
John Lloyd

Letter to *The Field*, 7 September 1867

More on the Dangers of Wading

For my part, during the summer season, when the waters are warm, I am in the constant habit of wading without any protection whatever, and I never feel the slightest inconvenience from it; but I will by no means take upon me to say that everybody could do it with the same impunity, as it is a well-known fact that many people of weakly constitution have entailed upon themselves a life of misery from rheumatism and other diseases, by indiscreetly exposing their legs and feet to wet. And, as the safer practice, it will be better for the angler to avoid, if possible, both wet legs and all waterproof contrivances whatever, and content himself with enjoying his sport as best he can, 'from mossy bank or pebbly shore.' And though his creel may not exhibit so many trophies of his skill, he will at least be free from the disagreeable prospect of being condemned to swallow bushels of Blair's pills, endure the perpetual scalding of mustard-plasters, and the necessity for calling in the aid of a Bath-chair for the remainder of his life.

A.S. MOFFAT, *The Secrets of Angling*, 1865

How to Revive a Drowned Angler

A bellows should be applied to one nostril, whilst the other nostril and the mouth are kept closed, and the lower end of the prominent part of the wind-pipe is pressed backward. The bellows is to be worked in this situation; and when the breast is swelled by it, the bellows should stop, and an assistant should press the belly upward to force the air out. The bellows should then be applied as before, and the belly again pressed; this process should be repeated twenty to thirty times in a minute, so as to imitate natural breathing as nearly as possible, as the trachea is always open through the glottis; air conveyed through the mouth, the nostrils being closed, would necessarily pass into the lungs. If the cartilages of the larynx (throat) be pressed against the vertebrae (bones of the neck) so as to close the aesophagus (gullet) and prevent the passage of air into the stomach, and at the same time the mouth and left nostril be closed, and the pipe of the bellows inserted into the right nostril be closed, the air will pass into the lungs through the wind-pipe, because that is the only opening through which it can pass; its passage into the oesophagus, or its egress through the mouth or left nostril being prevented in the manner above described.

If there be any signs of returning life, such as sighing, gasping, twitching, or any convulsive motions, beating of the heart, the return of the natural colour and warmth, opening a vein in the arm or external jugular of the neck, may prove beneficial; but the quantity of blood taken away should not be large. The throat should be tickled with a feather, in order to excite the propensity to vomit, and the nostrils also with a feather, snuff, or any other stimulant, so to provoke sneezing. A tea-spoonful of warm water may be administered now and then, in order to learn whether the power of swallowing be returned; and if it be, a table spoonful of warm wine, or brandy and water may be given with advantage; and not before, as the liquor might pass into the trachea before the power of swallowing returns. The other methods should be continued with ardour and perseverance for two hours or upwards, although there should not be the least symptom of life.

In the application of stimulants, electricity has been recommended; and when it can be easily procured, its exciting effects might be tried in aid of the means already recommended; but the electrical strokes should be given in a low degree, and gradually as well as cautiously increased.

T.F. SALTER, *The Angler's Guide*, 1815

J.R. Hartley Introduces Miss Craigie to Fishing

I had now to meet my side of the bargain and introduce Miss Craigie to the allure of angling. I sounded out her wishes and she suggested we should go down to the river one lunchtime with a picnic; and afterwards she'd watch me for a bit to see how it was done and then perhaps have 'a wee go' herself. I could hardly take exception to this – indeed it was something of a relief that she hadn't opted to attend the evening rise and expose me to an anxious walk home in the gloaming.

The day was fixed for a Sunday in June when I knew Mr Congleton was on duty and couldn't come spying on us. Not wishing to be seen leaving the school with Miss Craigie, I told her at the last minute that I had to dash into Winsham on my motor cycle. If she could set off with the picnic, I'd join her by the river. I let her see me speed away down the drive and turn out of the gates.

Then I stopped in a lay-by for ten minutes before coming back into the grounds.

Miss Craigie had arrived with the picnic. She spread out the rug under a tree and subsided like a languorous puncture on to the ground. As she unpacked the food, which in those days of rationing was a rare spread for two, I noticed uneasily that some exotica from Fortnum and Mason were included in the bill of fare; I hoped that Miss Craigie hadn't on my account made inroads into young Alexander Russell's food parcel which she had taken into safe keeping a day or two before.

'Majestic,' I said as we finished our meal.

'Did you like it?' she asked eagerly.

'Majestic,' I repeated.

I lay back with my head on my arms to endorse the impression of satisfaction. She made a sudden lunge towards me but I instinctively hunched my knees over my body and she went first bounce into the picnic basket.

I got to my feet to discourage a second attempt. 'Time for your fishing lesson,' I said, and began to set up my rod.

She watched me for a while in silence, her head on one side – whether in a consciously wistful pose or because she'd hurt her neck on the picnic basket, I couldn't be sure. Then she asked, 'How big are the fish?'

'Normally about a pound to a pound and a half.'

'That's titchy,' she said.

'It's not enormous,' I conceded, 'but we're not fishing for survival, we're pursuing the angler's art.'

I opened my fly box and went through the patterns for her: Black Gnat, Blue Dun to match the Medium Olive, Little Marryat to match Pale Watery, Red Palmer for the Cinnamon Sedge. I lectured her briefly on Caenis, the 'Angler's Curse', the tiny pale cream up-winged fly which trout love, but which is virtually impossible to represent on a hook.

She looked impressed.

'Did you tie those yourself?' she asked.

'Some of them.'

'Fiddly, aren't they?' she said.

Yes, I said, you had to concentrate.

'Which one are we going to use?'

'I think perhaps a Red Palmer.' I pointed to it. 'It's a traditional Axe fly.'

'Who's Red Palmer when he's at home?'

I explained that Red was in this context a shade rather than a Christian name, and that as far as I knew Palmer was a colonel.

'You really know about fishing, don't you?' she said admiringly.

With the rod set up, a conventional split-cane eight-and-a-half-footer, I attached my small Hardy Perfect reel and paid out the silk line, dressing it with grease to make it float. Then I tied on the gut cast, supple from being soaked in my cast wallet. Miss Craigie watched dutifully. Her neck seemed all right again.

'Not very like Highland dancing, is it?' she said.

Comments rose to my lips that would have hurt her feelings. I restrained myself and said with a smile, 'Less music.' Then I told her to stay where she could see what was happening and moved cautiously towards the bank.

Before too long I saw a fish rise towards the far side. He looked really solid. I pointed towards him for Miss Craigie's benefit and raised my finger to my lips. She acknowledged her excitement with a wave of the hand.

I cast, and he rose short to me. I remained kneeling, watching the water intently. Smack – up he came again. I raised my arm to alert Miss Craigie that this was action stations and flicked the Red Palmer in front of his nose. I had him. Though I say it myself, it was a passable demonstration of the dry fly art.

I was fishing with light tackle, and for all Miss Craigie's surprise at the 'titchiness' of the trout, these things are relative. He was evidently an exceptionally good fish, and though my light rod and my three-pound breaking strain cast were quite sufficient for my purpose, they weren't by any means a telegraph pole and a hawser. Besides, with Miss Craigie wearing the L plates behind me I wasn't going to take any chances.

He'd gone quite deep and made for the reeds. Once he wrapped me round them and I thought I'd lose him, but somehow I got back in contact and eased him clear. Only when I had him almost ready for the net did I look round to court Miss Craigie's approval. As I did so she flew past me like a giant blancmange and crashed unclothed into the river. A descending plume of water soaked my head and shoulders.

The fish quite soon regained the ascendancy as Miss Craigie joined in at its end of the line and began dragging me down the bank. With my rod bent double I implored her to give me some idea of what she thought she was doing. The question seemed only to amuse her.

It was now, just when I had fallen on my side and my line was festooned in huge loops all around me, that the headmaster, rod in hand, came strolling up the bank to join us. He looked at the undignified scene for a while without comment, possibly believing himself the victim of hallucination. Miss Craigie's bosom, bouncing like a cavalry ride past, was competing for his attention, but it was the fisherman in him that finally prevailed.

'Big Craigie?' he asked. 'Size 42?'

'J.R. HARTLEY', *Flyfishing*, 1991

Driven Mad by the Pursuit of Pike

Now there is nothing remarkable in seeing a rod and reel in Ireland, but these particular weapons made me open my eyes and mouth in amazement. The rod at its point was thick as my little finger, the reel not less than 8 inches in diameter and the line – shades of Izaak Walton! What a line was there. I have towed a canoe up the Thames with cord less thick.

I was on the point of enquiring into the particular uses of this remarkable tackle, when the door of the cabin opened and a short, wiry old man with deep set, piercing eyes, iron-grey hair and clad in a shabby suit of tweeds, came in wearily, bearing just such another rod and reel and a huge basket which I instinctively felt contained fish. He took no notice of me, but gasped out, in a voice which told of his exhausted condition: 'The steelyard, the steelyard!'

With trembling hands he opened the rush basket and turned out of it one of the largest pike I had ever seen. Mrs O'Day who seemed in no way surprised, produced an ancient rusty instrument and proceeded in a businesslike manner to weigh the fish. The old man's excitement while she did this was painful to witness.

'Is it? Is it?' he commenced.

'No, it isn't,' said Mrs O'Day calmly. 'He's 5 lb short.'

I was looking at the fish, but, hearing a groan, turned my eyes to the old fisherman and saw him lying on the floor of the shebeen. He had fainted.

'Poor ould man,' said Mrs O'Day. 'It's disappointed he is and weak too for devil a bit of food has he touched this day since yesterday. Undo his collar sir, and I'll mix him a timperance drink.'

And so her tongue ran on. Meanwhile the old fellow came to himself and sat up, but his eyes went at once to the pike, which still lay on the floor.

'Only 35 lb,' I heard him mutter to himself. 'But I will have him soon. I will have him soon.'

Mrs O'Day's 'timperance' drink was in the nature of an egg flip. It acted like charm on the old man, who five minutes after drinking it rose, kicked the fish to the side of the cabin and for the first time appeared to be aware that a stranger was in the shebeen. Mrs O'Day noticed the questioning look he cast at me.

'It's a gentleman who lost his way in the bog,' she said.

'Not fishing?' he asked rather anxiously.

'No, snipe shooting,' said I, and he seemed to me greatly relieved at the intelligence. Mrs O'Day now turned out the stew on to a large dish and apologised for having no plates, remarking that she was 'not used to the gentry'. We were both of us more or less famished and talked but little during the meal, after which, Mrs O'Day having provided us with a second edition of the 'timperance' drink, we drew the settle close to the peat fire, and commenced to chat over our pipes.

My new acquaintance, from what I could gather, was an Englishman who had lived for many years in Ireland and apparently passed his whole time in fishing. But I was able to tell him of certain modern methods of pike fishing of which he had heard nothing. By and by he began to get communicative and finally I ventured to ask him why the weighing of the pike had so disturbed him. Without hesitation he told me the following story.

'From a boy ... I was an enthusiastic fisherman, I need not trouble to tell you how I caught salmon in Norway, gudgeon in the Thames, trout in the Test, and enormous grayling in the

Hampshire Avon. I fished whichever and wherever I could and nothing, however large or however small, came amiss to me. But one thing I had never caught – a really large pike. Even in Sweden I never took one over 30 lb. This nettled me, for many were the tales I read of monsters, particularly in the Irish lakes.

'One morning I read in a sporting paper a letter from an Irishman – a tackle dealer so I afterwards ascertained – asking why English anglers did not come more over there. In the lakes in his neighbourhood there was fine pike fishing. Thirty-pounders were common, and they got a forty-pounder or two every season. Here was exactly the information I wanted. I told some friends about it, but they only smiled. I said I would catch a forty-pounder before long. They replied that there was no such thing as a forty-pounder, alive or stuffed. Well, the end of it was I made a bet that I would go to Ireland and before I returned I would catch a fish of that weight.'

I here interrupted his story to tell him of a strange coincidence. It was that very tacklemaker's letter which had first brought me to Ireland. 'But go on,' I said. 'Finish your story and then you shall have mine.'

'I began badly,' he continued, 'I wrote to the man for details of these loughs he mentioned and received a reply from his widow, he having died soon after writing the paragraph. From the poor woman I could get no information. She said she had no idea to which waters her husband referred; in fact, she knew of none. Then I put a letter of enquiry in the sporting papers and received many replies from persons, some of whom were possibly not altogether disinterested in the matter.'

'I have suffered in the same way myself,' I interjected. 'I came to Ireland armed with tackle such as would hold the largest pike that ever lived.' He continued, not noticing my interruption.

'At first I was hopeful. What tales they told me to be sure. There was one of a big pike caught in Lough Derg or, I should say, was killed by some workmen who were digging drains near the lake. The bishop of Killaloo was reputed to be fond of pike, and to him the fish was taken. It was so large that half its body dragged on the ground as two men carried it, slung on a pole, to the bishop's palace. When the bishop saw it, he told them to give it to the pigs. "I am fond of pike," said he, "but distinctly decline to have anything to do with sharks." Ah! What would I not have given to have caught that fish. 'Well, I fished here and I fished there, first trying all the large Shannon Lakes, and then visiting Corrib and Cullen. Thence I went to the north of Ireland, catching now and then some fine fish, but never even a thirty-pounder. The more difficult I found it to attain my object, the more determined I became to succeed. And I shall succeed yet. Let me see. It is now twenty-five years since I came to Ireland. I must have caught thousands of pike in that time – that one there on the floor is the largest of the lot; in fact, the largest I have seen caught by myself or anybody else. This is my second great disappointment. At Athlone I thought I had succeeded. That was a big fish. I took him to the station and weighed him there. 'Forty-three pounds,' said the station master.

'A Major Brown who was looking on began to prod the fish with his stick. "Something hard there", he said. "Let's cut him open and see what he had for dinner."

'I would not agree to this as I wanted the skin entire, but the major squeezed him a bit and up came a lot of swan shot which my scoundrel of a boatman had evidently poured down his throat so that he might earn the reward I had promised him if I caught a heavy fish.

'But at last I really have found a monster pike – the catching of him is only a question of time. Not a quarter of a mile from this cabin [here he lowered his voice to a whisper] is a deep reedy lake. The priest has a boat on it, which he lends me. I was rowing along the other evening when something struck the boat with such force that I was thrown from the seat and nearly capsized. It was in deep water and there are no rocks in the lake. I had rowed right on to a pike as large as a calf.'

He said the last sentence slowly and earnestly. I expect I showed great interest in the statement for, like the old man, it had long been my ambition to catch a really immense pike.

'Well,' said I, 'let us go and try the lake together. I should like to help you land such a monster.'

'Ah, but you might catch him and not I. How then?' And he gave me a very unpleasant look out of his deep-set eyes.

We said nothing for a while, when my companion suddenly startled me by asking if I was aware that he was the Emperor of Germany. I said I was not, and another unpleasant silence ensued.

Mrs O'Day had made up two heather beds for us on the mud floor and without undressing we each stretched ourselves on our moorland couches.

Just as I was dropping off to sleep, my companion got up on his elbow and said gravely: 'Hang me if I don't believe you are a pike. I'll have a triangle into you tomorrow morning. Good night.'

There was no doubt about it. He was mad. I dared not go to sleep. I made a pretence of it until the old man began to snore and then sat by the fire until daybreak when, leaving some money on the table for Mrs O'Day, I sped away over the moor.

Years afterwards I was telling the tale of the demented angler who, I felt certain, had lost his wits in his unavailing search after a big Irish pike, when I was interrupted by Rooney, of the Irish Bar, who burst into a peal of laughter, swearing that he knew my pike-fishing acquaintance well and that there was no saner man in Ireland.

'Fact is Johnny,' said he, 'the old boy was fearful you would get that big fish before him and so he thought he would frighten you home.'

Rooney may say what he likes, but I decline to believe in the sanity of any man who expatriates himself during a quarter of a century in the endeavour to catch a 40 lb pike.

JOHN BICKERDYKE, *Wild Sport in Ireland*, 1895

Evasive Action

Bulls, even the most savage, can be halted and even put to flight. Roll about on the ground and make uncouth noises. It takes nerve to do this but is effective. Wasps, if you should happen to unwittingly trespass on their nesting site, can be very vindictive, even dangerous. Little can save you if you have the whole swarm after you unless you emulate the moorhen, diving into the water and coming up to breathe under a lily pad. Bees may be baffled by seeking refuge in a dense thorn bush but not so wasps. Wasps will thread a dense thicket once they get their blood up.

You can land a pike by grasping him by the eye sockets but the chances are you will find your hand inside his mouth if he is a big fish and then you will realise how difficult it must be for a roach to escape once it is seized by a pike. You will certainly bear honourable scars as a memento for many days to come.

Don't poach. I know many fishermen, and shooting men too, who have no qualms about trespassing on forbidden ground. Make sure of the limits of your beat beforehand.

If you are caught by an irate keeper and you have no loose change, speak rapidly in a foreign tongue. It works sometimes. If the owner catches you this ruse will not avail you and you deserve to feel uncomfortable. Remember there are two things which are guaranteed to make an Englishman very angry: 1, if you abuse or threaten his dog; 2, if you are trespassing in pursuit of game on his ground.

'B.B.', *Fisherman's Folly*, 1987

Chief Moose Heart

At the end of August 1921, I was fishing black bass in the lakes of the State of Maine.

One evening, in the hardware store at Mount Kineo, the usual meeting place of the fishermen of the district, one of the locals said to me: 'Since you're here, you ought to go and fish with a fly in the waters north of the lake near the Canadian Frontier, where the landlocked salmon gather in shoal before the frost. I guarantee you won't regret it!'

Fortunately, I had with me a fly rod, bought for five dollars from a pawnbroker in New York. I had cut and refashioned it. It was my first attempt at working in split bamboo. The rod had been transformed and was powerful, supple and, so far, virgin. Here was the opportunity of trying it out! I sought information and discovered that it took one day to get there, one day to return and that I could have two days' fishing. A big canoe was essential for crossing the lake which was always subject to storms. It was necessary to take food and the most important thing of all was to have a good guide.

Someone said: 'Ask Chief Moose Heart, who's smoking his pipe by the stove, if he'll go with you. You'll have the best guide in the district. He wins the canoe races on the lake every year and he's a famous fisherman, but his wife Carabou is expecting her sixth child and I am afraid he may refuse to leave her.'

I turned and saw a young Indian, about thirty years old, with ebony hair hanging in long locks, a superb specimen of his race, with no trace of degeneracy, wide shoulders, a powerful body and narrow hips, dressed in a black and red check shirt, doe-skin trousers and moccasins embroided with coloured beads. On his head, he wore a black felt hat with a large brim covered with the bright and variegated hues of innumerable salmon flies.

An expedition with an Indian chief by canoe into the wilds, and an opportunity to try out my rod, what a piece of luck! But would he agree?

My heart beating, I said to him:

'How's the fishing?'

He looked at me, smiled and replied 'Sometimes good, sometimes bad, it depends.'

Fortunately, the American came to my assistance and said: 'Chief, the Frenchman wants to go fishing.'

He looked me up and down, then addressed me in Canadian French: 'You want to catch fish on the lake?'

Thinking that we had better get down to brass tacks, I said: 'I want to try out my fly rod.'

I took my treasure out of its case to show him. I saw at once that he was interested. I put it together and handed it to him. With an expert hand, he made it bend two or three times, turned it about in all directions and then ran his eye along it.

'A good stick to take silver fish.'

Was I going to be lucky? I was now pretty certain that he coveted my rod, because he didn't give it back to me but made the other men present try it. The conversation began again: 'You French, many fish in your hunting grounds? I, Paris with Buffalo Bill, much beautiful women, much drink, good firewater, French *pinard*.'

'I'm Swiss, Chief.'

'Cheese with big holes, I been Zürich too, no speak, no understand, much mountains touch sky!'

'You like fly fishing, and I see that my rod pleases you; I made it myself but it has not caught anything as yet. I should much like to try it on your silver fish! Will you take me to where I can catch them?'

He looked at me for a moment before replying, hesitated, and said: 'Not possible, awaiting little chief.'

'If you consent, I shall stay there only two days, I merely want to try out my rod.'

'Pity, good stick, but can't catch fish before little chief arrives.'

It was no good! Death in my heart, I dared insist no further. Yet, there was a gleam of hope! He had taken up my rod again and was examining it. Well, it was worth the sacrifice.

'The rod's yours if you'll come with me and see that I get some fish.'

His eyes suddenly brightened; he got to his feet and went to the door. How tactless of me! I must have insulted him! I had heard that the Indians, and particularly the chiefs, were proud and independent.

'Wait, I come back.'

At that moment, the American winked, smiled and put a finger to his lips.

The door banged; doubtless he was going to find a friend. But the American said: 'You're in luck! I know him, and you can thank your rod! He's been wanting a rod like that for a long time, but with all his children and his wife, who's constantly pregnant, he's still waiting to save up enough dollars. He has to content himself with an old steel Bristol. Last year, he broke the tip and replaced it by two umbrella ribs bound together!'

After a wait of half an hour, Moose Heart came back smiling.

'See the medicine chief, allowed to go for three moons only; if you agree, be at landing place tomorrow morning six o'clock!'

The next morning, I met Moose Heart who was waiting for me by a huge canoe. He was looking at the sky and seemed anxious.

'Bad weather, cross lake very quickly, dangerous!'

He took my precious rod and rolled it up in blankets. The canoe was full to the bulwarks with tents, sleeping bags, pots and pans, two huge axes, a long pole and a tarpaulin covering the whole. He handed me a paddle and off we went!

During the journey, we talked and became good friends. This was the moment to ask the great question.

'Chief, do these silver fish only take a fly when it's cast? Do you think you can make them take by trolling?'

'Impossible. Where we going to fish, must cast.'

'I've practised fly casting in New York, but I've only fished with black bass rods!'

He looked at me but did not seem surprised.

'Fish take well, easy, me accustomed make beginners fish. Paddle harder, quick, storm coming, still an hour crossing lake.'

The wind rose, the storm broke, the waves grew higher and licked dangerously at the sides of our frail craft. We paddled like madmen, shipping a little water, while the rain whipped our faces and soaked us. Finally, towards midday, we drew near the land.

Moose Heart showed me to our left the mouth of a splendid river bordered by birch trees, its strong current washing furiously against the rocks in its bed.

'Leave paddle, me pole rapids.'

He stood up, seized the huge pole and punted the canoe, choosing with wonderful dexterity the best channels between the rocks.

About two o'clock we ate and then, after going about another three miles, I saw a magnificent pool. The Indian signed to me to put my rod together.

'Look, here many fish for beginner, get up in bows.'

There we were in position, all about us landlocked salmon were rising and jumping; I could see their backs and their fins breaking the surface. I went into the attack, casting and casting again without success. Then, suddenly, I felt a formidable take on an enormous fish, who shouted: 'Oy!' I turned about, startled, and saw that my Silver Doctor was anchored in Moose Heart's ear! He smiled and, without a word, tore the hook with a sudden jerk from his ear, detached it from my leader and stuck it in his hat, which he then pulled down over his ears.

CHARLES RITZ, *A Fly Fisher's Life*, 1959

Deschutes River

This sky, for instance:
closed, gray,
but it has stopped snowing
that is something. I am
so cold I cannot bend
my fingers.
Walking down to the river this morning
we surprised badger
tearing a rabbit.
Badger had a bloody nose,
Blood on its snout up to its sharp eyes:
       prowess is not to be confused
       with grace.

Later,
eight mallard ducks fly over
without looking down. On the river
Jack Sandmeyer trolls, trolls
for steelhead. He has fished
this river for years
but February is the best month
he says.
Snarled, mittenless,
I handle a maze of nylon.
Far away,
another man is raising my children,
bedding my wife bedding my wife.

from RAYMOND CARVER, *At Night the Salmon Run*, 1976

375

Rafferty

It was Rafferty who turned up; Rafferty with a silly grin across his face, astride a flea-bitten hack. 'Yeeaauoo,' he screeched at me a hundred yards away. At a distance he looked like nothing so much as Don Quixote. A scraggy horse with a big man on its back. Two rods and a gaff slung round his neck; Rafferty twice as large as life.

'I had a mind to borrow a bicycle, but the man was away,' he began, clambering off its back. 'So you pinched his horse?' I enquired. Rafferty looked pained. 'This foine horse belongs to a gintleman hereabouts and I'll be sending him back right now.' He gave it a slap across its quarters and the beast plunged across the field, swung round and turned and stared at us.

It was still there when we walked down to the river with the tackle, and I began to be a little anxious for the gintleman hereabouts. 'Devil take it, the beast is entirely without sense at all,' rumbled the Rafferty, and vaguely hurled a piece of wood in its direction. It trotted up the road as we got down to the first pool. I never saw it again, but often wondered who had been foolish enough to leave his horse unguarded when the pride of Ballanamallard was in the vicinity.

The first three streams yielded two brace – three to Rafferty, one to me. By eleven o'clock he had got four brace and I had two; an hour later he made it six and a half brace. They were all good trout, several were over the pound mark, and if I had been by myself, I should have considered it a day of days.

Rafferty's fishing was entirely in keeping with his character. He had a wonderful eye for a good stretch of water, but it was a case of spotting a run, cast, catch and land . . . another run upstream, half-a-dozen more casts, a strike and the whole procedure over again. Sometimes he would pause a moment, put his bean pole of rod on the ground and run up the bank until he reached a point where he could stare back down the river. He seemed to be looking for someone, and I wondered if the borrowed horse had anything to do with it.

'Devil take the horse,' said the Rafferty when I mentioned it to him. 'But a man should be after keeping his eyes open whether he's fishing or not.' And no more would he say.

The car had been moved up twice. On the second occasion I drove it well upstream, perhaps two miles, and spent a very agreeable hour alone on a ragged stretch of water until he came up. Throughout the morning I had used a variation of a home-tied Partridge and Orange as there were a few March Browns on the water. After lunch there was a definite hatch of Olives. They were duns with wings the colour of a thunder cloud, and I went over to the ubiquitous Greenwells Glory.

It was not at all successful at first – which was surprising as rises were commonplace. I flogged two pools and then got an unexpected pluck at my line – made by something really good. The line tightened, there was a vortex where the flies ought to have been, and a first-rate trout porpoised over in the water twenty yards away. That fish knew his business. He came out twice and tried to fall back towards me. I gave line, I let him have all the slack for the jumps and put the spine of the rod against him when he started to bore in deep water. Rafferty came up in time to gaff him for me.

Now Rafferty with a gaff was a wonderful sight. His casting was effective but ragged; shooting the line never occurred to him; his technique of playing a fish gave me a gripping pain, but with the gaff he was an angel. He put the steel into the water beside the fish. He never hurried. He moved it forward imperceptibly and then – with a turn of the wrist – the point went straight under the gill plates. A light jerk – and the trout was out on the bank.

He gaffed mine with the remark that it was not a bad fish but he had got one in his bag which would make two of it. I swallowed hard and deigned to look over his catch.

Eleven brace!

He suggested they should go in the car. Maybe I would like to drive farther along the track? I asked how far. Oh – perhaps a mile. We should get into deep water then and the fish would be moving at dusk. There would be some real fishing.

'Seen the horse lately?' I asked maliciously.

It was wasted sarcasm. He never looked up. No, he said slowly. The horse had moved on somewhere. It was probably trotting right home at the moment. Didn't I understand they were all friends of his in these parts. And what was the loan of a horse to a friend?

What indeed?

Rafferty handed over nearly twenty-five pounds of fish in a calico bag, and I walked up in the valley, towards the track. Behind me the fish killer was already rolling his line across the water with that unvarying half Spey switch. I felt sure he had another brace before I crested the rise.

As I approached the car there was a mournful hoot down valley and the pride of the Donegal State Railway chuffed past. The little mechanic would probably be on board with his cash or his car parts, the nuns too, and the usual complement of livestock. It passed on towards Stranolar, and there was no sound again but the falls of the River Finn.

Magnificent river! My own fish, eleven of them, were spread out on the grass. Rafferty's were already in the back of the car, and I put my rod in beside them. It was not worth while dismantling it. The tail fly stuck in the cork handle and the rod point stuck out of the sunshine roof, far over the bonnet.

A great bellow from the river broke the silence.

I listened. Another bellow and something like a strangled cry. Rafferty must have fallen in or maybe he had caught a bigger fish than he could handle. It suddenly occurred to me that he probably wanted my help. I scrambled down the side of the track, cleared the first level of heather, and ran till I came to the rocks above the river.

There was an amazing sight below. By the side of the pool where I had caught my big fish, there was a man lying on his back and Rafferty and somebody else were milling into each other a few yards from him. The second man lashed out with something that looked like a gaff, Rafferty ducked and landed a haymaker on the side of his head. There were two men on the floor, but the first casualty was getting to his feet again. Rafferty didn't wait for any more. He grabbed his rod in the middle, like a spear, roared again and galloped up the valley towards the track.

I shouted to him and he changed direction.

'Get that plurry car going,' he puffed. 'Have you got my other rod? They snaked up on me, the low down snivellin' bastes.'

'Your pals with the horse I suppose,' I said, as we bumped round in reverse. But I was wrong, bless his heart. He said they were only bailies.

JOHN HILLABY, *Within the Streams*, 1949

Catching a Cow

It must be clearly understood that I am not at all proud of this performance. In Florida men sometimes hook and land, on rod and tackle a little finer than a steam-crane and chain, a mackerel-like fish called 'tarpon,' which sometime run to 120 pounds. Those men stuff their captures and exhibit them in glass cases and become puffed up. On the Columbia River sturgeon of 150 pounds weight are taken with the line. When the sturgeon is hooked the line is fixed to the nearest pine tree or steamboat-wharf, and after some hours or days the sturgeon surrenders himself, if the pine or the line do not give way. The owner of the line then states on oath that he has caught a sturgeon, and he, too, becomes proud.

These things are mentioned to show how light a creel will fill the soul of a man with vanity. I am not proud. It is nothing to me that I have hooked and played seven hundred pounds weight of quarry. All my desire is to place the little affair on record before the mists of memory breed the miasma of exaggeration.

The minnow cost eighteenpence. It was a beautiful quill minnow, and the tackle-maker said that it could be thrown as a fly. He guaranteed further in respect to the triangles – it glittered with triangles – that, if necessary, the minnow would hold a horse. A man who speaks too much truth is just as offensive as a man who speaks too little. None the less, owing to the defective condition of the present law of libel, the tackle-maker's name must be withheld.

The minnow and I and a rod went down to a brook to attend to a small jack who lived between two clumps of flags in the most cramped swim that he could select. As a proof that my intentions were strictly honourable, I may mention that I was using a light split-cane rod – very dangerous if the line runs through weeds, but very satisfactory in clean water, inasmuch as it keeps a steady strain on the fish and prevents him from taking liberties. I had an old score against the jack. He owed me two live-bait already, and I had reason to suspect him of coming up-stream and interfering with a little bleak-pool under a horse-bridge which lay entirely beyond his sphere of legitimate influence. Observe, therefore, that my tackle and my motives pointed clearly to jack, and jack alone; though I knew that there were monstrous big perch in the brook.

The minnow was thrown as a fly several times, and, owing to my peculiar, and hitherto unpublished, methods of fly throwing, nearly six pennyworth of the triangles came off, either in my coat-collar, or my thumb, or the back of my hand. Fly fishing is a very gory amusement.

The jack was not interested in the minnow, but towards twilight a boy opened a gate of the field and let in some twenty or thirty cows and half-a-dozen cart-horses, and they were all very much interested. The horses galloped up and down the field and shook the banks, but the cows walked solidly and breathed heavily, as people breathe who appreciate the Fine Arts.

By this time I had given up all hope of catching my jack fairly, but I wanted the live-bait and bleak-account settled before I went away, even if I tore up the bottom of the brook. Just before I had quite made up my mind to borrow a tin of chloride of lime from the farm-house – another triangle had fixed itself in my fingers – I made a cast which for pure skill, exact judgement of distance, and perfect coincidence of hand and eye and brain, would have taken every prize at a bait-casting tournament. That was the first half of the cast. The second was postponed because the quill minnow would not return to its proper place, which was under the lobe of my left ear. It had done thus before, and I supposed it was in collision with a grass tuft, till I turned round and saw a large red and white bald faced cow trying to rub what would be withers in a horse with her nose. She looked at me reproachfully, and her look said as plainly as words: 'The season is too far advanced for gadflies. What is this strange disease?'

I replied, 'Madam, I must apologize for an unwarrantable liberty on the part of my minnow, but if you will have the goodness to keep still until I can reel in, we will adjust this little difficulty.'

I reeled in very swiftly and cautiously, but she would not wait.

She put her tail in the air and ran away. It was a purely involuntary motion on my part: I struck. Other anglers may contradict me, but I firmly believe that if a man had foul-hooked his best friend through the nose, and that friend ran, the man would strike by instinct. I struck, therefore, and the reel began to sing just as merrily as though I had caught my jack. But had it been a jack, the minnow would have come away. I told the tackle-maker this much afterwards, and he laughed and made allusions to the guarantee about holding a horse.

Because it was a fat innocent she-cow that had done me no harm the minnow held – held like an anchor-fluke in coral moorings – and I was forced to dance up and down an interminable field very largely used by cattle. It was like salmon fishing in a nightmare. I took gigantic strides, and every stride found me up to my knees in marsh. But the cow seemed to skate along the squashy green by the brook, to skim over the miry backwaters, and to float like a mist through the patches of rush that squirted black filth over my face. Sometimes we whirled through a mob of her friends – there were no friends to help me – and they looked scandalized; and sometimes a young and frivolous cart-horse would join in the chase for a few miles, and kick solid pieces of mud into my eyes; and through all the mud, the milky smell of kine, the rush and the smother, I was aware of my own voice crying: 'Pussy, pussy, pussy! Pretty pussy! Come along then, puss-cat!' You see it is so hard to speak to a cow properly, and she would not listen – no, she would not listen.

Then she stopped, and the moon got up behind the pollards to tell the cows to lie down; but they were all on their feet, and they came trooping to see. And she said, 'I haven't had my supper, and I want to go to bed, and please don't worry me.' And I said, 'The matter has passed beyond any apology. There are three courses open to you, my dear lady. If you'll have the common sense to walk up to my creel I'll get my knife and you shall have all the minnow. Or, again, if you'll let me move across to your near side, instead of keeping me so coldly on your off side, the thing will come away in one tweak. I can't pull it out over your withers. Better still, go to a post and rub it out, dear. It won't hurt much, but if you think I'm going to lose my rod to please you, you are mistaken.' And she said, 'I don't understand what you are saying. I am very, very unhappy.' And I said, 'It's all your fault for trying to fish. Do go to the nearest gate-post, you nice fat thing, and rub it out.'

For a moment I fancied she was taking my advice. She ran away and I followed. But all the other cows came with us in a bunch, and I thought of Phaeton trying to drive the Chariot of the Sun, and Texan cowboys killed by stampeding cattle, and *'Green Grow the Rushes, O!'* and Solomon and Job, and 'loosing the bands of Orion,' and hooking Behemoth, and Wordsworth who talks about whirling round with stones and rocks and trees, and 'Here we go round the Mulberry Bush,' and 'Pippin Hill,' and 'Hey Diddle Diddle,' and most especially the top joint of my rod. Again she stopped – but nowhere in the neighborhood of my knife – and her sisters stood moonfaced round her. It seemed that she might, now, run towards me, and I looked for a tree, because cows are very different from salmon, who only jump against the line, and never molest the fisherman. What followed was worse than any direct attack. She began to buck-jump, to stand on her head and her tail alternately, to leap into the sky, all four feet together, and to dance on her hind legs. It was so violent and improper, so desperately unladylike, that I was inclined to blush, as one would blush at the sight of a prominent statesman sliding down a fire escape, or a duchess chasing her cook with a skillet. That flopsome *abandon* might go on all night in the lonely meadow among the mists, and if it went on all night – this was pure inspiration – I might be able to worry through the fishing line with my teeth.

Those who desire an entirely new sensation should chew with all their teeth, and against time, through a best waterproofed silk line, one end of which belongs to a mad cow dancing fairy rings in the moonlight; at the same time keeping one eye on the cow and the other on the top joint of a split-cane rod. She buck-jumped and I bit on the slack just in front of the reel; and I am in a position to state that that line was cored with steel wire throughout the particular section which I attacked. This has been formally denied by the tackle-maker, who is not to be believed.

The *wheep* of the broken line running through the rings told me that henceforth the cow and I might be strangers. I had already bidden good-bye to some tooth or teeth; but no price is too great for freedom of the soul.

'Madam,' I said, 'the minnow and twenty feet of very superior line are your alimony without reservation. For the wrong I have unwittingly done to you I express my sincere regret. At the same time, may I hope that Nature, the kindest of nurses, will in due season –'

She or one of her companions must have stepped on her spare end of the line in the dark, for she bellowed wildly and ran away, followed by all the cows. I hoped the minnow was disengaged at last; and before I went away looked at my watch, fearing to find it nearly midnight. My last cast for the jack was made at 6.23 p.m. There lacked still three and a half minutes of the half-hour; and I would have sworn that the moon was paling before the dawn!

'Simminly someone were chasing they cows down to bottom o' Ten Acre,' said the farmer that evening. ''Twasn't you, sir?'

'Now under what earthly circumstances do you suppose I should chase your cows? I wasn't fishing for them, was I?'

Then all the farmer's family gave themselves up to jam-smeared laughter for the rest of the evening, because that was a rare and precious jest, and it was repeated for months, and the fame of it spread from that farm to another, and yet another at least three miles away, and it will be used again for the benefit of visitors when the freshets come down in spring.

But to the greater establishment of my honour and glory I submit in print this bald statement of fact, that I may not, through forgetfulness, be tempted later to tell how I hooked a bull on a Marlow Buzz, how he ran up a tree and took to water, and how I played him along the London-road for thirty miles, and gaffed him at Smithfield. Errors of this kind may creep in with the lapse of years, and it is my ambition ever to be a worthy member of that fraternity who pride themselves on never deviating by one hair's breadth from the absolute and literal truth.

RUDYARD KIPLING, *On Dry-cow Fishing as a Fine Art*, 1911

Jogging with a Bull

I am hail-fellow-well-met with any cow that does not splash among the rising fish. But, when there is a bull about, I have no sort of doubt as to which is the better side of the river. Sometimes, even to be on the better side of the river is an insufficient precaution. It is an altogether insufficient precaution in the presence of a bull who is definitely interested in the difference between wet and dry flies. I have recently met such a bull. Inspirited by rain, the trout had begun to rise as they often do just before the becks begin to colour the river. I had done nothing earlier in the afternoon and knew that I must make the most of the rise while it lasted. Heavy rain far up the valley promised a spate. I had got a brace of half-pounders on Waterhen and Yellow and was casting to a third, who was rising in a little eddy on the far side of the river, when this bull became suddenly an important feature of the landscape. He came to the bank opposite me and looked down into the eddy, young, powerful, impatient and, as it appeared, inquisitive. I failed to get that fish and moved up. I got another fish on the Waterhen when the bull observed in a decidedly truculent voice that my proceedings displeased him. I did not care, because I was on the better side of the river. I got a fish on the Blue Hawk. The bull tried to toss a clump of grass. Just then, looking back, I saw the trout in the eddy rise again. He had refused my wet flies, so I changed my cast for a tapered one with a fluffy grey fly on the end of it. The changing of casts interested the bull exceedingly. He followed when I worked down the river again until I was in a position to cast across to the eddy. The first cast was a failure, dropping below the trout. At the second up he came, down went my fly and a few minutes later I was putting the best fish of the day into the creel. The bull was beside himself with interest in this change of technique. He came lumbering down the bank into the water and finding it deep went up river along his own side. By this time there was a good deal of water in the river and it had begun to colour. I had hardly replaced my wet flies before I perceived that I was no longer on the better side of the river. That bull, wishing to know the difference between wet and dry flies, had swum the river higher up and was approaching me grimly, inevitably, like a thunder-cloud, along my own bank. There are those who in such circumstances advise presence of mind in the form of an impenetrable calm, which, they say, will disarm the most ferocious of bulls. For my part I think that sort of presence of mind is best which most rapidly produces absence of body. I retired. The bull followed. I cut a corner. The bull foresaw that manoeuvre and did the same. I quickened, slightly, my pace. So did he. A split cane of Hardy's is an excellent weapon, but not for all purposes. That beast crossed three stone walls and lost interest only at the fourth. And there are those who say that fishing is the recreation of the contemplative man.

ARTHUR RANSOME, *Rod and Line*, 1929

A Dictionary Defines Persecution

clegs The North-country term for *horseflies*, deriving from ON *kleggi* (cf. Mod. Norwegian *klegg*), and being first attested in English in 1449 ('The unlatit woman . . . pungis as the cleg').
Horseflies are ugly, vicious, bloated, biting insects which suck blood from the exposed parts of fishermen, usually in Scotland or Ireland. They are impossible to deter with insect repellent; insect repellent attracts them. They should be smacked dead before they bite, if possible. Cleg-smacking is an alternative pursuit to fishing during long, hot, sweaty and windless days when the fish are as sulky as the weather.

From *Fly-Fishing: A Book of Words*, C.B. MCCULLY, 1993

Enjoying Scottish Midges

Wading now became necessary, for I had either caught or 'put down' most of the fish within casting distance of the shore. I had no waders, but, having confidence in the hot sun, took off boots and stockings and waded in. Then the midges found me out, and soon, from the edge of the tucked-up knickerbockers to the waterline, my legs were covered with a black band of the venomous insects. They were so thick that they jostled one another, and I verily believe interfered with each other's feeding arrangements. Not that they failed to bite, but the punishment was less than I should have expected. The experience was unique and satisfying.

About this time the gillie returned, saying M. was fishing the lower lake, and hoped I should not be long. People in mosquito countries are said to get quite hardened in the matter of mosquitoes, but this Highlander, though born and bred near the place, had a bad time of it with the midges. For a while he stood quietly, landing-net in hand, only uttering an exclamation every now and then when a midge found out a tender spot; but finally he gave up the unequal battle, cast down the net, and, fleeing a little inland, took off his coat, wrapped up his head in it, and buried himself as deeply as possible in the heather. I had too much to do to look after the fast-rising trout to mind those little pests, which, making due allowance for difference in size, are infinitely more poisonous than rattlesnakes.

JOHN BICKERDYKE, *Days of My Life*, 1901

Self-decapitation

Amongst my memorandums of singular incidents, I find one which even now affords me as much amusement as such a circumstance can possibly admit of; and as it is, at the same time, highly characteristic of the people amongst whom it occurred, in that view I relate it. A man *decapitating himself by mistake* is indeed a *blunder* of true Hibernian character.

In the year 1800, a labourer dwelling near the town of Athy, County Kildare, (where some of my family then resided) was walking with his comrade up the banks of the Barrow to the farm of a Mr Richardson, on whose meadows they were employed to mow; each, in the usual Irish way, having his scythe loosely wagging over his shoulder, and lazily lounging close to the bank of the river, they espied a salmon partly hid under the bank. It is the nature of this fish that, when his *head* is concealed, he fancies no one can see his *tail* (there are many wise-acres, besides the salmon, of the same way of thinking). On the present occasion the body of the fish was visible.

'Oh Ned – Ned dear!' said one of the mowers, 'look at that big fellow there: isn't it a pity we ha'nt no spear?'

'May be,' said Ned, 'we could be after piking the lad with the scythe-handle.'

'True for you!' said Dennis: 'the spike of yeer handle is longer nor mine; give the fellow a dig with it at any rate.'

'Ay, will I,' returned the other: 'I'll give the lad a prod he'll never forget any how.'

The spike and their sport was all they thought of: but the *blade* of the scythe, which hung over Ned's shoulders, never came into the contemplation of either of them. Ned cautiously looked over the bank; the unconscious salmon lay snug, little imagining the conspiracy that had been formed against his tail.

'Now hit the lad smart!' said Dennis: 'there now – there! rise your fist: now you have the boy! now Ned – success!'

Ned struck at the salmon with all his might and main, and that was not trifling. But whether 'the boy' was piked or not never appeared: for poor Ned, bending his neck as he struck at the salmon, placed the vertebrae in the most convenient position for unfurnishing his shoulders: and his head came tumbling splash into the Barrow, to the utter astonishment of his comrade, who could not conceive *how* it could *drop off* so suddenly. But the next minute he had the consolation of seeing the head attended by *one of his own ears*, which had been most dexterously sliced off by the same blow which beheaded his comrade.

The head and ear rolled down the river in company, and were picked up with extreme horror at the mill-dam, near Mr Richardson's, by one of the miller's men.

'Who the devil does this head belong to?' exclaimed the miller.

'Whoever owned it,' said the man, 'had three ears, at any rate.'

SIR JOHN BARRINGTON, *Personal Sketches of his Own Times*,
1827

A Most Unfortunate Attachment

It may not be inapplicable to term it a most *unfortunate* attachment with those classes of society who have no property but their *trades*, and to whom *time* alone must be considered a kind of freehold estate: such time lost by a river side, in the frivolous and uncertain pursuit of a paltry plate of fish, instead of being employed in business, has reduced more men *to want*, and their families to *a workhouse*, than any species of sport whatever. Racing, hunting, shooting, coursing, and cocking, (destructive as the latter has been,) have never produced so long a list of *beggars* as the sublime *art of angling*; in confirmation of which fact, the eye of observation need only turn to any of those small country towns near which there happens to run a *fishing stream*, when the profitable part of the pleasure may be instantly perceived by the poverty of the inhabitants.

WILLIAM TAPLIN, *The Sporting Dictionary*, 1803

The Safety of Not Fishing

I knew how dangerous a sport fly fishing for trout can be. I have since come to know personally some of its casualties – and to shudder. I speak not of the physical dangers – though every sufficiently old fishing club has on its wall one or more coiled leaders with a fly attached and a label that reads, 'Tom Smith's last cast,' meaning the one he had on when they found him and fished him out, drowned while wading, or the victim of heart stoppage, possibly brought on by excitement over the biggest fish of his life. Such cases, however, are comparatively uncommon; the danger I refer to is more widespread, and more insidious. It is mental, emotional. Fly fishing for trout has wrecked men's marriages, their careers; when begun early enough in life it has prevented them from ever getting around to either marriage or a career and turned them into lifelong celibates and ne'er-do-wells. I have known some. Two whom I know had the strength of will to cure themselves of chronic alcoholism, but not of their addiction to fly fishing. Theodore Gordon threw up his job at an early age, sponged off his relatives, remained a lifelong bachelor, neglected his old, dying mother, and did nothing but two things with himself: fish for trout and, out of season, tie flies to fish through the coming one. There are, incidentally, a great many fishermen who think his was an exemplary life. The danger of becoming that kind of addict not only scared me, it appalled me. Before all excess the healthy, well-balanced mind draws back in distaste and fright; such zeal for a mere sport is particularly unbecoming. I both pity and despise any person who makes a passion out of a pastime. I know that, like everything else, moderation can be carried to excess; nonetheless, I am a firm believer in moderation.

That is my belief – in practice I am excessive in everything I do, and I had long suspected that my failure to master fly fishing had been a blessing in disguise, like the man prevented from becoming a lush because he could never hold down the stuff.

WILLIAM HUMPHREY, *My Moby Dick*, 1979

CHAPTER EIGHT

Fish That Bit Back

*T*hat the odds are not stacked against the fish should be obvious by now. If it were not so, it wouldn't be much of a sport. For the most part, the revenge of the fish on the angler is indifference. Not the scorn which pitches lovers into hormonal gloom, but something altogether grander, a sort of disdain, expressed through a flick of the tail as the fish turns away from your lure without the slightest interest.

Occasionally, though, the fish may wreak some greater revenge. Plenty of fishermen have lost bits of fingers in the jaws of a pike. Every child who's ever seen an octopus has heard or made up stories about people being dragged to a watery grave. No one takes lightly a live – and angry – conger eel in the boat with them. The long, curving teeth of moray eels have torn chunks out of fishermen who were silly enough to wait a few seconds before killing them. Hundreds of people a year are wounded by stingrays, occasionally fatally. Pearl divers are wary of the giant cod which live in dark caves among the coral with their mouths wide open, ready to swallow the head of a swimmer. In South America, electric eels have sent enough power through rivers to kill men and horses.

The revolting stonefish, a small sea-dweller covered in warts and slime, will lie on a rocky or coral bottom, indifferent to the greatest commotion in the water, virtually invisible in its camouflage, until an unlucky wader steps on its poisonous spine. Medical accounts describe one overwhelming symptom: staggering pain. It can last for twelve hours and there is no antidote to the venom. Victims are so overcome by the agony that it frequently takes four or five men to hold them down as they froth at the mouth deliriously.

Anyone fishing at night in places like the Gulf of Mexico should be on guard for the Needlefish. These can grow to a length of five feet or so and spend their lives at or near the surface of the sea. When they get confused – for example by the light of a night-fisherman's lamp – they show an astonishing ability to leap clear of the water at great speed. A Captain William Gray of the Miami Seaquarium found himself nailed to his boat when a needlefish ran its beak straight through his leg.

Equally nerve-wracking is the candiru or toothpick-fish. This little chap is attracted to the taste of uric acid and will cheerfully swim up the stream of urine from anyone peeing into the Amazon and thence into the urethra. Once there, it raises its gill-cover and sticks out a set of spines. It is then a race to get to hospital before your bladder explodes. Once there, having a surgeon wield a knife is blessed relief.

Most fabled of all freshwater fishes of course, is the piranha, described by President Theodore Roosevelt as 'the fish that eats men when it can'. Descriptions of shoals of piranha, with their vice-like jaws and razor-sharp teeth, being drawn to a victim by the sound of splashing or the smell of blood, occur in one adventure story after another. Roosevelt's account of the man who put his toe in the water only to have it bitten off is typical of the genre. Well-documented, factual cases are another matter. One expert I consulted was pretty certain that piranhas were scavengers more than preda-tors. If this is so, it merely proves the adage that the bigger the politician, the bigger the necessary pinch of salt.

The so-called Killer Whale labours under the misfortune of a name to which it does not really live up. Whaling boats have found themselves battered by Killer Whales, but authenticated accounts of people being eaten by them are rare indeed. Swordfish too have only rarely been known to attack man, although there is an account of someone sitting on a boat off Sierra Leone a number of years ago who was speared through by one. And big game fishermen tend to treat swordfish with a great deal of caution once they have hauled them onto the deck.

Barracuda are unpredictably vicious. The spectacularly sharp teeth which fill their huge mouths can kill in a single bite. Most sinisterly, they will attack in the shallowest waters. There are dozens of cases in which anglers or paddlers standing up to their knees in water have been savaged by single fish stripping the flesh from the leg.

Wreaking Havoc – Grandville, *Petites Misères*, 1843

Most feared of all are sharks. Not all these sleek creatures are dangerous. But those that are, like the great white shark with its triangular teeth, are enough to invest the whole species with a peculiar terror. The eyewitness accounts of shark attacks are so numerous and detailed, the medical and autopsy reports so precise, that no one can have any doubts about the terrifying savagery of these beasts. Some reports even speak of bodies in armour or an entire horse being found inside sharks. In the grip of bloodlust a shark will snap at anything: fishermen who have tried to gaff one from a boat have discovered it so enraged by the smell of blood that it will tear at its own entrails.

Sharks can't swallow humans whole. That privilege belongs, uniquely, to whales. They are not, of course, fish. But their huge size, the fact that these are about the only creatures on the planet capable of doing it, has led to endless fascination about what would happen if an adult were swallowed by a whale. Even at the time when humans were most mercilessly hunting them down, the whale exercised an extraordinary hold over the imagination. The whale-hunter's account of being swallowed by a whale on p. 409 must have seemed at the time as remarkable as a meeting with aliens would seem nowadays.

From this brief digest, then, the following rules seem sensible:

If you haul into the boat anything long and snake like, kill it at once or throw it back over the side.

Don't wear anything silvery while wading in barracuda territory – you might be mistaken for a fish.

Don't wade in bare feet on coral.

Don't hunt whales. But if you get swallowed by a whale, at all events keep calm and prepare yourself for a new career as a snowman (see p. 410).

If you're fishing the Amazon, don't pee in the water.

Late on the evening of the second day of our trip, just before midnight, we reached Conçepción. On this day, when we stopped for wood or to get provisions – at picturesque places, where the women from rough mud and thatched cabins were washing clothes in the river, or where ragged horsemen stood gazing at us from the bank, or where dark, well-dressed ranchmen stood in front of red-roofed houses – we caught many fish. They belonged to one of the most formidable genera of fish in the world, the piranha, or cannibal fish, the fish that eats men when it can get the chance . . . They are the most ferocious fish in the world. Even the most formidable fish, the sharks, or the barracudas, usually attack things smaller than themselves. But the piranhas habitually attack things much larger than themselves. They will snap a finger off a hand incautiously trailed in the water; they mutilate swimmers – in every river town in Paraguay there are men who have been thus mutilated; they will rend and devour alive any wounded man or beast; for blood in the water excites them to madness. They will tear wounded wild fowl to pieces, and bite off the tails of big fish as they grow exhausted when fighting after being hooked. Miller, before I reached Asunción, had been badly bitten by one. Those that we caught sometimes bit through the hooks, or the double strands of copper wire that served as leaders, and got away. Those that we hauled on deck lived for many minutes. Most predatory fish are long and slim, like the alligator-gar and pickerel. But the piranha is a short, deep-bodied fish, with a blunt face and a heavily under-shot or projecting lower jaw which gapes widely. The razor-edged teeth are wedge-shaped like a shark's, and the jaw muscles possess great power. The rabid, furious snaps drive the teeth through flesh and bone. The head, with its short muzzle, staring malignant eyes, and gaping, cruelly armed jaws, is the embodiment of evil ferocity; and the actions of the fish exactly match its looks. I never witnessed an exhibition of such impotent, savage fury as was shown by the piranhas as they flapped on deck. When fresh from the water and thrown on the boards they uttered an extraordinary squealing sound. As they flapped about they bit with vicious eagerness at whatever presented itself. One of them flapped into a cloth and seized it with a bulldog grip. Another grasped one of his fellows; another snapped at a piece of wood, and left the teeth-marks deep therein. They are the pests of the waters, and it is necessary to be exceedingly cautious about either swimming or wading where they are found. If cattle are driven into, or of their own accord enter, the water, they are commonly not molested; but if by chance some unusually big or ferocious specimen of these fearsome fishes does bite an animal – taking off part of an ear, or perhaps of a teat from the udder of a cow – the blood brings up every member of the ravenous throng which is anywhere near, and unless the attacked animal can immediately make its escape from the water it is devoured alive. Here on the Paraguay the natives hold them in much respect, whereas the caymans are not feared at all. The only redeeming feature about them is that they are themselves fairly good to eat, although with too many bones. . . .

One of the most extraordinary things we saw was this. On one occasion one of us shot a crocodile. It rushed back into the water. The fish attacked it at once and they drove that crocodile out of the water back to the men on the bank. It was less afraid of the men than of the fish. . . . I happened to mention that one of our naturalists, Miller, had been bitten by a piranha, and the man-eating fish at once became the subject of conversation. Curiously enough, one of the Brazilian taxidermists had also just been severely bitten by a piranha. My new companions had story after story to tell of them. Only three weeks previously a twelve-year-old boy who had gone in swimming near Corumbá was attacked, and literally devoured alive by them. Colonel Rondon during his exploring trips had met with more than one unpleasant experience in connection with them. He had lost one of his toes by the bite of a piranha. He was about to bathe, and had chosen a shallow pool at the edge of the river, which he carefully inspected until he was satisfied that none of the man-eating fish were in it; yet as soon as he put his foot into the water one of them attacked him and bit off a toe. On another occasion, while wading across a narrow stream, one of his party was attacked; the fish bit him on the thighs and buttocks, and, when he put down his hands, tore them also; he was near the bank, and by a rush reached it and swung himself out of the water by means of an overhanging limb of a tree; but he was terribly injured, and it took him six months before his wounds healed and he recovered. An extraordinary incident occurred on another trip. The party were without food and very hungry. On reaching a stream they dynamited it, and waded in to seize the stunned fish as they floated on the surface. One man, Lieutenant Pyrineus, having his hands full, tried to hold one fish by putting its head into his mouth; it was a piranha, and seemingly stunned, but in a moment it recovered, and bit a big section out of his tongue. Such a haemorrhage followed that his life was saved with the utmost difficulty. On another occasion a member of the party was off by himself on a mule. The mule came into camp alone. Following his track back, they came to a ford, where in the water they found the skeleton of the dead man, his clothes uninjured, but every particle of flesh stripped from his bones. Whether he had been drowned, and the fishes had then eaten his body, or whether they had killed him, it was impossible to say. They had not hurt the clothes, getting in under them, which made it seem likely that there had been no struggle. These man-eating fish are a veritable scourge in the waters they frequent.

THEODORE ROOSEVELT, *Through the Brazilian Wilderness*,
1924

Missing Fingers

Romilio was a wiry, silent little man. He wore a curious square red beret which gave him the look of a cardinal. Two fingers of his right hand were missing, and a deep scar ran from wrist to elbow. Two years earlier, when he had brought a shark alongside, clubbed it, and was beginning to haul it aboard, the fish turned and with a final effort tore away half his forearm.

'Sharks aren't hard to kill,' Romilio explained to me, 'and this was quite a little one. The hook was right down in his stomach. But it's after you're sure they're dead that you've got to start being careful.'

El tiburón is a carrion-eater, and the wounds it makes very quickly become infected. If Romilio had delayed his return to port by a few hours he would have had to lose half his arm.

I was to find later that many shark-fishers are similarly maimed. Alvarez, another Cojimar man, had his hand pierced one night by the bill of a swordfish. He had hauled the great creature within a few yards of the boat when it broke free. For some seconds it remained motionless on the surface of the water. Alvarez was leaning over the side and hauling in the line when an astonishing thing happened: instead of vanishing at once into the depths, as these fish usually do when they get off the hook, the swordfish attacked the boat. And Alvarez' hand, braced against the hull a few inches below the gunwale, received the thrust.

Such incidents are fairly common. A case is known of men being attacked in the middle of the night by five or six swordfish at once, and at Cojimar one of these creatures pierced the hull of a boat in its struggles, after being brought alongside with a hook tearing its stomach.

FRANÇOIS POLI, *Sharks Are Caught at Night*, 1958

Pike Attacks

The best-authenticated instance of attempted *man*slaughter on the part of a Pike is one which occurred, within a comparatively recent date, in Surrey. The particulars are given by Mr Wright:-

'In the Reading Mercury a statement appeared 'that a lad aged fifteen, named Longhurst, had gone into Inglemere Pond, near Ascot Heath, to bathe, and that, when he had walked in to the depth of about 4 feet, a huge fish, supposed to be a Pike, suddenly rose to the surface and seized his arm. Finding himself resisted, however, he abandoned it, but still followed, and caught hold of the other hand, which he bit very severely. The lad, clenching the hand which had been first bitten, struck his assailant a heavy blow on the head, when the fish swam away. W. Barr Brown, Esq., surgeon, dressed seven wounds, two of which were very deep, and which bled profusely.'

'I wrote to this gentleman, who very politely obtained, and sent this day, Sept. 18, 1857, the whole account, in writing, from the young man's father (Mr George Longhurst, of Sunning Hill), which I give as I received it:-

'"*Particulars of an Encounter with a Fish in the month of June* 1856. — One of my sons, aged fifteen, went with three other boys to bathe in Inglemere Pond, near Ascot Race-Course; he walked gently into the water to about the depth of 4 feet, when he spread out his hands to attempt to swim; instantly a large fish came up and took his hand into his mouth as far up as the wrist, but, finding he could not swallow it, relinquished his hold, and the boy, turning round, prepared for a hasty retreat out of the pond; his companions, who saw it, also scrambled out of the pond as fast as possible. My son had scarcely turned himself round when the fish came up behind him and immediately seized his other hand, crosswise, inflicting some very deep wounds on the back of it; the boy raised his first-bitten, and still bleeding, arm, and struck the monster a hard blow on the head, when the fish disappeared. The other boys assisted him to dress, bound up his hand with their handkerchiefs, and brought him home. We took him down to Mr Brown, surgeon, who dressed seven wounds in one hand; and so great was the pain the next day, that the lad fainted twice: the little finger was bitten through the nail, and it was more than six weeks before it was well. The nail came off, and the scar remains to this day.

'"A few days after this occurrence, one of the woodmen was walking by the side of the pond, when he saw something white floating. A man, who was passing on horse-back, rode in, and found it to be a large Pike in a dying state; he twisted his whip round it and brought it to shore. Myself and my son were immediately sent for to look at it, when the boy at once recognized his antagonist. The fish appeared to have been a long time in the agonies of death; and the body was very lean, and curved like a bow. It measured 41 inches, and died the next day, and, I believe, was taken to the Castle at Windsor.'

'There can be no doubt,' Mr Wright adds, 'that this fish was in a state of complete starvation. . . . If well-fed, it is probable it might have weighed from 30 to 40 lbs.'

The same gentleman also mentions that he was himself on one occasion a witness, with Lord Milsington and many other persons, to a somewhat similar occurrence, where, during the netting of the

Bourne Brook, Chertsey, one of the waders was bitten in the leg by a Pike which he had attempted to kick to shore. This fish, which was afterwards killed, weighed 17 lbs.

I am indebted for the following to Dr Genzik: – 'In 1829 I was bathing in the Swimming-School at Vienna with some fellow-students, when one of them – afterwards Dr Gouge, who died a celebrated physician some years ago – suddenly screamed out and sank. We all plunged in immediately to his rescue, and succeeded in bringing him to the surface, and finally in getting him up on to the hoarding of the bath, when a Pike was found sticking fast to his right heel, which would not loose its hold, but was killed, and eaten by us all in company the same evening. It weighed 32 lbs. Gouge suffered for months from the bite.'

H. CHOLMONDELEY-PENNELL, The Angler Naturalist, 1868

Grim the Pike Has Her Revenge

Grim has taken the bait, and is now darting about with it. She had been hungry after three days' storm and wind, and had therefore rushed blindly at the lure. Alas, it is another of those prickly fish, she notices at once, one of those confounded tit-bits that are only to be looked at, but which neither teeth nor throat are ever glad to deal with; and she opens her mouth and chokes and spits.

She gets rid of the fish she had snatched; she sees it, half dead and with long rents in its sides from her teeth, floating on its side with a reddish yellow eye turned up towards her through the water. But the prickly thorn that she took in at the same time is fixed in her jaw.

She darts hither and thither, turning and twisting. Now she is down in deep water, rubbing her wounded mouth upon the bottom, now she darts, with the bubbles in her wake rising above her, round a clump of water-lilies.

The angler sees an island of leaves as big as a dining-table disappear.

Then she is off again. The reel shrieks and hums as if a giant grasshopper sat chirping in it. All at once, Grim leaps out of the water high into the air, so that her golden, black-streaked body, with the panther-like spots and the trickling waterdrops, casts a gleam over the lake.

Never had the good man seen such a fish! The very waves that it raises as it returns to the water, breaking the surface like a submarine, show him that it is – as he is accustomed to express it – 'one of the good old-fashioned sort.' He continues to gaze open-mouthed at the place where it disappeared, while a flurry of rings spreads out in all directions.

A little later a whirlpool appears on the seething water, and he catches a glimpse of a dorsal fin with the hinder point missing. Then the old fisherman rejoices. A marked fish, one of his oldest, perhaps his biggest!

He winds in, lets the line run out, and winds in again. His big body is perspiring with his exertions, and he has to stand with his legs wide apart and his feet firmly fixed whenever the mighty fish gives one of its sudden jerks.

While this is going on there are bites on two of the perch-lines, and the angler can see they are not small fish either. The lines, which are lying loose over the gunwale, run out at a great pace, so that the winders hop and dance about at the bottom of the boat. One of them is jerked over the edge, so that fish, hooks, and line are lost; the other he tries to make sure of by setting his foot upon it.

Like the back of a cat about to spring, the rod bends under its floundering burden. The old man has to keep on incessantly slacking and tightening the line; hoping to tire out the fish that was dragging his rod from one side to the other.

He notes the smallest movement of his captives. It is still in full vigour, and there are many water-plants and stalks in the way. Will he be able to draw his captive from the deep water with his fine, fragile line?

Suddenly Grim turns and darts in beneath the boat with such force that the rod must either break or follow her. The angler chooses to let it go in the hope of picking it up on the other side.

It happens as he expected: the rod appears, floats up; he leans over and reaches it.

The fight and nervous excitement recommence – the quick, exciting contest between man and fish.

The wind plays its autumn hymn upon the rushes, and ruffles the water between the yellow-spotted water-lily leaves, while the sun's rays, as they come and go, light flaming torches among the trees and reeds. They gleam, they sparkle, they flash; and great, heavy, September clouds drift over the lake.

At last the shrewd fisherman has the upper hand, and cautiously draws his captive close up to the boat. He bends down, with his knees upon the gunwale, and leans over with the landing-net in his right hand.

Grim suddenly finds herself close to the great 'water-bird,' and gives a violent jerk. The fisherman reaches out with his arm, and the upper part of his body as far as they will go; but he forgets that he is in a boat and on unsafe ground, loses his balance, and falls overboard with a splash, upsetting the boat as he does so.

No one sees the accident, and his heavy waders drag him quickly down.

Grim darts this way and that, winding the line round him and drawing him to the bottom. And then, among the rocks of the reef, the line breaks; the angler's body drifts in among the reeds.

SVEND FLEURON, *Grim, the Story of a Pike*, 1920

How Hiawatha Caught the Sturgeon

FORTH upon the Gitche Gumee,
On the shining Big Sea-Water,
With his fishing-line of cedar,
Of the twisted bark of cedar,
Forth to catch the sturgeon Nahma,
Mishe-Nahma, King of Fishes,
In his birch canoe exulting
All alone went Hiawatha.

Through the clear, transparent water
He could see the fishes swimming
Far down in the depths below him;
See the yellow perch, the Sahwa,
Like a sunbeam in the water
See the Shawgashee, the crawfish,
Like a spider on the bottom,
On the white and sandy bottom.
At the stern sat Hiawatha,

With his fishing-line of cedar;
In his plumes the breeze of morning
Played as in the hemlock branches:
On the bows, with tail erected,
Sat the squirrel, Adjidaumo;
In his fur the breeze of morning
Played as in the prairie grasses.

On the white sand of the bottom
Lay the monster Mishe-Nahma,
Lay the sturgeon, King of Fishes;
Through his gills he breathed the water
With his fins he fanned and winnowed,
With his tail he swept the sandfloor.

There he lay in all his armour;
On each side a shield to guard him,
Plates of bone upon his forehead,
Down his sides and back and shoulders
Plates of bone with spines projecting!
Painted was he with his warpaints,
Stripes of yellow, red, and azure,
Spots of brown and spots of sable;
And he lay there on the bottom,
Fanning with his fins of purple,
As above him Hiawatha
In his birch canoe came sailing,
With his fishing-line of cedar.
'Take my bait!' cried Hiawatha
Down into the depths beneath him,
'Take my bait, O Sturgeon, Nahma,
Come up from below the water,
Let us see which is the stronger!'
And he dropped his line of cedar
Through the clear, transparent water,
Waited vainly for an answer,
Long sat waiting for an answer,
And repeating loud and louder,
'Take my bait, O King of Fishes!'

Quiet lay the sturgeon, Nahma,

Fanning slowly in the water,
Looking up at Hiawatha,
Listening to his call and clamour,
His unnecessary tumult,
Till he wearied of the shouting;
And he said to the Kenozha,
To the pike, the Maskenozha,
'Take the bait of this rude fellow,
Break the line of Hiawatha!'
    In his fingers Hiawatha
Felt the loose line jerk and tighten;
As he drew it in, it tugged so
That the birch canoe stood end wise,
Like a birch log in the water,
With the squirrel, Adjidaumo,
Perched and frisking on the summit.
    Full of scorn was Hiawatha
When he saw the fish rise upward,
Saw the pike, the Maskenozha,
Coming nearer, nearer to him,
And he shouted through the water,
'Esa! esa! shame upon you!
You are but the pike, Kenozha,
You are not the fish I wanted,
You are not the King of Fishes!'
    Reeling downward to the bottom
Sank the pike in great confusion,
And the mighty sturgeon, Nahma,
Said to Ugudwash, the sun-fish,
'Take the bait of this great boaster,
Break the line of Hiawatha!'
    Slowly upward, wavering, gleaming
Like a white moon in the water,
Rose the Ugudwash, the sun-fish,
Seized the line of Hiawatha,
Swung with all his weight upon it,
Made a whirlpool in the water,
Whirled the birch canoe in circles,

Round and round in gurgling eddies,
Till the circles in the water
Reached the far-off sandy beaches,
Till the water-flags and rushes
Nodded on the distant margins.
  But when Hiawatha saw him
Slowly rising through the water,
Lifting his great disc of whiteness,
Loud he shouted in derision,
'Esa! esa! shame upon you!
You are Ugudwash the sun-fish,
You are not the fish I wanted,
You are not the King of Fishes!'
  Slowly downward, wavering, gleaming,
Sank the Ugudwash, the sun-fish,
And again the sturgeon, Nahma,
Heard the shout of Hiawatha,
Heard his challenge of defiance,
The unnecessary tumult,
Ringing far across the water.
  From the white sand of the bottom
Up he rose with angry gesture,
Quivering in each nerve and fibre,
Clashing all his plates of armour,
Gleaming bright with all his warpaint;
In his wrath he darted upward,
Flashing leaped into the sunshine,
Opened his great jaws, and swallowed
Both canoe and Hiawatha.
  Down into that darksome cavern
Plunged the headlong Hiawatha,
As a log on some black river
Shoots and plunges down the rapids,
Found himself in utter darkness,
Groped about in helpless wonder,
Till he felt a great heart beating,
Throbbing in that utter darkness.
  And he smote it in his anger,

With his fist, the heart of Nahma,
Felt the mighty King of Fishes
Shudder through each nerve and fibre,
Heard the water gurgle round him
As he leaped and staggered through it,
Sick at heart, and faint and weary.
    Crosswise then did Hiawatha
Drag his birch canoe for safety,
Lest from out the jaws of Nahma,
In the turmoil and confusion;
Forth he might be hurled and perish.
And the squirrel, Adjidaumo,
Frisked and chattered very gaily,
Toiled and tugged with Hiawatha
Till the labour was completed.
    Then said Hiawatha to him,
'O my little friend, the squirrel,
Bravely have you toiled to help me;
Take the thanks of Hiawatha,
And the name which now he gives you;
For hereafter and for ever
Boys shall call you Adjidaumo,
Tail-in-air the boys shall call you!'
And again the sturgeon, Nahma,
Gasped and quivered in the water,
Then was still, and drifted landward
Till he grated on the pebbles,
Till the listening Hiawatha
Heard him grate upon the margin,
Felt him stand upon the pebbles,
Knew that Nahma, King of Fishes,
Lay there dead upon the margin.
    Then he heard a clang and flapping,
As of many wings assembling,
Heard a screaming and confusion,
As of birds of prey contending,
Saw a gleam of light above him,
Shining through the ribs of Nahma,

Saw the glittering eyes of sea-gulls,
Of Kayoshk, the sea-gulls, peering,
Gazing at him through the opening,
Heard them saying to each other,
"'Tis our brother, Hiawatha!'
  And he shouted from below them,
Cried exulting from the caverns,
'O ye sea-gulls! O my brothers!
I have slain the sturgeon, Nahma;
Make the rifts a little larger,
With your claws the openings widen,
Set me free from this dark prison,
And henceforward and for ever
Men shall speak of your achievements,
Calling you Kayoshk, the sea-gull,
Yes, Kayoshk, the Noble Scratchers!'
  And the wild and clamorous sea-gulls
Toiled with beak and claws together,
Made the rifts and openings wider
In the mighty ribs of Nahma,
And from peril and from prison,
From the body of the sturgeon,
From the peril of the water,
Was released my Hiawatha.
  He was standing near his wigwam,
On the margin of the water,
And he called to old Nokomis,
Called and beckoned to Nokomis,
Pointed to the sturgeon, Nahma,
Lying lifeless on the pebbles,
With the sea-gulls feeding on him.
'I have slain the Mishe-Nahma,
Slain the King of Fishes!' said he;
'Look! the sea-gulls feed upon him,
Yes, my friends Kayoshk, the sea-gulls;
Drive them not away, Nokomis!
They have saved me from great peril
In the body of the sturgeon.

Wait until their meal is ended,
Till their craws are full with feasting,
Till they homeward fly at sunset,
To their nests among the marshes;
Then bring all your pots and kettles,
And make oil for us in Winter.'
    And she waited till the sunset,
Till the pallid moon, the Night-sun,
Rose above the tranquil water,
Till Kayoshk, the sated sea-gulls,
From their banquet rose with clamour,
And across the fiery sunset
Winged their way to far-off islands,
To their nests among the rushes.
    To his sleep went Hiawatha,
And Nokomis to her labour,
Toiling patient in the moonlight,
Till the sun and moon changed places,
Till the sky was red with sunrise,
And Kayoshk, the hungry sea-gulls,
Came back from the reedy islands,
Clamorous for their morning banquet.
    Three whole days and nights alternate
Old Nokomis and the sea-gulls
Stripped the oily flesh of Nahma,
Till the waves washed through the rib-bones,
Till the sea-gulls came no longer,
And upon the sands lay nothing
But the skeleton of Nahma.

HENRY WADSWORTH LONGFELLOW, *The Song of Hiawatha*,
1855

Jonah

A cream of phosphorescent light
Floats on the wash that to and fro
Slides round his feet – enough to show

FISH THAT BIT BACK

Many a pendulous stalactite
Of naked mucus, whorls and wreaths
And huge festoons of mottled tripes,
With smaller palpitating pipes
Through which some yeasty liquor seethes.

Seated upon the convex mound
Of one vast kidney, Jonah prays
And sings his canticles and hymns,
Making the hollow vault resound
God's goodness and mysterious ways,
Till the great fish spouts music as he swims.

ALDOUS HUXLEY, 1917

A Victorian Whale-hunter Recalls Being Swallowed By his Quarry

I remember very well from the moment that I fell from the boat and felt my feet strike some soft substance. I looked up and saw a big-ribbed canopy of light pink and white descending over me, and the next moment I felt myself drawn downward, feet first, and I realized that I was being swallowed by a whale. I was drawn lower and lower; a wall of flesh surrounded me and hemmed me in on every side, yet the pressure was not painful and the flesh easily gave way like soft india-rubber before my slightest movement.

Suddenly I found myself in a sack much larger than my body, but completely dark. I felt about me; and my hands came in contact with several fishes, some of which seemed to be still alive, for they squirmed in my fingers, and slipped back to my feet. Soon I felt a great pain in my head and my breathing became more and more difficult. At the same time I felt a terrible heat; it seemed to consume me, growing hotter and hotter. My eyes became coals of fire in my head, and I believed every moment that I was condemned to perish in the belly of a whale. It tormented me beyond all endurance, while at the same time the awful silence of the terrible prison weighed me down. I tried to rise, to move my arms and legs, to cry out. All action was now impossible, but my brain seemed abnormally clear; and with a full comprehension of my awful fate, I finally lost all consciousness.

This fascinating narrative was written by 35-year-old James Bartley, an English sailor on the *Star of the East*, who on 25 August 1891, while whaling in the South Atlantic off the Falkland Islands, was reportedly swallowed by a whale. What is so extraordinary is not so much that Bartley was swallowed by an enraged sperm whale in the midst of the hunt – there have been a few other such reports – but that he lived to tell the story.

According to this widely published account of the incident, within a couple of hours of the whale's swallowing Bartley, it was killed and brought to the mother ship. There, after hours of butchering, the stomach section was opened and the astonished crewmen found the lost Bartley: unconscious, bleached to a deathly white by the gastric acids, but still living. For two weeks Bartley remained in a near delirious condition, but apart from his almost albino state (which remained with him all his life), he made a full recovery.

DAVID DAY, *Whale War*, 1987

A More Plausible Account of What Happens to Those Swallowed by Whales

SIRS:

I was greatly interested in the letter, appearing in your April publication, concerning the incredible incident of the unfortunate seaman, Jas. Bartley, who was swallowed by a sperm whale and lived to tell the tale. My interest is in a sense personal because of my small part in a similar though not so fortunate accident . . .

It was in February or March of '93 or '94 when, as a young surgeon, I was attached for the season to the sealing fleet out of St. Johns, Newfoundland, as much for the adventure as for my "sealers' share" of the trip. We sailed on the schooner "Toulinguet," one of a considerable fleet of wooden ships bent on the winter's take of seal pups.

One of the lads on another ship had the misfortune, in full view of his comrades, to become isolated from the others on an ice pan, from which he fell into the icy waters in the proximity of a huge sperm whale. The whale was apparently as lost and out of season in those Arctic waters as he was confused and angered by the sudden appearance of a fleet of ships and men.

Somehow the poor fellow was swallowed by the whale, which then made straight for one of the smaller sealers. A lucky shot from the small cannon mounted on her stern mortally wounded the huge mammal and served to change his course, though he traveled a full three miles out to sea before his final death thrashing. The next day he was found floating belly-up by one of the longboats as it was searching for seals; and though it was impossible under those conditions to bring him in, the men, by a valiant effort and many hours of hard labor, were able to hack their way through his abdomen below the diaphragm and isolate his huge gas-filled "upper stomach," which apparently contained their comrade. This was severed with some difficulty at the cardia and in the first portion of the duodenum. They brought it to me for inspection and also for preservation of the man's body, as it was hoped he could be returned to his native Argentia (Newfoundland) for burial.

At first I attempted the dissection with my scalpel but quickly gave it up in favor of one of the sharpest galley knives. The stomach was finally opened and gave off an overpowering stench. A fearsome sight met our eyes. The young man had apparently been badly crushed in the region of his chest, which may have been enough to kill him outright. (In any event an examination of his lungs revealed a general atelectasia with marked hemorrhage throughout.) The most striking findings were external, however; the whale's gastric mucosa had encased his body (particularly the exposed parts) like the foot of a huge snail. His face, hands, and one of his legs, where a trouser leg had been pulled up or torn, were badly macerated and partially digested . . . It was my opinion that he had no consciousness of what happened to him. Curiously enough some lice on his head appeared still to be alive.

The appearance and odor were so bad that all save I were forced to turn away, and we were obliged to consign him to the briny deep – the last resting place of many a good sealer – rather than to carry him back to his rocky homeland.

EGERTON Y. DAVIS, JR.
Boston, Mass.

Letter in *Natural History* (Journal of the American Museum
of Natural History), June 1947

A Modern Captain Ahab

The 543-ton *Tonna* entered the pirate armada of the North Atlantic in a series of devious transformations typical of all pirate whaling vessels. She was once the Japanese trawler *Shunyo Maru*. Then she appeared in Curaçao in the Caribbean as the *Southern Fortune*. By the time she finally joined the *Sierra* (her now notorious sister pirate vessel) in the Canaries, she was named the MV *Tonna* and had been converted into a whaler. Typically, she was registered not as a whaler but as a fishing boat under the dummy company Red Mullet Fishing and flew the Netherlands Antilles flag-of-convenience – or, more to the point, flag-of-confusion. By chance, its managers happened to be the now familiar Sierra Fishing Agency, a division of the quotable Andrew M. Behr of South Africa.

The *Tonna* combined operations with the *Sierra*, sometimes acting as the *Sierra*'s factory ship because of her larger slipway and sometimes killing and slaughtering the whales herself. The result was that the ships had doubled their killing range and doubled their tonnage. Together they continued to kill every species they encountered, and cut only the prime meat from them, dumping the rest back into the sea.

On 27 June 1978 the *Tonna* made a solo whaling voyage; the *Sierra* was laid up in port with repairs. By 22 July she was returning to the Canaries with her freezers packed with 450 tons of whale meat. Weighted down as she was, the *Tonna* rode very low in the water. Some 220 miles off Portugal, at about five o'clock in the evening, the *Tonna* sighted a sleek 70-foot fin whale. Her Norwegian captain, Kristhof Vesprhein, succumbed to pure greed. He accelerated the engines to full diesel power and overtook the enormous fin whale. The harpooner fired into the beast and played the steel line with the powerful winch as the whale dove and thrashed in the water, slowly dying.

As the whale fought on, and the *Tonna* struggled to pull in her prey, deep sea swells rapidly rose up and began to pitch the heavily laden ship from side to side. Suddenly, while the crew attempted to drag the 50-ton whale on to the slipway, the whale's weight and a large swell pulled the ship far over to one side. The overladen *Tonna* keeled over, the rail was pushed under water, the scuppers were awash. Because of the tropical heat, several hatches and portholes had been carelessly left open in the stern, and the sea poured in. The engine room flooded, blowing out all the electrics. Not only was there no engine power but the winches were immobilized. The crew could neither release their catch nor cut it loose.

The ship became the captive of the captured whale, the two wrapped in a fatal embrace. The swift fin whale, known as the greyhound of the sea, was now a deadly 50-ton anchor pulling the destroyer down with it. As its grey back rolled away, its long white belly turned up. The weight of the fin whale tugged the line again, the sea rushed in faster, the speed of descent accelerated, and that colourful international cast of 42 pirate whalers rushed for the lifeboats.

What happened next cannot be easily explained. Captain Kristhof Vesprhein refused to give up the fight, and despite appeals from his crew would not abandon his ship. Like one in a dream, mesmerized, he refused to leave the bridge. Something else tugged at him as the whale tugged on the ship. Did he see in the white belly of the whale an old tale, its time come around again: the great whale pulling him and all the machinery of death at his command into the beckoning vortex of oblivion? Adamant, resigned to fate, he remained on the bridge – a beer bottle in his hand – and waved his crew away.

The *Tonna* pitched again and the 50-ton whale pulled the ship, her 450-ton cargo, her arsenal of harpoons and cannon and her pirate captain down to a watery grave. And just as Melville concluded his tale over a century before, when the whirling vortex of the ship subsided, 'the great shroud of the sea rolled on as it rolled five thousand years ago'.

For the pirates of the Atlantic, it was an ill omen. It was a warning of worse to come. The tide of their war had changed, and all their luck was gone. The 42 survivors of the *Tonna* were rescued that same night just before midnight by a Greek freighter to which had been relayed the *Tonna*'s distress call. On her decks, the orphaned crewmen told their rescuers a strange variation of that old tale of Moby Dick, and how they had lost their own Ahab and his ship to the whale.

DAVID DAY, *Whale War*, 1987

Stonefish Poisoning

In March, 1956 an Indian youth of 15, well-built and athletic, was swimming there [Pont Larus, Mahé, Seychelles] and came towards the rocks. As he trod he felt a stab in the sole of his foot. He pulled himself up, sat on the rock and then saw three punctures. By this time intense pain had developed at the site of the punctures, which spread rapidly up the leg to the body. In a short time he was in agony and showing signs of collapse. Alarmed by his appearance the others managed to find a pirogue in which he was taken to shore. By this time he had turned blue and was frothing at the mouth. He was at once put in a car that set out for the hospital, but he died on the way there.

According to the medical officer who examined the body, this was greatly cyanosed, and the apparent cause of death was a cardiac or respiratory poison that had been injected. His medical attendant reported that he had not suffered from heart trouble.

At Pinda, Mozambique, on the 23rd September, 1956, two men went out in a canoe to the margin of the reef, close on 5 miles from land, and near low tide went wading, hunting for fishes with spears. The elder soon noted that the other had collapsed in the water. Hastening over, he found his companion almost delirious, but able to say that he had been stabbed in the foot by a 'sherowa' (*Synanceja*). Others came to help; the wounded man, now unconscious, was carried to the nearest canoe, and the stonefish was found and killed, cut open and the gall-bladder extracted, for the natives believe this, swallowed, to be an antidote to the poison. The victim was by then unconscious and, well within an hour was dead.

I examined the corpse later. There was only one stab in the front of the second toe of the right foot. It was close on $\frac{3}{4}''$ deep and went along the bone. The man must have kicked against the stonefish from behind. There was neither discoloration nor swelling in the toe or foot and from the rapidity with which he succumbed the toxin may well have been injected directly into a blood vessel. The victim was between 30 and 40 years of age and apparently, as well as from enquiry, strong and in good health.

DR J.H.B. SMITH, in *Copeia*, 1957

Forget the Video!

KEY WEST, Fla. (AP) – Barracudas generally don't attack people unless provoked. But don't tell that to Nadine Cloer, who received nearly 200 stitches after an 8-foot (2½-meter) barracuda leaped into a houseboat and bit her hand and leg.

'I saw him come out of the water like a bullet,' the Tampa-area woman said from her Key Largo hospital bed Sunday. 'It was like a torpedo right out of the water. It looked like it was diving straight for me.'

Family members rushed to help Cloer after the fish lunged at her Saturday off the Florida Keys. They pushed it overboard with poles.

'When I arrived she was in a pool of blood with everyone trying to stop the bleeding,' said Capt. Mitch Schacter of Sea Tow Marine Services, who responded to the distress call.

Cloer, 46, said she had to have tendons replaced and skin grafts to cover the wounds. She is able to hobble around a little and hoped to be released Monday.

Cloer's doctor was unavailable, but nursing supervisor Greg Vignone at Mariner's Hospital said he saw the wounds.

'It was definitely a fish bite,' he said.

Barracudas, long, thin predators with razor-sharp teeth, do not usually attack unless speared or provoked by divers or snorkelers.

Cloer, a school bus driver, was spending the weekend in a rented houseboat fishing with her husband, two sisters and a brother-in-law.

She said her brother-in-law hooked a 5-foot barracuda and she saw it pass under the boat. She went inside the cabin to get a video camera and as she was walking out the door, a much larger one cleared the deck and lunged at her.

'I still can't believe the force that it hit me with,' she said. 'It was unreal.'

The cabin of the 40-foot vessel is set back about 8 feet from the edge. Family members say the fish jumped some 12 to 15 feet. The force knocked Cloer back into the cabin with the fish on top of her.

'I don't have any idea why it attacked me,' she said. 'It is possible the bigger one could have been chasing the one that my brother-in-law had on the line.'

Cloer's doctor told her the fish came within a thumb's width of severing an artery in her pelvis, which almost certainly would have killed her.

ASSOCIATED PRESS DESPATCH, 12 July 1993

An Octopus and a Fisherman

I was wading at low tide one calm evening on the lip of the reef at Ocean Island when a Baanaban villager, back from fishing, brought his canoe to land within twenty yards of where I stood. There was no more than a show of breaking seas, but the water was only knee deep, and this obliged the fisherman to slide overboard and handle his lightened craft over the jagged edge. But no sooner were his feet upon the reef than he seemed to be tied to where he stood. The canoe was washed shorewards ahead of him; while he stood with legs braced, tugging desperately away from something. I had just time to see a tapering, greyish-yellow rope curled around his right wrist before he broke away from it. He fell sprawling into the shallow water; the tapered rope flicked writhing back into the foam at the reef's edge. The fisherman picked himself up and nursed his right arm. I had reached him by then. The octopus had caught him with only the tip of one tentacle, but the terrible hold of the few suckers on his wrist had torn the skin whole from it as he wrenched himself adrift.

ARTHUR GRIMBLE, *A Pattern of Islands*, 1952

A Cruising Rogue Shark

The series of attacks by what was described as the 'mad shark' began on 2nd July 1916 at Beach Haven, New Jersey, a popular summer resort, about 70 miles south of New York and not far from Atlantic City.

A 24-year-old man named Vansant was swimming in about five feet of water at 5 p.m. There were only a few others with him. The nearest was about 40 feet away. Sheridan Taylor saw Vansant standing alone shoulder deep in the sea. He heard Vansant scream and saw him wildly beat the water. Taylor was almost immobilized for a second. Then he saw the water turn red and rushed towards Vansant. Taylor saw the shark clearly. Its fin and part of its back were well out of the water. Taylor grabbed Vansant and with the aid of others, who formed a human chain, began pulling him in. The shark came too, its jaws on its victim's leg.

Taylor could have touched it without any effort. They came right in until they stood in about eighteen inches of water. The shark was still there. Then it turned and made off. On the sand a medical student applied a tourniquet above severe injuries on the man's left leg, but Vansant died a few hours after reaching hospital. This killer, observers said later, was bluish-grey and about 10 feet long.

On 6th July, four days later, Charles Bruder lost his life in a similar manner at Spring Lake, 35 miles farther north. His right leg was taken off just below the knee and the left leg amputated by the shark's teeth at the ankle. They were horrible injuries, and Bruder died a few minutes after being rescued.

Hundreds of men and women and many children were on the beach on the afternoon when Bruder, far out beyond the outer life lines, raised a cry for help. Two lifeguards, George White and Chris Anderson, who had been watching the swimmer closely because of his distance from the shore, launched a lifeboat and started for Bruder while the crowd on the beach watched. As the lifeguards drew near, the water about Bruder was suddenly tinged with red. When White and Anderson reached Bruder, he cried out that a shark had bitten him. He then fainted.

On the beach an attempt was made to bandage his wounds while a doctor was called. Before one arrived, Bruder was dead.

This second attack horrified people in the area. Motor-boat patrols were instituted in a number of resorts. Wire-netting enclosures were set up. The entire coastal area went into a kind of systematic and organized panic.

Bruder's death renewed the controversy that had raged for years as to whether a shark would attack a man. It was suggested at the time that a turtle or huge mackerel had killed him. In support of that theory it was pointed out that the victim's legs were torn and chewed as though something had hacked them, and not bitten with the clean, sharp bite supposed to be characteristic of a shark. Colonel W.G. Schauffler, Surgeon-General of the National Guard of New Jersey, and a member of Govenor Fielder's staff, who attended Bruder just before his death, described the wounds on the young man's body. Because of the question raised by some as to whether or not Bruder had really been attacked by a shark, Colonel Schauffler's description of the wounds is detailed.

Bruder's right leg, he said, had been taken off so that the bone stuck out to a point halfway between the knee and the ankle. The foot and ankle had been bitten off and were missing. The flesh was ripped as high as the knee, and the bone was denuded of flesh. The left leg had been bitten off at the ankle, the lower ends of the two leg bones protruding from the flesh fully one-third of the length of the leg. There was a very deep circular gash above the left knee, extending down to the bone. On the right side of the abdomen a piece of flesh had been gouged out.

After the attack at Spring Lake experienced surf men and fishermen ridiculed the elaborate precautions taken, asserting that sharks had never been sighted although some small blue-nosed sharks had been caught near the fish pounds at Asbury. . . .

Two days after the attack, Captain Frank Claret of the liner *Minnehaha* made a statement. He was astounded, he said, that man-eating sharks had been seen at Jersey beaches. It was the first time he had ever known man-eaters to go north of the Bahamas. . . .

Reports from incoming steamers supported a theory that man-eaters along the Jersey coast had been driven north by hunger. Skipper of the vessel *Atlantic* (Captain Brewer), said he had seen sharks swimming northward. Off Cape Hatteras his steamer had passed the largest school of sharks he had ever seen. Some were huge monsters.

After the attacks were investigated, Dr J.T. Nichols, Curator of the Department of Fisheries of the American Museum of Natural History, retracted a statement he made on 8th July that there was very little danger of a shark attacking anyone.

Of course – it happens everywhere – bathers quickly forgot about sharks. Then on 12th July the nation was galvanized. The rogue-shark cycle was completed. On that day a 10-year-old boy and a young man were torn to death by the ravages of a shark. Another youngster was torn from hip to knee by the same monster. It was this third and final tragedy that shook the nation and caused President Wilson to summon his Cabinet to consider the menace.

Early on 12th July, Captain Thomas Cottrell, a retired mariner, saw a dark grey shape swimming rapidly in the shallow waters of Matawan Creek. The creek was only 30 miles by sea north of Spring Lake, but it was 20 miles from the ocean. Captain Cottrell recalled the two swimmers killed by sharks on the New Jersey coast. He hurried to town and spread the warning among the 2000 residents that a shark had entered Matawan Creek.

Everywhere they laughed at him. How could a shark get 20 miles away from the ocean, swim through Raritan Bay, and enter the shallow creek? Thus the townfolk reasoned, and grown-ups and children flocked to the creek as usual for their daily dip.

But Captain Cottrell was right. That night a body lay in the Long Branch Memorial Hospital. A dead child lay somewhere in the dark water and in St Peter's Hospital, New Brunswick, doctors worked throughout the night maintaining the life of another lad torn about the hip.

It was unfortunate that the first victim, 10-year-old Lester Stilwell, suffered from fits. When he was convulsed in the water and went below the surface, Stanley Fisher, son of the retired Commodore of the Savannah Line, assumed the boy had taken a fit and raced to the centre of the creek to his aid. Young Stilwell came to the surface as Fisher approached. The lad screamed and yelled and waved his arms wildly. His body swirled round and round in the water. Fisher was warned it might be a shark. 'A shark here?' he said incredulously. 'I don't care, anyway. I'm going after that boy.'

When he got to the centre of the stream there was no sign of the lad. Fisher dived once, twice. At last he came up with the blood-stained figure in his arms.

He was nearer the opposite shore and struck out in that direction, while Arthur Smith and Joseph Deulew put out in a motor boat to bring him back. Fisher was almost on the shore. When his feet touched bottom, the onlookers heard him utter a cry and saw him throw up his arms. Stilwell's body slipped back into the stream. With another cry, Fisher was dragged after it.

'The shark! The shark!' cried the crowd ashore, and other men sprang into motor boats and started for the spot where Fisher had disappeared. Smith and Deulew were in the lead, but before they overtook him Fisher had risen and dragged himself to the bank where he collapsed.

Those who reached him found the young man's right leg stripped of flesh from above the hip at the waist line to a point below the knee. He was senseless from shock and pain, but was resuscitated by Dr G.L. Reynolds after Recorder Arthur Van Buskirk had made a tourniquet of rope and staunched the flow of blood from Fisher's frightful wounds.

Fisher said he was in less than three or four feet of water when the shark grabbed him, and he had had no notion of sharks until that instant. If he had thought of them at all, he said, he had felt himself safe when he got his feet on the bottom. He had felt the nip on his leg, and looking down, had seen the shark clinging to him. Others ashore said they saw the white belly of the shark as it turned to seize him. Fisher was carried across the river and hurried by train to the hospital at Long Branch. He died before he could be carried to the operating table.

At the creek, meantime, dynamite had been procured. Arrangements were being made to detonate it off, when a motor boat raced up to the steamboat pier. At the wheel was J.R. Lefferts. In the craft lay 12-year-old John Dunn. With his brother William and several others, he had been swimming off the New Jersey Clay Co. brickyards at Cliffwood, about half a mile below the spot where Stilwell and Fisher were attacked.

News of the accident had reached the boys and they had hurried from the water. Dunn was the last to leave, and as he drew himself up on the brick company's pier, with his left leg trailing in the water, the shark struck. Its teeth shut over the leg above and below the knee and much of the flesh was torn away. He was taken to a factory near by, where Dr H.J. Cooley, of Keyport, dressed his wounds, and then by car to St Peter's Hospital, New Brunswick, where the torn leg was amputated. Two days later they found Lester Stilwell's body resting against the shore 100 yards upstream from the place where he was attacked. There were seven wounds, four on the body, two on the left leg and one on the right.

After this tragedy one of the most intensive shark hunts in history began. Hundreds of hunters scoured the area in boats. They used nets, they laid steel meshes across the creek and they fired thousands of rounds of ammunition into spots where sharks might be hiding. Hourly catches were made and many sharks writhing and threshing were dragged ashore.

Two days later, Michael Schleisser, a taxidermist, caught an eight and a half footer off South Amboy, New Jersey, about 4 miles north of Raritan Bay. When he opened the shark he found in its stomach a mass of flesh and bones weighing about 15 lbs. The bones were identified as human. They included portion of a shin bone which apparently belonged to Charles Bruder, who had been attacked nine days previously. Mr Schleisser mounted the skin and placed it on exhibit, where Dr J.T. Nichols, of the American Museum, saw it and positively identified the shark as the great white shark, *Carcharodon carcharias*.

After the capture of this killer, shark attacks ceased. Mr Murphy, of the Brooklyn Museum, and Dr Nichols investigated this remarkable series of tragedies and concluded that Schleisser's shark was a solitary one and the sole attacker of the men and boys.

There was no lack of theories to account for these killings. Some said it was a shark season. Others suggested the brute must have been suffering from a kind of shark rabies like a mad dog. There was another suggestion that owing to the interference with shipping – nobody had forgotten there was a world war on – the sharks missed the food they were used to getting from ocean liners and sought other victuals. There was a theory that recent naval disasters had given sharks an acquired taste for human flesh.

V.M. COPPLESON, Shark Attack, 1958

Shark in the Boat

The lengths to which the sharks will go in search of fish are incredible. Urged on by the struggles of the fish, whether caught on lines or in nets, the sharks often attack fishing craft. The smell of fish around the boat, bait in the boat, or even the sound of fish flapping on the floorboards is enough to excite them. Apparently frantic with hunger, sharks have even at times been known to leap bodily into the boats.

Just before Christmas 1946 Harry Lone, a well-known fisherman of Gladstone, Queensland, left his fishing launch moored alongside a jetty while he went to lunch. Later he was about to step into the craft when, to his amazement, he saw a 400-lb. shark lying in the cockpit. It had obviously taken a flying leap from the water during his absence. Lone and a friend took a knife to it. The shark retaliated so violently with snapping teeth and flying tail that after it was finally killed, Lone spent some time sadly examining the launch's bent tail shaft, a broken clutch and smashed floorboards.

Fortunately for fishermen, such marine gymnastics are rare, but when, however, an enterprising monster hurls itself into a small boat occupied by fishermen, fishing becomes really exciting.

With two others, 35-year-old Doug Miller was fishing from a 16-foot dinghy at Seaholme, Victoria, one fine day in December 1949. Miller was not feeling particularly fit – in fact he was lying in the bottom of the dinghy feeling very much out of sorts. Up to this point any amateur fisherman could feel sympathy for Doug Miller. Later he told his story, short and to the point. He said:

One minute I was lying there, wishing I was dead. I felt terrible. Suddenly I heard a scream and a yell and an eight-and-a-half foot grey nurse landed fair on top of me. For a second I didn't know what it was. Then I knew and nearly blacked out. I fought to get to my feet and as soon as I did I was knocked down by its tail. Three times I stood up and three times I landed back in the bottom of the boat. I felt like going overboard, but I couldn't leave the other two.

All three in the boat had great difficulty in avoiding injury from the snapping teeth and threshing tail before they finally killed the shark with a mighty blow from the tiller.

All kinds of craft have been damaged and sunk and in some cases lives have been lost by sharks' ramming tactics. Even sturdily built boats have been attacked. Some of the attacks by hooked sharks have been particularly savage. At Cronulla, New South Wales, in March 1934, two fishermen caught a 12-foot shark on a line about 6 miles off the coast. The enraged monster immediately speared into an attack on the solid 18-foot launch. Several times it drove its great weight at the launch, snapping viciously at the rudder and bow, causing the boat to rock violently. The two men were mightily relieved to be taken aboard a larger launch. Meanwhile the shark continued its attack on the smaller boat. The shark fought every inch of the way for an hour before it was landed. Several mako shark's teeth were later extracted from the launch's timber.

v.m. coppleson, *Shark Attack*, 1958

What to Do If A Shark Attacks

... you can kick or stiff-arm an oncoming shark, swim aside, or even try going straight at it – a method of defence practised by divers centuries before the birth of Christ. It's also a good idea to lie prone, so as to offer the most difficult target and to force the shark to attack on the surface, where you can see it better. In this regard, it's worth noting that lifejackets are death traps, for they virtually immobilize the castaway and force him to remain upright and unable to defend his legs.

If you're on a raft and happen to have a survival manual handy, try tearing it up and sprinkling the pieces in your wake. This worked at least twice during the war, causing sharks assaulting a raft to veer off and chase the paper. They never came back.

Slapping the surface with a cupped hand, shouting underwater, and blowing bubbles are time-honoured devices that have occasionally worked with lesser sharks but may not be much more reliable against big ones than yellow dye or the pellets of the military. The reason is simple: not all sharks are easily intimidated. One can hardly expect a primitive, hungry fish, twenty feet long, to be impressed by one man's slaps or bubbles. In fact, making a commotion may backfire by exciting the shark and attracting others.

It has scared off yard-long reef sharks, to be sure, but when it comes to big, dangerous species, slapping the water may be tantamount to an explosion or chumming with blood: it draws them like magnets. . . .

It should be noted in passing, though, that noise and splashing will *sometimes* have the desired effect and make aggressive sharks turn away. Four R.A.F. crewmen clinging to a one-man rubber raft off Ceylon beat off repeated attacks for six hours by kicking and splashing furiously whenever a shark ran in at them. A man in the raft acted as spotter, alerting them for each assault. When they looked over the side of the ship that rescued them, they saw 'what looked like hundreds and hundreds of sharks waiting in layers below the dinghy'. Undoubtedly they had been attracted by the commotion.

Noise and splashing, coupled with the jabs of sharp spears, kept a twelve-foot grey nurse at bay for several hours near Sydney, Australia, after it had come upon seven spear-fishermen hunting together and tossed one in the air as it chased a fish below him. The divers banded together and drove the shark off with spears and thrashing, despite repeated rushes at them. They then posted a guard to watch it as it circled restlessly forty or fifty yards away. The divers speared 140 pounds of fish before the day was done – in full view of the shark, which stayed with them to the end.

Shouting underwater and blowing bubbles probably have even less value than slapping the water with a cupped hand, though some helmet divers in full suits use bubbles to frighten sharks away and other people claim that bubbles from Aqua Lungs have the same effect. Still others say that bubbles are worthless. Again, the result depends on the particular circumstances and the size, spirit, species, and hunger of the shark. Bubbles are certainly worth trying when all else has failed; anything is.

A deep-sea shout reportedly saved the lives of three survivors of a German submarine sunk off French West Africa in 1943. Charged and bitten, they put their heads below the surface and roared at their assailants. The sharks ran away. . . .

If the worst comes to the worst and a shark slams in at you in a dreadful lunge, wait till the last instant, then duck quickly aside. This is the time, if you have the wit, strength, knife, and courage, to try to stab it in the gills or rip its belly open. Considering the thick armour of the hide, the latter feat is difficult to perform, especially by a heavily-clad man in a life-jacket. Nevertheless, it *has* been done – by people who grew up in the sea, were thoroughly familiar with their adversary and its method of attack, and took good care to pick their sharks. Other men could do it too. . . .

The United States Navy once advised readers in an earlier (and grossly misleading) version of *Shark Sense* to grab a fin when a shark charges and hitch a ride, so that 'when he turns for another attack, you aren't there, you are riding with him, behind his mouth and out of danger from his teeth. Hold tight and hang on as long as you can without drowning yourself. In the meantime,' the Navy alleged, 'after missing his target, the shark may lose his viciousness and become his usual cowardly self again.' The idea certainly has exciting possibilities, but unfortunately, no examples were cited of persons who had done this and lived to tell the tale.

On the other hand, Hawaiians are said to have ridden ashore in this manner from shipwrecks at sea, so perhaps it's worth trying. In one instance, two Hawaiians literally jumped ship from a whaler thirty miles off Oahu in 1859, swam for twenty hours, then grabbed the dorsal and pectoral fins of a large shark that came up at them and rode the remaining ten miles to land. They steered the shark by slapping its face.

A pearl diver in the Tuamotus who bumped into a twelve-foot shark on the bottom and retreated to an underwater cave had to mount the shark's back to escape when his air ran out. He held on by digging his fingers into its gill slits – and got the ride of his life. The shark shot to the surface and high into the air, rolled over once, and took the diver down again. Shortly afterwards, it beached itself on a coral reef. The bleeding, battered rider staggered ashore and then, as an afterthought, returned and swung his fist at the shark's snout. It snapped its head up and bit off his hand.

Hitting a shark's nose is, nevertheless, sometimes recommended as a last resort for those fortunate enough to be armed with a pistol, club, or some other heavy object. Others say to refrain from such action, since it won't kill a shark and may infuriate it. Sharks that may flee from a nose-tapping may also endanger you with their tails; Florida sponge divers, who carry a metal hook for removing sponges, purposely refrain from hitting sharks' noses for fear they'll be slammed by their tails when the startled fish wheel about in retreat.

Skin divers armed only with spears can take heart, however, from Don Ide, a Corona, California, music teacher. He stopped a nine-foot hammerhead off La Jolla that had made several passes at him and his friend, Joe Turner, by firing a spear straight down the shark's throat. This incapacitated it enough for them to drag it ashore.

Fishermen on boats, it should be added, despatch sharks by shooting them in the eye, stabbing them repeatedly in the gills, or smashing their snouts with hatchets. But for swimmers without hardwear, it is difficult indeed to take such action.

In short, if a twelve-foot tiger shark grows fond of you and moves in for a closer acquaintance, do what you can to repel it, but don't be too optimistic about the outcome, for the shark is in its element and is considerably stronger and more durable than a human being. Your brain is almost four times as large as its, though, and if properly applied, may help prolong the struggle until help arrives or you win through to safety.

DAVID WEBSTER, *Myth and Maneater*, 1962

CHAPTER NINE

Fishing Inns and Fishing Accomplices

The fishing experience is not confined to what happens out fishing. There is the smell of mothballs on a winter's night when you open the case full of feathers and fur for fly-tying; the elaborate preparations on the riverbank and the late-night discussions of tactics which get thrown to the winds once you start fishing; the chance meetings with other fishermen, keepers and poachers. I even have fond memories of the truly dreadful pub my brother and I stayed in while we spent all night fishing for sea-trout. It turned out to have a main road thundering below the bedroom windows when we were trying to sleep during the day, food you could hardly swallow and the most unpleasant landlord in Britain. The fact that we caught nothing at all in three nights' fishing and then had a four-hour drive back to start work on the Monday morning somehow gave the weekend a symmetry.

This chapter is a small selection of writings about fishing pubs, keepers and, most of all, gillies. The gilly's role is a curious one. The essence of fishing is solitude. You can spend a pleasant enough day in a boat with a friend, being blown gently down a lake or following the seagulls tracking shoals of mackerel. But, like travel, fishing is best done alone. Yet in taking a gilly on a river or lough (and not taking one may not only be counterproductive but positively dangerous), you sign up for a day in the close company of a complete stranger. He is your accomplice, assistant, mentor, tutor and moral guardian. His job is to help you catch fish, and what the best of them don't know about fishing isn't worth knowing. If they feel bloody-minded, like the notorious gang on a stretch of the Spey, they can be a positive nuisance. The smartest, like the Duke of Roxburghe's, are turned out in identical tweeds, from their breeches to their deerstalkers. Others look like people turfed out of a Salvation Army hostel for being too scruffy. As in all things, appearances are deceptive. One of the poshest gillys I ever fished with had such an air of upholstered substance in his tweed livery that he was regularly mistaken for one of the 'rods', who had paid handsomely for the privilege of his assistance. He turned out to have been a Mother's Pride delivery man in Berwick-on-Tweed the previous month. What he didn't know about fishing was definitely worth knowing.

The scruffiest I have shared a hut with was called Patsy. He had a fearsomely filthy red beard, shoulder-length hair tied back in a greasy ponytail, a vast beerbelly and smelt like a pub parlour the morning after. This hell's-angel appearance concealed a fishing talent which had enabled him, so he claimed, to land 250 salmon from the Irish Blackwater the previous summer.

The gilly's job is to help the fisherman to catch a fish. It begins with advising which fly to tie on and ends with slipping the landing net under the salmon once the fisherman has brought it to the bank. In between these two events he may dispense advice, observations on wildlife, observations on life, jokes or oaths. He is, of course, an enthusiast, but even enthusiasm has limits when the bloke you're stuck with for the day can't cast a fly or the river is swollen the colour of hot chocolate and the rain is driving horizontally into your face. It is invariably at times like this that you lose your casting rhythm, thrash the water fruitlessly and turn around to see the face of the gilly registering . . . absolutely nothing. That blank expression is the mark of his professionalism: he will stay there as long as the fisherman wants to continue his utterly futile attempt. But you know that he knows there isn't a cat-in-hell's chance of catching anything. And he knows you know he knows. He's waiting for you to say it yourself.

The first gilly I ever met was Mr Thompson. I was eleven or twelve, he about fifty, although he seemed immeasurably ancient. Mr Thompson, the head gilly on the Yorkshire Flyfishers water on the Eden, was a man of few words. Those few tended to come in such a bass Cumberland growl that you could hardly make them out. He had huge feet, always encased in enormous rubber boots, a black oilskin which reached his calves, a walrus moustache which entirely covered his mouth, boiled-sweet glasses and an old-fashioned cap on which the front stood up from the peak. Once, seeing him trudge wearily through the driving January snow towards the pub, I plucked up the courage to ask him whether he'd caught anything, to which he replied 'Not a sausage,' and plodded on dourly up the hill. It was a world in which small boys were not expected to ask damnfool questions.

Since those days I have fished at odd times and in odd places with a variety of gillies. It is still a rare event – most of my salmon fishing is done on small rivers where you are left entirely to your own devices. But on the big rivers and some of the big loughs, you have no choice: you must have a gilly. So, when, in the early June mayfly hatch, trout fishermen from all over the world converge on Lough Corrib, it is a chance to renew old friendships. If you're lucky enough to stay at the delightfully eccentric Currareavagh House (it has been serving the same dinners on the same nights of the week for the last fifty years), you may be there on the day the proprietor, Harry Hodgson, offers his annual prize for the best day's fishing. The smallprint of this contest includes points awarded for, among other things, the boat which makes the 'most stylish start' to a day's fishing.

Of all the Currareavagh gillies, the most fearsome was Matty Mons. Setting out in the morning in his extraordinary outfit – bloodspattered trousers, ankle-length black plastic coat and one of his selection of ancient, encrusted hats, he had that purposeful air you only find in four-year-olds determined to pull the tablecloth off the table. Or avenging psychopaths.

On the morning of the great competition, Matty Mons could be seen walking with his determined expression up and down the mooring jetty, loading one killer device after another into his boat. When his angler arrived, Matty seated him in the back of the boat, and, as everyone else muddled about throwing things into boats, gunned up the outboard engine, cast off and described a full-power arc around the bay, as if towing a waterskier.

This would certainly have won the prize for the most stylish start, had he not forgotten to fill up with petrol. Two minutes later the engine spluttered to a stop and Matty began the long and humiliating row back to shore.

By choice, one fishes alone. But it is curious to think how many of the happiest days of your life have been spent in the company of more-or-less complete strangers, united only by an obsession. But without it, I should never have met James, the Lough Beltra boatman who would have preferred to make a living farming, but whose entire herd of livestock consisted of one cow. Nor should I have heard the longest, most implausible and yet somehow believable story I have ever heard about a horse which drank potcheen, collapsed drunk, was skinned, discovered to have been merely unconscious and then reclothed with a collection of knitted-together sheepskins. I'd just about believed all of it until Pat claimed that they had taken a crop of wool from the horse for the next ten years.

That story was told over a brew of tea at lunchtime, but something almost as implausibly plausible might as easily have been heard any night in the bar of a decent fishing pub. Arthur Ransome thought it easy enough to sort out the good ones from the bad. At the decent ones you stood a chance of catching fish. All the rest were swindles.

While the distinction holds true today, there can be compensations to make up for indifferent fishing. The old Lake Vyrnwy hotel in north Wales was that sort of place. It was stuck at the end of one of the bleakest patches of water in Britain and presided over by a retired colonel who thought that if you failed to answer the gong for dinner you deserved to go hungry (he once discovered that someone had, in ignorance, written their modest catch in the fishing book themselves and scrawled alongside 'Put This Man On A Charge!' Most of the year, the fishing was pretty dour, but there was a shabby peace about the place which more than made up for it.

Still, some of these old inns lumber on into the twenty-first century, scarcely having noticed the twentieth. There is one in the Borders where the clientele look as if they've been there since the nineteenth, periodically dusted off and carried from one table to another in the dining room to give the appearance of change. Some of the best of the old inns – the places where they serve large breakfasts, turn you out with a packed lunch, have masses of hot water and don't mind if you turn up for dinner two hours late because suddenly there was a wonderful trout rise (or don't turn up at all until midnight for the same reason) – survive, but they are a dying species.

Mostly, the owners of fishing inns have realized that a nation of motoring weekenders offers richer pickings. The next time you go, there is Laura Ashley wallpaper in the bedrooms. After that come the locks on bedroom doors, where none existed before. And then a bar with a grill manned by some idiot who hasn't the faintest interest in fishing. Previously, you drank all night, signing a chit in increasingly indecipherable hand as the theories became ever more complicated and the ones that got away ever bigger. Now, the bored barman shouts last orders around midnight and pulls down the shutter.

But I am, like everyone who writes about fishing, getting nostalgic. There do still exist a few old-fashioned fishing hotels and anyone unlucky enough to pitch up at a once-fine hotel like the one on the River Blackwater, to discover that he is being charged £1 just for a flask of hot water, has only to resolve never to go there again. And, anyway, there was nothing particularly special about fishing all morning and opening your lunch to discover nothing better than a pork pie which had turned green a fortnight ago.

Because of the way fishing has evolved in Britain, the ambience at these places is, it goes without saying, masculine. The smell of fishing establishments is the smell of tobacco smoke, mothballs, old leather and whisky. There are still a few sporting lodges in the Scottish Highlands in which the world of *John Macnab* lives on, where the armchairs are scuffed and the horsehair and ticking mattresses are worn to the consistency of a Sunday paper minus the supplements. It's hard to tell whether the old claw-footed cast-iron baths are genuinely rusted or merely stained that colour from a century of taps dripping peaty water the colour of armagnac. It doesn't matter – they are the last baths in Britain in which an adult can lie back, legs straight and water lapping around the ears. After spring days in which the rain has run down your neck for six hours solid, there is no comfort to beat it.

If the walls are adorned with any dead creatures, they tend to be stags' heads, otters and the like. Stuffed fish (actually plaster casts), in which there is now a thriving market, are nowadays found in places which are trying to pretend to be something they are not. If in doubt, check to see whether there is an inscription with the date and place of capture. If in further doubt, visit the gents'. In the genuine old fishing inns the loos are either indescribably acrid or grand affairs with urinal pillars which reach the armpit. The sort of place in which the cook who was sacked from a London club for using the loo with one hand while whacking a trout to death on the pillar with the other might have learned his trade and his bad habits.

Yet angling is not, for all that, a *male* sport. True, at one end it tends to be wreathed in cigar smoke, at the other, the stink of cheap, thin cigarettes. Holinshed's *Scottish Chronicle* related the belief that 'if a woman wade through the one fresh river in the Lewis, there shall be no salmon seen there for a twelvemonth after.' Because the great flowering of British fishing came in Victorian/ Edwardian days, the caricature ambience is that of the three bored gentlemen who became the most celebrated poacher in fiction, *John Macnab*. They sit in a Pall Mall club, talkin' of fishin' and dashed well finding a challenge to their ennui. But it has many times been remarked how many of the most successful catchers of fish in the last hundred years have been women. Lady Jane Joicey held the record for several years for the most salmon (twenty-eight) and sea trout (two) caught in a single day, an almost unimaginable total which would nowadays be much more likely to raise eyebrows than applause. Georgina Ballantine's 64 lb salmon on the Tay, Miss 'Tiny' Morrison's 61 lb monster from the Deveron or Doreen Davey's 59 lb spring salmon from the Wye were all taken between 1922–24, before *John Macnab* was written.

Various crackpot theories have been advanced to explain their success, including the suggestion that large male fish are attracted to the scent of female pheromones. One or two of the hypotheses even sound slightly plausible. But, in the end, salmon fishing is largely a question of luck. And if, as happens with many women anglers, you fish more delicately, more painstakingly and more methodically than irascible men, you tend to make your own luck. It is also noticeable that two of these three monster fish were taken late in the day, when the sun had gone off the water. Perhaps it was only then that the men were prepared to allow the women to have the run of the best pools.

The Hostess at the Ale-House – Izaak Walton,
The Compleat Angler, 1824

Fishing inns are of two kinds, good ones and downright swindles. As the holiday months draw to an end, most fishermen have something to say about one or other. It is noticeable that they say a good deal more about the downright swindles than about inns of the other kind. This is not because there are more of them, but because a good fishing inn is something that is not often given away. The man who has found such an inn is inclined to keep it to himself, lest by becoming too well known it should come to hold more visitors than there are fish in its waters, and so deteriorate into one of the downright swindles. These everybody knows. Their advertisements are shameless anachronisms, since they describe as good fishing the depleted waters that were well enough fifty years ago. For them the fishing is merely what the feathers are to the bare hook, a means to attract, but a travesty of what is promised. The visitors to these places are always new to the water, for no man would ever go there twice. The new-comer finds himself among other new-comers, bamboozled like himself, and, like them, hearing from the landlord of the great catches that have been made there in some golden age, lingers from day to day until his holiday is gone and he is himself almost out of conceit with the sport that has filled his dreams for months before. There is no one to undeceive him. All are new and full of hope, and do not realize until it is too late that the only successful angling in that place is done by the landlord, and that they are themselves the poor fish who rose to a lie in an advertisement, were played and landed, and will at last be 'put back', wise enough at least not to rise to that particular advertisement again. That is, indeed, their only revenge, for they have been fed and bedded, and if they have paid an extravagant price for board and lodging on account of the fish which, not being in the river, are not to be caught, no one to whom they complain will understand their bitterness or put down their empty baskets to anything but their inadequate skill. It will be a long time before the *Anglers' Diary*, for example, that invaluable guide to fishing, good and bad alike, has the courage to copy Baedeker and to distribute stars to those hotels where the fishing is really good and whole constellations to those whose fishing deserves it. When that day comes we shall judge fishermen with more accurate regard to the waters in which they fish, and the man who gets his brace of half-pounders from the waters of a fishing inn with one star will hold up his head with the man who has got his dozen brace from the ten-starred water elsewhere. Meanwhile there is nothing to be done, except to demand some more accurate description of the fishing than the word 'good', which, in the interests of an inn-keeper, is sometimes applied to the barrenest waters in the kingdom.

Good fishing inns are easily defined. They are inns the guests of which have the opportunity of good fishing. If they give us that, we can forgive them all else. Their beds may be boards, their food uneatable except at the close of a good day, when a fisherman will swallow anything. One of the best I ever knew was not an inn at all, but a peasant's barn, inhabited by rats and chickens and such an enormous quantity of fleas that the sleepiest of men could count on being on the water at sunrise. The food was black bread and the fish we caught, with plenty of eggs and plenty of milk. We washed in the river, for there was nowhere else for that purpose. To get to that place we drove for thirty miles along a bad road and nearly as many where there was no road at all, but we drove with delight, laughing at the bumps which on any other journey would have been no laughing matter, for we were going to the river or coming back from it, and on that river we counted it a poor day if we had not our ten brace of trout and grayling apiece. Perhaps that old barn, on the cliff above the river, is no fair example. But there are plenty of such places in England. If the fishing is good, nothing else matters much. If I were writing a guide to fishing lodgings and fishing inns I should give that barn five stars, whereas I should give no star at all to the famous — at —, where the beds would satisfy the princess in the fairy tale and they serve a six-course dinner at night and a five-course luncheon in the middle of day. Luncheon in the middle of the day betrays a bad fishing inn (unless on one of those sea-trout rivers that are fished at night). In a good fishing inn they have forgotten how to make luncheons, for all their guests grab sandwiches, rush out immediately after breakfast and come back hungry for dinner with the sandwiches still in their pockets, because they have never had time to eat them. An inn that expects its guests to come in for luncheon in the middle of the day is an inn with a bad conscience, which knows that its water is not worth fishing.

It is best, of course, if the people of the inn are a little interested in fishing. They should know enough to say the right things. I do not much like it if the landlord himself fishes. If he fishes too well he is apt to be a bore. If he fishes too badly he is apt to be a butt. We can do well without either. The widow of a fisherman makes a good hostess for a fishing inn. Her relationship to actual fishing is near enough but not too near. She will not think that it is a good fishing day because the rain is coming down, and she will have learnt not only to accept excuses for failure but even to feel when they are necessary and to offer them herself. A good fishing inn is enhanced by a picture or two by Rolfe or some stuffed fish, but these should have the dates and places of their capture clearly visible inside the cases. There are bad fishing inns, I have been told, that buy stuffed fish and hang them in their halls as a sort of ground bait. Lastly, of course, a good fishing inn has the right visitors. These are simple, kindly fellows, not desperate 'eye-wipers' of the kind so delicately described by William Caine. They may disagree on all subjects but one. That one is a rhyme known as the Fisherman's Prayer. On that they should be unanimous. If any mutton-headed purveyor of second-hand wit should so much as begin to lead up to the quotation of that rhyme, they should be the sort of men who, without a word said, would arise all together and take that man and drown him in the river.

ARTHUR RANSOME, *Rod and Line*, 1929

The Offending Item

Lord, suffer me to catch a fish,
So large that even I,
When talking of it afterwards,
May have no need to lie.

And Another Version

I pray that I may live to fish until my dying day.
And when it comes to my last cast, I then most humbly pray;
When in the Lord's great landing net and peacefully asleep
That in his mercy I be judged . . . good enough to keep.

SEEN ON A PUB WALL IN CONNEMARA

A Perfect Fishing Inn

There are many kinds of fishing inns, some are not 'inns' at all, but hotels, which serve six course dinners every night and the best of wines and where the boot boy, the chambermaid, the waiter, the head waiter and the commissionaire all expect a tip when you depart.

These hotels are patronised by the wealthy fishermen, thick-set, tweedy, red-faced men in knickerbockers and two-way hats. Their tackle is the best that money can buy, they consume great quantities of whisky, they are not concerned with what happens to their fish once their gillies have landed them. Often they are accompanied by their wives, likewise tweed-clad, beautifully groomed and with loud exquisite voices.

These places are not true fishing inns. I knew a fishing inn in Bedfordshire which I will call the Three Chubs. The first time I saw the place I realised that this was the real thing. I knew nothing about the fishing which, after all, was the most important adjunct, but that was investigated later and found to be beyond my highest expectations.

It was a very small inn, the only one in the very small village. It lay back from the road with a small triangle or green grass before it on which stood the sign of the Three Chubs, three huge chubs standing on their tails. The sign was faded but attractive, those chub really *were* chub, they looked appetising too, which every good angler knows chub are not; it is the most bony, tasteless, freshwater fish that swims, whatever Izaak Walton has to say.

But there was something in that rude painting which warmed my heart, these were *big* fish, worthy of your skill, their fins faded red, their eyes still golden, their painted scales still suggesting a silver and green lustre.

Before inspecting the inn I leant over the three-arched bridge which was also very old. Under the arch nearest the bank the river ran shallow and quite swift, wagging cushions of poa grass. Three lusty chub, a trifle more modest of girth than those on the sign hard by, but nevertheless undoubted three-pounders, were lying, one behind the other, close to the waving tresses. Under the other two arches the river was dark and deep, and silver water beetles gyrated just in the back wash of the current as it crinkled against a stone buttress covered with bright green moss.

Up-river was a charming June evening glimpse of wet meadow and willows and hawking swallows, a frieze of ruminating red cattle by a pollarded tree and seven white ducks processing down-river towards a shallow ford. The place smelt of fish, big ones.

I turned and crossed the little green under the sign of the Three Chubs. The inn was thatched, coral-pink roses embowered the windows and bushed them in, they almost hid the top of the door so that it was like the entrance to a wren's nest. The windows were (of course) mullioned, and martins had their nests under the wide thatched caves.

Over the door, almost invisible because of the roses, was a notice, lettered in old and graceful characters more suitable to a tombstone, 'Ernest Small, licensed to sell wines, spirits, and tobacco.'

On opening the door I found myself in a flagged passage of rose-red quarries. In front of me was a door labelled BAR, on the left another under a beam labelled, very grandly, LOUNGE, I opened this and went in. It was very different from other lounges I have known in other fishing inns.

Over the fireplace was a faded photograph in a very heavy wood frame. It depicted two gentlemen, holding rods, wearing straw hats and long, drooping moustaches. One was in his shirt sleeves. At their feet was a fishmonger's array of victims, some of them vast bream, larger, apparently, than the old-fashioned leather bellows. I thought this picture was very proper and right – now for the stuffed fish. Yes, there it was, sure enough, regarding me with affrighted stare from behind its curved glass front. A bream, a very large one, indeed I thought it was the largest I had ever seen, dead or alive. On the opposite wall, likewise regarding me with affrighted stare was a perch, a three-pounder, and one of his pectoral fins had dropped off and was lying on the silver sand under his belly.

Close by was a faded photograph of Lord Kitchener, in a topee, and farther along the wall an oleograph of Queen Victoria entitled 'Gentlemen, The Queen!'

At this juncture the door opened and the landlord stood before me. He was most appropriately, on this warm June evening, in his shirt sleeves. I recognised him as one of the straw-hatted gentlemen in the photograph, though the drooping moustache was missing and the years had given him more fat. And never in my life have I seen a man so like a chub!

He had a round face, pink and rubicund, his eyes were slightly protruding, with a merry twinkle in them, but his mouth, which should have been thick-lipped and large to complete the smile, was like a cherub's. He had no teeth. He reminded me of a medieval serving-man, or something out of Chaucer, he certainly should have been clad in jerkin and hose. I intimated that I had a thirst upon me and accordingly he led me down the passage to where three stone steps led into a cellar. There against a whitewashed wall was a cask and stooping down he turned a tap and there came to me the gratifying sound of beer trinkling into a pewter pot.

And *what* beer it was to be sure! Ice-cold and full of nutty flavour, I have not tasted beer like it since.

I was hungry, so Mrs Small, a plump body with a beaming face, spotless in a snowy apron, ushered me into the parlour and bustled off to prepare the meal. Meanwhile mine host stood by the door and talked, he rolled his words as though they were bread pellets, Pike? Yes, there were very big pike. Chub? Ah, there was no better place for chub in the whole of the Ouse valley. Had he not caught one himself the day before, a fish of four pounds? 'Why, sir, the place smells on 'em.' I remembered the smell on the bridge and agreed.

Soon came Mrs Small bearing a tray loaded with plates, a crusty cottage loaf, fresh lettuce plucked a minute ago from the garden, a dish of freshly caught gudgeon fried in bread crumbs and laced with watercress, and a flap of Small-cured ham on which was enthroned two 'half apricots' of fried eggs still sizzling! It was unbelievable!

Host and hostess then retired and I was left to discuss my supper. The mullioned window was wide open and the roses peeped in at me. It looked on to the garden and a small green lawn where two black-and-white rabbits were hopping about in a wire pen. Beyond was a low wall, a few apple trees and – the river. I glimpsed silvery willows and pallisades of sedge and there came to me the perfume of meadowsweet and river water. Somewhere a hidden weir was making a low murmur and patrolling martins and swallows kept up a continual twitter.

Beyond were water meadows and black poplars. You will always find black poplars in the haunts of big chub. My meal finished at last I strolled down the garden and leant my elbows on the low wall.

The June evening was softening, sedge warblers chattered and grated among the willows of a little island in mid-river, exactly opposite to me, and in the crinkling deeps beyond the sedge beds fish were rising after the dancing gnats.

It was all so perfect, all too good to be true, the whole scene – inn, landlord, supper, beer, river, and evening had something unreal about it, something not far removed from a fisherman's idea of paradise. Not far off were the remains of an old watermill and it was from there that the sound of rushing water came, a low, soothing murmur which later would lull me to sleep.

'B.B.', *Fisherman's Folly*, 1987

The Perfect Fishing Tea

And now for the first time we fished as high as Mindrum Mill. While fishing near the mill an old man approached me with a kindly good-day, and a hope that I had good sport. He was a fresh complexioned man, of apparently more than three score years and ten, and somewhat feeble in his walk. A few more words passed, and he enquired at what time I expected to return. Having named five o'clock, I passed on thinking no more of the matter. Our fishing ended, my friends and myself were wending our way back along the river-side when the old man came forward and said courteously, 'My wife's waiting for you, and all's ready, come away.' We could not resist such unaffected kindness, and followed him into the house. Here he introduced us to his very counterpart in age and simple gentleness. Dressed in plain homespun but with cap and collar white as drifted snow, this aged mistress of the farm entered on her hospitable task. We were ushered into a charming little room in which to make our toilette, and then into the best sitting room, where we found a table spread with meat hot and cold, eggs, honey, tea, and O! such cream and butter. The old lady sat down and presided at the feast, but her husband would only walk about the room pleased to ask us questions and to join his wife in urging us to every possible effort in eating and drinking.

WILLIAM HENDERSON, *My Life as an Angler*, 1879

More Food

Of all eating and drinking connected with fishing I remember best the suppers that we came home to after the evening rise at Wrackle-ford. They were simple enough – good Dorset ale in plenty; a salad of lettuce and tomatoes that one made and dressed oneself with olive oil and vinegar; crisp, well-flavoured celery from the garden, where it grew in banked rows like steeplechase fences; white bread and golden Jersey butter with all the richness of the meadows we had walked in our fishing; and blue vinny cheese. There is no other cheese to equal blue vinny at a time like that. Stilton is noble, but rich and clinging for such a late meal; Cheddar is a grand cheese, mellow and clean and full of flavour. But the Dorset cheese puts no restraint on the appetite, because it is made from skim milk, with no soft richness in it; yet the flavour is full and smooth and satisfying, with a slight dryness that reminds one suitably often that a glass is waiting to be refilled. After cheese and salad, perhaps a great ripe peach, fresh from the greenhouse, or a bunch of black grapes, Madresfield Court for preference, and currant cake to go with them.

Cheese and beer and the fruits of summer and fall fit naturally into any picture of fishing days. But a winter fisherman has other delights as good: after a January day of hard wading, good Irish whisky, sparkling by artificial light, and a fire of alder wood or maple leaping up the chimney; five or six hours to talk and a dinner of roast beef or roast saddle of venison somewhere in them, the inward warmth spreading slowly out to meet the surface warmth already built by a bath and the fire.

All these things – fish caught, problems solved, the sights and scents and sounds of woods or meadows, the quiet ease of companionship, good food on a sharpened hunger, comfortable warmth built from cold and a measure of discomfort – are satisfactions. Some are physical, some mental, some, no doubt, spiritual.

RODERICK HAIG-BROWN, *A River Never Sleeps*, 1942

Bent Bailiffs and Blindfolds

In times when water bailiffs in Tweed had very small salaries, they themselves were by no means scrupulous about the observance of close time, but partook of the good things of the river in all seasons, lawful or unlawful. There is a man now, I believe, living at Selkirk, who in times of yore used certain little freedoms with the Tweed Act, which did not become the virtue of his office. As a water bailiff he was sworn to tell of all he saw; and indeed, as he said, it could not be expected that he should tell of what he did not see.

When his dinner was served up during close time, his wife usually brought to the table in the first place a platter of potatoes and a napkin; she then bound the latter over his eyes that nothing might offend his sight. This being done, the illegal salmon was brought in smoking hot, and he fell to, blindfolded as he was, like a conscientious water bailiff – if you know what that is; nor was the napkin taken from his eyes till the fins and bones were removed from the room, and every visible evidence of a salmon having been there had completely vanished: thus he saw no illegal act committed, and went to give in his annual report at Cornhill with his idea of a clear conscience.

WILLIAM SCROPE, *Days and Nights of Salmon Fishing*, 1843

Some Really Bad Advice for Young Anglers

If at any time you happen to be overheated with walking, or other exercise, avoid small liquors, especially water, as you would poison; but rather take a glass of rum or brandy, the instantaneous effects whereof, in cooling the body, and quenching drought are amazing.

THOMAS SHIRLEY, *The Angler's Museum, or the Whole Art of Float and Fly Fishing*, 1784

Myths About Patience

On a blank day one can think about fishing. My mind keeps going back to the people who talk about patience. Put it like this. A man who is fishing for salmon has a whippy piece of wood, attached to the end of which there is a bit of string perhaps as long as a cricket pitch. He has got to wave his piece of wood in such a way as to extend the string behind him and then drop it in front of him in an absolutely straight line. Many people have difficulty in managing a crop, whose lash is only about four feet long. He repeats this delicate feat perhaps seven hundred times in a day, speculating every time about the exact place where he wants the string to land, and he is content to do this for three days running without killing a fish, provided that he kills one on the fourth. This looks to me like a good tribute to the excitement of the kill.

People seem to think that a fisherman sits in the shade of a pollard willow watching his float, whilst the countryside dreams about him, the cuckoo sings, and the cattle draw the grass. It has snowed or sleeted almost every day that I have been here. I have walked perhaps ten miles a day, and been at it nearly twelve hours a day – in the sleet. This is not because I am tough or obstinate, but because the joys are so *thrilling* (a queer word to use about an art that has nothing to do with steeplechases or motor-racing) that it would be unthinkable to do anything else. The fisherman fishes as the urchin eats a cream bun, from lust. You might as well talk about the patience of Tarquin.

T.H. WHITE, *England Have My Bones*, 1936

Solitary Vice

The true fisherman is essentially a solitary. He goes back to the time when humanity had not spread over all the world. He loves the seclusion in which his primitive instincts have full play. I take it that the first fisherman, who went out alone as on some secret errand and came back with fish, astonished the world and his savage wife with shining and unlooked for gifts.

Yes, the truth is that we who fish are a savage race. Our philosophy is a kind of solipsism. When I fish I am the universe. There is none but me. We may club together as against others, but by the water we divide. A true fisherman cannot bear another human within a mile of him, unless he has something noble to show him. I am apt to suspect a stray shepherd of being a fisherman in disguise. I desire to hear no human sound. The distant bark of a dog I can endure, or the baa of sheep, though I own that sheep by the river's bank are often offensive. Cattle in a stream are also troublesome, though at times they help us by rendering it turbid and thus rendering trout less cautious, less far-seeing. But as for man – why, Swift himself could scarcely feel as we feel. A stranger on our water is worse than a yahoo. We wish to be alone. Our wives and sweethearts, our mistresses, may exist. They cease to be while we fish. If, greatly daring, any such come and speak to us they should be firmly checked. If not there is no end to their interference. They expect to be answered. They urge a man to take an untimely lunch. They will even bring tea-baskets and expect him to leave the milk and cream of the afternoon rise. If he has caught nothing they ask how many he has caught. If he has caught much he has rarely caught enough. They wish to send some to their mothers and their aunts, and keep telling him that he will miss the post. I have even heard of a wife who, wishing her husband to come back to tea, pushed a knitting needle through his waders before he left the house. The wise fisherman, if he has a wife or a mistress, goes fishing without her. The wisest will be celibate, for he can then leave home, or at least the place in which he keeps his tackle, whenever he pleases. There will be none to prevent him starting for the north of Scotland or for Finland at a minute's notice. The best fishing may be where the inns are dreadful and without hot water or baths, where the food is appalling and terrible to all women, where beds are vile and lumpy and apt to creak.

It seems clear, then, that a fisherman belongs to a peculiar species of humanity. No man of science can define a species or a specific difference with any accuracy. But man as a rule is a social animal. A fisherman is not properly a social animal. There is no other kind of man who welcomes rain on a holiday. There is no other kind of man who luxuriates in the fact that the whole of the moorland is a bog which holds water for weeks at a time. There is no other human being who can be perfectly happy five miles from home when he is wet through, tired out, hungry and carrying a bag, or creel, which weighs ten pounds. He is the only creature existing whose joy is an increasing burden, a heavier handicap.

MORLEY ROBERTS, *A Humble Fisherman*, 1932

A Verse of Proverbial Excuses

Sometimes too early, sometimes too late,
Sometimes too small, sometimes in spate,
Sometimes too windy, sometimes too calm,
Sometimes too frosty, sometimes too warm,
Sometimes too dirty, sometimes too clear,
There's aye something wanting, when I'm fishing here.

G.P. BUDDY QC, in a Hotel Visitor's Book

An Introduction to Guides

No wonder normal people can't stand fishermen. Fishermen can't stand each other. They have to pay people to keep them company.

Guides are people who can stand anybody. For seven dollars a day and their keep, they will associate with fishermen. For eight dollars a day, who knows *what* they would do?

In the evening, guides sit around the campfire and spit in it. They like to hear the sizzle. After a day of fishing, it makes sense.

My friend Lyman Clark went moose-hunting. He asked his

Indian guide what he should do. The guide took him to a clearing, and said,

'You sittum down on stump. Me blow in birchbark horn, makum noise like cow moose in heat. Bull moose, he hearum. Run like hell ketchum cow. Me keep on blowum horn. Bull moose runnum in clearing. You shootum. You shootum good. You no shootum, bull moose rapum guide.'

Fishermen call guides 'picturesque.' Guides call fishermen 'sports.'

The other guides know what they mean.

ED ZERN, *To Hell with Fishing,* 1945

An Englishman Patronizes Irish Gillies

Every Irish gillie worthy of the name is an enthusiatic sportsman; he will drop the last or the plane for the sake of the sport which is the breath of his nostrils, and if he is attached to a reasonably-minded master will serve him with unflagging fidelity. He knows every stone in the river, has a keen eye for the conditions that make pools fishable, and will cast a fly with unerring accuracy to within an inch of the spot where a fish lies. Salmon-angling is hard work, but the gillie is never tired, and is always ready to mitigate the toil by taking a hand at the rod. He has a perfect talent for misleading his compatriot gillies when there is a rush for pools, and will tell Tim Sullivan that his governor is to be on the spot at 6 a.m., two hours later than the time arranged.

His poaching proclivities make him an early riser, and one must not complain if he is awakened at three o'clock instead of four by a shower of pebbles hurled at his dormitory window. To know that he has been a poacher is a commendable grace. It is generally alluded to as one of the cardinal virtues.

On one occasion, in summing up the merits of a new gillie, I was informed that he was the biggest poacher on the river, and with an air that showed that the vice was counted to him for righteousness. The accomplishment, however, has its drawbacks, and the poaching fever in the blood on occasion shows itself in ugly spots. Once I had arranged to fish a pool on Monday morning, which was full of salmon. The nets had been off from six o'clock on Saturday morning, and on Sunday afternoon the salmon were freely showing in the pool. At four o'clock the gillie was to call me. I awoke with a start at six, and, thinking that my attendant had overslept, I set out for the river. On calling at his house I was informed that he had started at daybreak, and was supposed to have gone in quest of me. I proceeded to the pool, and on reaching it found the gillie fishing with all his might!

But the principal vice is whiskey. This is even worse than the weakness for poaching. The free use of the flask on the part of English anglers robs many a fisherman of a valuable servant. The taste of liquor to these hot-headed Celts is like blood to the tiger. They will have more of it. One of the finest gillies I have known – a splendid fly-tyer and an out-and-out enthusiast – was lost to me for a week through lending him for a day to a brother angler. When he turned up again, full of apologies and regrets, I ventured to lecture him, and, with the best intentions of appealing to his better nature, asked, 'Why do you touch it at all? You know the very taste of it means a week's drinking.' But he was equal to the occasion, and replied, 'Arrah, sir, it was a mistake altogether; I thought it was a bottle of Kops the gintleman offered me.' Anglers, if they are to retain their men, must avoid offering them whiskey. Years ago a novel method of securing the gillie's sobriety is said to have been adopted on the Galway River. At the close of a day's fishing, the moment the gillie left the fishery he usually disappeared for two or three days for an obvious reason. The police-station was close to the river, and a constable was bribed to arrest the gillie the moment he passed through the gates. He was straightway taken to the guard-room and provided with a bed for the night. Thus his sobriety was assured.

When the gillie fails to turn up, drink, as a rule, is the explanation. His friends will assign plausible and even virtuous reasons for his disappearance. One, who was a carpenter by trade and an angler by profession, was missing one morning. The run of the grilse was at its height, and the prospects of a day's angling were unusually promising. I determined to hunt him up, and called at the house where he lived. His father opened the door, and when I inquired for Dan – which was not his name – I was informed that he was in bed.

'Drinking again!' I ejaculated. 'No, indeed, sir,' came the reply, in a half-indignant tone; 'the drink had nothing to do with it; he was up all night making a coffin.' I hastily apologized and withdrew, meditating on the virtues of the man whom I had been mentally maligning. I had not gone far before I encountered the virtuous Dan emerging from a public-house in an advanced stage of intoxication. Evidently he had been up all night making his own coffin.

It is advisable to study this phase of the gillie's character to prevent being victimized by it. He is conscious of it himself, and by no means indisposed to enter into your plans for insuring sobriety. If one is fishing for three or four weeks a gillie's payment will amount to a considerable figure, and he will be ready to agree that payment should be deferred to the end of the engagement. Tips after a successful day's angling are dangerous. The attendant regards it in the light of an extra to be spent in a jubilant fashion. An angler will sometimes say, 'Now, Dan, half a crown extra for every salmon we catch today.' A crown may be due at the end of it, but no gillie will turn up next morning in all probability. It is far wiser to add all extras to the sum total at the end of the visit. I have known gillies who feared the danger of handling money during their engagement so much as to ask a local tradesman to be treasurer for them.

The optimism of the gillie is unbounded. The graphic description of the prospects, when one feels disposed to 'chuck' sport after a series of bad days, is stimulating. 'Where's the use,' you exclaim, 'in going on thrashing the river? The water is too low for a run of fish, and there is nothing in the pools but old stagers.' 'No run of fish! It's entirely mistaken you are, sir. Sure, when they want to come up the river it isn't the height they'd be mindin'. They'd travel if the river was dry when they set their mind to it; and, sure the pool by the wood is teemin' wid fish. I went down late last night, and they were so thick that you could walk across the river on their backs without wettin' your boots!' Then would come a touching appeal at the possible consequences of wandering about the town and the temptations of the public-house.

'It's yerself that's kept me sober for the last month, and the divil a ha'penny o' pay I'll take today if I don't give ye a tight line.' Who could resist this? And the gillie will have his way in the end.

After a blank couple of hours you feel disposed to comment on the obdurateness of the fish. 'They don't seem to be stirring, Dan.' 'No, sir; there's thunder in air, and when it's like that it's hard to move them; but it'll clear presently, and the rise will come on at such a rate that if ye throw a copogue – Anglice, dock leaf – to them they'd take it.'

But, with all his faults, something like a genuine affection springs up between master and man. There is no use in setting up a high standard of consistency and expecting these gillies to conform to it. To be a little blind to their follies is a wise course. The chances are, from an angler's point of view, that the balance is in favour of redeeming qualities. There is no prouder man than the gillie when he leads the way to the hotel with a brace of fish slung by the gills. He receives the tidings of your leaving with a look of genuine regret, and, as he puts it, 'will be counting the days till yer honour returns. Sure, the sport ye've had is nothing to what it'll be then, for this was the worst season ever known on the river.' He will be down in the morning to take the rods to the station – 'it isn't himself that'll be trusting them to them divils of jarvies.'

So he hovers round you to the end, insists on shaking hands for the second time, and, as the train steams out of the station, the last pathetic object standing on the platform and waving his adieu is the person of the faithful gillie.

JOSEPH ADAMS, Salmon and Trout Angling, 1923

And An Irishman Praises One

River fishing is one-man pursuit, lake fishing a partnership. There may be a partnership of three, if the second rod is a friend with similar views, but the ideal is two: the angler and his boatman. The boatman supplies the knowledge of local conditions while the angler decides the method of fishing. It takes time to perfect such a partnership, for every angler has his own theories and methods, which necessitate the boat being handled in the way which suits his style, and the boatman must learn to do this without continual direction. Some boatmen will not learn and some try to dictate. The wise angler will accept suggestions from an intelligent boatman but he must never tolerate dictation.

I have had many fruitful partnerships but none so ideal as that with Miley Costello of Fermoyle. Speech was unnecessary, and indeed Miley seemed to have a mistrust of speech, doling out his rare remarks as if he was dispensing a dangerous medicine. It was a point of pride with him to be able to read the mind of his angler and take the appropriate action before he was told. Nothing escaped his observation. A turn of the head, a glance at the sky, a shift of position, the opening of a fly box, these gave him the clues to what was going on in my mind. Yet there must have been something more than quick observation. I would think 'I wonder is the salmon which I saw move by the big rock last Saturday still in the same place?' and Miley would take up the oars and row me to the most favourable point for drifting the big rock. To fish with Miley was to have four eyes. Battling up against half a gale he would suddenly stop the boat and point out a direction for me to cast and as often as not the flies would be taken by a fish whose movement he had spotted despite the roughness of the wave. I can recall his making only one error, and then the real fault was mine. While he was away gathering heather for the luncheon fire the wind died and I changed to a thin and rather worn cast, but kept on the same flies. I was so accustomed to Miley seeing everything that I forgot to tell him about the change when he came back. As soon as we started again after lunch, a big white trout took the tail fly and charged straight in towards the boat. The orthodox counter is for the boatman to pull half a stroke, allow the fish's rush to take him past the stern and so avoiding the danger of a dropper catching on the keel. With any other angler Miley would have done this automatically, but he knew that with a cast of normal thickness I preferred to take in line with my hand and direct the fish by side pressure clear of the stern. The weak cast did not take the strain of so large a fish, and parted. Miley picked up the broken end, examined it and flushed. 'To think I never noticed,' was all he said.

T.H. KINGSMILL MOORE, *A Man May Fish*, 1979

A Typical Gilly's Tale

'You hear a lot of stories about anglers catching strange things, but I'll tell you one of the strangest, and if you don't believe me, then the gentleman who was with me at the time will be happy to confirm that what I'm saying is true.

'I was fishing the Till here, and after getting my gentleman started, I followed him down the pool. Now the river is only some thirty yards wide, and I was so busy watching how my gentleman was getting on that I made a foolish cast and the flies landed in the long grass on the far bank of the river.

'When I tightened there came a terrible commotion. I'd hooked a partridge under the wing! The bird rose in the air squawking and yelling blue murder. There wasn't much I could do about it, so I pulled it out of the grass, off the bank and into the river.

'Half-way across the river there came this great swirl, and a 12 lb salmon rose and grabbed the dropper. The salmon shot off upstream like a rocket, dragging the partridge after him. At times the salmon and bird were both in the air. When the fish ran, the partridge flapped after him, splashing along the surface; when the salmon sulked, the bird flew helplessly round and round above.

'It took me nearly an hour, but eventually I landed them both. My gentleman was standing watching, mouth agape. He claimed that if he hadn't seen it with his own eyes, he would have called anyone who told him such a story a damned liar. But there you have it, as true as I am sitting here.

BRUCE SANDISON, *The Sporting Gentleman's Gentleman*, 1986

A Fine Scottish Gilly

Sunday. Fishing illegal. I was woken at 4 a.m. by two blackbirds, singing like angels, and worked at another book. Now that some of yesterday's horror has worn off I can record a story of Macdonald's which amused me. It was about a short-sighted gentleman who was a bad fisherman, but he enjoyed it. Macdonald swears that he once fished the whole of the Mill Pool with his fly caught in the knee of his plus-fours. 'He could hear the line splashing into the water,' says Macdonald, 'and that keepit him happy.' 'But why didn't you tell him?' I asked. 'Ah,' says Macdonald, putting his finger by the side of his nose, ''twas safest there.'

I shall remember a lot of things about Macdonald: how he always said that the water was in good or bad 'orrder': how collectedly he moved his tough body, which in a townsman would have lumbered, over boulders that kept me lagging behind, and up slopes of one in one, carrying rods and game bag with two or three heavy fish in it: how he did not suffer from the bugbear of 'getting his feet wet,' but walked in the water as cheerfully as on the land, knowing that an active man cannot catch cold: how philosophically he replied, when I asked him whether the local labourers didn't hate him for stopping their poaching, 'Well, I'm no weel likit.' He was the loyalest, neatest, gentlest person. He was impossible to tire, always good-humoured, and loved his work: the kind of man who is neither weak nor hard. When he was at leisure he enjoyed his shirt sleeves, like a soldier out of uniform: on Sundays he went religiously to chapel: he was a fine man for his food.

God bless him and his place anyhow; and good-bye to Scotland, the loveliest country in the world.

T.H. WHITE, *England Have My Bones*, 1936

An Irish Boatman Reveals a Secret

When we were clear of the little bay but still in shallow water, I asked where I was to begin fishing. Patsey's answer is among our classics. It came as a matter of course – 'Where you are, sir; fish away, there's tons of them below you.' I laughed and repeated the phrase in mocking disbelief. 'There's tons of them below you!' My scepticism hurt Patsey, but he bided his time. Two years later he took his kindly revenge. Again it was May, but later in the month. It was a warm and balmy evening with scarcely a breath of wind. Patsey had gone home, as I thought, and we were finishing dinner when the maid came to me and whispered that Patsey was in the hall and wished to speak with me. When I joined him he was a trifle excited. 'Put on your coat, sir, and come in the boat; I have something to show you.' I protested that a dinner-jacket was hardly the costume for a fishing excursion, but as there was to be no fishing I put on the coat and went with him. It was a perfect spring night; the lake was a polished mirror reflecting the light of the moon, almost at the full. He pulled swiftly to the southern shore and paused. 'Listen, sir!' All about us were feeding fish – one circle flowing into the next; their 'chopping' could be heard distinctly and among them were some very heavy fish. They were feeding along the shore up to the very edge of the grass. Then away he pulled to one of the islands, halting in the shadow of the overhanging trees; chop, chop, chop; everywhere it was the same – under the overhanging bushes, at the ends of the oars, out in the deep as far as we could see. Then he carried me off to a shallow, rocky bay, and there it seemed as if all the trout in the lake were congregated – it was unbelievable! As we crossed the lake on the way home he paused again, in the deepest part, and as far as one could see there were feeding trout. Then he spoke and his voice was very serious. 'Do you remember, sir, the first day you were here? You were after asking me where you should fish, and I told you – "Where you are, there's tons of them below you" – you laughed at me, sir, and thought I was telling what wasn't true. Well, sir,' – and here he spoke with a new firmness – 'was I right?' Then I made the best apology I was able. He had been right, perfectly right. He had not overstated the facts by so much as a pound. When I had made my apology he merely said, 'Very good, sir' – and the boat sped back where the lights shone out from unshaded windows and the sound of the piano came sweetly across the stillness.

F.D. BARKER, *An Angler's Paradise*, 1929

An Irish Gillie

Jamesie was willing to be helpful, even forthcoming, in a discussion on flies, but when it came to the business of catching fish, he was a different man. He liked fishing, liked better to catch fish, but best of all he liked to show his superiority over rival boatmen. This was a necessity for his complete happiness. He would rather bring back a mediocre catch which was larger than that of any other boat, than a really good bag which only took second place. So far so good. Anyone fishing with Jamesie could be certain than he would leave nothing undone to get fish. But it did not end there. He craved also the personal triumph of beating the other rod in his own boat, and to make sure of this he was willing to use devious methods. He did draw a line. I have heard him refer with disapproval to leaving his companion's fly-box behind or weakening his gut by the touch of a cigarette. Physical interference was a foul, but when it came to a contest of wits anything was permissible.

It took me a couple of days to smell mischief. Most boatmen are only too glad to set the boat on along straight drift and leave it so. Not Jamesie. From the bow came a continual murmur of directions to Jimmy. 'Pull a stroke now' – 'Back her a couple' – 'Pull easy, easy' – 'Back half a stroke' – and so on. This called for no particular comment. I knew that Jamesie had fished the lake for fifty years, and had an eye on him like a travelling rat. All parts of the shallow sliding past under the keel might look equally enticing to me, one part of the bay as good as another, but to his observation, backed by experience and a most remarkable memory, there might be a significant difference. He was always recalling past victories. 'Twenty throut did I get to my own rod on the shore of that island in an easht wind and a shining sun, and all of them on a Grey Monkey. It was the September of the year that the ould Queen died and maybe the throut were still in half mournin'.' With such a precedent, the wind east and the sun bright, what was I to do but put on a Grey Monkey and let Jamesie control the drift? And sure enough the trout took it, even though no royalty had lately deceased.

I began to work out the effect of his orders. 'Pull easy' and 'Back easy' kept the boat working diagonally to left or right across the natural line of drift, and were explicable on the assumption that there was an underwater bank running obliquely to that line. 'Pull a stroke' and 'Back a stroke' or 'Pull two' and 'Back two' shifted the boat two or four lengths to right or left of the line she was on and set a new drift parallel to, but some distance from, the old. Each of these manoeuvres gave both rods fresh water, no doubt, in Jamesie's judgment, better water. But what about 'Back half a stroke' or 'Pull half a stroke'? The result of the first was to allow Jamesie to fish the line I had been fishing, and of the second to put me on Jamesie's line and give him new water. I became suspicious that Jamesie would not take my line, or give me his, unless he thought the change was to his advantage.

On the morning of the third day a trout took a daddy directly down wind of me and about forty yards away. If the boat were left to her natural drift I was bound to fish the spot where the trout had risen; but when we had gone about twenty yards there came the order for which I was waiting. 'Back half a stroke.' It was time for me to act. 'Do no such thing, Jimmy,' I said 'If anyone is going to fish that trout it will be me and not Jamesie.'

The effect of my remark on Jimmy was startling. For two days he had been following directions, comprehending perfectly that Jamesie was trying to get the better of me, amused and yet a little disapproving, for he was naturally loyal to his employer. Still, it was none of his business to interfere. Let me find out for myself if I was able. Now that I had found out he was free to enjoy the biting of the biter. He shipped both oars carefully, put his two hands on his knees, and laughed out to the heavens. 'Begob, Jamesie, you're losht. The gentleman has ye discovered.' Jamesie looked at us both with dignity, and then delivered a rebuke addressed to Jimmie but aimed at me. 'Ye should know by this, Jimmy McDonagh, that that was a thravellin' throut and wherever he is now he is not where he rose lasht.'

Jamesie had saved his face but he had been warned. 'Pull half a stroke' and 'Back her half' ceased to figure in his instructions. He still held the trumps. He knew the lake and I did not. If he said 'Pull two strokes,' or gave any command which gave both rods a new line, I was helpless. Automatically to halve his order might do us both harm, and anyhow Jamesie would have been quick enough to counter by directing the boat to be moved twice the distance he wanted. I felt sure I was being foxed and could not prove it. I tried bluff. 'Look here, Jamesie, either you play fair or there will be only one rod fishing in this boat.' Jamesie looked at me. His moustache moved. His eyes creased. Then he in his turn broke into laughter. He had had his fun, and it was time to stop. 'Very well Sir. I'll play fair.' And play fair – or very nearly fair – he did from that on.

T.H. KINGSMILL MOORE: *A Man May Fish*, 1979

But Your Life May Depend on Him ...

Courage and coolness are great qualities in a gillie, and you do not really know your man till you have been with him in a storm. Nothing tests a man like danger to life. I knew a boatman on Lough Mask who went as white as a sheet when a stiff nor'wester blew down Mountrasna Bay, and the waves were topped with white. It was no place for him, and he was not typical. Most gillies have cool heads and hearts of oak. They must have these qualities; to be cool and courageous is part of their job. Anglers want fish, and are often willing to take a chance. Whatever precautions are taken, you may be caught at a disadvantage. Storms arise suddenly; winds swing round, and plans 'go all a'gley'. When that happens, the courage required is not the active heroism of the soldier in action; but it is resolution, the ability to be calm and cool and collected. On a stormy lake there is little one can *do*; man cannot pit his puny strength against wind and wave; he cannot *fight* the forces of nature; he must *use* them; and that means keeping calm and cool, and doing the right thing at the right time.

Michael and I have shared not a few anxious moments – moments that to me were anxious; but I never once saw him flustered, much less frightened; in a tight corner he always seems to have something in reserve. His worst day on the lake is worth describing. He has often told me about it in general terms, such as, 'The lake went up in smoke that day, Sir.' The angler who was with him in the adventure wrote an account of it at the time, and he has shown me the record, and it is frightening still.

It was the day of an angling competition in April, 1943. The rendezvous was Coryosla Bay at the Pontoon end of Lough Conn, some eight miles by water from Cloghans, where Michael lives. It was wartime, and there was no petrol for outboard engines or for driving round by road. After breakfast Frank, a young engineer, and Michael set off in their good, solid nineteen-foot boat; it was a calm morning, and Brendan, Michael's son, decided to go, too, in Michael's dinghy on the chance of a job as gillie. The dinghy was little more than a canoe, about twelve feet long, as light as a cork, with an up-turned prow at either end, like a Viking ship; it was meant for coasting about in sheltered bays in fair weather. They reached Coryosla without incident in a couple of hours; but clouds were piling up in the south; the wind was freshening; and the men knew that they were in for it. The competition gun was fired, and the anglers started work; but almost immediately the storm broke, and very soon fishing was out of the question. Lashed by wind and rain the boats ran for the nearest shelter, and tied up; anglers and gillies took refuge in hospitable cottages, where they found a welcome, warmth and tea. All the afternoon the storm raged, but lulled off about 6 p.m. Then Frank, Michael and Brendan forgathered at Coryosla and held a council of war. The issue was simple – eight easy-looking miles by water, or a trudge of twice that distance on a rough and stony road, with the prospect of returning on the morrow for boats and gear. The wind was still strong, but southerly; it should be with them all the way; rowing would be easy, and if all went well, they would be safe and sound at home within an hour and a half. That is better than a four hours' trudge, is it not? The *ayes* have it. They decided that all three should go in the big boat, and take the dinghy in tow.

For a while they were in sheltered water, and all went well; but as they drew out into the open lake, the wave was longer, and the dinghy began to misbehave. Towing is never easy in a wave; in a high and following wave it is almost impossible. Now the light dinghy would overrun and bump; now it would act as a sail and confuse the steering. To weight it and control it Michael volunteered to enter the towed dinghy and guide it with an oar. He did so, and found that he could guide it up to a point, but not control it; for as the wave grew steeper, the dinghy would poise like a surf-board on the white crest of a breaking wave, and then come sliding down the forward slope and crash against the boat. It was a terrible position for them all. Frank and Brendan shouted to Michael to come back into the comparative safety of the boat and cut the dinghy adrift. He would not hear of it; he stayed in the dinghy, cut the tow rope, and pulled clear. It was a high act of cool and calculated courage. The two men were in a solid boat with a good keel and considerable freeboard, and if they shipped a sea, the one could bale, while the other rowed; but Michael was alone in a cockle-shell, alone in the middle of an angry lake; his craft had little or no freeboard; it could spin round at a touch, and if it met a breaker broadside on, it would swamp instantaneously. But Michael never relaxed for a moment; he kept his head, and, watching every wave like a lynx, by sheer boatcraft he remained in full control of his frail barque.

An hour passed, and now in the gathering gloom the following wind had brought boat and dinghy to a point within half a mile of Rinmore Point, and if they could round that headland, there lay safety and a lee shore. Suddenly the wind failed them, and veered; the south wind that had blown all day dropped, and there was for a few moments an oily calm, an ominous calm, more fearsome than the storm; away to the west, high up in the sky over the shoulder of Mount Nephin, appeared the lurid red glow that told of a change of wind and of a hurricane on the way. They pulled frantically; for they were abreast the long, pitiless Brackwanshagh Reef. The last few yards made all the difference. They had just cleared the reef, and had entered Storm Bay, when they heard a rumble; and with a roar like an express train a tornado from the west struck the lake. Then (in the words of Frank's record) 'the squall hit us in a cloud of spray. It enveloped us completely and sent us hurtling towards the shore. All I could do was to keep our stern square to the wind. I kicked my rubber boots off. Soon the boat was travelling at such speed that I feared she would split in two when the crash came. A thole-pin broke, and I lost the last vestige of control. Suddenly Brendan started; he saw the line of white breakers ahead. I felt the keel grating on the rocks. Then a great wave took us up and hurled us broadside-on right over the rocks and into the sandy pool beyond. Twenty yards away we could dimly see Michael calmly tying up his tiny dinghy.'

A.A. LUCE, *Fishing and Thinking*, 1959

Oola of the Alta

I had taken bigger fish on the Alta, while fishing as Tony Pulitzer's guest on the Jöraholmen farm, but never under circumstances as bizarre as the day I found myself being ghillied by a girl.

This came about by chance, as it was my day to fish a very fine salmon pool, adjoining a great rocky point, which is ordinarily fished by boat. But I had offered my boat to a friend who was leaving for home that evening. His fishing had been unlucky and we all wanted to give him a last chance. My host concurred, and suggested that I try fishing the pool from the rocky promontory, as long as I would have no boat at my disposal until after 2 p.m. when the other guest would have to leave.

This was challenging, as if I did succeed in hooking a fish, casting from the rocks, the only possible gaffing place would be on the lower part of the rocky point, where the footing for gaffing is on a narrow ledge, about three feet wide and twelve feet long and some three feet above the water level.

I pondered the problem through a late breakfast and at 11 a.m. decided to go look at this difficult landing spot, to see if I could figure out a way to cope with a fish there with nobody around to gaff it for me.

The cook was busy in the kitchen, the Jöraholmen family was out on the farm, the chauffeur had left with Tony Pulitzer, and I was about to give up the idea when suddenly I remembered that in passing the house I had seen somebody hanging up the laundry out in back. That would be Oola, I realized, the young Lapp girl who had only a few days before begun working as kitchen helper and laundress.

Nobody knew much about Oola, who was short and stocky and very round, except that young as she was she already had several children, back in the village of Kaiteno, from lumberjacks, village boys and slate quarry workers. She had explained, in applying for the job, that she needed money to send back to the Lapp woman who was taking care of her kids, the result of her too great kindness to mankind. Oola was high in the front and low in the rear, with a very round face, dark but extremely smooth skin and Asiatic eyes. She was a very sweet girl, with a most comprehensive viewpoint, always looking at us men hungrily, I thought, and we all felt sorry for the poor creature.

'Hello Oola, how would you like to go fishing with me for an hour?'

She jumped up in the air saying, 'Yes, yes.'

I picked up my rod and the gaff and we started for the trail, of about half a mile, that led to the pool, Oola following along behind me until we reached the first barbed wire fence.

I snaked under it, as it was too high to climb over, and when I reached the other side Oola passed me the rod and the gaff and started to imitate me. She stopped with a yell, as the barbed wire caught in her skirt. I managed to get her loose and urged her on and just as she started to crawl again there was another, louder yell, reflecting a more serious problem. This time the wire was taut and stretching almost to the limit across that area of Oola which resembled two honeydew melons. After several failures I finally succeeded a second time in giving her full freedom of movement and Oola was at last able to pass and join me.

This she did, however, in such a confused and excited state that she threw her arms around me and I had to explain with many gestures that this was not part of salmon fishing and I almost told her I did not want to increase her little tribe. So off we went again towards the pool through the mossy grass and the birch trees.

When we reached the top of the rock, I decided to show Oola what I expected her to do and exactly how to use the gaff. She became more and more excited and I stepped away from her so as to keep clear of her weapon which she was waving frantically. We went to the rocky point and I started casting. 'Oola: all you have to do is to hold the gaff and keep away from my line while I am casting and always stay a reasonable distance behind me until I have the salmon at the foot of the rock, ready for gaffing.' She was holding the gaff and started to dance around me, again waving her weapon dangerously. I somehow managed to calm her and get her back to normal. After a few minutes I located two salmon just where the slack and fast waters met. This was a very good sign. I decided to use a medium size Arctic wolf hair tubefly and started casting.

All of a sudden I thought my fly had caught in a tree and when I turned I noticed the leader wrapped around the gaff and Oola standing close behind me. I stared at her and said: 'Now Oola, come and sit on the rock and leave the gaff on the ground and if you don't obey, you will have to go back to your chores.'

On the third cast, I was into a good fish. He immediately jumped twice and made for deep water and then up again for another jump as he tried to reach the current and swim downstream. He succeeded in doing this and took out a lot of line. I had to follow him trying to prevent the line from breaking on the jagged edges of the rock. I finally managed to stop the fish, then heard some wild yells, just as I had a slack line and the fish turned upstream. Suddenly I saw Oola, gaff in hand, doing some kind of a wild Lapp dance. By that time, my nervous system had almost reached its peak and I had the hardest time to control myself, the fish and Oola. At the end, in despair, I threatened to throw Oola in the pool. She began to cry and, gaff still in hand, started to return to the camp.

'Oola, come back at once, otherwise I will have to send you home to Kaiteno.'

She stopped, came back and sat down on a big stone. I was then able to concentrate on the salmon. Three more runs then he started to show signs of fatigue and I began to think that my usual luck was back. The fish tried twice to swim downstream and reach the current, but without success. He was finally almost still. I could start to bring him close enough for the gaffing. Then the great tragedy of my fisherman's life happened. I had decided I could not trust Oola with the gaff and the only solution was to hand her the rod realizing that any additional delay would increase the chances of the fly tearing loose. I could see it on the edge of the mouth. Now I explained to Oola how to handle the rod.

'Oola, here is the rod, hold it high with both hands, one on the reel and don't move. Remain as still as a statue!'

I took the gaff and immediately had it fast into the fish and lifted him out of the water, on to the rocky ledge. But the salmon was still lively and got off the gaff while I was trying to grab him with my hands. Oola then pulled on the rod with all her strength and broke the leader which had already been frayed on the rocks.

As I was scared of losing him, I did the only logical thing that came to my mind. I flopped down on the salmon. All of a sudden, I felt a tremendous weight on me. Oola was so excited and wanted to be so helpful that she lay on top of me. When the fish had quietened down and I managed to get Oola off me, I looked around for a stone to kill the poor salmon but not seeing one, I sent Oola to find a suitable stone. She soon returned with a rock of about twenty pounds which she wanted to drop on the salmon and probably on me also. I ordered her to lay it down and succeeded in making her understand the need to find a small stone. Soon she returned with a smaller stone, but still too heavy. On the third trip she brought the right sized stone. I killed the poor salmon and finally he was ours! We were shaking and then looked at each other and I felt like giving her a brotherly kiss, but at the last moment I changed my mind because she was looking at me with such spawning eyes.

The salmon tipped the scales at twenty-nine pounds. From that day on every time I saw Oola she gave me such a hungry look that I always had to tell her to stick to her laundry and that I had a French Oola waiting for me in Paris.

Upon my return to Paris, Ludwig Bemelmens was staying with us at the Ritz and when I told him Oola's story, he said: 'Charles, if you write about it, I will gladly make a sketch for you,' which he very kindly did.

But all my friends could say was: 'Oola indeed. Ooh-la-la, you wicked old Frenchman!'

And what kind of remark is that to make to a Swiss?

CHARLES RITZ, *A Fly Fisher's Life*, 1959

The Gentleman's Gentleman

These are the *real* gentlemen, the keepers, stalkers, and gillies: men who have spent a lifetime caring for their stags, salmon, grouse and game; who have devoted all their energies to providing their guests with sport and pleasure.

My strongest impression is one of admiration for the vast knowledge they have of their sport; my strongest feeling, one of disappointment at the ill-usage they so often receive at the hands of their 'gentlemen'.

Without exception, these men deplore the destruction being meted out to Atlantic salmon stocks through overfishing at sea and in the estuaries. Viewing the present situation against a background of more than sixty years' day-to-day experience, they presage with one accord the passing of the 'good old days', when each morning brought the chance of a few fish, or maybe more.

They have presided helplessly over the demise of one of the world's great sporting fish, while their 'gentlemen' stood idly by, allowing it to happen. It is little wonder that many of my gillies were bitter and not too sorry to hang up their rods and be done with it.

Yes, times change, and the fortunes and conditions of employment of present-day keepers have vastly improved. But it is still a completely demanding, twenty-four hour job, and the modern keeper is just as much at the beck and call of his master as ever a keeper was before.

As to the 'gentlemen', they are more demanding than ever. Having paid dearly to obtain even second-rate fishing or shooting, they expect value for money, and at times they are not over particular about the methods they use to achieve it.

I suppose that is the nature of the beast, but it seems to me that fishing and shooting are becoming more and more professional and commercialised. Much of the simple pleasure of being out on hill or loch, like a lightly hooked salmon, have gone forever.

BRUCE SANDISON, *The Sporting Gentleman's Gentleman*, 1986

The Invention of John Macnab

'You fellows beat me,' he cried. 'Here you are, every one of you a swell of sorts, with everything to make you cheerful, and you're grousin' like a labour battalion! You should be jolly well ashamed of yourselves. It's fairly temptin' Providence. What you want is some hard exercise. Go and sweat ten hours a day on a steep hill, and you'll get rid of these notions.'

'My dear Archie,' said Leithen, 'your prescription is too crude. I used to be fond enough of sport, but I wouldn't stir a foot to catch a sixty-pound salmon or kill a fourteen pointer. I don't want to. I see no fun in it. I'm *blasé*. It's too easy.'

'Well, I'm dashed! You're the worst spoiled chap I ever heard of, and a nice example to democracy.' Archie spoke as if his gods had been blasphemed.

'Democracy, anyhow, is a good example to us. I know now why workmen strike sometimes and can't give any reason. We're on strike – against our privileges.'

Archie was not listening. 'Too easy, you say?' he repeated. 'I call that pretty fair conceit. I've seen you miss birds often enough, old fellow.'

'Nevertheless, it seems to me too easy. Everything has become too easy, both work and play.'

'You can screw up the difficulty, you know. Try shootin' with a twenty bore, or fishin' for salmon with a nine-foot rod and a dry-fly cast.'

'I don't want to kill anything,' said Palliser-Yeates. 'I don't see the fun of it.'

Archie was truly shocked. Then a light of reminiscence came into his eye. 'You remind me of poor old Jim Tarras,' he said thoughtfully.

There were no inquiries about Jim Tarras, so Archie volunteered further news.

'You remember Jim? He had a little place somewhere in Moray, and spent most of his time shootin' in East Africa. Poor chap, he went back there with Smuts in the war and perished of blackwater. Well, when his father died and he came home to settle down, he found it an uncommon dull job. So, to enliven it, he invented a new kind of sport. He knew all there was to be known about *shikar*, and from trampin' about the Highlands he had a pretty accurate knowledge of the country-side. So he used to write to the owner of a deer forest and present his compliments, and beg to inform him that between certain dates he proposed to kill one of his stags. When he had killed it he undertook to deliver it to the owner, for he wasn't a thief.'

'I call that poaching on the grand scale,' observed Palliser-Yeates.

'Wasn't it? Most of the fellows he wrote to accepted his challenge and told him to come and do his damnedest. Little Avington, I remember, turned on every man and boy about the place for three nights to watch the forest. Jim usually worked at night, you see. One or two curmudgeons talked of the police and prosecutin' him, but public opinion was against them – too dashed unsportin'.'

'Did he always get his stag?' Leithen asked.

'In-var-i-ably, and got it off the ground and delivered it to the owner, for that was the rule of the game. Sometimes he had a precious near squeak, and Avington, who was going off his head at the time, tried to pot him – shot a gillie in the leg too. But Jim always won out. I should think he was the best *shikari* God ever made.'

'Is that true, Archie?' Lamancha's voice had a magisterial tone.

'True – as – true. I know all about it, for Wattie Lithgow, who was Jim's man, is with me now. He and his wife keep house for me at Crask. Jim never took but the one man with him, and that was Wattie, and he made him just about as cunning an old dodger as himself.'

Leithen yawned. 'What sort of a place is Crask?' he inquired.

'Tiny little place. No fishin' except some hill lochs and only rough shootin'. I take it for the birds. Most marvellous nestin' ground in Britain barrin' some of the Outer Islands. I don't know why it should be, but it is. Something to do with the Gulf Stream, maybe. Anyhow, I've got the greenshank breedin' regularly and the red-throated diver, and half a dozen rare duck. It's a marvellous stoppin' place in spring too, for birds goin' north.'

'Are you much there?'

'Generally in April, and always from the middle of August till the middle of October. You see, it's about the only place I know where you can do exactly as you like. The house is stuck away up on a long slope of moor, and you see the road for a mile from the windows, so you've plenty of time to take to the hills if anybody comes to worry you. I roost there with old Sime, my butler, and the two Lithgows, and put up a pal now and then who likes the life. It's the jolliest bit of the year for me.'

'Have you any neighbours?'

'Heaps, but they don't trouble me much. Crask's the earthenware pot among the brazen vessels – mighty hard to get to and nothing to see when you get there. So the brazen vessels keep to themselves.'

Lamancha went to a shelf of books above a writing-table and returned with an atlas. 'Who are your brazen vessels?' he asked.

'Well, my brassiest is old Claybody at Haripol – that's four miles off across the hill.'

'Bit of a swine, isn't he?' said Leithen.

'Oh, no. He's rather a good old bird himself. Don't care so much for his family. Then there's Glenraden t'other side of the Larrig' – he indicated a point on the map which Lamancha was studying

– 'with a real old Highland grandee living in it – Alastair Raden –
commanded the Scots Guards, I believe, in the year One. Family as
old as the Flood and very poor, but just manage to hang on.
He's the last Raden that will live there, but that doesn't matter so
much as he has no son – only a brace of daughters. Then, of
course, there's the show place, Strathlarrig – horrible great house as
large as a factory, but wonderful fine salmon-fishin'. Some
Americans have got it this year – Boston or Philadelphia, I don't
remember which – very rich and said to be rather high-brow.
There's a son, I believe.'

Lamancha closed the atlas.

'Do you know any of these people, Archie?' he asked.

'Only the Claybodys – very slightly. I stayed with them in
Suffolk for a covert shoot two years ago. The Radens have been to
call on me, but I was out. The Bandicotts – that's the Americans –
are new this year.'

'Is the sport good?'

'The very best. Haripol is about the steepest and most sportin'
forest in the Highlands, and Glenraden is nearly as good. There's
no forest at Strathlarrig, but, as I've told you, amazin' good salmon
fishin'. For a west coast river, I should put the Larrig only second
to the Laxford.'

Lamancha consulted the atlas again and appeared to ponder.
Then he lifted his head, and his long face, which had a certain
heaviness and sullenness in repose, was now lit by a smile which
made it handsomer and younger.

'Could you have me at Crask this autumn?' he asked. 'My wife
has to go to Aix for a cure and I have no plans after the House
rises.'

'I should jolly well think so,' cried Archie. 'There's heaps of
room in the old house, and I promise you I'll make you comfortable.
Look here, you fellows! Why shouldn't all three of you come? I can
get in a couple of extra maids from Inverlarrig.'

'Excellent idea,' said Lamancha. 'But you mustn't bother about
the maids. I'll bring my own man, and we'll have a male establishment, except for Mrs Lithgow. . . . By the way, I suppose you can
count on Mrs Lithgow?'

'How do you mean, "count"?' asked Archie, rather puzzled.

Then a difficulty struck him. 'But wouldn't you be bored? I can't show you much in the way of sport, and you're not naturalists like me. It's a quiet life, you know.'

'I shouldn't be bored,' said Lamancha, 'I should take steps to prevent it.'

Leithen and Pallister-Yeates seemed to divine his intention, for they stimultaneously exclaimed. – 'It isn't fair to excite Archie, Charles,' the latter said. 'You know that you'll never do it.'

'I intend to have a try. Hang it, John, it's the specific we were talking about – devilish difficult, devilish unpleasant, and calculated to make a man long for a dull life. Of course you two fellows will join me.'

'What on earth are you talkin' about?' said the mystified Archie. 'Join what?'

'We're proposing to quarter ourselves on you, my lad, and take a leaf out of Jim Tarras's book.'

Sir Archie first stared, then he laughed nervously, then he called upon his gods, then he laughed freely and long. 'Do you really mean it? What an almighty rag! . . . But hold on a moment. It will be rather awkward for me to take a hand. You see I've just been adopted as prospective candidate for that part of the country.'

'So much the better. If you're found out – which you won't be – you'll get the poaching vote solid, and a good deal more. Most men at heart are poachers.'

Archie shook a doubting head. 'I don't know about that. They're an awfully respectable lot up there, and all those dashed stalkers and keepers and gillies are a sort of trade-union. The scallywags are a hopeless minority. If I get sent to quod –'

'You won't get sent to quod. At the worst it will be a fine, and you can pay that. What's the extreme penalty for this kind of offence, Ned?'

'I don't know,' Leithen answered. 'I'm not an authority on Scots law. But Archie's perfectly right. We can't go making a public exhibition of ourselves like this. We're too old to be listening to the chimes at midnight.'

'Now, look here.' Lamancha had shaken off his glumness and was as tense and eager as a schoolboy. 'Didn't your doctor advise you to steal a horse? Well, this is a long sight easier than horse-stealing. It's admitted that we three want a tonic. On second thoughts Archie had better stand out – he hasn't our ailment, and a healthy man doesn't need medicine. But we three need it, and this idea is an inspiration. Of course we take risks, but they're sound sporting risks. After all, I've a reputation of a kind, and I put as much into the pool as anyone.'

His hearers regarded him with stony faces, but this in no way checked his ardour.

'It's a perfectly first-class chance. A lonely house where you can see visitors a mile off, and an unsociable dog like Archie for a host. We write the letters and receive the answers at a London address. We arrive at Crask by stealth, and stay there unbeknown to the country-side, for Archie can count on his people and my man in a sepulchre. Also we've got Lithgow, who played the same game with Jim Tarras. We have a job which will want every bit of our nerve and ingenuity with a reasonable spice of danger – for, of course, if we fail we should cut queer figures. The thing is simply ordained by Heaven for our benefit. Of course you'll come.'

'I'll do nothing of the kind,' said Leithen.

'No more will I,' said Palliser-Yeates.

'Then I'll go alone,' said Lamancha cheerfully. 'I'm out for a cure, if you're not. You've a month to make up your mind, and meanwhile a share in the syndicate remains open to you.'

Sir Archie looked as if he wished he had never mentioned the fatal name of Jim Tarras, 'I say, you know, Charles,' he began hesitatingly, but was cut short.

'Are you going back on your invitation?' asked Lamancha sternly. 'Very well, then, I've accepted it, and what's more I'm going to draft a specimen letter that will go to your Highland grandee, and Claybody and the American.'

He rose with a bound and fetched a pencil and a sheet of notepaper from the nearest writing-table. 'Here goes – *Sir, I have the honour to inform you that I propose to kill a stag* – or a salmon as the case may be – *on your ground between midnight on* – *and midnight* –. We can leave the dates open for the present. *The animal, of course, remains your property and will be duly delivered to you. It is a condition that it must be removed wholly outside your bounds. In the event of the undersigned failing to achieve his purpose he will pay as forfeit one hundred pounds, and if successful fifty pounds to any charity you may appoint. I have the honour to be, your obedient humble servant.'*

'What do you say to that?' he asked. 'Formal, a little official, but perfectly civil, and the writer proposes to pay his way like a gentleman. Bound to make a good impression.'

'You've forgotten the signature,' Leithen observed dryly.

'It must be signed with a *nom de guerre.*' He thought for a moment. 'I've got it. At once business-like and mysterious.' At the bottom of the draft he scrawled the name 'John Macnab.'

JOHN BUCHAN, *John Macnab*, 1925

Poacher's Logic

By opening the fender at Steep Weir I had annoyed certain salmon poachers, who came from the town with gaffs, twisted brass nooses on poles, and even dung-forks. Four of them eyed me sullenly as I arrived by the fender, which I found closed on my second visit. These men were out of work, through no fault of their own: at that time two million in Britain were permanently without jobs. I talked with some of them, who had fought in the war. I said that the flesh of the purple and brown fish in the river was poor: that some were kelts, which needed to clean themselves in the sea. They were not good to eat.

'But what about they green-backs? They'm clane enough! They'm what you water-whipping gentry call clean-run. The lice be still upon 'm! They green-backs kick up the eggs already laid, and put down their own, for what purpose? Shall I tell 'ee? For to breed more green-backs, to do the same thing, and kick up more eggs, and take their place, until all you rod-and-line men will have is green-backs to catch by whippin' water in winter. Then where's your spring sport, with a nice packet o' sandwiches and a nip o' whiskey? Can yew answer me that, tho'?'

I could not; so I gave them a few shillings each for this information, saying that I was a writer, and paid for information; and at least they had not condemned me to a watery death when I had re-opened the fender. I gave them a lift back to the town, where they entered a butcher's shop to buy pork chops, with which they set off for their homes, seeming to be as pleased as I was.

HENRY WILLIAMSON, *A Clear Water Stream*, 1958

Staying Solvent in Tackle Shops

It is as mistaken to think that we go to tackle-shops only because we need tackle as to think that we go fishing only because we want to eat fish. Most fishermen dislike eating fish and do their best not to buy tackle. It is just because the tackle-dealer is a fisherman himself that he can be so extraordinarily tolerant of his customers. For there are two distinct kinds of visits to tackle-shops, the visit to buy tackle and the visit which may be described as Platonic when, being for some reason unable to fish, we look for an excuse to go in and waste a tackle-dealer's time. Of this the tackle-dealer is well aware. He knows, at once, as one of us comes through the door what kind of visit is intended. The man who looks at his watch, raps out his order in accurate detail, half a dozen each of Brunton's Fancy and Little Marryat with two casts tapered to 4x, is going grayling fishing and wants from the dealer nothing but efficiency. That other, a little shy, whose eyes wander from the rods in their khaki cases to the glass-fronted cupboard of reels, from the artificial minnows to the flies, from them to the labelled boxes on the shelves, who modestly suggests that another customer shall be served before himself (to give him an excuse for staying longer in the shop) is in a different category. The one has come because he is going fishing. The other is there because, alas, he is not. The one wants tackle, the other a course of mental treatment. Such is the noble nature of tackle-dealers that in most cases he gets it.

In this matter the really good tackle-dealer can put doctors and even solicitors to shame. He could give lessons to diplomatists. None, so well as he, knows how to suffer fools. Everyman, while at his tackle-dealer's, is made to feel that he is something of a fisher, that his praise of this or that is praise worth having, that he is, indeed, the very man the tackle-dealer is glad to talk fishing with. And if Everyman does, at his tackle-dealer's, spend rather more than the small amount he had decided to stand himself when he came in, why he comes out with a moral tonic that is worth the money many times over, and he has the tackle too. It is the moderation of the tackle-dealer that is so admirable, for he has his visitor at his mercy. Of course, he must not be tempted too far. The visitor, if he is wise, will keep his talk to the safe subjects. It is not safe to mention reels and, if the conversation approaches the point at which rods begin to come out of their cases, he had better remember an appointment; or, if he really wants to play with fire, announce firmly that he does not mean that day to buy a rod. The tackle-dealer will tell him that he need not think of buying one, but will let him handle the magic wands just the same. Magic they are and the dealer knows it and so should Everyman, who must in this crisis continually count over in his mind the long row of rods he has already. A rod bought on one of these Platonic visits to a tackle-shop is never the pleasure that a rod is which has been bought, so to speak, on purpose. The Platonic visit should retain its character to the end. There is no harm in paying for it by the purchase of a few flies (which will always 'come in some time'), or some gut or a packet of hooks. But major purchases introduce an element that may destroy the otherwise salutary effect of the visit. A packet of flies can be hidden in the pocket and from the conscience, but to have to carry through the streets a brand-new rod as a proof that you have needed comfort on account of an inability to go fishing is a searing experience, not to be easily forgotten. This is, of course, well known to the superlative tackle-dealer, who will even put a rod away rather than take advantage of a customer's weakness (and we are often very weak) to inflict upon him a humiliation difficult to forgive. Bad tackle-dealers, who are not fishermen, take their chance and lose their customers. No man likes to revisit the scene of a public loss of his self-control.

ARTHUR RANSOME, *Rod and Line*, 1929

CHAPTER TEN

The Ethics of Fishing

$\mathcal{A}$t some time or other all thoughtful anglers have wondered how they can justify inflicting pain for their own pleasure. That electrifying convulsion of the rod is a creature struggling for its life. The fish you lift from the water is bright silver, serpentinely alive as it writhes in the net. You knock it on the head, once, twice, perhaps three or four times to make sure you've killed it, and wonder at its beauty.

A fish fresh from the water is a form of perfection. Its body is hydrodynamically flawless, from its rounded nose to the thickest point at the dorsal fin, tapering down to the base of its fan-like tail. Try lifting a live salmon by that tail and you realize that every fibre of the creature is pulsing with kinetic energy, twisting, writhing and strong enough to shake your arm in its shoulder socket. 'No human being, however great or powerful, was ever so free as a fish,' Ruskin once said.

But now the fish is dead. In an hour or so, the filmy mucus on the body will have thickened into a viscous glue. In three or four hours, the corpse will have darkened and stiffened. All lustre is gone. What had been a vibrant, silver enigma is just a lump of dead matter.

Of course, no one who eats fish can feel too many qualms. The fishmongers are stocked with the proceeds of mass slaughter. Dragged into a near-invisible net in their thousands and then either drowned or gutted alive in the bowels of some stinking factory ship, fish caught to satisfy the huge demand for human food have a miserable end.

But the fish killed by rod-and-line dies because it has been deceived, as a consequence of its own greed, hunger or aggression. The angler respects the quarry he tries to trap; the fish has free choice. The Spanish trawlerman sees so much dead meat or so many pesetas.

Yet this is precisely what seems most to bother the little band of fanatics who try to bully fishermen into giving up their sport. They cannot bear the thought that people are enjoying themselves. They are a new breed of puritans. Their case presupposes that fish feel pain like any warm-blooded creature. One wonders, then, at the numerous stories of trout risen and pricked three or four times before they are finally taken, at the carp which may be caught a dozen times if the fisherman is guileful enough. If it felt pain would it really continue taking the same bait? Hunger, the campaigners reply. But then what of a salmon, which eats nothing at all in fresh water? And what are we to make of the fish which swallowed a hook on which was impaled its own eye?

But common-sense is no bar to the purple-haired saboteur hysterically screaming 'murderer!' as an angler called Humphrey reels in his catch on a Tyneside reservoir. When she asked him whether he believed fish felt pain, he sucked on his pipe and replied thoughtfully, 'I really don't know, lovey. Why don't you ask one?'

Fishing people have had to put up with this sort of assault for generations. Byron's famous remark of this 'cruelest, coldest and stupidest of pretended sports', that 'no angler can be a good man', should be taken with a bucket of salt. What Byron objected to was the sport's apparent cruelty, specifically Walton's humbug about treating frogs lovingly while threading hooks through them. Yet we learn from his own letters that Byron's objection is humbug too: he was happy to go fishing himself.

In fact, far from the antis' caricature, it is noticeable how much writing about fishing is taken up with ethics. The very first book in English on the sport, the *Treatyse of Eysshynge with an Angle*, is full of advice about not poaching, not taking more fish than you need, even closing gates behind you.

If their attitudes were ever seriously questioned in the following centuries, anglers could respond with the verse from the very first chapter of the very first book of the Bible, that having created man in his own image, God gave him 'dominion over the fish of the sea and over the fowl of the air and over every living thing that moveth upon the earth' (Genesis, 1, v.28). As numerous seventeenth-century writers pointed out, the first four disciples, Peter, Andrew, James and John, were all fishermen.

There is a strong environmental argument, too. No group of people is more concerned to improve the cleanliness of rivers, streams and lakes than anglers. If it were not for the lobbying of organizations from local angling associations through to the Atlantic Salmon Trust, many more of the country's waterways would be stinking, filthy and stagnant. No one more wants a healthy supply of healthy fish.

But if fishermen have never really had much of a problem justifying their sport in general terms, they have constructed a vast, complicated filigree of dos and don'ts since then. The hierarchy of fishing is built upon the idea that the harder the method, the more worthwhile the catch. The fly-fisherman disdains the angler who uses a prawn. Both look down on the person who tries to catch his fish by 'snigging' or foulhooking. Even poachers moan about driftnets on the high seas.

Every angler has had at some time to put up with having the damnation attributed to Dr Johnson quoted back to him. 'Fly-fishing, Sir, may be a very pleasant amusement; but angling or float-fishing I can only compare to a stick and a string, with a worm at one end and a fool at the other.' The fact that the old bombast had probably plagiarized the remark from Martial Guyet deters them not the slightest. The sniffiness about 'angling' as opposed to game fishing certainly belongs more to the nineteenth century. Although some Jacobean authors suggested there was a hierarchy in fishing, it took the Victorians, with their fine nose for orders of being, to create the full range of class distinctions. Before then, anglers had been happy enough to use worm, maggot or fly, just as long as they caught a fish or two. The advent of mass travel and mass recreation, the Victorians' romantic obsession with the Scottish Highlands, the development of the idea of 'gentlemanly pursuits', all of it egged on by writers and tackle manufacturers, left us with the caste-system we have today.

The sheer cost of fishing for salmon and chalkstream trout has, I think, something to do with the way that rules are made about what are legitimate tactics. On many of the best salmon rivers, the use of the shrimp is banned. This is usually said to be because it is 'unsporting', although it is hard to see why it is any more illegitimate than dragging a bit of metal through the water on the end of a spinning line. To fish a spun prawn, feeling for a take on the tip of the index finger, or a prawn hung from a float, where you have constantly to mend the line to bring it down the right drift, all the time watching for the hint of a nudge, takes a good deal more skill than spinning, which many of the posher waters will allow quite happily when the river is high.

The plain fact is that the shrimp is a deadly weapon. The objection is that it is simply *too* deadly. To be worthwhile, fishing has to be hard, and sophistication is all about making it more difficult. The greatest consideration is that the predator have some respect for his quarry. When a couple of anglers take seventy fish in the same pool with a prawn, it isn't sport but slaughter. They are fishmongers. When it's too easy, there's no challenge. When there's no challenge, there's no dignity.

The most recent ethical revolution in fly-fishing, the introduction of 'catch-and-release', has turned much traditional practice upside-down. On many of the swankiest American rivers, the idea of killing the trout you have caught is looked down upon with a disdain greater than that of the dry-fly purist to the maggot-dangler. Worse, it is seen as immoral.

'Catch-and-release' seems certain to grow, perhaps to become the norm in time. But we shouldn't be under any illusion that its supposed superiority is anything to do with consideration for the fish. Lee Wulff, the great American fly fisherman who coined the idea in 1938, hadn't a thought about the welfare of his quarry. The belief that 'gamefish are too valuable to be caught only once,' is built on the explicit premise that the creatures are there only to give pleasure to the angler. If fish *do* feel pain, it is a policy of allowing them to continue living in order that we can inflict more pain on them, again and again.

Of course, it makes for better, more difficult fishing as the trout get wilier as the years go by – five times bitten very shy indeed. It removes the need to keep restocking rivers with bloated, stew-pond-bred trout-slugs. It may be the only way to keep rivers closer to their natural state when the number of people fishing – thirty-six million men and eighteen million women in America – has become so great. It may save the best American waters from the fate which has overtaken some of the most famous English chalk streams, ruined by trying to meet the pressure with farmed fish. Whether it is innately superior, or another version of Walton's guff about treating frogs you have maimed 'lovingly' is another matter.

This chapter shows how writers have tackled these questions of ethics – and other pressing ethical questions, like whether all fishermen are always and inevitably liars.

A Salmon Poacher Caught Red-handed

A fly fisherman's knowledge is compounded of many things. It grows out of imagination, curiosity, bold experiment and intense observation. A fly fisherman must always be picturing to himself what is going on under the water; he must try to understand what his fly means to the fish and so he must choose it or tie it with meaning, he must try to make it move in or on the water with meaning. He must look for new ideas, try them out when they come to him and watch closely to see their effect and find others.

A mark of all the best fishermen I have known has been power of concentration, and this, perhaps, is the most important single quality a fisherman can have. This does not mean that fishing must become a strain. I like nothing better than to tempt fate by slinging my rod under my arm with a full line out while I take time to watch some ducks circle or to fill a pipe and light it. But it does mean that every cast should have an idea behind it and should be fished out to the end with the expectation of catching a fish. The men who do this are those who have a close knowledge of fish and water, who know where a fish is likely to be lying, how he will be feeding, what the current will do to the fly, and, not least, who realise that their knowledge is imperfect and that the unexpected can happen. All this knowledge will force concentration on a man almost in spite of himself.

To take proper advantage of his opportunities, a fly fisherman needs reasonably quick and sure reactions and fair control over his emotions – many a fish has sampled an artificial fly with impunity because the fisherman was slow to respond to the sight or feel of the rise, and many another has gone off with the fly in his jaws because of a jumpy strike. On this purely physical side of things, a fisherman may sometimes need endurance – a long day in cold water can test it – and perhaps even courage, for bold wading and climbing often enough put a fly in a place it would not otherwise have reached. . . .

We are civilised men, not merely fishers for meat. Our tradition is that of the first man who sneaked away to the creek when the tribe did not really need fish, a tradition developed for us through thousands of years and millions of river lovers. We fish for pleasure, and fishing becomes pleasure from within ourselves in proportion to the skill and knowledge, to the imagination and flexibility of soul that we bring to it. Like the hunter, the hawker and the fowler, the fisherman takes life in finding his pleasure. It is reasonable to ask of him that he make it as keen and thorough and satisfying, as productive of growth in himself as he reasonably can. For only then can it be the strong and sensitive pleasure of a civilised man.

RODERICK HAIG-BROWN, *A River Never Sleeps*, 1942

'A Procurer of Contentedness'

It is remarkable that among the Twelve Holy Apostles there were four of them fishermen, whom our Saviour elected and inspired to preach the Gospel. And the reason that some give for this choice is that he knew and found the hearts of such men naturally more fitted for contemplation and quietness, having spirits mild, sweet and peaceable.

Besides, our Saviour seems to have a more than common respect for their occupation, for two reasons. First, he never reproved them for their profession, as he did others, viz the scribes and the money-changers. Next, he dignified these poor fishermen with the priority of nomination in the Catalogue of the Twelve Apostles. Nay, that which is more observable is this, that our Saviour took only three of these Fishermen with him when he ascended the Mount to bear him company at his Transfiguration.

Now, as to the lawfulness of Fishing, I think none can speak against it, since our Saviour himself commanded St Peter to fish to pay Caesar his tribute.

And as the Ancients have highly applauded and approved of this ingenious exercise, several of the Heroes of old, in the height of their glory, having exercised themselves herein; as Dr Whitaker, learned Perkins, Dr Nowell, Dean of St Pauls London, and the incomparable Sir Henry Wotton, Provost of Eton College, who was a great lover of Angling and would frequently say thereof, that it was after his study a Rest to his mind, a cheerer to his Spirits, a diverter of Sadness, a calmer of Unquiet thoughts, a Moderator of Passions, a procurer of Contentedness; and that it begot habits of Peace and Patience in those that possess and practise it.

NICHOLAS COX, *The Gentleman's Recreation*, 1697

And a Purifier of Thoughts

It has been gravely said that a good angler must also be a good Christian. Without literalizing the assertion, it may well be admitted that there is much in the contemplative character of his pursuit, and in the quiet scenes of beauty with which it brings him face to face, to soften and elevate, as well as to 'humanize.' The rushing of white water, and the deep greenery of woods and fields, seem incompatible with what is base or sordid. They act like a tonic on mind and body alike, and the fisherman, solitary with his own thoughts, shut out from the world, 'shut in, left alone' with himself and perfection of scenery, can hardly fail to be penetrated with the spirit that haunts solitude and loveliness. A chord is touched that must find an echo in every heart not utterly dead to gentle influences – awakening what is good, silencing what is bad; directing the thoughts into purer channels, and leading them almost instinctively to 'look through Nature up to Nature's God.'

H. CHOLMONDELEY PENNELL, *The Practical Angler*, 1870

The Qualities Necessary in an Angler

Various are the attributes which a good angler must possess. He must be a philosopher – must know something of astronomy – must have quickness of intellect, great perseverance, good temper, decision and sharp sight; he ought to be a good rower, and swim well; for he may at times have occasion to exert his aquatic energies for self-preservation. How often is philosophy necessary! A hook gets beyond the barb into your hand, finger, or perhaps your nose or lip. You can't get it out; if you are alone, bad enough; if in company, you must get the tying carefully cut off, after which the hook must be turned out point foremost, and the other way; all here depends on the goodness of the hook, for it can't be extricated the way it went in, without barbarous cutting, and, perhaps, not in the exact place; but when turned out properly, it is easily drawn forth, and no bad effects will follow, except the loss of the fly. Again, how often may you have a fine fish almost within reach, when your fly or hook flies into the air, or some bungler pulls the gaff across the line, and breaks all! Again, you set off from home in a great hurry, to get to a lake or river some miles distance, and find that you have left flies, trolling hooks, and all tackling at home, and what a pleasant walk you have back, cursing and growling the whole way; and devoting some person, who caused your inadvertence, to the especial custody of Satan! Again, you go with a party; the fishing is bad in the early part of the day; but when the sun declines, becomes excellent, when one of your companions takes his watch out, and declares for an immediate return, as you are expected at a certain hour, and the dinner will be spoiled; on this latter occasion, if you don't possess a good portion of philosophy, the temper of your mind may be guessed at pretty easily. So much for philosophy.

You must know the changes of the moon, and the particular times, when it has on fish, in the opinion of many, a very direct influence. . . .

Several persons say they have not patience for angling: this is truly ridiculous; we must have patience on all occasions; but I think the word ought to be altogether expunged from the vocabulary of sportmen, and the word *perseverance* substituted. If this quality is not inherent in a sportsman, he will be a bad hand at either shooting or fishing. How often after many hours of fruitless exertion without success, when all seems blank, may not a fine scull of trout with fins and tail over water, make their appearance, when, if a good angler, you pick up three or four of them in a few minutes, and bless your stars that you persevered to the end! . . .

You must have decision, particularly if you angle for large fish where weeds and rocks abound. . . . You must, or ought to have good temper, particularly if you fish with bunglers or beginners; and though you feel many mental pangs at their frequent and gross mismanagement of fish, cracking off flies, entangling constantly with you, perhaps destroying the sport altogether, you should have pity and forbearance; should direct and advise them, and recollect the days of your youth, when you were, most probably, a fruitful source of annoyance to others under similar circumstances. Various are the additional vexations sportsmen may be subjected to; such as wet and stormy weather, breaking of oars, often obliged to land on a lee shore, having several miles to walk, without remedy, perhaps wet to the skin; drunken boatmen, . . . all these, and many more crosses unnecessary to state, are the lot of anglers, to all of whom I recommend a quiet and thankful temper; though my *preaching* may, I doubt not, be better than my *practice*, as some of my friends, perhaps justly, imagine. And so much for good temper.

I will now conclude this long chapter by a cursory notice of anglers, as men; and I do assert, that I have almost invariably found them persons of good and charitable dispositions, possessing mild, though firm tempers, sharp and intellectual minds; incapable of committing base and ungenerous actions; much inclined to the heavenly passion of love; free from the debasing vice of avarice; lively and lighthearted; agreeable and intelligent. The very pursuit, while it demands the possession of intellect, must sharpen it. Were I to select the professions among the members of which I have met the best men, and the most skilful anglers, I would certainly name the army and the law. I mean the highest branch of the latter; as for the attorneys, with many honourable exceptions, they are an incorrigible race. Indeed I have rarely seen any of them who could angle at all, perhaps, only one; and he was a sinister biped (left-handed.) They are, for the most part, devoted to worldly gain; and . . . will never give a direct answer to a question.

JAMES 'THE' O'GORMAN, *The Practice of Angling*, 1845

The Earliest Rules of Fishing

I charge and require you in the name of all noble men that ye fish not in no poor man's several water as his pond, stew or other necessary things to keep fish in without his licence and goodwill; nor that ye use not to break no man's gins lying in their weirs and in other places due unto them; ne to take the fish away that is taken in them, for after a fish is taken in a man's gin if a gin be laid in the common waters, or else in such waters as he hireth, it is his own proper goods, and if ye take it away ye rob him, which is a right shameful deed to any noble man to do that that the thieves and [vagabonds] do which are punished for their evil deeds by the neck and otherwise when they may be espied and taken. . . . Also that ye break no man's hedges in going about your disports; ne open no man's gates but that ye shut them again. Also ye shall not use this foresaid crafty disport for no covetousness to the increasing and sparing of your money, only, but principally, for your solace and to cause the health of your body and specially of your soul; for when ye purpose to go on your disports in fishing ye will not desire greatly many persons with you, which might let you of your game, and then ye may serve God devoutly in saying affectuously your customable[3] prayer. And thus ye shall eschew and void many vices, as idleness, which is [the] principal cause to induce man to many other vices as is right well-known. Also ye shall not be too ravenous in taking of your said game as too much at one time, . . . as when ye have a sufficient [measure] ye should covet no more as at that time. Also ye shall busy yourself to nourish the game in all that ye may and to destroy all such things as be devourers of it. And all those that do after this rule shall have the blessing of God and Saint Peter, which He them grant that with His precious blood us bought.

from the *Treatyse of Fysshynge With an Angle*, attributed to
Dame Juliana Berners, 1496

Some Eighteenth-century Fishing Laws

The laws of England being all public, ignorance of their contents excuses no offender. It will not be amiss therefore to say something of those which concern the angler, that he may have a certain knowledge, how, without offence, to demean himself amongst his neighbours, when he goes about his sport. . . .

If any person shall keep any net, angle, leap, piche, or other engine for taking fish, (except the makers or sellers of them, or the owners or occupiers of rivers or fisheries) such engines, if they shall be found fishing without the consent of the owner, shall be seized; and any person, by a warrant under the hand and seal of a Justice of the Peace, may search the houses of persons prohibited and suspected, and seize to their own use, or destroy such engines.

No servant shall be questioned for killing a trespasser within his master's liberty, who will not yield, if not done out of former malice: yet if the trespasser kills any such servant, it is murder.

None shall erect a weir or weirs along the seashore, or in any haven or creek, or within five miles of the mouth of any haven or creek, or shall willingly take or destroy any spawn, fry or brood of any sea-fish, on pain of ten pounds, to be divided between the king and the prosecutor. Neither shall any fish in any of the said places, with any not of a less mesh than three inches and a half between knot and knot, (except for Smoulds in Norfolk only) or with a canvas net, or other engine, whereby the spawn or fry of fish may be destroyed, on pain of forfeiting the said net or engine, and ten shillings in money, to be divided between the poor and the prosecutor.

Barbel is not to be taken under twelve inches long; the penalty is twenty shillings, the engine, and the fish.

Herrings are not to be sold before the fishermen come to land, and must not be brought into Yarmouth Haven between Michaelmas and Martinmas; the penalty is imprisonment, and forfeiture of the herrings.

Lobsters must not be taken under ten inches; the forfeiture is twenty shillings, the fish, and the engine they are taken with.

Salmon is not to be sent to London to fishmongers, or their agents, weighing less than six pounds; and every person that buys or sells such, shall be liable to forfeit five pounds, or be sent to hard labour for three months.

In the Rivers Seven, Dee, Thame, Were, Tees, Ribble, Mersey, Dun, Air, Ouze, Swale, Caldor, Eure, Derwent, and Trent, no person is to lay nets, engines, or other devices, whereby the spawn or small fry of salmon, or any keeper or shedder salmon, under eighteen inches long from the eye to the middle of the tail, shall be taken, killed or destroyed. Nor shall they make, erect, or set any bank, dam, hedge, stank, or nets, cross the said rivers, to take the salmon, or hinder them going to spawn: nor shall they kill salmon in the said rivers, between the twelfth of August and the twenty-third of November, or fish with unlawful nets, under the penalty of five pounds for every offence: and for want of distress, to be sent to hard labour for not less than one month, nor more than three months. . . .

No one shall enter into any park or paddock fenced in and inclosed, or into any garden, orchard, or yard adjoining or belonging to any dwelling-house, in or through which park or paddock, garden, orchard, or yard, any river or stream, pond, pool, moat, stew, or other water, and by any ways, means, or device whatsoever, shall steal, take, kill, or destroy any fish bred, kept or preserved, in any such river or stream, pond, pool, moat, stew, or other water aforesaid, without the consent of the owner or owners thereof; or shall be aiding or assisting in the stealing, taking, killing, or destroying, any such fish as aforesaid; and being thereof indicted within six calendar months next after such offence or offences shall have been committed, before any judge or justices of gaol delivery for the county wherein such park or paddock, garden, orchard, or yard, shall be, and shall on such indictment be, by verdict, on his or their own confession or confessions, convicted of such offence or offences as aforesaid, the person or persons so convicted shall be transported for seven years.

RICHARD BROOKES, *The Art of Angling*, 1790

(The last paragraph, from the first Act of 1765, is accurate. The licence to kill, in the third paragraph, attributed to the law of Queen Elizabeth I, is pure wishful thinking – ED.)

The Laws of Fishing, 1803

By the 5th Eliz. c. xxi. s. 2, it is provided, That if any person shall unlawfully break or destroy any head or dam of a fish pond, or shall wrongfully fish therein, with intent to take or kill fish, he shall, on conviction at the assizes or sessions, at the suit of the King, or the party injured, be imprisoned three months, and pay treble damages; and after the expiration of the said three months, shall find sureties for good behaviour for seven years to come.

By 31st Henry Eighth, c. ii. s. 2, If any evil-disposed persons shall fish in the day-time, from six in the morning till six in the evening, in any ponds, stews, or moats, with nets, hooks, or bait, against the will of the owners, they shall, on conviction thereof, at the suit of the King, or the party aggrieved, suffer imprisonment for the space of three months, and find security for their good behaviour.

By 22d and 23d Charles Second, c. xxv. s. 7, it is enacted, That if any person shall, at any time, use any casting-net, drag-net, shove-net, or other net whatever; or any angle, hair, noose, troll, or spear; or shall lay any wears, pots, nets, fish-hooks, or other engines; or shall take any fish by any means whatsoever, in any river, stew, moat, pond, or other water, or shall be aiding thereunto, without the consent of the owner of the water, and be convicted thereof before a justice, by confession, or the oath of one witness, within one month after the offence committed, such offender shall give to the party injured such satisfaction as the justice shall appoint, not exceeding treble damages; and shall, over and above, pay down presently unto the overseers of the poor, such sum, not exceeding 10s. as the justice shall think fit: and in default of payment, the said penalties to be levied by distress; and for want thereof, the offender to be committed to the house of correction, for a term not exceeding one month, unless the party offending enter into bond, with surety, to the party injured, in a sum not exceeding 10l. never to offend in like manner.

Justices are also authorized to take, cut in pieces, and destroy, all such articles as before recited and adapted to the taking of fish, as may be found in the possession of offenders when taken. Persons aggrieved may appeal to the quarter sessions, whose judgment shall be final. Although this power is vested in a magistrate, yet the owner of the water, or fishery, cannot justify such a measure, but can only take them damage feasant, as is particularly expressed in various clauses of different acts of Parliament upon this subject. And by the 4th and 5th William and Mary, it is enacted, That no person (except makers and sellers of nets, owners of a river or fishery, authorized fishermen, and their apprentices) shall keep any net, angle, leap, pike, or other engine for taking of fish.

The proprietor of any river or fishery, or persons by them authorized, may seize, and keep to his own use, any engine which shall be found in the custody of any person fishing in any river or fishery, without the consent of the owner or occupier. And such owner, occupier, or person, authorized by either, sanctioned by the consent of any justice, in the day-time, may search the houses, or other places, of any person prohibited to keep the same, who shall be suspected to have such nets, or other engines, in his possession, and the same to seize, and keep to their own use, or cut in pieces and destroy.

By the 5th George Third, c. xiv. s. 1, it is enacted, That if any person shall enter into any park or paddock inclosed, or enter into any garden, orchard, or yard, belonging to, or adjoining to, any dwelling-house, wherein shall be any river, pond, moat, or other water, and, by any means whatsoever, (without the consent of the owner,) steal, kill, or destroy, any fish, bred, kept, or preserved therein, or shall be assisting therein, or shall receive or buy any such fish, knowing them to be such, shall, upon conviction, be transported for seven years. Persons making confession of such offence, and giving evidence against an accomplice, who, in pursuance thereof, shall be convicted, will be entitled to a free pardon.

And by the same Act, s. 3, it is enacted, That if any person shall take, kill, or destroy, or attempt to take, kill, or destroy, any fish in any river or stream, pool, pond, or other water, (not being in any park or paddock enclosed, or in any garden, orchard, or yard, belonging or adjoining to a dwelling-house, but in any other enclosed ground, being private property,) such person, being thereof convicted by confession, or the oath of one witness before a justice, shall forfeit five pounds to the owner of the fishery of such river or other water; and in default thereof, shall be committed to the house of correction for a time not exceeding six months.

Stealing fish in disguise is made felony by the 9th George the First, c. xxii. If any person armed and disguised, shall unlawfully steal, or take away, any fish, out of any river, or pond, or (whether armed or not) shall unlawfully and maliciously break down the head or mound of any fish-pond, whereby the fish shall be lost and destroyed, or shall rescue any person in custody for any such offence, or procure any other to join him therein, he shall be guilty of felony, without benefit of clergy.

WILLIAM TAPLIN, *The Sporting Dictionary*, 1803

Lord Byron's Celebrated Contempt for Fishing

And angling, too, that solitary vice,
Whatever Izaak Walton sings or says;
The quaint, old, cruel coxcomb, in his gullet
Should have a hook, and a small trout to pull it.

It would have taught him humanity at least. This sentimental savage, whom it is a mode to quote (amongst the novelists) to show their sympathy for innocent sports and old songs, teaches how to sew up frogs, and break their legs by way of experiment, in addition to the art of angling, the cruelest, the coldest, and the stupidest of pretended sports. They may talk about the beauties of Nature, but the angler merely thinks about his dish of fish; he has no leisure to take his eyes from off the streams, and a single *bite* is worth to him more than all the scenery around. Besides, some fish bite best on a rainy day. The whale, the shark, and the tunny fishery have somewhat of noble and perilous in them; even net fishing, trawling, etc., are more humane and useful. But angling! – No angler can be a good man.

BYRON, note to Don Juan, Canto xiii

An Angler's Riposte

For our parts we have always smiled at the noble poet's indignation against the cruelty of anglers, and the more so, since that indignation is expressed in a work, the hero of which is a model of refined cruelty – one of those lax, yet interesting young gentlemen, who think less of breaking a woman's heart – be she maid, wife, or widow – than poor quiet old Izaak would of paining a grasshopper. Angling a 'solitary vice'! Gambling, dog-fighting, boxing, intrigues, both with married and with single, are certainly not 'solitary' vices; but that is the only negative praise that can attach to them; and he who has been known to indulge in and to patronize them, must have been in rather a maudlin mood when he spun the above verses.

WILLIAM SHIPLEY, A True Treatise on the Art of Fly Fishing,
1838

Halieus and Physiecus Debate the Ethics of Fishing in 1828

I can find authorities of all kinds, statesmen, heroes, and philosophers; I can go back to Trajan, who was fond of angling. Nelson was a good fly fisher, and as a proof of his passion for it, continued the pursuit even with his left hand. Dr Paley, the great moral philosopher, was ardently attached to this amusement; so much so, that when the Bishop of Durham enquired of him, when one of his most important works would be finished, he said, with great simplicity and good humour, 'My Lord, I shall work steadily at it when the fly-fishing season is over,' as if this were a business of his life.

PHYS. – I do not find much difficulty in understanding why warriors, and even statesmen, fishers of men, many of whom I have known particularly fond of hunting and shooting, should likewise be attached to angling; but I own, I am at a loss to find reasons for a love of this pursuit amongst philosophers and poets.

HAL. – The search after food is an instinct belonging to our nature; and from the savage in his rudest and most primitive state, who destroys a piece of game, or a fish with a club or spear, to man in the most cultivated state of society, who employs artifice, machinery, and the resources of various other animals, to secure his object, the origin of the pleasure is similar, and its object the same: but that kind of it requiring most art may be said to characterise man in his highest or intellectual state; and the fisher for salmon and trout with the fly employs not only machinery to assist his physical powers, but applies sagacity to conquer difficulties; and the pleasure derived from ingenious resources and devices, as well as from active pursuit, belongs to this amusement. Then as to its philosophical tendency; it is a pursuit of moral discipline, requiring patience, forbearance, and command of temper. As connected with natural science, it may be vaunted as demanding a knowledge of the habits of a considerable tribe of created beings – fishes, and the animals that they prey upon, and an acquaintance with the signs and tokens of the weather and its changes, the nature of waters, and of the atmosphere. As to its poetical relations, it carries us into the most wild and beautiful scenery of nature; amongst the mountain lakes, and the clear and lovely streams that gush from the higher ranges of elevated hills.

PHYS. – All these enjoyments might be obtained without the necessity of torturing and destroying an unfortunate animal, that the true lover of nature would wish to see happy in a scene of loveliness.

HAL. – If all men were Pythagoreans and professed the Brahmin's creed, it would undoubtedly be cruel to destroy any form of animated life; but if fish are to be eaten, I see no more harm in capturing them by skill and ingenuity with an artificial fly, than in pulling them out of the water by main force with the net; and in general, when taken by the common fishermen, fish are permitted to die slowly, and to suffer in the air, from the want of their natural element; whereas every good angler, as soon as his fish is landed, either destroys his life immediately, if he is wanted for food, or returns him into the water.

PHYS. – But do you think nothing of the torture of the hook, and the fear of capture, and the misery of struggling against the powerful rod?

HAL. – I think it cannot be doubted that the nervous system of fish, and cold-blooded animals in general, is less sensitive than that of warm-blooded animals. The hook usually is fixed in the cartilaginous part of the mouth, where there are no nerves; and a proof that the sufferings of a hooked fish cannot be great, is found in the circumstance, that though a trout has been hooked and played for some minutes, he will often, after his escape with the artificial fly in his mouth, take the natural fly, and feed as if nothing had happened; having apparently learnt only from the experiment, that the artificial fly is not proper food. And I have caught pikes with four or five hooks in their mouths, and tackle which they had broken only a few minutes before; and the hooks seemed to have had no other effect than that of serving as a sort of *sauce piquante*, urging them to seize another morsel of the same kind.

SIR HUMPHREY DAVY, *Salmonia*, 1828

Why it's All Right to Kill Fish

Ancient man's sport was dangerous. He slew or was slain by the mammoth, the sabre-toothed tiger, by strange and monstrous growths of swamps, or secret terrors haunting mountain and forest. It was kill or be killed. His prey was for ever seeking prey. But now what fox will kill a man? Will a pheasant slay him? And do these seek to kill? They are not savage, not cannibals, but harmless and, apart from their sexual combats, very peaceable. The fox himself is a gentle and most faithful husband. There is no divorce but death for him. But fish are essentially savage. They eat each other. There is something devilish and brutal in the grab a salmon makes at a spun minnow. He does not even want to eat it. He cannot eat when in fresh waters. He means to kill a harmless little fish just for fun. But all fish are like that, if we except the tropical calipeever, which, so I am told, eats nothing but one water weed, and is the strictest vegetarian, turning a pitying, disdainful eye upon the best bait the unskilled offer him. Personally, I now hate killing and there have been times when I felt that nothing but this ceaseless desire of fish to slay justified me in deceiving them. They live by killing, and are without mercy. And I, too, catch the savagery from them and put them into my bag without remorse. Never yet have I picked up a soft-feathered, delicate bird without grief, and no one now shall get me to kill so much as a rabbit. But fish are the merest cannibals.

MORLEY ROBERTS, A Humble Fisherman, 1932

Evidence in Support

And now I am speaking of this sort of fish give me leave to tell you a true story concerning the voracity of it, from whence in Latin it is called the water-wolf. A gentleman whom I know and whose word I dare rely upon assured me that as he was fishing for pike in a river called Brosnach in this county he hooked a pretty large one which required some play in the water before he could pull him out without hazard of breaking his tackle, but when he found his fish more manageable and thought he had almost tired him, of a sudden and much to his surprise he found the weight of it mightily increased, which after some wary skill he pulled out of the river and saw the pike which he had hooked half swallowed up by another larger fish of the same kind, who was so very greedy of his prey, or so incapable of disengaging himself from it that both fell into the fisher's hands.

Letter from John Donton, *The Rawlinson Collection*, Bodleian Library, Oxford

Who, Precisely, is the Aggressor?

'Let us see how the case stands. I take a little wool and feather, and, tying it in a particular manner upon a hook, make an imitation of a fly; then I throw it across the river and let it sweep round the stream with a lively motion. This I have an undoubted right to do, for the river belongs to me or my friend; but mark what follows. Up starts a monster fish with his murderous jaws, and makes a dash at my little Andromeda. Thus he is the aggressor, not I; his intention is evidently to commit murder. He is caught in the act of putting that intention into execution. Having wantonly intruded himself on my hook, which I contend he had no right to do, he darts about in various directions, evidently surprised to find that the fly, which he hoped to make an easy conquest of, is much stronger than himself. I naturally attempt to regain this fly, unjustly withheld from me. The fish gets tired and weak in his lawless endeavours to deprive me of it. I take advantage of his weakness, I own, and drag him, somewhat loth, to the shore, where one rap on his head ends him in an instant.

WILLIAM SCROPE, *Days and Nights of Salmon Fishing*, 1843

The Ancient Fear

At around six-thirty the other morning my daughter awoke me with the news that a heron was on the pond. He is a rogue which has been clearing up all the goldfish ponds in the neighbourhood and I saw on my lawn one large 2 lb goldfish with a stab wound, a fish I have had for over ten years. The trouble with a rogue heron is that he will come again and again until he has cleared a pond, and he will come under the moon, or in the early morning, just when it is getting light. I let off a blank cartridge and he flapped away over the boundary hedge. Ever since, I have kept a storm lantern burning on the lawn each night.

Herons are expert poachers. Last year an owner of a trout farm told me that if there was the smallest hole in the netting a heron would find its way through; they are a pest on trout farms. What struck me was how the fish in my pond were shocked into immobility. Usually they cruise about in full view, and come to be fed, including two magnificent golden orfe which must weigh close on 3 lbs and which I have had for fifteen years. Looking at the water you would not have guessed there was a fish in the pond and for two days they remained hidden in the mud and weeds. This shows what I call the 'Ancient Fear'. Man is not feared like the predators of the wild because we appeared on earth long after the birds of prey and the heron.

At my old home we had a large outdoor aviary in the grounds which contained a pair of hawfinches and other birds. It was planted up with thick bushes and they bred there. One day when I was looking out of the window a sparrowhawk made a swoop at the wire. The birds scattered in panic and for quite an hour afterwards they remained like little stuffed dummies, perched in the bushes, eyes wide in a sort of hypnotic trance. When sparrowhawks were common I often witnessed the same thing when one made a swoop at finches. They rushed into the hedge, and one could almost pick them off the branches.

Even man has something of the 'Ancient Fear' when a sudden sound, a breaking stick, or even a pheasant bursting from underfoot like a bomb, can make the heart jump if one is alone in the wilds.

We have enormous fun with our moorhen family. The parents stayed with us all through the winter, only leaving when the pond was frozen over. When the ice covers the pool they are vulnerable, for foxes prey on them. They then roost in hedges and trees like pheasants, for the water is no longer a protection. Foxes dislike swimming, and vermin, like stoats and cats, will not enter water if they can help it.

The most feared of all winged predators are, of course, the peregrine and sparrowhawk. I was once waiting in a wood for pigeon and was startled when literally, out of the blue, there fell into the wood, and I mean fell, some twenty or forty pigeon. They came through the upper branches like stones and I glimpsed a peregrine sweep overhead. This was a wonderful example of the ancient fear, for even when the pigeon saw me down on the wood floor, they were loth to take wing; like the hunted finches and sparrows they seemed to be carved in stone.

I remember, too, standing beside a haystack sheltering from a shower. All at once numbers of sparrows, cheeping with frantic fear, descended all round me, and a sparrowhawk came sweeping round the angle of the stack and snatched a sparrow close beside me.

Likewise, fish in a pool seem to know instinctively when an otter is about. At my old home, where we had a lake stocked with trout and carp, if there was an otter about, the pool went dead, and not a fish was to be seen. Even worms, hunted by their ancient enemy the mole, can often be seen surfacing, though, like a rabbit pursued by a stoat, they have little chance of escape. The fisherman, requiring worms, knows that to stick a fork in the ground and to work it to and fro will often persuade worms to surface, for they think a mole is active.

Man may be feared by wild creatures, but this fear is nothing compared with the 'ancient fear' which goes back such a long way into the dim past.

'B.B.', *The Naturalist's Bedside Book*, 1980

Judgement on Matters of Which we Know Nothing

If trout were wanted for human food, a net would have answered the purpose with less trouble to the man and less annoyance to the fish. Throughout creation man is the only animal – man, and the dogs and cats which have learnt from him – who kills, for the sake of killing, what he does not want, and calls it sport. All other animals seize their prey only when hungry, and are satisfied when their hunger is appeased.

Such, it can only be answered, is man's disposition. He is a curiously formed creature, and the appetite for sport does not seem to disappear with civilisation. The savage in his natural state hunts, as the animals hunt, to support his life; the sense of sport is strongest in the elaborately educated and civilised. It may be that the taste will die out before 'Progress.' Our descendants perhaps, a few generations hence, may look back upon a pheasant battue as we look back on bear-baiting and bull-fighting, and our mild offspring, instructed in the theory of development, may see a proof in their father's habits that they come of a race who were once crueller than tigers, and will congratulate themselves on the change. So they will think, if they judge us as we judge our forefathers of the days of the Plantagenets and Tudors, and both we and they may be perhaps mistaken. Half the lives of men in medival Europe was spent in fighting. Yet from medieval Europe came the knightly graces of courtesy and chivalry. The modern soldier, whose trade is war, yet hates and dreads war more than civilians dread it. The sportsman's knowledge of the habits of animals gives him a kindly feeling towards them notwithstanding, and sporting tends rather to their preservation than their destruction. The human race may become at last vegetarians and water-drinkers. Astra may come back, and man may cease to take the life of bird, or beast, or fish. But the lion will not lie down with the lamb, for lambs and lions will no longer be; the eagle will not feed beside the dove, for doves will not be allowed to consume grain which might have served as human food, and will be extinct as the dodo. It may be all right and fit and proper: a world of harmless vegetarians may be the appropriate outcome of the development of humanity. But we who have been born in a ruder age do not aspire to rise beyond the level of our own times. We have toiled, we have suffered, we have enjoyed, as the nature which we have received has prompted us. We blame our fathers' habits; our children may blame ours in turn; yet we may be sitting in judgment, both of us, on matters of which we know nothing.

J.A. FROUDE, *Cheneys and the House of Russell*, 1879

Do Fish Feel Pain?

Anglers are not, as a rule, men given to cruelty in the affairs of life, and yet the fear of possible cruelty in fishing does not impress them as a real one. Some cruelty must be involved in causing the death of any creature, and so long as humane men and women desire to eat slaughtered sheep, cattle, poultry, game, and fish, the angler need not much concern himself beyond proving that his sport involves no greater cruelty than this. A great accumulation of instances in which fish seem to have shown an almost complete indifference to wounds or injuries that would cause extreme agony to warm-blooded animals, seems to establish as a fact that fish are comparatively insensible to pain.

I have myself hooked a fine spring salmon of about 18 lbs., which, after taking the fly with a firm pull, merely sank with it to the bottom of the river, and gave no sign of feeling anything unusual. As I was wading in deep and difficult water, the first thing was to get into the shallows and shorten the line, and then I gave a good sharp pull at the fish. Nothing happened. I gave another and a more severe pull, now almost doubting whether the fish was still on, or whether by any chance it had left the fly in some new and uncharted snag. That doubt did not last long. At the third pull the fish bolted past me up the deep stream, then turned and dashed slanting across to the far side of the river, repeatedly rising to the surface and wallowing along half out of the water at every few yards. Off ran the forty yards of casting line, but still the fish held on for some rocky shallows, whilst the thin silk backing cut the forefinger that was trying to check it. He won. No sooner did he get amongst the boulders than he got the line round one of them, and, with a few splashing plunges, he broke me and departed. Luckily the line came free, and with it came back the large claret fly that he had taken, but with the hook now snapped off just at the tail of the fly. It must have gone firmly into some pretty tough spot to break at such a place.

From his behaviour it is hard to think that this fish felt much pain from the hook, and his vigorous and effective line of action after the third pull was given to him may have been due quite as much to realising that some fisher had got hold of him, as to any feeling of pain from the extra pull at the hook, when he had shown none at the first or the second pull.

Another instance I know of, which happened to an angler who was fishing some water below me. He hooked a fish which went straightway back to his lying-place on the bottom and sulked there for an hour before he could be induced to move. Then, in due time, he was landed and was found to weigh 28 lbs. He was hooked in the point of the lower jaw. One cannot imagine any warm-blooded animal, hooked in the nose or mouth or ear or in any other place, however gristly, which could without a single preliminary struggle calmly stay where he was and allow his captor to tug and pull at him to his heart's content. One would suppose that 'sulking' would be almost impossible if the salmon felt acute pain from the repeated tugging at the hook. Yet fish do sulk often enough – although, in fact, it has never happened to me to have one do so. And people who, in clear water, have been able to see the sulking fish, say that he may be seen poised head downwards, with his nose on the gravel and his tail gently waving to keep him down against the pull of the rod. Such conduct does not suggest any acute pain.

One knows, too, that a salmon will frequently take a fly several times, and sometimes even after he has had a very sharp prick. Once in the month of August 1890 I was fishing a quiet glassy pool, bent on catching a large fish weighing, as I judged, close on 30 lbs., that I had seen and tried so often that I knew his position almost to a yard. The river was low and clear, and I had to wade out with great care to avoid making a ripple. Just as I got to the place from which I had hoped to cover him, I saw a wasp fall into the river and go drifting down, buzzing upon the surface of the water straight over the salmon. As I watched it in the bright sunshine, a big shoulder rose quietly out of the water, followed by a black tail, and down went my friend the wasp, and he certainly did not come to the surface again. Thereupon I changed my tiny silver fly for a small black and orange fly with dun turkey wings known as a 'Gipps,' and with it at once hooked my friend. Now that fish had no fear of a wasp. Of course he may have crushed it instantly in his jaws, but it is an experiment that no warm-blooded animal cares to try twice, although every puppy has generally tried it once.

A.H. CHAYTOR, *Letters to a Salmon Fisher's Sons*, 1910

An Eye for an Eye

A very singular, though I believe, not unparalleled instance of the voracity of the perch occurred to me when fishing in Windermere. In removing the hook from the jaws of the fish, one eye was accidentally displaced and remained adhering to it. Knowing the reparative capabilities of piscine organisation, I returned the maimed perch, which was too small for my basket, to the lake and, being somewhat scant of minnows, threw the line in again with the eye attached as bait, – there being no other of any description on the hook. The float disappeared almost instantly; and on landing the new comer, it turned out to be the fish I had the moment before thrown in, and which had thus been actually caught by *his own eye*.

This incident proves, I think, conclusively, that the structure of cold blooded animals enables them to endure very severe injuries and wounds without experiencing material inconvenience; a fact which may tend to remove any qualms of conscience felt by anglers on the score of the sufferings supposed to be inflicted on their captives.

This incident appears on the face of it so very much like one of the flights of fancy of Baron Munchausen, that were it not that it took place in the presence of not less than half-a-dozen witnesses I should have hesitated to mention it.

H. CHOLMONDELEY-PENNELL, *Fishing Gossip*, 1866

Some Seventeenth-century Theology

But I fancy that some prevaricating Zoilist[1] will stigmatize anglers (and the art) with those black blemishes of barbarity and cruelty, when only design'd to kill a fish. To which I reply, that the creatures in the creation (by divine appointment) were appropriated for use, and what may that use be, if not the refreshment and nourishment of mankind? Adam had a commission from the King of Heaven, impowering him lord over all sublunary creatures: Will any one question this privilege? And Peter was commanded to arise, kill, and eat; when doubting with himself the legality of the thing, who disputes this commission? Now for any man to question these divine truths, (except a Banian,[2]) he questions the Scriptures, the authority of truth. The creatures in the creation (we must grant)

[1] Critic
[2] Vegetarian

were design'd for nutrition and sustentation; yet no man had a commission so large to take away life upon no other account than to gratify his lust. Then the next question arising will be, whether the rod or the net is rather to be approved of? I have only this to answer, (since both contribute to health and maintenance,) the apostles themselves they used the one, why then may not the angler plead for the other?

RICHARD FRANCK, *Northern Memoirs*, 1658

Biblical Symbols and April Fools

Angling, although it is termed 'the gentle art', is, I suppose, a sort of relic of primitive hunting. But it is termed 'the gentle art', and there is something holy about it. At any rate, there would be something holy if sporting instincts didn't swing uppermost, and the angler felt no joy in a fish's fight for life. That's the real wasp in the font. The fish must struggle, and struggle hard, or there will be little or no fun in catching him. The harder he struggles the better the fishing, and yet the harder he struggles the more certain it is that he objects to being caught. But probably he doesn't feel the hook too painfully. How can he, when he pulls like that! The instinct of a man with a pair of dental forceps jammed in his mouth is to clasp the dentist round the waist, and not push himself furiously backwards in his chair.

But cruelty or no cruelty – and why did God create hunters and sportsmen? – there is something in fishing that is relative to holiness. It makes men good-tempered and quiet-minded. It steadies the nerves and sweetens the understanding. It undermines vulgarity, and prompts simplicity of thought and manners. All this it does in spite of the fact that an unfortunate angler is apt to let forth rushing cascades of bad language. But the total effect of his days by river- or pond-side is to improve both his manners and his language, not to speak of his general disposition and humour. He has had to be by himself and take stock of himself, whether he wanted to or not. A bad man was never a good fisher, and probably never a fisher at all, undesirous even of wetting a line.

The fish, indeed, enters into the ritual of Christianity, for its first prominent symbol was the sign of the fish and not the sign of the Cross. The early Christians scrawled the design of a fish in the catacombs of Rome – a secret sign by which they knew one another. Moreover, in primitive Christian and medieval Christian art the picture of a fish signified Christ. I do not know Greek, but I understand that the origin may be discovered in 'the initial letters of the names and titles of Jesus in Greek – Jesus Christ, Son of God, Saviour, which spell together the Greek word for fish'. Added to this it must be remembered that some of Christ's early disciples were fishers: Simon Peter, who holds the keys of the gates of heaven, the most important of them.

Another holy fisher was Saint Wilfrid, who was instrumental in converting the heathen inhabitants of Sussex through his knowledge of fishing. When he visited the country the exceedingly ignorant and unskilful people were dying of famine; but St Wilfrid pointed out that there was abundance of food in their waters and showed them how to come by it. 'By this benefit the bishop gained the affection of them all, and they began more readily to hope for heavenly blessings, since by his help they had already received those which are temporal.'

It is probable that the only sport in which the medieval monks frequently indulged was the sport of fishing. No one, who has not his entire living to make by it, can fish without enjoyment; for fishing, at any rate angling, is like playing tennis with God. Fish was the monks' only permissible flesh food on Fridays and other fast days. At least once a week they had to fish with nets or rod and line. On the Continent, the carp pond was a common feature of the monastery preserves. And, as a relic of all this, Puritan Protestants have generally sat down to fish lunches on Good Fridays.

Fish, too, played an important part in one of the most inexplicable of Christ's miracles – the Feeding of the Five Thousand. And in St Matthew we read that when Christ was asked to pay tribute He told Simon Peter to procure the money in this wise: 'Go thou to the sea, and cast an hook, and take up the fish that first cometh up; and when thou hast opened his mouth thou shalt find a piece of money: that take, and give unto them for me and thee.' All of which was probably a parable (slightly distorted in its committal to writing), and a way of telling Simon Peter to earn the necessary money by catching fish.

For a long time the fish seems to have figured as a religious symbol. Medieval church pilgrims, called 'palmers', who made pilgrimages to the Holy Land, wore the armour of a shell-fish as the symbol of their material aloofness. The cockle-shell or scallop-shell was the insignia of their withdrawal from all riot of worldliness.

But the French, sad to relate, out of their inborn passion for mockery and profanity, have made of the fish a symbol of foolishness and reproach. Medieval French thieves and blackguards, called 'coquillards' (a fraternity to which that wild but great poet François Villon belonged), adopted cockle-shells and scallop-shells as symbols of their independence and rascality; while in modern France any kind of finned fish has become the symbol of April Fool's Day, 'un poisson d'avril', signifying an April fool. On April the first an unwary person may walk the length of the town with a stale herring dangling down his back, pinned there by the *enfant terrible* when he was unobservantly staring too intently in front of him. Also on that day it is usual to receive a post card with the picture of a fish on it, though most of these post cards are quite inoffensive and just sent 'pour rire'. Mockery may be mingled with sentimentality – the first of April turned into a sort of St Valentine's Day, and above the symbolical fish a pair of clasped hands, male and female, display themselves. But *la blague* may develop rather too much into *la blague*, and a fish a month old, wrapped up in innumerable pieces of paper with the information that it is valuable and fragile, be carefully delivered by the postman. To be hoaxed in this way or any way is to 'swallow the fish.'

HERBERT PALMER, *The Roving Angler*, 1933

The Character-forming Benefits of Fishing

Most Coarse Fishermen are humble, poor men, of somewhat idle disposition, albeit they may work well enough and hard enough at their respective callings. Unlike the fly-fisher their time is limited, and because of this, they value it the more and take a keener pleasure in their craft. For are not the best Anglers to be found among the artisans and publicans and grooms and gentlemen's body servants? Pedagogues also make good fishermen for they are naturally idle men, who like to take Life as smoothly as the streams they fish in. But none are knaves; I repeat, none are knaves, their wants are simple, their needs few. We must admit however that fishermen are prone to jealousy, they are as particular over their respective pitches as a dog over his bone and barrel. They have also earned a reputation for telling untruths and verily it is understandable, (this weakness which they undoubtedly do possess) for no man can prove them wrong, or very rarely.

And often it is that much of what they say contains truth, for is it not always the big fishes, which, by their very weight, and girth, and power of tail, break free and leave the angler to mourn and to be miserable? For I say that there is no misery quite so keen as that experienced by an angler, who, after many hours of patient waiting and perhaps of a playing of his fish, loseth it at the bank side. It is enough to make any man mourn, in all truth, and even if he catch another fish just as large, soon after, that first grief, like a man's first disappointment in matters of the heart, takes much forgetting.

Your true angler enjoys what he snares, he eats what he catches, and his fish hath an added relish thereby which no man may gainsay. Most anglers are not over-particular of their attire, yet they are not ragged nor slovenly in their habits and appearance, for the very reason that they school themselves to be careful of their tackle and to take a pride in it, keeping it clean and drying their lines when they have had done. Anglers make good Husbands and Fathers, and women do well to marry anglers, knowing that in each there is something of the boy. They must take heed however to make much of their husband's catch and know how to prepare it, however bemired the fishes may be. But such women must be content to be left alone and at home on Holydays, for fishermen do not want their wives with them when they go a-fishing, unless they be quiet women, which few are. But for their part they know that their men are at no mischief with other women, nor frequenting ale-houses unduly. Yet, I must say your true angler hath a healthy liking for *good ale*, when his day's fishing be done, for then he likes jolly company and ballads and discourse on fishes. They are men of peace and quiet places, they sleep soundly in their beds (with their wives) and are good trencher-men and, being always by the sweet rivers when their work be done (instead of in low taverns, a dicing and card-playing, and telling bawdy stories), they are as guile-less as cows. Therefore your true Angler is no knave, but an Honest Man.

'B.B.', *Fisherman's Folly*, 1987

Patience

The late Dr Franklin observed, that of all the amusements, which the ingenuity of Man had devised, none required the exercise of Patience so much as Angling, and he enforced his remark by reciting the following: that setting out from Philadelphia at six o'clock on a summer's morning, to go about fifteen miles, he passed a brook where a Gentleman was angling, he enquired what sport, and was told none, but added the Gentleman, I have only been here *two hours*. The Doctor continued his journey, and on his return in the evening, found the Angler at the same spot, and repeated his enquiry, Very good sport was the reply. The query was naturally resumed, by asking how many fish he had caught? None at all, answered the Gentleman, but about the middle of the day I had a *most glorious nibble*.

To the Doctor's anecdote, that of the river Lea Angler, may be added: this person being daily seen at one particular spot, a brother Angler conceived it must be the resort of abundance of fish, and there one morning at day-break, began his operations. The usual attendant of the place arrived some hours after, and threw in his line, a long silence ensued, when the first comer remarked, that he was out of luck in not having caught any fish in this favourite hole, which, says he, I am convinced it is with you, from the constant attention I have seen you pay to it. Sir, replies the Gentleman, I confess long custom has rendered me extremely partial to the spot, but as for the fish, I assure you that *here* have I angled for *forty years*, and never had *a bite yet*. Without expecting the modern Angler's patience will equal that of either of the above persons, it is absolutely requisite he should be possessed of a full stock.

THE REVEREND WILLIAM DANIEL, *Rural Sports*, 1802

Calmness in the Face of Adversity

Some have said that an angler must be a man of no thinking, because say they, he is constantly busy on such trifles, as that of catching a trout, and can spend a whole day, or perhaps a day and night, nay many days and nights, on so mean an affair, and they would therefore compare him to the Lord Rochester's countryman who 'whistled as he went for want of thought.'

On the other hand, I take it to be rather a token of a thinking retir'd disposition, or else a meer want of employment; and they might then more justly apply it to those who the same Lord Rochester represents as profess'd thinkers, 'who retire to think because they've nought to do.'

It must be allow'd that as it is a kind of still life, (as the painters call it) it is most suitable to retir'd minds; 'tis a pleasing kind of diversion to a person who loves to be alone, and yet I do not think it is at all of kin to any thing of what they call Melancholy; for 'tis a mistake when we think that a truly melancholy man, can apply himself with such calmness and such a sedate mind, as is required to make Angling a sport; for the mind of a melancholy man, is far from being in repose, on the contrary, there is nothing farther from it; a melancholy man has his spirits always in agitation, and in a hurry; and therefore you find him the most easy of any man in the world to be put in a passion, and to fly out in the most dangerous extreams of it upon every trifling occasion; such a man is not fit to be an angler, nay is not fit to be trusted by the river side with an angle rod in his hand. On the contrary, he that angles, must have all his passions at his command, he must govern his temper with an absolute sway, and be able to sustain his mind under the greatest disappointments.

Alas the sport of angling is liable to the greatest vicissitudes, and to the most provoking incidents; Job's loss of his children by the fall of the house, was a very great trial indeed, but what is all that to a man having taken a charming trout, or a large pike, and brought him with the utmost dexterity to the very landing net, or perhaps just to the rivers bank, and at one spring have him get from him and recover the river again, who he was as it were in his hands; if the angler does not stamp and stare, swearing an hundred oaths, or pull the hair off his head, nay if he does not throw himself into the very river after it, he must be allowed to be a man of great temper, and have the command of himself to a wonder.

Whereas on the contrary, the true angler takes all this as calmly and quietly as if it had been nothing; but goes, and new fits his tackle, new baits his hook, and throws it into the river again, with as much calmness, as if nothing had happened; only *by the way*, he does not throw his hook again in the same place, for reasons we shall see, as we go on.

JAMES SAUNDERS, *The Complete Fisherman*, 1724

Be Duly Grateful

We fished for years, my Uncle and I, down where the sea met the river and such was the remoteness of the place that never once did we see another man or child crossing the wide flat sands of the estuary. Never, that is, until one year's end long ago.

We had spent the day repairing the house which stood alone, bleached and whitened by centuries of wind and salt. Even the furniture was centuries old by then, it was as old as the house and each piece so heavy and crooked, but each piece a part of our lives.

So we had spent that day repairing the weatherboarding with odd planks that we found washed up on the beach. They made the house look more ramshackle year by year, but since no one else ever saw it what did that matter? When occasionally we stopped to exchange a few words we automatically looked out over the distant waters in case a ship was passing. But it was years since anything had passed this way.

Then, in the early afternoon, Uncle suggested that we try fishing. It was a bad day for it, too cold and the wind all wrong, but I didn't like to argue with Uncle. We took out the heavy rods and the great brass reels and tramped down to the water's edge. Uncle could cast beautifully and though I watched him for many years I never really learned the art. He threw our lines eighty, perhaps one hundred yards out into the low, angry surf, and then we waited.

The thick cane rod tops nodded gently towards the water keeping time with the movement of the waves, but no fish disturbed their rhythm. As usual, we watched out to sea, saying nothing to each other because long silences were our way. If we had spent some time watching back over the flat lands behind us we might have seen the stranger coming. But it would have made no difference. We would have stayed and waited for him because there was nothing else to do.

'Anything doing?'

The voice behind us, not startling, but strong and confident. The owner of the voice wore an old, greasy jersey over his head in the strangest fashion.

The ends of the two sleeves were tied with string and a drawstring had been fitted to the waist. The jersey had then been stuffed with newspaper, the two thickly filled sleeves tied under the man's chin, the body of the garment riding fat and high above his head. The rest of his clothes appeared to be made from a million layers of rags and scarves and tatters of old coats and jackets. He was almost emaciated, to judge by his face, but he wore so many layers of clothing that he looked like a giant. Uncle and I only stared at him.

'Anything doing?' he said again. 'Perhaps it's not such a good day for fishing. Perhaps you should be home by the fire, with the doors locked against the wind.'

Then, looking at me, he said: 'Try casting that bit closer into the gullies where the poor fish lie to escape the coldest waves.'

'We don't know you,' my Uncle almost shouted. He looked at the stranger with undisguised ill-feeling, then he turned and faced back out to sea.

'Your uncle won't take an old man's advice,' said the stranger to me.

Not knowing what to say in reply, I said nothing, but I knew something had made Uncle angry. When I reeled in to check my hooks I couldn't resist trying a short cast into the foam; it suited me since I could never hope to compete with a champion caster like my Uncle. Almost as soon as my bait hit the water I caught a fat cod and then another and another.

The stranger watched with a calm face, saying nothing, but all the while watching Uncle's back. Soon I had a basketful of fish, but I couldn't bring myself to thank the stranger in front of my Uncle, who all the while had stayed silent and kept his face to the sea.

Evening was coming in and still we three stood on the edge of the sea as if we were the only people in the world. Then, without a word, Uncle lifted his great rod and reeled in. He had caught nothing. As we packed away our things, the stranger came closer and asked if we would give him a fish. I looked at Uncle, wondering what I should do. He took no notice and packed our fish into his bag.

'Would you give me a fish?' said the stranger once again, but this time directly to my Uncle who, suddenly and without a word, struck the man hard across the face. He fell and as he lay there my Uncle pushed me past him, across the sands and back towards the house.

That night we ate the cod and listened in silence to the wind. In the morning my Uncle was dead.

ROBERT GREEN, *Tales of the Sea*, 1890

Is Fishing a Disease?

Diagnosis is easy, since the symptoms are well marked. . . . At the annual recrudescence of the disease the patient begins to exhibit a dislike to the ordinary business routine, and, if watched at this time, he will be found to be taking a morbid interest in insects of all sorts, his eagerness in their study and in attempts to imitate them by fashioning flies, for instance, of feathers of birds and of hair from the smaller mammals, would be amusing were it not pathetic. His efforts in this direction almost amount to mania, some of his productions being ludicrous in their wide divergence from the shape or colour of any insect known to entomologists. To some of these freak productions he loves to give the name of 'lure'.

The calls on his purse at this season will be very heavy, and sufferers have been known to imperil their financial position by prodigal outlays on the implements of what they may be heard to call their 'craft'; for these the disease gives them a morbid craving.

Perhaps the most serious and distressing symptom of the malady is the brain degeneration which it engenders: this may be correctly classed as one of the sequelæ. 'Fishermen', as those who suffer from it are known, have an inherent difficulty in restricting themselves to anything approximating the exact truth when recounting their experiences. The tendency to embroider would appear to be irresistible. This is so well known that efforts have been made to segregate them in clubs where this tendency is recognized and allowed for. Thus herded together, wonder inspiring anecdotes told by sufferers who may be otherwise men of high moral rectitude, fall harmless on accustomed ears.

The disease is interesting, and one that will repay careful study, but the interest of such study cannot, it should be stated, fail to be damped to a certain extent by the fact that all treatment has failed, and that it must therefore be pronounced incurable.

Journal of the Flyfishers' Club, 1918

The Art of Lying

I am not a good fisherman myself. I devoted a considerable amount of attention to the subject at one time, and was getting on, as I thought, fairly well; but the old hands told me that I should never be any real good at it, and advised me to give it up. They said that I was an extremely neat thrower, and that I seemed to have plenty of gumption for the thing, and quite enough constitutional laziness. But they were sure I should never make anything of a fisherman. I had not got sufficient imagination.

They said that as a poet, or a shilling shocker, or a reporter, or anything of that kind, I might be satisfactory, but that, to gain any position as a Thames angler, would require more play of fancy, more power of invention than I appeared to possess.

Some people are under the impression that all that is required to make a good fisherman is the ability to tell lies easily and without blushing; but this is a mistake. Mere bald fabrication is useless; the veriest tyro can manage that. It is in the circumstantial detail, the embellishing touches of probability, the general air of scrupulous – almost of pedantic – veracity, that the experienced angler is seen.

Anybody can come in and say, 'Oh, I caught fifteen dozen perch yesterday evening' or 'Last Monday I landed a gudgeon, weighing eighteen pounds, and measuring three feet from the tip to the tail.'

There is no art, no skill, required for that sort of thing. It shows pluck, but that is all.

No; your accomplished angler would scorn to tell a lie, that way. His method is a study in itself.

He comes in quietly with his hat on, appropriates the most comfortable chair, lights his pipe, and commences to puff in silence. He lets the youngsters brag away for a while, and then, during a momentary lull, he removes the pipe from his mouth, and remarks, as he knocks the ashes out against the bars:

'Well, I had a haul on Tuesday evening that it's not much good my telling anybody about.'

'Oh! why's that?' they ask.

'Because I don't expect anybody would believe me if I did,' replies the old fellow calmly, and without even a tinge of bitterness in his tone, as he refills his pipe, and requests the landlord to bring him three of Scotch, cold.

There is a pause after this, nobody feeling sufficiently sure of himself to contradict the old gentleman. So he has to go on by himself without any encouragement.

'No,' he continues thoughtfully; 'I shouldn't believe it myself if anybody told it to me, but it's a fact, for all that. I had been sitting there all the afternoon and had caught literally nothing – except a few dozen dace and a score of jack; and I was just about giving it up as a bad job when I suddenly felt a rather smart pull at the line. I thought it was another little one, and I went to jerk it up. Hang me, if I could move the rod! It took me half an hour – half an hour, sir! – to land that fish; and every moment I thought the line was going to snap! I reached him at last, and what do you think it was? A sturgeon! a forty pound sturgeon! taken on a line, sir! Yes, you may well look surprised – I'll have another three of Scotch, landlord, please.'

And then he goes on to tell of the astonishment of everybody who saw it; and what his wife said, when he got home, and of what Joe Buggles thought about it.

I asked the landlord of an inn up the river once, if it did not injure him, sometimes, listening to the tales that the fishermen about there told him; and he said:

'Oh, no; not now, sir. It did used to knock me over a bit at first, but, lor love you! me and the missus we listens to 'em all day now. It's what you're used to, you know. It's what you're used to.'

I knew a young man once, he was a most conscientious fellow and, when he took to fly-fishing, he determined never to exaggerate his hauls by more than twenty-five per cent.

"When I have caught forty fish," said he, "then I will tell people that I have caught fifty, and so on. But I will not lie any more than that, because it is sinful to lie."

But the twenty-five per cent plan did not work well at all. He never was able to use it. The greatest number of fish he ever caught in one day was three, and you can't add twenty-five per cent to three – at least, not in fish.

So he increased his percentage to thirty-three-and-a-third, but that, again, was awkward, when he had only caught one or two; so, to simplify matters, he made up his mind to just double the quantity.

He stuck to this arrangement for a couple of months, and then he grew dissatisfied with it. Nobody believed him when he told them that he only doubled, and he, therefore, gained no credit that way whatever, while his moderation put him at a disadvantage among the other anglers. When he had really caught three small fish, and said he had caught six, it used to make him quite jealous to hear a man, whom he knew for a fact had only caught one, going about telling people he had landed two dozen.

So eventually he made one final arrangement with himself, which he has religiously held to ever since, and that was to count each fish that he caught as ten, and to assume ten to begin with. For example, if he did not catch any fish at all, then he said he had caught ten fish – you could never catch less than ten fish by his system; that was the foundation of it. Then, if by any chance he really did catch one fish, he called it twenty, while two fish would count thirty, three forty, and so on.

It is a simple and easily worked plan, and there has been some talk lately of its being made use of by the angling fraternity in general. Indeed, the Committee of the Thames Anglers' Association did recommend its adoption about two years ago, but some of the older members opposed it. They said they would consider the idea if the number were doubled, and each fish counted as twenty.

If ever you have an evening to spare, up the river, I should advise you to drop into one of the little village inns, and take a seat in the tap-room. You will be nearly sure to meet one or two old rod-men, sipping their toddy there, and they will tell you enough fishy stories in half an hour to give you indigestion for a month.

George and I – I don't know what had become of Harris; he had gone out and had a shave, early in the afternoon, and had then come back and spent full forty minutes in pipeclaying his shoes, we had not seen him since – George and I, therefore, and the dog, left to ourselves, went for a walk to Wallingford on the second evening, and, coming home, we called in at a little riverside inn, for a rest, and other things.

We went into the parlour and sat down. There was an old fellow there, smoking a long clay pipe, and we naturally began chatting.

He told us that it had been a fine day to-day and we told him that it had been a fine day yesterday, and then we all told each other that we thought it would be a fine day tomorrow; and George said the crops seemed to be coming up nicely.

After that it came out, somehow or other, that we were strangers in the neighbourhood, and that we were going away the next morning.

Then a pause ensued in the conversation, during which our eyes wandered round the room. They finally rested upon a dusty old glass-case, fixed very high up above the chimney-piece, and containing a trout. It rather fascinated me, that trout; it was such a monstrous fish. In fact, at first glance, I thought it was a cod.

'Ah!' said the old gentleman, following the direction of my gaze, 'fine fellow that, ain't he?'

'Quite uncommon,' I murmured; and George asked the old man how much he thought it weighed.

'Eighteen pounds six ounces,' said our friend, rising and taking down his coat. 'Yes,' he continued, 'it wur sixteen year ago, come the third o'next month, that I landed him. I caught him just below the bridge with a minnow. They told me he wur in the river, and I said I'd have him, and so I did. You don't see many fish that size about here now, I'm thinking. Good night, gentlemen, good night.'

And out he went, and left us alone.

We could not take our eyes off the fish after that. It really was a remarkably fine fish. We were still looking at it, when the local carrier, who had just stopped at the inn, came to the door of the room with a pot of beer in his hand, and he also looked at the fish.

'Good-sized trout, that,' said George, turning round to him.

'Ah! you may well say that, sir,' replied the man; and then, after a pull at his beer, he added, 'Maybe you wasn't here, sir, when that fish was caught?'

'No,' we told him. We were strangers in the neighbourhood.

'Ah!' said the carrier, 'then, of course, how should you? It was nearly five years ago that I caught that trout.'

'Oh! was it you who caught it, then?' said I.

'Yes, sir,' replied the genial old fellow. 'I caught him just below the lock – leastways, what was the lock then – one Friday afternoon; and the remarkable thing about it is that I caught him with a fly. I'd gone out pike fishing, bless you, never thinking of a trout, and when I saw that whopper on the end of my line, blest if it didn't quite take me aback. Well, you see, he weighed twenty-six pound. Good night, gentlemen, good night.'

Five minutes afterwards a third man came in, and described how *he* had caught it early one morning, with bleak; and then he left, and a stolid, solemn-looking middle-aged individual came in, and sat down over by the window.

None of us spoke for a while; but, at length, George turned to the newcomer, and said:

'I beg your pardon, I hope you will forgive the liberty that we – perfect stangers in the neighbourhood – are taking, but my friend here and myself would be so much obliged if you would tell us how you caught that trout up there.'

'Why, who told you I caught that trout!' was the surprised query.

We said that nobody had told us so, but somehow or other we felt instinctively that it was he who had done it.

'Well, it's a most remarkable thing – most remarkable,' answered the stolid stranger, laughing: 'because, as a matter of fact, you are quite right. I did catch it. But fancy your guessing it like that. Dear me, it's really a most remarkable thing.'

And then he went on, and told us how it had taken him half an hour to land it, and how it had broken his rod. He said he had weighed it carefully when he reached home, and it had turned the scale at thirty-four pounds.

He went in his turn, and when he was gone, the landlord came in to us. We told him the various histories we had heard about his trout, and he was immensely amused, and we all laughed very heartily.

'Fancy Jim Bates and Joe Muggles and Mr Jones and old Billy Maunders all telling you that they had caught it. Ha! ha! ha! Well, that is good,' said the honest old fellow, laughing heartily. 'Yes, they are the sort to give it *me*, to put up in *my* parlour, if *they* had caught it, they are! Ha! ha! ha!'

And then he told us the real history of the fish. It seemed that he had caught it himself, years ago, when he was quite a lad; not by any art or skill, but by that unaccountable luck that appears to always wait upon a boy when he plays the wag from school, and goes out fishing on a sunny afternoon, with a bit of string tied on to the end of a tree.

He said that bringing home that trout had saved him from a whacking, and that even his schoolmaster had said it was worth the rule-of-three and practice put together.

He was called out of the room at this point, and George and I turned our gaze upon the fish.

It was really a most astonishing trout. The more we looked at it, the more we marvelled at it.

It excited George so much that he climbed up on the back of a chair to get a better view of it.

And then the chair slipped, and George clutched wildly at the trout-case to save himself, and down it came with a crash, George and the chair on top of it.

'You haven't injured the fish, have you?' I cried in alarm, rushing up.

'I hope not,' said George, rising cautiously and looking about.

But he had. That trout lay shattered into a thousand fragments – I say a thousand, but they may have only been nine hundred. I did not count them.

We thought it strange and unaccountable that a stuffed trout should break up into little pieces like that.

And so it would have been strange and unaccountable, if it had been a stuffed trout, but it was not.

That trout was plaster of Paris.

JEROME K. JEROME, *Three Men in a Boat*, 1880

The Guiding Principle of Fishermen's Tales

My next general rule is the Recitative: A rule of singular use to an unfertile invention; it requires no great skill to become master of it, and extends only to the marvellous. It is of great use to coffee-house politicians, and news mongers in general, and chiefly depends upon enumeration: it is indeed a sort of branch to the ambiguous. . . . I have known it practised with success by a friend of mine frequently who has laughed, and been heartily laughed at, for the fruitfulness of his imagination. If you tell a story which happened in one country, he immediately repeats the same, with a trifling variation, that happened in another. If you carry it to the possible he extends it to the probable; if you sink it to the improbable, he lowers it to the impossible; in short it is the art of refining epitomised. Example: One said he saw a pike in a small pond in Kent, weighing 40 pounds, and that one of 30 pounds was taken out of its belly. My friend immediately replied, That was nothing; he had seen in Wiltshire one of 50 pounds weight, and a pike of 40 pounds taken out of its belly; and not only that, says he, but another entire pike was taken out of the belly of it, which weighed 27 pounds and a half. This was between the probable and possible. The gentleman, finding himself outdone, replied, It was strange, but yet he had heard something beyond that; he had a friend of his in Northampton-shire, who stopped at a little public house, and called for a bottle of ale; it was set on the table, and, being ripe, forced out the cork, which went through the ceiling and roof of the house, and hit a small bird which was that instant flying along; the bird dropped perpendicularly down into the bottle, the cork followed plump into the neck again, stopped the bottle and drowned the bird. My friend very gravely replied, that was nothing; for he had heard his father say, that, by such an accident in Wiltshire, he caught a covey of partridges, consisting of eight brace and a half of birds, and at one blow, with this addition only, that it was a two quart bottle they fell into &c.

An Introduction to the Art of Lying, appended to *The Art of Angling*, in *A Collection of Scarce, Curious and Valuable Pieces*, Ed. W. Ruddinan, 1773

Dubious Monsters

A pike weighing 53lb. 11oz. is said to have been caught recently in Lough Sheelan by Mr Patrick Kenny, of Ross, co. Meath. The story runs that Mr Kenny saw a tame duck go under, one of many, so set a small barrel afloat with a spoon bait and two phantoms attached. The fish took the spoon, battled with the barrel for an hour and twenty minutes, and was then landed. The measurements are given as 4ft. 5¾in. length, 29½in. thickest girth. The method by which the pike is said to have been caught is manifestly impossible. We are making further inquiries into the subject. On July 30, 1898, we published an account of a 52lb. pike caught by one Thomas Kenny, of the Constabulary, in Lough Macnean, Fermanagh, but failed to obtain satisfactory verification of its alleged weight.

from *The Field*, 7 September 1901

Another Likely Story

'As Mr John Wane, a Penrith grocer, was angling in the River Eamont some time ago, after taking a quantity of trout, he found an unusual attack made on his bait, and discovered that he had hooked an otter of 7 lb. in weight, and apparently about 4 months old.

'No sooner did he bring it within reach of his landing-net, than the young savage bit the rim of it in two, though made of brass wire about ¾ inch in circumference. He, nevertheless, contrived to throw it over his head on to the bank, and after repeated attacks, he managed to seize upon it.

'Finding himself in a very unusual element, the animal made a loud whistling noise which brought to it the parents, and along with them five or six young ones, which, swimming to the edge of the water, set themselves in battle array by rearing themselves on their hind legs, and following the example of the captive, by setting up a loud whistling noise and spurting water at Mr Wane, whilst showing every symptom of savage ferocity.

'Mr Wane carried off his prisoner, and afterwards returned to the river and made his bag up to 67 lb. The otter, in time, became domesticated.'

from the *Coventry Herald*, 1816

And Another

In the year of our Lord 1180, near Orford in Suffolk, there was a
fish taken in the perfect shape of a man; he was kept by Bartholomew
de Glanville in the Castle of Orford above half a year; but at
length not being carefully looked to, he stole to the sea and was
never seen after. He never spake, but would eat any meat that
was given him, especially raw fish, when he had squeezed out the
juice: He was had to church, but never shewed any signe of
Adoration.

NICHOLAS COX, *The Gentleman's Recreation*, 1674

Three Fisherman's Tales

I was forcing a greased line into the wind; and as I was wading deep
the late drive required to extend the line against the gale caused the
rod point to strike the water at each cast. Imagine my surprise when
a salmon's head emerged just as the rod point hit the water, and
seizing the tip gave it a good pull.

On another occasion I was acting as gillie for a friend, who was
playing a salmon from the bank where the water was deep at the
edge. There was a ripple and the light was bad, but his fish was
close into shore. Seeing a salmon turn and glint, I took a chance and
sinking the gaff drew it out, and there was the fish – or so I
thought. But my friend was still playing his fish! I had gaffed
another which had been keeping his fish company.

One day I hooked a fish on a threadline minnow. Meanwhile my
greased-line fly was hanging a rod's length from the stem of my
boat for the cast to soak. No sooner was the first fish hooked when
another took the fly. Seizing the second rod, there I stood a rod in
each hand, a salmon on each and both reels screaming – two to one!
The boatman took one rod and killed the salmon, but mine came
unstuck – one to two!

G.P.R. BALFOUR-KINNEAR, *Catching Salmon and Sea-Trout*, 1938

An Irish Hare Plays a Salmon

'Hear the major,' says the priest; 'he'll tell the story.'

'By the sowl of me, and I'll tell it any how.'

'Tell it right, major.'

'Is there a man would say that to me but your own good-looking self, now, Father?'

I begged to hear the story.

'You *must* believe it,' said the priest.

'And who doesn't?' said the major, gulping down his third tumbler of punch, and slamming the glass on the table. Then, turning to me – 'Sir, everybody knows the fact – I caught a hare and a salmon at one cast of the fly!'

'Oh, Benedicite,' says the priest.

'None of your holy bother, now, Father. I'm after relating to the gentleman this remarkable adventure. Give me the materials.'

The needful was soon prepared; and the major, directing his conversation exclusively to me, proceeded to say that, while fishing in the Lee, not far from Macroom, he saw a fine fish rise under the opposite bank. He immediately drew out his line, so as to enable him by a cast to reach the exact spot. He had previously put on two large flies, such as are commonly used for salmon in high water. He drew back the line which would extend thirty or forty yards behind him. On endeavouring to make the cast, he found he had, as fishermen call it, 'hitched behind'. At this moment the salmon rose again in the same spot, and, in his eagerness to cover him, he gave a strenuous jerk, with the intent of breaking one fly, and covering the salmon with the other. Splash into the river went something heavy, which immediately took to swimming towards the opposite bank, close to the spot where the salmon had risen. The action of the animal so effectually played the other fly before the salmon, that he forthwith seized it, and both were well hooked. The major continued to relate that hereupon commenced a hard struggle; sometimes the salmon was on the surface, and sometimes the other was drawn under water, till, by judicious management, both were safely landed, and proved to be a fine hare, hooked by the leg, and a salmon of twenty pounds weight!

R. ALLEN, *The Sportsman in Ireland*, 1840

A Retrieving Salmon

Colonel Cane, who was a keen fisherman and an artist with the prawn, told me a salmon story which I should not have believed from anyone else. He said that one day when the water was low he was sitting above the fall and saw two fish lying below him. He threw his prawn above them and beside them, time after time, and they paid no attention. Finally he put it in front of one of the fish and let it lie there. Then the salmon slowly approached it, lifted it with the edge of its lips, swam with it to an adjacent flat rock just covered with water, left it there, and swam back to its original position. Colonel Cane's theory was that it was just bored with the perpetual reappearance of the prawn, and wished to remove the annoyance as soon as it could be done without danger. I wonder.

MAURICE HEADLAM, *Irish Reminiscences*, 1947

Cleopatra Sees Through Antony

On a time Antonius went to angle for fish, and when he could take none, he was as angrie as could be, bicause Cleopatra stoode by. Wherefore he secretly commaunded the fisher men, that when he cast in his line, they should straight dive under the water, and put a fishe on his hooke which they had taken before: and so snatched up his angling rodde, and brought up fish twise or thrise. Cleopatra found it straight, yet she seemed not to see it, but wondred at his excellent fishing: but when she was alone by her selfe among her owne people, she told them howe it was, and bad them the next morning to be on the water to see the fishing. A number of people came to the haven, and got into the fisher boates to see this fishing. Antonius then threw in his line and Cleopatra straight commaunded one of her men to dive under water before Antonius' men, and to put some old salte fish upon his baite, like unto those that are brought out of the contrie of Pont. When he had hong the fish on his hooke, Antonius thinking he had taken a fishe in deede, snatched up his line presently. Then they all fell a laughing. Cleopatra laughing also, said unto him: Leave us (my Lord) Ægyptians (which

dwell in the contrie of Pharus and Canobus) your angling rodde:
this is not thy profession: thou must hunt after conquering of
realmes and contries.

PLUTARCH (AD 46–120), *Parallel Lives*, translated by Sir
Thomas North, 1579

Lloyd George Cheats on His Wife

The Newton breakfast table was shaken again on 31 August when
the newspapers announced that the Prime Minister had reached the
Highlands accompanied not only by Mrs Lloyd George but by that
dreadful Miss Stevenson: their friend, his mistress – who could tell
– and in either case how could his wife put up with it? They came,
this ménage à trois, to stay with the Duke of Atholl at Blair Castle
in Perthshire and then advanced by motor car to the Station Hotel
of Inverness, from which the Prime Minister went shopping for
fishing rods, reels and feathery flies which were supposed to appeal
to West Highland fish. The party then went on to Flowerdale
House at Gairloch to which Kenneth Mackenzie had invited them.
The weather was bad. The fish would not rise. But as they had been
invited to stay for several weeks, until parliament re-assembled, they
had hope.

The best fishing, below the fifty foot waterfall of the river Kerry,
was shared by the Mackenzies of Flowerdale and the Mackenzies of
Shieldaig and these two had made an agreement to fish there with
their guests on alternate days. Lloyd George was 'as disappointed as
a schoolboy' to hear on the first fine day that it was Shieldaig's turn.
He and his friends had to go to the source of the river where it
flows out from Loch Bad-na-Scalaig, and where the water was
muddy from weeks of rain. No one caught anything, not even Miss
Stevenson 'who casts quite a dexterous line'. Lloyd George left
them at it flogging their hopeless flies and went downstream alone
where, unseen, he put on a worm and landed a twenty ounce brown
trout, the only catch of the day, thereby adding to his sins in all the
eyes of Newton, where fishing with a worm was taboo. And then,
'happy as a schoolboy' he hurried through the long grass to Miss
Stevenson 'and proudly exhibited the catch on the palms of his

extended hands'. Then Mrs Lloyd George who had spent the morning in the house arrived by motor-car with a luncheon basket.

DAVID THOMSON, *Nairn in Darkness and Light*, 1987

The Art of Excuses

THE angler's lies are of two kinds. First we have those which he tells in order to excite the admiration and envy of his fellows. Such lies are concerned with the huge size, portentous weight, and inconceivable number of the fishes which in the glorious past he has destroyed. Secondly, we have those which he tells, day by day, in order to explain his failure to bring anything whatever home in his creel. It is this second kind of lie which I propose here to consider.

On most trout waters there is a limit of size – say, seven inches – which fishes that are taken must reach or be returned to the stream. Where such a rule prevails one says, on one's arrival at the hotel, something like this: 'I must have had fifty trout to-day if I had one – and not a blighter of the lot reached the seven inches. A most exasperating day.' This is the lie which I myself commonly tell.

Another very valuable falsehood can be told in some such words as these: 'No, I've brought nothing back. The fact is I had forty-seven nice fishes, but I was rather a long way from the hotel when I knocked off, and I didn't much fancy lugging twenty pounds' weight of fish home on my back. So I handed them in, half a dozen at a time, at each of the cottages I passed, and so got rid of them, and jolly glad to do it I was, too.'

I have heard an angler very ingeniously narrate how, just as he was about to leave the water, with close on 100 trout to his score, he, working his way through some bushes on the bank, had the misfortune so to engage the straps of his creel with a projecting twig that the whole thing was inverted, and its entire contents poured out into a very rapid piece of water which swept every fish away, beyond all hope of recovery, into the midst of a large and prodigiously deep pool.

Lies of this nature are astonishingly effective, but it is well not to overwork them. A hotel may reasonably be expected to accept one such misfortune a week, but not more. Personally I make a point of restricting the number of such wholesale losses to two in three weeks, and for the rest of the time make out with my undersized fishes' story or with one or more of the standard excuses, those sound, well-tried *clichés* which have served anglers from the beginning of time, and will, I have no doubt, continue to do so during the rest of it. Of these the most usual is the weather. The sun, for instance, has been too bright; the wind has been too cold; the rain has been too wet; the hail too round; the snow too white; the mist has been too thick; the thunder has been too loud; the lightning has been knocking one about too much.

Or you can blame your tackle. Your gut has been too thick (or too weak), your flies too small (or too large), your rod too stiff (or too limber). Or the river may have been too full or too low, the water too clear or too muddy, the rise of natural fly too meagre or too abundant, or the trees have been too green. Or you can say that if you had only had on wading trousers, instead of stockings, you could have filled your basket twice over; or that if you had only had ham sandwiches for lunch instead of beef you could have filled it ten times over.

You can also blame the trout. They were coming short, they were coming long, they were smutting, they were minnowing, they were sulking, there weren't any. Or you can blame the birds for putting you off with their loud, incessant singing. Or the rabbits for goring you with their horns.

The only thing you must never do (if you are a true fisherman) is to blame yourself. For this would be to tell the truth.

WILLIAM CAINE, *Fish, Fishing and Fishermen*, 1927

It's All Relative, After All

That we fishermen are all liars is the grossest libel. Some are, there is no doubt of that. So in any hundred men there is a percentage of thieves. Among a hundred bishops there are a few who steal umbrellas and Elzevirs. But most of us are honest and even painfully desirous of speaking the truth. I say painfully because sometimes as mere human beings we should like to adorn the truth. The struggle to be exactly honest as to inches and ounces may be too much for us. Those who accuse us never think of the power of the imagination, and how hard it is for the artist to control it. Every fisherman knows that only too well. He is continually trying to curb his own. He can sympathize with imaginative artists of other orders, such as those who play golf and drive balls with exactness to incredible distances. For all of us who fish are either born psychologists or become such. We understand the relativity of the soul. We know that we are all subject to illusions, even to delusions. We may think the false true and the truth false. How else can we hope to account for a fish having three different weights, and even a fourth when it is foul-hooked? A fish is one weight when it first takes the fly, another when it is grassed, and another lesser weight half an hour afterwards. And if it is lost it weighs as much as all its other weights together. This can perhaps be explained by Post-Relativity physics. I wonder if Einstein is a fisherman. If so he may thus have reached his notion of gravitation depending on some wonderful way on the curves of space. In some parts of space I understand that something may weigh nothing and in others become heavier than any metal imaginable. Why not the same with fish? Let us remember that a fish of three different weights is being estimated by the fisherman when at three different points in space.

MORLEY ROBERTS, *A Humble Fisherman*, 1932

Keeping a Sense of Proportion

Killing is beginning to become clear to me. It came as an inspiration. Before, I had been puzzled at liking to kill things, because I am generally more humane than most people: certainly than the warmongers, the flogging magistrates, the snake killers, and most schoolmasters. I cannot remember when I last killed a fly, or a wasp, or a mouse. It is, as I discovered yesterday, a question of art. When it is difficult to kill the thing, when skill and achievement come into it, I find that the killing is worth while. You forget the dead salmon in the ecstasy of creation: you have perfected something yourself, even more perfect than the dead fish. This must sound silly to anybody who has not shared the perfection; who has not created a cast, or a shot, or a run, himself. But it is rock bottom.

To triumph over difficulties is the essence of sportsmanship. This is what the dear old colonels mean, the colonels whose apparent brain weight would give the common vole a sensation of volatility in his head, when they talk about the 'sporting chance.' Such-and-such a sport, they say, is not a decent one, because the such-and-such doesn't get a 'sporting chance.' They are absolutely right. They mean that the sport is not sufficiently difficult to make the kill worth while. The pleasure of surmounting the difficulty is not enough to counteract the displeasure of killing a beautiful thing.

This is why I stopped fishing on the 24th of April. It was worth killing the silver superlative of a salmon when it took a day to do it: three in one day lowered the achievement, so I stopped. It was becoming a slaughter, not a sport.

This, also, is why the Englishman kills his trout with a dry fly and imposes a limit. . . . Anybody can catch a trout on a worm. If you use a worm, except for the pot-fishing, you have nothing to achieve and to congratulate yourself upon.

Hence the, to the foreigner, astonishing spectacle of an Englishman handicapping himself. I read in a book once that an Englishman even handicaps his drink. He puts brandy into his port, waits fifty years for the brandy to work itself out again, and then drinks it, in exactly the same state as it started, with reverence and exultation. In Canada, apparently, they kill salmon by the daily score. In England even, I was sorry to see that some woman or other has killed between sixteen and twenty in one day.[1] That was not sport, not achievement over difficulty: it was butchery. It cannot have been difficult to raise those fish: a question merely of dolloping in the fly, and walking up and down the bank for ten minutes, and gaffing the

---

[1] Which is by no means a record. The best example I know, of this astonishingly stupid attitude towards sport, is that of Franz Ferdinand. His, however, was an achievement with the gun. He used to shoot at Konopišt with no less than seven weapons and four loaders, and he once killed more than 4,000 birds, himself, in one day. [*A propos* of statistics, and quite beside the point: a Yorkshireman once drank 52½ pints of beer in one hour.] Now why did Franz Ferdinand do this? Even if he shot for twelve hours at a stretch, without pause for luncheon, it means that he killed six birds in each minute of the day. The mere manual labour, a pheasant every ten seconds for twelve successive hours, is enough to make a road-mender stagger; and there is little wonder that, by the time the unhappy archduke had accumulated his collection of 300,000 head of game, he was shooting with rubber pads on his coat and a bandage round his ears. The unfortunate man had practically stunned himself with gunpowder, long before they bagged him also at Sarajevo.

fish. Give her, at an underestimation, ten minutes per fish. She must have been actually playing the fish she killed for nearly three and a half hours of her day. If I know anything of the gentry, and she was a titled woman, she did not start before 10.30, nor fish after 6, and took at least an hour off for luncheon. This leaves her about six fishing hours, with fish on for more than half the time – provided that she really did kill her fish in ten minutes, a fact of which I am doubtful. Where is the difficulty, where the achievement, where the sport? I can't help feeling that I should have gone home after the first four.

This is why the stories of Canadian abundance leave me unmoved: why I can reasonably abominate snake-killers whilst myself killing partridges: why my heart moves for a dead mouse but exults over a dead pheasant in his pride. After all, there is a lot of blank air for the shot to go into, besides the pheasant.

T.H. WHITE, England Have My Bones, 1936

It Shouldn't Be Too Easy

Said a witty friend: 'It is extraordinary with what contempt your true angler looks upon any method which will really catch fish.' The wit pierces near the heart of the matter. Any method which will only catch fish? Yes. The true angler is not he whose pole is but the weapon of his predatory instinct. The love of the art must be above the greed of prey. With the boisterous fisherman and the picnicker with a fishing-rod, we have no concern. But among actual sportsman-like anglers the manifestations of the enjoyment of the recreation are as various as temperaments. Each exaggerates some of its pleasures; but he best realizes them whose rod is a divining wand, who has the widest sympathy with the outer world – whether it touch him through his scientific insight, his artistic sensibility, or that nameless poetic feeling which longs for the sunshine, the wind, and the rain. We may for a moment envy him who tells of great game taken from some far-off lake, but our hearts go out to him who bids us share his little brook 'when the Sanguinaria is in bloom.'

LEROY YALE, Getting Out the Fly Books, 1897

Lenin Was a Sportsman, Stalin Wasn't

Although Lenin preferred the gun to the rod, both Gorki and Trotsky have borne witness to his love of fishing. Like Chekhov, he was no angling artist, and to him the joy of capture was everything. In his *Days with Lenin*, Gorki tells how the little man, then an exile from Tsarist Russia, went sea-fishing with the Italian fishermen of Capri. Here for the first time he learnt to catch fish 'with his finger', that is, with a rodless line. The Italians explained to him that the fish must be struck as soon as the fingers felt the vibration of the line. They gave him a practical demonstration and exclaimed, 'Cosi, drin, drin. Capisce?' A second or two later Lenin felt a bite, struck savagely, and hauled in a fish with a child-like joy and a shout of 'Drin-drin'. The Italians laughed and thereafter christened him Signor Drin-Drin. When he left Capri, they remembered him and used to ask Gorki, 'How is Drin-Drin getting on? The Tsar hasn't caught him yet, has he?' In perhaps the finest piece of invective that he ever wrote, Trotsky refers to Lenin's fishing exploits in Siberia and extols him as a true sportsman. Then Trotsky adds, 'Stalin also fished in Siberia. He set traps.'

SIR ROBERT BRUCE-LOCKHART, *My Rod My Comfort*, 1949

Mr Theodore Castwell

Mr Theodore Castwell, having devoted a long, strenuous and not unenjoyable life to hunting to their doom innumerable salmon, trout, and grayling in many quarters of the globe, and having gained much credit among his fellows for his many ingenious improvements in rods, flies, and tackle employed for that end, in the fullness of time died and was taken to his own place.

St Peter looked up from a draft balance sheet at the entry of the attendant angel.

'A gentleman giving the name of Castwell. Says he is a fisherman, your Holiness, and has "Fly-Fishers' Club, London" on his card.'

'Hm-hm,' says St Peter. 'Fetch me the ledger with his account.'

St Peter perused it.

'Hm-hm,' said St Peter. 'Show him in.'

Mr Castwell entered cheerfully and offered a cordial right hand to St Peter.

'As a brother of the angle –' he began.

'Hm-hm,' said St Peter. 'I have been looking at your account from below.'

'I am sure I shall not appeal to you in vain for special consideration in connection with the quarters to be assigned to me here.'

'Hm-hm,' said St Peter.

'Well, I've seen worse accounts,' said St Peter. 'What sort of quarters would you like?'

'Do you think you could manage something in the way of a country cottage of the Test Valley type, with modern conveniences and, say, three quarters of a mile of one of those pleasant chalk streams, clear as crystal, which proceed from out the throne, attached?'

'Why, yes,' said St Peter. 'I think we can manage that for you. Then what about your gear? You must have left your fly rods and tackle down below. I see you prefer a light split cane of nine foot or so, with appropriate fittings. I will indent upon the Works Department for what you require, including a supply of flies. I think you will approve of our dresser's productions. Then you will want a keeper to attend you.'

'Thanks awfully, your Holiness,' said Mr Castwell. 'That will be first-rate. To tell you the truth, from the Revelations I read, I was inclined to fear that I might be just a teeny-weeny bit bored in heaven.'

'In h-hm-hm,' said St Peter, checking himself.

It was not long before Mr Castwell found himself alongside an enchantingly beautiful clear chalk stream, some fifteen yards wide, swarming with fine trout feeding greedily: and presently the attendant angel assigned to him had handed him the daintiest, most exquisite, light split-cane rod conceivable – perfectly balanced with the reel and line – with a beautifully damped tapered cast of incredible fineness and strength, and a box of flies of such marvelous tying as to be almost mistakable for the natural insects they were to simulate.

Mr Castwell scooped up a natural fly from the water, matched it perfectly from the fly box, and knelt down to cast to a riser putting up just under a tussock ten yards or so above him. The fly lit like gossamer, six inches above the last ring; and next moment the rod was making the curve of beauty. Presently, after an exciting battle, the keeper netted out a beauty of about two and a half pounds.

'Heavens,' cried Mr Castwell. 'This is something like.'

'I am sure his Holiness will be pleased to hear it,' said the keeper.

Mr Castwell prepared to move upstream to the next riser when he noticed that another trout had taken up the position of that which he had just landed, and was rising. 'Just look at that,' he said, dropping instantaneously to his knee and drawing off some line. A moment later an accurate fly fell just above the neb of the fish, and instantly Mr Castwell engaged in battle with another lusty fish. All went well, and presently the landing net received its two and a half pounds.

'A very pretty brace,' said Mr Castwell, preparing to move on to the next string of busy nebs which he had observed putting up around the bend. As he approached the tussock, however, he became aware that the place from which he had just extracted so satisfactory a brace was already occupied by another busy feeder.

'Well, I'm damned,' said Mr Castwell. 'Do you see that?'

'Yes, sir,' said the keeper.

The chance of extracting three successive trout from the same spot was too attractive to be forgone, and once more Mr Castwell knelt down and delivered a perfect cast to the spot. Instantly it was accepted and battle was joined. All held, and presently a third gleaming trout joined his brethren in the creel.

Mr Castwell turned joyfully to approach the next riser round the bend. Judge, however, his surprise to find that once more the pit beneath the tussock was occupied by a rising trout, apparently of much the same size as the others.

'Heavens,' exclaimed Mr Castwell. 'Was there ever anything like it?'

'No, sir,' said the keeper.

'Look here,' said he to the keeper, 'I think I really must give this chap a miss and pass on to the next.'

'Sorry, it can't be done, sir. His Holiness would not like it.'

'Well, if that's really so,' said Mr Castwell, and knelt rather reluctantly to his task.

Several hours later he was still casting to the same tussock.

'How long is this confounded rise going to last?' inquired Mr Castwell. 'I suppose it will stop soon.'

'No, sir,' said the keeper.

'What, isn't there a slack hour in the afternoon?'

'No afternoon, sir.'

'What? Then what about the evening rise?'

'No evening rise, sir,' said the keeper.

'Well, I shall knock off now. I must have had about thirty brace from that corner.'

'Beg pardon, sir, but his Holiness would not like that.'

'What?' said Mr Castwell. 'Mayn't I even stop at night?'

'No night here, sir,' said the keeper.

'Then do you mean that I have got to go on catching these damned two-and-a-half pounders at this corner forever and ever?'

The keeper nodded.

'Hell!' said Mr Castwell.

'Yes,' said his keeper.

G.E.M. SKUES

Fishing for Sport Not For Glory

Angling's problems are never solved. They rise anew with each new pool and each new day.

The difficulty lies not in just being able to fool the fish. Their intelligence is far inferior to our own. Deceiving them is a much easier problem than guessing where they will be at any given time under an ever-changing-and-never-quite-the-same set of weather and water conditions. To the fish three things are of prime importance: food, safety and comfort. If it is food the fish are seeking the angler must concern himself with the kind of food and where they will go to look for it. With that problem decided he can concentrate on making his lure effective. If it is safety the fish are seeking he must find his fish before he can tempt him. And if it is comfort he must know where a fish will seek it and put his lure within easy reach of his quarry.

There will be no end to angling controversies for there is no one best way for everyone to fish. One angler may take a certain phase of angling and through his mastery of the single side of the game claim fishing success. Among such fishermen are those who fish with but a single lure. Through their knowledge of fish habits and their ability to put their single lure where feeding fish will take it they often outdistance others with more suitable lures but without the same knowledge of fish and fishing waters. There are too many conditions, varying constantly, that must be balanced for any set solution to be devised. The problem itself alone remains constant, to find the fish and make them strike. It is seeking the answer that absorbs years of men's lives and gives them in return the blessing of peace of mind and the health that follows hours spent in the open.

Increasing populations and the decrease in the amount of fishable water due to pollution and the inroads of civilization as we know it have lifted the value of our inland fish for sport far above their value as food. The day of the great catches is passing. Hatcheries, operated by funds from the license fees of anglers, turn out millions of fish to stock the lakes and streams. Over the years the fish have developed a new wariness, angling has become an art requiring great skill, and the catching of many fish is a privilege lavished on the few whose opportunity or skill is great.

There is a growing tendency among anglers to release their fish, returning them to the water in order that they may furnish sport again for a brother angler. Game fish are too valuable to be caught only once. Fish from the markets, though not so rare, are just as nourishing and just as tasty as the game fish of our lakes and streams. It seems logical to buy our food fish where they are much cheaper than those we buy for sport by way of license, tackle, transportation and time . . . and return our catches to the waters we, as anglers, hope will always be well stocked.

It is a long step from the day when the fisherman's catch meant life and health to himself and his family to our present day where anglers fish for sport alone. Even the day of the fisherman who consistently hangs up his trophies to brag about is passing, too. Pride in accomplishment will always remain but, seemingly, angling is reaching a new high plane when a fisherman can spend a day on the lake or stream, catching fish and returning them to the water again, unharmed, to come home empty handed. That angler keeps no trophy to show his fellow men as proof of his prowess but contents himself with the pleasure of hours well spent in the surroundings he loves. He has fished for sport and not for glory.

LEE WULFF, *The Handbook of Freshwater Fishing*, 1939

The Redneck Apostle

Through no fault of Mr Wulff's, a great injustice has flowed from that sentence. Scores of angling writers, many of them Mr Wulff's cronies, have given him credit for establishing catch-and-release fishing as the nationally accepted practice that it is today. And there is no question that catch-and-release was Wulff's *idea*.

But it took a slip-sliding, fast-talking apostle of the Redneck Way to put catch-and-release into the head of every potbellied Texas bassin' man and every worm-slinging Vermont trout murderer. To find this man, you must leave such storied waters as the Restigouche and the Little Codroy of Newfoundland, the Laxa of Iceland and the Dee of Scotland – this last being where according to the British sporting press, Wulff in 1962 caused 'something like a sensation' among the bloodthirsty natives by releasing his salmon unharmed.

You must travel into the heart of deep Alabama, down below Montgomery, crossing the slack, catfish-blessed waters of Catoma Creek and passing through the sun-blasted hamlet of Pintlala, before you find the lakeside home of Ray Scott.

It is hard to imagine two men more different than Ray Scott, born in 1933 in Montgomery and founder of the tournament-fishing movement that brought us the red-metal-flake bass boat, and Lee Wulff, who was born in 1905 in Valdez, Alaska, and spent his last years trying to protect the Atlantic salmon from extinction.

Lee Wulff graduated from Stanford University in engineering. He studied art in Paris, invented the modern fishing vest, created an important family of dry flies, pioneered light-rod fly fishing for salmon and wrote several elegant books.

Ray Scott set out at nineteen to emulate the success of a Montgomery insurance salesman whom he admired as a 'classy dude' who 'strutted when he walked.' He wrote possibly the worst book ever written by a major figure in American sport fishing, *Prospecting and Selling: From a Fishing Hole to a Pot of Gold*. It is devoted only in passing to fishing, but deals mainly with popularizing Scott's 'Wheel of Fortune' concept of salesmanship, which rests on such key principles as 'Definitizing Appointment.' The book also contains the breathtaking – and, thankfully, shamefaced – revelation that Scott's own sales techniques include telling 'bald-faced lies to poor unfortunate [black] people' in order to collect on their twenty-cents-a-week burial policies.

Still, Ray Scott *is* a major figure in American sport fishing. His decision in 1972 to impose catch-and-release rules in the tournaments of his Bass Anglers Sportsman Society (BASS) has probably saved the lives of more fish than any other regulatory step since state governments first began putting legal limits on catches in the 1870s.

This step popularized 'catch-and-release fishing for the vast majority of American freshwater anglers,' according to Gene Mueller, a veteran outdoor writer in Washington, D.C. 'Sure, trout purists have turned fish loose for centuries, paying more attention to outsmarting the wily critter than frying it later in the day, but it was Scott's BASS group that made live releasing of fish truly popular. Now there isn't a backwoods kid in the U.S. that doesn't practice it at least part of the time.' . . .

I went to see Ray Scott at his big house overlooking a heavily stocked fifty-acre lake where stumps, tree limbs and rocks had been professionally installed to make the best possible habitat for large-mouth bass. Scott had sold his interest in BASS to a group of Montgomery investors in 1986 for a rumored $17 million. He didn't seem to care much for fishing anymore, but he doted on his role as a personal friend and fund-raiser for President Bush and took an almost childlike joy in Bush's semiannual fishing visits. As for what inspired him to try catch-and-release, there was a short answer: 'It was good business. I am first and foremost a businessman. I work for money.'

By 1972, Scott was making a lot of money from the tournaments he started in 1967 and from *Bass Master Magazine*, started in 1968 to plug the tournaments and the products made by the tackle companies that bought space in the magazine. But he ran into 'a gnawing problem.'

While the motel owners and fish camps were always glad to have a bass tournament on the big lakes that dot the South and Southwest, local fishermen and sportswriters were infuriated by the bass carnage that was on view when Scott would turn up in his cowboy hat to preside over the weigh-in.

'We were catching these fish and putting them in a johnboat behind the weigh-in, and after they all flopped themselves to death, we'd give them to a children's home or an old ladies' home or whatever.'

At first, Scott relied on scientific quotations to calm the yokels. He cited biologists who 'tell me that when you've got twenty-five thousand acres and you take a ton of bass out, that's like a grain of sand. They can show me on paper that the lake could regenerate that much poundage before you could weigh them in.'

This did not work. 'I can still picture those chubby old men with the gray hair with their hands tucked down in the bib of their overalls, looking down on those fish, mumbling to each other, "By God, that's why we ain't catching no more fish."'

So Scott told the highly skeptical 'tour fishermen' that if they wanted to participate for tournament dollars they had to install aerated live wells in their boats. Scott himself built a giant aquarium where the captured bass were displayed before being weighed and released into the lakes from whence they came.

Two years later, in 1974, Scott noticed that what began as a public-relations tactic was altering the attitudes of the fishermen themselves. This happened when a burly, sunburned contestant appeared at the weigh-in with four live fish and one dead one.

'He said, "Ray, I'm sorry, I don't know why that fish died. I did everything I could to keep him alive." And he got a big tear in the corner of each eye. I thought, "My God, I just wanted to give the guy a little religion. I didn't mean for him to become a priest."'

The catch-and-release gospel spread quickly enough among warm-water fishermen to force makers of bass tackle to drop their historical practice of advertising lures by showing a stringer of dead fish. Editors of saltwater publications got angry letters for pictures of fish being landed with a killing stroke of the gaff. All up and down the East Coast, guides like Mark Kovach on the Potomac and Bob Clouser on the Susquehanna altered their policies of allowing a customer to keep one or two trophy fish and went to complete no-kill fishing.

What caused this tidal wave of acceptance? No one, including Ray Scott, had counted on the proliferation of cable television shows starring tournament fishermen. Each Saturday, viewers could see a Jack Nicklaus lookalike named Roland Martin, or Jimmy Houston, an Oklahoma hustler with a hyena laugh, or Rick Clunn, the most radical environmentalist on the tournament trail, throwing fish back right and left.

'The same thing happened with fishing that happened with golf,' Scott said. 'A golfer sees Jack Nicklaus on television and when he goes out to the course, he wants to wear the same kind of clothes and use the same clubs and try to hit the ball the way he saw Nicklaus do it. A fisherman sees Roland Martin throwing back a seven-pound bass and he decides that's what you do if you're a real fisherman.' . . .

The prophet of catch-and-release and its popularizer never met. But their luck went sour at about the same time. Wulff flew his airplane into a hill near Hancock, New York, on April 28, 1991. Almost exactly a year later, Ray Scott flew his foot into his own fast-moving mouth. A Georgia newspaper carried an interview in which Scott spoke this paragraph in describing the guesthouse beside the lake where George Bush often came to fish:

'You ever been to an old nigger house? Smell that kinda old ashen kind of smell coming from the fireplace? You know, you've got that smell in the house. Bush walked in there the first time like this [sniffing]. He said, "Man, I could stand some of this."'

Ray Scott's public – particularly the black members of BASS – proved more interested in his racist language than in his accounts of President Bush's fondness for the smell of wood smoke. Scott issued a forlorn statement of the sort that white Southerners and politicians of every region issue when they get caught talking that way: 'I am not a racist,' he said. 'I am ashamed to have carelessly made reference to a racial epithet.' The presidents of two black fishing clubs – the Original East Atlanta Bass Anglers and the

Golden Rod Bassmasters of Birmingham – came forward to say that they were satisfied with Scott's apology. But you will not be surprised to know that in the dashing to and fro of the 1992 campaign, President Bush did not stop off again at Ray Scott's pond. Late in the campaign, Scott was allowed to stand near the President on the speakers' platform at an outdoor rally in Montgomery. He managed to get hold of a microphone and assure the crowd that, having once seen Bill Clinton in a men's room, he could attest that the Democratic nominee was not a manly man. Even the seasoned slurmeisters of the Bush campaign thought this public discussion of penis size went a tiny bit too far.

So, as I said, Ray Scott is hardly in Lee Wulff's league when it comes to eloquence or, for that matter, minimally civil behavior. Moreover, as one who lived his boyhood surrounded by the ugliness of a racist society, I have made it a policy never to feel sorry for people who get caught using 'nigger' or 'Jap' or 'kike' or any other word designed to wound people in their identities.

Still, when I think of old motor-mouth Ray sitting down there in his big house beside the pond where George Bush used to fish, I cannot help feeling a twinge of pity. I say, all hail the elegant Mr Wulff for his role as prophet. Long may we remember him in our prayers. But don't forget to say a few for Ray Scott, too. In fishing, at least, he rerouted his people from the Redneck Way.

HOWELL RAINES, *Fly Fishing Through the Mid-Life Crisis*, 1993

Why Anglers Make Fine Old People

Escaping to the Stone Age by the morning train from Manchester, the fisherman engages in an activity that allows him to shed the centuries as a dog shakes off water and to recapture not his own youth merely but the youth of the world.

He may not know that this is his aim. Indeed if he were too conscious of it he would not be able to achieve it. But, if we watch him we notice a number of signs that show clearly enough that when he goes fishing his primary reason is not the need of fish. He imposes on himself unwritten laws that betray his real intention. He has a better reason than hunger for being a fisherman. He is not moved by a primitive instinct for slaughter. If he were he could satisfy it better by using a hand-grenade, poison or a net. His unwritten laws give the fish approximately the same chance that they had against the hungry savage. Most fishermen are secretly dissatisfied with themselves if they feel that they owe too much of their success to the mechanical perfection of their equipment. For example, I have yet to meet a man who has done much spinning and fly-fishing who would not agree at once that he would rather catch his two-pounder on a fly than with the help of one of the ingenious modern spinning reels. The fisherman sets the highest value on those fish which have made the highest demands on his personal prowess, his knowledge of nature, his watercraft and his skill. A fish caught on a home-made fly is a greater satisfaction to the fisherman than one which has been tricked by a fly bought in a shop. Why? Because it better satisfies the fisherman's instinctive desire to re-create conditions in which he depends on himself alone in his voluntary contest with nature. There is no hostility in this contest. The trout chasing minnows or picking flies from the surface of the stream is contesting with Nature in the same way as the fisherman chasing trout. Neither trout nor fisherman are opposed to Nature in their several activities. Quite the contrary. The home-made fly gives the fisherman a better right to say, 'Alone I did it.' That is why he prefers it. . . .

We return in fishing not to the Stone but to the Golden Age. Historical accuracy is happily denied to us. We do not feel it necessary to go fishing in a wolf's skin instead of in a Burberry. The character of our return to this mythical age is far deeper than can be expressed by any fancy dress. What we are doing is to exchange an elaborate and indirect for a simple and direct relationship with Nature. This latter relationship is very hard to put into words. Is the fisherman returning to the Golden Age to enjoy aptitudes in himself which he might otherwise lose? Is he reassuring himself by happy experiment that he can still climb *down* his family tree? Fishing cannot be explained simply as a means of escape from our over-elaborate life, for it is enjoyed by men who have lived all their lives on the river bank as well as by those who escape to their fishing from the towns. The happiness of Walton's fishing was as keen as our own, but the country was then at a Londoner's back door. The truth, I think, is, that we resume 'palaeolithic life' not because of preference for any past age but to seek a relationship with Nature which is valuable in all ages. . . .

The good fisherman is always engaged in the active exercise of his imagination. He is the fish he catches. He, as that fish, feels the currents in the pool and pushes his way to shelter in a pocket of still water. The fish that go into his creel are so many testimonials to his right reading of nature. The power of vision that he develops while fishing persists when the rod is in its case. The fisherman knows what is happening in the river when he is not there. As the rain pours down on autumn streets, he is conscious, as he buttons his coat about his neck, of the fish running up the Eden from the Solway Firth. The pavements are soft grass under his feet, the stone walls of the houses are no prison for him and through the roar of the towns he can hear running water. It is this that distinguishes fishing from such pursuits as golf, cricket, football, billiards, or chess. These games do not affect a man's relationship to nature. Fishing does. In looking round for another pursuit of which this can be said, I think of gardening. The gardener, like the fisherman, 'resumes palaeolithic life without the spur of palaeolithic hunger.' Like the fisherman he becomes so much a part of Nature that he is reconciled to the changes of the year. He welcomes the seasons as they come and no longer wishes to put a spoke in the wheel of time. It is generally said that gardeners and fishermen make fine old men. This is not surprising. They have been caught up into Nature, grow old with a good will and no hanging back, and are without misgivings about their own mortality.

ARTHUR RANSOME, *Rod and Line*, 1929

The Fisherman

Although I can see him still,
The freckled man who goes
To a grey place on a hill

In grey Connemara clothes
At dawn to cast his flies,
It's long since I began
To call up to the eyes
This wise and simple man.
All day I'd looked in the face
What I had hoped 'twould be
To write for my own race
And the reality;
The living men that I hate,
The dead man that I loved,
The craven man in his seat,
The insolent unreproved,
And no knave brought to book
Who has won a drunken cheer,
The witty man and his joke
Aimed at the commonest ear,
The clever man who cries
The catch-cries of the clown,
The beating down of the wise
And great Art beaten down.
Maybe a twelvemonth since
Suddenly I began,
In scorn of this audience,
Imagining a man,
And his sun-freckled face,
And grey Connemara cloth,
Climbing up to a place
Where stone is dark under froth,
And the down-turn of his wrist
When the flies drop in the stream;
A man who does not exist,
A man who is but a dream;
And cried, 'Before I am old
I shall have written him one
Poem maybe as cold
And passionate as the dawn.'

W.B. YEATS, from *The Wild Swans at Coole*, 1919

A Sense of Priorities

I do not defend sport for any of its extraneous advantages: health, scenery, natural history, or any such. I pay my opponents the compliment of crediting them with the highest principles, and I ask the same concession in return. They say that sport degrades the sportsman, and, if this is so, it is no rebuttal to say that it carries with it certain advantages. Similarly those who plead for the indissolubility of Christian marriage are quite rightly unmoved by the miseries it may cause. These cannot make wrong right. And it is on this ground that I want to meet my opponents. And certainly I shall indulge in no abuse or contempt, for I have a passion for essential truth, and there must be truth in what a great many people believe. On both sides there are many believers: both sides must contain truth, and each is shocked by the action of the other, considering it untruth. If I revolt some by shooting so noble an animal as a stag, I felt an equal horror on reading that money was to be spent on looking after horses in Abyssinia during the war, when there was unending need for money, and more money, in caring for the sick and the wounded, the women and the children. They say I am cruel. I retort, you put the lower above the higher, horses before children. I say, first things first. Which is right, either, both or neither?

I believe that Mr Hemingway is right[1] and that people may be divided into two groups, those who identify themselves with animals and those who identify themselves with human beings. He goes on to say that those who identify themselves with animals 'are capable of greater cruelty to human beings than those who do not identify themselves readily with animals.' A hard saying, this, though no harder than those which animal lovers are accustomed to fling at sportsmen. But what I want to know is whether it is true. Let me take a few examples, general and particular. The English are admittedly the greatest animal lovers in the world. The English are not kind to children. We are not: we put it in another way, saying that French and Italian mothers spoil their children. That really admits the charge. An English mother can entrust her child to almost any Italian nurse, but she has to choose carefully an English nurse. I

---

[1] *Death in the Afternoon.*

constantly read the Press of other countries. I know of no Press which reports so many barbarities to children as does the English Press. If you were to shake savagely a dog in any London park you would immediately have an angry crowd round you. You can shake a child as much as you like and nobody interferes. I once discussed vivisection with an English lady who was opposed to it. We came to the question of the right to inflict pain. She said you may have to thrash a child. I answered that not only would I not do so, but I would not use the word. That brilliant American who wrote under the name of O. Henry tells a story of which the climax is a Kentucky proverb: Kind to animals, cruel to women. A friend of mine watched a bullfight. On seeing a horse killed she hid her face in her hands. A Spanish woman leant over her. 'Oh, you English,' she said, 'you hide your eyes at the death of a horse, but you applaud the death of a man.'

J.W. HILLS, *My Sporting Life*, 1936

Heaven

Fish (fly-replete, in depth of June,
Dawdling away their wat'ry noon)
Ponder deep wisdom, dark or clear,
Each secret fishy hope or fear.
Fish say, they have their Stream and Pond;
But is there anything Beyond?
This life cannot be All, they swear,
For how unpleasant, if it were!
One may not doubt that, somehow, Good
Shall come of Water and of Mud;
And, sure, the reverent eye must see
A Purpose in Liquidity.
We darkly know, by Faith we cry,
The future is not Wholly Dry.
Mud unto mud! – Death eddies near –
Not here the appointed End, not here!
But somewhere, beyond Space and Time,
Is wetter water, slimier slime!

And there (they trust) there swimmeth One
Who swam ere rivers were begun,
Immense, of fishy form and mind,
Squamous, omnipotent, and kind;
And under that Almighty Fin,
The littlest fish may enter in.
Oh! never fly conceals a hook,
Fish say, in the Eternal Brook,
But more than mundane weeds are there,
And mud, celestially fair;
Fat caterpillars drift around,
And Paradisal grubs are found;
Unfading moths, immortal flies,
And the worm that never dies.
And in that Heaven of all their wish,
There shall be no more land, say fish.

RUPERT BROOKE, 1913

BIBLIOGRAPHY

Adair, James: *The History of the American Indians* (London, E. & C. Dilly, 1775)

Adams, Joseph: *Salmon and Trout Angling* (London, Hutchinson, 1923)

Alexander, Karen: *The Changing Year* (Windsor, Harmsworth Active, 1993)

Aksakoff, Serge: *A Russian Schoolboy* (trans. J.D. Duff, Oxford University Press, 1924)

Ayrton, Elisabeth: *The Cookery of England* (London, André Deutsch, 1974)

Bainbridge, George C.: *The Fly-fisher's Guide* (Liverpool, 1816)

Balfour-Kinnear, G.P.R.: *Catching Salmon and Sea-Trout* (London, Thomas Nelson, 1958)

Barker, Fred: *An Angler's Paradise* (London, Faber & Gwyer, 1929)

Barker, Thomas: *Barker's Delight, or The Art of Angling* (London, 1657)

Barrington, Sir Jonah: *Personal Sketches of His Own Times* (London, Henry Colburn, 1827)

Barry, W.: *Moorland and Stream* (London, Tinsley Brothers, 1871)

Bates, H.E.: *Sugar For the Horse* (London: Michael Joseph, 1957)

'B.B.': *The Fisherman's Bedside Book* (London, Eyre and Spottiswoode, 1945)

'B.B.': *The Idle Countryman* (London, Eyre and Spottiswoode, 1955)

'B.B.': *The Wayfaring Tree* (London, Hollis & Carter, 1948)

'B.B.': *Fisherman's Folly* (Woodbridge, Boydell, 1987)

'B.B.': *The Naturalist's Bedside Book* (London, Michael Joseph, 1980)

Berners, Dame Juliana (attrib.): *The Treatyse of Fysshynge with an Angle* in *The Boke of St Albans* (London, Wynkyn de Worde, 1496)

Best, Thomas: *A Concise Treatise on the Art of Angling* (London, 1787)

Bickerdyke, John: *The Book of the All-Round Angler* (London, 1899)

Bickerdyke, John: *Wild Sport in Ireland* (London, Upcott Gill, 1897)

Bickerdyke, John: *Days of My Life* (London, Longman, Green, 1901)

Bishop, Elizabeth: *The Complete Poems* (New York, Farrar Strauss and Giroux, 1955)

Blakey, Robert: *Historical Sketches of the Angling Literature of All Nations* (London, John Russell Smith, 1856)

Bowlker, Richard & Charles: *The Art of Angling* (Birmingham, 1774)

Blunden, Edmund: *The Face of England* (London, Longman's, 1932)

'Boz' (Charles Dickens) ed.: *Bentley's Miscellany* (London, Richard Bentley, 1851)

Brautigan, Richard: *Trout Fishing in America* (San Francisco, Four Seasons Foundation, 1967)

Bromley-Davenport, Walter: *Sport* (London, Chapman & Hall, 1885)

Brookes, R.: *The Art of Angling* (London, Wm Lowndes, 1790)

Browne, G.F.: *Off The Mill* (London, Smith Elder, 1895)

Bruce-Lockhart, Sir Robert: *My Rod My Comfort* (London, Dropmore Press, 1949)

Buchan, John: *John Macnab* (London, Penguin Books, 1956)

Buckland, Frank: *The Logbook of a Fisherman and Zoologist* (London, Chapman & Hall, 1875)

Burroughs, John: *Locusts and Wild Honey* (Boston, Houghton Osgood & Co, 1879)

Caine, William: *An Angler at Large* (London, Kegan Paul, 1911)

Caine, William: *Fish, Fishing & Fishermen* (London, Philip Allen, 1927)

Cameron, L.C.R.: *Rod, Pole and Perch* (London, Martin Hopkinson, 1928)

Canaway, W.H.: *A Creel of Willow* (London, Michael Joseph, 1957)

Canaway, W.H.: *A Snowdon Stream* (London, Putnam, 1958)

Caras, Roger: *Dangerous to Man* (London, Barrie & Jenkins, 1976)

Carver, Raymond: *At Night the Salmon Run* (Santa Barbara, Capra Press, 1976)

Chalmers, Patrick: *At the Tail of the Weir* (London, Philip Allan, 1932)

Chalmers, Patrick: *The Angler's England* (London, Seeley Service, 1938)

Chaytor, A.H.: *Letters to a Salmon-fisher's Son* (London, John Murray, 1910)

Chekhov, Anton: *The Culprit* in *The Portable Chekhov* (New York, Viking Press, 1947)

Chetham, James: *The Angler's Vade Mecum* (London, 1681)

Cholmondeley-Pennell, H.: *Perch Fishing* (London, Routledge, 1884)

Cholmondeley-Pennell, H.: *The Modern Practical Angler* (London, Routledge, 1870)

Cholmondeley-Pennell, H.: *Fishing Gossip* (London, A&C Black, 1866)

Cholmondeley, Pennell, H: *The Angler-Naturalist* (London, John Van Voorst, 1868)

Coppleson, V.M.: *Shark Attack* (London: Angus & Robertson, 1958)

Courtney Williams, A.: *Angling Diversions* (London, Herbert Jenkins, 1945)

Couch, Jonathan: *A History of Fishes of the British Islands* (London, Groombridge & Sons, 1863)

Cox, Nicholas: *The Gentleman's Recreation* (London, 1674)

Daniel, Revd William: *Rural Sports* (London, 1802)

Davies, the Revd William: *Rural Sports* (London, Bunny and Gold, 1812)

Davy, Sir Humphry: *Salmonia, or days of Fly-fishing* (London, John Murray, 1828)

Day, David: *Whale War* (London, Routledge and Kegan Paul, 1987)

Dennys, John: *The Secrets of Angling* (London, 1613)

Dickie, John M.: *Great Angling Stories* (London, W. & R. Chambers, 1941)

Dudgeon, John: *A Modest Day's Fishing* (London, Excalibur Press, 1992)

Dunne, J.W.: *Sunshine and the Dry Fly* (London, A. & C. Black, 1924)

Fallon, Niall: *The Irish Game Angler's Anthology* (Dublin, Country House Books, 1991)

Farson, Negley: *Going Fishing* (London, Country Life, 1942)

Faulkner, William: *The Sound and the Fury* (New York, Jonathan Cape & Harrison Smith, 1931)

Fedden, Romily: *Golden Days: From the Fishing Log of a Painter in Brittany* (London, A. & C. Black, 1919)

Fleuron, Svend: *Grim, the Story of a Pike* (London, Gyldendal, 1920)

Fox-Strangways, V.: *Wandering Fisherman* (London, Arthur Barker, 1955)

Francis, Francis: *A Book of Angling* (London, 1867)

Franck, Richard: *Northern Memoirs* (London, 1658)

Froude, J.A.: *Cheneys and the House of Russell* (London, *Fraser's Magazine*, September 1879)

Gammon, Clive: *A Tide of Fish* (London, Heinemann, 1962)

Gammon, Clive: *The Fisherman's Bedside Book* (London, Heinemann, 1961)

Gay, John: *Rural Sports* (London, 1713)

Gibbs, Arthur: *A Cotswold Village* (London, John Murray, 1898)

Gibbs, A. Hamilton: *Rivers Glide On* (London, Hutchinson, 1934)

Gierach, John: *Trout Bum* (Boulder, Colorado: Pruett Publishing 1986)

Gilbert, H.A.: *The Tale of a Wye Fisherman* (London: Methuen, 1929)

Gilbert, William: *The Angler's Delight* (London, 1676)

Gingrich, Arnold: *The Fishing in Print* (New York, Winchester Press, 1974)

Glasse, Mrs: *The Art of Cookery Made Plain and Simple* (London, 1803)

Gray, L.R.W. (Lemon Grey): *Torridge Fishery* (London, Nicholas Kaye, 1957)

Grey, Sir Edward: *Fly Fishing* (London, J.M. Dent, 1899)

Grey, Zane: *Tales of the Angler's Eldorado* (New York, Harper Bros, 1926)

Grey, Zane: *Adventures in Fishing* (New York, Harper Bros, 1952)

Grey, Zane: *Tales of Freshwater Fishing* (New York, Harper Bros, 1928)

Grigson, Jane: *English Food* (London, Ebury Press, 1992)

Grimble, Arthur: *A Pattern of Islands* (London, John Murray, 1952)

Haig-Brown, R.L.: *Pool and Rapid* (London, A. & C. Black, 1932)

Haig-Brown, R.L.: *Return to the River* (London, Collins, 1942)

Haig-Brown, R.L.: *A River Never Sleeps* (London, Collins, 1948)

Halford, F.M.: *An Angler's Autobiography* (London, Vinton & Co, 1903)

Halford, F.M.: *Dry Fly Fishing in Theory and Practice* (London, Sampson & Low, 1889)

Halford, R.M.: *An Angler's Autobiography* (London, Vinton & Co, 1903)

Hamilton, R.: *A History of British Fishes* (London, Hardwicke & Bogue, 1890)

Hammond, Bill: *An Irish Salmon Gilly* (Fermoy, Cameo Publications, 1984)

Hargreaves, Barbara: *The Sporting Wife* (London, H.F. & G. Witherby, 1971)

Harpur, Merrily: *Pig Overboard! . . . and other strange letters to* The Field, (London, Robson, 1984)

Hastings, Macdonald: *Country Book* (London, George Newnes, 1961)

Hastings, Macdonald & Carole Walsh: *Wheelers' Fish Cookery Book* (London, Michael Joseph, 1974)

Headlam, Maurice: *Irish Reminiscences* (London, Robert Hale, 1947)

Headlam, Maurice: *A Holiday Fisherman* (London, Christopher's, 1934)

Heaney, Seamus: *Seeing Things* (London, Faber and Faber, 1991)

Hemingway, Ernest: *Byline* (New York, Charles Scribner's Sons, 1967)

Hemingway, Ernest: *The Old Man and the Sea* (New York, Charles Scribner's Sons, 1952)

Henderson, William: *My Life as an Angler* (London: W. Satchell, 1879)

Henn, T.R.: *Shooting a Bat* (Cambridge, Golden Head Press, 1964)

Herodotus: *The Histories* (trans J.A. Prout, London, Kelly, 1858)

Hiaasen, Carl: *Double Whammy* (London, Century Hutchinson, 1987)

Hillaby, John: *Within the Streams* (London, Harvey & Blythe, 1949)

Hills, J.W.: *A Summer on the Test* (London, Philip Allen, 1924)

Hills, J.W.: *A History of Flyfishing for Trout* (London, Philip Allen, 1921)

Hills, J.W.: *My Sporting Life* (London, Philip Allan & Co., 1936)

Hintz, O.S.: *Trout at Taupo* (London, Max Reinhardt, 1955)

Hobbs, A.E.: *Trout of the Thames* (London, Herbert Jenkins, 1943)

Hofland, T.C.: *The British Angler's Manual* (London, Whitehead & Co., 1834)

Holder, Charles Frederick: *The Log of a Sea Angler* (London, Constable, 1906)

Holder, Charles Frederick: *The Big Game Fishes of the United States* (New York, Macmillan, 1903)

Holder, Charles Frederick and David Jordan: *Fish Stories* (New York, Henry Holt & Co., 1909)

Howitt, Atkinson, *et al*: *Foreign Field Sports, Fisheries and Sporting Anecdotes* (London, Edward Orme, 1814)

Hudson, W.H.: *Idle Days in Patagonia* (London, Chapman & Hall, 1893)

Hudson, W.H.: *Far Away and Long Ago* (London, Longman, 1918)

Humphrey, William: *My Moby Dick* (London, Chatto and Windus, 1979)

Hughes, Ted: *The River* (London, Faber and Faber, 1983)

Huxley, Aldous: *Jonah* (Oxford, Holywell Press, 1917)

Irving, Washington: *The Sketch Book of Geoffrey Crayon, Gent* (London, Nelson, 1819)

Jackson, John: *The Practical Fly-Fisher, more particularly for grayling or umber* (London, George Bell, 1853)

Jardine, Alfred: *Pike and Perch* (London, Lawrence & Bullen, 1898)

Jefferies, Richard: *The Gamekeeper at Home* (London, 1878)

Jerome, Jerome K.: *Three Men in a Boat* (London, 1880)

Johnson, Stephen: *Fishing from Afar* (London, Peter Davies, 1947)

Jukes, H.R.: *Loved River* (London, Faber & Faber, 1935)

Kelson, George: *The Salmon Fly* (London, privately printed, 1895)

Kingsley, Charles: *Chalkstream Studies*, in *Collected Works* (London, Macmillan, 1903)

Kingsmill Moore, T.C.: *A Man May Fish* (Gerard's Cross, Colin Smythe, 1979)

Kipling, Rudyard: *Dry-cow Fishing as a Fine Art* (reprint, Cleveland, The Rowfant Club, 1926)

Lane, Joscelyn: *Fly-Fisher's Pie* (London, Herbert Jenkins, 1956)

Lang, Andrew: *Angling Sketches* (London, Longmans, Green & Co, 1891)

Leitch, A.: *A Scottish Fly-Fisher* (Paisley, Alexander Gardner, 1911)

Longfellow, Henry: *The Song of Hiawatha* (London, Macmillan, 1855)

Luard, G.D.: *Fishing Fortunes and Misfortunes* (London, Faber & Faber, 1942)

Luce, A.A.: *Fishing and Thinking* (London, Hodder and Stoughton, 1959)

Lyons, Nick: *Fisherman's Bounty* (London, W.H. Allen, 1973)

Macdonald Robertson, John: *In Scotland with a Fishing Rod* (London, Herbert Jenkins, 1935)

Mackenzie, Gregor: *Memoirs of a Ghillie* (Newton Abbot, David and Charles, 1978)

McClane, A.J.: 'Song of the Angler', in *Field and Stream* (October 1967)

Maclean, Norman: *A River Runs Through It* (Chicago, University of Chicago, 1976)

MacLysaght, Edward: *Irish Life in the Seventeenth Century* (Dublin, The Talbot Press, 1939)

McCully, C.B.: *A Dictionary of Fly-Fishing* (Oxford, Oxford University Press, 1993)

Mainwaring, Arthur: *Fishing and Philandering* (London, Heath, Cranton & Ouseley, 1914)

Manchester Anglers' Association: *Anglers' Evenings* (Manchester, Abel Heywood, 1880)

Marshall, Howard: *Reflections on a River* (London: H.F. & G. Witherby, 1967)

Martin, J.W.: *My Fishing Days and Ways* (Plymouth, Brendon & Sons, 1906)

Marvell, Andrew: *Complete Poetry* (New York, Modern Library College eds, 1968)

Maurice, Henry: *Sometimes an Angler* (London, Chapman and Hall, 1947)

Mitchell Hedges, F.A.: *Battles with Giant Fish* (London, Duckworth, 1923)

Moffat, A.S.: *The Secrets of Angling* (Edinburgh, A&C Black, 1865)

Mottram, J.C.: *Thoughts on Angling* (London, Herbert Jenkins, 1948)

Mottram, J.C.: *Fly-Fishing – Some New Arts and Mysteries* (London, *The Field* and *Queen*, 1915)

Munchausen, Baron (Rudolf Erich Raspe): *Gulliver Revived* (London, G. Kearsely, 1787)

Nobbes, Robert: *The Compleat Troller* (London, 1682)

Norris, Thadeus: *The American Angler's Book* (Philadelphia, G.H. Butler, 1865)

O'Gorman, James ('The' O'Gorman): *The Practice of Angling, particularly as regards Ireland* (Dublin, Wm Curry Jun. & Co, 1845)

O'Neil, Paul, 'Excalibur: The Steelhead', in *Sports Illustrated* (11 March 1957)

Oliver, Stephen: *Scenes and Recollections of Fly-fishing in Northumberland, Cumberland and Westmoreland* (London, 1834)

Orwell, George: *Coming Up for Air* (London, Victor Gollancz, 1939)

Palmer, Herbert: *The Roving Angler* (London, J.M. Dent & Sons, 1933)

Parker, Eric (ed.): *An Angler's Garland* (London, Philip Allan & Co, 1920)

Paterson, Wilma & Peter Behal: *Salmon and Women* (London, H.F. & G. Witherby, 1990)

Pearson, Anthony, *Fisherman* (London, Pelham Books, 1970)

Pierce, Roger: *Fishing with my Father* (Chinnor, The Children Agency, 1993)

Piscatorial Society, The: *The Book of the Piscatorial Society, 1836–1936* (Piscatorial Society, 1936)

Pliny The Elder: *Natural History*, trans. John Healy (London, Penguin Books, 1991)

Plunkett Greene, Henry: *Where The Bright Waters Meet* (London, Philip Allen, 1936)

Plutarch: *Lives*, trans. by Bernadotte Perrin (London, Heinemann, 1920)

Poli, François: *Sharks Are Caught At Night* (London, Rupert Hart-Davis, 1958)

Pollard, Major Hugh: *The Sportsman's Cookery Book* (London, *Country Life*, 1926)

Pownall, David & Gareth: *The Fisherman's Bedside Book* (London, Windward Books, 1980)

Profumo, David and Swift, Graham: *The Magic Wheel* (London, Heinemann, 1985)

Radcliffe, William: *Fishing From The Earliest Times* (London, John Murray, 1929)

Raines, Howell: *Fly Fishing Through The Midlife Crisis* (New York, William Morrow, 1993)

Ransome, Arthur: *Mainly About Fishing* (London, A. & C. Black, 1959)

Ransome, Arthur: *Rod and Line* (London, Jonathan Cape, 1929)

Ritz, Charles: *A Fly Fisher's Life* (London, Max Reinhardt, 1959)

Robb, James: *Notable Angling Literature* (London, Herbert Jenkins, 1947)

Roberts, Morley: *A Humble Fisherman* (London, Grayson & Grayson, 1932)

Robertson, John: *Handbook of Angling* (London, Houlston & Wright, 1856)

Ronalds, Alfred: *The Fly-Fisher's Entomology* (London, 1836)

Roosevelt, Theodore: *Through The Brazilian Wilderness* (London, John Murray, 1924)

Ruddiman, W.: *A Collection of Scarce and Curious Pieces* (Edinburgh, 1773)

Sage, Dean: *Salmon Fishing on the Ristigouche* (Edinburgh, D. Douglas, 1888)

Salter, T.F.: *The Angler's Guide* (London, T. Tegg & Co., 1815)

Sandison, Bruce: *The Sporting Gentleman's Gentleman* (London, George Allen & Unwin, 1986)

Saunders, James: *The Compleat Fisherman* (London, William Brown, 1724)

Sawyer, Frank: *Keeper of the Stream* (London, A. & C. Black, 1952)

Scrope, William: *Days and Nights of Salmon Fishing* (London, 1843)

'Jock Scott': *Fine and Far Off* (London, Seeley, Service and Co., 1952)

'Jock Scott': *Game Fishing Records* (London, H.F. & G. Witherby, 1936)

Sharp, Arthur: *An Angler's Corner* (London, Herbert Jenkins, 1930)

Sharp, Arthur: *Rod and Stream* (London, Herbert Jenkins, 1928)

Sheringham, H.T.: *Elements of Angling* (London, The Field Press, 1930)

Sheringham, H.T.: *Fishing: A Diagnosis* (London, Field and Queen, 1914)

Sheringham, H.T.: *Coarse Fishing* (London, A. & C. Black, 1913)

Shipley, William: *A True Treatise on the Art of Fly-fishing* (London, 1838)

Shirley, Thomas: *The Angler's Museum, or the Whole Art of Float and Fly Fishing* (London, 1784)

Skues, G.E.M.: *Minor Tactics of the Chalkstream* (London, A. & C. Black, 1910)

Skues, G.E.M.: *Sidelines, Sidelights and Reflections* (London, Seeley, Service, 1932)

Skues, G.E.M.: *The Way of a Trout with a Fly* (London, A. & C. Black, 1921)

Skues, G.E.M.: *Itchen Memories* (London, Herbert Jenkins, 1951)

Skues, G.E.M.: *Nymph Fishing for Chalk Stream Trout* (London, A. & C. Black, 1939)

Smith, George (attrib.): *The Gentleman Angler* (London, 1726)

Stevenson, Robert Louis: *An Inland Voyage* (London, Kegan Paul, 1878)

Stewart, W.C.: *The Practical Angler* (Edinburgh, A. & C. Black, 1857)

Stoddart, Thomas Tod: *An Angler's Rambles* (Edinburgh, Edmonon and Douglas, 1866)

Stuart, John: *Lays of the Deer Forest* (London, 1869)

Taplin, William: *The Sporting Dictionary* (London, Vernor & Hood, 1803)

Thomas, Henry: *The Rod in India* (Mangalore, Stoltz, 1873)

Thomson, David: *Nairn in Darkness and Light* (London, Hutchinson, 1987)

Thompson, Leslie P.: *Fishing in New England* (London, Eyre and Spottiswoode, 1957)

Thornton, Col. Thomas: *A Sporting Tour Through the Northern Parts of England and great part of the Highlands of Scotland* (London, 1804)

Thoreau, Henry: *Walden, or life in the Woods* (New York, 1854)

Traver, Robert: *Trout Magic* (New York, St Martin's Press, 1960)

Trench, Charles Chevenix: *The Poacher and the Squire* (London, Longmans, 1967)

Trench, Charles Chevenix: *A History of Angling* (London, Hart-Davis, Macgibbon, 1974)

Tuohy, Frank: *Live Bait* (London, Macmillan, 1978)

Turner, L.M: *Contributions to the Natural History of Alaska* (Washington, Government Printing Office, 1886)

Turrell, W.J.: *Ancient Angling Authors* (London, Gurney and Jackson, 1910)

Twain, Mark: *More Tramps Abroad* (London, Chatto & Windus, 1897)

Unett, John: *Fishing Days* (London, Cassell, 1957)

Various authors: *The One That Got Away* (London, Merlin Unwin Books, 1991)

Venables, Robert: *The Experienced Angler* (London, 1662)

Venner, Tobias: *Via Recta ad Vitam Longam* (London, 1620)

Voss Bark, Conrad: *A History of Fly Fishing* (London, Merlin Unwin Books, 1992)

Walker, Richard: *No Need To Lie* (London, E.M. Art & Publishing, 1961)

Walker, Richard: *Still Water Angling* (Newton Abbot, David & Charles, 1975)

Walton, Izaac & Charles Cotton: *The Compleat Angler* (London, 1676)

Watson, John: *Confessions of a Poacher* (London, Leadenhall Press, 1890)

Webster, David Kenyon: *Myth and Maneater* (London, Peter Davies, 1962)

Wetzel, Charles: *American Fishing Books* (Newark, privately printed, 1950)

Wheatley, Hewett: *The Rod and Line or practical hints and devices for the sure taking of trout* (London, 1849)

White, Ellington: *Striped Bass and Southern Solitude*, in *Sports Illustrated* (10 October 1966)

White, T.H.: *England Have My Bones* (London, Collins, 1936)

Whitney, John: *The Genteel Recreation, or the Pleasure of Angling* (London, 1700)

Wiggin, Maurice: *The Passionate Angler* (London, Sylvan Press, 1949)

Williams, Courtney: *Angling Diversions* (London, Herbert Jenkins, 1946)

Williamson, Henry: *Salar the Salmon*, (London, Faber & Faber, 1936)

Williamson, Henry: *A Clear Water Stream* (London, Faber & Faber, 1958)

Wulff, Lee: *Handbook of Freshwater Fishing* (New York, J.P. Lippincott, 1939)

Yale, Leroy M. (ed.): *Angling* (New York, Charles Scribner's Sons, 1897)

Yates, Christopher: *Casting at the Sun* (London, Pelham Books, 1986)

Younger, John: *River Angling For Salmon and Trout* (Kelson, J. & J. Rutherford, 1864)

Zern, Ed: *To Hell With Fishing* (New York, Appleton–Century, 1945)

INDEX

Adair, James 131–2
Adams, Joseph 177–8, 446–9
Addison, Joseph 98–100
Aelfric, Abbot of Eynsham xvi
Aelian xvi
Africa 109–10, 423
Akaba, Gulf of 52–3
Aksakoff, Serge 316–17
Alaska 110–12, 133–4
Allen, Alec 318–23
Allen, R. 517
Alta, river, Norway 458–62
Alvie, Loch 333–4
America, modern sport fishing in 530–4; shark attacks 415–20
American dream 14–16
American Indians, British Columbia 134–5; Chief Moose Heart 371–5; taking catfish 131–2
'Ancient Fear', the 492–4
Angler's Prayer 318, 436, 437
angling, as opposed to game fishing 475, 501–3, see also coarse fishing
'antis' (anti-bloodsports) 474
Antonius (Antony) 518–19
Apostles, fishermen among 479–80, 500–1
April Fool (poisson d'Avril) 501
Ardgalleys, river 8, 19
Atbara river, Abyssinia 275–7
Ausable, river 245
Australia, sharks 420–1, 422–3
autopsies 182–4
Azores, whale-hunting in 285–90

badger, stuffed 357; trout fishing 172
Bainbridge, George 228–9, 238
bait 65–7, 170, 224–5, 226; brains as 4–5; for carp 225–6, 233; chocolate biscuits 231–3; for chub 4–5, 151–2, 304–5; for crocodiles 195; grasshoppers 245–6; hippopotamus as 275; limpet 231; live frogs for pike 143–7;

for mahseer 112, 113; ram's member 231; salmon roe 226–7; shrimps and prawns 476, 518; spoon 112, see also flies; maggots; worms
Baker, Sir Samuel 275–7
Balfour-Kinnear, G.P.R. 516
Ballantine, Georgina 301–3, 432
Barker, F.D. 452–3
Barker, Thomas 184
barracuda 393, 413–14
Barrington, Sir John 386–7
Bartley, James 409–10
bass, American sport fishing 530–4; frogs as live bait for 144–7; night fishing 58–61
Bass Anglers Sportsman Society (BASS) 531, 533
Bassus, Cassianus 231
Bastard, Thomas xv, 349
Bates, H.E. 269–73
'B.B.' 27, 74–5, 161–2, 228, 284–5, 371; on character of fishermen 501–3; fishing inns 437–40; night fishing 249–52; on predators 492–4
Bedfordshire, fishing inn 437–40
Belize 70–1
bells, to summon fish 83–4, 159
Beltra, Lough 430
Berners, Dame Juliana 65, 182–3, 205, 474
Bessarabia, sturgeon in 155–7
Best, Thomas 170
Bible, fishing in 475, 479, 500–1
Bickerdyke, John 366–70, 385–6
birds 34–6, 492–4
biscuits, chocolate 231–3
Bishop, Elizabeth 44–6
black poplars 440
black-fish (Dallia Pectoralis) 110–12
Blackwater, river, Co. Cork 284–5, 428
Blakey, Robert 132–3
blindfolds 442
Blunden, Edmund 39–40, 116–17

INDEX

Boecxken, Dit 162

Bohemia 117

Borders 67–8, 430; leistering in 135–6, *see also* Scotland; Tweed, river

Bourne Brook, Chertsey 400

bow and arrow, for shooting pike 138–41

Bowlker, Charles 115, 233

Bowlker, Richard 233

boys, small 93, 310–14, 316–17

Brautigan, Richard 53–8

breakfasts, small boys' 93

Bristol, Bishop of (G.F. Browne) 273–5

Brittany 17–19

Bromley-Davenport, Walter xviii, 46–7, 253–6

Brooke, Rupert 539–40

Brookes, Richard 106–7, 197, 229; on carp 94–5, 225–6; fishing laws 483–5; on whales 97–8, 137–8

Browne, C.C.L. 119–20

Browne, G.F. (Bishop of Bristol) 273–5

Bruce-Lockhart, Sir Robert 525

Buchan, John, *John Macnab* 431, 432, 463–9

Buddy, G.P. 445

bulls 350–1, 371, 384–5

Burroughs, John 65–7

Bush, President George 531, 533, 534

Byron, Lord 474, 488

Caine, William 218–20, 520–1

California 307–10, 340–3

Canada 41–2; salmon fishing 134–5, 263–6

Canaway, W.H. 347–9

candiru (toothpick fish) 392

Cane, Colonel 518

Caras, Roger 86–7

Caribbean, turtles 133

carp, bait for 225–6, 233; British records 326–33; explained 94–5; lost 259–60; revived by brandy 121–2; summoned by bells 83–4

carp fishing 292, 310–14, 316–17

Carron Wellington, V. 358–60

Carver, Raymond 13–14, 375

casting a fly 177–8; for salmon 185–6

Castwell, Theodore 525–8

'catch-and-release' 476, 529, 530–4

catches, unusual 357–8

catfish 131–2

Cauvery, river, S. India 112

chalk streams 28–32, 33–4

Chambers, Patrick 105–6

Chaytor, A.H. 495–7

Chekhov, Anton 277–82

Cheneys (Chenies), Bucks. 21–6

Cheshire, Barn-Meer 115

Chetham, James 222

Chevenix-Trench, Charles 164–5, 169–70

Chile, rainbow trout in 323–5

Cholmondeley-Pennell, H. xviii, 187, 398–400, 480; curious fish 83–4, 109, 121–2, 497–8

Christianity, fish symbol in 499–500, *see also* Bible

Christmas, chub fishing 3–7

chub 101, 437–8, 439, 440; baits for 151–2; large 303–6

chub fishing 3–7; with fly 149–50

Clapton, Eric xvii

clegs (horseflies) 385

Cleopatra 518–19

Cleveland Wrecking Yard 53–8

Cloer, Nadine 413–14

clothing 214–16, 360–1

coarse fishing xv, 501–3

cod 120–1, 391

Colan, Maj H.L. 112

Columbia, river 13

commandments, for anglers 199–200

conger eels 119–20, 391

Conn, Lough 456–8

Coppleson, V.M. 417–23

Corrib, Lough xv, 114, 429

Cotton, Charles 205, 220

cow, catching a 357, 379–83

Cox, Nicholas 479–80, 516

cranes 152–4

crocodiles 194–6

crosslines, for salmon fishing 194

Cubbany, river, S. India 112

Currareavagh House, Lough Corrib 429

dace, at Isleworth 61–4

Daniel, Revd William 103–5, 147, 152, 197–9, 221–3, 503

Danube delta 155–7

Davey, Doreen 336–8, 432

Davy, Sir Humphrey 489–90

Day, David 97, 409–14

decapitation, self- 386–7

Dennys, John 215, 224–5

Derg, Lough 38–9
Deschutes river 375
Diala River, Iraq 112
dipper's nest 34–6
dogs 352; fishing 161, 171–2
dolphins, to catch mullet 173–4
Donton, John 147–8, 491–2
Dorset, food in 441–2
Doubleday, Thomas 196–7
drink, for fishing 235, 443
drugging fish 162
dry-fly fishing xvi, 48–50, 176, 177; for dace
  62–3; superiority of 126–7, 178–81
dynamite 189–90

Edam, Holland 79
eel-pout (Chekhov) 277–82
eels 120; enigma of 105–9; means of catching
  157–60
Egypt, crocodiles in 194
environmental arguments 475
Eskimo fishing methods 133–4
Esmonde, Sir Thomas Grattan 38–9
Ettrick, river 67
Euphrates, river 113
evening 39–40
Ewes, river 136
excuses xv, 436, 445, 520–1
Exmoor, fishing on 218–20

falling in 349–50, 358–60
Farson, Negley 134–5, 144–7, 155–7, 323–5
Fedden, Romilly 17–19
Ferrari, Luigi 52–3
Finn, river 378
first aid, for drowned anglers 362–3; for fish
  121–2
fish, alternatives to cooking 95–6; are predators
  490–2; as Christian symbol 499–500; cruelty
  to 474, 488, 495–9; decline of xiv–xv, 349;
  farmed 476–7; fascination of xii, 77–9,
  539–40; as killers 391–3; lost 243–4, 245–9;
  procreation 96; record size of 291–2; St
  Anthony's sermon to 98–100; tame 83–5, see
  also individual species
Fisherman's Prayer 318, 436, 437
fishermen 536–7; commandments for 199–200;
  drowned 362–3, 400–2; the duffer 354–7;
  necessary attributes of 479–82, 501–3,

504–6; Paul's last day 71–4; relationship with
  Nature 480, 534–6; as solitary 444–5;
  thinking like fish 160; trepanning of 16–17
fishermen's tales 509–14, 515–16
fishing, American dream 14–16; American
  sport 530–4; class structure of 175–7, 476;
  company for 160–1; cost of 206–7, 211–12;
  dangers of 345–6, 349, 351–3, 370, 388–9;
  ethics of 473–7, 489–90, 494–5; joys of 65,
  478–9; Laws on 483–7; masculinity of
  431–2; in Middle Ages 500–1; as obsession
  203, 347–9, 366–9, 388–9, 508–9; opponents
  of 474, 488; rules of (oldest) 482–3; as time-
  wasting 387–8; types of xv–xvi, see also
  coarse fishing; fly fishing
fishing advice 125–8, 200–2, 506–8
fishing cars 208–10, 213
fishing inns 427, 430–2, 434–6
fishing literature xvi–xx; American xix; to hold
  flies in 210–11
fishing records 306–7
Fleuron, Svend 400–2
flies xvi, 206, 207, 235–6; approximations 236–
  8; Black alder 22; Black Dog 256; Black
  spider 11, 62; Blue Dun xiii; broken 23, 24;
  Bulldog 19; for chub 150; Coachman 237;
  Dotterel dun 237; for Exmoor 219;
  Governor 22; Greenwell's Glory xiii, 11, 13;
  Iron-blue dun 236, 237; J.W. Dunne's dry
  12; Kessler's Fancy 8; Little Chap 237;
  McGinty 43; March Brown xiii, 22, 24;
  Mayfly 25; Mole fly (sedge) 236; Olive Quill
  236; Purple xiii; quill marryat 181; quill
  minnow 379–80; Red Palmer 365; Red
  Spinner 22, 23; Royal Coachman 43; for
  salmon 256, 268, 358; Snipe xiii; for tarpon
  70; Tay Rose (salmon) 358; teasing with
  large 189; trimmed down 188; Tup's
  Indispensable xiii, 32; Wickham's Fancy xiii;
  Wilkinson (salmon) 268; Yellow Sally xiii,
  see also bait
Florida, barracudas in 413–14
fly fishing xvi, 475; for chub 149–50; class
  structure of 126, 175–7; first principles
  174–5; zen and the art of 478–9, see also dry-
  fly fishing; flies; salmon; trout
fly-tying, in winter 10–13
food, for fishing 234, 235; fishing teas 235,
  440–1

INDEX

Forth, Firth of 291
Fox-Strangeways, V. 109–10, 231–3
Francis, Francis 148–9, 179, 185–6
Franck, Richard xix, 93–4, 101–2, 498–9
Franklin, Dr. Benjamin 503
Franz Ferdinand, Archduke 523
frogs, as bait 143–7, 304–5; revenge on pike 117
Froude, J.A. 21–6, 494–5

Gaius, Emperor 80
Galway, river 178
Gammon, Clive 58–61
Gaul, lampreys in 81
Gay, John 170–1
geese, to catch pike 147–8
George V, King 129
Gierach, John 160–1, 238–42, 243
Gilbert Islands 130–1, 154–5
Gilbert, William 226, 234, 235–6
gillies 427–30, 445–6, 450–1, 462–3; Irish 193–4, 446–50, 452–8; Oola (Lapp girl) 458–62; Scottish 451–2
gin, for fishing 235
Golden Age, lament for xiv–xv, 349
Gorki, Maxim 525
gratitude, for advice 506–8; of pike 118
Green, Robert 505–7
Greenwell, Canon William xiii
Grey, Sir Edward (Lord Grey of Fallodon) xvii, xviii, 48–50, 206
Grey, Zane 206, 260–3, 292
Grimble, Arthur 130–1, 154–5, 416
gudgeon 170; power of 80
guides see gillies

Haig-Brown, Roderick 152, 441–2, 478–9
Haja, Egypt 53
Halford, Frederick 126–7, 178–80
Hall, John Inglis 189
Hallahan, Maurice 284–5
Hammond, Bill 193–4
Hardy Brothers catalogue 306–7
hare, hooked 517
Harpur, Merrily 51, 357–8
Hartley, J.R. 363–6
Hastings, Macdonald 100–1
Hawaii, sharks 424
Headlam, Maurice 157–8, 518

Heaney, Seamus 21
Heaven 539–40
Hell 526–8
Hemingway, Ernest 41–4, 245–9
Henderson, William 440–1
Herodotus xvii, 96, 194–5
herons 492–4
Hiawatha's sturgeon 402–8
Hillaby, John 376–9
Hills, J.W. 180–1, 538–9
Himalayas 267
Hobbes, Robert 172–3
Hofland, T.C. 84–5, 164, 226–7, 228
Holder, Charles 307–10, 340–3
Holinshed, Scottish Chronicle 432
Holland, George 181–2
Homer xvi
horseflies (clegs) 385
Howitt, Atkinson 85–6
Hughes, Robert 70–1
Hughes, Ted 83
Humphrey, William 175–7, 388–9
hunting, shooting and fishing 51
Huxley, Aldous 408–9

idyllic days 1–3
India, whistling for eels 159–60, see also mahseer
Inglemere Pond, Ascot Heath 398–400
inns 427, 430–2, 434–6
Iraq 112–13
Ireland, eel-switching 157–8; gillies 193–4, 446–50, 452–8; Lough Beltra 430; Lough Conn 456–8; Lough Corrib xv, 114, 429; Lough Derg 38–9; Lough Mask 266–7, 455–6; pike fishing 114, 147–8, 266–7, 366–70, 515; salmon fishing 193–4; trout fishing 376–9
Isleworth, dace at 61–4
Itchen, river 181–2

Jardine, Alfred 118
Jefferies, Richard 141–3, 168–9
Jerome, Jerome K. 508–13
Johnson, Dr Samuel 475
Johnson, Stephen 151
Joicey, Lady Jane 432
Jonah 408–9
June, trout in 49–50

INDEX

Kennet, river 30
Kerry, river 519
Kildare, Co. 386
Kilmorac, Falls of 164
Kingsley, Charles 24, 28–32, 149–50
Kingsmill Moore, T.H. xiv–xv, 449–50, 453–5
Kipling, Rudyard 379–83
knitting, as alternative to fishing 348–9

Laja river, Chile 323–5
Lake Vyrnwy hotel 430
Lamb, Dana 245
lampreys 81
Lane, Joscelyn 159–60, 267–9
Lane, Maj F.B. 112
Lang, Andrew xv, 67–8, 354–7
Lang's Pot, Scotland 20
Law, and fishing 483–7
Lawrence, D.H. 77–8, 114
leisters, to catch salmon xvi, 135–6
Lenin, V.I. 525
letters, carried by cod 121
Lewis, Edwin 320
Liddel, river 136
lightning 352
lime, chloride of 163
limpet, as bait 231
lines 204–5, 222–3; horsehair 222, 223–4; silk
   gut 224; telephone cable 113
Lloyd George, David 519–20
Lloyd, John 360–1
Lobb, A.E. 112
Longfellow, Henry Wadsworth 402–8
Longhurst, George 398–9
Luard, G.D. 282–4
Luce, A.A. 455–8
lying, the art of 509–14, 521–2, see also
   fishermen's tales
Lyons, Nick 36

McCully, C.B. 385
Macedonians xvi
Maclean, Norman 71–4
maggots 228–9, 234
Magnus, Olaus, Bishop 78
mahseer (Indian fish) 112–13, 338–40; lost
   267–9; taming 165–6
Mainwaring, Arthur 189–90
man, fish in shape of 516

Martial xvi
Martin, J.W. 3–7
masculinity of fishing 431–2
Mask, Lough (Ireland) 266–7, 455–6
Maurice, Henry 36–7
Mauritius 119
mayfly 25; hatch 27
Medway, river 233
mermaids 78–9
midges, Scottish 385–6
Mocha Dick, whale 294–301
Moffat, A.S. 64–5, 217–18, 361–2
money 206–7, 211–12
monks, and fishing 500
Mons, Matty 429–30
Monteith, Loch of 147
Moose Heart, Chief 371–5
moose hunting 445–6
Morrison, Miss 'Tiny' 432
moths, for night fishing 238
motor cars, for fishing 208–10, 213
Mottram, J.C. 34–6, 182–4
Mozambique 413
Mrs Beeton's cookery book 357
mullet, catching with dolphins 173–4
Mundus, Frank, shark fisherman 86–7
myths 78–9

needlefish 392
Nelson, Horatio, Lord xvii
New Jersey, rogue shark off 415–20
newspaper, swallowed by shark 92
night, pond at 40–1
night fishing, bass 58–61; moths for 238; for
   pike 252–3; for tench 249–52
nightlines, for trout 164–5
Nile, river 96, 176; crocodiles 194–5
Norris, Thadeus 14–16, 224, 234–5
Norway 78, 79, 120–1; salmon fishing in
   253–6, 458–62
Nyasa, Lake (Nkata Bay) 231–3

Ocean Island 414–15
octopus 129–31; attack by 414–15
O'Gorman, The xviii, 210–11, 480–2
oil, from potatoes 269
Oliver, Stephen 215–16
O'Neil, Paul 81–3
Orford, Suffolk 79, 516

INDEX

Orwell, George 310–14
otters 68–9, 494, 515
Ouse, river 303–6

pain, do fish feel? 474, 488, 495–8, 499
Palmer, Herbert 499–501
Paraguay, piranhas in 395–7
Parker, Sir Hyde 253
Parsifal (Parsifalian quest) 36
partridge, hooked 451
patience 443, 481, 503
Pearson, Anthony 52–3
perch 109, 176, 497–8
peregrine falcon 493–4
Phayre, Lt Col R.B. 112–13
philosophy, of fishing 479–82
pike 46–7, 103, 116–17, 272–3, 491; appetite of
    114–15; attacks by 398–402; frog's revenge
    on 117; a grateful 118; 'Grim' 400–2; Irish
    114, 147–8, 266–7, 366–70, 515; large
    113–14, 333–4; live bait for 143–4, 170;
    means of catching 138, 141–3, 147–8, 172–3;
    night fishing for 252–3
piranha 392, 395–7
pirates, whaling 410–12
Placid, Lake 245
Plata, river (Argentina) 171–2
Pliny the Elder 80–1, 129–30, 173–4
Plunkett Greene, Henry 335–6, 349–50
Plutarch 518–19
poachers 163, 469; John MacNab 463–9
poaching 371, 446; by tickling 167–70; pike
    141–3; trout 164–5, see also fishing, Laws on;
    leisters
poetry, reciting 189
poisoning 163–4
Poli, François 397–8
Pollard, Maj Hugh B.C. 93
ponds, at night 40–1; emptying 46–7, 103
Portugal, and the Portuguese 100, 101
Pound, Ezra 102–3
predators 492–4
Preston Lake, near Norwich 252–3
Price, Alderman David 319–22
proverbs 445
pubs see inns
Pulitzer, Tony 458, 459

quietness 16

rabbit, rolling 36–7
Rafferty 376–9
rainbow trout 41–6, 81–3, 323–5
Raines, Howell 530–4
rams xiii, 231
Ransome, Arthur xvii, 384–5, 430; on
    fishermen 534–6; fishing inns 434–6; fly-
    tying 10–13; tackle shops 469–71
recipes, gudgeon 439–40; very small roach 93
Redmire lake 326–9
reed, bobbing 32–3
reels see tackle
relativity, in fish weights 522
Reynolds, J.N. 294–301
Rhodes, Cecil 89–93
Ritz, Charles 371–5, 458–62
river gods 30–2
river keepers xiii, 23, 25, 33–4
Rivett-Carnac, Col J.S. 112
roach 93, 101–2, 152
Roberts, Morley 444–5, 490–1, 521–2
Robertson, R. Macdonald 138–41
rods 204–5, 220; making 221–2
Rogers, Byron 318–23
Rogue River, Oregon 81
Ronalds, Alfred 177
Roosevelt, President Theodore 392, 395–7
Rotterdam, carp in 83–4
Roxburghe, Duke of, gillies 428
rudd 93, 102
Ruddinan, W. 514
ruffe see perch
Ruskin, John 473
Russia, carp fishing 316–17; Danube delta
    155–7; eel-pout 277–82

Sacramento River 81
Sage, Dean 263–6
St Anthony of Padua 98–100
St Peter 525–6
St Wilfrid 500
salmon 102–3, 184, 291–2, 518; British record
    301–3, 336–8; first 7–10; leistering for
    135–6; life story 93–4; lost 253–6, 263–6,
    273–5, 282–4; poaching 163, 169–70; Salar
    the 256–9; self-poaching 164; striking for
    151, 187
salmon fishing 184, 185–6, 314–16, 371–5, 432;
    in Canada 134–5, 263–6; Norway 253–6,
    458–62; with worms 190–3

Salter, T.F. 362–3
Sandison, Bruce 450–1, 462–3
sardines, laying down 100–1
Sargasso Sea 106
Saunders, James 504–5
Sawyer, Frank 33–4, 122–3, 167–8
Scotland 114, 147, 218, 333–4, 431; river Spey 349–50, 428; river Tay 301–3, 358–60; salmon fishing 7–10, 19–20, *see also* Borders
Scott, Ray 530–4
Scrope, William xvi, xviii, 205, 216–17, 442, 492
sea-monsters 78–9
seatrout 83
Seychelles, stonefish 412
shad, River Plata fish 171–2
sharks 154–5, 393, 397–8; attacks by 415–21; blue 86–7; Cecil Rhodes's fortune from a 87–93; defence against 422–5; feeding frenzy 86–7; tiger 154–5, 424–5; white 85–6
sheep, to feed trout xii, xiii
shell-fish 501
Sheringham, H.T. 227, 235, 259–60; dace 61–4; dangers 350–3; essentials 211–14
Shipley, William 488
Shirley, Thomas 443
shooting 523
Sicily 132–3
Simon Peter, the apostle 500–1
Skues, G.E.M. 27–8, 32–3, 127, 181–2; flies 237–8; Theodore Castwell 525–8
sluices 33–4
Smith, Dr J.H.B. 414–15
Snake River 81
snares, for pike 141–3
solitude 444–5
song, to attract fish 132–3
Soo, river, Canada 41–2
sparrowhawk 494
spears, for salmon fishing 135–6, 163
Spey, river 349–50, 428
sport, analysis of 494–5, 524; not glory 528–30; or slaughter 522–4
spring 64–5, 74–5
spurge, to drug fish 162
Stalin, Joseph 525
steelhead trout 81–3
Stevenson, Robert Louis xii, 16–17
Stewart, W.C. 126

Stoddart, Thomas Tod 47–8, 190–3, 314–16
Stoics, the 255
stonefish 391–2, 412–13
stones, throwing 71, 188, 190
Stuart, John 68–9
sturgeon 155–7, 318–23, 402–8
swordbearer fish 132–3
swordfish 392, 398

tackle 203–7, 218, 345; essential 211–14; exotic 238–42
tackle shops 203–7, 469–71
Taplin, William 387–8, 485–7
tarpon fishing 70–1, 260–3
Tay, river 301–3, 358–60
Taylor, R. 107–9
tea, for fishermen 235, 440–1
tench 103–5, 148–9; night fishing 249–52; tickling 168–9
Test, river 335–6
Thames, river 61–4, 105
Thomas, Henry Sullivan 165–6, 195–6
Thomas, Peter 326–9
Thomson, David 519–20
Thoreau, Henry 40–1
Thornton, Colonel Thomas 333–4
Thornville Royal, Yorkshire 103–5
Three Trouts (Three Fishes), St Paul's churchyard 203, 236
tickling for fish 167–70
tiger shark 154–5
tiger-fish 109–10
tigress, hooked 357–8
Tigris, river 112
Towy, river 318–23
toys, use of 161–2
Traver, Robert 1–3, 200–2, 208–10
Treatyse of Fysshynge with an Angle 65, 474, 482–3
Trent, river 4
Trotsky, Leon 525
trout 27–8; death by starvation 122–3; diet of 183–4; large 245–9, 335–6; poached 164–5, 167–8; rainbow 41–6, 81–3, 323–5; stuffed 432, 511–13; tame 84–5, *see also* flies; fly-fishing
trout stream, used, for sale 54–8
tuna 307–10, 340–3
Turner, L.M. 110–12, 133–4

turtle fishing 133, 276–7
Twain, Mark 87–93
Tweed, river xvi, 67–8, 151, 442

'Uncle Silas' 269–73
United States Navy 423
Ure, river xi

Venables, Bernard 285–90
Venables, Robert xvi, 158, 174–5, 229–31
Vesphrhein, Kristhof 411–12
Vienna, Swimming School 400
Vishnu, Hindu god 79
voles 33–4

wading 205–6, 216–17, 349–50; boots 217–18;
    dangers of 358–62; fishing trousers 360–1
Walker, Richard 292, 303–6, 326–9
Walton, Izaak xvi, xvii, 16, 103, 205; dyeing
    lines 223–4; frogs and pike 117, 143–4
water bailiffs 378–9, 442
Watson, John 163–4
weather, and predictions 197–8
Webster, David 424–6
whales, fin 411–12; hunting 137–8, 285–90,
410–14; killer 97, 392; love life of 97–8;
    man-swallowing 393, 408–10; sperm 97, 285;
    various 97; white (Mocha Dick) 294–301
Wheatley, Hewett 202
whistling, for eels 159–60
White, T.H. xviii, 7–10, 19–20; on gillies 443,
    451–2; on killing 522–4
Whitney, John 233–4
Williamson, Henry 256–9, 469
winter 3–7, 74–5
women, successful anglers 432–3
worms 170–1, 227, 228–31; in pyjamas 228; for
    salmon 190–3
Wulff, Lee 188–9, 476, 528–34
Wye, river 336–8

Yale, Leroy 524
Yates, Christopher 329–33
Yeats, W.B. 152–4, 536–7
Yeovil, Somerset 107–9
Yorkshire Flyfishers gilly 428–9

zen and the art of fly fishing 478–9
Zern, Ed 95–6, 160, 445–6